Konstantinos D. Politis (ed.)

The World of the Nabataeans

ORIENS ET OCCIDENS

Studien zu antiken Kulturkontakten
und ihrem Nachleben

- -

Herausgegeben von
Josef Wiesehöfer

in Zusammenarbeit mit Pierre Briant,
Amélie Kuhrt, Fergus Millar und
Robert Rollinger

Band 15

The World of the Nabataeans

Volume 2 of the International Conference
The World of the Herods and the Nabataeans
held at the British Museum, 17–19 April 2001

Edited by Konstantinos D. Politis

Franz Steiner Verlag 2007

Bibliografische Information der Deutschen Nationalbibliothek
Die Deutsche Nationalbibliothek verzeichnet diese Publikation in der Deutschen Nationalbibliografie; detaillierte bibliografische Daten sind im Internet über <http://dnb.d-nb.de> abrufbar.

ISBN 978-3-515-08816-9

ISO 9706

Gedruckt auf säurefreiem, alterungsbeständigen Papier.

Druck: Printservice Decker & Bokor, München
Printed in Germany

Contents

Prologue

The idea of holding an international conference concerning the 'World of the Herods and Nabataeans' was originated by Drs Nikos Kokkinos and Konstantinos Politis. Their respective researches into these closely-related subjects inspired them to plan an assembly of the most eminent academics to discuss the varied issues generated by the study of the Herodian Dynasty and the close familial relationship they shared with their Nabataean neighbours.

Their efforts were greatly assisted by the enthusiasm of Sam Moorhead who facilitated the arrangements for this unique conference to be held in the Clore Education Centre which is part of the newly-built Great Court of the British Museum in London. This was the inaugural academic congress to be held in this centre at the beginning of the new century. The venue, combined with the attendance of all the invited scholars, ensured the success of this extraordinary event.

With the exception of Jacqueline Studer's, the papers in this volume are presented by authors who attended the conference. It should be noted however, that five of the original contributions do not appear here, as it has been decided that they would be published elsewhere: Petra Depicted, 1812–1847 by Bryony Llewellyn; Recent Excavations at the 'Great Temple' in Petra by Leigh-Ann Bedal; A Group of 120 Clay Bullae from Petra with Titles of the City by Haim Gitler; The Date of the al-Khasneh at Petra: A New Approach by Karl Schmitt-Korte; and, Conservation of the Textiles and Leather from Khirbet Qazone, Jordan: From Excavation to Display by Pippa Cruikshank, Anna Harrison and John Fields.

In addition to the British Museum sponsoring and hosting the conference, several other institutions made valuable contributions to the symposium. They were the Hellenic Society for Near Eastern Studies, the Palestine Exploration Fund, the Karim Rida Said Foundation and the Kress Foundation. The Wingate Foundation also helped with the costs of editing.

The stimulating insights gained by the participants, engendered by the informative papers given by the speakers, encouraged Drs Kokkinos and Politis to separately edit the proceedings in what has become two volumes.

With appreciation of the efficiency of the publishers Steiner Verlag and gratitude to all the contributors I now proudly present this, the second volume encompassing the 'World of the Nabataeans'.

Konstantinos D. Politis,
Hellenic Society for Near Eastern Studies, Athens

The Rediscovery of Petra, 1807–1818

Norman N. Lewis

This paper is concerned with three early nineteenth century travellers and the contributions they made to our knowledge of Petra. They were U.J. Seetzen, who guessed that the ruins in Wadi Musa might be those of Petra but was not able to get there, J.L. Burckhardt who reached Wadi Musa and tentatively identified the ruins as those of Petra, and W.J. Bankes who was the first to make drawings of some of the monuments and to copy inscriptions there. The section on Bankes differs from those on Seetzen and Burckhardt in that it is largely based upon Bankes' own papers many of which have only recently been thoroughly studied.

U.J. SEETZEN was the pioneer explorer of the country beyond the River Jordan and the Dead Sea. He was the first European in modern times to visit Jerash and Amman and to identify the ruins there as those of Gerasa and Phila-delphia. From time to time since his day it has been suggested that he was also the first European to reach the ruins of Petra in Wadi Musa.[1] In fact his travel journals and letters, summarised below, make clear that although he tried to reach Wadi Musa he failed to do so.

Seetzen's first journeys south of Damascus were made in December 1805. In January 1806 he left Damascus for the last time and made a wide ranging tour which included Jerash, Amman and Kerak.[2] He 'enquired for Petra' at Kerak but obtained no useful information.[3] Having rounded the southern end of the Dead Sea he reached Jerusalem on 6th April 1806 and spent most of that year west of the Jordan. In December he explored the western side of the Dead Sea and in the following January made a second tour of the eastern side and returned to Jerusalem.[4]

On 13th March 1807 he set off from Jerusalem on a journey which was to take him via Sinai to Suez and Cairo.[5] At Hebron, as he prepared for the desert stages ahead of him, local people talked to him about the country to the south and south-east and gave him the names of places, inhabited or deserted, which were to be found there. Among them were Wadi Musa, 'Pharaūn' and 'Seyyidna Harūn'. Later, as Seetzen travelled south from Hebron, his guide took up the theme,

[1] Gage, for example, who published an abridged translation of Ritter's *Erdkunde* (Gage 1866 I, 419) wrote that 'I cannot doubt that Seetzen is to be considered the true modern discoverer of Petra', and as recently as 1972 an article in the Archaeological Encyclopaedia of Israel stated not only that Seetzen was the first European traveller to reach Petra but also that he 'had no idea of its true identity' (This statement was replaced in subsequent editions of the Encyclopaedia by another in which Burckhardt was identified as the discoverer).

[2] Monat. Corr. XVIII 331–367, 417–448; Brief Account 7–47; Reisen I, 362–426.

[3] Monat. Corr. XVIII 434; Reisen II, 356; Burckhardt 1822, 387.

[4] Reisen II, 217–274, 293–385.

[5] Monat. Corr. XVII 132–153; Reisen III, 3–163.

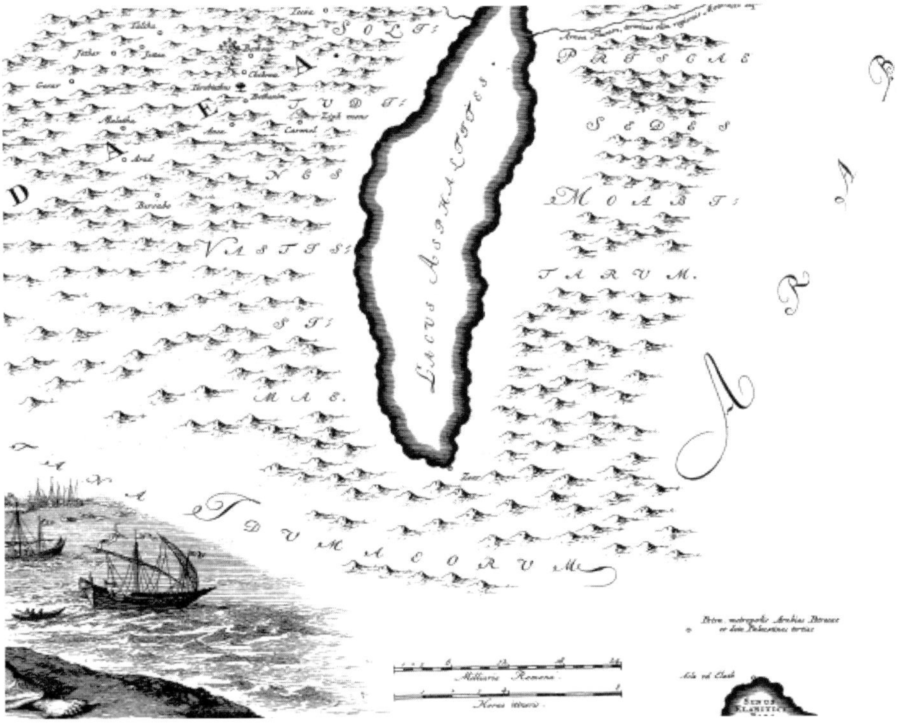

Fig 1. Part of the frontispiece map in Reland's Palæstina, 1714.

telling him that he was unlikely to find interesting ruins in the area through which they were then passing; he should go east to the Jibal and the Sharah where there were marvellous ruins. Fired by enthusiasm the guide exclaimed 'By God, when I behold the ruins of Pharaūn I could weep!' and he went on to say more about Wadi Musa and its environs. It became clear to Seetzen that the ruins of 'Pharaūn' were in Wadi Musa and that the *mazar* of Harūn, to which Muslims made pilgrimage, was on a rocky mountain above the Wadi. Seetzen speculated at length about all this; he knew that Harūn was the Arabic name for Aaron and wondered whether the eminence above the Wadi could really be Mount Hor and whether Pharaūn might be Pharan, or perhaps Petra.[6] He thought about it a great deal and would have liked to follow up the information, but he could hardly change his plans at this point. He pursued his chosen route via Beersheba and the Tih desert to western Sinai and thence to Suez and Cairo, where he arrived on 24th May 1807.

[6] Monat. Corr. XVII, 136–139; Reisen 1855 III 16–19

Little more than a year after this he decided to try to find the mysterious 'Pharaūn' which, as he told von Hammer in a letter from Cairo dated 10th July 1808, was said to be in Wadi Musa, a well watered valley near which on a high rock was the reputed tomb of Aaron. It might possibly be the site of Petra, he continued, but whether or not that were so the association of the Israelites with that area made it so interesting to him that he felt he must try to get there. He did not know where it was but guessed it to be a day or two east or north east of Aqabah. 'Pharaūn' was only one of three places he hoped to reach; the others were 'Midian on the Red Sea three days' journey south of Aqabah', and the ruins of Medain Saleh in Hijaz on the route of the Syrian Hajj. [7]

In making his plans Seetzen seems not to have taken fully into account the difficulties of travelling in the Hijaz and adjacent areas which were now more or less controlled by the Wahhabis. The great Syrian and Egyptian pilgrim caravans no longer travelled each year to and from the Holy Cities, and Wahhabi raiding and tribute collecting parties ranged far to the north – even the people of Kerak 'became Wahabis' for a time from 1808.[8] We have no details of what attempt, if any, Seetzen made to reach Wadi Musa or the other places he had mentioned in his letter of 10th July 1808; in a later letter, dated 29 July 1809, he described his further exploration of Sinai and sent von Hammer a sheet of Sinaitic inscriptions he had copied, but all he said about Aqabah or Petra was that he had been unable to get to them, his plans having been frustrated by the Wahhabis.[9]

Seetzen had no further chance of finding Petra. He travelled to Mecca later in 1809, to Mocha in 1810, and never returned to the north. He died, almost certainly of poison, near Mocha in 1811.

J L Burckhardt's 'Description of a journey from Damascus through the mountains of Arabia Petræa and the desert El Ty to Cairo, in the summer of 1812' begins with the following words:

> 'Wishing to obtain a further knowledge of the mountains to the east of the Jordan, and being still more desirous of visiting the almost unknown districts to the east of the Dead sea, as well as of exploring the country which lies between the latter and the Red sea, I resolved to pursue that route from Damascus to Cairo, in preference to the direct road through Jerusalem and Ghaza, where I could not expect to collect much information important for its novelty.'[10]

[7] Fundgruben I, 43–45. Burckhardt was sent a copy of this first, 1809, issue of Fundgruben in 1811, when he was in Aleppo. He mentioned this, and Seetzen's letter of 10th July, 1808 which was published in it, in a letter he wrote to his friend G.C. Renouard on 3rd May, 1811 (B.L. Add. Ms. 27620), but did not mention Seetzen's speculations about Wadi Musa; the only part of the letter which interested him seems to have been that in which Seetzen described his book-buying successes in Cairo, contrasted ruefully by Burckhardt with the modest results of his own efforts in Aleppo. It would appear that he either did not read the rest of the letter or read it without much interest and soon forgot it. He would not, at that time, have heard of Wadi Musa and had probably not yet considered the route he might eventually follow to Cairo. So far as is known there is no indication in anything else Burckhardt wrote that he was aware of Seetzen's speculations concerning Wadi Musa or Petra.

[8] Burckhardt, 1822, 283

[9] Fundgruben II, 474

[10] The summarised narrative which follows is based on Burckhardt 1822, 311–456 and

Wearing 'the most common Bedouin dress' and mounted on 'a mare that was not likely to arouse the cupidity of the Arabs' Burckhardt rode out of Damascus on the 18th June 1812. He took a south-westerly route, crossed the Jordan at Jisr Banat Yaqub and reached Tiberias on 23 June.[11] From here he intended to go to Al-Salt, the place from which he planned to start his journey east of the Dead Sea, but he chanced to meet Lady Hester Stanhope's companion Michael Bruce who 'easily prevailed' on him to accompany him to Nazareth where Lady Hester was staying.[12] After meeting her Ladyship he joined a little caravan of petty merchants who were going to Al-Salt.

He reached Al-Salt without difficulty but was delayed there while he looked for, bargained with and eventually engaged a man to accompany him to Kerak. Not all the time was wasted; one day, tiring of Al Salt, he rode over to Al Fuhays, nearby, and there 'was so fortunate as to find a guide who five years ago had served in the same capacity to Mousa, the name assumed by M. Seetzen' who agreed to take him to Amman.[13] There Burckhardt was able to make notes and to sketch a plan, as he had done at Jerash in May; the resultant lengthy and informative descriptions of the two sites eventually appeared on pp. 252–265 and 357–360 of Burckhardt 1822. From Amman he returned to Al-Salt and, on 13th July, got away to the south.

At Kerak another twenty days of delay ensued because Yūsuf Majali, the Shaykh of Kerak, would not let him go further on his own or with a single guide; he himself was going southward in a few days, he said, and Burckhardt should go with him. While Burckhardt was in Kerak he enjoyed the hospitality of many of the Christian townsmen and from them obtained much information about the country round about. Finally on 4th August Shaykh Yūsuf accompanied by forty horsemen started for a tour to several villages south of Kerak and Burckhardt

except where otherwise stated all page references in the text and notes of this section are to Burckhardt 1822.

[11] At first sight it seems surprising that Burckhardt should go to Tiberias, west of the Jordan, when his objective was Al-Salt. This was probably due to the fact that in May he had been unable to reach Al-Salt from Jerash because of the unsettled state of the country, the Bani Sakhr in particular constituting a menace to travellers (p. 264). Now, a month later, he did not want to be obliged to turn back again, and calculated correctly that he would be more likely to find other people going to Al-Salt from Tiberias or other towns west of the Jordan than from the sparsely populated and dangerous area to the east. That the diversion to Tiberias was not due to any sudden change of plan is shown clearly by a letter he wrote on 16th May 1812 – soon after his return from the Hauran and almost a month before he left Damascus again – in which he outlined the route he proposed to take, and did in fact take (Letter to J. Fiott, B.L. Add. Ms. 47490).

[12] Burckhardt's description of the meeting with Lady Hester is in his pages 335–337. A commentary on it with reference to other sources is in Lewis 2001, 57–69, and particularly 68–69.

[13] This was the second time that Burckhardt found a man who had guided Seetzen. During his tours of the Hauran and the country south of it, in 1810 and 1812, his paths several times crossed those followed by Seetzen in 1806. (p. 57, 71, 211, 268, 362, 374, 387, 390) He came to admire Seetzen, whose name was often mentioned by the country people, and who Burckhardt concluded, had been 'indefatigable in his researches'. (Letter to G C Renouard, 3rd May 1811, BL Add. Ms 27620)

went with him. Although Burckhardt had paid the Shaykh an agreed amount for his guidance and protection the latter now demanded more and as they travelled subjected Burckhardt to various impositions and humiliations. It was not until the Shaykh and his men turned back to Kerak on 12th August that Burckhardt was able to make his own way with a succession of beduin guides. He sold his mare in order to buy provisions and went barefoot. Having stopped briefly at Shaubek he followed the Aqaba road for a day or so but then turned a little towards the south-west. He did so because he wanted to avoid Aqabah with its soldiers and officials and more immediately because he was 'particularly desirous of visiting Wadi Mousa, of the antiquities of which I had heard the country people speak in terms of great admiration; and from thence I ...hoped to cross the desert in a straight line to Cairo' (p. 418). The 'country people' he referred to were probably his informative hosts at Kerak and the 'terms of great admiration' which they used almost certainly resembled the information which Seetzen had been given at Hebron four years earlier. Listening to them Burckhardt may have wondered, as Seetzen did, if the ruins might be those of Petra, or he might have remembered something of what Seetzen had written in his letter of 10th July 1808, but he gives no indication of this.

He determined to make the detour to Wadi Musa, but he needed an excuse for so doing; as he said, to have left the Aqabah road 'out of mere curiosity to see the Wady would have looked very suspicious in the eyes of the Arabs'. Fortunately he knew that Aaron's tomb was situated 'at the extremity of the valley'[14]; and he therefore 'pretended to have made a vow to slaughter a goat in honour of Haroun (Aaron)... and by this stratagem I thought that I should have the means of seeing the valley on my way to the tomb. To this my guide had nothing to oppose; the dread of drawing upon himself, by resistance, the wrath of Haroun, completely silenced him' (p. 419)

At Al-Ji near the head of Wadi Musa he hired another guide to conduct him to the tomb and evidently told him the same story. He and this man walked, carrying a goat and a waterskin, through the Siq, past the Khazneh, the theatre and Qasr al Bint and then turned away from the valley to climb towards Jabal Harun. Just before sunset they reached a high plateau from which the tomb was clearly visible, and there they immolated the goat. They slept at the place of sacrifice and in the morning returned to Al-Ji by the way they had come. The 'stratagem' had succeeded admirably.

Three days later Burckhardt threw in his lot with a party of eight beduin, with twenty camels, making for Cairo. They crossed the Arabah and the Tih desert ('the most barren and horrid tract of country I have ever seen') in a series of forced marches, and reached Cairo before sunrise on September 4th.

Burckhardt announced his arrival in Cairo to his 'employers', as he called the Association for Promoting the Discovery of the Interior Parts of Africa, by a letter dated 12th September, telling them amongst much else that he had visited

[14] This was an uncharacteristically inaccurate statement; in fact he knew that the tomb was on Jabal Harun.

Wadi Musa 'and the remains of an ancient city which I conjecture to be Petra, the capital of Arabia Petræa, a place which, as far as I know, no European traveller has ever visited'. After a short description of the ruins he mentioned the tomb of Aaron and added, in parentheses, '(if I remember right, there is a passage in Eusebius, in which he says that the tomb of Aaron was situated near Petra)'[15]. In the next few weeks Burckhardt wrote letters to his family and friends telling them about his discovery, as well as a full account for the Association.[16] In one of the letters, written on 18th October 1812 to Renouard, he added to a brief description of the ruins the following words: 'I am ignorant whether Mr Seetzen has seen Wady Moosa; if not, the discovery is mine, and I pride myself a little on it because the spot is difficult of access, especially from the North. From Akabah it may perhaps be visited with less danger.[17] In the same letter he wrote that 'among several circumstances which strengthen my opinion, [that the ruins were those of Petra] is the authority of Eusebius who says that Aaron was buried near Petra (v. Reland geog. sacra)'[18]

[15] Burckhardt 1819, xlvi.

[16] Some of the letters Burckhardt wrote at this time are cited below, others are in Burckhardt-Sarasin 1956, 139, and in Otter 1824, 598–604. Other people also wrote spreading the news, not always very precisely. Lady Hester Stanhope, for example, told her cousin that 'Sheick Ibrahim, the traveller, after leaving me at Nazareth, went God knows where into the desert, and has discovered a second Palmyra...' (Cleveland, 1914, 151)

[17] B.L. Add. Ms 27620. Burckhardt was, of course, correct. No other traveller was able to reach Petra from the north (i.e. using Burckhardt's route) until the Turkish military occupation of the region in the 1890s (although Bankes and his companions did the journey in the reverse direction in 1818). Following Linant and Laborde's pioneering journey from Egypt, Sinai and Aqabah in 1828, however, hundreds of tourists used this route to reach Petra in succeeding decades.

[18] A difference between the phraseology of Burckhardt's letter of 12th September 1812, on the one hand, and the words used in the letter of 18th October and in his full report to the African Association is of some interest. In the letter of 12th September he writes, 'if I recollect right there is a passage in Eusebius...' whereas it is clear from the letter of October 18th and from his full report that he had consulted Reland's *Palaestina* (a compendium of geographical and other information derived from the works of classical authors) and that it was this from which he took Eusebius' statement. We do not know why he expressed himself differently in each of the three documents but a probable explanation is as follows. When he arrived in Cairo he was in rags and carrying almost nothing – certainly no books or notes on books, and when he wrote his first letter he must have been relying on an uncertain memory. It is most unlikely that he had a copy of Reland with him in Syria (he explains in another letter – Otter 1824, 597 – that he had few classical books there), and his reading of Reland must have been done before he left England in 1808. It is not surprising that four years later he could not remember where he had read the 'passage in Eusebius'. (It is, perhaps, more surprising that he did not remember Reland's bold and challenging map, Fig 1 above). We know from the letter of 18th October 1812 that he had papers sent from Damascus to Cairo and he probably also arranged to have others sent from England to await his arrival in Cario. By the time he wrote his letter of 18th October to Renouard and started to write his full account for the African Association he would have been able to collect his belongings, to have notes ready to hand and to be somewhat more definite and specific in his references. It is likely that he had notes from Reland with him rather than the two-volume book; if he had had the latter he would have been able to quote Eusebius' words as given by Reland:

'Mons Hor in quo mortuus est Aharon erat juxta urbem Petram.' (Reland 1714 Lib. III, 930)

Burckhardt finished the full account of the journey from Damascus before the end of 1812 and sent it off to London. The conclusion of his description of Petra is admirably short, precise and modest; it reads as follows:

> 'In comparing the testimonies of the authors cited in Reland's Palæstina, it appears very probable that the ruins in Wady Mousa are those of the ancient Petra, and it is remarkable that Eusebius says the tomb of Aaron was shewn near Petra. Of this at least I am persuaded, from all the information I procured, that there is no other ruin between the extremities of the Dead sea and Red sea, of sufficient importance to answer to that city. Whether or not I have discovered the remains of the capital of Arabia Petræa, I leave to the decision of Greek scholars'. (p. 431)

Unfortunately the Association made no announcement about Burckhardt's discovery until 1819, when they published his letter of 12th September 1812 in the 'Memoir on the Life and Travels of John Lewis Burckhardt' which appeared as a Foreword to his *Travels in Nubia*. This was followed in 1822 by his *Travels in Syria* containing the full account – ten years after Burckhardt's death.

W J BANKES and Burckhardt first met in Cairo towards the end of 1815 and immediately became good friends, Burckhardt describing Bankes in a letter as 'a very superior man.... indefatigable and accurate in his researches' and adding that 'he draws beautifully and is besides well stocked with learning'.[19] (Bankes was equally complimentary; he wrote in his journal that Burckhardt was 'made on purpose for a traveller, full of energy and enterprize', and praised his mastery of Arabic and his knowledge of the East).[20] They exchanged information and discussed further plans and when Bankes left Egypt for Syria at the end of the year he took with him 'invaluable information and advice' given him by Burckhardt. They continued their discussions by correspondence until 1817. In what proved to be Bankes' last letter to Burckhardt he wrote of his plans to explore the country beyond the Dead Sea; the letter was dated October 15th, 1817, the date of Burckhardt's death.[21]

In November, 1817 Bankes stayed in Aleppo for a few days and there met Charles Irby and James Mangles, two naval officers who like him had travelled extensively in Egypt and Nubia and who were now 'exploring' Syria. They met again on March 2, 1818, at Tiberias, where Bankes renewed a suggestion he had made in Aleppo that the three of them should travel together, and more specifically that the others should join him in a tour east of the Jordan and the Dead Sea and they 'embraced the opportunity of accompanying him'.[22] Ten days later they forded the Jordan and made for Jerash where they spent several days taking measurements and drawing plans. They then paid some beduin to guide them to Al Salt and Kerak, but things went badly. They reached Al Salt with some difficulty but having fallen out with their guides were obliged to retreat across the

[19] Burckhardt's letter to Clarke, 28th June 1816, in Otter 1824: 617–624.

[20] Bankes' journal of his journey from Alexandria to Cairo, August 1815, pp. 23–24, Egyptian Department, British Museum.

[21] Dorchester Record Office, Bankes papers, ref. no. HJI/75.

[22] Irby and Mangles 1823, 296.

Jordan and to find their own way to Jerusalem.[23] They stayed in Jerusalem for over a month, making more careful preparations than they had for their first attempt and adding to their numbers. Thomas Legh who had recently arrived in Jerusalem having travelled from Moscow, joined them and so did Giovanni Finati who had served Bankes as personal servant and interpreter in Egypt and Nubia.[24] Attended by other servants, guides and guards they made a party which at least initially numbered eleven men. Bankes had tried to persuade officials in Istanbul, Damascus, Jerusalem and elsewhere to authorise the journey, but finding none of them helpful, he and his companions 'determined to proceed, trusting to our numbers and force, and to try our fortune with the sheikh of Hebron' and with others beyond.[25] They left Jerusalem on May 6th, 1818.

There could have been no greater contrast between Burckhardt's deliberately unobtrusive manner of travelling and that of Bankes' party. Although as a matter of convenience they put on Arab dress they did not pretend to be other than Europeans. They had good horses, firearms and plenty of money and had phenomenally good luck in finding the right people to guide and protect them, foremost amongst whom was Yūsuf Majali, the shaykh of Kerak. (They evidently did not know that Shaykh Yūsuf had ill treated and cheated Burckhardt six years earlier. At first he seemed to them to be 'a plain, blunt, honest old man' and despite the faults in him which they discovered as they went he served them well; they realised that they could not have reached Wadi Musa without his help).[26] They found their way from Hebron to Kerak without much difficulty, and then Shaykh Yūsuf took them in charge. He led them to the tents of Muhammad Abu Rashid, a Shaykh of the Huwaytat tribe, who agreed without hesitation to take them to Wadi Musa. Unfortunately Abu Zaytun, the Shaykh of Wadi Musa, was present when Muhammad Abu Rashid undertook to do this, and he fiercely objected to the plan.[27] This was the prelude to five days of arguments, quarrels and negotiations. The situation became very tense and inter-tribal strife and bloodshed were feared, but eventually some sort of agreement was reached, 'peace was

[23] The beduin were of the same tribe, the Bani Sakhr, as those who were indirectly responsible for Burckhardt's retreat from his area in May, 1812 and for his decision in June to take the route west of the Jordan as far as Salt; see p. 12 and Note 11 above, and Finati 1830, II, 271–2.

[24] As a result of this accession to their numbers the journey of Bankes and his companions from Jerusalem to Petra and beyond is extraordinarily well documented; Bankes in his journal which commences with the departure from Jerusalem (the ms. of which is in the County Record Office at Dorchester, ref. no. HJ4/19 and 20, cited below as 'Journal'), Irby and Mangles 1823, 335–486 (most but not all of which is an edited version of Bankes' journal), Legh in MacMichael 1819, 187–267 and Finati 1830, II 234–278 all left accounts of it. Use is made of all these in the following summary; citations are given only when extracts are quoted.

[25] Irby and Mangles 1823, 338.

[26] Irby and Mangles 1823, 367.

[27] This was Muqabil Abu Zaytun, who continued to make difficulties for travellers at Petra until his death in or about 1848. We do not know exactly why he so strongly opposed the entry of the Bankes party; in his later encounters with visitors his object was primarily to ensure that they paid as much as possible for the privilege of entering 'his' territory. (At least a dozen published accounts by travellers between 1837 and 1849 mention him, some of them at length).

Fig 2. Bankes' sketch, no title. Probably Brünnow no. 825. Dorset Record Office ref. no. D/ BKL;IV/A8

proclaimed' and on 24th May Shaykh Muhammad was able to lead the travellers through the Siq and into Petra.

Shaykh Muhammad was apparently nervous that further trouble might develop while the travellers remained in Wadi Musa and he insisted that they must leave after two full days. During that short period, however, they were allowed to do whatever they wished (even to climb Jabal Harun and to enter Aaron's tomb) and Bankes, assisted by the others, produced an impressive body of work. Bankes was observant and perceptive and the portion of his journal devoted to Petra (much of which was written out by Irby at Bankes' dictation) contains over 11,000 words of information, comment and speculation. The journal and his sketches complement each other.[28] To take one example, Bankes commented at

[28] The reproductions of Bankes' sketches in this paper are from originals in the Archive of the Bankes family of Kingston Lacy and Corfe Castle held by the Dorset Record Office and owned by the National Trust. The author gratefully acknowledges permission to reproduce them. Dorset Record Office reference numbers are given in the caption to each illustration.

Fig 3. Bankes' sketch, 'Petra. The Nubian Geographer Nubicus Climat III says the houses at Petra were excavated in the rock' Dorset Record Office ref. no. D/BKL: IV/A9

length on the 'features of a sort of architecture that was new to me and is perhaps not elsewhere to be found', and he noted in particular the 'peculiar and indigenous style' of the tomb facades of the type shown in Fig. 2. At the angles of many of these, he continued, are 'pilasters with a considerable diminution upwards whose capital is very peculiar. I had already seen it at Bostra and at Shohba and had supposed it always the rough draft of an unfinished Ionic capital as it comes from the quarry. It is, however, almost universal on these tombs, and is certainly

Fig 4. Bankes' sketch, no title. View of Khubtha ridge from the West. Dorset Record Office ref. no. D/BKL: IV/A6

the Arabian order…'[29] (He would doubtless have been pleased to know that late nineteenth and twentieth century scholars would also recognise the affinity of the 'horned' capitals at Bosra and elsewhere in the Hauran with those at Petra and would call them, not 'Arabian' but 'Nabataean'.[30]

Similarly, on his sketch of troglodyte dwellings in Wadi Siyagh, (Fig. 3) he noted that 'the Nubian Geographer Nubicus Climat 3d. says that the houses at Petra were excavated in the rock.'[31] In his journal he describes some of these 'grottos'… which, he wrote, were certainly not sepulchral; they were residences, some large and roomy, others 'small and mean'. He also pointed out, however, that it was not 'universally true' that the people lived in excavated houses, as was 'evident from the great quantity of stones employed in the lesser kind of edifices which are scattered over the whole site which are no doubt the remains of dwellings of the inferior sort'.[32]

[29] Journal, II, 2. Irby and Mangles 1823, 409, judiciously substituted 'may be called' for 'is certainly'.

[30] Butler, 1919, wrote of 'a new architectural order' much as Bankes had. Cf. Dentzer-Feydy, 1986, 279–286 and McKenzie 1990, 185 and 190.

[31] Bankes was evidently familiar with *Geographia Nubiensis*… the title under which G. Sionita and J. Hesronita in 1619 had published their translations into Latin of an abridgement of the work of the twelfth century Arab geographer al-Idrisi, of whose name they were apparently unaware. Thereafter, until P. A. Jaubert published his *Geographie d'Edrisi* in 1836–40, the unknown author was commonly known as 'the Nubian Geographer'. (Some scholars, however, were familiar with al-Idrisi's name and work before Jaubert published; Reland, for example, and Renouard, who was to become Professor of Arabic at Cambridge in 1815 and who introduced Burckhardt to al-Idrisi's work in 1808. Burckhardt was particularly interested in what al-Idrisi wrote on Africa; see his notebooks in Cambridge University Library, Add. Ms. 282 and his letters to Renouard of 21st August 1808 and 3rd May 1811, British Library Add. Ms. 27620.

[32] Journal, II, 18.

Fig 5. Bankes' sketch, no title. The Khazneh. Dorset Record Office ref. no. D/BKL: IV/A7

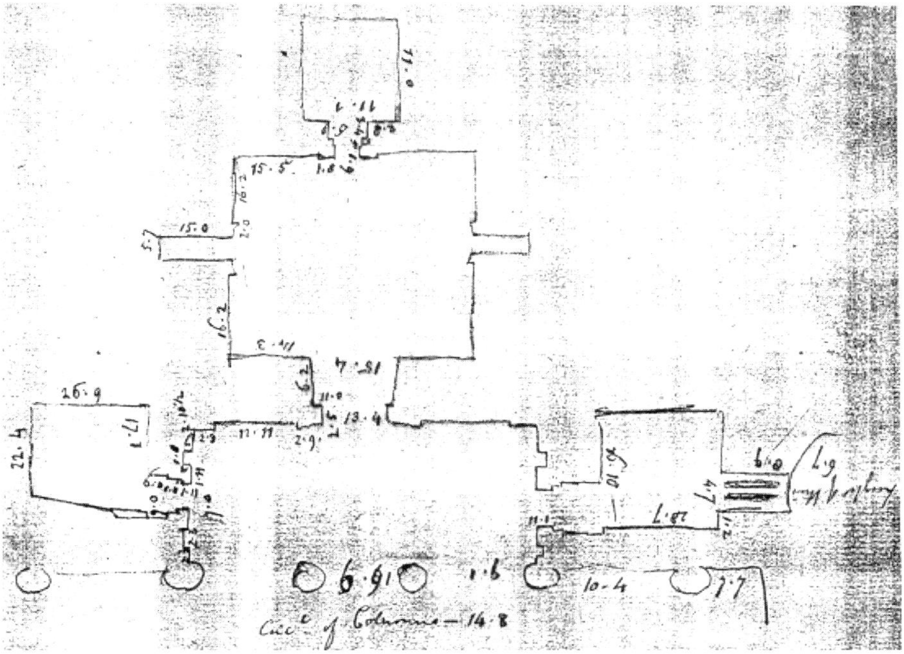

Fig 6. Bankes' sketch, 'Petra. Ground plan of gt. Tomb or Temple'. Dorset Record Office ref. no. D/BKL: IV/A5

Many of Bankes' sketches, like Fig. 4, are rough, but bold and effective. His fine drawing of the Khazneh (Fig. 5) is very different; it was, said Finati, 'the work of many hours'.[33] In style it resembles many of the drawings he did in Egypt, Syria and Asia Minor: beautifully drawn, realistic and accurate. He made no attempt to embellish his subjects or to hazard reconstructions. The plan of the interior, with its detailed measurements, (Fig. 6) must have been produced by several of the party working together. It stands comparison with Dalman's, done eighty years later.[34] Similarly, their measurements of the 'Turkmaniyah' tomb appear closer to the true dimensions than those of Brünnow and Domaszewski.[35] The plan and elevation of Qasr al Bint are, however, faulty in several respects.

All of the inscriptions which Bankes copied in Petra are shown, numbered and annotated on a lithograph printed in England after his return home in 1820 (Fig. 7) No. 2 on the lithograph is from the inscription on the rear wall of the Urn tomb, which, as Bankes noted, 'proves the establishment of Christianity at Petra'. No. 3 is an excellent copy of the Arrianos epitaph which was inscribed on a

[33] Finati 1830, 263. We are fortunate to have the drawing; it was purloined on the journey back from Petra to Acre, but Bankes was able to buy it back from the thief a few days later – Irby and Mangles 1823, 481.

[34] Dalman, 1911, plate xv.

[35] Brünnow and Domaszewski 1904–09, 363.

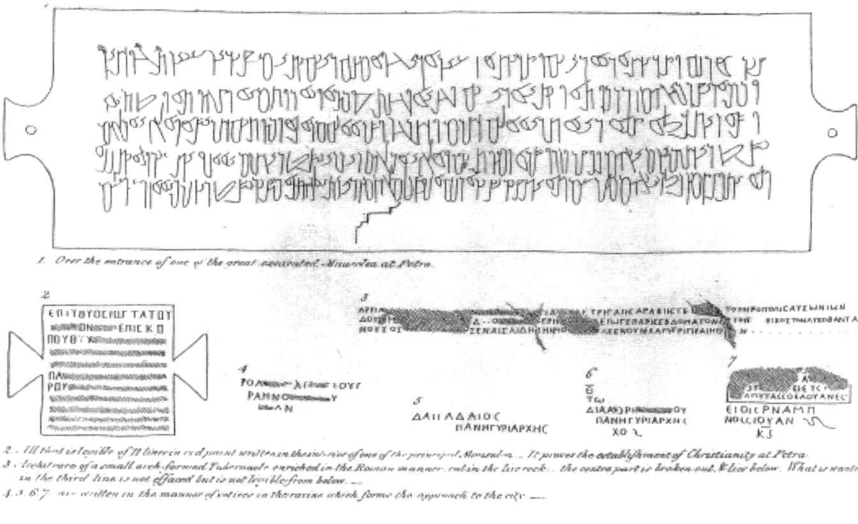

Fig 7. Lithograph of Bankes' copies of inscriptions at Petra

monument near the theatre which collapsed in 1847. The most important text is that at the top of the lithograph, the 'long inscription in some strange character which it was a great labour for my master to copy' as Finati put it.[36] This was the Nabataean inscription on the front of the Turkmaniyah tomb. The inscription is in five long lines, high up, and difficult to transcribe, but, as Bankes noted, the letters are cut 'with much neatness and precision and are in a state of wonderful preservation' and he was able to make an extraordinarily accurate copy. He also pointed out that the letters were 'exactly similar to those scratched upon the rocks in the Wadi Makutub and about the foot of Mount Sinai'.[37] In his journal and in a note on his fair copy of the inscription he appears to suggest that the script of the inscription might be the same as or related to that of the letter sent by the Nabataeans to Antigonus the One-eyed after his attack on them in 312 B.C. Thus he was not only the first person to record a Nabataean inscription in Petra and to recognise that this and the Sinaitic graffiti were in the same script, but also to attribute it to the Nabataeans and to put it into its correct historical context. [38]

At daybreak on 26th May the party started the long return journey to the north and after putting in a little more work on the survey of Jerash which Bankes had started in 1816 they reached Acre on June 25, soon after which they dispersed.[39]

[36] Finati 1830, 263.

[37] Journal II, 4–5.

[38] I owe the foregoing observation on the Turkmaniyah inscription to M.C.A. MacDonald. A more complete discussion of the subject will appear in a joint paper by Mr MacDonald and myself in the journal SYRIA, forthcoming.

[39] Irby and Mangles 1823, 479–486

After Bankes' return to England in 1820 friends and colleagues eagerly expected him to publish some of the work he had done in Egypt, Syria and elsewhere during his travels.[40] He did in fact take the first step by having a number of lithographs made, including the one of the Petra inscriptions; he must have intended to publish these but never did so. Part of the explanation is apparent in a letter he wrote to Byron in 1822 in which he said 'As for publication, I am always thinking of it, and from a strange mixture of indolence with industry always deferring it…'[41] and although he continued for some years to think about publishing some of his material, the only book which appeared under his name was the '*Narrative of the Life and Adventures of Giovanni Finati*' (1830) of which he was the translator and editor. In a footnote to p.148 of that book he wrote that he hoped to publish some of his Syrian material 'in the course of the present year', but he did not do so. Three years later he was accused of committing a homosexual offence. He was acquitted but when, in 1841, he was faced with a similar charge he fled to Italy where he remained until his death. His papers, on which the foregoing account is largely based, remained unregarded in his house, Kingston Lacy in Dorset, until nearly the end of the 20th Century. They may now be consulted at the Dorset County Record Office in Dorchester.

References

R. E. BRÜNNOW and A. von DOMASZEWSKI
1904–09 *Die Provincia Arabia.* Strasbourg

J. L. BURCKHARDT
1822 *Travels in Syria and the Holy Land.* London

C. BURCKHARDT-SARASIN and HANSRUDOLF SCHWABE-BURCKHARDT
1956 *Scheik Ibrahim (Johann Ludwig Buckhardt) Briefe an Eltern und Geschwister.* Basel.

H. C. BUTLER
1919 *SYRIA, Publication of the Princeton University Archaeological Expeditions to Syria in 1904–05, Div IIA.* Leyden

CLEVELAND, DUCHESS OF
1914 *The Life and Letters of Lady Hester Stanhope.* London

G. DALMAN
1911 The Khazneh at Petra. *Palestine Exploration Fund Annual.* London

J. DENTZER-FEYDY
1986 *Hauran I*, part 2, 279–286. Paris.

[40] See, for example, Legh in MacMichael 1819, 220, Turner 1820, II, 454, Leake in Burckhardt, 1822, iv.

[41] Letter, Bankes, Jan 2nd 1822, to Byron, in the archives of John Murray, Publishers, whose permission to publish this extract is greatly appreciated.

G. FINATI
1839 *Narrative of the Life and Adventures of Giovanni Finati.* (Translated and edited by W. J. Bankes.) London

W. L. GAGE
1866 *The Comparative Geography of Palestine and the Sinaitic Peninsula by Carl Ritter, Translated and adapted to the Use of Biblical Students.* Edinburgh.

C. L. IRBY and J. MANGLES
1823 *Travels in Egypt and Nubia, Syria and Asia Minor during the years 1817 and 1818.* London. (Printed for private distribution; reprinted London 1985)

P. A. JAUBERT
1836-40 *Géographie d'Édrisi*, 2 vols. Paris.

FR. KRUSE. See Seetzen

LEGH, T See MacMichael, 1819

N. N. LEWIS
2001 The Anger of Lady Hester Stanhope: some letters of Lady Hester, John Lewis Burckhardt and William John Bankes. *Travellers in the Levant*, ed. S. Searight and M. Wagstaff. Durham.

W. MacMICHAEL
1819 *A Journey from Moscow to Constantinople in the Years 1817, 1818.* London. (The last chapter of this book, p. 188f., is an account of T. Legh's journey to Petra with Bankes, Irby and Mangles, as told by Legh to MacMichael.)

J. McKENZIE
1990 *The Architecture of Petra.* London

W. OTTER
1824. *The Life and Remains of the Rev. E. D. Clarke.* London.

H. RELAND
1714 *Palaestina ex Monumentis Veteribus Illustrata.* Trajecti Batavorum

U. J. SEETZEN
1810 *A brief account of the Countries adjoining the Lakes of Tiberias, the Jordan and the Dead Sea.* Published for the Palestine Association of London. Bath. [Seetzen's name appears on the title page as M. Seetzen.]

U. J. SEETZEN
1854-55 *Reisen durch Syrien, Palästina, Phönicien, die Tranejordan-Länder, Arabia Petræa und Unter-Aegypten.* Ed. Dr. Fr. Kruse. 3 vols. Berlin.

G. SIONITA and J. HESRONITA
1619 *Geographia Nubiensis...* Paris.

W. TURNER
1820 *Journal of a Tour in the Levant* (3 vols). London

Periodicals

Fundgruben des Orients (Mines de l'Orient), Vol. 1, 1809, Vol 2, 1911. Wien.

Monatliche Correspondenz beförderung der Erd-und Himmelskunde, herausgegeben vom Freyherrn F. von ZACH, Vols. 13f. Gotha.

The Nabataeans in History

Robert Wenning

What is possible to write the history of the Nabataeans was done about twenty years ago by Glen W. Bowersock in his *Roman Arabia*. Recent research, excavations, inscriptions and other finds have changed the picture to some degree, but in general, Bowersock's treatment is still the best history of the Nabataeans available today. I neither want to repeat this nor give just an overview, but like to discuss a few of the problems[1]. The history which can be reconstructed from Greek and Roman sources is more or less the history of the contacts of the Greeks, Romans and Jews with the Nabataeans and it is their view of the Nabataeans. It is so to speak a history of Nabataean foreign affairs and this is only one part of their history. There is no Nabataean literature. The few, longer Nabataean inscriptions, coin legends and other archaeological evidence do not really fill the gap. Being a tribal society of nomadic tradition the Nabataeans could have had an oral tradition. This 'history' cannot be reconstructed.

There are more problems involved in writing a history of the Nabataeans. The period which can be described best is the first century B.C. and the first century A.D. This is supported by rich archaeological evidence. In A.D. 106 the Nabataean kingdom was transformed into *provincia Arabia*. The Nabataeans lost their influence in the area. The history of the second and third centuries A.D. is no longer a history of the Nabataeans, but of the Roman *provincia Arabia*, although the Nabataean population and their culture survived into the Late Roman period.

The step into history

What happened before the first century B.C. and what happened before 311 B.C. when the Nabataeans are undoubtedly mentioned in historical sources for the first time, is still unknown. I do not want to speculate on the origins of the Nabataeans, the area they occupied, and the date of their origins[2]. In my opinion, all suggestions given so far are problematic to indicate where one should look for the

[1] I would like to thank the organizers of the conference for all the help they offered and especially for the wonderful opportunity of this conference. Many colleagues gave me value comments on my paper, I express my thanks to G. W. Bowersock, S. Dar, D. F. Graf, H. Gitler, J. F. Healey, N. Kokkinos, M. C. A. Macdonald, K. D. Politis, P. Parr, J. Patrich, I. Shatzman, and F. Zayadine. M. Neujahr and K. D. Politis kindly proof-read the English of my draft; any remaining mistakes are mine. The article was transmitted in 2002 and up-dated February 2004.

[2] Cf. Milik 1982; Knauf 1986; Graf 1990; with some critics Macdonald 2000, 47–48; Hackl-Jenni-Schneider 2003, 15–19.

origins of the Nabataeans. All that can be said with certainty is that the Nabataeans are known in the sources since the fourth century B.C. Up to that time the Qedarites, the dominant Arab tribe of the Persian period, controlled the south from the Hejaz and all of the Negev into southern Palestine with a local center at Lachish. The Qedarites are known as the immediate neighbours of the Achaemenid province, Yehud, from biblical and other sources[3]. They must have controlled the frankincense trade in their realm.

It now seems that there is some evidence for the time when the Nabataeans appeared in history and when they became the main traders of frankincense from the Arabia peninsula to the Mediterranean World. Aramaic ostraca finds indicate that the Persian province Idumaea must have been established before 363 B.C.[4]. The historical context was after the revolt of the Pharao Hakoris and King Euagoras from Salamis in 385/80 B.C. For some reason the Qedarites joined the coalition against the Persians[5], probably after Hakoris won the Mediterranean coast around 383 B.C., and when Euagoras needed help to resist a new attack by the Persians in 381 B.C. After the Euagoras revolt was put down it is assumed that a reorganisation of Arabia took place by the Persians before the Persian campaign against Egypt in 373 B.C. Beside the establishment of Idumaea, which meant the loss of a large territory, the Qedarites obviously lost of their privileges of the frankincense trade. It can be assumed that they were replaced by the Nabataeans[6]. Arabia did not become a Persian province and enjoyed still a large degree of autonomy. It might be that the Nabataeans lived in the Hejaz or lived in southern Jordan and therefore were chosen by the Minaeans or the Persians to become their middlemen and by this rose to influence and power in the area. On the other hand it has been argued that the Persians lost their interest in the former area of the Edomite Kingdom after about 400 B.C., which allowed the Nabataeans to gain importance in this area[7]. All these changes contributed to the process by which the Nabataeans gained control of the frankincense from Dedan to Gaza. Gaza, the final destination of the frankincense route was granted special status as a Persian garrison[8]. It allowed the Persian King to control both the incense trade as well as the routes to Egypt by water and overland.

There seemed to be other evidence for this early period of the Nabataeans, the so-called Philisto-Arabian coins and some theophoric names. Both groups turned out to be of no such relevance. One of the consequences of the reorganisation of the area seems to be the introduction of coinage minted at Gaza, the so-

[3] Knauf 1985a, 96–108.

[4] Lemaire 1999.

[5] Diod. Sic. 15.2.3–4.

[6] Nabataeans are listed as traders of the frankincense route in the younger sources and not the Qedarites. Concerning the relationship between Qedarites and Nabataeans I do not follow the assumption of Knauf 1985a, 106–108 who takes the Nabataeans as a subtribe of the Qedarites. The punishment of the Qedarites would loose its sense, if the privilegies were turned to a subtribe in such a tribal system. Furtheron, there are differences between the Qedarites and the (later) Nabataeans concerning language, religion, trade routes etc.

[7] Knauf 1988, 76–77.

[8] Mildenberg 1990.

called Philisto-Arabian coins[9]. These coins are divided into two groups of minting authorities by Mildenberg, the first he attributed to city of Gaza, the second to regional non Persian rules of northern Arabia[10]. He described some heads on the coins as portraits of bedouins[11], among which one would expect Nabataeans following the above considerations. There is more than one problem with this interpretation and with the identification made by Mildenberg. It is not easy to trace a particular prototype; some of the 'portraits' seem to belong to a completely different context. At present, these coins do not contribute to the understanding of the Nabataeans.

A continuity from Edomites to Nabataeans is often stated, but there is a gap of some centuries between Edomite and Nabataean settlements[12]. There does not seem to be any more Edomite settlement in Edom after around 400 B.C. Nabataean settlement of Edom barly started before the second century B.C., but took place mainly in the first century B.C. and first century A.D. Petra with some finds of the second half of the third century B.C. is at the beginning of this process[13]. Nevertheless, Bartlett is not completely wrong in assuming a kind of continuity from Edomites to Nabataeans[14], but in a more complex development. Those Edomites who had not left their homes to go merging with the Idumaean population, probably returned to a nomadic life and may have joined tribes in the Hisma or other desert areas[15]. Could these parts of the regional population have preserved the memory of Qaus, venerated by Nabataeans as Qos four hundred years later? Or is Qos passed on to the Nabataeans by the Hellenistic Idumaeans, among whom Qos was a prominent deity? One way or another there is a continuity.

Petra in 311 B.C.

One gets the impression from the famous report of Hieronymus of Cardia about Petra and the Nabataeans[16] that Petra in 311 B.C. was not yet the seat of the tribe and certainly not the religious center of the Nabataeans. Therefore, one should not misinterprete the site during this period. It may be described as a camp site

[9] Gitler 2000; Mildenberg 2000.

[10] Mildenberg 2000, 382–283 pls. LVIII–LX. Cf. Knauf 1985b, 24–28.

[11] Mildenberg 2000, 385, 390–391 nos. 71, 75, 79, 80, 83, 85. Nos. 71, 75 rather portray the Great King or Persian officials because of the *kidaris*. No. 80 is of greater importance. The obverse could show a ruler, a male head crowned with a diadem. Contrary to Mildenberg it is not a cap, because the curls overlap the diadem. The reverse shows a warrior riding a dromedary. He sits in the so-called shadad-saddle and is clad with a sword. There is a thymiaterion in front of him. Therefore one may assume a warrior deity of the desert people rather than a fighting king. Any name and context given to the rider and the ruler remain hypothetical.

[12] Hart 1986; 1987a–b; Schmid 2000a, 109.

[13] Wenning 1987, 200–201.

[14] Bartlett 1979; but cf. Bartlett 1990.

[15] Knauf 1988, 76–77; Knauf 1995.

[16] His report is found in the Geography of Diodorus Siculus 2.48–49; 19,94–100.

with a few people in charge of the frankincense stores and the herds of dromedaries in the surrounding area.

Concerning the year 311 B.C., instead of the common 312 B.C., one should follow the reconstruction of Errington 1977 and Winnicki 1989 describing the activities of the *diadochs* in Syria in the years 312 to 311 B.C. They date the battle at Gaza between Demetrios Poliorketes and Ptolemy in the autumn instead the spring of 312 B.C. Demetrios lost and went back to Tripolis in Phoenicia. Ptolemy established his interest up to Sidon. In the following spring of 311 B.C. Antigonos Monophtalmos occupied the Phoenician coastal cities. From here he sent two expeditions against the Nabataeans, the first under the command of Demetrios, the second under Athenaios. Both campaigns which were intended to subjugate the Nabataeans, or at least to bring back booty[17], failed. The information comes from the above mentioned Greek officer and historian Hieronymus of Cardia, who led a third expedition to the Dead Sea.

Concerning the identification of 'Petra' (in Greek literal 'the rock') by Diodorus Siculus is debated among scholars[18]. The continuity of the place-name seems to be a good argument to identify the famous Petra with the 'Petra' in the ancient report. If one looks for the easily defendable rock with only one access where the Nabataeans tried to hide their goods, as described in the report, Umm al-Biyara is the best candidate[19]. Nevertheless, this identification does not seem to be correct if one takes the data of Diodorus seriously. In chapter 95 he gives the distance of 2,200 stades from the district of Idumaea, that is about 250 miles. This is often misstated as it is thought that the figures are wrong. But Diodorus did not describe the distance between Gaza and Petra[20] (about 130 miles), but rather the distance from Phoenicia to Idumaea. The situation is more clear in chapter 98. After plundering 'Petra' Demetrius tried to go as far as possible before camping near the Dead Sea at a distance of 300 stades to 'Petra', that is about 34 miles. The distance from the famous Petra to the Dead Sea would be about 74 miles. The distance reported in Diodorus locates the site of Khirbet es-Sela^{c}. Therefore the 'Petra' of Hieronymus and Diodorus should be identified with Khirbet es-Sela^{c}[21]. The site also fits the description in Diodorus as a natural refuge with an easibly defendable ascent.

The early material found so far at the Petra we know today identifies this site as one of various places to store goods by the Nabataeans. Gradually this site became more established. This may be due to the fact that the plateau of Khirbet

[17] It might be that the Greeks noticed the Nabataeans and their wealth for the first time during the conquest of Gaza in 332 B.C., although the sources mention only Arabs (Arrian 2.25–27; cf. Plutarch, Alexandros 25.6; Pliny, Hist. Nat. XI.33.62). The rumour about their wealth could easily have influenced these later campaigns.

[18] Starcky 1966, 886–900, 943; Lindner-Hübner-Gunsam 2001, 273–275. This discussion is connected with the debated identification of Old Testament Sela (= rock) in the Edomite mountains.

[19] Horsfield 1938,3–4. I do not agree with Knauf 1997, 21–22, who identified "Petra" with Jebel el-Hubtha.

[20] The attacks of the Greeks on 'Petra' did not happen during the siege of Gaza.

[21] Zayadine 1999, 89–90; Lindner-Hübner-Gunsam 2001 (description of the site).

es-Sela^c was difficult to reach, as opposed to the valley of Petra, where the Umm el-Biyara could have served as a refuge[22]. For the Greeks the 'capital' of the Nabataeans remained to be a 'Petra', a rocky site in the mountains of Edom. They did not care about the changes in that area as they had no other knowledge about it before the second century B.C. The Nabataeans, on the other hand, had names for both sites. *Raqmu* was the name for the Petra we know today[23]. The Greeks had no problem to connect their 'Petra' with Raqmu, the 'capital' of the Nabataeans since the second century B.C. Probably they did not even realised that the name shifted from one site to the other.

The account of Hieronymus of the way of life of the Nabataeans is more idealistic than it seems at first. One can romanticise the wild and freedom-loving nomads of this account. But here a more general picture of nomads was constructed by using common topoi[24]. The account should be read with caution. There is no reason to deny the nomadic nature of the Nabataeans. Archaeological evidence demonstrates that the Nabataeans lived predominantely in tents and possibly in rock-cut caves until the Augustan period, when they started to build houses[25]. Petra should be seen as a great tent site for a long time during the earlier periods.

Petra, the seat of the tribe

There are a few inscriptions referring to Nabataean traders or Nabataean slaves in the Hellenistic world[26]. The oldest reference for *Petraioi* is probably an inscription from Miletus from the middle of the third century B.C.[27]. Others belong to the second half of the second century. A few literary sources of the Hellenistic period[28] show some Nabataeans at different places in the third and second centuries B.C., but do not contribute to the question of the sedentarisation of the Nabataeans, rather illustrate their nomadic way of life. The sedentarisation of the Nabataeans or at least of parts of Nabataean society is understood as a longer process which started when Petra was chosen to become the seat of the tribe, that is the residency of the royal family and the nobility of the tribe. Dealing with a tribal Arab community in a process of transition from nomadism to sedentarism which follows traditions other than Greek poleis, this kind of sedentarisation does not mean urbanisation, but representation of the upper class. Living in tents did not exclude luxury. A royal court was established at Petra, and became known as the capital of the Nabataeans in the Greek world[29]. Among the earliest evidence

[22] So far no finds from the earlier Hellenistic periods are reported from Umm el-Biyara.

[23] The Nabataean name of Khirbet es-Sela^c remains unknown.

[24] Hornblower 1981; Graf 1990, 51–53.

[25] Stucky 1992, 139; Kolb 1997, 62–63; 2000, 229–230.

[26] Cf. Wenning 1987, 22–23; Roche 1996.

[27] Rehm 1997, no. 140/37 (cf. no. 174).

[28] Papyri of the Zenon archives, Poseidippos of Pella, Agatharchides of Cnidus in Diod. Sic., 1/2 Macc.

[29] Cf. Josephus, AJ 14,1,4.

for it is an inscription from Priene. The city of Priene in Asia Minor sent an embassy to Petra in about 129 B.C.[30]. Petra also seems to be mentioned in Chinese sources in 126 B.C.[31]

The regional and local deity Dushara[32] became the tutelar deity of the tribe, of many tribal clans and of the Nabataean dynasty. Whether the name Dushara is related to the mountains of Edom or describes a deity of the wilderness is debatable[33]. Being the deity of Petra, the seat of the tribe, Dushara became the most prominent of the deities venerated by the Nabataeans. Petra became the political and religious center of the Nabataeans living either at Petra or elsewhere in the Nabataean realm. Nabataean clans assembled at Petra for their festivities. The area around the center of the city is full of such places and the clans buried their dead under the protection of Dushara in the famous rock-cut tombs at Petra[34].

The transfer of the tribal seat to Petra and the gradual emergence of the capital might be dated into the second half of the second century B.C. when there is more archaeological evidence[35]. Stucky dated the beginning of a tent settlement at Az-Zantur to the end of the second century B.C.[36]. Nabataean pottery and coins developed not much before 100 B.C.; the need for these indicates a growing population. One should not forget that this development would be the background for the struggle between the Nabataeans and the Hasmonaeans concerning territories on the east of the Dead Sea and Jordan River.

The Nabataean tribe settled at Petra sometime before 96 B.C. when Dushara is mentioned in the oldest dated Nabataean inscription at Petra in the Bab as-Siq sanctuary. The well-hewn large triclinium of the Bab as-Siq sanctuary[37] indicates that one could expect such rock-cut living-rooms, cultic cellae, triclinia and tombs some decades before, though there are no archaeological criteria identifying such early rooms and tomb façades. The same is true for the dating of the betyls, the aniconical representations of Nabataean deities at Petra[38].

The First Century B.C.

The earliest concrete genuine Nabataean works of arts are coins and pottery. What is typical for the beginning of Nabataean art is a direct, though simplified imitation of Hellenistic prototypes. This can be demonstrated in coinage[39] as well

[30] Hiller von Gaertringen 1906, 84–91 No. 108, V 168; cf. Bowersock 1983, 22.

[31] Discussed by Graf 1996, 209.

[32] Macdonald 1993, 345; AAE 2000, 48.

[33] Dyma 1999; Healey 2001, 85–107; Wenning 2003b.

[34] McKenzie 1990; Wenning 2003c.

[35] Wenning 2003d.

[36] Stucky 1992, 137–139.

[37] Cf. McKenzie 1990, 170f.; Zayadine-Farajat 1991, 275–278.

[38] Cf. Wenning 2001.

[39] Wenning 2003d, 145–147. Cf. coins of Aretas II; Kushnir-Stein-Gitler 1992/93 with convincing early dating against the late dating by K. Schmitt-Korte.

as in pottery[40]. While in minor art this kind of influence is more obvious, in monumental art, particularly the tomb façades, eastern traditions continued and adopted Hellenistic forms relatively late, but then culminated dramatically in the Khazneh, an almost pure Alexandrine style façade of the third quarter of the first century B.C.[41]. Social institutions adopted Hellenistic forms and behaviour as well, as can be seen from later coin legends and titles in inscriptions. Among the social elements where Arab and ancient Near Eastern traditions and Hellenistic institutions converged is the banquet/symposium and the *marzeah*, an assembly of a particular group to carry out the veneration of their tutelar deity or to have a memorial meal[42]. Nabataean society remained a tribal organisation and the sheikhs/kings of the tribe seem to have followed the behaviour of Hellenistic eastern kings only within the constraints the tribal rules allowed them[43].

One should not overemphasise the Hellenistic influence on the Nabataeans in the late Hellenistic period. No doubt, the Nabataeans were hellenized by the end of the second century B.C., but as far as this development is reflected in the arts, Nabataean culture seems to gradually change by about the middle of the first century B.C. One cannot speak of a substantial Hellenisation before the last third of the first century B.C. The development of an unique Nabataean style in the arts follows the same gradual transition phases[44]. Characteristic Nabataean art can be found from the Augustan period onwards.

Often the coins of Aretas III, minted at Damascus during the years 84–72 B.C.[45], are seen as evidence for a greater Hellenisation of Petra. It is doubtful, though, that this conclusion can be made on the basis of these coins. They continue in style and legend of his predecessors coins. The coin legend calling Aretas 'Philhellenos' might reflect a legitimate story that he took the crown of Coele Syria to help the people of Damascus because he was chosen as King of Coele Syria by the citizens of Damascus. First in line was Aretas the legal successor of the Syrian King Antiochus XII Dionysus who was defeated and killed by the Nabataeans in the battle of Motho. Aretas did not establish a Nabataean power at Damascus, but continued the policy of his Seleucid predecessors and acted as King of Coele Syria[46]. It is difficult to establish what benefit the Nabataeans gained from his rule at Damascus. Aretas defeated Alexander Iannaeus but did not get back any 'Nabataean' cities or areas occupied by the Hasmonaeans. He could not stop him to conquer cities east of the Jordan, such as Pella. It is interesting that the Damascus coins did not appear at Petra under Aretas III. Here,

40 Schmid 2000a, 110–125, 133, 147–150, 157.

41 Cf. Schmid 2000a, 157–158; Schmid 2000b, 486–492; Wenning 2003d, 150–161 (with new photographs of the reliefs).

42 Cf. Wenning 1997, 181–182; McLaughlin 2001.

43 Wenning 1997, 179–181. See below the description of a banquet by Strabo. Cf. furtheron the critics of Macdonald 1991 on the understanding of the Nabataean society as a Bedouin state by E. A. Knauf.

44 Schmid 2000a, 24, 37–38, 147–150, 157–159; Wenning 2003d.

45 Meshorer 1975, 12–16 pl. 1; Schmitt-Korte-Price 1994, 93–94.

46 Cf. Bowersock 1983, 25.

the peculiar imitations of Hellenistic coins of Aretas II continued. True Nabataean coins did not appear before the reign of Obodas II in 62–60 B.C.[47].

During his last year, Aretas III had to accept Roman sovereignty. Even the Nabataean kings kept their autonomy until A.D. 106. The decision of how to organise the Roman East was taken by Pompey in 63 B.C. with the new *provincia Syria* and the client kingdoms of the Hasmonaeans and Nabataeans. The realisation to make the Nabataeans Roman clients was concluded when M. Aemilius Scaurus undertook an expedition against the Nabataeans in 62 B.C. and accepted their submission together with a large amount of money from Aretas III before reaching Petra[48]. In 58 B.C. Scaurus issued a coin at Rome to commemorate the subjugation of Aretas[49].

Malichus I (59–30 B.C.) being mostly a loyal client to Rome (aside from the alliance with the Parthians in 41/40 B.C.) supported the triumvir Marc Antony, the legal Roman representative in the East. The love-affair of Antony with Cleopatra VII and her attempts to recreate a Ptolemaic empire is well-known. She demanded great parts of the Roman East. Antony did not grant her as much, but nevertheless gained territory in 34 B.C. This probably included the lucrative balsam groves on the Dead Sea shores and the control of the Red Sea, which was more strategic for Nabataean trade. Cleopatra made the Herodian and Nabataean kings to fight each other in order to weaken them. The battles resulted with a major defeat of the Nabataeans near ‘Amman in 31 B.C. causing the Nabataeans to accept Herod as their *prostates*, their overlord[50]. But little resulted of this defeat as Octavian's victory of Actium and the death of Antony and Cleopatra completely changed the situation.

The Augustan period

Octavian confirmed the autonomy of both kings. He changed not the previous border between the two kingdoms apart from the fact that he gave the important harbour city of Gaza to Herod and allowed him to keep the conquered city Esbous. At that time he did not cut off other Nabataean territories. In 23 B.C. Herod became protector of the Batanea, the Trachonitis and the Auranitis, and in 20 B. C. of the Gaulanitis, areas which were of greater interest to the Nabataeans and settled by Arab tribes[51] if not partly by Nabataeans. The Herodian protector-

[47] The existence of this king is much debated. The numismatic evidence seems to support the assumption (cf. Wenning 1993b, 32–33; Schmitt-Korte-Price 1994, 96–97) and as well the Tell esh-Shuqafiya inscription (Fiema-Jones 1990), if the crucial number in the dating, year 18 or year 14 of Cleopatra, can unambiguously be read as ‘year 18’ as it seems.

[48] After 62 B.C. Aretas III is not mentioned in the sources. One should not exclude the possibility that Aretas III lost his crown by decision of the tribal assembly because of these events. Obodas II followed him in 62/61 B.C. Kokkinos 1998, 95 note 40 prefers to lower the reign of Aretas III to 60 B.C., directly followed by Malichus I in 60/59 B.C.

[49] Schmitt-Korte 1991, 145–146 nos. 67–70.

[50] Cf. Bowersock 1983, 40–43.

[51] Cf. Schottroff 1982; Macdonald 1993; Wenning 1994; Knauf 1998.

ate of these regions meant there was a kind of Jewish-Roman buffer zone between Syria and the Arab groups to the east, and the south[52], and the control of Nabataean trade into Syria to the displeasure of the Nabataeans[53].

These events did not affect the Nabataean art, though the fall of the Ptolemaic kingdom in 30 B.C. probably did. There might have been an interest in Alexandrian art for a longer period. The Khazneh may be part of this as it can be assumed that Alexandrian influence became one prominent factor after the fall of the Ptolemaic kingdom when Alexandrian artists were seeking employment. During this phase the formulation of Nabataean type column capitals, the Isis-niche from the Wadi Siyyagh dated to 26/25 B.C.[54], the dual-portraits of king and queen on the coins of Obodas III (since 29/28 B.C.) and possibly somewhat later wall-paintings and Alexandrine prototypes among the sculptures and the terracotta figurines[55]. How the great building projects and their decorations are influenced by Alexandrian influence[56] needs more study. If the first phase of the so-called 'Great Temple' was indeed an *oecus corinthius*, a peristyle building and a monumental reception hall[57], such influence is possible[58].

While an approach towards Hellenistic forms continues over a longer period amongst Nabataean artifacts, by the last third of the first century B.C. a new style was created, which is today called 'Nabataean'. This new style affected all genres of art but culminated in the great cultic and public buildings of the Augustan period in the centre of Petra which have been described as a conception of a new Nabataean identity[59]. Such a splendid new style of monumental art can be found elsewhere in the Roman East of that period[60]. Concerning Petra, the expedition by Aelius Gallus into Arabia Felix in 25/24 B.C. reactivated the frankincense route for the Nabataeans to an extent not seen before, and created immense wealth. The acceptance of temples and figural sculpture by the Nabataeans, and living in built structures, exhibiting of wealth and a hospitable royal court with many foreigners, as described by Strabo, is not only embedded in the overall

[52] Bowersock 1983, 50; Kasher 1988, 160–161, map 15.

[53] There are three aspects to understand this decision. The main reason as given by Josephus is that Augustus gave the areas to Herod, because he trusted in Herod to bring peace to the area (Josephus, AJ 15.10.1) and because Herod was highly regarded by him (Josephus, BJ 1.20.4). On the other hand, Rome did not agree to the Ituraean-Nabataean demands concerning the regions (cf. Kasher 1988, 157–160). At least, concerning the date 23 B.C. it should not be excluded, that the decision is to be taken as a concealed punishment of the Nabataeans after the failure of the Aelius Gallus expedition into Arabia Felix in 25/24 B.C. Because of the vague circumstances no official measures were taken in the first years after the expedition (Bowersock 1983, 49). Later, Syllaeus, the Nabataean advisor, was accused of treachery concerning the expedition and was beheaded at Rome for this (Strabo, Geogr. 16.4.23–24).

[54] Merklein-Wenning 1998.

[55] Wenning 2003d, 161–164.

[56] Cf. McKenzie 1990, 85–104, 124–126; Tholbecq 1997, 13–14 (cf. his contribution to the conference).

[57] Cf. Förtsch 1996, 83–87.

[58] Schluntz 1998, 221–222; Wenning 2003a.

[59] Freyberger 1998, 25, 103.

[60] Freyberger 1998, 26, 121–123.

cultural development of the east during this period, but seems to be a product of the particular political and economic situation of the Nabataeans.

Strabo on the Nabataeans

Strabo is the main literary source for some of our insights into the social and cultural order of Petra and the Nabataeans during this period[61]. Postdating the execution of Syllaeus in 6 B.C. the report of the Nabataeans seems to be written before 3/2 B.C.[62]. Strabo was told about that by his friend, the philosopher Athenodorus of Tarsus[63]. His report is very illuminating. On the other hand, one must be cautious with particular information of Athenodorus, who does not understand the tribal aspects of Nabataean society very well. For example, if he admires the Nabataean government because the Nabataeans were not engaged in lawsuits with one another, contrary to the many Romans and foreigners at Petra, he seemed not to know that the judicature was the responsibility of the king and tribal organisations, usually during the great assembly of the tribe.

Athenodorus describes King Obodas as a man who did not care much about public and particularly military affairs, a trait, as he remarks, common to all Arabian kings. Attributing his prejudice to a misunderstanding of how the Nabataean King held court and left the handling of public affairs to his vezir, he influenced old[64] and current scholarship describing Obodas as a weak and lazy king[65]. The great building programme at Petra and elsewhere in the Nabataean Kingdom and other developments which took place under Obodas, contradict such a statement as these activities cannot be attributed only to Syllaeus, inspite of his ambitious.

According to Strabo the Nabataeans publicly fined anyone who has diminished his possessions. This again reflects tribal law. While herds of camels or sheep might belong to a family, pasture land and water rights are owned by the tribe. A single member of the tribe was not allowed to give up part of it. The tribal assembly could punish members violating the law and honour all who contribute to assets of the tribe[66].

Athenodorus claims that the Nabataeans did not have many slaves since they were served by their relatives; once again reflecting an element of tribal structures. Concerning slaves Athenodorus may be correct since various inscriptions indicate that there were some slaves, though their number seems rather small.

In this context Athenodorus describes the Nabataean King as *demotikos*, acting as the man of the people (often incorrectly translated as 'democratic'),

[61] Strabo, Geogr. 16.4.21–26.

[62] Cf. Bowersock 1983, 55.

[63] Probably Athenodorus, son of Sandon, and not the older Athenodorus Kordylion. He was one of the teachers of Octavian.

[64] Josephus, AJ 16.7.6.

[65] Bowersock 1983, 46, 50.

[66] Tribal rules of modern Bedouin societies might be different, cf. Henninger 1989, 83–138.

because the king himself serves his guests at communal meals. It is important to note the context in which this is said[67]. Athenodorus mentions banquets of groups of thirteen people, each banquet with two girl-singers, organised by the king in a magnificent style. The custom was that no one drink more than eleven cupfuls, each time using a different golden goblet. This indicates that it was a particular event with clear and possibly formal or ritual regulations. In the next sentence Athenodorus speaks about the account that the king has to give in the tribal assembly (*demos*), where even his mode of life is scrutinised. This fits very well with the position of the tribal leader, in spite of any title, to be *primus inter pares*. He is supported by the nobility of the tribe. Even though leadership is dynastic, the king depends on the nobility. He will be jugded by a successful rule and he must give benefits to the nobility. Along with positions and estates, and sharing in trade profits, he has to give communal meals in a magnificent style at his own cost. Here he acts as the *rab marzeah*, personally serving his guests, to show them that he is of no higher rank than them. A similar institution is known from the Graeco-Roman world, where a *symposiarches* or a *quinquennalis* headed an association. This was an important social element but does not seem to be a *demotikos* in the sense Athendorus indicated the Nabataean custom.

Athenodorus correctly describes that Nabataean cities such as Petra had no protective walls. This was not on account of the *pax Augusta*, as he states, but according to the tradition of tent sites and Arab-Semitic settlements[68]. When he declares that the land produces no horses, and camels afford the service they require instead of horses, he probably mixed it with his impression of caravans. From literature concerning battles as well as from archaeological evidence, it is known that riding horses was common amongst Nabataeans[69].

Another prejudice of Athenodorus was to characterise the Nabataeans as businessmen and traders, but not very good warriors. Indeed, the way they used the desert for military tactics was quite different from the Roman way of trying to win on the traditional battlefield or by laying siege to towns. The Nabataeans required a strong military power to protect their trade routes and caravans. They fought many battles against Hasmonaeans and Herodians. They participated in Roman armies as clients and at least as a dromedary unit after A.D. 106. Therefore one should be cautious to see them as such bad warriors[70]. Petra itself was not the place to show much of a military presence as opposed to Rome and other Roman capitals and cities, such as Caesarea.

Athenodorus describes Nabataean dwellings as houses built of stone and being costly. The new excavated wealthy mansion of az-Zantur IV[71] seem to be later than the houses visited by Athenodorus at Petra, but it becomes clear from

[67] Wenning 1997, 180–181.

[68] Cf. a tent site at Oboda (Negev 1983, 46, fig. p. 73) and the open settlements of the first centuries B.C./A.D. in the Decapolis and the Hauran (Wenning 1994, 12–14).

[69] Cf. Macdonald 1997, 74–75, who suggested that Athenodorus/Strabo could have received this information from Aelius Gallus.

[70] Graf 1994.

[71] Kolb 2000; Kolb 2001; Kolb-Keller 2001.

the source, that at his time there must have been more than one such house. Living in built houses had become a normal dwelling form. Athenodorus does not mention tent or cave dwellings which also must have existed, and which were also costly to decorate. It might be that he only liked to compare these rich Nabataean mansions with houses he was familiar with. Nevertheless, his statement is important for the dynamic changes which had taken place at Petra within only a few decades[72].

A well-known misunderstanding is Athenodorus' statement that the Nabataeans regard their dead as dung burying their kings beside dung-heaps. He confuses the similar-sounding words for dung and tomb[73]. No archaeological evidence indicates such a custom which Athenodorus claimed. On the contrary, most Nabataeans or at least the nobibilty of Nabataean clans are buried in huge rock-cut tombs with large façades. Among them are the Khazneh and the so-called Urn Tomb, which may be royal. There are also hundreds of shaft tombs and simple graves (some of which are of later date). There is nothing dishonourable amongst the many burials.

Athenodorus listed locally produced and imported products. Local products included gold, silver[74] and most of the aromatics, despite the fact that Nabataeans were actually trading, and not producing these. Imports are brass, iron, purple garb, styrax, crocus, costaria, embossed works (*toreuma*), paintings (*graphe*) and moulded works (*plasma*). In at least one case, *plasma*, that is sculptures, Athenodorus is again wrong. There are various Nabataean sculptures at Petra worked in the local sandstone pre-dating A.D. 106[75].

In general, Athenodorus described more what he believed to see than reality. It is apparent that he was so proud of his own Greek culture be superior, that he was asthonished to find such a rich culture among a people he considered barbarians. Nevertheless, his report describes Petra as a splendid part of the Graeco-Roman world during the late first century B.C. without any unusual feature, characterised by the previous reports of Hieronymus of Cardia.

The enigma of the Nabataeans in the Hauran

Good relations between Hasmonaeans and Nabataeans during the second century B.C. are reflected in the Books of Maccabees as indicated above. This concerns the Hauran and the Galaaditis. At that time Bosra was not yet a Nabataean settlement. There is little information about other Arab tribes in the Galaaditis and Moabitis. It seems that the Moabitis, Ammonitis and Galaaditis were neither settled nor controlled by Nabataeans. Probably the Nabataeans did not expand north of Wadi el-Hesa or of Wadi el-Mǒjib before the Hasmonaeans started to occupy territories in Coele Syria east of the Jordan during the late second/early

[72] Stucky 1992, 137–139; see above.
[73] Wright 1969.
[74] Rosenthal-Heginbottom 1997.
[75] Hübner 1997; Weber 1997, 114–121; Wenning 1999; Wenning 2004.

first century B.C. That does not mean that the Nabataeans could not have used the old 'Kings's Highway' to reach Syria with their trade-goods beside the more important route through the great Wadi Sirhan to the east. But the early presence of Nabataeans in the Hauran probably did not resulted in this trade. There is no reason to assume an immigration of Nabataeans into the Hauran from southern Jordan in the third century B.C. The evidence for Nabataeans in the Hauran from the well-known Zeno papyri from 259 B.C. cannot be taken to state the presence of Nabataeans in the region as a regular part of the population[76]. Probably these Nabataeans lived like others, as nomadic groups in the region. What seems to be remarkable, is the fact that the early sources call these groups 'Nabataeans'. Nevertheless, it is difficult to see any dominant role of the Nabataeans in the region at this time.

The situation changed dramatically in the early Roman period. During the last 20 years there has been a discussion of the so-called 'Nabataean evidence' from the Hauran in the early Roman period in terms of differences in language, art and culture from the evidence in Arabia Petraea[77]. What was described as 'Nabataean' in the past should be characterised better as 'Hauranite'. The inscriptions are currently labelled as 'Aramaic'[78]. The differences are greater than can be explained as regional features alone, and rather, point to a separate development and different traditions, among them the stronger being Aramaic[79]. Although one cannot and should not exclude Nabataeans being among the Hauranite population, it seems that according to the inscriptions there was a greater activity of various tribes, clans and groups arriving in the Hauran and moving in the area in the first century B.C. It may be assumed that some clans invaded the Hauran directly from Aramaic-speaking areas of Mesopotamia or the Persian Gulf or somewhere with strong Aramaic influence. While the Nabaṭu of the south formed a kingdom based on the frankincense trade, the Hauranite people lived as more independent smaller tribes and clans or became partly settled benefitting from the fertile land. One of the first greater settlements was Qanawat.

In 23 B.C. the southern Hauran was cut off from the Auranitis which was given to Herod by Augustus. It is not very difficult to describe the border between the two parts[80], but more difficult to understand this division. One reason might be that the southern part was far less fertile. Another reason could be that the south did not yet have a settled population in the late first century B.C. The northern Auranitis developed under stronger Hellenistic and Roman influence; inscriptions are dated according the reigns of the Roman emperors. The south

[76] Graf 1990, 54.

[77] The interpretation of Wenning 1987, 25–51 (regions B–F) is outdated by the new researches in the Hauran; cf. Dentzer 1985/86; Macdonald 1993.

[78] Scholars have just started more systematically and profoundly to establish regional differences of the 'Nabataean' and other languages of the Near East and started to discuss the consequences of that for the history of the 'Nabataeans'. Cf. Macdonald 2000; Healey, this conference.

[79] The Aramaic tradition was emphazised by J.-M. Dentzer 2003.

[80] Cf. Dentzer-Feydy 1988, Fig. 1.

was also closely connected with the Nabataean kingdom, at least since Malichus II, when inscriptions are dated according the reigns of the Nabataean kings[81]. The people living in the south between Bosra and Umm el-Jimal with cultic centres at Salkhad and Bosra, seek support and agreement with the Nabaṭu, then the most important Arabic tribe of the Near East. Probably this was not accidental. According to epigraphical evidence one can almost be sure that one of the tribes living here, the Rawahu, was related to the Nabataeans[82].

Nabataeans and Jews

In view of the of the 'World of the Herods and the Nabataeans' a few remarks on the relationship between Jews and Nabataeans should be added. The main source is Flavius Josephus. He describes the many conflicts the Nabataeans had with the Hasmonaeans and the Herodians. They had also some family relations. Often and following the literary sources, the conflicts have been emphasised in modern scholarship[83]. Contrary to politics and conflicts there were close interactions in neighbourly relations, trade exchange, activities in real estate and intermarriages.

At the beginning the good relations between the two peoples during the second century B.C. are reflected in the Book of Maccabees[84]. Petra was the destination of many who try to flee persecutions in Jerusalem, among them the Jewish high priest Jason in 168, Herod the Great in 40 and Hyrkan II in 30 B.C. Masada was chosen as the refuge for the Herodian Dynasty not only because it was distant from Jerusalem, but also because it was the nearest route to Nabataea crossing the Lisan peninsula. One reason to seek exile amongst the Nabataeans was the fact that Herodian and Nabataean royalty were related and that there had been a history of good relations for many years. The rich Idumaean noble man Antipater, the father of Herod, had married a Nabataean princess, Kufra/Kypros[85]. Their children were sent to Aretas III during the war with Aristobulus II. The Nabataean king supported Hyrkan II and Antipater in the siege of Jerusalem in 65/64 B.C., which was stopped by the legate of Pompey. Antipater put 300 talents at Aretas' disposal to avoid the invasion of M. Aemilius Scaurus in 62 B.C. Nevertheless, when Herod fled the invading Parthians in 40 B.C. and attempted to seek refuge at the Royal court at Petra, he was not accepted as a refugee by Malichus I for political reasons. This resulted in a break-down in the good relationship between both rulers.

Later, one finds Syllaeus, the vizir of Obodas III, at the Herodian court seeking to marry Salome, the sister of Herod. Herod set the condition that Syllaeus had to became Jewish, an impossibility for Syllaeus, making him an enemy of Herod. On the other hand, Herod's son Antipas married a Nabataean

[81] CIS II 174 from A.D. 50/51.

[82] Macdonald 1993, 358f.

[83] Cf. among others Kasher 1988; Kokkinos 1998.

[84] 1 Macc. 5.25; 9.35.

[85] Josephus, BJ 1.8.9.

princess, a daughter of Aretas IV, possibly Phasaelis[86]. After many years Antipas disowned his wife in A.D. 33/34 when Herodias, the wife of his brother Philip developed a passion for him. Phasaelis escaped from Machaerus to her father's court. Aretas IV took revenge with a great military victory over Antipas in A.D. 36.

Despite personal relationships between the dynasties and nobilities, and probably other people, there seems to be little evidence for Jews in the Nabataean Kingdom and for Nabataeans in the Herodian Kingdom. And there does not seem to be much evidence that one side had much influence over the other. Rather, both looked for Graeco-Roman ideas and monuments, and both were shaped partly in the same way by this cultural influence. This was lately demonstrated by a comparison of architectural features of dwellings[87]. What Jewish evidence can be found is a Jewish(?) name at Petra[88], a tomb of a Jew at Hegra from A.D. 42/43[89] and some other Jewish names and Hebrew graffiti in the neighbourhood of Hegra[90], though not precisely datable, but probably later than the tomb. Looking into the Herodian Kingdom, not a single Nabataean inscription is found there. Nabataean coins have been found at 24 sites[91], but this cannot be taken for an exclusive presence of Nabataeans. There are only a few places where Nabataean pottery is recorded[92]. Eight places are listed with pseudo-Nabataean pottery from the Herodian period made in Jerusalem[93]. It is interesting to see this imitation of Nabataean pottery. We can only speculate as to what it means[94].

The main source for an intermingling between Jews and Nabataeans are the documents from the well-known archive of Babatha from A.D. 93 to 132, concerning the latest phase of the Nabataean Kingdom and the first decades of *provincia Arabia*. Her property near Mahoza[95] was situated in the Nabataean territory southeast of the Dead Sea, the greater area in which the Khirbet Qazone Nabataean cemetery[96] is situated. While the burial customs are different, the type of the graves of the Khirbet Qazone cemetery are of the so-called 'Qumran type' and demonstrate that the same regional features can be found on both sides of the

[86] Kokkinos 1998, 229–232, 268.

[87] Cf. Kolb 2000, 277–283, 295–296; Kolb 2001.

[88] Starcky 1965, 48 no. 12. There is no proof, that this name cannot be Aramaic/Nabataean. The context of the inscription does not support the interpretation as a Jewish name.

[89] Healey 1993, 95–97 no. 4 (A.D. 42/43).

[90] Jaussen-Savignac 1909/1914, inscriptions nabatéennes nos. 172bis, 315, 386, 387 and Hebrew inscriptions II 641–644 nos. 1–8; T. J. Milik in Winnett-Reed 1970, 163 nos. 1–2 (Hebrew); Noja 1979, 288–314.

[91] Not limited to the Herodian kingdom there are 45 sites in Israel with Nabataean coins known to me. An article about these coins and others from Jordan with a stratigraphical context is in preparation.

[92] Cf. Wenning 1987, 134–137.

[93] Jerusalem, Jericho, Herodium, Masada, Qumran, Ein Feshka, Nahalat Yehuda, Sepphoris(?) and Nabataean Oboda; cf. Schmid 2000, 115–116.

[94] Schmid 2000, 116.

[95] Cotton-Greenfield 1995; Yadin-Greenfield-Yardeni-Levine 2002. It has been suggested that Babatha may have been an Idumaean Jewess (Kokkinos 1998, 294).

[96] Politis 1998.

Dead Sea[97]. The archive also demonstrates that border zones are strongly subjected to the process of contacts and exchanges.

From Kingdom to Province

Milik assumed that Rabbel II transferred his capital from Petra to Bosra in the Hauran[98]. Most scholars agree with this position though the arguments are not the strongest[99]. Changes in the frankincense trade routes resulting in less income for the Nabataeans happened earlier and did not necessitate the transfer of the capital nor a change towards agriculture instead of trade[100]. The greater importance of agriculture in the first century A.D. can be explained by an increasing sedentarisation, a growing population and the expanding kingdom. There is no reason to assume a decline of Petra or in Nabataea during the reign of Rabbel II as Petra flourished as city. The thesis of the transfer is based mainly upon a single Nabataean inscription, later Roman coin finds and the assumption that Bostra was the capital of the new *provincia Arabia*. A Nabataean inscription from Imtan of A.D. 92/93 was read as saying Dushara is 'the god of our lord who is in Bosra'. Other inscriptions indicate that the formula is related to the god who is in Bosra, not to the king.

Concerning the latest phase of the Nabataean kingdom I have put forward the idea of a religious and possible national (re)novation under Rabbel II some years ago[101]. This programme I connected indirectly with the end of the Nabataean kingdom by conquest and occupation by Rome instead of a peaceful annexation or heredity[102]. It is not very likely that Rome acted in this way because of the death of Rabbel II, moreover the assumption of the death of the last Nabataean king in A.D. 106 is totally hypothetical[103]. If Bostra was the capital of the new province[104] or just the garrison town of the *legio III Cyrenaica* is debatable[105]. The new *provincia Arabia* was officially accepted as '*adquisita*' only five years after the occupation of the former Nabataean Kingdom. Petra probably remained the administrative center of the new province as '*metropolis Arabiae*'[106].

[97] Zangenberg 1999.

[98] Milik 1958, 233–235.

[99] Cf. Wenning 1993a, 94–95; Fiema 2003.

[100] The *Periplus* of the Red Sea, dated to the middle of the first century A.D. demonstrates that the trade was still running well; cf. Bowersock 1983, 70–71. Another result of the changes in the trade seems to be a more intensive contact with the Golf area since the Augustan period; cf. Schmid 2000, 129–130. Further arguments by Fiema 2003, 39–43.

[101] Wenning 1993a, 86–93.

[102] Cf. as well Schmid 2000, 139–146.

[103] Wenning 1993a, 97–98.

[104] Based on an inscription from Madeba from A.D. 108 before the official recognition of the province; cf. Milik 1958, 244; but Fiema 1988, 112; Fiema 2003, 44.

[105] Bowersock 1983, 82–86; Sartre 1985; Fiema 1987; Fiema 1988; Fiema 2003, 44–47.

[106] The title is found in inscriptions and coins legends since A.D. 114. Furtheron, Petra seems to have been the *caput viae* for the *Via Nova Traiana*, cf. Graf 1995, 242–243; Fiema 2003, 45–46.

Bibliography

Bartlett, J. 1979. "From Edomites to Nabataeans: A Study in Continuity", *PEQ* 111, 53–66.

– 1990. "From Edomites to Nabataeans: the Problem of Continuity", *Aram* 2, 25–34.

Bowersock, G. W. 1983. *Roman Arabia*, Cambridge, Mass.: Harvard University Press.

Cotton, H. M. – Greenfield, J. C. 1995. "Babatha's *Patria*: Maḥoza, Maḥoz 'Eglatain and Ẓo'ar", *ZPE* 107, 126–134.

Dentzer, J.-M. 1985/86. *Hauran. Recherches archéologiques sur la Syrie du Sud à l'époque hellénistique et romaine* I, 1–2, Paris: Paul Geuthner.

Dentzer, J.-M. 2003. Le Jebel al-ʿArab à l'époque <hellénistique>: Repères chronologiques et Identité Culturelle, in K.S. Freyberger – A. Henning – H. von Hesberg (eds.), *Kulturkonflikte im Vorderen Orient*. Orient-Archäologie 11, Rahden: Verlag M. Leidorf 181–217.

Dentzer-Feydy, J. 1988. "Frontières et matériel archéologique en Syrie du Sud: politique et culture du Ier siècle av. notre ère au IVe siècle de notre ère", in P.-L. Gatier – B. Helly – J.-P. Rey-Coquais (eds.), *Géographie historique au Proche-Orient*, Paris: CNRS.

Dyma, O. 1999. *Der Gott Dūšarā' im Spiegel der nabatäischen und subnabatäischen Primärquellen*. Unpublished degree dissertation Tübingen University.

Errington, R. M. 1977. "Diodorus Siculus and the Chronology of the Early Diadochoi, 320–311 B.C.", *Hermes* 105, 478–504.

Fiema, Z. T. 1987. "The Roman Annexation of Arabia: A General Perspective", *The Ancient World* 15/1–2, 25–35.

– 1988. "The Era of Bostra. A Reconsideration", *Corso di cultura* 35, 109–120.

– 2003. "Roman Petra (A.D. 106–363). A Neglected Subject", *ZDPV* 119, 38–58.

Fiema, Z. T. – Jones, R. N. 1990. "The Nabataean King-List Revised: Further Observations on the Second Nabataean Inscription from Tell Esh-Shuqafiya, Egypt", *ADAJ* 34, 239–248.

Förtsch, R. 1996. "The Residences of King Herod and their Relations to Roman Villa Architecture", in K. Fittschen – G. Foerster (eds.), *Judaea and the Greco-Roman World in the Time of Herod in the Light of Archaeological Evidence*, AbhAkWissGött 215, Göttingen: Vandenhoeck & Ruprecht, 73–119.

Freyberger, S. K. 1998. *Die frühkaiserzeitlichen Heiligtümer der Karawanenstationen im hellenisierten Osten*. DamForsch 6, Mainz: Verlag Philipp von Zabern.

Gitler, H. 2000. "Achaemenid Motifs in the Coinage of Ashdod, Ascalon and Gaza from the fourth Century BC", *Trans* 20, 73–87.

Graf, D. F. 1990. "The Origin of the Nabataeans", *Aram* 2, 45–75.

– 1994. "The Nabatean Army and the *cohortes Ulpiae Petraeorum*", in E. Dabrowa (ed.), *The Roman and Byzantine Army in the East*, Krakow, 265–311.

– 1995. "The Via Nova Traiana in Arabia Petraea", *JRA Suppl.* 14, 241–267.

– 1996. "The Roman East from the Chinese Perspective", *AAAS* 42, 199–216.

Hackl, U. – Jenni, H. – Schneider, C. 2003. *Quellen zur Geschichte der Nabatäer*.Textsammlung mit Übersetzung und Kommentar. NTOA 51, Freiburg/Schweiz – Göttingen: Universitätsverlag – Vandenhoeck & Ruprecht.

Hart, S. 1986. "Some preliminary Thoughts on Settlement in Southern Edom", *Levant* 18, 51–58.

– 1987a. "Five Soundings in Sothern Jordan", *Levant* 19, 33–47.

– 1987b. "The Edom Survey Project 1984–85: The Iron Age", *SHAJ* 3, 287–290.

Healey, J. F. 1993. *The Nabataean Tomb Inscriptions of Mada'in Salih*. Journal of Semitic Studies Suppl. 1, Oxford: University Press.

– 2001. *The Religion of the Nabataeans. A Conspectus*, Religions in the Graeco-Roman World 136, Leiden-Boston-Köln: Brill.

Henninger, J. 1989. *Arabica Varia. Aufsätze zur Kulturgeschichte Arabiens und seiner Nachbargebiete*, OBO 90, Freiburg/Schweiz – Göttingen: Universitätsverlag – Vandenhoeck & Ruprecht.

Hiller von Gaertringen, F. 1906. *Inschriften von Priene*, Berlin: Verlag G. Reimer.
Hornblower, J. 1981. *Hieronymus of Cardia*, Oxford: University Press.
Horsfield, G. and A. 1938. "Sela-Petra, the Rock, of Edom and Nabatene (I)", *QDAP* 7, 1–42.
Hübner, U. 1997. " 'Dem König, was des Königs ist'. Die Selbstdarstellung des nabatäischen Könighauses", in Weber-Wenning 1997, 111–114.
Kasher, A. 1988. *Jews, Idumaeans, and Ancient Arabs*, Texte und Studien zum Antiken Judentum 18, Tübingen: J.C.B. Mohr (Paul Siebeck).
Knauf, E. A. 1985a. *Ismael. Untersuchungen zur Geschichte Palästinas und Nordarabiens im 1. Jahrtausend v. Chr.* ADPV 7, Wiesbaden: Otto Harrassowitz.
– 1985b. "Philisto-arabische Münzen", *BiblischeNotizen* 30, 19–28.
– 1986. "Die Herkunft der Nabatäer", in M. Lindner (ed.), *Petra. Neue Ausgrabungen und Entdeckungen*, München – Bad Windsheim: Delp Verlag, 74–86.
– 1988. "Edom und Arabien", *Biblische Notizen* 45, 62–81.
– 1995. "Edom: The Social and Economic History", in D. V. Edelman (ed.), *You Shall Not Abhor An Edomite For He Is Your Brother*, Atlanta: Scholars Press, 93–117.
– 1997. "Der sein Volk liebt", in Weber-Wenning 1997, 14–24.
– 1998. "The Ituraeans: Another Bedouin State", in H. Sader – T. Scheffler – A. Neuwirth (eds.), *Baalbek: Image and Monument 1898–1998*, Beiruter Texte und Studien 69, Beirut, 269–277.
Kokkinos, N. 1998. *The Herodian Dynasty*, Journal for the Study of the Pseudepigrapha Suppl. Series 30, Sheffield: Academic Press.
Kolb, B. 1997. "Petra – eine Zeltstadt in Stein", in Weber-Wenning 1997, 63–66.
– 2000. *Die spätantiken Wohnbauten von ez Zantur in Petra und der Wohnhausbau in Palästina vom 4.–6. Jh. n. Chr.* Petra Ez Zantur II,2, Mainz: Philipp von Zabern, 200–311.
– 2001. "A Nabataean Mansion at Petra: Some Reflections on ist Architecture and Interior Decoration", *SHAJ* 7, 437–445.
Kolb, B. – Keller, D. 2001. "Swiss-Liechtenstein Excavation at az-Zantur/Petra: the Eleventh Season", *ADAJ* 45, 311–324.
Kushnir-Stein, A. – Gitler, H. 1992/93. "Numismatic Evidence from Tel Beer-Sheva and the Beginning of Nabataean Coinage", *INJ* 12, 13–20.
Lemaire, A. 1999. "Der Beitrag idumäischer Ostraka zur Geschichte Palästinas im Übergang von der persischen zur hellenistischen Zeit", *ZDPV* 115, 12–23.
Lindner, M. – Hübner, U. – Gunsam, E. 2001. "Es-Sela^{c} – 2500 Jahre Fliehburg und Bergfestung in Edom, Südjordanien", *Das Altertum* 46, 243–278.
Macdonald, M. C. A. 1991. "Was the Nabataean Kingdom a "Bedouin State"?", *ZDPV* 107, 102–119.
– 1993. "Nomads and the Ḥawrān in the Late Hellenistic and Roman Periods. A Reassessment of the Epigraphic Evidence", *Syria* 79, 303–413.
– 1997. "Hunting, Fighting, and Raiding: The Horse in Pre-Islamic Arabia", in D. G. Alexander (ed.), *Furusiyya: The horse in the art of the Near East*, Vol. 1, Riyadh, 72–82.
– 2000. "Reflections on the linguistic map of pre-Islamic Arabia", *AAE* 11, 28–79.
McKenzie, J. 1990. *The Architecture of Petra*, Oxford: University Press.
McLaughlin, J. L. 2001. *The Marzēaḥ in the Prophetic Literature. References and Allusions in Light of the Extra-Biblical Evidence.* VTS 86, Leiden – Boston – Cologne: Brill.
Merklein, H. – Wenning, R. 1998. "Ein Verehrungsplatz der Isis in Petra neu untersucht", *ZDPV* 114, 162–178.
Meshorer, Y. 1975. *Nabataean Coins.* Qedem 3, Jerusalem: The Hebrew University of Jerusalem.
Mildenberg, L. 1990. "Gaza von 420 bis 332 nach den Sachquellen", in *Akten des XIII. Internationalen Kongresses für Klassische Archäologie Berlin 1988*, Mainz: Philipp von Zabern, 431–432.
– 2000. "Über die Münzbildnisse in Palästina und Nordwestarabien zur Perserzeit", in Ch. Uehlinger (ed.), *Images as media. Sources for the cultural history of the Near East and the*

Eastern Mediterranean (1st millenium BCE). OBO 175, Freiburg/Schweiz – Göttingen: Universitäts Verlag – Vandenhoeck & Ruprecht, 375–391.
Milik, J. T. 1958. "Nouvelles inscriptions nabatéenes", *Syria* 35, 227–251.
– 1982. "Origines des Nabatéens", *SHAJ* 1, 261–265.
Negev, A. 1983. *Tempel, Kirchen und Zisternen*, Stuttgart: Calwer Verlag.
Noja, S. 1979. "Testimonianze epigrafiche di Giudei nell'Arabia settentrionale", *Bibbia e Oriente* 21, 283–316.
Politis, K. D. 1998. "Rescue Excavations in the Nabataean Cemetery at Khirbat Qazone 1996–1997", *ADAJ* 42, 611–614.
Rehm, A. 1997. *Inschriften von Milet, Teil 1, A*. Inschriften n. 187–406; P. Herrmann, Nachträge und Übersetzungen zu den Inschriften n. 1–406, ed. by V. von Graeve, Berlin – New York: Walter de Gruyter.
Roche, M.-J. 1996. "Remarques sur les Nabatéens en Méditerranée", *Semitica* 45, 73–99.
Rosenthal-Heginbottom, R. 1997. "Gold und Silber mag ich sehr", in Weber-Wenning 1997, 140–144.
Sartre, M. 1985. *Bostra des origines à l'Islam*, BAH 117, Paris: P. Geuthner.
Schluntz, E. L. 1998. "The Upper Temenos and the Great Temple", in M. Sharp Joukowsky, *Petra Great Temple Vol. I: Brown University Excavations 1993–1997*. Providence: E. A. Johnson Company, 209–224.
Schmid, S. G. 2000a. *Die Feinkeramik der Nabatäer. Typologie, Chronologie und kulturhistorische Hintergründe*. Petra Ez Zantur II,1, Mainz: Philipp von Zabern, 1–199.
– 2000b. "The "Hellenistic" Tomb Façades of Nabataean Petra and their Cultural Background", in V. Christides – Th. Papadopullos (eds.), *Proceedings of the Sixth International Congress of Graeco-Oriental and African Studies Nicosia 30 April – 5 May 1996*, Nicosia, 485–501.
Schmitt-Korte, K. 1991. "Die Nabatäer im Spiegel der Münzen", in M. Lindner – J. P. Zeitler (eds.), *Petra, Königin der Weihrauchstrasse*, Fürth: VKA-Verlag, 135–148.
Schmitt-Korte, K. – Price, M. 1994. "Nabataean Coinage – Part III. the Nabataean Monetary System", *Numismatic Chronicle* 1994, 67–131.
Schottroff, W. 1982. "Die Ituräer", *ZDPV* 98, 125–152.
Starcky, J. 1965. "Nouvelles stèles funéraires à Pétra", *ADAJ* 10, 43–49.
– 1966. "Pétra et la Nabatène", *SDB* VII, 886–1017.
Stucky, R. A. 1992. "Das nabatäische Wohnhaus und das urbanistische System der Wohnquartiere in Petra", *Antike Kunst* 35, 129–140.
Tholbecq, L. 1997. "Les Sanctuaires des Nabatéens: État de la question à la lumière de recherches archéologiques récentes", *Topoi* 7, 1069–1095.
Weber, T. 1997. "Die Bildkunst der Nabatäer", in Weber-Wenning 1997, 114–125.
Weber, T. - Wenning, R. 1997. *Petra. Antike Felsstadt zwischen arabischer Tradition und griechischer Norm*, Mainz: Philipp von Zabern.
Wenning, R. 1987. *Die Nabatäer – Denkmäler und Geschichte*, NTOA 3, Freiburg/Schweiz – Göttingen: Universitätsverlag – Vandenhoeck & Ruprecht.
– 1993a. "Das Ende des nabatäischen Königreichs", in A. Invernizzi – J.-F. Salles (eds.), *Arabia antiqua. Hellenistic Centres around Arabia*, Roma: Is.M.E.O.
– 1993b. "Eine neuerstellte Liste der nabatäischen Dynastie", *Boreas* 16, 25–38.
– 1994. "Die Dekapolis und die Nabatäer", *ZDPV* 110, 1–35.
– 1997. "Bemerkungen zur Gesellschaft und Religion der Nabatäer", in R. Albertz (ed.), *Religion und Gesellschaft*. AOAT 248, Münster: Ugarit Verlag, 177–201.
– 1999. "Gods in stone – Gods on stone – stone as God: The case of the Nabataean deities", paper read at the *First Conference on Nabataean Research and Studies*, 21–23 June, 1999, Petra-Jordan.
– 2001. "The Betyls of Petra", *BASOR* 324, 79–95.
– 2003a. Review of M. Sharp Joukowsky, Petra Great Temple Vol. I: Brown University

Excavations 1993–1997. Providence: E. A. Johnson Company, 1998, in *Antike Welt* 34, 109–110.

– 2003b. " 'Das ist Dushara!' Zu den Problemen der Interpretation der Quellen und Denkmäler nabatäischer Religion", in M. Gielen – J. Kügler (eds.), *Liebe – Macht – Religion. Interdisziplinäre Studien zu Grunddimensionen menschlicher Existenz. Gedenkschrift für Helmut Merklein*, Stuttgart: Herder, 143–160.

– 2003c. "The Rock-Cut Architecture of Petra", in G. Markoe (ed.), *Petra Rediscovered. Lost City of the Nabataeans*, New York: H. N. Abrams – Cincinnati Art Museum, 133–144.

– 2003d. "Hellenistische Denkmäler aus Petra. Überlegungen zum Hellenisierungsprozess der Nabatäer", in G. Zimmer (ed.), *Neue Forschungen zur hellenistischen Plastik. Kolloquium zum 70. Geburtstag von Georg Daltrop*, Eichstätt – Wolnzach: Universitätsverlag – Kastner, 141–164.

– 2004. "Nabatäische Büstenreliefs aus Petra – zwei Neufunde. Mit einem Beitrag von U. Hübner", *ZDPV* 120, 157–181.

Winnett, F. V. – Reed, W. L. 1970. *Ancient Records from North Arabia*, Toronto: University of Toronto Press.

Winnicki, J. K. 1989. "Militäroperationen von Ptolemaios I. und Seleukos I. in Syrien in den Jahren 312–311 v. Chr.", *Ancient Society* 20, 55–92.

Wright, G. R. H. 1969. "Strabo on Funerary Customs at Petra", *PEQ* 101, 113–116.

Yadin, Y. – Greenfield, J. C. – Yardeni, A. – Levine, B. 2002. *The Documents from the Bar Kokhba Period in the Cave of Letters. Hebrew, Aramaic and Nabatean Aramaic Papyri.* Judean Desert Studies 3, Jerusalem.

Zangenberg, J. 1999. "The 'Final Farewell'. A Necessary Paradigm Shift in the Interpretation of the Qumran Cemetery", *The Qumran Chronicle* 8, 213–218.

Zayadine, F. 1999. "Le relief néo-babylonien à Sela^{c} près de Tafileh, interprétation historique", *Syria* 76, 83–90.

Zayadine, F. – Farajat, S. 2001. "Excavation and Clearance at Petra and Beiḍa", *ADAJ* 35, 275–311.

Crawford, G. A. 2003. Petra and the Nabataeans. A Bibliography. ATLA Bibliography Series 49, Lanham – Oxford: Scarecrow Press.

Nabataean Inscriptions: Language and Script

John F. Healey

The aim in this short paper is to survey the question of the language or languages used by the Nabataeans and the Nabataean script in its various forms. It is not possible here to enter into detail in relation to either topic. Instead I try to give a summary of the facts and the consensus of scholarly opinion, but I will also explore some newly emerging aspects of these topics and also comment on the content of the Nabataean inscriptions, speculating a little on what might be found in the future.

Preliminary

Before launching myself into this ambitious plan, I have to draw attention to some difficulties which constantly arise in the study of Nabataean inscriptions, important factors which must always be kept in mind if we are to avoid making nonsense of the evidence.

Firstly, the Nabataean Kingdom had geographical limits at any particular time and disappeared in 105/6 C.E. when it was incorporated into the Roman Province of Arabia. Many of the inscriptions in what we call for convenience and by scholarly convention the "Nabataean" script were produced outside these geographical and chronological limits. Some are post-Nabataean, even if they are from Petra; others are contemporary with the Nabataean kingdom but were manufactured outside its geographical boundaries.

Secondly, in order to avoid clumsy expressions, scholars have to use a certain amount of shorthand in referring to the languages of the area. So when we write here of the "Nabataean" language, it should be understood that we are referring to the local Nabataean dialect of Aramaic. When we speak of Arabic, even more care is needed. We know Classical Arabic properly only from the seventh century C.E. onwards, i.e. the early Islamic period. Some form of "pre-Arabic" was, however, in use among some peoples even in the first centuries of the Common Era. It is important not to confuse this with the Arabic we know from much later and, when we refer by a kind of shorthand to "Arabic" influence, to keep in mind the fact that, as far as we can tell, Classical Arabic as such did not exist in the period of the Nabataean Kingdom.

By keeping these points in mind we may avoid distorting the evidence.

The Nabataean Language

The Nabataean inscriptions were first fully deciphered by Eduard Beer in 1840 on the basis of copies of texts from Sinai (Beer 1840). From a very early stage of their study it became clear that the language involved was a form of Aramaic. It is not Hebrew (which some eccentric Victorian fundamentalists would have liked: in one group of "Nabataean" inscriptions Forster could hear the "voice of Israel from the rocks of Sinai" [Forster 1851; see discussion in Healey 1994, 84–91]), nor is it Arabic (which some Arab linguistic nationalists would like). Aramaic is *related to* Hebrew and Arabic, but it has linguistic features which set it completely apart from these sister languages. Most obvious linguistically is the lack of any prefixed definite article ("the"). Aramaic had long been widely used in the Middle East, becoming an important diplomatic and commercial *lingua franca* under the Achaemenid Persian empire (Beyer 1986, 14–19). It functioned a bit like Latin in medieval Europe.

Although the Nabataean inscriptions are written in a form of Aramaic, from an early stage of their study note was made in some inscriptions of the presence of Arabic-type vocabulary and grammatical intrusions. There are pieces of un-Aramaic vocabulary like *walad*, "child, children", *nasīb*, "kinsman", and the verb *la*ᶜ*ana*, "to curse". Nöldeke and other nineteenth century philologists were alert to these intrusions (Nöldeke 1885; O'Connor 1986; Healey 1995). It came to be widely accepted that these intrusions arose because the Nabataeans must have spoken Arabic in everyday speech, but when they wrote their inscriptions they used the already established *lingua franca*, Aramaic.

There are other linguistic arguments which could be used to bolster this view that the Nabataeans spoke Arabic on an everyday basis, but used Aramaic for public purposes, such as the fact that the actual Aramaic of the inscriptions is rather archaic and old-fashioned by comparison with the contemporary dialects of Aramaic which are used in inscriptions from Palmyra, for example: the Aramaic of Nabataea might have preserved its archaic features through being basically a non-spoken language (Beyer 1986, 26–27; Healey 1993, 59–63). There are also non-linguistic arguments in favour of this idea that the Nabataeans spoke some form of Arabic, including the widely held view that the Nabataeans were in fact a bedouin Arab tribe who had settled in southern Jordan to form a state. Caution is needed here, however, since non-linguistic arguments of this kind do not prove much about linguistic matters. But at least it could be argued that the hypothesis that the Nabataeans spoke some early form of Arabic fits with the idea that the Nabataeans were Arabs.

However, apart from the quite separate argument over whether the Nabataeans *regarded* themselves as Arabs (and what the term "Arab" meant in the first century C.E.: see Healey 1989; 2001b), recent discussions of linguistic questions have now at least raised some questions about the view that they spoke Arabic while writing in Aramaic.

Most importantly, the supposed Arabic influences in the Nabataean inscriptions of the first century C.E. are mostly limited geographically to the southern area of Nabataea, especially around Ḥegra/Madāʾin Ṣāliḥ in Saudi Arabia (O'Connor 1986, 220 and generally). We should not, however, be too dogmatic here: there is *some* evidence of Arabic influence further north towards the end of the 1st century C.E. (e.g. in the Nabataean papyri of Naḥal Ḥever [see Greenfield 1992]), and it is possible that the impression of stronger Arabic influence in the south is a function of the fact that the southern inscriptions, especially those from Ḥegra/Madāʾin Ṣāliḥ, are of greater length.

We do, however, have to keep chronology as well as geography in mind. Some of the other evidence of Arabic influence is in inscriptions from Sinai dated after the end of the Nabataean Kingdom: again not all inscriptions in Nabataean script have anything to do with the Nabataeans of Petra and they cannot be regarded as indicative evidence for the linguistic and ethnic situation of first century C.E. Petra (Healey 2001b and 2002). Second and third century C.E. inscriptions from Sinai tell us about Sinai at that period, not about Petra 150 years earlier.

The idea that it was *necessary* for speakers of an early form of Arabic to resort to Aramaic for public inscriptions also needs to be questioned, since contemporary peoples of a supposedly similar background to that of the Nabataeans, like the Lihyanites in north-west Arabia (centred on Dedan/al-ᶜUlā), spoke and wrote their own North Arabian dialect, using the South Arabian script. And that such a possibility would have been available to the Nabataeans further north is evident from the fact that the authors of the Safaitic inscriptions of eastern Jordan and southern Syria, some of them people attached to the Nabataean state (as we know from their basileophoric personal names incorporating the names of Nabataean kings), also wrote in a North Arabian language using a form of the South Arabian script. Given these facts it is not easy to explain why *other* Nabataeans, those in Petra and the other main cultural centres, used Aramaic.

It may also be noted that certainly in the post-Nabataean period, and probably also in the Nabataean period, completely informal inscriptions, graffiti, are written in Aramaic: i.e. Aramaic is used in circumstances which do not demand the formality of adopting an official tongue rather than the vernacular. Why did the Nabataeans write these graffiti in Aramaic if some form of Arabic was their daily language? (Here, however, we have come full circle logically – the Arabic intrusions into the graffiti of Sinai may be taken to point to the idea that the writers were normally speakers of Arabic.)

Taking all of the above into account – both the consensus view that the Nabataeans spoke Arabic and the reservations I have noted – we may have to adopt a more nuanced view of the linguistic situation of the inhabitants of Nabataea. The Nabataean élite, the royal family and its closest associates, may well have been of north Arabian stock. The kings' devotion to Arabian religious practices and deities and their personal names suggest this (Healey 2001a). The main god of the Nabataeans is Dushara and his name is of a distinctively Arabic type, with the prefix *dhū-*. There were probably also other sections of the Nabataean population who could be called "Arabian" from a linguistic and cultural point of view. The Safaitic subjects of the Nabataean kings are the most visible (because of their use of a distinctive script to write in an Arabic-related language). But this does not mean that *all* the population of Nabataea were Arabic-speakers. Rather, Nabataean hegemony covered many areas where Aramaic was dominant, as is best known from nearby Judaea, the Dead Sea Scrolls and the Persian-period Wādī al-Dāliyyah documents, texts from Idumaea, etc. (Beyer 1986, 16; Lemaire 2001, 7–8). In the more remote areas of Nabataean influence extending into southern Syria, the Aramaic tradition is even stronger and there is no trace of Arabic linguistic influence in the Aramaic used there until much later. So we are left with the possibility that many but by no means all of the population of Nabataea spoke a language akin to Arabic: possibly the élite, probably some of the population of the southern provinces of Nabataea, and certainly those writers of Safaitic inscriptions who owed their allegiance to the Nabataean state. Others probably spoke Aramaic, the Nabataean kingdom being multilingual and "multi-scriptal".

The best explanation of the choice of the Aramaic language and script for official purposes, both formal public inscriptions and legal documents, remains the supposition that the newly established state, even if its leaders spoke some sort of Arabic, wanted to assert its status by adopting an established prestige language, Aramaic, along with the other trappings of statehood.

Before moving on, it may be worth reflecting very briefly on the role of Greek and the significance of bilingual inscriptions. While Greek inscriptions and bilinguals are common in the Ḥawrān area, in fact Greek was not in wide use in Nabataea until after 105/6 C.E. Of the documents of the Babatha archive none of the Greek texts predate 105/6 (Lewis 1989, 29). We may contrast the case of Palmyra, which was under heavier Roman influence. There are, however, some Greek-Nabataean bilinguals of the period of the Nabataean kingdom. Those which occur outside Nabataea, within the Roman world, are easily explicable in terms of the locations in which they were set up: thus the Nabataean bilinguals from Delos and Miletus dated 9 B.C.E. (Roussel and Launey 1937, ID 2315; Rehm and Kawerau 1914, no. 165) and one from Cos dated 9 C.E. (Levi della Vida 1938). More interesting in terms of the implications for Nabataean society is the Bāb es-Sīq triclinium inscription from the reign of Malichus II (40–70 C.E.) (Healey 1993, 243–44; Sartre 1993, 89–91: no. 54), the only Greek text from the area securely dated before 105/6 C.E. In this inscription, a man with a purely Nabataean name (^{c}Abdmanku) is the son of a father with an apparently Greek name, *Achaios*. There are some peculiarities in the formulae used in this inscription by comparison with other tomb texts and one might suspect that this is a special case of a Petran particularly proud of his Hellenism! The peculiarities of the inscription were debated by Milik, who concluded that ^{c}Abdmanku was a foreigner (Milik 1976), a view opposed by Sartre (1993: 89-91).

The Nabataean Script

In turning to the Nabataean script, I begin with another reminder that many of the inscriptions called Nabataean in the scholarly tradition have nothing immediately to do with the Nabataeans of the Nabataean kingdom: many come from peripheral areas and post-date the kingdom. The Nabataean script is a characteristic artefact of the Nabataean kingdom and had its origin and main centre there, but it is not exclusive to it. To use the Latin analogy again, not every individual or state using the Latin script can be labelled Roman or uses Latin or even inhabits territory formerly held by the Romans.

We also need to be wary of other weaknesses in the scholarly tradition in this regard. There has been a general lack of care in distinguishing different script-forms and texts are sometimes included in collections of "Nabataean" inscriptions which are quite distinctive and could arguably be better included in a different category. This applies to some of the inscriptions from southern Syria (see Starcky 1966, cols 930–31; see also on the inscriptions from Sīᶜ, Healey 2001a, 66) and to some of the later inscriptions from Sinai. Even some of the inscriptions from what is arguably the Nabataean heartland, such as those from Khirbat al-Tannūr (Starcky 1966, col. 930; Healey 2001a, 60), are arguably different in script from the standard Nabataean style. A new typology and classification is needed.

We do, however, have a substantial number of dated or datable inscriptions on stone which were definitely made by Nabataeans of the Nabataean Kingdom, using a standard type of script which we can legitimately call "Nabataean". This script is one of the several local variants of the Achaemenid Persian Aramaic script: the local variants emerged when local post-Achaemenid rulers and élites were writing Aramaic inscriptions for local consumption, i.e. not as part of the world-wide administration of the Persian Empire. Aramaic's role as a *lingua franca* was disappearing. There is a Latin analogy again, in that local versions of the Latin script developed as states formed in Europe after the demise of the Roman Empire.

This classical Nabataean script in the time of the Nabataean Kingdom appears to have been used in at least two forms, a monumental form and a cursive form. The monumental script is used on stone for the writing of public inscriptions, whether religious or funerary, and is typically represented by the tomb inscriptions of Madāᵓin Ṣāliḥ (Healey 1993). The cursive script was used in legal, diplomatic and commercial documents for writing on papyrus or parchment (see the Nabataean texts in the Babatha archive, now available in Yadin et al. 2002). In fact this division into two styles may be over-simple, since there are some written materials which are hard to classify, such as graffiti, which, as in virtually all script traditions, tend to be written in a hybrid of formal and informal styles (see Healey 1990–91). Typically the graffito-writer tries to make his inscription look more formal than his ordinary handwriting. There is also some variation in the papyrus documents: some appear to be rather formal, in a style you might use for a legal document, while others are more casual. There are also texts written on plaster which are a little different again (see Savignac and Horsfield 1935, 265–70 and plate x).

Worthy of note here is the fact that the more formal inscriptions and documents clearly aspire to a certain calligraphic elegance: i.e. there is an element of display. The inscription on the Turkmaniyyeh tomb at Petra and the tomb of Kamkam at Madāʾin Ṣāliḥ are notable examples (*CIS* II, no. 350; Healey 1993, 238–42, and no. H16). In the case of tomb inscriptions there is clear evidence that the legal details inscribed on a tomb-facade were also lodged in papyrus form in a local registry (Healey 1993, no. H36:9). We can guess, though the evidence is indirect, that the stone mason might have been an expert in lettering, but not a literate and legally trained scribe. He might well have copied his text from a manuscript original. This may explain the occasional intrusion of unexpected cursive letter-forms, and it certainly makes sense of the several cases where the stone mason runs out of space and has to squash up the lines or run over onto the tomb-façade (e.g. Healey 1993, no. H9, H16).

The continued use of the script in the post-Nabataean period is important in the search for the origins of the Arabic script known to us from the early Islamic period. This is not the place to discuss this later history in detail (see Gruendler 1993). Suffice it to report that there is a consensus view, despite a dissident minority, that the cursive Nabataean script lies at the origin of the later cursive Arabic script known to us from about 640 C.E. Essentially the evidence consists of a number of distinctive Arabic letter-forms which cannot be easily explained in any other way than by assuming a link with Nabataean. Our assumption is that the cursive form of the Nabataean script continued in use in the post-Nabataean period in commercial and perhaps legal contexts. There is very limited evidence in the period between 105/6 C.E. and the seventh century (though see Healey 1990–91), but this cursive script then re-emerged in the early Islamic period as the script adopted for most practical purposes for the writing of Arabic.

I would just draw attention to three things. Firstly, one of the earliest texts in something approaching Classical Arabic, the Namārah inscription dated 328 C.E., is written in the Nabataean script (recent detailed discussion in Briquel-Chatonnet and Robin 1997). Secondly, there are several types of early Arabic script, including the beautiful Kufic script, and not all of them may have been direct descendants from the Nabataean. Other influences may have been at work. And thirdly, it is to be noted that some of the features of the Arabic scripts might be accounted for as being derived from or inspired by the Syriac script (which originated in northern Syria). The incoming Muslim Arabs will certainly have seen and been impressed by fine Syriac calligraphic manuscripts in cities like Damascus (Healey 2000).

The Content of the Inscriptions

The inscriptions and documents for the most part fall into the following categories:

(a) religious, mostly minor inscriptions, usually referring to dedications of statues and altars, identifying places, *loci*, for particular cults, occasionally referring to religious laws and regulations (e.g. the inscriptions at ᶜAyn al-Šallālah and the inscription from the Temple of the Winged Lions: see Healey 2001a, 56–59, 162–63, with further references);

(b) tomb-inscriptions, mostly of a legal character, referring to ownership, authorization for burials, fines on rule-breakers (most of these from Madāʾin Ṣāliḥ: Healey 1993);
(c) informal inscriptions, often of a commemorative character and difficult to date. A common formula for these is "Remembered be so-and-so for good before the god so-and-so" (Healey 1996);
(d) legal and administrative texts and letters on papyrus and leather (Yadin et al. 2002; Starcky 1954).

The inscriptions are very numerous, numbering several thousands if we include all the Sinai texts (Stone 1992–94) and even those from the period of the Nabataean Kingdom probably number more than a thousand. But what do they tell us? Unfortunately the answer is "disappointingly little" except in one or two areas of life! They *do* tell us
(a) quite a lot about the most immediate and concrete aspects of religion (like names of gods, religious practices), but nothing at all about mythology or higher-level aspects of religion. There is enough, just about, to enable us to reconstruct some general ideas about Nabataean religion (Healey 2001a);
(b) quite a lot about social structures, though these are often difficult to interpret: so, for example, we have information on inheritance matters, administration, some aspects of the legal tradition and the status of women (al-Fassi 2000);
(c) quite a lot about the Nabataean tradition of personal names (but again the evidence is hard to interpret) (Negev 1991; Macdonald 1999).

We learn virtually nothing about the trade on which the Nabataeans built their power!

What of the Future?

More inscriptions are always appearing, but they are rarely significant enough to change our perceptions. Most important, especially for linguistic, script and legal studies is the full publication of the Nabataean papyri from the Naḥal Ḥever texts, the so-called Babatha Archive. These were published in a preliminary way on microfiches as part of the Dead Sea Scrolls (Tov 1993) and recently in definitive form (Yadin et al. 2002).

What might the archaeologists find in the future? My own wish-list is a little optimistic:
(a) the Nabataean myth of creation – surely there was one;
(b) a Nabataean national epic – again there must have been some sort of story accounting for the establishment of the Nabataean state and where its rulers came from;
(c) examples of Nabataean court poetry.

All the analogies with what we know of pre-Islamic Arabia suggest that these probably existed, at least in oral form. Whether they were written down we do not know, though it seems likely. Such prizes can appear unexpectedly, as we know from the discovery of the Dead Sea Scrolls and the Petra Greek papyri, and such discoveries would put us in a much better position to understand the Nabataeans.

References

Beer, E. F. F., 1840. *Inscriptiones Veteres Litteris et Lingua Incognitis ad Montem Sinai Magno Numero Servatae*, Leipzig: J. A. Barth.
Beyer, K., 1986. *The Aramaic Language. Its Distribution and Subdivisions*, Göttingen: Vandenhoeck & Ruprecht.
Briquel-Chatonnet, F. & C. Robin, 1997. "Linteau inscrit: AO 4083", in Y. Calvet & C. Robin (eds), *Arabie heureuse, Arabie déserte*, Paris: Réunion des Musées Nationaux, 265–69.
al-Fassi, H. A., 2000. *Women and Power in Ancient Northern Arabia: Nabataea*. University of Manchester Ph.D. (unpublished).
Forster, C., 1851. *The One Primeval Language Traced Experimentally through Ancient Inscriptions in Alphabetic Characters of Lost Powers from the Four Continents*, London: R. Bentley.
Greenfield, J. C., 1992. "Some Arabic Loanwords in the Aramaic and Nabatean Texts from Naḥal Ḥever", *Jerusalem Studies in Arabic and Islam* 15, 10–21.
Gruendler, B., 1993. *The Development of the Arabic Scripts*, Atlanta, Georgia: Scholars Press.
Healey, J. F., 1989. "Were the Nabataeans Arabs?" *Aram* 1, 38–44.
–, 1990–1991. "Nabataean to Arabic: Calligraphy and Script Development among the Pre-Islamic Arabs", *Manuscripts of the Middle East* 5, 41–52.
–, 1993. *The Nabataean Tomb Inscriptions of Mada'in Salih (Journal of Semitic Studies Supplement 1)*, Oxford: Oxford University Press.
–, 1994. "The Decipherment of Alphabetic Scripts", in K. J. Cathcart (ed.), *The Edward Hincks Bicentenary Lectures*, Dublin: Glendale, 75–93.
–, 1995. "Lexical Loans in Early Syriac: a Comparison with Nabataean Aramaic", *Studi Epigrafici e Linguistici* 12, 75–84.
–, 1996. " 'May he be remembered for good': an Aramaic Formula", in K. J. Cathcart & M. Maher (eds), *Targumic and Cognate Studies. Essays in Honour of Martin McNamara*, Sheffield: JSOT, 177–86
–, 2000. "The Early History of the Syriac Script: a Reassessment", *Journal of Semitic Studies* 45, 55–67.
–, 2001a. *The Religion of the Nabataeans: a Conspectus (Religions in the Graeco-Roman World 136)*, Leiden: E. J. Brill.
–, 2001b. " 'Romans Always Conquer'. Some Evidence of Ethnic Identity on Rome's Eastern Frontier", in N. J. Higham (ed.), *Archaeology of the Roman Empire. A tribute to Professor Barri Jones* (BAR 940), Oxford: Archaeopress, 167–72.
–, 2002. "Nabataeo-Arabic: Jaussen-Savignac nab. 17 and 18", in J. F. Healey & V. Porter (eds), *Arabian Studies in Honour of G. Rex Smith*, Oxford: Oxford University Press, 81–89.
Lemaire, A. 2001. *Nouvelles Tablettes Araméennes (Hautes Études Orientales 34; Moyen et Proche-Orient 1)*, Geneva: Droz.
Levi della Vida, G., 1938. "Una bilingue Greco-Nabatea a Coo", *Clara Rhodos* 9, 139–48.
Lewis, N. (ed. with contributions by Y. Yadin & J. C. Greenfield), 1989. *The Documents from the Bar Kokhba Period in the Cave of Letters: Greek Papyri*, Jerusalem: Israel Exploration Society/Hebrew University/Shrine of the Book.
Macdonald, M. C. A., 1999. "Personal Names in the Nabataean Realm: A Review Article", *Journal of Semitic Studies* 44, 251–89.
Milik, J. T., 1976. "Une inscription bilingue nabatéenne et grecque à Pétra", *ADAJ* 21, 143–52.
Negev, A., 1991. *Personal Names in the Nabatean Realm*, Jerusalem: Institute of Archaeology of the Hebrew University.
Nöldeke, T., 1885. "Noten zu den nabatäischen Inschriften", in J. Euting, *Nabatäische Inschriften aus Arabien*, Berlin: G. Reimer, 73–80.
O'Connor, M., 1986. "The Arabic Loanwords in Nabatean Aramaic", *JNES* 45, 213–29.
Rehm, A. & G. Kawerau, 1914. *Milet. Ergebnisse der Ausgrabungen und Untersuchungen seit dem Jahre 1899 III. Das Delphinion in Milet* (ed. T. Wiegand), Berlin: G. Reimer.

Roussel, P. & M. Launey, 1937. *Inscriptions de Délos (Nos 2220–2879)*, Paris: Librairie Ancienne Honoré Champion.
Sartre, M., 1993. *Inscriptions de la Jordanie. Tome IV. (Inscriptions grecques et latines de la Syrie. Tome XXI)*, Paris: P. Geuthner.
Savignac, R. & G. Horsfield, 1935. "Le Temple de Ramm." *RB* 44, 245–78.
Starcky, J., 1954. "Un contrat nabatéen sur papyrus", *RB* 61, 161–81.
–, 1966. "Pétra et la Nabatène." *Dictionnaire de la Bible, Supplément* 7, cols 886–1017.
Stone, M. E., 1992–94. *Rock Inscriptions and Graffiti Project* 1–3, Atlanta, Georgia: Scholars Press.
Tov, E., 1993. *The Dead Sea Scrolls on microfiche: a comprehensive facsimile edition of the texts from the Judean Desert,* Leiden: E. J. Brill.
Yadin, Y. *et al.* 2002. *The Documents from the Bar Kokhba Period in the Cave of Letters: Hebrew, Aramaic and Nabatean-Aramaic Papyri*, Jerusalem: Israel Exploration Society / Institute of Archaeology, Hebrew University / Shrine of the Book, Israel Museum.

Nabataean Religion

John R. Bartlett

In some ways I have drawn the short straw. Understanding other people's religions is always difficult; understanding one's own religion is difficult enough. Understanding the religion of a people who lived two millennia ago is almost impossible. We hardly know what the Nabataeans believed, what they thought about their beliefs, how they prayed, or how they worshipped. They left no scriptures, no liturgical texts, no religious writings, no books of theology or philosophy, not even any historical writings. We have very limited references from other ancient writers. Herodotus, from the fifth century BC, says of the pre-Nabataean Arabs that they keep their pledges more religiously than almost any other people; that they swear friendship by daubing seven stones with their mixed blood, calling on the gods Bacchus and Urania; 'Bacchus they call in their own language Orotal, and Urania, Alilat' (Hist. 3.8). Herodotus thought that they had two gods, one male, one female. The first century BC historian Diodorus Siculus, drawing on Hieronymus of Cardia (fourth century BC) and Agatharcides of Cnidus (second century BC), has much to say about the Nabataeans, but says nothing at all about their religion (Diod. Sic. 2.48, 1–6; 19.94, 95). The geographer Strabo, a contemporary of the Nabataean king Aretas IV, says that the Nabataeans have the same regard for the dead as for dung, and bury even their kings beside dung-heaps; and that 'they worship the sun, building an altar on top of the house, and pouring libations on it daily and burning frankincense' (Strabo Geog. 16.4.26). We can accept that they burnt incense and poured libations; they perhaps also had altars on temple roofs. Strabo's 'sun worship' is vague, and not supported by the iconography available to us. The reference to burying the dead beside dung-heaps may refer to a practice of exposure of corpses (cf. Wright 1969). Perhaps the most useful ancient description of Nabataean religion comes from the Lexicon of Suidas, a late Byzantine (tenth century) anthology of earlier snippets. This lexicon gives an entry for Theus-Ares, 'Theus-Ares: this is the god Ares in Petra of Arabia, for they honour him especially. The image is a black stone, square, unshaped, four feet high, two wide. It is placed on a gold-plated base. To this they sacrifice and pour out the blood of sacrificial victims. This is for them the libation. The whole building is rich in gold and there are many dedications' (translation from Healey 2001, 96). Clement of Alexandria in the second century (Protrepticus 4.46,2; see Patrich 1990, 51 n. 2) had noted that the Arabs worshipped a stone, and his contemporary Tertullian knew that the god of Provincia Arabiae was Dusares (Apologeticum 24.8; see Patrich 1990, 52 n. 6); a little earlier Maximus Tyrius (c.AD 125–185) said that he did not know whom the Arabs worshipped but that he had seen their image: it was a square stone

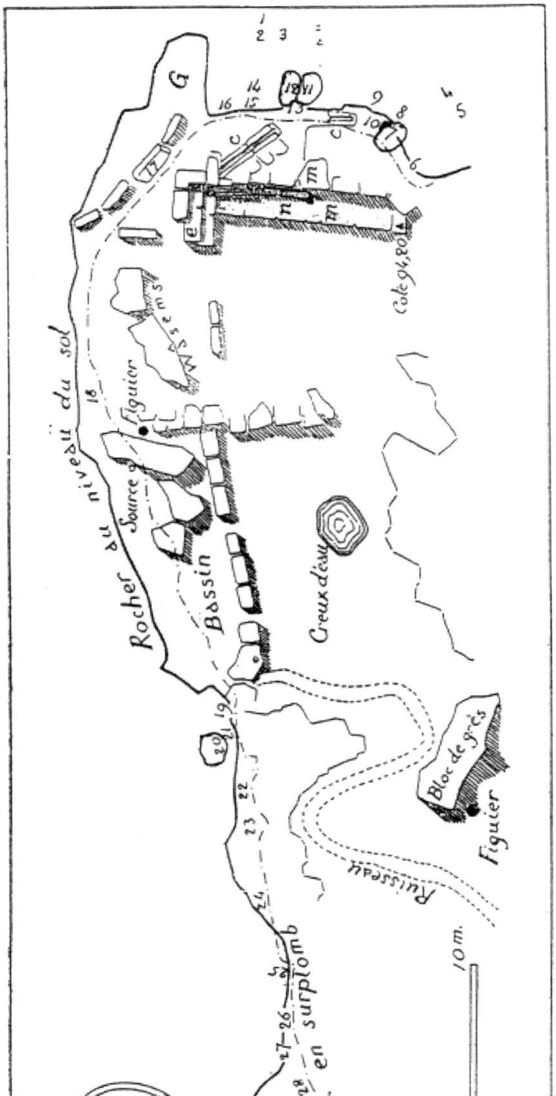

1. Plan of 'Ain esh-Shellāleh (Savignac, RB 43 [1934], p. 573, fig. 1)

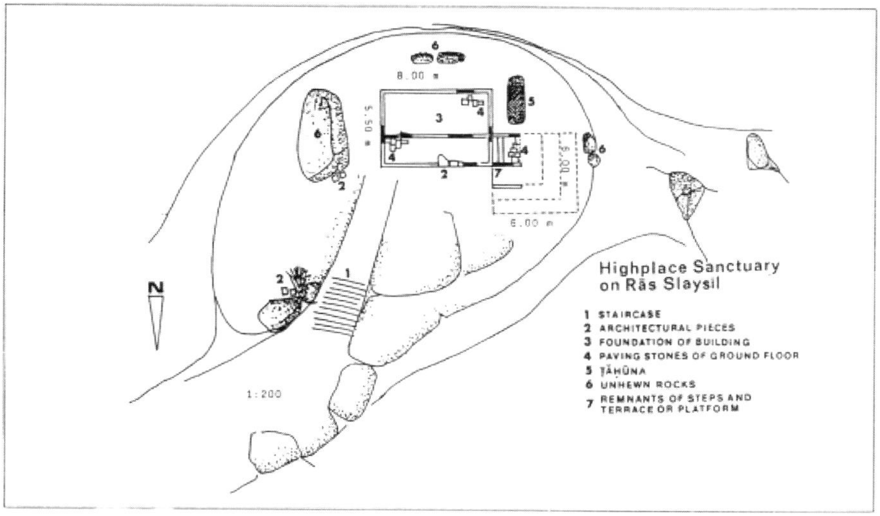

2. Plan of sanctuary of Rās Slaysil (Lindner, ADAJ 39 [1995], p. 272, fig. 5)

Philosophoumena 2.8; see Patrich 1990, 51 n. 3). Clearly, some ancient writers knew of Dusares as the Nabataean god, and of the use of a square stone as an image of deity.

Our own knowledge of Nabataean religion is largely based on examination of the ancient monuments and inscriptions. Almost the first things one sees on descending from el-Ji to Petra are the large, solid blocks of stone, commonly known as Dushara blocks, cut away from the surrounding sandstone. If they indeed represent the chief Nabataean deity, what did they convey to the Nabataean devout? A sense of mystery, or power? The presence of the deity? What did Nabataean worshippers do at them or round them? They appear in smaller versions in the betyls which stand in niches carved into the rock faces round Petra, sometimes individually, sometimes in groups, and sometimes accompanied by inscriptions. The word betyl itself derives via the Greek from the Hebrew word Beth-el, house of God, which was the name given to the place where, according to Genesis 28.19, Jacob, fleeing from Esau, had set up a pillar and poured oil on the top of it. The setting up of a stone pillar in honour of the deity was a very ancient practice indeed in this part of the world, as anyone who has visited Gezer in Israel or Lejjun in Jordan knows. Most of these betyls are plain, and rectangular, standing in the shallow recess of the niche; sometimes there are two blocks side by side, or even three; sometimes one is larger than the other. But, unless there is an inscription beside them, they are anonymous. If they represent a deity, they are aniconic, suggesting no figuration of the deity (see Mettinger 1995). Some of these betyls, however, have inscribed a pair of squares indicating eyes, or two squares and a vertical line between them representing eyes and nose; or even occasionally a mouth as well. The basic form, plain, rectangular, and severe, is

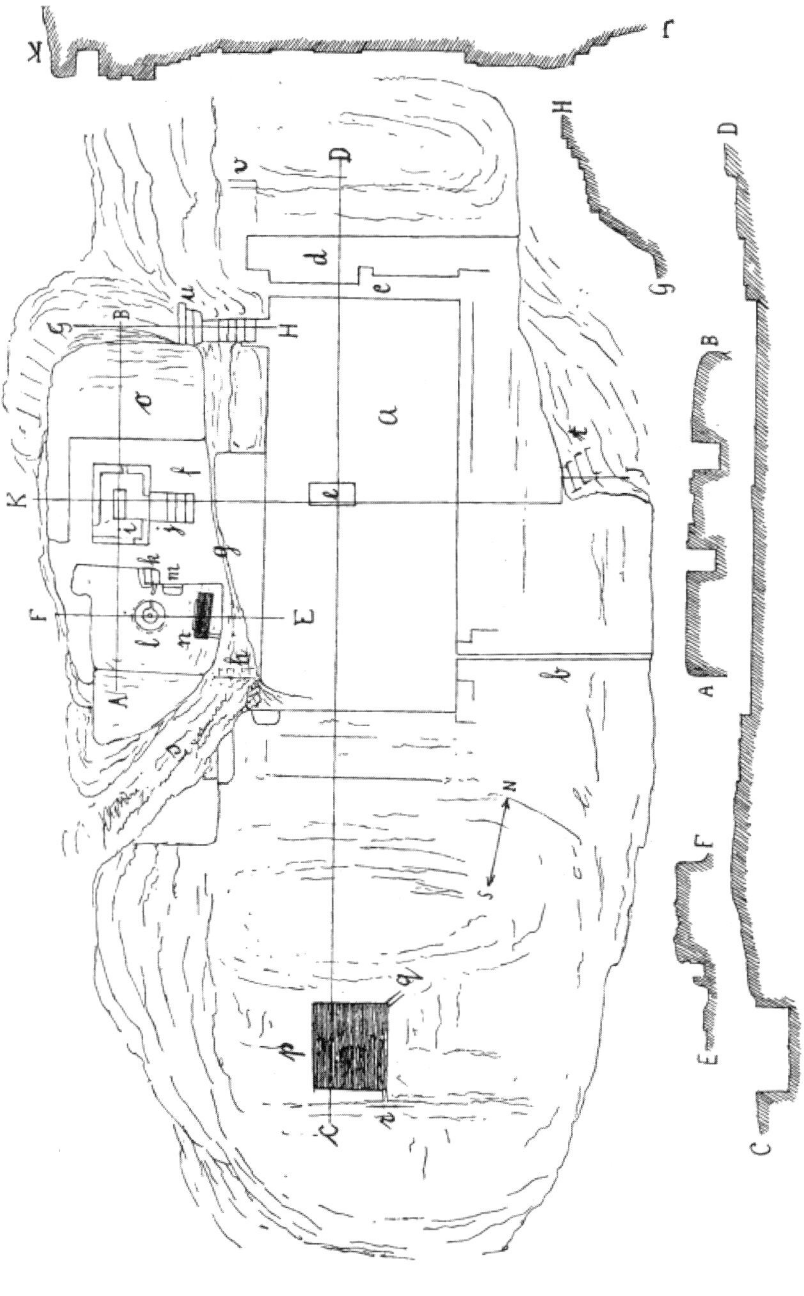

3. Plan of the Great High Place, Petra (Dalman, *Petra und seine Felsheiligtumer* [1908], abb. 83)

preserved; yet there seems to be some concession to representing the deity concerned in something approaching human form. This is perhaps intended to represent a god who observes, who smells the sacrifices, and who perhaps even speaks, presumably through natural phenomena like thunder or through human, prophetic figures.

Also observable are areas which seem to have been sanctuaries, set aside for corporate worship of some kind. Betyls in their niches alongside a path may have been cut by individuals, to meet individual needs of prayer or thankoffering or the like; but the wider spaces of sanctuaries were surely intended for public, communal rituals. Pere Savignac identified a sanctuary at Ain Shellāleh in Wadi Ramm (fig. 1); here a length of rock face was covered with niches and inscriptions, and a small aqueduct channelled water from the spring (Savignac 1932, 1933, 1934). Manfred Lindner discovered a high place at Rās Slaysil north west of Petra (fig. 2), with a structure built against a huge rock high above a Nabataean temple 450 metres below (Lindner and Gunsam 1995); he also identified a 'garden sanctuary' above the Sidd el-Ma'ajin, which is a narrow ravine in the north-eastern corner of Petra, full of cultic niches. The sanctuary above also contained niches, both rectangular and arched, water basins for lustrations, a triclinium and biclinium (dining halls with stone benches), sherds of broken bowls for offerings, and a processional way. Lindner sees such a sanctuary as catering for religious needs quite different from those satisfied by the major temples such as the Qasr al Bint (Lindner 1990). Most famous of all, there is the great high place of Petra (fig. 3), cut from the rock at the summit of Jebel Madbah (Wenning 1987, 217–20). The processional route up from Wadi Farasā led the worshippers to a slightly sunken court measuring 16 m north-south by 7 m east-west; in the middle is a raised platform 1.55 x .85 m.; this faces a 3 m x 2 m altar block approached by three steps and separated from the surrounding rock by a narrowly cut passage. Some water tanks and drainage channels (for washing away the messier aspects of sacrifice?) complete the ensemble, though two nearby obelisks, formed by cutting the rock away on all sides, may have been related in some way, perhaps as symbols of the gods whose site this was. This sanctuary has been well known for a century, but the ceremonies enacted here, and their religious meaning, remain hard to determine.

The other obvious signs of Nabataean religion are the temples. Among others, we might mention the temples at Si^c, Sūr and Sahr in the Hauran area (Wenning 1987, 31–38, 27–28, 26–27); at Gerasa (ibid. 54–56); at Dibon, at Dhāt Rās, and at Qasr Rabba in the region of ancient Moab (ibid. 62–64, 73, 67–68); at Lehun in Moab (Homès-Fredericq 1989, 575–80); at Kh et-Tannūr (Wenning 1987, 76–81) , Kh. edh-Dhariḥ (ibid. 82–84), the Qasr al Bint (ibid. 234–245) and the Temple of the Winged Lions (Hammond 1986) (fig.4) and the 'Pond temple' (Lindner and Gunsam 1993) in Petra itself, all in the region of ancient Edom; and the temple at er-Ramm in the W. Ḥismah region (Wenning 1987, 101–105; Tholbecq 1998). In Egypt there is the temple at Qasrawet (Oren 1982) (fig. 5). Abraham Negev has brought to light a large Nabataean temple at Avdat (Wenning 1987, 159–72). There appear to be two basic types of Nabataean

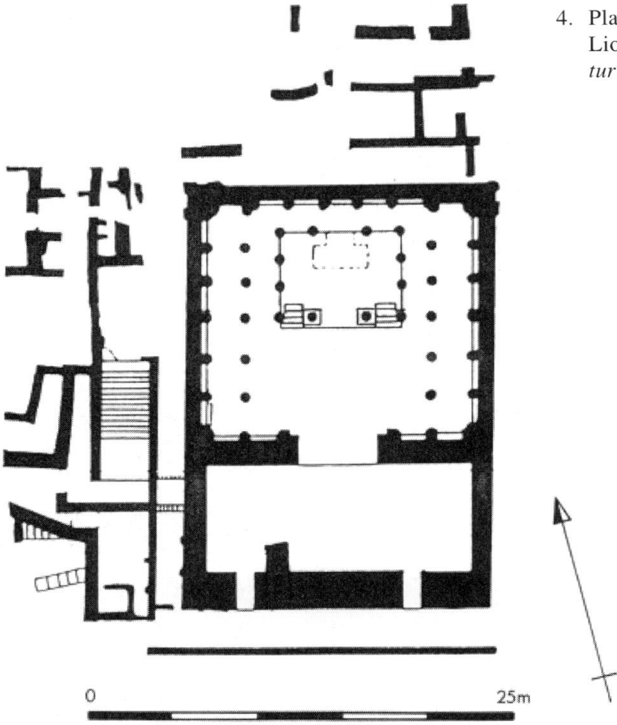

4. Plan of Temple of the Winged Lions (McKenzie, *The Architecture of Petra* [1990], Pl. 78b)

temples (cf. Mettinger 1995, 66–7). The first (fig. 6) is based on a square cella, or shrine, sometimes with a pillar at each corner, sometimes walled, perhaps with niches containing cult statues on the front; round this shrine an outer wall has been built; the effect is of one box inside another. This basic plan is seen in the temples at Siʿ, Sūr and Sahr in the north, and also at Kh. Et-Tannūr, Kh. Edh-Dhariḥ, the Petra Temple of the Winged Lions, and Er-Ramm in the south, so this is not simply 'the northern type' of temple, as Negev suggests (Negev 1977, 617,

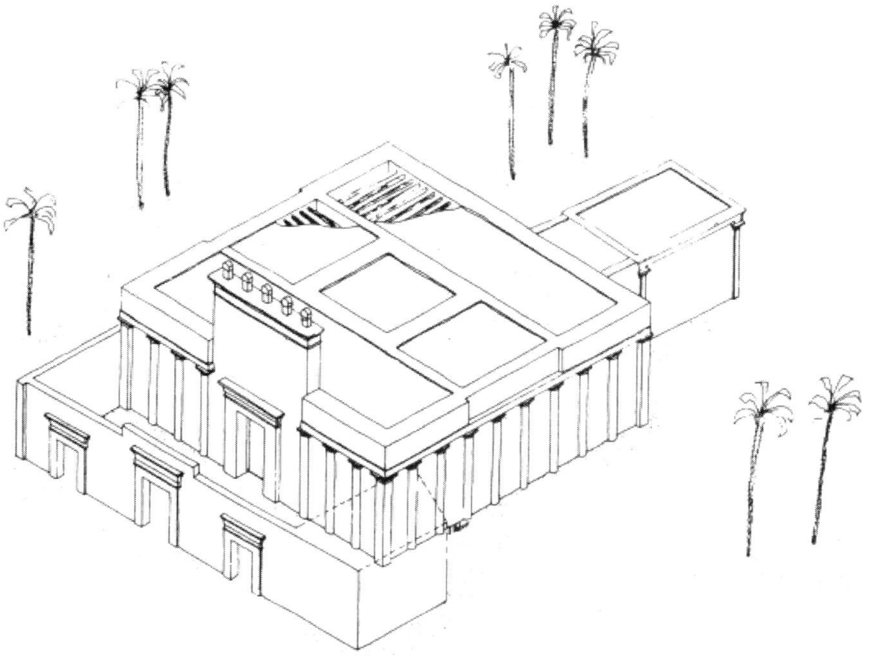

5. Nabataean temple at Qasrawet: isometric view from north-west (Oren, IEJ 32 [1982], p. 207, fig. 4)

619). It is not clear just what the inner constructions were – whether altars or platforms for altars, or shrines containing idols. Stairs, internal or external, led up to an altar, or perhaps to a roof altar, on which according to Negev (Negev 1977, 617; cf Sheila Gibson's drawing of Kh. et-Tannūr, fig. 7) incense was burned. In the second type (fig. 8), seen particularly at Qasr al Bint (fig. 9), Dibon, and Qasr Rabba, the temple building perhaps is nearer the usual Greek pattern: a wide stairway in front leads to a pillared pronaos, and then to the main cella, with an adyton, usually tripartite, at the rear. In the first type, the worshipper could move round the central shrine, perhaps even process round it; in the second, the worshipper could approach the adyton and the image displayed in it, and worship before it. Both types had access to the roof, but presumably, with narrow staircases, access was for priests or officials or workmen rather than for the worshipping public. How the second type relates to the first is not clear. Was it a development of it, the original free-standing shrine being moved to the back wall, thus creating three chambers at the temple's rear? If the central room was used for the cult statue or stone block, what were the side rooms used for? Both types, however, were entered through a large forecourt, or *theatron*, surrounded with colonnades on three sides, with benches on the rear walls, and an altar somewhere in the middle. This was surely where the crowds gathered for major religious festivals or other national occasions.

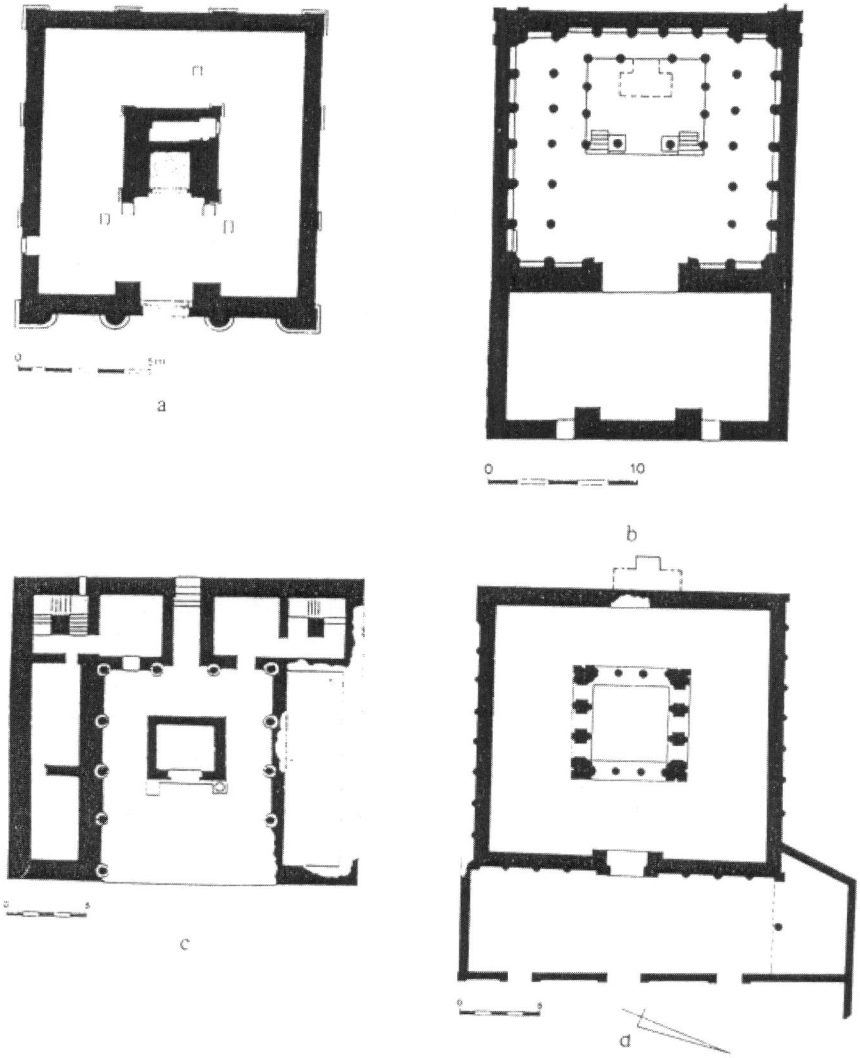

6. Nabataean temples with square ground plan (Patrich, *The Formation of Nabataean Art* [1990], p. 44, ill. 2)

All this is only general observation; we need more specific information about the deities worshipped through these stone blocks, betyls, high places and sanctuaries, and temples. This further information can come from inscriptional and iconographical evidence. A stele found on Jebel et-Tannur, on the northern border of the earlier Iron Age kingdom of Edom, bears an inscription reading '[stele] which Qosmalak made for Qos, god of ḤWRW' (Savignac 1937, 408–9,

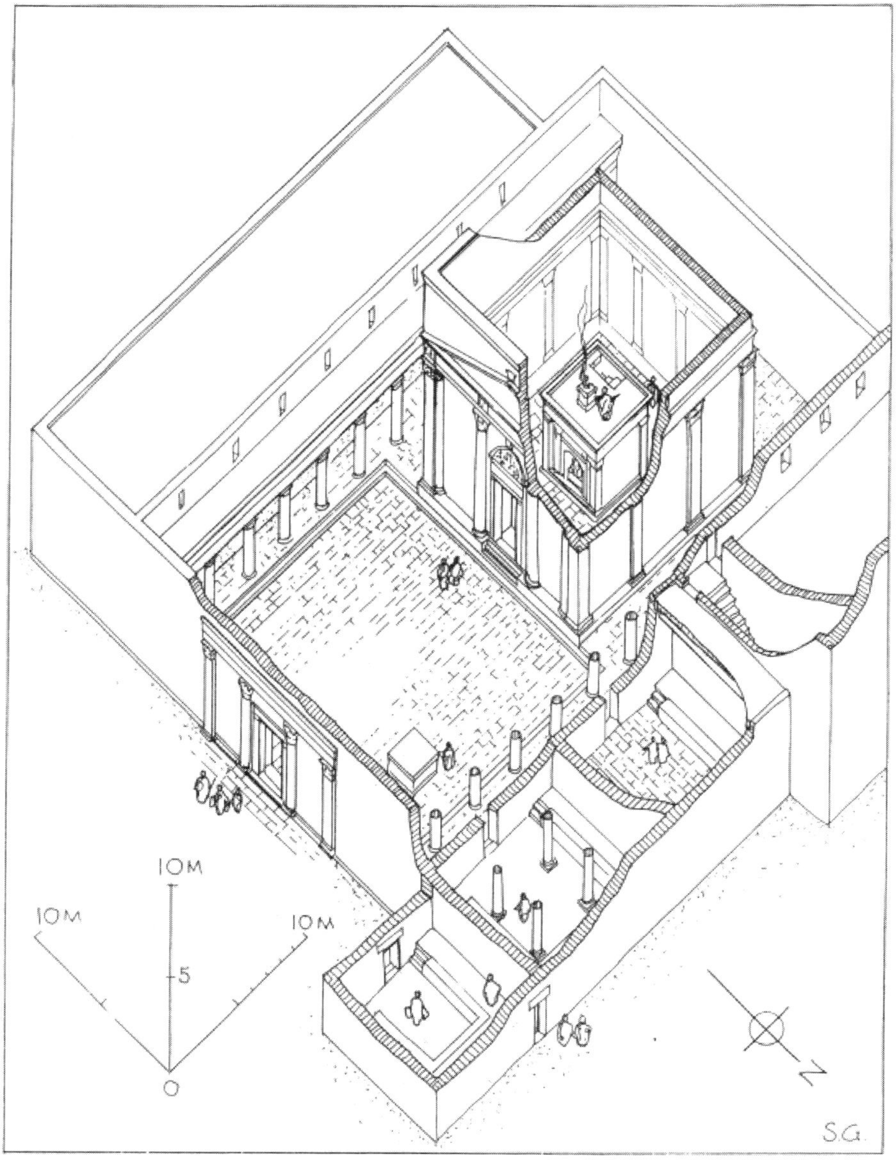

7. Axonometric reconstruction of temple complex at Khirbet et-Tannūr (S.Gibson, J.McKenzie, PEQ 134.1 [2002], p. 70, fig. 21)

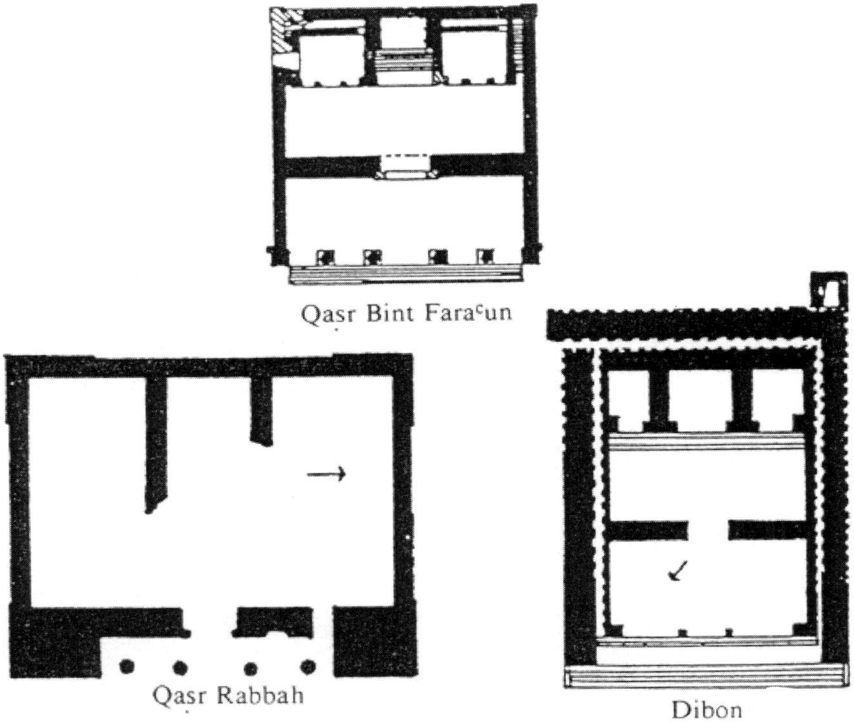

8. Nabataean temples with tripartite adyton (Patrich, *The Formation of Nabataean Art* [1990], p. 46, ill. 3

pl. IX.3, X; Milik 1958, 237–39; Healey 2001, 61, 127). ḤWRW may be the original name of the location of this sanctuary; Qos was certainly the name of the god worshipped here by the Edomites before the Nabataean civilisation developed (Bartlett 1989, 200–207). Also at Jebel et-Tannūr Glueck found a statue (fig. 10) showing a god holding a thunderbolt, seated between two bulls, perhaps representing Qos but carved in the form of the Syrian god Hadad, who was also identified in the hellenized east with the Greek Zeus (Glueck 1966, 93–94, 195–209, pls 41, 42). A bilingual Greek-Nabataean inscription at Bosra in Syria records that 'Muaino son of Zabdai has made the eagle in honour of Qos' (Milik 1958, 235–4; Healey 2001, 126–7). The worship of Qos is thus evidenced through both the Edomite and the Nabataean periods, and into the third century. The most helpful evidence for Nabataean deities comes from the sanctuary at Ain esh-Shellāleh, the spring of the waterfall below Jebel Ramm, in the Ḥismeh region of Jordan. T.E. Lawrence visited this spring in the course of his campaign in the First World War, and comments on the inscriptions (Lawrence 1940, 363). Père Savignac of the Ecole Biblique in Jerusalem visited this site in April 1932, and reported finding a sanctuary, with inscriptions, niches and betyls on the rock

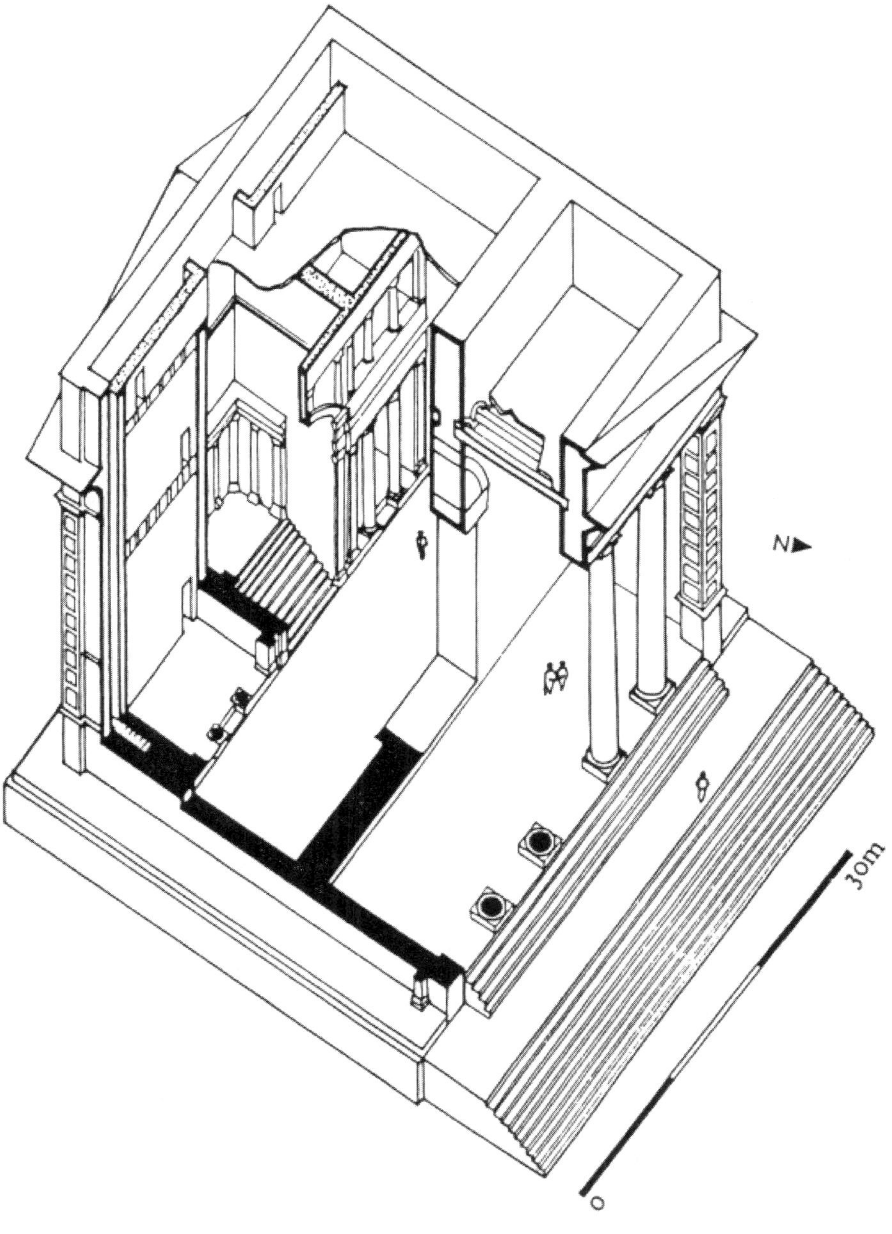

9. Axonometric reconstruction of Qasr el-Bint (McKenzie, *The Architecture of Petra* [1990], Pl. 68b)

10. Statue of Qos-Hadad-Zeus at Kh. Et-Tannur (Glueck, *Deities and Dolphins* [1966], p. 94, pl. 42)

face round the spring (Savignac 1932, 1933, 1934). First, a rectangular niche, with pilasters indicated on either side, contained a rectangular plain betyl with a sphere above it, set above a square block with arms extending upwards like horns – presumably some sort of throne or *motab* (betyl no. 7) (fig. 11). An inscription to the left reads, 'This is the goddess Allat of Bosra' (Savignac 1932, 587; 1934, 582–5, Pl. xxviii, and fig. 7). The same goddess was worshipped at the nearby temple in Wadi Ramm, where an inscription refers to 'the great goddess who is at Iram' (Savignac and Horsfield 1935, 245–78; pl x., 1a & b); another local inscription is a memorial to Hayan 'before Allatou the goddess who is at Iram' (Savignac 1932, 593). Another niche at Ain esh-Shellāleh contained two rectangular stelae, one plain, and the other, larger, stele with two squares representing

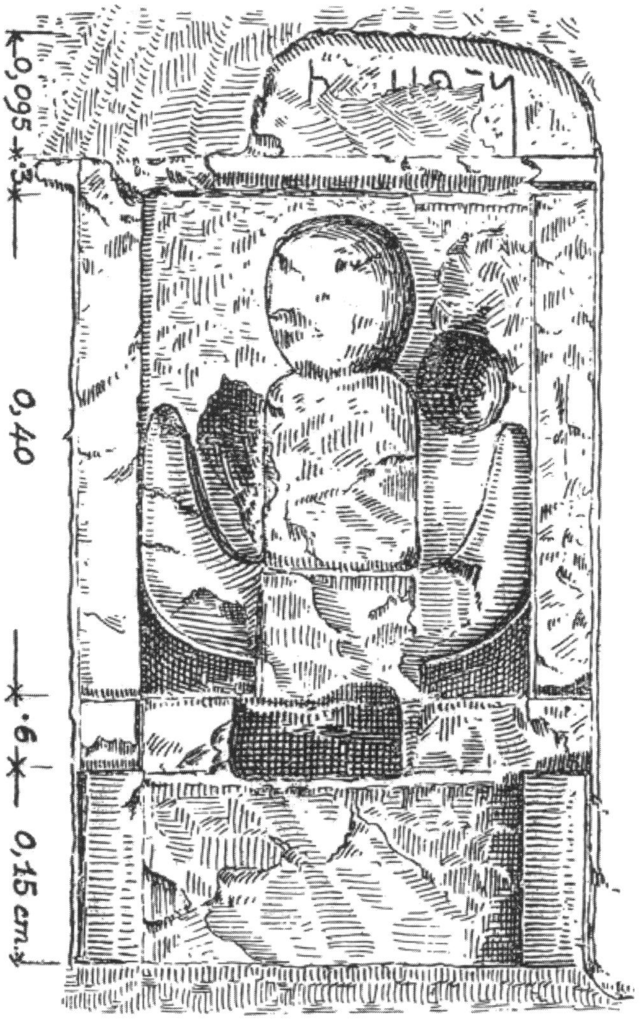

11. Betyl of Allat of Bosra, at Ramm (Savignac, RB 43 [1934], p. 584, fig. 7)

eyes; this had the accompanying inscription 'This is al-'Uzza and the Lord of the House' (Savignac 1933, 413f., Pl. xxiv, and fig. 5) (fig. 12). A similar inscription was found on the path up to el-Hubta in Petra alongside an empty niche, perhaps designed to receive portable betyls of the two gods brought by pilgrims (Torrey 1907, 349; 1908, 197ff.). Al-'Uzza is female; her apparent consort is 'The Lord of the House', that is, presumably, the god of the temple, probably the god Dushara. Al-'Uzza is coupled with another god named as al-Kutbā of Gaia in an inscription accompanying a pair of stelae at Ain esh-Shellāleh (Savignac 1934, 574–5 [no. 17]) (fig. 13). Both these two stelae are 'eye-idols', with slightly star-shaped eyes and a vertical, rectangular bar for a nose. The inscription below them

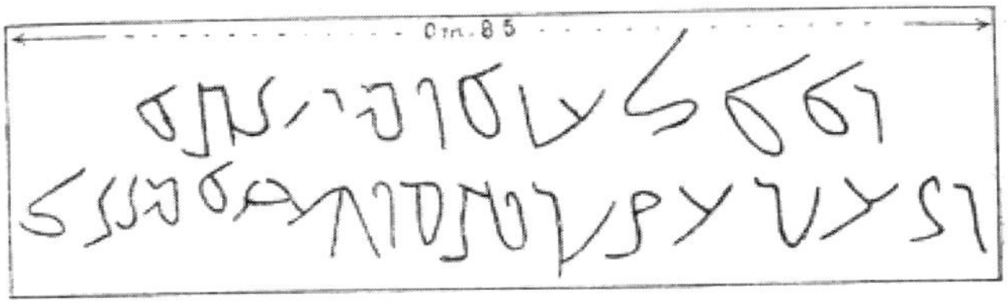

12. Inscription, *al-'Uzza and Lord of the House* (Savignac, RB 42 [1933], p. 414, fig.5)

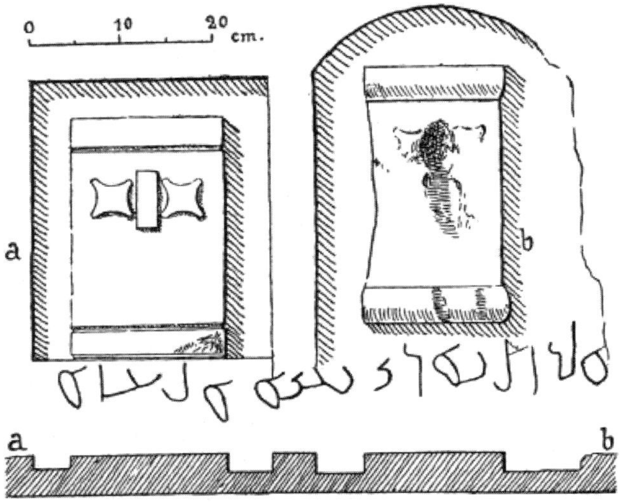

13. Inscription, *al-Kutba' of Gaia, al-'Uzza* (Savignac, RB 43 [1934], p. 587, fig. 10)

reads 'al-Kutbā of Gaia, el-'Uzza'. Al-Kutbā is usually taken to be male, and el-'Uzza female. Al-Kutbā is identified as being at home at Gaia, i.e., el-Ji, outside Petra, but had temples at Tell esh-Shuqafiya and at Qasrawet in Egypt (Strugnell 1959, Patrich 1990, 61, Zayadine 1990, 35–51). Two other eye-idols should be noticed here: first, the eye-idol from Petra (fig. 14) accompanied by the inscription *'TR'T' MNBGYT'*, i.e., the Syrian goddess Atargatis of Membidj (Hierapolis, on the Euphrates) (Brunnow and Domaszewski 1904, 323, fig. 358 no 428k,1 = CIS II, 422f.; Patrich 1990, 82–3; Lindner and Zangenberg 1993). And second, the beautifully cut stela (fig. 15) from the Temple of the Winged Lions in Petra (Hammond 1981), whose inscription reads 'the goddess of Haiyan, son of Nayibat' – but which goddess was this? The obvious possibility is the goddess al-'Uzza, and a temple dedicated to her at Petra, directly across the wadi from the Qasr el-Bint, which is generally associated with Dushara, would make sense. Al-'Uzza was identified in the Greek world with Aphrodite; we know this principally from a bilingual inscription found on the island of Cos (Levi della Vida 1938), but also from some gold ear-rings found at Mamshit in Israel. One pair bears a design reminiscent of the eye-idols, with two eyes and a nose; a very similar ear-ring, also from mamshit, has much the same design but with a recognisable Aphrodite in place of the nose (Patrich 1984; 1990, 137–9). But another possibil-

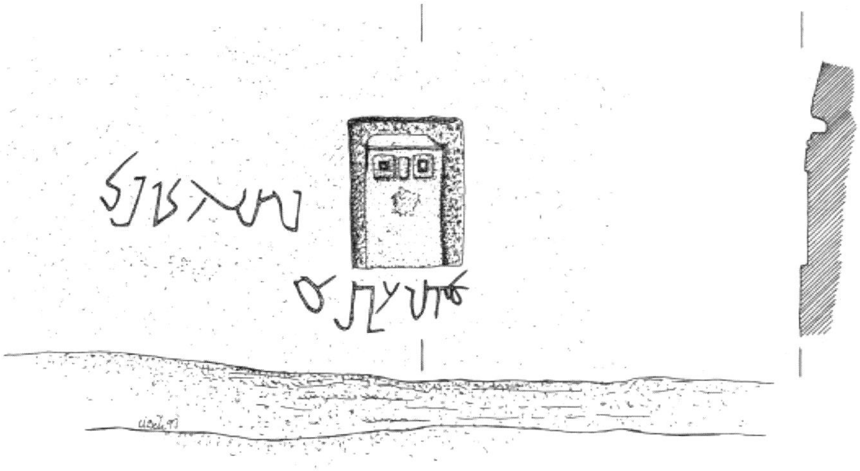

14. Inscription, 'TR 'T' MNBGYT' (Lindner and Zangenberg, ZDPV [1993], p. 144, fig. 1)

15. Stele of the goddess of Haiyan, son of Nayibat (Hammond, BJB 180 [1980], p. 139, fig. 1)

ity for the goddess is the Syrian Atargatis, for an eye-idol with her name attached was found in the Wadi Siyyagh in Petra (see above) (Lindner and Zangenberg 1993). But Atargatis was not a Nabataean goddess in origin and was not at home in Petra (cf Hammond 1990, 119–20), and it is hard to believe that the local Nabataeans would build a major, central temple to her there. More recently Hammond has suggested identifying her as the important Nabataean goddess Allat (Hammond 1990) – but though Allat was at home at er-Ramm, she was not at home in Petra, and is not mentioned by any inscription so far found in Petra (as Zayadine points out in a note appended to Hammond's article, p. 127), so that this identification also seems unlikely. Recently, Healey (2001, 141) has collected evidence of the influence of the Egyptian goddess Isis in the Temple of the Winged Lions at Petra, and notes Isis decoration (cf. Hammond 1981) on the stele from the temple, and describes the stele as an 'Isis figurine' (caption to Plate IVa). However, Healey does not see the stele as portraying the goddess of the temple. The most convincing identification of the goddess of Haiyan son of Nayibat may yet be al-'Uzza, 'the powerful one'.

More should be said about al-Kutbā and Dushara. Al-Kutbā's name probably derives from the Semitic root *ktb*, to write (Zayadine 1990b, 35), and so perhaps means 'the scribe'. A triclinium inscription from Petra, 'before Kutbā [KWTB'], this god', suggests that this god is masculine (not feminine, as Strugnell [1959, 29–36] argued) (Milik and Teixidor 1961, 22–25). Healey (2001, 122–4), however, points out that the masculine KWTB' of the Petra inscription is spelled differently from the more common 'LKTB', and he regards the two as 'distinct deities, perhaps male and female aspects of the same planetary deity, Mercury' (ibid. 123). Fawzi Zayadine has argued, 'as a scribal god, Al-Kutba is to be equated with the Egyptian Thot, Assyrian Nabu, Palmyrene Arsu, Safaitic Ruda and Graeco-Roman Hermes-Mercury' (1990b, 38). These identifications would link Al-Kutbā with the Orotal of Herodotus; Orotal was the male god of the two gods Herodotus credited to the Nabataeans' Arab precursors. The point is, not that these various deities are be identified, but that they have sufficient similarities for ancient Nabataeans or Greeks or others crossing borders to identify them. Just how the Nabataeans perceived al-Kutbā's role in their lives is hard to say; but if he was associated in their minds with Nabu he was perhaps a divine scribe who wrote down people's destinies; and if he was associated with the Greek Hermes, he was the god of writing and astronomy, an interpreter of the divine will, the one who accompanied the spirits of the dead, the one who protected travellers and shepherds in this life. Al-Kutbā' is known to have been worshipped at el-Ji next to Petra, at Qasrawet and at Tell esh-Shuqāfiyeh, where a temple was built to him, in Egypt (cf. Zayadine 1990b, 37–38), all stations on important trade routes, and al-Kutbā' was perhaps revered as the protector of travelling Nabataeans (Strugnell 1959, 29–36). But though there is plenty of sculptural evidence of the popularity of Hermes-Mercury at Petra and at Jebel et-Tannūr (Glueck 1966, 465–70, pls 145–52), there is little if any hard evidence directly associating al-Kutbā with Hermes-Mercury. L'Abbé Starcky identified al-Kutbā rather with the chief Nabataean god Dushara himself, both al-Kutbā and Dushara being versions of Herodotus' Orotal, the Safaitic or North Arabian god Ruḍā (Starcky 1966, cols 993–6). Both gods are associated in inscriptions with Gaia (el-Ji) near Petra (see Savignac 1934, 574–5; Healey 2001, 90). The names al-Kutbā and Dushara are both descriptive names – 'the scribe', and 'he of Shara' (the mountain area around Petra) – and both may therefore be titles applied to a god with a proper name, e.g., the North Arabian Ruda, Graecised as Orotal. However, there are two difficulties here: Ruda does not appear in Nabataean inscriptions or personal names, and al-Kutbā' is probably feminine, not masculine; Starcky's proposed identification of Dushara and al-Kutbā', therefore, must probably be rejected (Healey 2001, 94, 123–4).

Dusares (Drijvers 1986) is a Greek version, perhaps influenced by the name of the Greek god of war, Ares, of the Arabic form Dushara, 'he of Shara': inscriptions in his honour and other evidence of his cult have been found as far west as Puteoli in Italy (where a sanctuary was dedicated to him; Wenning 1987, 22–3), at Miletus on the Aegean coast of Turkey (ibid. 23), at es-Suweda in Syria (ibid. 39), at Bosra and Imtan in the Hauran region (ibid. 44, 47), at Susita (Hippos?) and Der'a in the Decapolis (ibid. 53–4), at Medeba (ibid. 59) and Lejjun (ibid. 76) in Moab, at el-Sil' (ibid. 86–7) and el-Ji (ibid. 91) in Edom, at Jebel Ramm in the Wadi Hismah (ibid. 102), at al-Jauf in the Wadi Sirhan (ibid. 115), at Madā'in Ṣāliḥ in the Hegra (ibid. 120), at Wadi Mukatteb in Sinai (ibid. 194), at Sobata (ibid. 155) and Oboda (ibid. 169) in the Negev, and in other places. Dushara was obviously widely known, over a long period (Bowersock 1990), and easily linked with other gods. An inscription from Imtan in the Hauran (RES 83), dated to Rabbel's twenty-third year (AD 93), bears a dedication 'to Dushara Aʿra, who resides at Bosra, god of our Lord Rabbel'; here Dushara has been identified with a local god, Aʿra (see Healey 2001, 97–9). At Ain esh-Shellāleh, there is a dedicatory inscription 'to Dushara A'[ra],... to Ba'alshamin, gods of our lord [Rabbel]' (Savignac 1934, 576f.), which puts Dushara alongside another important god of Syria, Baalshamin. But Dushara's real home was nearer Petra: an inscription from Jauf refers to a sanctuary built by one Ganimu 'for Dushara the god of Gaia who is at Dumat [i.e., Jauf]' (Savignac and Starcky 1957, 198), and another inscription from Avdat similarly describes Dushara as 'the god of Gaia' ('LH G'Y') (Negev 1963, 113, no. 10). Dushara's associations with Gaia, which is el-Ji (Petra), and Bosra, and with king Rabbel II, who according to some scholars moved the seat of his kingdom from Petra to Bosra, make it clear that Dushara was publicly presented as the patron of the Nabataean royal house, the Nabataeans' chief god. He was represented by a plain rectangular betyl or by the large stone blocks at the entrance to the Siq at Petra; the black stone mentioned in Suidas' lexicon may have been the representation of Dushara in his temple in Petra, the Qasr al-Bint – though some argue that the fragmentary hand from a large statue found there is evidence for an anthropomorphic statue of the god in the adyton (Parr 1968). The 'medallion and block' relief (fig. 16) on the way up to the high place perhaps illustrates a development from an aniconic to an anthropomorphic way of representing the god – the medallion perhaps represented Dionysus (Zayadine 1989, 115)) or a fertility/vegetation goddess from

16. Medallion and block relief (Hammond, BASOR 192 [1968], p. 17, fig. 1)

17. Coin of Antoninus Pius from Der'a (Hill, *BMC Arabia* [1922], pl. xlix.2)

18. Coin from Bosra (Hill, *BMC Arabia* [1922], pl. xlix. 13)

Kh et-Tannūr (Hammond 1968, 16–21); Dushara became associated with the Greek gods Dionysus and Zeus (especially in the Hauran, where Dionysus was popular). But the aniconic tradition continued; a mid-second century coin (fig. 17) of Antoninus Pius (138–61) from Der'a (Adraa) in Syria shows an oval dome on a raised platform, with pillars either side; the Greek inscription round the coin's edge says 'Dousares, god of the people of Der'a' (Hill 1922, xxii–xxiv, pls iii.5, xlix.2; Patrich 1990, 70–71, ill. 14). A slightly later coin (fig. 18) from Bosra, Syria, however, shows on one side a beardless male head crowned with a diadem – perhaps representing Dusares –, and on the other side a raised platform, reached by a ladder, with three stelae on top of it, and two human figures

19. Figures of goddess Isis at Petra (Roche, Syria 64 [1987], p. 219, figs 1,2)

apparently involved in a ritual act before them. The inscription says 'Dousares of the people of Bosra' (Hill 1922, xxvi. Pl. xlix.13; Patrich 1990, 71–4, ill.15). The plate-like objects on top of the stelae are much debated – loaves, perhaps, or stones have been suggested. The three stelae may represent Dusares (in the middle) with two other gods – Al-Uzza? Allat? – on either side.

The importance of Dushara must not blind us to the evidence that foreign deities were known and venerated at Petra – we have already mentioned Syrian Atargatis and Baalshamin, and their presence is not surprising given that Nabataean power extended into Syria in the mid-first century of this era, as St Paul found to his cost (2 Cor. 11.32). But the Egyptian goddess Isis was also well-known at Petra (Roche 1987; for a recent survey of evidence, see Healey 2001, 137–40). Most obviously, there is the relief of the goddess Isis-Tyche on the tholos of the Khazneh, and an Isis-crown on the central akroterion of the middle gable (see on this especially Lyttelton 1990, 21–22); as the Khazneh was probably a tomb for Obodas III or Aretas IV, these features suggest a royal interest in the Egyptian goddess (Milik and Starcky 1975, 123; Zayadine 1991, 301. A headless female figure, seated on a throne, with an Isis knot between her breasts, found at a Nabataean sanctuary near Jebel Harun, was probably a statue of Isis (Parr 1962, 21–3) (fig. 19, 2). A cultic niche near the mouth of the Wadi Siyagh dated in the fifth year of Obodat, i.e., 25 BC, holds a small carved figure of an enthroned Isis (fig. 19, 1), with an inscription reading (A) 'This goddess/is Isis/

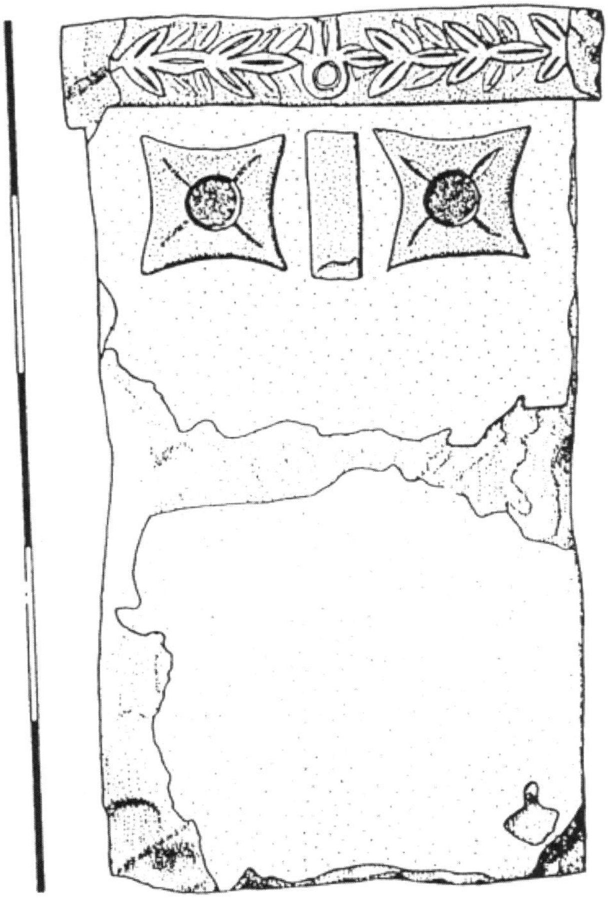

20. Al-Uzza-Isis-Stele from ez-Zantur (Lindner, AfO 40/41 [1933/4], p. 316, figs 26, 27)

which was made by the sons of Bar/H..LYR Qaiuma/and....LMNB' '; (B) 'On the first (day) of (the month) Iyyar,/ in year/ five/ of Obdas/ the king' (Milik and Starcky 1975, 120–24, pl. 45; Merklein and Wenning 1998, 166–8; Healey 2001, 138). This is the oldest datable anthropomorphic figure so far known in Petra; it is also apparently the work of Nabataeans, not Greeks or Egyptians. (One might note also the presence in Petra of an Egyptian votive statue of a priest of Osiris, found in the cellar area of the Temple of Winged Lions [Meza 1993]; this is unlikely to indicate any Nabataean cult of Osiris at Petra, but Meza suggests the statuette might have been deposited in an Isis temple on the site of the later Temple of Winged Lions [Meza 1996, 174–5].) Other fragments witness to Isis' presence in Petra, for example, the stele found by Manfred Lindner in 1988 at ez-Zantur (fig. 20) which combines the Isis emblem with the features of an eye-idol (Lindner 1993/4, 316–18). This suggests that there was – perhaps in the first century AD – some identification of Isis with al-'Uzza. Al-Uzza was a goddess, the powerful one; Isis herself represented the female principle, controlling the transformation of things, ruling the sea, the fruits of the earth, and the dead, and she was widely popular in the Graeco-Roman world. If the Khazneh suggests that Nabataean royalty was interested in her, the niche and its idol by the Wadi Siyagh suggest that her cult extended further down the social scale.

In this brief overview of Nabataean religion, there is no time to examine other, less influential deities like Hubalu and Manōtu and Shai' el-Qaum (see Healey 2001, 127–32; 132–35; 145–47; Gawlikowski 1990, 2668–71). More should be said about Jebel et-Tannūr and the iconography revealed by Nelson Glueck's excavations in 1937 (Glueck 1966). Why, for example, did a Nabataean ruler set up on that remote peak a statue of a Hellenistic Tyche holding up a circular zodiac (fig. 21) (Glueck 1952, McKenzie 2002)? The only inscription at Jebel et-Tannūr naming a deity is from the Nabataean stele dedicated to the god Qos (Savignac 1937, 408f., pl.X; Milik 1958, 237). Perhaps Jebel et-Tannūr was originally a sanctuary of the Edomite god Qos, developed in its second, main, phase by king Rabbel II, anxious to present his kingdom as part of the wider cultural world of hellenised Syria. Perhaps more typical of popular religious sentiment are the tomb inscriptions of Medāin Ṣāliḥ, where, for example, Kamkam daughter of Wa'ilat together with her own daughter Kulaybat made a tomb for themselves and added this imprecation at the doorway 'May Dushara and his throne' – note that the throne, the *motab*, is conceived to have divine powers – 'and Allat of 'Amnad and Manōtu and her Qayshu curse anyone who sells this tomb or who buys it or gives it in pledge or who makes a gift of it or removes from it body or limb or who buries in it anyone other than Kamkam and her daughter and their descendants' (Healey 1993, 154). Though it is sometimes tempting to think that the Nabataeans really had only three or four chief gods, the gods Dushara and al-Kutbā' (both associated with Gaia), and the goddess Allat, possibly to be identified with the goddess al-Uzza/Aphrodite (Healey 2001, 113, 116), the evidence of such inscriptions as Kamkam's and of the several gods worshipped at Ain esh-Shellāleh make clear that the popular mind ignored sophisticated theology and venerated a wider pantheon. Strabo (Geog. 16.4.26) says that the Nabataeans worshipped the sun on their rooftops; perhaps Dushara was identified in the minds of some with Zeus Helios (for possible evidence see Healey 2001, 102–4). Reliefs of the sungod Helios have been found at et-Tannūr (Glueck 1966, 144, 454–5, pl.136), Qasr al-Bint, Qasr Rabba (Glueck 1966, 58, 287, pl. 137a) and elsewhere, and in Syria certainly the Greeks assimilated Baalbek's chief god to their Helios (Teixidor 1977, 59). There was clearly some association of Nabataean gods with Graeco-Roman gods, as, for example, of Dushara with Dionysus, Zeus and Helios (cf. Herod. Hist. 3.8; Zayadine 1989, 116; Healey 2001, 100–106), or of al-'Uzza with Aphrodite (L. della Vida 1938, Zayadine 1984, 1991, Healey 2001, 117), or of Allat with Athene (Zayadine 1989, 119, Healey 2001, 113), and there was some use of hellenistic iconography. But one must ask, in which social context did this take place? One suspects that while the plebeian heart of Nabataean religion remained fiercely Semitic and somewhat uncompromising (witness the surviving aniconism of the god Dush-

21. Nike, supporting Tyche with zodiac (Glueck, *Deities and Dolphins* [1966], p. 110, pl. 48)

ara), the Nabataean rulers were glad to adorn their temples with softer and more pleasing effects from the Graeco-Roman world. In the harsher world of ordinary daily life, however, men and women carved niches, erected idols, travelled on pilgrimage, climbed to rocky sanctuaries, and offered gifts of grain and blood to gods representing the unanswerable powers of heaven and fate, the forces of nature and fertility, and life and death; surrounded by so many tombs and memorials they were clearly very aware of the ever-present mystery of death. But in the absence of documents, we have to admit that the Nabataean mind remains largely closed to us, and that Nabataean religion remains something of a mystery.

Bibliography

Bartlett, J.R., 1989. *Edom and the Edomites*, Sheffield: Sheffield Academic Press.

Bowersock, G.W., 1990. "The cult and representation of Dusares in Roman Arabia", pp. 31–36, in Zayadine 1990a.

Drijvers, H.J.W., 1986. "Dusares", LIMC III.i, 670–72.

Gawlikowski, M., 1990. "Les Dieux des Nabatéens", *ANRW* II Principat, Band 18, Religion 4, 2659–77.

Glueck, N., 1952. "The zodiac of Khirbet et-Tannûr", *BASOR* 126, 5–10.

–, 1966. *Deities and Dolphins*, London: Cassell.

Hammond, P.C., 1968. "The medallion and block-relief at Petra", *BASOR* 192, 16–21

Hammond, P.C., 1981. "Ein Nabatäisches Weiherelief aus Petra", pp. 137–41 in G.H.Salies (ed.), *Die Nabatäer: Erträge einer Ausstellung im Rheinischen Landesmuseum Bonn*, Köln: Rheinland-Verlag (= Bonner Jahrbücher 180 [1980]).

Hammond, P.C., 1986. "Die Ausgrabung des Löwen-Greifen-Tempels in Petra (1973–1983)", in M.Lindner (ed.), *Petra: Neue Ausgrabungen und Entdeckungen*, Munich: Delp), 16–30.

Hammond, P.C., 1990. "The Goddess of the 'Temple of the winged Lions' at Petra (Jordan)", pp. 115–30 in Zayadine 1990a.

Healey, J.F., 1993. *The Nabataean Tomb Inscriptions of Mada'in Salih* (JSS Supp. 1), Oxford: Oxford University Press for the University of Manchester.

Healey, J.F., 2001. *The Religion of the Nabataeans: A Conspectus*, Leiden: Brill.

Hill, G.F., 1922. *Catalogue of the Greek Coins of Arabia, Mesopotamia and Persia*, London: British Museum.

Homès-Fredericq, D., 1989. "Un temple nabatéen à Lehun (Jordanie)", in *Archaeologia iranica et orientalis* II, 575–80, ed. de Meyer, L., and Haerinck, E., Gent: Peeters.

Lawrence, T.E., 1940. *Seven Pillars of Wisdom*, 2nd ed., London: Cape.

Levi della Vida, G., 1938. "Una bilingue Greco-Nabatea a Coo", *Clara Rhodos* 9, 139–48.

Lindner, M., 1993/1994. "An Al-Uzza-Isis-Stele from Ez-Zantur", AfO 40/41, 316–17.

Lindner, M, and Gunsam, E., 1995. "The unique Nabataean high place of Rās Slaysil northwest of Petra and its topographical context", *ADAJ* 39, 267–80.

–, 1995 "A newly discovered Nabataean temple near Petra: the 'Pond Temple'", SHAJ 5, 199–214.

Lindner, M., and Zangenberg, J., 1993. "The re-discovered *Baityl* of the goddess Atargatis in the *Siyyag* gorge of Petra (Jordan) and its significance for religious life in Nabataea", ZDPV 109/2, 141–51.

McKenzie, J.S., 2002. "The sculpture of Petra and Khirbet Tannur", pp. 169–195 in G. Morhoe (ed.), *Splendors from a Caravan Kingdom*, Cincinnati: 2002.

Merklein, H., and Wenning, R., 1998. "Ein Verehrunsplatz der Isis in Petra neu untersucht", *ZDPV* 114, 162–78.

Mettinger, T.N.D., 1995. *No Graven Image? Israelite Aniconism in its ancient Near Eastern Context*. Coniectanea Biblica, Old Testament Series 42, Stockholm: Almqvist and Wiksell.
Meza, A.I., 1993. "An Egyptian statuette from Petra", *ADAJ* 37, 427–31.
–, 1996. "The Egyptian statuette in Petra and the Isis cult", *ADAJ* 40, 167–76.
Milik, J.T., 1958. "Nouvelles inscriptions nabatéennes", Syria 35, 227–51.
Milik, J.T., and Starcky, J., 1975. "Inscriptions récemment découvertes à Pétra", *ADAJ* 20, 111–30.
Milik, J.T. and Teixidor, J., 1961. "New evidence of the North-Arabic deity Aktub-Kutbâ'", *BASOR* 163, 22–25.
Negev, A., 1963. "Nabataean inscriptions from 'Abdat (Oboda) [II]", *IEJ* 13, 113–24.
Oren, E.D., 1982. "Excavations at Qasrawet in North-Western Sinai. Preliminary report", *IEJ* 32, 203–11.
Parr, P.J., 1962. "A Nabataean sanctuary near Petra: a preliminary notice", *ADAJ* 6/7, 21–23.
Parr, P.J., 1968. "Découvertes récentes au sanctuaire du Qasr à Petra", Syria 45, 1–24.
Patrich, J., 1984. "'Al-'Uzzā' Earrings", *IEJ* 34, 39–46.
–, 1990. *The Formation of Nabataean Art. Prohibition of Graven Images among the Nabataeans, Leiden*: Brill; Jerusalem: Magnes Press.
Roche, M.-J., 1987. "Le culte d'Isis et l'influence Egyptienne à Pétra", Syria 64, 217–22.
Savignac, R., 1932. "Notes de voyage: Le sanctuaire d'Allat à Iram", *RB* 41, 581–97.
–, 1933. "Le sanctuaire d'Allat à Iram" (1), *RB* 42, 405–22.
–, 1934. "Le sanctuaire d'Allat à Iram (suite)", *RB* 43, 572–89.
–, 1937. "Le Dieu nabatéen de La'aban et son temple", *RB* 46, 401–16.
Savignac, R., and Horsfield, G., 1935. "Le temple de Ramm", *RB* 44, 245–78.
Savignac, R., and Starcky, J., 1957. "Une inscription nabatéenne provenant du Djôf", *RB* 64, 196–217.
Starcky, J., 1966. "Pétra et la Nabatène", *DBS* 7, cols. 886–1017.
Strugnell, J., 1959. "The Nabataean goddess el-Kutba' and her sanctuaries", *BASOR* 156, 29–36.
Teixidor, J., 1977. *The Pagan god. Popular Religion in the Greco-Roman Near East*, Princeton, N.J.: Princeton University Press.
L.Tholbecq, 1998. "The Nabataeo-Roman site of Wadi Ramm (Iram): a new appraisal", *ADAJ* 42, 241–54.
Wenning, R., 1987. *Die Nabatäer – Denkmäler und Geschichte: Eine Bestandsaufnahme des archäologischen Befundes* (Novum Testamentum et Orbis Antiquus 3), Göttingen: Universitätsverlag Freiburg Schweiz, Vandenhoeck und Ruprecht.
Wenning, R., and Merklein, T., 1997. "Die Götter in der Welt der Nabatäer", pp. 105–110 in T.Weber and R.Wenning (eds), *Antike Felsstadt zwischen arabischer Tradition und griechischer Norm*, Mainz am Rhein: Verlag Philipp von Zabern.
G.R.H.Wright, 1969. "Strabo on funerary customs at Petra", *PEQ* 101, 113–116.
Zayadine, F., 1984. "Al-'Uzza Aphrodite", *LIMC* II.i, 167–69.
–, 1989. "Die Götter der Nabatäer", pp. 113–23 in M.Lindner (ed.), *Petra und das Königreich der Nabatäer*, 5th ed., Munich/Bad Windsheim: Delp.
–, (ed.), 1990a. *Petra and the Caravan Cities*, Amman: Department of Antiquities.
–, 1990b. "The god(dess) Aktab-Kutbay and his (her) iconography", pp. 37–51 in Zayadine 1990a.

Nabataean Art Between East and West: A methodical assessment

Joseph Patrich

One of the difficulties in properly evaluating the historical evidence in studying the ancient Near East, is that modern Europeans or westerners approaching it cannot help doing so with a host of confused and half-formed preconceptions about the 'Orient'.[1] The preconceptions inherent in western scholarship about the Orient is a principal point in Edward Said's *Orientalism*.[2] Such difficulties exist also in the particular study of Nabataean history and culture.[3]

Preconception lies, in my opinion, at the basis of scholarly preoccupation with tracing Greco-Roman or Oriental traits in this art, defining it as eclectic rather than original, speaking about a gradual process of Hellenization/Romanization, as against conservatism and adherence to ancestral tradition, or in defining the principal characteristic of Nabatean art in the rock carved facades and in the painted pottery, as "excessive ornamental."[4] This is a correct observation, of course, but the contemporary Greco-Roman baroque architecture was no less loaded with ornaments.

But another difficulty should be acknowledged in the study of the evolution of Nabatean art and the transformation it underwent in both the public realm and the private domain during the approximately seven centuries of its existence, and this is the modest number of final archaeological reports, presenting all records in full, and enabling the reader to examine the various finds in the correct chronological context, and evaluate all statements critically.[5]

[1] F. Millar, *The Roman Near East 31 BC – AD 337*, Harvard University Press, Cambridge Massachusetts and London 1993, p. 1. This assessment of Millar is derived from his prologue, entitled: "In Search of the Orient," where the author examines a dedication of a Roman soldier, in Greek, "to Zeus Betylos, the ancestral god of those by the Orontes."

[2] E. W. Said, *Orientalism*, 1978 (rev. ed., Harmondsworth 1995).

[3] This warning of Millar should be borne in mind with regard to a claim that the aniconic representation of the god among the Nabateans, in the context to be discussed below, "should be assigned to the field of art only with considerable reservations" (K. Parlasca, *Israel Exploration Journal* 43 (1993), p. 279). In modern times there is much more awareness of the abstract and conceptual dimensions in art, not just of iconography and style.

[4] J.Starcky, 'Pétra et la Nabatène', *Supplément au Dictionnaire de la Bible*, VII (1966), cols. 981–985.

[5] In the 12 years since the critical review by P.J. Parr, "Sixty Years of Excavation in Petra: A Critical Assessment." *Aram* 2 (1990), 7–23, when only one final report was at hand (Ph. C. Hammond, The Excavation of the Main Theater at Petra, 1961–1962: Final Report, London 1965), only few final reports have appeared in print: N. Khairy, *The 1981 Petra Excavations: Vol. 1*, Wiesbaden 1990; Ph. Hammond, *The Temple of the Winged Lions, Petra, Jordan, 1974–*

More than ten years have elapsed since my book, *The Formation of Nabatean Art: Prohibition of a Graven Image among the Nabateans*, was published, in which I tried to present a balanced evaluation of Nabatean art.[6] This is therefore an opportunity to examine the thesis again, in respect of the results of more recent finds and studies.

In evaluating Nabatean art (as well as the art of any other culture), its original features should be scaled against external influences. Diffusion and fusion of styles and motifs were inevitable in the open Hellenistic and Roman world, a world of religious tolerance and syncretism, and in a society of kings and rich merchants, eager to expose their wealth by artistic patronage. But this society was open not only to the Greco-Roman (mainly Alexandrian and Pergamene) west, it was also open to the Parthian and Mesopotamian east and to the Arabian south. Nor should we forget the neighborhood of Herodian Judaea, with its own religious customs and ancestral traditions, which underwent a somewhat similar process of acculturation vis à vis the Hellenistic and Early Imperial Roman world. And while weighting external influences, adaptation should be considered as against adoption, acculturation as against assimilation. There is also the issue of the relationship between center and periphery. A Greco-Roman influence on prestigious architecture is to be expected more in the capital Petra than in peripheral sites such as Mada^{c}in Saleh in the farthest south or Oboda in the Negev. On the other hand, the peripheral sites may better define the local, traditional affinities.

In this connection, following Hammond, it would also be proper to cite Leonard Wooley's words: "... the measure of a nation's culture is its capacity to

1990, Fountain Hills, Arizona 1996; A. Bignasca et al., *Petra, Ez Zantur I: Ergebnisse der schweizerisch-liechtensteinischen Ausgrabungen 1988–1992* [Terra Archaeologica II]. Mainz: Philip von Zabern 1996; S. G. Schmid and B. Kolb, *Petra, Ez Zantur II: Ergebnisse der schweizerisch-liechtensteinischen Ausgrabungen* [Terra Archaeologica IV]. Mainz: Philip von Zabern 2000. Recently the final report on the Qasr Bint Faraun, by F. Zayadine, F. Larché and J. Dentzer-Feydy was published, and that on Kh. adh-Dharih, by F. Villeneuve and Z. al-Muheisen, is due soon. The precise date of several key structures in the city center, namely the Colonnaded Street, the Temenos Gate, the first Qasr, and the ‚Great Temple' are still debatable issues as they were in 1990. See also: P. Parr, "The Architecture of Petra: Review Article," *PEQ* 128 (1996): 63–70.

[6] J. Patrich, *The Formation of Nabatean Art: Prohibition of a Graven Image among the Nabateans*, The Magnes Press, The Hebrew University, Jerusalem and E.J. Brill, Leiden 1990. For reviews see: *Liber Annuus* 41 (1991) 541–542 (by Michele Piccirillo, Studium Biblicum Franciscanum, Jerusalem); *Journal of Roman Studies* 82 (1992) 279 (by Judith McKenzie, Oxford); *Society of Old Testament Studies Booklines* (1992) 119–120 (by John Healey, University of Manchester); *Israel Exploration Journal* 43 (1993) 279–281 (by Klaus Parlasca); *Journal of American Oriental Society* 114 (1994) 665–666 (by H. Liebowitz). Contrary to Parlasca's comment (p. 281), G. Dalman (*Petra und seine Felsheiligtümer*, Leipzig 1908, p. 275, and fig. 218 on p. 276), indeed speaks about a two-humped camel ("zwei-höckeriges Kamel;" "doppelte Höcker des Kamels"). So he is wrong in this comment. His other comments are a result of the preconceptions referred to above. An attempt to refute these preconceptions was one of the major objectives of my book. The studies that he mentions, which had skipped my notice, pertaining mainly to the veneration of Isis among the Nabataeans, would not have altered, or modified my arguments.

borrow and so to assimilate its borrowings that its individuality is enhanced by them."[7]

But there were also internal factors at work, resulting from the heterogeneous ethnicity of the kingdom.[8] The Nabatean population was originally composed of desert-born Arabs – caravaneers, nomads, and semi-nomads, and an indigenous sedentary population of the fertile lands – the descendants of the Edomites, and Moabites, whose cult and culture were agricultural. All intermingled to form Nabatean society, but each ethnic component inherited its own ancestral deities, religious customs, and artistic tradition. Therefore, any attempt at a cultural evaluation of Nabataean art should take into account not only acculturation between the Nabataeans and the surrounding external cultures, but also the various ethnic contributions. In order to evaluate it properly all these streams – "classical" external, and "sub classical" and Arab internal – should first be differentiated, and then evaluated. If possible, we should try to attribute each work of art found in the Nabataean territory to its appropriate ethnic source or local cultural tradition. Then the extent of external influences, from the Greco-Roman west, mainly via Alexandria, Pergamon, Rhodes and Rome, or from inner Syria and Parthian-Mesopotamian East; from the Arabian peninsula, or from the neighboring Jewish state, should be examined. Each component should be evaluated qualitatively and quantitatively, and examined along the axis of time, throughout the history of the Nabataeans. Since the Arab component in this society was the most important social and political one, it is primarily their art and culture that we should define. Such a detailed study is far beyond the present methodical survey, the scope of which is much more limited.

What should be considered a Nabataean work of art? The most general answer is anything that was produced in their country by local artists or by foreign artists employed by them, no matter to what extent it is "contaminated" by foreign influences. These works of art can be divided by their media into major categories, each of high artistic standards: public and private architecture and rock-carved facades, relief, sculpture, and molded figurines, stucco and fresco, pottery, jewelry, and numismatics.

Due to the exceptional un-iconic representation of the deity among the Nabataeans, I maintain that a rewarding clue for a more refined classification of the influences at work, and a better comprehension of their art and culture as a whole, is the presence or dearth of figurative anthropomorphic representations in all the categories mentioned above. This, in addition to iconographic and stylistic analyses, makes it possible not only to differentiate Greco-Roman and Oriental groups in Nabataean figurative art, but also to define, in between, another group, a non-figurative one, which might be attributed to the Arab component in the Nabataean society.

[7] L. Wooley, *Middle East Archaeology*, Oxford 1949, cited by Ph. Hammond, "The Excavations at Petra, 1974: Cultural Aspects of Nabataean Architecture, Religion, Art, and Influence," in *SHAJ*, vol. I, 1982, 231–238, p. 231.

[8] Patrich, *supra*, n. 6, pp. 31–35.

Sedentarization

In the late 4th century Arabs called *Nabataeans* inhabited the northern parts of Arabia, the land between Syria and Egypt which, to a large extent, was a waterless desert. They were herders and caravan traders. They lived in the open air, were forbidden to drink wine, till the soil, or construct a house. Anyone who transgressed these traditions was put to death.[9] In a course of some 300 years a tremendous transformation took place in Nabataean society, a process of sedentarization. By the mid-1st century BC the Nabataeans of Petra are depicted as materialistic and acquisitive. They lived in costly stone houses and enjoyed local supply of all kinds of foods and aromatics. Yet despite their materialism they preserved tribal modes of egalitarian behavior. The royal ceremony and court style differed greatly from that encountered in Hellenistic royal courts. From time to time a popular assembly was called, at which the king would often account for his kingship and his way of life might be examined.[10] The Petra ez-Zantur excavations had indicated that the process of sedentarization at Petra was gradual, and that even when the urban center at Petra became more and more monumental, traditional tents still existed side by side with elaborate stone houses.[11] Interestingly, even in the moreelaborate phase of ez-Zantur houses, the dwelling wing remained simple, and next to it there was a more luxurious, stately-representational wing, decorated with western stucco and fresco (see below).

Rock-carved facades: Mesopotamian Influences

The neo-Babylonian (probably 6th c.) rock relief found near the village of Selᶜa in the district of at-Tafilah, 50 km north of Petra, near Busayra, indicates the neo-Babylonian domination over Edom, and the extent of its presence in this region,

[9] Diodorus of Sicily (*Bibliotheca Historica*, II, 48, 1–9; 49, 1; XIX, 94, 1–10; 97, 1–4; 100, 1–2), following Hieronimus of Cardia, an officer in the service of Antigones Monophthalmus in the military expeditions launched by him against the Nabataeans in 312 BC.

[10] Strabo of Amaseia, *Geographica* XVI. 4. 26.

[11] S. G. Schmid, "Nabataean Fine Ware Pottery and the Destructions of Petra in the Late First and Early Second Century AD," *SHAJ* VI (1997) 413–420, p. 414, gives the following sequence for the three major phases at the site during the Nabataean period: Tent phase: early and middle 1st c. BC; House I (simple): last quarter of the 1st c. BC; House II (bigger and more luxurious): very early 1st c. AD. On the development and components of the dwelling complex at EZ I see *supra*, n. 5, *Petra, Ez Zantur I*, pp. 13–46; R.A. Stucky, "The Nabataean House and the Urbanistic System of the Habitation Quarters in Petra," *SHAJ* V (1995), pp. 193–198, B. Kolb, „Excavating a Nabataean Mansion," NEA 65/4 (2002), pp. 260-264; idem., „Petra – From Tent to Mansion: Living on the Terraces of Ez-Zantur," in: G. Markoe (ed.), *Petra Rediscovered: The Lost City of the Nabataeans*, New York 2003, pp. 230–237. Settlement in the lower parts of the valley, under the paved street and the colonnade started ca. 50 years earlier, as simple houses built of wadi stones and clay; these were replaced later in the 1st c. AD by ashlar structures. The street, first with gravel surface, is still later. See Parr, *supra*, n. 5 (1990), with references on p. 15, note 24.

not just in the Oasis of Teima, Nabonidus' place of retirement, where he spend ten years of his life. The relief, covering an area of ca. 3x2m, is carved high on a vertical sandstone cliff. It depicts a standing figure, presumably Nabonidus (556–539 BC), three divine symbols, and a cuneiform inscription of about 30 lines, heavily eroded.[12]

Most of the facades at Petra are simple 'eastern', types, with Assyrian crowsteps (crenellations) or a pair of stepped, horn-like projections serving as crowning elements. Only 34 out of the 512 tomb facades at Petra reflect Alexandrian, Greco-Roman influence. Putting the emphasis on the study of just the "principal monuments" in the necropolis may distort our evaluation of the Nabataean culture.[13]

But the Assyrian motifs crowning most of the Nabataean tomb facades at Petra, and Madain Saleh, were not necessarily derived directly from Mesopotamia. Crenellations occur in several monuments of the Persian period in Phoenicia (such as the Ma^{c}abed of ^{c}Amrit) and in Palmyra (the Temple of Bel), and they topped some temples of the Roman period in Syria (Slem; Demer, temple of Zeus).[14]

Another Mesopotamian motif in the Nabataean rock-carved facade was recently recognized by McKenzie, Reyes and Schmidt-Colinet.[15] They identified the bearded face with long flowing hair at each end of the attic of Tomb 649 (Heger type) at Moghar en-Nasara, the so-called "Tomb with the Armor" (the only oriental facade in Petra having figural decorations on its attic), with the cut-off head of Humbaba, the Sumerian hideous-faced demon, the guardian of the Cedar Forest. He was killed by Gilgamesh and Endiku, who cut off his head.

[12] For the relief see: S. Dalley and A. Goguel, "The Sel^{c}a Sculpture: A Neo-Babylonian Rock Relief," *ADAJ* 41 (1997), 169–174; F. Zayadine, "Le relief à Sela^{c} près de Tafileh: interprétation historique," *Syria* 76 (1999), 83–90; E. Raz, T. Raz, and A. Uchitel, "Sel^{c}a – the Rock of Edom," *Cathedra* 101 (2001), 19–38 (Hebrew). For the other archaeological remains at the site see: S. Hart, "Sel^{c}a: The Rock of Edom?" *PEQ* 118 (1986), 91–95; M. Lindner, "Sel^{c}a (el/es- Sel^{c}a)," in: D. Homès-Fredericq and J. Hennessy (eds.), *Archaeology of Jordan*, [*Akkadica Supplementum* 8], Leuven 1989, pp. 557–559. On Nabonidus' career see: P.-A. Beaulieu, *The Reign of Nabonidus, King of Babylon 556–539 BC*, New Haven 1989.

[13] R.E. Brünnow and A. von Domaszewski, *Die Provincia Arabia*, pp. 137–173. Starcky, *supra*, n. 4, cols. 951–973; F. Zayadine, 'Die Felsarchitektur Petras', Lindner (ed.), *Petra und das Königreich der Nabataer,* Bad Windsheim 1980, pp. 212–248; A. Schmidt-Colinet, 'Nabataische Felsarchitektur', *Bonner Jahrbücher,* 180 (1980), pp. 189–230; Judith McKenzie, *The Architecture of Petra* [British Academy Monographs in Archaeology #1]. Oxford: Oxford University Press 1990. At the focus of this study are the "principal monuments." See also: K. Matthiae, "Die Fassade von Ed-Der in Petra: Ein Beitrag zur nabatäischen Felsarchitektur," *Klio* 71 (1989) 257–279; *idem*, "Die Fassade des Bab es-Siq-Trikliniums in Petra: Bemerkungen zu ihrer Gestaltung," *ZDPV* 104 (1989) 74–83; *idem*, "Die nabatäische Felsarchitektur in Petra," *Klio* 73 (1991) 226–278; E. Netzer, *Nabatäische Architektur*, Mainz 2003, pp. 13–66, and especially the suggestive chart of the chronological-typological evolution of the facade types, given there as Abb. 53, on pp. 46–47.

[14] R. Amy, "Temples à escaliers," *Syria* 27 (1950) 82–136.

[15] J. S. McKenzie, A. T. Reyes and A. Schmidt-Colinet, "Faces in the Rock at Petra and Medain Saleh," *PEQ* 130 (1998), 35–50.

According to the authors, the iconography of Humbaba influenced the iconography of the Gorgon Medusa, killed by Perseus in Greek mythology. This iconographical relationship between the Humbaba and Medusa heads was recognized by them also in the rock-carved facades of Petra, and Mada^{c}in Saleh, where the earlier tombs, up to ca. AD 50, depict an iconography more similar to the eastern Humbaba than to the western Gorgon Medusa. Both heads served as an apotropaic motif. The crowsteps are no longer an isolated example of local survival of a Mesopotamian decorative motif, as the authors pointed out in their concluding sentence.[16]

Stucco faces

Faces, in stucco, have been uncovered in various excavations in Petra and beyond. The largest group came from the Temple of the Winged Lions. The group consists of architectural stucco affixes, most less than 10 cm high, 24 of them in a relatively good state of preservation. The find location suggests that they were displayed on the lower frieze of the altar platform of the temple. Male and female individual portraits were recognized, except for one, which might have been a 'tragic mask.' According to Hammond and Mellott-Kahn all seem to have certain Oriental facial features in common: rounded cheeks, bulbous eyes, and pouting lips, which suggests local Nabataean manufacture. At the same time, the individuality of the faces indicates that actual persons were being portrayed, and that individual sculpting preceded the molding and casting of a reduced size.[17] Another face in stucco, ca. 14 cm high, came from Kh. adh-Dharih, but so

[16] Other than these faces, J. R. Green, in an appendix to the article mentioned in the previous note, counted seven architectural members with masks in relief from Petra characterized by their open mouth (including a new block depicting five masks, found in the Petra Church excavations; all the others were already known for some time). Most seem to belong to the period of the Nabataean Kingdom, rather than to the period of the Roman province. One is held by a Muse depicted in high relief, another adorns the abacus of a Type 2 Nabataean floral capital, one is from as-Sabra, and several had adorned the frieze of the Khasneh. Seven more masks, six female and one male, were found more recently in the excavations of the so called "Great Temple" at Petra. They were attributed to the theater phase there (mid 1st c. AD). See: E.L. Schlunz, "The Architectural Sculpture of the 'Great Temple' – The Masks," in: Martha S. Joukowsky, *Petra Great Temple,* Vol. 1, Rhode Island 1998, pp. 232–233, Figs. 5.53–5.57. In May 2005, 22 stone heads were uncovered in the Beidha suburb of Petra. Some are in the Greco-Roman style, others – in the Oriental style. They were tentatively assigned to capitals of columns that had decorated the 1st c. AD triclinium. See: Rana Dino, "22 stone heads of ancient gods unearthed in Petra," *Jordan Times*, May 18, 2005; ACOR's Beidha (Little Petra) Excavation Project, in: http://www.caorc.org/news/highlights/acor/acor-2005-06-01.htm; *ACOR Newsletter* 17.1 – Summer 2005, p. 11.

[17] Ph. Hammond and T. Mellott-Khan, "Nabataean Faces From Petra," *ADAJ* 42 (1998), 319–30. The authors suggest (p. 324) that they represent Temple's recognition of donations from the individuals, thus "blessed" by the privilege of being displayed within the Temple. A facial mold was recovered long ago by M.A. Murray and J.C. Ellis, *A Street in Petra*, London 1940, pp. 30–31 and pls.

far it has been just provisionally published.[18] Yet another human plaster-head affix, 30 cm high, i.e., about life size, and much larger than those of the contemporary Temple of the Winged Lions, came from a private domain. It was found in Room 1 in the stately wing of the house with the frescos excavated by the Swiss-Liechtenstein ex-cavations at az-Zantur IV in 1996.[19] The *terminus post quem* of its construction is AD 20, and it was destroyed in the 363 earthquake. It is assumed that the plaster-head affix was part of the upper wall decoration of that room.

The oriental elements

The major study of the oriental elements in Nabataean art in the wider context of the ancient Oriental art is still that of Michael Avi Yonah.[20] His concern was the art of the oriental-indigenous component in the Nabataean realm, as expressed in the 2nd and 3rd phase statuary at Kh. Tannur, dated to the provincial period, and produced when political and cultural conditions had changed. Somewhat similar statuary was found by Villeneuve and Muheisen in the adjacent contemporary Nabataean temple at Kh. adh-Dharih, that also presents Greco-Roman iconography in oriental style.[21]

In his study Avi Yonah attributes the introduction of Greco-Roman art into the Nabataean kingdom to the dominating class, of Arab origin, and the production of the oriental-style statuary to the indigenous agricultural population.[22] Hence it turns out that no original Arab Nabataean art ever existed. It is this conclusion that I would like to re-examine.

[18] Z. al Muheisen and F. Villeneuve, "Khirbbet adh-Dharih: A Nabataean Site in Wadi al-La'ban," *ADAJ* 34 (1990), Arabic section, p. 12.

[19] B. Kolb *et al.*, "Swiss-Liechtenstein Excavations at az Zantur in Petra 1996 – the Seventh Season", *ADAJ* 41 (1997), p. 239, fig. 10. A fragmentary floral Corinthian capital similar to those of the Temple of the Winged Lions, with plastered details, was found there as well.

[20] M. Avi Yonah, *Oriental Art in Roman Palestine*, Rome, 1961, pp. 34–57.

[21] J. Dentzer-Feydy, "Khirbet edh-Dharih: Architectural Decoration of the Temple." *Aram* 2 (1990), 229–234; eadem, in: F. Zayadine, F. Larché and J. Dentzer-Feydy, *Le Qasr al-Bint de Petra. L'architecture, le décor, la chronologie et les dieux* [Édition Recherche sur les Civilisations], Paris 2003, p. 69, Pls. 40–43; F. Villeneuve, "Khirbet edh-Dharih," *RB* 92 (1985), 421–426; *RB* 93 (1986), 247–252; *idem* and Z. al-Muheisen, "Fouilles à Khirbet edh-Dharih (Jordanie), 1984–1987: un village, son sanctuaire et sa nécropole aux époques nabatéenne et romaine," *CRAI* (1988), 458–479. See also *infra*, n. 82; and *iidem*, "Dharih and Tannur: Sanctuaries of Central Nabataea," in: Markoe, *supra*, note 11, pp. 83–100.

[22] These were Avi-Yonah's concluding words pertaining to Tannur statuary (*op. cit.*, p. 57): "... it seems that the Nabataean art was not 'Nabataean' at all, but an evolution – under Hellenistic influence – of the art of the Arameans, Israelites and Edomites. All these remained in the Nabatene under the domination of a small group of Arab traders, who imposed their rule upon the peasants of Transjordan. The rulers themselves quickly became Hellenized, as is attested by the rock-cuttings of Petra, while the earthy art of Tannur, Seia and the Hauran was the work of their subjects, the tillers of the soil and growers of wheat, oil and vine."

Classification of Nabataean works of art

Works of art from the Nabataean realm should be divided into two main groups, the first non-figurative and the second figurative. The first includes most of the tomb facades and plain-faced Nabataean capitals associated with them: Corinthian, pseudo-Ionic or Doricized;[23] painted pottery, oil lamps, most of the jewelry[24] and of course, the betyls, or stelae, representing the Nabataean deities.[25] All these works of art should be ascribed to the Arab Nabataeans, since they served in their cult of the gods and of the dead, and their distribution is restricted mainly to the southern part of the kingdom.

The figurative group may be subdivided stylistically into two main subgroups. The first reflects decisive influences of Alexandrian and Pergamene Hellenistic culture. It includes seven out of 512 burial monuments,[26] the Petraean statuary, [27] and figurative works in stucco and fresco, as depicted in the prestigious monuments such as the temple of Qasr Bint Faraun, the Temple of the

[23] J. Patrich, "The Formation of the Nabatean Capital," in: K. Fittschen and Gideon Foerster (eds.), *Judaea and the Greco-Roman World in the Time of Herod in the Light of Archaeological Evidence*, Göttingen 1996, pp. 197–218; J. McKenzie, *supra* n. 12, p. 190, Diagram 14; *eadem*, "Keys from Egypt and the East: Observations on Nabataean Culture in the Light of Recent Discoveries," *BASOR* 324 (2001) 97–102; A. Schmidt-Colinet, "Dorisierende Nabatäische Kapitelle," *Damaszener Mitteilungen* 1 (1983) 307–312.

[24] Patrich, *supra*, n. 6, pp. 137–139; Renate Rosenthal-Heginbottom, "Goldschmuck," in: Th. Weber and R. Wenning (eds.), *Petra, Antike Felsstadt zwischen arabischer Tradition und griechischer Norm* [Sonderhefte der antiken Welt, Zaberns Bildbände zur Archäeologie], Mainz 1997, pp. 140–144.

[25] Patrich, *supra*, n. 6, pp. 50–104; M.J. Roche, "Les Betyles," *Le Monde de la Bible,* 14 (1980) 33–35; *eadem*, "Les niches cultuelles du Sadd al-Ma`jan à Pétra," *ADAJ* 33 (1989) 327–334; L. Nehmé, "Nouvelles gravures rupestres à Pétra: techniques, religion, épigraphie," SHAJ V (1995), pp. 427–435; U. Avner, "Nabataean Standing Stones and Their Interpretation," *Aram* 11–12 (1999–2000). 97–122; R. Wenning, "The Betyls of Petra," *BASOR* 324 (2001) 79–95.

[26] A detailed description is to be found in: McKenzie, *supra* n. 13; see also: *eadem*, "The Dating of the Principal Monuments at Petra: A New Approach," *SHAJ* III (1987), pp. 295–306; *eadem*, "The Chronology of the Principal Monuments at Petra," *Levant* 19 (1987) 145–165.

[27] G.R.H. Wright, "Some Aspects Concerning the Architecture and Sculpture," *ADAJ* 12–13 (1967–68), 20–29, Pls. XII–XIII = *Syria* 45 (1968), 25–40, Pls. VI–VII; J. Starcky, "Les figures divines à Petra," *Le Monde de la Bible* 14 (1980), pp. 30–32; J. S. McKenzie, "The Development of Nabataean Sculpture at Petra and Khirbet Tannur," *PEQ* 120 (1988), 81–107; eadem, "Carvings in the Desert: The Sculpture of Petra and Khirbet Tannur," in: G. Markoe (ed.), *supra*, note 11, pp. 165–192; M. Lyttelton, "Aspects of the Iconography of the Sculptural Decoration of the Khazneh at Petra," in: F. Zayadine (ed.), *Petra and the Caravan cities*, Amman 1990, pp.19–30; M. Lyttelton and T. Blagg, "Sculpture from the Temenos of Qasr El-Bint at Petra," *Aram* 2 (1990), 267–286; M. Lyttelton and T. Blagg, "Sculpture in Nabataean Petra, and the Question of Roman Influence," in: M. Henig (ed.), *Architecture and Architectural Sculpture in the Roman Empire* [Oxford University Committee for Archaeology Monograph #29], Oxford 1990, pp. 91–107; U. Hübner and Th. Weber, "Götterbüsten und Königsstatuen. Nabatäische und römische Plastik im Spannungsfeld zwischen Konvention und Staatsraison," in: Weber and Wenning, *supra*, n. 24, pp. 111–125. On the Beidha busts see supra, note 16. On eight new reliefs from the 'Great Temple,' see: J.J. Basile, "Two visual languages at Petra: Aniconic and Representational Sculpture of the Great Temple," *NEA* 65/4 (2002), pp. 255–258.

Winged Lions, the Temenos Gate, and the so called Great Temple, which apparently proved to be the impressive royal reception hall, transformed into a bouleterion.[28] With these monuments are associated floral Corinthian capitals and zoomorphic capitals depicting winged lions, Indian elephant heads, goats or rams, and griffins.[29]

The second figurative subgroup is in the provincial Greco-Oriental style, typical of the Syrian interior, and reflecting Parthian influences. It includes mainly the statuary of Kh. Taunur and Kh. adh-Dharih, both of the provincial period. McKenzie recognized the iconographic influence of Petra on Kh. Tannur.[30] The god venerated at Tannur was Qos,[31] and that of Kh. ad-Dharih is still unknown. These sculptures have a purely zodiacal-astral and agricultural inspiration. Characteristic features are frontality, oversized heads, patterning of dress and hair, fixed expressions and pouting mouths, long faces, and large and prominent eyes. Although the style is oriented towards inner Syria,[31a] the iconography, the dress, and the accessories of the figures are Hellenistic.

[28] Martha S. Joukowsky, *Petra Great Temple*, Vol. 1, Rhode Island 1998, with a bibliography for earlier publications on pp. xxxv–xxxviii; See also: *eadem*, "1993 Archaeological Excavations and Survey of the Southern Temple at Petra, Jordan," *ADAJ* 38 (1994) 293–332; *eadem* and Erika Schluntz, "1994 Archaeological Excavations and Survey of the Southern Temple at Petra, Jordan," *ADAJ* 39 (1995) 241–266; *eadem*, "Brown University 1997 Excavations at the Petra Great Temple", *ADAJ* 42 (1998), pp. 293–318; *eadem*, „The Petra Great Temple: A Nabataean Architectural Miracle," *NEA* 65/4 (2002), pp. 235-248; *eadem*, "The Great Temple," in: Markoe, *supra*, note 11, pp. 214–222; E. Schlunz, *From Royal Palace to Public Assembly Space: the Transformation of the "Great Temple" Complex at Petra, Jordan*, Ph.D. dissertation, Brown University 1999; Martha S. Joukowsky, "Exploring the Great Temple at Petra: The Brown University Excavations, 1993–1996," L.E. Stager *et al.* (eds.), *The Archaeology of Jordan and Beyond. Essays in Honor of James A. Sauer*, Indiana 2000, pp. 221–234; *eadem* and J.J. Basile, "More Pieces in the Petra Great Temple Puzzle," *BASOR* 324 (2001) 43–58; L.A. Bedal, "A Pool Complex in Petra's City Center," *BASOR* 324 (2001) 23–41.

[29] Patrich, *supra* n. 23; J. McKenzie, *supra* n. 13, pp. 94–96 and p. 190, Diagram 14 (goats and griffins in place of corner volutes are mentioned on p. 95); *eadem*, *supra* n. 23; Z. Safar, "Les Chapiteaux de Petra," *Le Monde de la Bible* 14 (1980.) 27–28; P.C. Hammond, "The Capitals from 'The Temple of the Winged Lions,' Petra," *BASOR* 226 (1977) 47–52; T. Blagg, "Column Capitals with Elephant-Head Volutes from Petra," *Levant* 22 (1990) 131–137 (goats or rams in place of corner volutes are mentioned on p. 136). For a capital of an engaged column with two intact elephant heads found in 2000 see: M.S. Joukowsky and J.J. Basile, "More Pieces in the Petra Great Temple Puzzle," *BASOR* 324 (2001) 43–58, p. 47, Fig. 4. Most came from the Lower Temenos. See also Joukowsky, *supra* n. 16, pp. 226–231 and 268–273. Those published by Blagg, found in the late 1950 in debris to the E of the Qasr al-Bint Temenos Gate, were attributed to the *propylon* of the Temple of the Winged Lions. See also: M.S. Joukowsky, "Rediscovering Elephants at Petra!" in: L.H. Lesko, *Ancient Egyptian and Mediterranean Studies. Iin Memory of William A. Ward*, Brown University Department of Egyptology 1998, pp. 133–48.

[30] McKenzie, *supra*, n. 27; J. McKenzie, S. Gibson and A.T. Reyes, "Reconstruction of the Nabataean Temple at Khirbet et-Tannur," *PEQ* 134 (2002), pp. 44–83.

[31] J. Starcky, "Le Temple Nabatéen de Khirbet Tannur," *RB* 75 (1968), pp. 206–235, Pls. 15–20. On the Kh. adh-Dharih temple, see *supra*, note 21, and *infra*, note 82.

[31a] See: J. Dentzer-Feydy, "Décor architectural et dévelopment du Hauran du Ier siècle avant J.-C. au VIIe siècle après J.-C.," in: J.M. Dentzer (ed.), *Hauran I. Recherches archéologiques sur la Syrie du Sud à l'époque hellénistique et romaine* [Bibliothèque archéologique et his-

In the figurative group should also be included a few rock-cut niches with anthropomorphic deities representing mainly Isis,[32] clay figurines[33] (some, again clearly associated with Isis), crude imitations of the Roman discus lamp, several works of jewelry, and Nabatean coins.

Nabataean figurines

Parr examined 182 figurines, 150 of which came from stratified context.[34] The date range spans throughout the 1st and 2nd century AD. Two thirds are zoomorphic, and only a third anthropomorphic. Similar relative proportions of 60% and 40% respectively were noted by Horsfield in his excavations. Their religious purpose is taken for granted, but according to Parr, only few depict deities and even fewer might be identified with certainty. These are Isis, Nike/Tyche, and Hathor/Astarte, but this minority can hardly be said to be typical of the Nabataean figurine repertoire. Most, especially the horses, camels, and sitting and standing

torique 124], 2 vols., Paris 1985, reviewed by D. Graf, *Journal of Roman Archaeology* 5 (1992), pp. 261–310.

32 M.J. Roche, "Le culte d'Isis et l'influence Égyptienne à Pétra," *Syria* 64 (1987), pp. 217–222; Patrich, *supra*, n.6, pp. 104–106; F. Zayadine, "L'iconographie d'Isis à Pétra," *MEFRA* 103 (1991), 283–306; A. I. Meza, "The Egyptian Statuette in Petra and the Isis Cult Connection," *ADAJ* (1996) 40, pp. 167–176. See also: H. Donner, *Isis in Petra*. Leipzig 1995; H. Merklein and R. Wenning, "Ein Verehrungplatz der Isis in Petra neu untersucht," *ZDPV* 114 (1998), 162–178; K. Parlasca, "Bemerkungen zum Isiskult in Petra," in: U. Hübner et al. (eds.), *Nach Petra und ins Königreich der Nabatäer. Notizen von Reisegefährten. Für Manfred Lindner zum 80. Geburtstag*. Bodenheim 1998, pp. 64–69; J. F. Healey, *The Religion of the Nabataeans. A Conspectus*, Leiden-Boston-Köln 2001, pp. 137–140. A Nabataean inscription in Sidd el-Mreriyyeh, next to the niche housing Isis enthroned (J.T. Milik and J. Starcky, "Inscriptions, récemment découvertes à Pétra," *ADAJ* 20 (1975), pp. 120–123, Pl. 44.1–2), suggests that the goddess was venerated by the clan of the Hobal (or Hubal). In the same gorge of Petra there are many rock-cut houses decorated with stucco and frescos related to the 2nd Pompeian style (Zayadine, *op. cit.*, pp. 289–291). Greco-Roman influences are evident in this zone of Petra. In-terestingly, according to the early Islamic author Ibn al-Kalbi, Hubal was one of the only two pre-Islamic deities that had a statue; all others were represented by stones or trees. See Healey, *op. cit.*, p. 188.

The popularity of Isis should be associated also with the decisive Alexandrian architectural influence evident in the Petraean monuments, as was comprehensively illustrated by Mckenzie (*supra*, n. 13). The Khazneh, on which Isis and her crown are depicted is the best illustration of this association. On the assimilationof Dushara with Osiris see: J. Patrich, "Was Dionysos, the Wine God, Venerated by the Nabataeans?" *Aram Periodical* 17 (2005), pp. 95–113.

33 Ingemarie Parlasca, "Die nabatäischen Kamelterrakotten," in: M. Lindner, *Petra. Neue Ausgrabungen und Entdeckungen*, Munich 1986, pp. 200–213; *eadem*, "Terrakotten aus Petra, ein neues Kapitel nabatäischer Archäologie," in: F. Zayadine (ed), *Petra and the Caravan Cities*, Amman 1990, pp. 87–106; P. J. Parr, "A Commentary on the Terracotta Figurines from the British Excavations at Petra 1958–64" in: F. Zayadine (ed.), *Petra and the Caravan Cities*, Amman 1990, pp. 77–86; Ingemarie Parlasca, "Probleme Nabatäischer Koroplastik: Aspekte der Auswärtigen Kulturbeziehungen Petras," A. Invernizzi and J.-F. Salles, *Arabia Antiqua. Hellenistic Centers Around Arabia* [*Serie Orientale Roma* LXX,2], Roma 1993, pp. 55–79; *eadem*, "Terrakotten," in: Weber and Wenning, *supra*, n. 24, pp. 126–131.

34 P.J. Parr, *op. cit.*

nudes, must have been produced to satisfy some religious popular and traditional need. Possible suggestions are household gods, votive offerings, or good-luck talismans, but these cannot be decided. Most were associated with domestic objects.

The types included in the standardized anthropomorphic group include standing nude males, with hand raised in worship and blessing, with collar of a pendant crescent worn around the neck (16%), and seated figurines (25%). Half seemed to be clothed, the rest nude. The zoomorphic figurines, for entertainment, ex votos, or good-luck charms, include horses (41%) and camels (28%), and the rest are birds, goats, a monkey, a donkey, and a pig.

In the inventory of Ingemarie Parlasca there are 400 items.[35] A noteworthy new type is a naked goddess on a throne, holding an apple or pomegrenate in her right hand, and her left is raised in blessing or supplication. She is identified as the Syrian Astarte/Atargatis, the counterpart of the Arab al-Uzza and the Greek Aphrodite. In addition to Isis in grief, Harpocrates is also represented. Another noteworthy type is a standing, naked lad, identified as the child Eros. His hands are depicted like those of the seated goddess, and on his neck he has a collar with a pendant crescent. There are also variants without a collar. A rare type is a figurine depicting three musicians. The zoomorphic figurines are similar to the other group.

Let us turn now to the non-figurative group.

Nabataean Stelae

The betylic representation of the Arab gods is known from all over the Nabataean realm, and it was of long duration. It seems fair to assume that such a representation was the Nabataeans' custom from their very inception as a national entity, though the earliest dated example is from the beginning of the first century BC. The latest examples were dated to the first half of the 4th century AD. After the Roman annexation, during the 2nd and 3rd centuries AD, stelae appeared on the city coins of Bostra, Adraa, Charachmoba, and Madaba.[36] There was no gradual abandonment of the non-figurative mode of representation in favor of the figurative as time elapsed. The reality was far more complex. The influence of this non-figurative conception was so strong that the great Syrian goddess, *Dea Syriae*, represented as a cone-like stele at her main temple in Hierapolis-Mabug, was represented at Petra as a rectangular eye idol (see below).[37] Similarly, the Edo-

[35] Ingemarie Parlasca, *op. cit.* (1990).

[36] Patrich, *supra*, n. 6, pp. 70–75; T. Mettinger, *No Graven Image?* [Coniectanea Biblica. Old Testament Series 42], Stockholm 1995, pp. 58–62. See also *supra*, note 25.

[37] R. E. Brünnow and A. von Domaszewski, *Die Provincia Arabia*, I, p. 323, fig. 358, no. 428k,l; Patrich, *supra*, n. 6, pp. 82–83, Ill. 26. For a certain reservation about the association between the two words of the inscription see Healey, *supra*, n. 32, pp. 140–141. See also: Ch. Clermont-Ganneau, "Maboug-Hiérapolis dans les inscriptions nabatéennes," *RAO* IV (1901) 99–112; M. Lindner and J. Zangenberg, "The Re-discovered *Baytil* of the Goddess Atargatis in

mite deity Qos was depicted as a stele in the first two phases at Kh. Tannur, while later he was represented anthropomorphically.[38] Betyls, in various shapes, are also known in Hellenistic Maresha, in Idumaea, to the south of Judaea, in Israel.[38a] Isis, generally represented anthropomorphically at Petra, as elsewhere, assumed a betylic shape in one case (ez-Zantur), where her head emblem was recognized by Lindner in the center of the diadem.[39] When some Hellenized Nabataean decided to assign to his deity, presumably Dionysos, an anthropomorphic shape, he still felt obliged to add the traditional stele. The result was the Medallion and Block relief, where the medallion can be interpreted as specifying the identity of the god, which was shaped as a stele underneath, instead of identifying it by an inscription.[40]

A particular type of stele is the so-called "eye idol" representing the Nabataean goddess al-'Uzza.[41] Tiny stone tablets, of matchbox size and shaped like "eye idols," indicate that they may have served as a substitute for the clay anthropomorphic figurines among the orthodox circles of the Arab Nabataean society.[42] At ez-Zantur I an eye idol was venerated as a household diety in the Nabataean house of the 1st century AD, while in the Late Roman phase it was an alabaster statuette of Isis.[43]

It is astonishing to learn that a similar "aniconic iconography," so to speak, of two schematic eyes and a nose, was applied in the fashioning of a pair of gold earrings found by Negev at the Nabataean necropolis of Memphis. A Romanized version can be seen in another earring from that site, where Aphrodite, the Greco-Roman counterpart of al-'Uzza, is depicted.[44]

the *Siyyagh* Gorge of Petra (Jordan) and Its Significance for Religious Life in Nabataea," *ZDPV* 109 (1993) 141–151.

[38] Starcky, *supra*, n. 31; Patrich, *supra*, n. 6, pp. 63–64, Ill. 10.

[38a] A. Kloner (ed.), *Maresha Excavations Final Report I, Subterranean Complexes 21, 44, 70*, [*IAA Reports 17*], Jerusalem 2003, p. 38, Fig. 3.14, Plan 3.5; p. 48, Fig. 4.10; pp. 56–57, Figs. 5.2, 5.4, 5.5, Plan 5.4.

[39] M. Lindner, "Eine al-ᶜUzza-Isis-Stele und andere neu aufgefundene Zeugnisse der al-ᶜUzza-Verehrung in Petra (Jordanien)," *ZDPV* 104 (1988), 84–91, pls. 2–11A.

[40] Ph. C. Hammond, "The Medallion and Block Relief at Petra," *BASOR*, 192 (1968), 16–21; F. Zayadine, "Une ouvrage sur les Nabatéens," *Revue Archéologique*, 70 (1975), 336–37; Patrich, *supra*, n. 6, p. 107, Ill. 33.

[41] The most detailed list of eye idols is to be found in H. Merklein and R. Wenning, "Ein neuentdeckter Augenbetyl in der Hremiye-Schlucht nebst einer Übersicht über die bekannten nabatäischen Augenbetylen," in: U. Hübner et al. (eds.), *Nach Petra und ins Königreich der Nabatäer. Notizen von Reisegefährten für Manfred Lindner zum 80. Geburtstag*, Bodenheim 1998, pp. 71–91, with updates in R. Wenning, "The Betyls of Petra," *BASOR* 324 (2001) 79–95, p. 87, note 18.

[42] Patrich, *supra*, n. 6, p. 83, Ill. 27.

[43] R.A. Stucky *et al.*, "Swiss-Liechtenstein Excavations at ez-Zantur in Petra 1993: The Fifth Campaign." *ADAJ* 38 (1994), pp. 275–279, Fig. 9 (eye idole); Weber and Wenning, *supra*, n. 24, p. 115, Fig. 126 (statuette); *Petra, ez Zantur I* (*supra*, n. 5), pp. 341, 344–345, Figs. 942–944.

[44] J. Patrich, "Al-Uzza Earings," *IEJ* 34 (1984), 39–46.

The non-figurative iconography adopted in the fashioning of these earrings is evidence for the vitality of this iconographic scheme among the Nabataeans. The Aphrodite earring was the result of a foreign, Greco-Roman, influence, while when influences from the Arabic Peninsula were at work – presumably from the Teima area, rather than from South Arabia – the result was the famous stele found by Hammond at the Temple of the Winged Lions, a unique representation of al-'Uzza/Atargatis.[45] The resemblance of this betyl to the funerary commemorative stelae in the Arabian Peninsula is evident.[46]

Nabataean pottery

The prohibition of a graven image is recognized in the painted pottery as well. Since it was first identified by the Horsfields in 1929, much progress has been achieved in the study of its technology, typology, chronology, and chemical composition of its clay.[47] During almost four centuries of production, it was decorated almost solely by floral motifs;[48] anthropomorphic motifs are extremely

[45] Ph. Hammond, "Ein nabatäisches Weihrelief aus Petra," *Bonner Jahrbücher des rheinischen Landesmuseums in Bonn und des Vereins von Altertumsfreunden im Rheinlande* 180 (1980), 265–269; *idem*, "The Goddess of the 'Temple of the Winged Lions' at Petra (Jordan)," in: F. Zayadine (ed.), *Petra and the Caravan Cities*, Amman 1990, pp. 115–130.

[46] See Patrich, *supra* n. 6, p. 85, with references.

[47] The most comprehensive study is S. G. Schmid, "Die Feinkeramik der Nabatäer. Typologie, Chronologie und kulturhistorische Hintergründe," in: S. G. Schmid and B. Kolb, *Petra, Ez Zantur II: Ergebnisse der schweizerisch-liechtensteinischen Ausgrabungen* [Terra Archaeologica IV], Mainz: Philip von Zabern 2000, Part 1, pp. 1–199, Ills. 1–438, and color figs. 1–12. Earlier noteworthy studies are: Ph. C. Hammond, "Pattern Families in Nabataean Painted Ware," *American Journal of Archaeology*, LXIII (1959), 371–382; *idem*, "A Classification of Nabataean Fine Ware," *American Journal of Archaeology* 66 (1962), 169–180; *idem*, "Pottery from Petra," *PEQ* 105 (1973), 27–49; P.J. Parr, "A Sequence of Pottery from Petra," J.A. Sanders (ed.), *Near Eastern Archaeology in the Twentieth Century*, New York 1970, pp. 348–381, pls.42–45; K. Schmitt-Korte, "Aufbau der Nabatäischen Keramikmuster," *Die Nabatäer, ein vergessenes Volk am toten Meer 312v – 106n. Chr.* [Ausstellung der prähistorischen Staatssammlung in Münchner Stadtmuseum 1970], pp. 44–47, pls. 22–27; A. Negev, *The Nabatean Potter's Workshop at Oboda*, Bonn 1973; N. Khairy, "The Painted Nabataean Pottery from the 1981 Petra Excavations," *Levant* 19 (1987), 167–181; S. G. Schmid, "Nabataean Fine Ware from Petra," in: *SHAJ* V, Amman 1995, pp. 637–647. On technical aspects see: N. Khairy, "Technical Aspects of Fine Nabataean Pottery," *BASOR* 250 (1983), pp. 17–40; Kh. 'Amr, "Instrumental Neutron Activation Analysis of Pottery and Clay from the Zurrabeh Kiln Complex," *ADAJ* 30 (1986), 319–328; *eadem*, *The Pottery from Petra: A Neutron Activation Analysis Study* [British Archaeological Reports, International Series # 324], Oxford 1987; J. Gunneweg, I. Perlman and F. Asaro, "The Origin, Classification, and Chronology of Nabataean Painted Fine Ware," *Jahrbuch des römisch-germanischen Zentralmuseums Mainz* 35 (1988), 315–345; J. R.B. Mason, "A Study of Nabataean Pottery Manufacturing Techniques: An Experiment for Reconstructing the Production of Fine Bowls," *Aram* 2 (1990), 287–307; J.R.B. Masom and Kh. ᶜAmr, "An Investigation into the Firing of Nabataean Pottery," in: *SHAJ*, V, Amman 1995, pp. 629–636. The plain Nabataean ware is not at our concern here.

[48] A noteworthy hypothesis is that this ceramic family is an imitation, in clay, of lost Nabataean gold vessels that were similarly decorated. See: M. Vickers, "Nabataea, India, Gaul,

rare (see below). Several Hellenistic ceramic groups were also similarly decorated, and no one will claim that prohibition of a graven image prevailed in that culture. Yet one may reach this conclusion in the case of the Nabataean painted pottery. Two exceptional bowls from Masada, and two others from Khairy's excavations at el-Katute, Petra, will make the point.[49] Tradition obliged the artist to adhere to the floral design. His only way of introducing a more personal expression into the conventional, dense, vegetal ornamentation was by combining several millipedes and floral motifs and fashioning them as anthropomorphous figures in a gesture of prayer or blessing. Other examples are known to depict birds, donkeys, and two human figures rendered in a naive, "childish" style.[50] Figurative depictions in a polychrome naturalistic style, like the single shard from ez-Zantur depicting a head, on a fine Nabataean bowl after its firing,[51] were very rare. Interestingly, the vessels painted in this style belong to phase 2, dated from 50 BC to AD 20. All the other shards with figurative floral motifs mentioned above belong to phase 3, dated from ca. 20 to AD 100. Naturalistic human depictions in the phase 2 style are not only rare, they were altogether rejected in the later phase. The figurative depictions in phase 3, rare as well, are in the conventional floral style, combining vegetal motives to obtain anthropomorphic or zoomorphic resemblance. It seems that the few naturalistic depictions of the previous style were no longer tolerated. This transformation in the attitude to figurative representations – an "iconoclastic" reaction in the Nabataean painted pottery – should not be underestimated.[52]

Another class of Nabatean ware, with impressed and rouletted decorations, and studied by Khairy, also depicts solely floral motifs.[53] A much rarer class is of molded vessels with figurative decorations. They are quite small in size – less than 10 cm high, made by mold, such as oil lamps and terracotta figurines, and dated to the 1st century AD.[54]

and Carthage: Reflections on Hellenistic and Roman Gold Vessels and Red-Gloss Pottery," *AJA* 98 (1994), pp. 231–248.

[49] Patrich, *supra*, n. 6, p. 128, Ill. 43; N. Khairy, *The 1981 Petra Excavations*, Vol. I [Abhandlungen des deutschen Palästinavereins # 13], Wiesbaden 1990, pp. 38–39, 118, 120, Figs. 40 and 42 (bowls nos. 5 and 8).

[50] Schmid, *supra*, n. 47 (2000), Figs. 377–385; R. A. Stucky *et al.*, "Swiss-Liechtenstein Excavations at ez-Zantur in Petra 1993: The Fifth Campaign," *ADAJ* 38 (1994), 284–286, Figs. 12–14.

[51] Schmid, *op. cit.*, Fig. 372, and color photo on the front cover. Two other shards, Figs. 373 and 374, belong to this category as well. An enlarged color photo of the head was published in: S. G. Schmid, "Die Feinkeramik der Nabatäer," in: *Petra und die Weihrauchstrasse* [Ausstellung in der Galerie 'le point' am Hauptsitz der Schweizerischen Kreditanstalt], Zürich 1993, p. 58.

[52] Schmid, *op. cit.*, pp. 84–88, esp. p. 86, note 375, is indeed fully aware to the significance of this transformation and its relation to developments in Nabataean art and culture at large.

[53] N. Khairy, "Fine Nabataean Ware with Impressed and Rouletted Decorations," *SHAJ* I, Amman 1982, pp. 275–283; *idem*, "Technical Aspects of Fine Nabataean Pottery," *BASOR* 250 (1983), 17–40.

[54] Khairy, *supra* n. 49, pp. 47–48 and 126–27, Figs. 48–49, Pl. 25, with further references; Patrich, *supra* n. 6, p. 130, note 36. Khairy remarks that earlier scholars referred to them as

Nabataean oil lamps

The avoidance of anthropomorphic representations in the painted pottery is also evident in the Nabataean oil lamps, and in this context I would like to cite Hammond, referring to finds in Petra:

"Only a few Nabataean lamps copied the pictorial Roman discus type, and these are generally crude imitations almost without exception. The scene-decorated lamps, so common to Petra, must be seen in as Roman imports and not local products. Why the local potters did not simply lift mold impressions and produced local copies is inexplicable in view of their mold-making skill."[55]

In light of the foregoing, this avoidance is quite explicable.

In Khairy's excavation of domestic complexes at al Katute, of the 38 oil lamps from the Nabataean period (1st c. AD), 19 are typical (non figurative) Nabataean, and only three are of the Roman rounded lamps with a sunken discus, depicting anthropomorphic scenes (one is an erotic scene and another a cultic one: divination by inspecting the entrails); the rest are non-figurative as well.[56] None of the 13 late Hellenistic (2), Nabataean (9), or early Roman (2) oil lamps from ez-Zantur depict figurative scenes.[57] Hammond's observation of 30 years ago concerning the avoidance of copying Roman scene-decorated lamps is still valid.

A unique local oil lamp, depicting the signs of the zodiac, was found in the Temple of the Winged Lions. The zodiac seems to be a popular motive, depicted also on the frieze of Kh. adh-Dharih temple, and on the facade, and held by Nyke, in Tannur. The assimilation of Dushara with Aion, attested by Epiphanius in the 4th c. AD, suggests that the zodiac was an attribute of Dushara. It may explain the popularity of this motive among the Nabataeans. In Roman art Aion was depicted holding the zodiac wheel.[58]

Fresco and stucco

Also in the private domain, the fresco and stucco found in most houses depict the layout of Hellenistic Masonry style, or the 1st and 2nd Pompeian styles, and area cover of geometric patterns.[59] The best preserved example was found by the

"miniature loving-cups" or "small cosmetic pots." A handle of a trefoil mouth-juglet with an applied Silenus head (Schmid, *op. cit.*, pp. 88–91), a separate class of local vessels, is so far a *unicum* in published Nabataean ceramics.

[55] Ph. C. Hammond, *The Nabataens: Their History, Culture and Archaeology*, Gothenburg, Sweden 1973, p. 90.

[56] Khairy, *supra*, n. 49.

[57] *Petra, ez Zantur I* (*supra*, n. 5), pp. 311–336 (studied by I. Zonani).

[58] On the zodiac oil lamp see: Ph. C. Hammond, in Markoe, *supra*, note 11, p. 229, Fig. 248. For the zodiac at Tannur, see McKenzie, *supra*, note 30; for the zodiac at Dharih, see Villeneuve and Muheisen in: Markoe, *supra*, note 11, pp. 92-96. For the assimilation of Dushara with Aion, and the representation of Aion in Roman art, see: Patrich, *supra*, note 32.

[59] F. Zayadine, "Decorative Stucco at Petra and other Hellenistic Sites," *SHAJ* III, Amman

Swiss-Lichtenstein expedition at ez-Zantur IV. A noteworthy point in the wall paintings of walls A and C in Room 1 is that the disk-shaped acroteria of the two lateral wings flanking the central pavilion of a segmented pediment depict two *gorgoneia*.[60] Their apotropaic function in Nabataean art was already mentioned above. Other than this, the illusionist architectural painted facades, each resembling the one depicted in stucco on the rear wall of the Qasr,[61] are covered with colorful two-dimensional, geometric motifs; there are no figurative motives. The upper zone was covered by stucco panels painted in geometric motifs as well. Corridor 2 and room 3 were decorated in the masonry style (1.7 m high), depicting alternating red and yellow panels set above a 0.3 m black plinth. It is similar to the decoration of the staircase in the so called "Bath" near the Qasr al-Bint Temenos Gate. However, a plaster human head affix, 30 cm high, life size, was also found in that room, and a figurative fresco in the private sphere was found on the vaulted ceiling in a rock-cut house in Siq el-Barid, depicting cupids and birds in a rich floral carpet.[62]

The stucco-work of the Qasr is very dense and elaborate. As a matter of fact, these decorations, with embossed gerlands, busts, and corner Nikae projecting from the plain stuccoed courses on which they are applied, are in this regard different than those of the contemporary, so called, ‚Great Temple'. As a matter of fact, those of the Qasr, unique in Petra, and assigned to the original construction program, are in variance with the Greco-Roman decorative system. Dentzer-Feydy notes that they present an encounter and fusion between the Oriental tendency for area cover, and the normative Greco-Roman decorative system.[63]

1987, pp.131–142; T. Safwan, "Frescos: From the Decapolis to the Umayyad Palaces," *SHAJ* V, Amman 1995, pp. 375–380; A. Barbet, "Les caracteristiques de la peinture murale à Pétra," *SHAJ*, vol. V, Amman 1995, pp. 383–389 (a rock-cut dwelling in Wadi as-Siyyagh depicting a row of blind doorways).

[60] B. Kolb *et al.*, "Swiss-Liechtenstein Excavtions at az Zantur in Petra 1996 – the Seventh Season," *ADAJ* 41 (1997), 231–254, pp. 234–39, Figs. 7 and 8. According to Kolb this and similar architectural wall paintings in Petra (discussed earlier by Zayadine and by Barbet: see previous note) are somewhat simple version related to the Second Pompeian Style, inspired by the Hellenistic architecture of Alexandria, as was vividly elucidated by McKenzie (*supra*, n. 13). Kolb also mentions the existence of an earlier phase of murals in the upper zone, and possibly also in the main zone, but its exact composition is yet unknown. For color illustrations of the ez-Zantur frescos see also: R. Wenning, B. Kolb and L. Nehmé, "Von Zeltlager zur Stadt. Profane Architektur in Petra," in: Weber and Wenning, *supra*, n. 24, 56–70, pp. 62–66, Figs. 69a and b; B. Kolb, in: Markoe, *supra*, note 11, pp. 235–237.

[61] H. Kohl, *Kasr Fira'un in Petra*, Leipzig 1910; F. Zayadine, "Recent Excavations at Petra (1979/81): Qasr al Bint," *ADAJ*, 26 (1982), pp. 374–380, Pls. CXXIII–CXXX. New and more accurate drawings and reconstructions, by Larché, were published in Zayadine *et al.*, *supra* n. 21. See also Weber and Wenning, *supra*, n. 24, pp. 74–75, Fig. 76a–c.

[62] F.M. Abel, "Le monument funerarire peint d'el-Bared," *RB* 15 (1906), 587–591; G. Dalman, *Petra*, p. 349, fig. 317, no. 850, p. 352; G. and A. Horsfield, "Sela-Petra I. The Topography of Petra," *QDAP* 7 (1938), 21–24; N. Glueck, "A Nabataean Painting," *BASOR* 141 (1956), 13–23; *idem*, *Deities and Dolphins*, pp. 5–6, and Pls. 202–206. For color photos of these ceiling decorations see also Weber and Wenning, *supra*, n. 24, p. 54, Fig. 52a–d.

[63] Dentzer-Feydy, *supra*, note 21, p. 74.

Devoid of paintings, they are more in line with the relieves of Kh. edh-Dharih facades (phase II, carved in stone, not molded in stucco). But this phase of Dharih was constructed only in the first half of the 2nd c., ca. a century after the Qasr.[64]

The stucco veneer of the 'Great Temple' (in both phases), also resembles the Late Hellenistic masonry style, but it lacks the dense embossed figurative patterns of the Qasr. Many gilded stucco fragments, along with others with delicate, skillfuly executed flowers, tendrils, leaves, partial inscriptions, and, in one case, a human face, were also discovered there. Noteworthy in its exceptional state of preservation is the painted and gilded stucco ceiling of the "Baroque Room", to the south of the structure, dated to the 1st c. CE, depicting an acanthus flower within a medallion. Its walls, and those of the adjacent 'chapel', were also covered by painted and gilded stucco.[65]

The works of fresco and stucco in the public and in the private sphere, were prestigious works, no doubt patronized by the royal house as well as by several rich, Hellenized merchants, all of them important members of the Arab component of Nabataean society. They reflect the degree of acculturation of these sectors of the Nabataean society, which was eccelerated since the second half of the first c. BC (see below).

Depictions on coins

The attitude of the royal house to figurative art is reflected in the Nabataean coins minted on its behalf.[66] Claiming authority internally and externally, they could not afford to neglect the universal custom of depicting the rulers' portraits on the obverse of the coins. For that same purpose statues of the royal family were erected in public places, to be admired by their subjects.[67] Obodas I was even deified, and cultic associations were established to commemorate him. But it is significant to examine the reverse of the coins, where we find another story. The earliest coins are of the Athene/Nike type of Aretas II (c.110–96 BC), and imitations of the Seleucid coins of Damascus, minted under Aretas III (ca. 84–62 BC), depicting a winged Nike, or a cornucopia-bearing Tyche, as well as Greek

[64] For the facades see *supra*, note 21, Pls. 40–43; For the chronology of this temple see: F. Villeneuve and Z. al-Muheisen, "Dharih and Tannur, Sanctuaries of Central Nabataea," in: Markoe, *supra*, note 11, pp. 82–100.

[65] M.S. Joukowski, "The Petra Great Temple," a Nabataean architectural miracle," *NEA* 65/4 (2002), 235–248, pp. 243–244; *eadem*, in: Markoe, *supra*, note 11, pp. 214–222, with human face and other painted stucco fragments depicted in p. 220, Figs. 240–241.

[66] Y. Meshorer, *Nabataean Coins* [*Qedem* 3], Jerusalem 1975; A. Negev, "Numismatics and Nabatean Chronology," *PEQ* 114 (1982) 119–128; K. Schmitt-Korte, "Nabataean Coinage, Part II: New Coin Types and Variants," *Numismatic Chronicle* 1990, 105–134; J.M.C. Bowsher, "Early Nabataean Coinage." *Aram* 2 (1990) 221–228; Alla Kushnir-Stein and H. Gitler, "Numismatic Evidence from Tel Beer-Sheva and the Beginning of Nabatean Coinage," *INJ* 12 (1994), pp. 13–20, Pls. 1–2; K. Schmitt-Korte, "Das Münzsystem der Nabatäer," in: Weber and Wenning, *supra*, n. 24, pp. 101–104.

[67] Patrich, *supra*, n. 6, pp. 134–135, note 52; U. Hübner and Th. Weber, *supra*, n. 24, pp. 111–114.

inscriptions.[68] But from the moment when, under Obodas II (62–59 BC), a Nabataean minting of a more nationalist character – bearing Nabataean inscriptions – emerged, figurative representations ceased to appear, in contrast to the almost universal custom at that time of depicting the deities anthropomorphically on the reverse of the coins. In its evolution, the Nabataean minting reveals a reaction against the Hellenistic culture from which it emerged, reflecting the injunction against graven images.

The introduction of statuary in the Greco-Roman style to Petra is archaeologically attributed mainly to Obodas III and Aretas IV.[69] Structures attributed to Aretas III "Philhellenos" are at present either scant or uncertain. However, it was his coins, first minted in Damascus, that bore figurative representations on their reverse, as well as Greek inscriptions.

Strabo's testimony on the avoidance of artistic figurative expressions

At this point Strabo's words should be recalled. Speaking about products which are imported to the country of the Nabataeans, he ends: "τόρευμα γραφή πλάσμα οὐκ ἐπιχώρια, namely embossed works, paintings, and moulded works are not produced in their country."[70] Strabo's words should be considered as authentic evidence that at that time, ca. 50 BC, works of art and architecture in the Greco-Roman figurative style were not yet found at Petra, or at least were very rare there. It is quite certain that Strabo is not referring to paintings on pottery vessels, or to the reliefs on the rock-cut tomb facades of the oriental types, both of which already existed in Petra at that time, to be seen by all. Strabo's source – Athenodoros, a philosopher[71] – certainly would not have made this statement if he had been living in Petra during the reign of Aretas IV. This testimony should therefore serve as a *terminus post quem* for the introduction of figurative statuary, fresco, and stucco into Petra's streets and private houses. The archaeological data are indeed in accord with this date.

Similarly, in the adjacent kingdom of Judaea, some members of the royal house were more open than the majority of their monotheistic subjects to figurative art. Drawn portraits of Aristobulus III and Mariamme were sent by their

[68] Meshorer, *op. cit.*, pp. 9–16; Alla Kushnir-Stein and H. Gitler, *op. cit.*

[69] *Supra*, n. 27. New reliefs, found more recently in the debris of the western exedra of the Qasr al Bint Temenos, include a bust panel depicting Tyche holding a cornucopia resembling the bust panels found in a fill in a vestibule to the south of the Temenos Gate. Inscription mentioning Marcus Aurelius and Lucius Verus was also found in this excavations. So far only a first note on these finds has been published: J. Dentzer and F. Renel, "Qasr al-Bint," *Le Monde de la Bible* 127, mai/ juin 2000, 61 = *Welt und Umwelt der Bibel* 19 (2001), 51.

[70] Strabo, *Geographica* XVI.4.26.

[71] On Athenodorus of Tarsus see: K.-H. Hülser, s.v. Athenodoros (no. 3 – Calvus), *Der Neue Pauly. Enzyklopädie der Antike*, ed. H. Cancik and H. Schneider, Vol. 2, Stuttgart 1997, col. 203; Daniella Dueck, *Strabo of Amasia. A Greek Man of Letters in Augustan Rome*, London and New York 2000, pp. 10–11 and farther references in n. 33, on p. 189. He lived in Rome since 44 BC, so his visit to Petra seems to occur earlier. He died ca. 13, or 3 BC.

mother Alexandra to Marc Antony in Egypt to impress him with their beauty and win his sympathy and support in her struggle against Herod the Great.[72] Statues of the daughters of Agrippa I stood in Caesarea or Sebaste.[73] Coins of the Herodian family, minted far from Jerusalem, bear figurative representations on their obverse as well as on their reverse. Herod's own status stood at the entrance to Ba^{c}al Shamin temple at Si^{c}a in the Hauran. Neither he, nor his successors, would dare to thus transgress the Jewish law in Jerusalem itself, although Herod erected a theater there, decorated with shields and armor, and placed a golden eagle above the entrance to the Jewish temple. Only after rumors of his death reached Jerusalem did two fanatics dare to climb up and remove this insulting figure.[74]

Nabataean iconoclasm?

Was a reaction of this kind taking place also in the Nabataean capital as a result of the overwhelming introduction of "western" influences into its urban space? The answer is definitely positive in the case of the Temple of the Winged Lions erected under Aretas IV (8 BC – AD 40). According to Hammond, the original decor of this temple was refurbished early in the reign of Malichus II (AD 40–70), all its previous figurative decorations in relief, fresco and stucco being plastered over.[75] The defacement of the busts in the metopes of the Doric frieze of Qasr al-Bint might have occurred in that same period. McKenzie put forward the proposal that after the earthquake of AD 48 works of restoration of the cornice and NE *anta* of the Qasr might have taken place.[76] Given the aniconic refurbish-

[72] Josephus, *Ant.* XVI.25–7; *War* I.439.

[73] *Ant.* XIX.357.

[74] *War* I.648–653; *Ant.* XVII, 149–155. On Herod's theater in Jerusalem see: J. Patrich, "Herod's Theater in Jerusalem – a new proposal," *Israel Exploration Journal* 52 (2002), 231–239.

[75] Hammond, *supra* n. 5 (1996), pp. 11–12. Hammond noted the discard of an inscription with the name of the former "iconophil" king – Aretas IV, on that occasion. (as noted, in Jerusalem "iconoclastic" youth had the guts to remove the Roman eagle from the temple facade only when rumors of Herod's death were first spread). The refurbishing of the Temple of the Winged Lions, as suggested by Hammond, predated the nationalistic religious *renovatio* under Rabel II, suggested by R. Wenning, "Das Ende des nabatäischen Königreichs," in: Jean-François Salles and Antonio Invernizzi (eds.), *Arabia Antiqua: Hellenistic Centres around Arabia* [*Serie Orientale Roma* Vol. 70.2], Rome 1993, 80–103, pp. 86–94, on the epigraphic evidence. See also Wenning and Merklein, "Die Götter in der Welt der Nabatäer", in Weber and Wenning, *supra* n. 24, p. 110. The effects of this *renovatio* are perhaps evident also in modifications in the painted pottery between phase 3a and 3b. See Schmid, *supra* n. 47, pp. 150–152 and 159–161. Doubts about Hammond's chronology were raised by K. Parlasca (*apud* Wenning, *op. cit.*, 1993), on stylistic grounds regarding stucco decorations.

[76] McKenzie, *supra* n. 13, p. 138 (but see Larché's reservation, *supra*, note 21, p. 75). On this earthquake see: D.H.K. Amiran *et al.*, "Earthquakes in Israel and adjacent Areas: Macroseismic Observations since 100 B.C.E.," *IEJ* 44 (1994) 260–305, p. 265; check: Emanuela Guidoboni, A. Comastri, and G. Traina, *Catalogue of Ancient Earthquakes in the Mediterranean Area*

ing of the Temple of the Winged Lions – one of the royal temples, at about that same time, if large-scale works of restoration indeed took place in the Qasr following this earthquake, it is only to be expected that its metope busts would be defaced in connection with these works. Actually, the iconoclasts could have used the scaffoldings of the restorers, reaching as high as the cornice. In this case AD 48 will constitute a *terminus post quem* for the defacement of the Qasr frieze busts.[77]

The embossed figurative stucco work of the Qasr was also defaced. This defacement, which seems to be deliberate, is very clear in the corner Nikai of the SE corner of the vestibule.[78] Here the defacement seems to be deliberate, and it seems that it was carried out throughout, leaving its marks, and resulting in obliterating all figurative motives. In this case as well high scaffoldings were needed.

The exact historical circumstances and background of the reformation reflected in the refurbishing of both temples early under Malichus II are meanwhile

up to the 10th Century (tr. from the Italian by B. Phillips), Rome 1994, p. 188, dating the tremor to AD 47.

[77] In addition to difficulties of accessibility to the metopes, the fact that the defacement of the busts was carried out without causing any damage to the rosettes or to any other member of the structure indicates that this was not an act of vandalism. Such a careful operation makes sense only as long as the temple was in use. The destruction of the temple is attributed to the Palmyrene invasion of AD 268–270, with farther destruction caused by the AD 363 earthquake, and by another tremor in the 6th c. [F. Zayadine, "Recent Excavation and Restoration at Qasr el Bint of Petra," *ADAJ* 29 (1985), 239–249; *idem*, in *supra*, note 21, pp. 65–67.]. Since it did not survive the advent of Christian rule, a Christian or Muslim defacement should be excluded (*face* Lyttleton and Blagg, *supra* n. 27, *Aram* 2, p. 269). And since an overall programmatic aniconism in the public seems to be unreasonable under the Roman regime, it should have rather occurred under the independent Nabataean monarchy.

On the entire affair of the Palmyrene invasion of Syria and Arabia see: D. Graf, "Zenobia and the Arabs," in: D.H. French and C.S. Lightfoot, *The Eastern Frontier of the Roman Empire* [BAR International Series 553(I)], Oxford 1989, pp. 143–167. On programmatic and tolerant aniconism see Mettinger, *supra* n. 36, pp. 18–27.

A bust medallion depicting Helios unearthed in 1960 (Wright, *supra* n. 27, p. 28, Pl. XIX.13) is regularly attributed to the Qasr frieze, although no archaeological context in which the stone was found has been provided. The fact that the bust is unscratched suggests, so it was argued, that the defacement of the other busts in the frieze metopes occurred after this block fell down, perhaps as a result of an earthquake. According to Zayadine et al., *supra* n. 21, p. 163 Fig. 29, p. 194 photo 7, p. 216 photo 82, and p. 222 photo 100; and McKenzie (*supra* n. 27, p. 91) and Lyttleton and Blagg, (*supra* n. 27, *Aram* 2, pp. 274 and 283, Pl. 6) the bust medallion under discussion is of limestone, while according to Weber and Wenning (*supra* n. 24, p. 119, and private communication with Prof. Weber), it is of sandstone. It seems that a better geological definition of this particular sandstone is required. The Qasr metopes were all of sandstone. I may add that to judge from the photos of the *in situ* metopes (McKenzie, *supra* n. 13, Pl. 40a), the defaced busts suggest that the original projection was less than 3/4 relief high, the background is flat, and without the rope pattern that surrounds the Helios bust. The overall thickness of the block, including the projection of the bust, is 34 cm. Its attribution to the Qasr frieze is far from certain. (The bearing of this particular bust medallion on the dating of the Qasr frieze defacement is left uncommented by Negev, next note).

[78] *supra*, note 21, Pl. 35.

obscure. However, the extent and nature of the iconoclastic activity show that the suggested movement had the backing of a large part of the population, and that there was no fear of royal punishment.

Thus we may now have not just one, but two prominent dated examples of iconoclastic activity in Petra. Given also the negative attitude of wide circles in the Arab-Nabataean society to figurative representation, I have suggested that the iconoclastic activity, which is so apparent throughout Petra, is to be dated within the kingdom period.[79] Traces of this activity are evident in all the figuratively decorated Petraean monuments and tombs. The despoilers took pains to reach even the remotest sites, they were zealous enough to risk their lives by reaching barely accessible reliefs on top of vertical walls and facades,[80] yet they were careful enough not to destroy more than was necessary. Floral scrolls and foliage or architectural reliefs were not touched. The purpose was not to disfigure the attractive shape of these monuments, only to remove the unacceptable ornaments. Such iconoclastic treatment seems to be inexplicable in a deserted city of the Islamic period.[81]

A two-peak graph is suggested for the introduction of figurative art into the Nabataean domain – one under Obodas III and Aretas the IV and one during the 2nd century, under the Roman provincial government. In between there are indications of iconoclastic activity firmly dated to the reign of Malichus II in at least one case: the Temple of the Winged Lions.[82]

[79] For details see Patrich, *supra*, n. 6, pp. 153–157. In line with my proposal is A. Negev, "Khaznet Fira'un at Petra – Iconoclasm Nabatean Style," *Aram* 6 (1994), 419–448. However, Negev confused my arguments. Contrary to what he ascribes to me (*ibid.*, pp. 422–423; the reference to my book there should have been to p. 165, not to p. 65), I maintain that the iconoclastic reaction evident in the monuments of Petra took place between two peaks of excessive figurative activity, one during the reigns of Obodas III and Aretas IV, and one after the annexation of the Nabataean kingdom to the Roman empire, and not *vice versa*, that these were two periods of iconoclastic reaction. I do not share the author's opinion (pp. 426–428) that the defacement of the Khazneh, as well as of the Qasr frieze, took place during the construction or immediately thereafter, using the same scaffolding. No new archaeological arguments are provided to sustain his arguments, and the refurbishing of the Temple of the Winged Lions, so far the only dated evidence in Petra of Nabataean defacement, is not associated by him with the iconoclastic phenomenon at the site.

[80] P.J. Parr, "The Investigation of some 'Inaccessible' Rock-Cut Chambers at Petra," *PEQ*, 100 (1968), pp. 5–15.

[81] On the poor condition of the site already at the end of the Byzantine period, see *idem*, "The Last Days of Petra," in: *Proceedings of the Symposium on Bilad al-Sham during the Byzantine Period*, Vol. II, Amman and Irbid 1986, pp. 192–205. For a different assessment, taking into consideration more recent finds, including the Petra papyri, see: Z. Fiema *et al.*, "Petra in byzantinischen Zeit," in Weber and Wenning, *supra* n. 27, pp. 149–160.

[82] The iconoclasm at Kh. adh-Dharih, constructed only in the 2nd c., under Roman regime, after the presumed iconoclasm in Petra, is dated, on good stratigraphic evidence, to after the mid 8th c. earthquake. Members of the zodiac frieze were still standing intact. On the excavations at the site see *supra*, n. 21, and Z. al-Muheisen and F. Villeneuve, "Jordanie: Dharih, un Sanctuaire Nabatéen," *Le Monde de la Bible* 89 (1994), pp.41–45; *iidem*, "Découvertes nouvelles à Khirbet edh-Dharih (Jordanie), 1991–1994: autour du Sanctuaire Nabatéen et Romain," *CRAI* (1994), 735–746; *iidem*, "Jordanie: Khirbet adh-Dharih – des dieux et des victoires," *Le Monde de la*

Is it a mere coincidence that more than six hundred years later, the Byzantine iconoclastic Emperor Leo III is referred to as "Nabataean" by his iconodulic opponents?[83] Reading Stephanus of Byzantium and other Byzantine Lexicographers, it is clear that the Byzantines possessed better literary sources on the Nabataeans than we do, and they might have had a clear reference to Nabataean iconoclastic activity.

The figurative Petraean works of art do not, therefore, refute the existence of an injunction against graven images among the Nabataeans, but rather support it, in being disfigured or refurbished.

Conclusion

The Arab-Nabataeans were very conservative in their centuries-long adherence to the aniconic representation of their gods, the floral motifs on their painted pottery, and the oriental facades of their tombs. The Khazne, dated to the beginning of the Imperial Age, is exceptional in the necropolis of Petra. Its general layout was imitated only in two other monuments, the Corinthian and ed-Deir tombs, but in both cases the heavy figurative and floral ornamentations were deliberately rejected. The Khazne did not inspire a general widespread new style of rock-carved architecture. The Greco-Roman clade, as reflected in ed-Deir, was adopted only to a certain extent, plain from any applied relief, to a measure that it would not affect the injunction against graven images.

The Nabonidus Selʿa relief, and the identification of Humbaba head behind the Gorgoneia as applied in Nabataean art, add another dimension to the Mesopotamian connection, so far recognized mainly in the crenellations, or crowsteps motif decorating the top of rock carved facades of pylon type, a motive that could have come from Phoenicia, rather than from Mesopotamia. The South Arabian connection is provided by the "Goddess of Hyn son of Nybt" eye-idol, from the Temple of the Winged Lions, resembling many South Arabian funerary stelae. The assimilation of the principal Arabian deity with Osiris, the Egyptian lord of resurrection,[84] adds another aspect – so far un-recognized – to Dushara, and permits a more profound understanding of the popularity of the Isis cult in Petra. This is expressed in several figural reliefs, clay figurines, and by the depiction of her crown on the Khazneh facade, and on several eye-idols, indicating that she was assimilated with al-ʿUzza.

Dense area-cover, like the stucco-work of the Qasr, and the relief-work of Dharih temple, is another oriental feature, though the iconography in the Qasr

Bible 116 (1999), 80; *iidem*, "Sanctuaire Nabatéen près de Pétra," *L'Archéologue* 41 (1999), 43–46; *iidem*, "Khirbet adh-Dharih," *Dos-siers d'Archéologie* 244 (1999), 54–59; *iidem*, *Khirbet adh-Dharih*, Université de Yarmouk 2000; *iidem*, "Dharih and Tannur: Sanctuaries of Central Nabataea," in: Markoe, *supra*, note 11, pp. 83–100.

[83] S. Gero, *Byzantine Iconoclasm during the Reign of Leo III*, Leuven 1973, p. 32 note 3. Healey, *supra* n. 32, p. 189, tends to conceive it as mere coincidence.

[84] Patrich, *supra* n. 32.

seems to bear western traits. Oriental features that pertains to inner-Syria, are better recognized in the figurative art of Dharih and Tannur. These works of art, dated to the early second century CE, imitate the more Greco-Roman figurative works of art of Petra, that was inspired by Hellenistic models from Alexandria and Pergamon.

But the aniconic tradition of the Arab component in the Nabataean society, remained valid throughout. This dual artistic language was noted in the so-called 'Great Temple',[85] as well as in the private sphere, where next to an elaboratre 'representational wing', there is always a more traditional living wing. The validity of the aniconic traditrion, expressed mainly in the betylic representation of the gods, is also evident in all domains of artistic creativity: rock-carved facades, the floral motifs of the painted pottery, the reverse of the Nabataean coins, the oil lamps, and even in some works of jewelry. This ancestral tradition ignited an iconoclastic reaction against western, figurative influaences.

My conclusion about the Arab-Nabataean art[86] is still valid. Prohibition of a graven image, suggested by their entire art, was the single ancestral law that caused this art to be such as it was: respectable and representative – to reflect their status and wealth, yet original and in accord with ancestral customs – to give expression to their national pride and self consciousness. Perceiving this, provides a key to proper appreciation of Arab-Nabataean culture at large.

[85] Basile, *supra* n. 27

[86] *Supra*, n. 6.

Nabataean Monumental architecture

Laurent Tholbecq

The study of Nabataean monumental architecture deals with two categories of monuments: a homogenous group of rock-cut tombs, geographically linked to Petra and Hegra (Medain Saleh) and a number of buildings, mainly religious, distributed over a large territory.

The inventory of the Nabataean rock-cut tombs was almost completed after the first expeditions[1]. The coherence of this group encouraged a typological approach which was quickly adopted[2]. However, although that method allowed for classification of the various monuments, it did not address the problematic question of their chronology. The assignment of a date to a particular type was difficult, because chronological information was lacking, and because various types of facades overlapped each other during the same period. It was concluded that these variations answered to other parameters: artistic ones (through the identification of individual rock-cutters signing their work in Hegra), sociological ones (the types reflect the social status of the owners and fashions reproduced by the local elites) as much as chronological ones[3].

If we consider the architecture *stricto sensu*, the catalogue contains a limited number of monuments, spread over time and space, with the exception of downtown Petra. Since 1929, the year of the first archaeological investigation in Petra, the digs have increased rapidly within the former Nabataean territory. Despite these numerous initiatives, a large amount of the architectural production remains totally unknown: villages in the Edom and Moab countryside are still greatly misunderstood and, on an archaeological level, central and northern Arabia remain, with a few exceptions, *terrae incognitae*. In the studied sites, pre-Roman settlements are often sealed by later occupations, as in the Negev (Elusa, Nessana, Rehovot, Sobata, Oboda, Mampsis), or in the Hisma area (al-Humayma), including the Hauran in such a very important site as Bosra[4]. Therefore, the

[1] Brünnow et von Domaszewski, 1904–1909; Jaussen et Savignac, 1914. A. Musil discovered other rock-cut tombs in Mugha'ir Shu'ayb (al-Bad/al-Bida, Saoudi Arabia): P.J. Parr et al, 1971, 30–34, ill. 12 à 17. They are illustrated in *An Introduction to Saudi Arabian Antiquities*, 1975, 88–89.

[2] The typology of Brünnow et von Domaszewski is still in use; discussion in Mc Kenzie, 1990, 2–3; for a full description of the types: Schmidt-Colinet, 1980, 189–230 and Matthiae, 1991, 226–278.

[3] Balty, 1983, 306, 316–318; Schmidt-Colinet, Weber et Zangenberg, 1997, 89–93. However, J.Mc Kenzie identified a general tendency towards simplification, when individual variations in the production of an artist exist, and continued for at least twenty years: Mc Kenzie, 1990, 14–25, 115–117.

[4] Elusa: Negev, 1993a, 379–383; Nessana: 1993b, 1145–1149; Rehovot: Tsafrir add Holum,

paucity of information is evident in the resulting publications. Inherently problematic within this large spatial distribution are several buildings belonging to the Nabataean world. For example, Nabataean dedications in a local sanctuary of the Hauran (Si') and in a temple along a Sinaïtic caravan track (small temple of Qasrawêt) are not sufficient evidence to identify these buildings as Nabataean. Another disparity is that this part of the catalogue is mainly represented by religious buildings. In fact, the public civilian architecture had been almost ignored until confirmed by the most recent excavations of the so-called Southern – or Great – Temple of Petra[5].

The comparison of the data from these two groups of monuments constitutes the basis of the analysis. In this field, the most successful work is that of J. McKenzie, who sought the internal evolution of the architectural production in Petra, through a detailed analysis of the decorative elements in her search for a chronology in both the freestanding and rock-cut monuments of Petra, Hegra and Alexandria[6]. Nevertheless, it appears that even if the rock-cut facades and the freestanding buildings belonged to the same artistic process, different techniques were employed. The tomb facades are not representative of proper construction techniques, but belong instead to monumental sculpture, and should be studied as such[7]. Consequently, another important debate arises resulting from the confrontation of these two types of monuments, related to the realistic or unrealistic character of the rock-cut production. Do these rock-cut tombs reflect existing buildings or, on the contrary, do they represent autonomous artistic creations which evolved independently from their freestanding neighbours?

The framework of this paper is derived from a recent article in which S. Schmid noted a parallel evolution among several Nabataean productions[8]. Starting from a limited material tradition related to their nomadic character, the Nabataean population produced, in parallel to its progressive sedentarization, artefacts reflecting surrounding Hellenistic models. According to Schmid's study, Roman influence manifested itself in numismatics during the reign of Obodas III, or in the architecture of the Deir, with an original identity appearing during the reignes of Malichos II in lamps and Rabbel II in ceramics and sculpture. Is it possible to follow this general evolution, which deserves detailed research, in the study of monumental architecture? In other words, can we identify the influences

1993; Sobata: Negev, 1993c, 1404–1405; Oboda: Negev, 1997; Mampsis/Kurnub: Negev, 1988; al-Humayma: Oleson, 2001, 570–572. Various architectural fragments dated to the Nabataean period were found reused in Byzantine structures and are attributed to a possible temple: Oleson et al, 1994, 548. For Bosra: J.-M. Dentzer, 1986, 62–87; id., 1993, 117–147; J.-M. Dentzer, J. Dentzer et P.-M. Blanc, 2001, 457–468.

[5] Apart from the complex situated south of the Great colonnade of Petra, civilian buildings present in the major cities of the Hellenistic and Roman East are mis-represented, with the exception of the theatres of Elusa and Petra: Negev, 1993a, 380–381; Hammond, 1965. Bath complexes discovered in various points of the Nabataean kingdom are part of private houses and belong to the domestic architecture (e.g. Wadi Ramm, Wadi Musa, Kh. edh-Dharih).

[6] McKenzie, 1990.

[7] Bessac, in Nehmé (forthcoming).

[8] Schmid, 2001a, 407–419.

upon the monumental production which lacked an indigenous architectural tradition? Moreover, do we have enough elements to identify an internal evolution which would establish a growing Roman influence and further autonomous developments?

According to literary sources, the Nabataeans were largely present in the Levant (Hauran, Ammanitid, Moab, Edom, Idumea, Gaza strip) during the fourth and third centuries BC, as nomads, shepherds and tradesmen[9]. That implies a progressive familiarisation with the local productions, and an awareness of Hellenistic patterns within the area. The first Nabataean archaeological evidence dates from the second century BC / early first century BC (ceramic, numismatic, domestic architecture). If the archaeological evidence places the sedentarization of the Nabataeans somewhere in the second century BC, it seems that less than a century later, the Nabataeans enjoyed an elaborate material civilization of which monumental architecture was the most spectacular aspect. Apart from the triclinium 21 of Petra, dated to the beginning of the first century BC, which does not display any unique, datable feature, the first firm date is of tomb B6 in Hegra, (1 AD). The oldest buildings in Petra, elaborated before the beginning of the first century AD, are recorded in Mc Kenzie's first group[10]. These architectural achievements which are – and this is the major point – technically very elaborate – would have occurred only a few generations after the settlement in the Petra region. This suggests that most of the monumental architecture resulted from imported artistic influence and technical skills.

This statement must be tempered by the fact that the nomadic Nabataeans were also under the influence of artistic traditions (along with architectural ones) specific to civilizations from which they derived. We know from current data that the Nabataeans emerged from an older population who occupied the north-western Arabian Peninsula, and whose material culture is poorly known. There would be, for example, much to learn from the material aspect of the Lihyanite civilisation that seems to vanish after the Nabataeans make their appearance. It is thus necessary to keep in mind that this nomadic civilization planted its roots in an area which had its own architectural traditions, a fact that is largely ignored today[11].

My second point concerns the technical aspect of this development, which is one of the more neglected characteristics. Nevertheless, and without entering into details, the relative precariousness of some constructions has been observed by scholars. For example, the substructures of domestic buildings in Kh. edh-

[9] For a recent point on the Nabataean presence in the Hellenistic Levant: Sartre, 2001, 411–424.

[10] The Temple of the Wing Lions, the Khazneh, the Qasr el-Bint, the "Baths" and the 1967 group of sculptures belong to that group: McKenzie, 1990, 134–143.

[11] Sartre, 1996, 533–552; Bowersock, 1996, 553–563; Salles, 1996, 565–607. On the connection between the Lihyanites and the Nabataeans, three Nabataean inscriptions (JS nab 334, 335 et 337) refer to "Mashudu, king of Lihyan", last Lihyanite king known through the sources. In these inscriptions, there is just one letter, the B of the inscription JS nab 334 that gives a chronological indication, and can be interpreted as archaic (pers. comm. L.Nehmé). Nevertheless, the end of the Lihyanite state is a controversial issue: Al-Ansary, 1999, 191–195.

Dharih, and in ez-Zantur, do not technically adjust for slope orientation, and the foundations of the public monuments, made up of ashlars, cannot compete with the well-constructed substructures of contemporary large Syrian or Egyptian buildings[12]. Similarly, Fr. Villeneuve notes that the facades of the temples of Kh. edh-Dharih and Kh. et-Tannur were crowned with the heaviest carved elements placed on their summit, in fact so precariously balanced that they defied the elementary rules of statics[13]. However, the Nabataeans also developed original building techniques, such as the extended use of wood beams in the walls of various sanctuaries, that might have originated in southern Arabia[14]. Whereas a Hellenistic origin is attributed to the arches supporting cistern ceilings, roofs and even monumental terraces[15]. Indeed, this technical aspect requires a study of its own but, at first sight, seems to suggest that this very dynamic creative process lacked an indigenous building tradition contrasting with the weight of architectural tradition in neighbouring civilizations.

A. The Rock-cut Facades: an influence of funerary architecture from adjacent areas

1. The Arabian Peninsula

The study of the peninsular architectural tradition former the Nabataean emigration to the Near-East is a relatively unknown field. However, fundamental comparative data has appeared recently in Qaryat al-Fau (Saudi Arabia) and Mleiha (Emirate of Sharjah)[16]. Recent excavations have unearthed the remains of monuments associating a funerary pit with a cubic mud-brick mass (fig. 1). These imposing monuments were decorated with lines of applied crowsteps. In Mleiha, the oldest of these funerary monuments belongs to the end of the third / early second century BC. Similar mud-brick cubic masses were described in Qaryat al-Fau, and dated to the same period[17]. These discoveries are of the utmost importance. First, they constitute the first convincing parallel to the Nabataean pylon tombs decorated with one or two rows of crowsteps. These cubic masses have been reproduced in Petra as rock-cut monuments. They are sometimes entirely carved, or visible on three or two faces, even if, in most cases, one single face of

[12] It is the case of the Qasr el-Bint and of the Temple of the Winged Lions, depite the remarks of Ph. Hammond: Zayadine, Larché and Denzer-Feydy, forthcoming; Hammond, 1996, 20–24.

[13] Nehmé and Villeneuve, 1999, 116–118.

[14] At the Qasr el-Bint (Petra): Larché, in Zayadine, Larché and Dentzer-Feydy, forthcoming; under the stylobate of the podium of the Temple of Kh. edh-Dharih: Villeneuve and al-Muheisen, 1988, 475; at the base of the inner chapel at the Temple of Wadi Ramm: Horsfield and Savignac, 1935, 247–248, in the latest temple of Qasrawêt (Sinaï): Oren, 1993, 1215 .

[15] Oleson, 1995, 717–718.

[16] Potts, 1990, 264–274; Boucharlat and Mouton, 1993, 278–287, fig. 2–4; Mouton, 1997, 87, pl. 6 et 8.

[17] *Ibid.*, 89; 91, fig. 11 et 12.

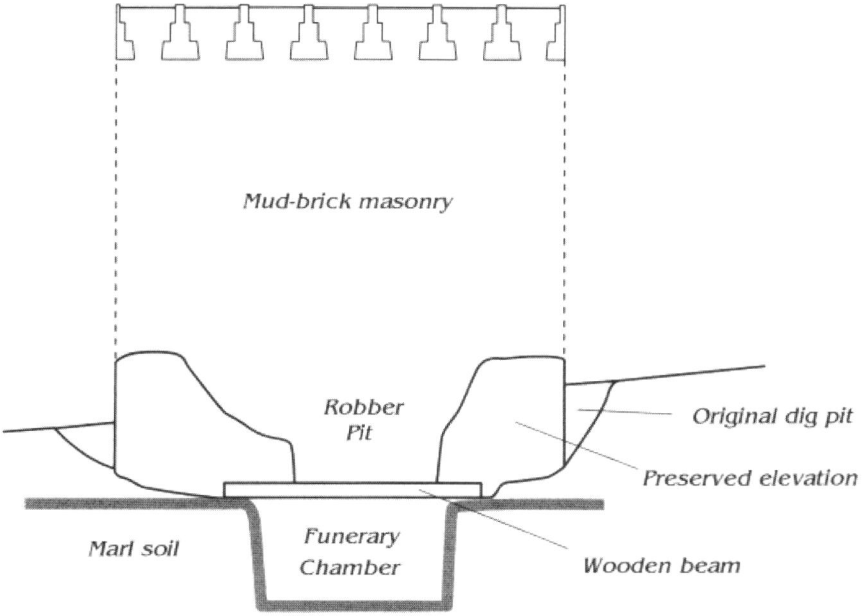

Fig. 1: Mleiha (Emitate of Sharjah). Reconstruction of a mud-brick funerary tower from cemetery C. End third, early second century BC. (after Potts, 1990, 265, fig. 16 b and Mouton, 1997, 87, fig. 6).

the monument is represented[18] (fig. 2). The rock-cut cubic masses are similarly decorated of rows of crowsteps. These examples testify that this type of Nabataean tomb belongs to an architectural tradition known from the end of the third century BC on the fringes of the Arabian Peninsula. At least one of the rock-cut cubic masses of Petra is surmounted by angular monumental crowsteps, similar to the ones that decorated the staircases of the temple of Bêl in Palmyra[19] (fig. 3–4). Therefore, the so-called steps decorating most of the proto-Hegra and Hegra types find a similar origin in elements decorating the top of freestanding buildings. Admittedly, the crowsteps decoration does not belong exclusively to the Nabataean vocabulary and is found in a scattered way after the Persian occupation of the Middle East, but the geographical proximity, the chronological relation and the functional similarity seem to confirm the idea of a direct affiliation,

[18] The most famous of these monuments stands at the Bab as-Siq, entirely carved out of the rock and decorated with a rank of crow-steps on each of its four faces: Brünnow et von Domaszewski, 1908, 203, n° 30; Paradise, 1998, 578, fig. 5. For the three faces monuments: Brünnow et von Domaszewski, 1908, 142, fig. 135, nos 71–74, 172, 173, 178.

[19] The half monumentalized crowstep found in Palmyra is restituted by R. Amy on the top of staircases reaching the roofed terrace of the temple of Bêl: Seyrig, Amy and Will, 1975, vol. 2, 116–118, 136–141. For a typology of the crowsteps in Palmyra, see Bounni, 1999, 511–512. For the other examples: Zayadine, 1974, 54–55.

Fig. 2: Petra. Wadi Farasah. Tomb BD 302. (Author's photo).

the examples of Arabian peninsula constituting the "missing link" between the Assyrian tradition where this motif is originated and Nabataean architecture[20].

This does not exclude the wish of certain members of the elite to command funerary monuments that, despite their massive aspect, are more akin to Hellenistic models. This is undoubtedly the case for one of the four monuments preserved located at the entrance of the Siq in Petra[21]. Its decorative dressing reflects the Hellenistic tendencies that find their expression in the first century BC in the Cedron valley, in Jerusalem or, in a different register, in the southern necropolis of Jerash[21a]. The same phenomenon is perceptible in inner Syria, where funerary architecture was a fertile interaction field between Semitic and Hellenistic data, as evidenced by mausolea of some Arab authorities at Hermel (Beqaa) or Suwaida (Hauran), located at the cross between the Hellenic tradition of mausoleum and its Semitic interpretation as monumentalized nephesh[22].

[20] Zayadine, 1974, 50–53; Bounni, 1999, 507–525. On the original function of the crowsteps: Duru, 1976, 69–74.

[21] Brünnow et von Domaszewski, 1908, 197–199, n° 9; Zayadine, 1979, 192–195, fig. 4; Fedak, 1990, 140–148. About Jerash:

[21a] Seigne and Morin, 1995, 175–191.

[22] That group was identified in 1949 by Er. Will: Will, 1949, 258–313, esp. 277–289. The Hermel hellenistic tomb is a cubic mass crowned by a pyramid: Perdrizet, 1938, 47–71. Closer to the Nabataean world, the mausoleum of Suwaida, today destroyed, is associated to a bilingual inscription (CIS, II, 162; IGLS XIV/1, 346) calling it nephesh (for the Greek word στήλη); Sartre-Fauriat, 2001, I, 196–198; id., II, 63–64. One should note though that this building does not directly belong to the Nabataean world but to a local pre-provincial culture of the Hauran: Starcky, 1985, 173, 179. Coming from a Greek inspiration, the pyramids crowning the funeral

Fig. 3: Petra. Wadi Farasah. Tomb BD 270. (Author's photo).

This discovery in the Arabian peninsula of a mud-brick funerary architecture is also significant, in that it answers to an intuition formulated long ago by H. Thiersh, for whom the truncated aspect of several rock-cut facades referred to

rooms are numerous in Syria (Sartre-Fauriat, 2001, II, 83–85), until the 4th c. AD, also in Christian contexts (e.g., Griesheimer, 1997, 188–189).

Fig. 4: Palmyra, Temple of Bêl, Angular monumental crowsteps. (Author's photo).

mud-brick antecedents, with the two inclined sides providing drainage after heavy rainfalls[23]. It is now established that the mud-brick architecture was not limited to Mesopotamia and northern Syria, but was widely used in other areas, like the Arabian peninsula, southern Nabataea and Egypt[24].

[23] Thiersch, 1911 (*n.v.*). A parallel with the Mesopotamian domestic architecture is suggested: Matthiae, 1981, 229–230, note 18. The truncated aspect of the façade justified the designation of "pylon-tomb": Brünnow et von Domaszewski, 1909, fig. 117–146.

[24] In the Nabataean world, mud-brick was used in domestic and public buildings in Aila (Aqaba): Parker, 1998, 378–384. Stone foundations for mud-brick walls have been discovered in al-Humayma: Oleson, 2001, 572. A similar conclusion was reached in Wadi Ramm by the author after the excavation of a building from the "Southern village" in 1998.

2. The Egyptian Necropolis from the Ptolemaic and Roman periods

This affiliation offers, I believe, an additional key in locating the origin of another type of rock-cut Nabataean tomb facade. Besides those decorated with rows of crowsteps, other types called "proto-Hegra" which are characterized by the presence of an Egyptian cornice surmounted by the two half monumentalized crowsteps, and the "Hegra" types, where the "plate bande" under the cornice is transformed into an architrave, supported by two side pilasters. If one can accept the affiliation between the Nabataean rock-cut facades decorated with rows of crowsteps and the quoted evidence of mud-brick funerary architecture, one can consider whether certain components of the latter two types also refer to other contemporary funerary architecture. The answer must be approached in two steps: to determine if such an architecture existed and, if it did, to determine if an influence is detectable.

Egypt, which offers a climatic environment close to that of the Arabian peninsula, developed a funerary architecture, partly in mud-brick, several of whose elements can be found in the Nabataean artistic vocabulary. Yet despite recent interest, the Egyptian necropolis from the Ptolemaïc and Roman periods remains poorly understood[25]. To illustrate this matter, the presentation will be limited to two exceptional cases: the cemetery of Ismant el-Kharab (Kellis), in the Dakhleh Oasis, which has important evidence of preserved mud-brick architecture, and the well-known Ptolemaic and Roman necropolis of Tehna el-Gebel (Hermopolis Magna) excavated in the early thirties[26].

In Ismant el-Kharab, about fifty mud-brick tombs were identified in two distinct necropoleis. In the northern one, about twenty funerary mud-brick chapels are aligned, apparently along a main access road to the site (fig. 5). They open out to a rectangular room, which is connected through a central doorway to one, two or three inner rooms. Their elevation, sometimes preserved to more than 5 m height, presents several decoration types that are found in the Nabataean area. First, the pylon-like entrance is faced with torus roll edgings, and surmounted by a cavetto cornice (e.g. tomb 2). In some cases, the facades are reinforced by four or more engaged semi-columns supporting an architrave and a cavetto cornice both in mud-brick (tomb 1, considered the oldest of the necropolis). The doorway received a distinctive decoration that emerged from an plain wall covered with white lime[27]. Although its dating is not yet established, as far as the site has been excavated, the oldest pottery found in Kellis goes back to the Roman period, the site being abandoned in the early Byzantine period.

The necropolis of Tehna-el-Gebel has about twenty preserved funerary chapels built from limestone. They represent the traditional succession of an anteroom leading to the principal chamber. Their facades display various types of decoration. The simplest one is a plain wall with the truncated edges limited by a

[25] P. Pensabene collected the main elements: Pensabene, 1993, 37–42, 221–272.

[26] The famous Christian necropolis of Bagawat provides good evidence for the use of a similar decorative tradition in mud-brick architecture, at a later period: Fakhry, 1951.

[27] Knudstad and Frey, 1999, 210–211.

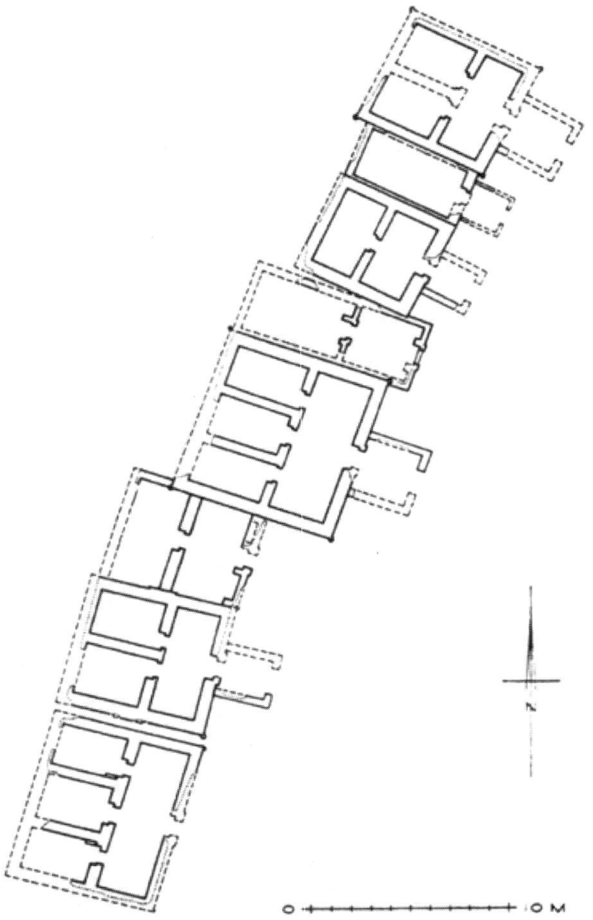

Fig. 5: Ismant el-Kharab. Northern Cemetery (from Knudstad and Frey 1999, 210, fig. 13.38).

torus roll and crowned by the Egyptian cavetto cornice (e.g. tomb 2, Fig. 6). More elaborated examples, presenting other important parallels with Nabataean types, will be cited later. Unfortunately, the date of this complex remains vague ("Ptolemaic and Roman periods")[28].

The fact remains that this funerary architecture displays several characteristics common to the Nabataean model: cavetto cornice, torus roll, truncated edges for the simplest types, and similar developments of the cavetto cornice surmounting an architrave supported by two edge pilasters and capitals, and entrance gate bordered by an applied decoration.

[28] Apart the Petosiris tomb that goes back to the fourth century BC, the chronological elements issued from the excavations of Gabra place the construction of the funerary chapels around the first century BC: Pensabene, 1993, 257–272.

Fig. 6: Tehna el-Gebel. Facade of tomb 2. (from Perdrizet 1941, pl. XXII).

Could this production have influenced Nabataean architecture? There is no reason to seek a Phoenician origin to the Egyptian cavetto cornice and the two half-monumental crowsteps of the Nabataean world[29]. As well as other Egyptian iconographic contributions, the cavetto cornice belongs, from long standing, to a Phoenician repertory, and is found on monumental altars in the Lebanese mountains, until the Roman period[30]. However, several occurrences of this motif appear apart from the Phoenician area. Culturally closer to the Nabataean world, the Temple of Bêl in Palmyra, dedicated in 32 AD, presents a cavetto cornice on its highest terrace, and also at the top of its stairways[31]. Even closer is the joint use of the cavetto cornice and row of crowsteps attested in the primitive state of the sanctuary of Zeus in Jerash. If this late-Hellenistic building might be compared once again to the group of cubic altars, the naos that succeeded (first century BC?) and seems to be destroyed around 65/70 AD answers to decorative conceptions close to the Nabataean ones[32]. These examples show, if necessary, that the Egyptian cavetto cornices, present in both rock-cut and freestanding Nabataean funerary contexts (the monumental tomb of Kh. edh-Dharih) and in religious buildings (Kh. et-tannur) are also represented in the Levant in some late-Hellenistic buildings.

All these arguments, the geographical proximity, the funerary nature of both ensembles, and the chronological correspondence, confirm the hypothesis of an influence, derived from the Egyptian necropolis, upon the Nabataean vocabulary. However, the major argument lies in the following development: the influence of the late-Ptolemaïc and early Roman architecture of Egypt can be detected in many Nabataean buildings, apart from the funerary context. It is thus time to evoke the more elaborate types of facade that show patterns, common to both funeral and religious architecture.

29 Hypothesis from J. Starcky, followed by other scholars: Starcky, 1966, col. 956; Zayadine, 1974, 59–60; Schmidt-Colinet, 1980, 201–202.

30 Concerning that group of monuments (main altar of Baalbek, altar of the temple B in Sfireh, second stage of the monument of Mashnaqa, altars and, if one follows Kalayan's reconstruction, the main tower of Qalaat Faqra): Collart, 1976, 88–94; Collart and Coupel, 1977, 61–70. To this partial list, one should add several unpublished isolated architectural fragments. For instance, in Umm el Amed : Dunand and Duru, 1962, n^{rs} 256, 287, 485 et 541. All these monuments owe much to the Phoenician naiskoi. The cavetto cornice can also top lintels, as in the case of the temple of Chrîm: Nordiguian, 1997, 946; Waliszewski, 1999, 596, ill. 603, fig. 2.

31 Seyrig, Amy and Will, 1975, vol. 2, 86; 116–118, 136–141.

32 Seigne, 1997, 996–997; Eristov, Seigne et al., 2002, 26–35. Another building, related by the excavators to two inscriptions, dated to 69/70 AD and mentioning the intervention of a man called Theon, shows a hybrid character: large monumental altar on a podium associated to stairs, hiding the earlier Hellenistic structures and various underground rooms: Seigne, 1997, 999. Elements of cavetto cornice have also been found in Damascus and in Bosra (person. comm. J. Dentzer-Feydy). It also appeared in the already mentioned Hellenistic tombs of Jerusalem.

B. The Hellenistic Influence: *Alexandria ad Aegyptum*?

The parallel between the design of the Khazneh and Pompeian wall-painting was established by I. Hittorf in 1866[33]. As far as I know, the first scholar to refer to Alexandrian parallels was H. Kohl who established in 1910 the Alexandrian origin of the Corinthian capitals of the Qasr el-Bint[34]. It is to the merit of J. McKenzie who skillfully demonstrated that both the Nabataean vocabulary and Second Style Pompeian wall-painting depended directly on Alexandrian models[35]. Through a detailed analysis of the decors, the affiliation of the Alexandrian model to the Petraean production is definitively established. However, it is now necessary to enlarge the debate as it appears that this influence, far from being limited to the decorative elements, might also be traced in the plans of the sanctuaries, as well as in the design of the rock-cut facades and the freestanding buildings. The comparative elements are not limited to Alexandria, but are also found throughout Egypt. It appears that several architectural innovations and tendencies, that occurred in late Ptolemaic and early Roman Egypt, will be reinterpreted in the Nabataean world. The first case presented here is the Nabataean sanctuary of which the origin of the plan will be discussed.

1. The Temple layout: an Egyptian origin

Despite an apparent heterogeneous spatial organisation, the Nabataean temples are concentrated around a common central element, the heart of the sanctuary, which generally contains a platform where the idols were exhibited[36]. This characteristic feature, equipped with two small staircases, was associated by E.Will to the "MWTB" from Nabataean inscriptions[37]. In Kh. et-Tannur, the top of this central element can be reached by a side staircase. In Wadi Ramm, this shrine looks rather like a chapel open towards the east[38]. However, several arguments seem to indicate that this original Nabataean feature is integrated within an imported framework. According to the present state of the documentation, if it is impossible to find a single model for each Nabataean temple, it should be established that the spatial organisation of several of these worship places was largely inspired by Egyptian models, in particular by monuments built in the years following the Roman annexation of Egypt. Among others, the most charac-

[33] Hittorff, 1866, 14.

[34] Kohl, 1910, 26.

[35] McKenzie, 1990, 100–101, 124–126.

[36] Qasr el-Bint, Temple of the Winged Lions, Kh. edh-Dharih.

[37] Aramaean: CIS, II, 114; Nabataean: CIS, II, 198 et 350. Will, 1986, 343–351. The actual meaning of the term MTB has been ignored. From the base of the root, one assumes that it means a throne, under its various forms. In the particular context of the temple, one can associate it with the characteristic platform of the Nabataean temples, but the meaning is neither firm nor exclusive: Starcky, 1966, col. 1010; Nehmé, 1998, 67–69; Gawlikowski, 1999, 498–499.

[38] Nothing indicates that its roof was used as an exposure area, unless one assumes that the worshippers used a ladder to reach it.

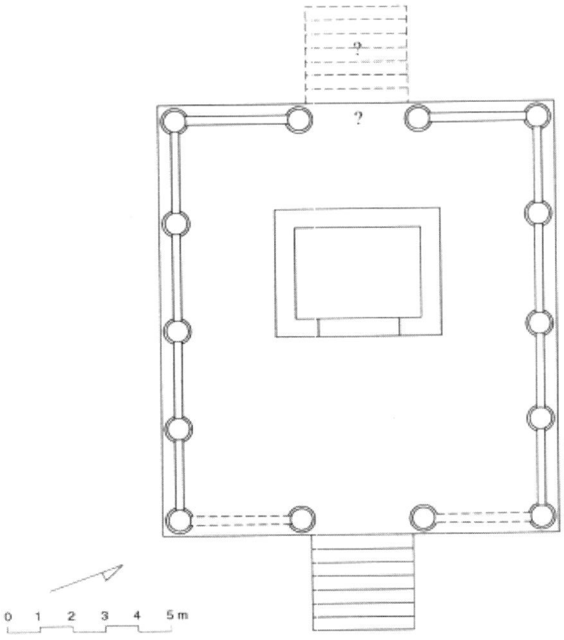

Fig. 7: Wadi Ramm. Temple, reconstruction of the first phase's layout. (L.Tholbecq).

teristic element, common to both Nabataean and Egyptian temples of this period, is the entrance antechamber, which, in Egypt, is characteristic of both temple and funerary chapel-plans.

After Actium, the new Roman power replaced the Ptolemaic administration by financing similar work in the most prestigious indigenous sanctuaries. The old architectural programs were completed by the addition of a pronaos, a courtyard, the building of a new gateway, or particular features like kiosks or birth-houses. At the same time, more modest constructions appeared in rural areas, besides the major religious centres[39]. These temples reflect a minimal program which fulfills the requirements of worship, reproducing the fundamental elements of the Egyptian sanctuary. The traditional succession of rooms devoted to defined rituals is adapted and reduced according to particular needs and the means. One shall see, through the following examples, how these buildings influenced the Nabataean religious architecture.

The Allat Temple in Wadi Ramm

The remains of the Allat temple in Wadi Ramm presents two major architectural phases. The first visible one, dated from the reign of Aretas IV at the latest,

[39] Derchain, 1974, 275–277.

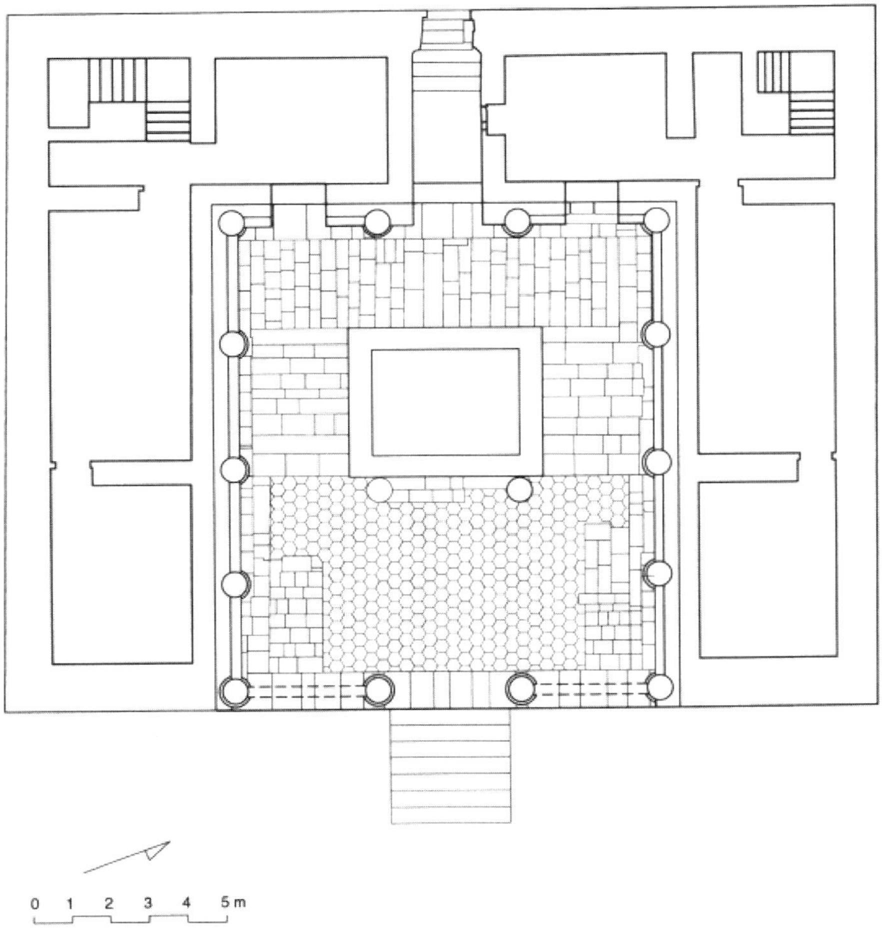

Fig. 8: Wadi Ramm. Temple, reconstruction of the second phase's layout (L.Tholbecq).

consists of a rectangular podium supporting sixteen columns crowned by Nabataean capitals and connected by screen-walls. That screen-wall still exists on three sides of the monument but was not identified on the façade, where it might be reconstructed, on both sides of the access facing the central stairs[40] (fig. 7).

A parallel with the Serapeion of Luxor was suggested in a preliminary report. But it is not absolutely convincing[41]. It is preferable to associate this first temple

[40] One might also suppose that a centred backdoor was connected by stairs on the western side of the temple, and eventually removed during the enlargement of the temple under Rabbel II.

[41] Tholbecq, 1998, 249. This building does not have screen-walls, and dates from the beginning of the second century AD.

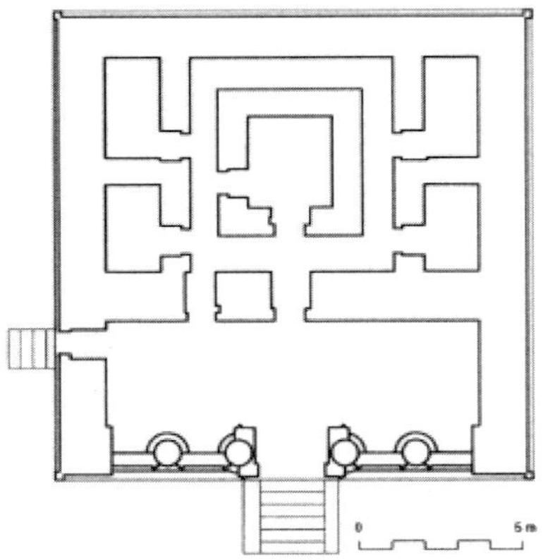

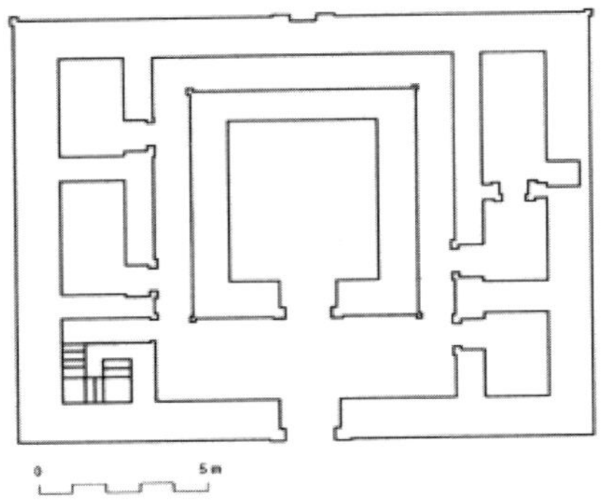

Fig. 9: Left: Philae. Temple of Harendotes. Plan. (after Lyons 1897, pl. 9). Right: Deir Chelouit. Temple. (after Zivie et al 1992, pl.11).

of Wadi Ramm with the layout of the Egyptian kiosk. This building is defined by a peripheral colonnade connected by screen-walls which creates half-opened intercolumniations. Its columns support a stone architrave bearing a wooden superstructure[42]. The screen-wall is a fundamental element of the Egyptian architectural vocabulary, present in kiosks, pronaoi and birth-houses. One sees its impact even more on the Alexandrine and consequently Nabataean decorative elements[43]. The more striking parallels to the first phase of the Allat temple in Wadi Ramm are the kiosk of Philae, formerly attributed to Trajan but actually now dated to the Augustan period[44], and the birth-house of the temple of Kalabsha dated to the same period[45].

Under Rabbel II, the Temple of Wadi Ramm was substantially altered, with the addition of eight rooms built along three of its sides. Two staircases were inserted in the posterior angles, providing access to a roof, at least partly terraced[46] (fig. 8). This latest stage finds close Egyptian parallels in Philae (temple of Harendotes), dated to the reign of the Emperor Claudius[47] and in Deir Chelouit (Western Thebes, Kôm el-Samak), where the earliest emperor mentioned, con-

[42] Arnold, 1999, 282–285.

[43] For the impact of the screen-wall on Greek architecture (Sélinonte, "Building C"; Ahtens, "Middle stoa" and "South Stoa"): Ginouvès, 1992, 24, note 57, pl. 11, fig. 3–4.

[44] Haeny, 1985, 229; Arnold 1999, 282, fig. 242 C.

[45] Siegler, 1970, 37–39, pl. 24, 28b.

[46] M. Gawlikowski suggests that both the temple of Wadi Ramm and the large temple of Qasrawêt were left unroofed: Gawlikowski, Forthcoming.

[47] Lyons, 1897, 31–32, pl. 22–24, plan 9; Heany, 1985, 229, Arnold, 1999, 252–3.

[48] The name of Augustus has been copied on a gate situated between the propylon and the temple, which is destroyed today: Zivie *et al.*, 1992, 2–11; the names of nine emperors have been identified in the temple, from Galba to Antoninus, which indicate that the temple decoration was done during the first and second centuries AD. One should keep in mind that several years can separate the erection of a building until the completion of its decoration: Zivie et al. , 1992, 71, note 208.

nected to the decoration of elements of the sanctuary, is Augustus[48] (fig. 9). The first temple, which was destroyed during the construction of a Byzantine church, has its square plan preserved *in situ*. A central staircase led up to the temple built on a square platform. The temple facade consisted of four columns connected by screen-walls, between two *antae*, and opened onto a *pronaos*, accessible through a secondary lateral doorway. Further, the *naos* was surrounded by a narrow ambulatory and four wing chambers.

The Temple of Deir Chelouit posseses several elements of the large sanctuaries: its central shrine is isolated from the rest of the masonry by an ambulatory, leaving some space in front of it, connected to a stairway giving access to the roof. The ambulatory is connected to the *wabet* ("pure-hall") and its crypt, fronted by a roofless courtyard (the "New Year" court), and various other rooms. Details of the eastern facade indicate that the temple was left unfinished[49].

The temple of Kh. edh-Dharih

The relationship between the temple of Kh. edh-Dharih (first half of the second century AD) and the Egyptian models is even more striking. This rectangular building opens on its southern side to a first rectangular ante-room (fig. 10). Recent excavation has confirmed that it was also accessible by a secondary lateral doorway. From the ante-room, a door gives access to the second room which opens into the main shrine. The characteristic Nabataean cultic platform is surrounded on three sides by a narrow corridor, and flanked by an additional three rooms and a staircase in the north-east. This temple seems to constitute a simplified version of two recently studied temples of the Theban area: the temple of El-Qalaʿa (Coptos) built under Augustus, and decorated under the emperors Caligula and Claudius[50], and that of Chenhour, also dating back to the Augustan period[51] (fig. 11). The elements present in Deir Chelouit are supplemented here by a rectangular entrance ante-room followed by a vestibule opening to an offering room and the naos. The periphery of the Egyptian world would also be aware of similar local adaptations like that of the Temple of Naga in modern Sudan (Naga 200, sixth cataract)[52].

[49] Zivie et al., 1992, 47, 69. With a *pronaos*, it would have resembled the Temple of Harendotes in Philae, and those of el-Qalaʿa and Shenhour in case of more important developments.

[50] Pantalacci and Traunecker, 1984–1985, 134–137; *id.*, 1990, 6.

[51] Traunecker and Willems, 1998, 111–146.

[52] Temple of Naga 200: Hinkel, 1997, 398, ill. 401, fig. 55. For other simplified versions of this pla : small temple south west of the temple of Khonsou, in Karnak: Laroche-Traunecker, 1982, 313–337; temple of Ain Amur: Arnold, 1999, 244–246, ill. 247, fig. 208. These minor buildings are, as yet, unstudied.

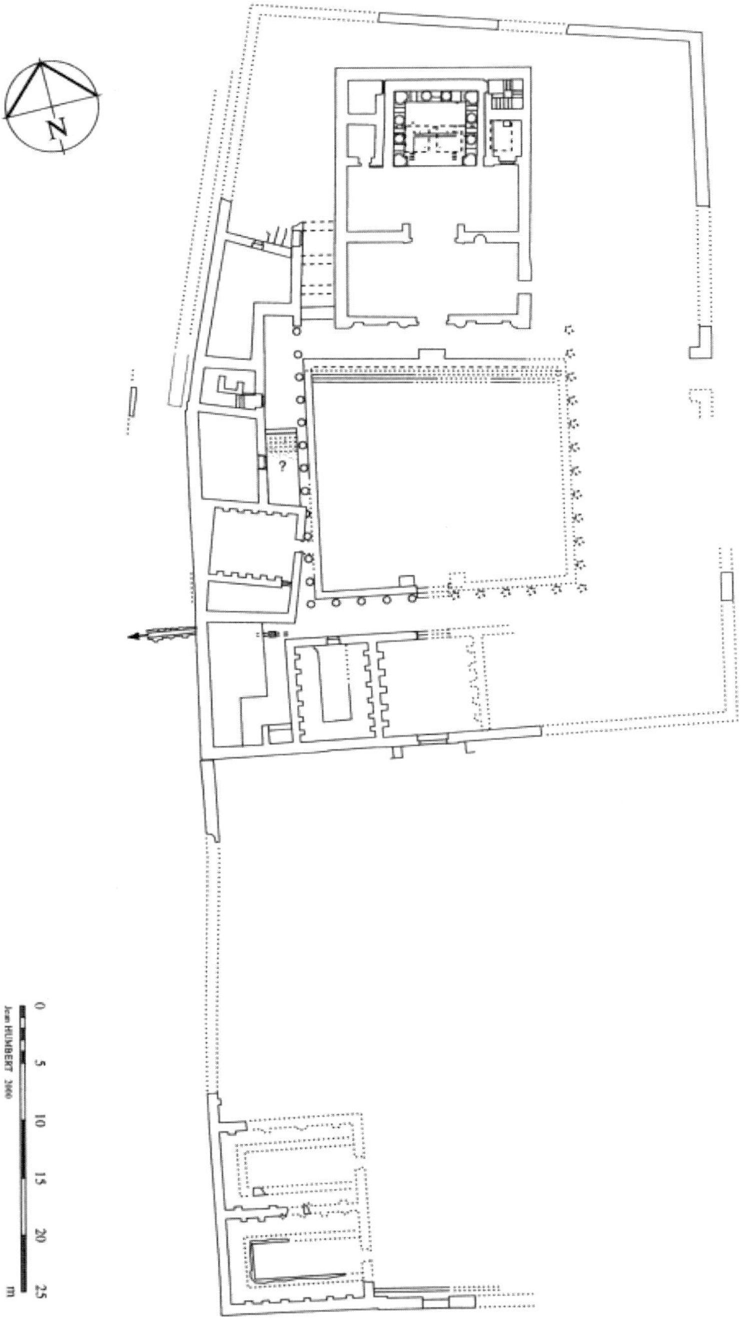

Fig. 10: Kh. edh-Dharih. Plan of the sanctuary (Drawing: J. Humbert.)

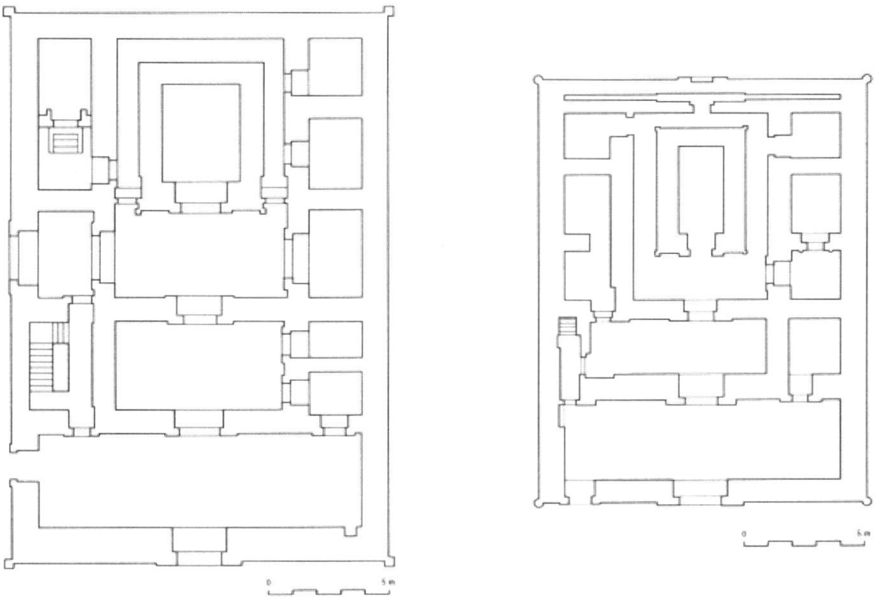

Fig. 11: Left: El-Qala'a. Plan of the Temple (after Pantalacci and Traunecker 1990, 7, fig. 2). Right: Shenhour. Plan of the Temple (after Traunecker and Willems 1998, 121, fig. 35).

The Qasr el-Bint of Petra

The Qasr el-Bint of Petra is a square *tetrastyle in antis* temple. Four columns create a porch, opening to a second large room directly connected to a centred *adyton* with platform for the divine images, and two lateral rooms whose function is as yet unknown. In Philae, the temple of Harendotes's layout evokes evident similarities with the Qasr el-Bint (fig. 10). Details also show parallels, like the central intercolumniation, wider than the lateral ones. Similarly, a remarkably thick wall separated the ante-room from the *cella*, supporting the ceiling joists of the Qasr el-bint, and, in Philae, where long flagstones were found reused in the church near the remaining foundations of the temple. According to F. Zayadine, the apparent division of the cella into three rooms is the consequence of the positioning of the main shrine against the center of the backwall of the inner sanctuary[53]. This makes sense, but it is important to note, however, that the Temples of Ruwwafa, presents the same division, as far as one can tell, with no specific arrangement of the *adyton*. Once again, this division into three comparable rooms, that open up to a large ante-room, is known in both Egyptian sanctuaries and funerary chapels[54]. Therefore, it is possible that the similar division

[53] Zayadine, Larché and Denzer-Feydy, forthcoming.

[54] In funerary contexts: Ismant el-Kharab : Knudstad and Frey, 1999, 209, fig. 13.36 à 39. In

within the Qasr el-Bint has its origin in an Egyptian model, within which the Nabataeans enclosed their characteristic platform. We will not review all the Nabataean temples here, but there are other buildings which show common characteristic features, that constitute isolated groups. One group of rectangular buildings that open up to a rectangular entrance ante-room, like the Temple of Kh. edh-Dharih, is found in Moab, at the temples of Dhiban and Nakhl, in Petra, in the temple of the Winged Lions, and in Negev, in the Temple of Oboda[55]. In other cases, this ante-room is transformed into a porch, opened by four columns, as in the Qasr el-Bint or in the temple of Qasr Rabbah.

However, the Egyptian affiliation to the Nabataean temple, ascertained by the layout of the plans, is consolidated by numerous other similarities. The access to the temple of Wadi Ramm by a narrow central stairway, or the presence of a secondary lateral doorway, leading to the ante-room in Kh. edh-Dharih, has Egyptian parallels[56]. The presence of crypts inside or under Nabataean cultic platforms evokes the Egyptian *wabet* platform[57], and indeed, J. Dentzer-Feydy identified the use of the Egyptian long cubit as a unit of measure in the Qasr el-Bint as well as in the Temple of Kh. edh-Dharih[58].

Religious architecture lends itself to defined rituals, and it is useful to mention the practices which show similarities in the two areas. For example, in both areas, the idols were, as far as we know, not permanently exposed, but taken out of the crypts at fixed hours[59]. Epiphanius of Salamis describes such a ritual in the sanctuary of Korè, in Alexandria, in the fourth century AD: "*They stay up all night singing hymns to the idol with a flute accompaniment. And when they have concluded their nightlong vigil, torchbearers descend into an underground shrine after cockcrow and bring up a wooden image (...). And they carry the image itself seven times round the innermost shrine with flutes, tambourines and hymns, hold a feast, and take it back down to its place underground. And when you ask them what this mystery means, they reply that today, at this hour, Core – that is the*

the Roman sanctuaries Birth-house of Isis in Dendera, (Augustus) ; Arnold, 1999, 187, 211, fig. 161 or temple of Deir el-Hagar (Nero), dedicated to the Theban triad: *id.*, 1999, 257–260, fig. 224–225.

[55] Tholbecq, 1997, 1069–1095, Negev, 1997, 24–38, 28, fig. 15.

[56] The nature of the cubic structure – access or altar – discovered under the monumental stairway of the Qasr el-Bint remains discussed, but it might be indeed some narrow original stairs built before the steps that are visible today: Zayadine and Farajat, 1991, 290–291, fig. 11, pl. XV, 2.

[57] For instance, the crypts inside the platform of Kh. edh-Dharih, the racks from the Temple of the Winged Lions, or even the small space reserved inside the main shrine of Kh. et-Tannur.

[58] Dentzer-Feydy, 1995, 162; Dentzer-Feydy, in Zayadine, Larché and Denzer-Feydy, forthcoming. The Egyptian long cubic is also used in the monumental tomb of Kh. edh-Dharih: Lenoble *et al.*, forthcoming. There is no systematic study available on this matter in the Nabataean world. Let us add that the Egyptian long cubic was used as the norm in the native architecture during the Roman period.

[59] The inscriptions from the temple of Zeus in Dmayr enlight similar practices in inner Syria in the third century AD: Roussel and de Visscher., 1942–43, 194–200; Millar, 1993, 317–319. Four hidden rooms found on the angles of the monument are interpreted as crypts where the idols were stored: Roussel and de Visscher, 1942–43, 199.

virgin – gave birth to Aco"[60]. Immediately after this description, Epiphanius adds "*This also goes on in the idoleion of the city of Petra. (…) And this is also done that night in the city of Elusa, as it is there in Petra, and in Alexandria*"[61]. In Egypt, the exposure of the divine image to the sun happened during the "New Year Festival" on the *wabet* platform, while various offerings were collected in the New Year unroofed court, in front of it. Once these ceremonies were completed, the procession started[62]. There are good reasons to think that, in the Nabataean world, the betyls could move apart from the sanctuary itself and be brought in procession to high-places, for symbolic reasons[63]. Undoubtedly one can imagine that kind of tie between the sanctuaries of Dharih and Tannur, and suppose that the idols of Dharih were moved in Tannur during festivals for prescribed religious purposes, which would justify the dedication of Netir'el, the curator of the source of La'aban, in Kh. et-Tannur. It is possible that the habit of exposing the idols to vital elements (water, sun) or to associate them to other divinities for theogonic unions known in the Egyptian tradition could justify in the Nabataean world a similar transfer of images to the top of the temple through the stairways, or in other sanctuaries and high-places through processions. That interpretation could be extended to Petra, and have associated in a similar manner sanctuaries and high-places.

I will close this chapter with a recent assumption by M. Gawlikowski concerning the distinctive Nabataean platforms. In analysing their upper sections and considering the possibilities for roof construction, he suggests that this area of the temple might have been left unroofed[64]. The question of roofing in ancient architecture is always debatable; however, it is interesting to note that the Egyptian sanctuary has such an open room in the "New Year" courtyard. Perhaps one might also see, in some particular features of the *wabet*, a possible origin of the development of the Nabataean cultic platform.

These examples demonstrate the importance of the Egyptian model in the conception of the Nabataean temples. It is thus clear that, as M. Gawlikowski identified local forms in the Syrian area (with various aspects of the "*thalamos*") under an Hellenistic dressing, the Nabataean temple integrated the betyl platform, heart of the sanctuary and a typical semitic feature, within an envelope imported from an other Hellenism, not Syrian but Egyptian, created from the meeting between Egyptian religious traditions and Hellenistic dynamics[65].

[60] Epiph., *Panar.*, 4, 22, 9–11, trad. F.Williams, 1987, 1, 51.

[61] There are numerous comments on the religious aspect of this text: Bowersock, 1990, 21–28; Healey, 2001, 103–104. However, the parallel between Alexandria and Petra (then Elusa) concerns the precise ritual described above as much as the religious comparison. I am grateful to Fr. Villeneuve who draw my attention to this passage.

[62] Watterson, 1998, 94–95.

[63] There is a famous example in Syrian context: every summer, the sacred image of the Emperor Elagabal left its temple on the Palatine hill for the *Palatium Sessorianum*, the large secondary residence built in Rome suburbs: Turcan, 1985, 137–138; Chausson, 1997, 65–66.

[64] Gawlikowski, 1998, 31–52.

[65] Gawlikowski, 1989, 345–346.

This association is not limited to the plans of the sanctuaries, and to some of their elements: as one will see in the following pages, it can also be identified in the forms of their elevations.

2. The Origin of the elaborated tomb facades with engaged orders

Numerous rock-cut and freestanding buildings present a common façade design which might be regarded as a distinctive feature of the Nabataean model. This facade is opened by a central doorway, and is framed by two engaged half columns or pilasters and bordered by two pilasters with engaged quarter columns[66]. The use of a similar engaged order finds its origin in Egypt. The Egyptian sanctuary developed progressively from the *naos* towards the exterior, each sovereign adding various elements to the prior complex. Most additions are concentrated within the front, which is underlined by porticoes or entrance kiosks. The engaged order has ancient precursors in the Egyptian architecture, but this tendency to project in two dimensions on the wall of the entrance pylon, with the frontal view of these buildings built in front of the complexes, underwent important developments during the Ptolemaic period[67]. This is the origin of the

Fig. 12: Tehna el-Gebel. Facade of tomb 4 (from Perdrizet 1941, pl. XXV)

[66] That facade does not occur in Hegra. In Petra: Urn Tomb, Tomb of the "Roman soldier", tombs 258 et 846, tomb of Sextius Florentinus, western face of the temenos gate of the Qasr el Bint; façade of the temple of Kh. edh-Dharih and eastern facades of the courts of Kh. et-Tannur.

[67] Arnold, 1999, 149–150, 284–285, fig. 242 ; for the antecedents: 55, fig. 28.

Fig. 13: Tehna el-Gebel. Facade of tomb 10 (from Perdrizet 1941, pl. XXX, 2).

Alexandrian illusionist architecture. The temple of Sobek at Qasr Qarun (*Dionysias*) shows, under the Emperor Nero, an impressive compromise – it was partially built in facade and partially engaged[68]. The development of these

[68] Arnold, 1999, 254, fig. 221. The Antoniadis Tomb of Alexandria and the small temple of Qasrawêt shown intermediate stages of this three-dimensional rythm, and two rooms separated by two columns and two half-engaged columns on both sides of the separation. About the Antoniadis Tomb: Mc Kenzie, 1990, pl. 195 b; Bernand, 1998, 246. Qasrawêt : Clédat, 1913, 152–153, fig. 2–3. See also the remarks of G.R.H. Wright and J. Starcky: Wright, 1961, 129; Starcky, 1966, col. 954–955.

Fig. 14: Tuna-el-Gebel. So-called "Roman Tomb" (from Holtoer and Ahlqvist 1974, 5, fig.1).

illusionist facades during the Ptolemaïc period favoured the use of this particular facade. The most elaborate types of Tehna el-Gebel display truncated edges, limited by a flattened surface, as a simplification of the torus roll[69] (fig. 12). A central doorway seems literally built against two columns, dividing the façade into three sections. These columns are crowned by composite capitals, supporting a false entablature (a flat surface continuing the surface of the external pilasters), and a cavetto cornice. Two pedestals, representing false screen-walls carved into the façade, frame the doorway[70] (fig. 13). In other words, all the elements of a *pronaos* or of a kiosk are represented on the façade. This organization, that is seen up to the Saïte period, is found in many later funerary monuments (e.g. Kôm Abu Billo / *Thermounthis*)[71]. Similarly, the so-called "Roman-temple" of Tuna-el-Gebel (*Akôris*) (not to be confused with the necropolis of Tehna el Gebel-*Hermopolis* just mentioned) is an exceptional rock-cut interpretation of the same facade[72] (fig. 14).

[69] Funerary chapel 1, 3 et 4: Perdrizet, 1941, 54–60, pl.19–25.

[70] M. Lyttelton used the facades of the funerary chapels of Tehna el-Gebel to explain the characteristics of the engaged order of the facade of the *adyton* and the main entrance of the temple of Bêl (Palmyra): Lyttelton, 1974, 96, pl. 107–108.

[71] Siwa, Temple of Amon, under Amasis (570–526 BC) : Arnold, 1999, 89–90, fig. 46–47; Kôm Abu Billo: Badawy, 1957, 52.

[72] Holthoer et Altvist, 1974, 4–24, fig. 1.

This affiliation between the Ptolemaic developments of that façade and the Nabataean examples is proven by another argument: it is, I think, the best way to explain the presence of the pedestals on both sides of the doorways in the temple of Kh. Edh-Dharih and in the Khazneh. Once again, Alexandria offers another parallel, in the triple storey underground tomb in the necropolis of Kom el-Shugafa, dated to the Roman period. The access to the main funerary chapel has on both of its sides, two trapezoidal bases, crowned by a cavetto cornice, and used as bases for supporting a representation of the *Agathodaimon*, reinterpretations of the screen-walls represented in two dimensions on a façade such as at Tehna el-Gebel[73]. The characteristic pedestals of the Khazneh and Kh. edh-Dharih are rock-cut and freestanding examples of the Nabataean importation of this pattern.

3. The Large developments of Hellenistic Origin

The obvious borrowings of the Nabataean monumental architecture from Alexandrian predecessors and the Hellenistic traditions that these models reflect, have been identified in the more elaborate tomb facades. It has been long discussed in the past, for instance, that the representation of a tholos on the first stage of several tombs (Khazneh, Corinthian Tomb and Deir) was related to Alexandrian architecture and the illusionist painting evoked by Vitruvius (7.5.5–7)[74]. Similarly, the "Palace Tomb" is named for its facade displaying several galleries on the higher floors[75]. We should also remember that the development of the upper gallery is described by the same Vitruvius as *Oecus Aegyptum*, as an open courtyard, in which the peristyle supports a second colonnade opened on the first storey (Vitruvius, 6.5). S. Schmid recently disclosed how the internal organisation of the tombs and their associated installations (platform, enclosure, portico) referred to a domestic hellenistic spatial concept[76]. Similarly, the integration of the pediment to the facade tomb may refer to Alexandrian models that have many Hellenistic antecedents (e.g. in the royal necropolis of Vergina).

4. Definition of an "Arabian Baroque"

The "Baroque" is characterized by "*the use of structural elements as surface decoration and the use of new forms of entablature and pediments*"[77]. The Nabataean vocabulary favoured the doubling of the orders (which established the

[73] Mc Kenzie, 1990, 68, pl. 196 b; Arnold, 1999, 227, fig. 181. On the necropolis : Bernand, 1998, 194–202, biblio. 388–389, pl.4.1 ; Empereur, 1998, 155–173.

[74] Schmidt-Colinet, Weber and Zandenberg, 1997, 92; Mc Kenzie, 1990, 92.

[75] The examples are numerous: palace of Hyrcan in Irak el Amir, floating palace of Ptolemaus IV after the description of Athenaios (restitution in Grimm, 1998, 60–63, fig. 54 a, b), tomb facades of Lefkadia, Thasos, palaces of Ctesiphon and Assur.

[76] Schmid, 2001b,159–197.

[77] Mc Kenzie, 1990, 87–88.

Fig. 15: Petra. Palace tomb. Detail of the false entablature topping the eastern entrance gate. (Author's photo).

difference between the so-called proto-Hegra and Hegra tombs), with a tendency to a layered order, as a purely decorative perspective[78]. The elevation of the cultic platform of Kh.edh-Dharih is a remarkable example of this tendency, reproducing on a freestanding building the succession of orders seen on several of the largest tombs of Petra[79]. Another example is the extraordinary stacking of orders visible in the niches crowning both lateral doorways of the "Palace Tomb" that finds an echo, albeit less dramatic, in the niches of the Nabataean arch of Bosra[80] (fig. 15).
Therefore, the interaction between the rock-cut and the freestanding monuments is quite evident. What is true for the monumental architecture, also appears in less spectacular examples, e.g., the rock-cut representation of betyls and the removable stones they imitate, are both objects of devotion[81], and the architectural framework, in which they are set, ranges from the simplest niche to complex developments imitating freestanding chapels, as testified by the two betyls of the Siq in Petra, placed against the front of an altar[82]. Also, the architectural framework surrounding the niche sculpted on the back-wall of room 468, located opposite the Deir in Petra, is a reproduction of the two encased successive stages of the altar at Kh. et-Tannur (fig. 16). Two external pilasters decorated with six square panels framed the pilasters of the earlier shrine[83]. Similarly, the internal decoration of rock-cut and freestanding rooms follow a common repertoire. For example, the internal articulation of the *triclinium* of the Roman soldier reflects that of the *cella* of the Temple of the Winged Lions[84]. Indeed, one can cite multiple examples.

I will not elaborate again on all the decorative elements common to the Alexandrian and Nabataean world, which the works of P. Pensabene, J. Mc Kenzie and A. Schmidt-Colinet cover thoroughly[85]. Among other major influenc-

[78] This tendency of multiplication of architectural orders appears in Transjordan in the 2d c. BC, in the palace of Irak el Amir; Dentzer-Feydy, *in* Will and Larché, 1990, 154–155.

[79] Dentzer-Feydy, 1990, 234, fig. 3; parallels in Petra, e.g.: Corinthian Tomb (No. 766), Bab el Siq Triclinium (No. 34), Palace Tomb (No. 765), Tomb of Sextius Florentinus (No. 763).

[80] Niche of the "Palace tomb": Mc Kenzie, 1990, 162–165, Pl.148 b; niche of the Nabataean arch of Bosra: Dentzer-Feydy, 1986, 281, fig. b.

[81] The same phenomenon occurs for the nephesh. For a recent synthesis, Wenning, 2001, 79–95.

[82] Zayadine, 1979, 195–196, fig. 5; McKenzie, 1990, 159; on that base, N.Glueck places the sandstone statue of Zeus-Hadad and its supposed counterpart of Atargatis in front of the altar of Kh. et-Tannur: Glueck, 1965, 94.

[83] Mc Kenzie, 1990, 150–151, pl. 111–112. This pattern is common to several public (Qasr el Bint, Temenos gate) and domestic buildings (az-Zantur). Similarly, various altars from the Alexandrian Museum represents a naiskos under a canopy: Pensabene, 1993, 134–135; pl. 117–118.

[84] That rhythm finds its antecedent in several alexandrian tombs : Lyttelton, 1974, 40-46; Hammond, 1996, 33–34. It is also found in the "Monumental building" of the "Lower Herodium", Förtsch, 1996, 103, fig. 20.

[85] P. Pensabene describes the elements of the Hellenistic vocabulary and their Alexandrian developments: Pensabene, 1993, 131–144.; J.Mc Kenzie describes the structural architectural features and the decoratives elements common to the Hellenistic (and particularly Alexandrian)

Fig. 16: Kh. et-Tannur. Reconstruction of the central altar (Drawing: L.Tholbecq).

es, the origin of the Nabataean capital has been sought in Alexandria, as well as similar capitals that developped in Egypt, in Cyprus and in the Herodian world[86]. I would like, however, to introduce a proposal that requires further analysis, namely the previously undetected impact of the Egyptian kiosk on the Nabataean architectural vocabulary, citing three particular aspects: the decorative pattern, the diffusion of the heart-shaped angle pillars and the origin of the Nabataean dwarf pilasters. During the Ptolemaic period, the kiosk underwent significant development. At this time, this building, freestanding or associated with a facade as an entrance kiosk, reproduced and replaced an originally wooden structure. The kiosk's influence on the development of engaged orders and the creation of illusionist architecture throughout the Ptolemaïc period has been demonstrated[87]. In addition, the shallow wooden barrel roof of the building was probably the origin of the segmental pediment in the Alexandrian architectural repertoire. Along the same lines, the sudden transformation of the kiosk came under later Alexandrian influences and adopted the heart-shaped pier in the third century BC[88]. The appearance of this feature is reflected in the cultic platform of the Temple of Kh. edh-Dharih, as in the centred space of the second Temple of Qasrawêt[89]. The third aspect concerns the recurring use of the dwarf pilaster which fills the vacuum created by the multiplication of architectural orders in Nabataean art, and whose origin has not yet received a satisfactory explanation[90]. A tomb in Hegra sheds some light on this matter. Tomb F4 from Hegra (dated from 64 AD), is given a three-dimensional depth by projecting from the rock face in an exaggerated manner, and this effect is enhanced by four dwarf-pilasters, set on the top of pillars, sculpted in three-dimensions[91] (fig. 17). This exposure provides a striking parallel to the upper sections of the Egyptian kiosk. Similarly, the elevation of the cultic platform of Kh. edh-Dharih integrate dwarf pilasters in its succession of architectural elements[92]. The relationship between elements of that platform and certain elements of the kiosk could support the idea of an affiliation. But this remains a proposal.

and Nabataean vocabularies, Mc Kenzie, 1990, 87-98. See also Schmidt-Colinet, 1991, 131–144; Schmidt-Colinet, 1993, 1–13.

[86] Mc Kenzie, 2001, 98–99. Is it necessary to attribute the origin of the "blocked-out" capitals to the decorated Alexandrian Corinthian types, or could they refer to more direct antecedents? One can mention here the spectacular parallels – precursors? – to the Nabataean capital found in the second century BC necropolis of Plinthine, in Alexandria's hinterland (Adriani, 1940–1950, 140–159; Empereur, 1998, 230) and in Marina el-alamein.

[87] Arnold, 1999, 294 and 98–100, fig. 50–54.

[88] In Alexandria, it is adopted in the "Mortuary chapel" of the Stanley Bay (east of Alexandria): Arnold, 1999, 151,152; ill. 103. For the other alexandrian examples: Pensabene, 1993, 126–127, fig. 105–106.

[89] Gawlikowski, forthcoming.

[90] About the origin of the dwarf pilaster, see Zayadine, 1974, 58.

[91] Jaussen and Savignac, 1909, 383, pl. 40, fig. 191; Nehmé and Villeneuve, 1999, 145, fig. 79.

[92] The adyton on the Qasr el-Bint shows the same order of dwarf pilasters as represented in stucco.

Fig. 17: Hegra. Tomb F4 (Photo: J.-M.Dentzer).

The arguments to prove the affiliation between Alexandrian models and the Nabataean data were, until now, based on what little evidence was available in Alexandria, namely the necropolis and isolated architectural fragments belonging to lost buildings. Following M. Lyttelton, the Alexandrian Baroque was integrated within a history of Greek architecture, as a consequence of a dynamic perceptible in its Hellenistic predecessors[93]. Is seems to me that this trend limits the Alexandrian phenomenon to its single Hellenic aspect. As mentioned in a recent conference, evaluating the interaction between indigenous and Hellenic elements in Alexandria is always difficult, whatever the field and the methods employed[94]. The native Egyptian element, identified in the Nabataean data, could testify that the Alexandrian Baroque – should we say late Ptolemaic architecture? – owes its vitality to both Greek and indigenous traditions.

One might, therefore, suggest two interpretations of the impact of late-Ptolemaic and early Roman architecture from Egypt on Nabataean architecture. First, could it be possible that the Alexandrian influence, transmitted by Gaza and the Sinaitic caravan roads, was less deterministic than it has been supposed[95] ? In assuming the geographically and politically Westernized idea that Alexandria was the privileged crossroads between Egypt and the Mediterranean world was recognized by the Nabataeans, one forgets that the Red Sea constituted the real boundary between both areas. Bearing this in mind, the Nabataean world could have been influenced by an architecture which developed not only in Alexandria, but elsewhere in Egypt at the end of the Ptolemaic and beginning of the Roman period. Or, is it more reasonable to consider that the Nabataean monumental architecture is indeed the reflection of its major Alexandrian model? If the latter is the case, the Nabataean data would give us information about a neglected aspect of this Alexandrian production, nourished by two traditions, and more indebted to Egyptian dynamics than the elements upon which our analysis was originally based.

C. The relationship with the Herodian world

It is time to turn towards the relation between Herodian and Nabataean architecture. Surprisingly, there is no systematic study on this matter. In the field of monumental architecture, the excavations carried out during the last decade, south of the colonnaded street of Petra, suggest new arguments about possible relationships. In 1998, a palatial interpretation of the "Petra Great Temple" was suggested by E. Schluntz: with the first building, being constructed towards the end of the first century BC, finding its best parallels in the triclinia of the Herodian palaces, multifunctional spaces, used together as banqueting halls an courts[96]. This view was confirmed by the discovery, on its eastern side, of a monumental basin, associated with an open garden, and interpreted as the *paradeisos* of the Hellenistic palaces[97]. This interpretation of the area goes along with

[93] Lyttelton, 1974; Mc Kenzie, 1990, 88–89.

[94] True and Hamma, 1996. Nevertheless, the juxtaposition of the Greek and the native elements seems to prevail, in both funerary practices and iconography, as revealed in the recent work carried out in the Alexandrian necropoleis: Empereur: 1998, 170–173.

[95] Humbert, 2000, especially the contributions of Th. Bauzou and I. Sachet, 47–54.

[96] Schluntz in Sharp Joukowsky, 1998, 220–222.

[97] Bedal, 1999, 227–239 ; id., 2001, 23–41. The interpretation is convincing, but one shall

F. Zayadine's opinion that the so-called Baths of Th.Wiegand were outbuildings of a larger unexplored palatial complex[98].

During the first century AD, a semi-circular *cavea* was integrated within the former "Petra Great Temple". One interpret this structure as a meeting room, or perhaps a bouleuterion[99]. In that case, the so-called "lower temenos" would have witnessed considerable assemblies. Indeed, the religious elements found among the ruins are scarce: two betyls found in a late collapse context, part of an altar (?) reused in the *propyleum*, and a meagre harvest of inscriptions found on the site, none of which are enough to establish the function of the building[100]. In addition, the layout of the complex does not evoke the religious schemes of the Nabataean sanctuary[101]. Why would the precinct, a sacred space supposently enclosed by a temenos wall, be opened on either side, flanked by two double lateral colonnades? As noted by J. Basile, the layout of the complex evoke a major public space as in the fora of Augustus or Trajan in Rome. Yet it is possible to compare this space to the forecourt of the Temple of Augustus, in Samaria-Sebaste[102], and the installation of important terraces over monumental arches and cryptoporticos finds a famous equivalent in the Temple of Jerusalem[103]. Although well-established, these parallels do not allow us to infer at this point whether there is a direct influence between the two kingdoms, or if they both refer to a common source.

It has also been suggested that the Roman phase of this complex could be the *Aphrodision* mentioned in the Babatha Archives[104]. The *Pap. Yadin 12*, dated to the first half of the Year 124 AD, mentions the *"verified exact copy of one item of guardianship from the minutes (apo aktôn) of the Boulè of Petra the metropolis, minutes displayed (prokeimai) in the Aphrodision in Petra"* [105]. Another hypothe-

keep in mind that Lucian described such a building in the centre of the sacred basin of the Atargatis temple of Hierapolis: Lucien, *De Dea Syria*, 45–46.

[98] Zayadine, 1987b,139. It is remarkable that these so-called baths present what seems to be the earlier example of pendentive dome (covering a square room) ever found in the Near-East, the other examples dating from the second and third centuries AD. The circular twin room finds one of its best parallels in a very similar room from the Herodion (24–15 BC): Corbo, 1989, pl. V.

[99] Bowersock, 2000, 60.

[100] Joukowsky and Basile, 2001, 48–51. The cult image from the south escarpment on the Upper temenos, might be isolated, and, therefore, does not give any clue as to the function of the building. Nevertheless, the building of a bouleutèrion within the limits of a former temple has been identified in the Artemis Temple of Dura-Europos: Leriche, 1999, 719–739.

[101] Except, perhaps, if the stage of the theater-like structure is, as was recentely assumed by the excavator, to be later than the cavea itself. In that case, the various Italian and Near-Eastern theater-like sanctuaries parallels can be taken into consideration.

[102] Basile in Joukowsky, 1998, 206. On the Temple of Augustus in Samaria-Sebaste: Avigad, 1993, 1307. It was also noted that all the spaces are dominated by a temple: Joukowsky and Basile, 2001, 52–53.

[103] Also in the precinct of the Temple of Augustus in Samaria-Sebaste: Hebsberg (von), 1996, 12–13, and 22, fig. 4.

[104] Nehmé and Villeneuve, 1999, 85.

[105] The document seems to be a Greek translation of an original in Latin: Lewis, 1989, no.12, 47–50.

sis might be that the Aphrodision, mentionned by the act, does not refer to a temple as such but to a building (namely the bouleuterion) placed under the protection of Aphrodite. Indeed, in the Hellenistic tradition, the Ptolemaic and Seleucid kings are under the personal protection of a Tyche, whose representation would have been simply veiled. However, when the Tyche appears with the turretted crown, as is generally the case in the iconography of the provincial cities, the Tyche does not symbolise protection to just a king or to a dynasty but a protection that is extended to the whole city or nation[106]. And such a representation of Tyche was rediscovered in the vicinity of the "Petra Great Temple". One might therefore tentatively suggest that the Artemis of the Babatha archives is the reinterpretation of Al-'Uzza, patroness of the Nabataean dynasty, who was probably represented in the public audience courtyard of the palace, and also of the turretted Tychè, a representation of the tutelary divinity of the city of Petra, who resided at the main seat of the authority, where decisions were made by the influential representatives of the former Nabataean capital, after the disappearance of royal power.

D. A living Art : Regionalism of the Roman period

It would be most beneficial to understand the architectural production of the 150 years that separate the creation of the *Provincia Arabia* from the dramatic earthquake of 363 AD. The colonnaded street in Petra, and the temenos gate of the Qasr el Bint were reorganized in the beginning of that period. The construction of the latter took place after the erection of the colonnaded street from which the oriental section is dated, based on coins and ceramics, of the late first, early second century AD, and might even be later than the annexation[107]. In other respects, the recent excavation of the monumental exedra that enclose the temenos of the Qasr el-Bint on its western side, provided archaeological and epigraphic evidence that seems to associate that structure to an imperial cult for the emperors Marcus Aurelius and Lucius Verus[108]. But, for the remainder, we lack information. The later two groups of monuments compiled by J. Mc Kenzie are associated, on one hand to the Deir (group E), to which a Roman date is generally given and, on the other hand, to the tomb of Sextius Florentinus (group F), the only Roman tomb in Petra dated by an inscription[109]. Indeed, the production of rock-cut tombs continues long after the annexation, but the chronological evidence is lacking.

One might expect to find more information from the Nabataean architectural production of the Roman period in Bosra, where the installation of a new administration generated urban developments, north and west of the ancient settle-

[106] Concerning the representation of Tychè in Provincia Arabia: Augé, 1990, 131–146.

[107] Parr, 1960a, 131–132; Fiema, 1998, 419; 2001, 435.

[108] Renel 2001, 29–30.

[109] Mc Kenzie, 1990, 52.

ment, and the creation of infrastructures were linked to the presence of a legio and civil servants. In addition to the military camp, characteristic monuments of a provincial city have been unearthed, such as a theatre, a monumental fountain, baths, a hippodrome and an amphitheatre, all absent, except – for the theatre – in Petra[110]. Unfortunately, our knowledge of the Nabataean Bosra is incomplete: the evidence is limited to the "Nabataean" arch and the associated religious complex on the east, to a building (temple?) within the western bath complex and a few isolated architectural fragments[111]. In common with Petra, the Nabataean arch, dated to the second half of the first century AD, seems to provide a monumental access to a large precinct, surrounded by a portico[112]. Similarly, the architectural fragments belong, with some variations, to the Petraean repertoire (Doric frieze, horned capitals, one fragment from a Nabataean Corinthian capital) . Therefore, as far as we can see, the Roman impact is clear in the urbanism and the appearance of new public buildings. If the study is extended to the entire region of the Hauran, a departure has been clearly identified in the field of architectural decoration during the second and third century AD, when the Roman vocabulary swept away the various pre-roman local tendencies that coexisted before the creation of *Arabia Provincia*[113].

In the southern part of the Province, such a departure is not evident. However, there is evidence of a vibrant local architectural production after the annexation. The sanctuaries of Kh. edh-Dharih, Kh.-Tannur and Qasr Rabbah are all rebuilt monuments, and evidence that important financial resources existed during the Roman period.

At Kh. Edh-Dharih, a first temple, smaller than the existing one, was destroyed during the second half of the first century AD. A coin of 152/153 AD, found in a foundation trench, gives a terminus *post quem* for the completion of the temenos wall. The second temple of Kh. edh-Dharih was therefore built sometime in the first half of the second century AD. Similarly the dating of the high-place of Kh. et-Tannur was recently reviewed, and there is no doubt that its last reconstruction was contemporary to the work done in Kh. edh-Dharih, in the second century AD. We have already discussed the origin of Kh. edh-Dharih's layout, with its facade heavily decorated with sculpted elements that belong to a provincial art form. This sculpted decoration belongs to the same Nabataean tradition represented more than a century earlier on the stuccos of the Qasr el-Bint. It imitates ashlar masonry decorated by figurative decorations, referring to mythology or local ritual[114]. Another remarkable characteristic of this example of late Nabataean art is the frieze of busts alternating with nikes, a local reinterpretation of the Doric frieze, which tops both the architraves on the Dharih and

[110] Sartre, 1985. The colonnaded streets are dated to the Severian period: Dentzer-Feydy and Blanc, 2001, 467.

[111] Dentzer-Feydy and Blanc, 2001, 449–467.

[112] Dentzer *et al.*, 1993, 119–126.

[113] Dentzer-Feydy, 1986, 286–299.

[114] Dentzer Feydy, forthcoming.

Tannur facades[115]. The last important feature, common to the general organization of the complexes, was the provision of numerous banqueting halls for visitors, a feature that was not specifically Nabataean, but which has not been formally identified in any other Nabataean free-standing sanctuary.

These sites are testaments to the vitality of the Nabataean architectural production of this period. Is it possible to elicit, from their building programs, the evidence of a cultural and religious reaction after the annexation, following the one identified under Rabbel II? Indeed, was the local elite responsible or did the Nabataean aristocracy (former royal family, tribes chiefs, influent businessmen) finance important work in sanctuaries, in order to emphasize their specific identity? This question remains open.

The last example is from Qasr Rabbah, where, based on the decoration, the temple is dated to the Antonine or even the Severian period[116]. The decoration is more clearly influenced by the Roman vocabulary than in Kh. edh-Dharih and Kh. et-Tannur. The layout of the building recalls a series of Near-Eastern buildings, identified by E.Will in his comparative study of Irak el Amir[117]. However, it is too soon to establish if the apparently Roman aspect of the decoration comes from a weakening of the local repertoire, to an eventual homogenisation or even to the impact of the administrative centre of Rabbat Moab.

Conclusion

The first part of this paper mainly focused on the origins of the Nabataean monumental architecture. I first attempted to expand the basis for the analysis of Nabataean architecture from Alexandria to Egypt, where examples of the Augustean period seemed to prevail. This affiliation is reflected on different aspects of the Nabataean production (in funeral and religious contexts, in both plans and elevation, and in rock-cut and freestanding buildings), and must be interpreted as the reflection of a specific Egyptian aspect from the architectural production of Alexandria. In counterpart, I tried to explain through several examples that the Nabataean production is not separated from general formulae that spread in the Near-East during that same period. Nevertheless, there is a danger of using the term "eclectic" while attempting to address the first missing shifts of this architecture. One should be cautious with the so-called "eclecticism", often referred to when qualifying the Nabataean production, as there is not yet clear evidence of direct influences between the Nabataean world and various other areas, like Phoenicia or the Parthian world. Similarly, direct influences from the Hellenistic world (e.g. Egea, Asia Minor, the Seleucid world) do not seem at this point firmly

[115] L. Tholbecq, "The Architecture of Khirbet et-Tannur: a new light on C.S.Fischer's work", al-Bayt University and Mutah University, *International Conference on the Nabataeans, Petra/Wadi Musa (Jordan), 21–23 June 1999*. The order of the busts remains unknown.

[116] Calzini Gysens and Marino, 1999, 849–856; *id.*, 2001, 496.

[117] Will and Larché, 1991, 270–277; Calzini-Gysens and Marino, 2001, 493–498.

established in the field of monumental architecture[118]. One should, on the contrary, consider that the Nabataean production is simply not isolated from a larger near-eastern artistic community, evidenced for example by the pre-Roman vestiges at Jerash, or, in the parallels with the Herodian world. Therefore, it appears that the Alexandrian influence, understood as the meeting point between the Egyptian and the Hellenic traditions, provided deep roots for Nabataean architecture and, along with a strong Semitic substratum, contributed to the development of an original creation[119].

Bibliography

Adriani, A., 1940–1950. "Nécropole et ville de Plinthine", *Annuaire du Musée gréco-romain d'Alexandrie*, 140–159.

Al-Ansary, A.-R.T., 1999. "The State of Lihyan: A New Perspective", Topoi, 9.1, 191–195.

An Introduction to Saudi Arabian Antiquities, Riyadh, 1975.

Augé, Ch., "Sur la figure de Tyché en Nabatène et dans la province d'Arabie", in Zayadine, F., (ed.), *Petra and the Caravan Cities, Proceedings of the Symposium organised at Petra in September 1985*, Amman, 131–146.

Avigad, N., 1993. Samaria (City), in *NEAEH*, 4, 1300–1310.

Arnold, A., 1999. *Temples of the Last Pharaohs*, New York – Oxford.

Badawy, A., 1957. "A Sepulchral Chapel of Greco-Roman Times at Kom Abu Billo", *JNES*, 16, 52–54.

Balty, J.-Ch., 1983. "Architecture et société à Petra et Hegra. Chronologie et classes sociales: sculpteurs et commanditaires", (Collection Ecole Française de Rome, 66), *Architecture et société de l'archaïsme grec à la fin de la République romaine*, Paris-Rome, 303–324.

Bedal, L.-A., 1999. "A Paradeisos in Petra: New Light on the "Lower Market"", *ADAJ*, 43, 227–239.

Bernand, A., 1998. *Alexandrie la Grande*, Paris.

Bernand, E., 1969. *Les Inscriptions grecques et latines de Philae*, Paris.

Bessac, J.-Cl., (Forthcoming). "Le travail de la pierre à Pétra", in Nehmé, L., *Atlas archéologique et épigraphique de Pétra, L'espace urbain de la capitale nabatéenne du IIIè siècle av. notre ère à l'époque byzantine*.

Bowersock, G.W., 1990. *Hellenism in Late Antiquity*, Ann Arbor.

–, 1996. "Exploration in North-West Arabia after Jaussen-Savignac", *Topoi*, 6, 553–563.

–, 2000. "La surprise du *Bouleutèrion*", Monde de la Bible, 127, mai–juin 2000, 60.

Bresciani, E. 1980. *Kom Madi 1977–1978. Le pitture murali del cenotafio di Alessandro Magno*, Suppl. EVO, II, 1979, Pise, Serie Archeologica, I, 1980, 17–52.

Brünnow, R.E. and von Domaszewski, A., 1904–1909. *Die Provincia Arabia*, 3 vol., Strasburg.

Boucharlat, R.. and Mouton, M., 1993. "Importations occidentales et influences de l'hellénisme

[118] More open tendencies towards the Mediterranean world (esp. Pergamon) can be isolated in sculpture: Schmidt-Colinet, 1980, 202–203; Lyttelton and Blagg, 1990, 91–107: nevertheless, nothing indicates that the influence was direct, and it is important to keep in mind that sculptors and painters moved with their stereotyped models.

[119] This text was entirely or partly read by J. Dentzer-Feydy, L. Nehmé, J. Mc Kenzie, M. Sharp-Joukowsky, Ch. Augé, Ch. Kanellopoulos and Fr. Villeneuve, who gave me their comments. D. Barrett, M. Perry and E. Bishop kindly corrected its English version. Thanks to all of them.

dans la péninsule d'Oman", in Invernizzi, A. and Salles, J.-F. (eds.), *Arabia Antiqua, Hellenistic Centres around Arabia*, Serie Orientale Roma, 70.2, Rome, 275–289.
Bounni A., 1999. "Couronnement des sanctuaires du Proche-Orient hellénistique et romain : origine et développement du merlon", Topoi, 9.2, 507–525.
Calzini-Gysens, J. and Marino, L., 1999. "L'architecture du temple de Qasr Rabba (Jordanie). Considérations préliminaires aux fouilles", Topoi, 9, 849–856.
–, 2001. "The Qasr Rabba Temple Project: Preliminary Remarks on the Architecture and State of Conservation", *SHAJ*, VII, 493–498.
Chausson, Fr., 1997. "Le site de la Vigna Barberini de 191 à 455", in *La Vigna Barberini, I. Histoire d'un site, Étude des sources et de la topographie*, Roma Antica, 3, École Française de Rome and Soprintendenza Archeologica di Roma, Rome, 1997, 31–85.
Clédat, J., 1913. "Fouilles à Qasr Gheit", *ASAE*, 12.2, 1913, 145–168.
Collart, P. and Coupel, P., 1977. *Le petit autel de Baalbek*, BAH 98, Paris.
Corbo, V.C., 1989. *Herodion, I. Gli edifici della reggia – Fortezza*, Studium Biblicum Franciscanum, Collectio Maior, 20, Jerusalem.
Dentzer, J.-M., 1986. "Les sondages de l'Arc nabatéen et l'urbanisme de Bosra", *CRAI*, 62-87.
–, 1993. "Nouvelles recherches franco-syriennes dans le quartier est de Bosra ash-Sham", *CRAI*, 117–147.
Dentzer, J.-M., Dentzer-Feydy, J. and Blanc, P.-M., 2001. "Busra dans la perspective des millénaires: la Busra nabatéenne", *SHAJ*, VII, 457–468.
Dentzer-Feydy, J., 1986. "Décor architectural et développement du Hauran du Ier s. av. J.-C. au VIIè s. ap. J .-C.", in Dentzer, J.-M., (ed.), *Hauran I*, Paris, 261–310.
–, 1990. "Khirbet edh-Dharih: Architectural Decoration of the Temple", *Aram*, 2, 229–234.
–, 1995. "Remarques sur la métrologie et le projet architectural de quelques monuments d'époque hellénistique et romaine en Transjordanie", *SHAJ*, V, 161–171.
Derchain, Ph., 1974. "Les temples secondaires des époques ptolémaïque et romaine", in *Textes et Langage de l'Égypte Pharaonique, Cent cinquante années de recherches, 1822–1972*, III, *Hommage à Jean-François Champollion*, Le Caire, Bibliothèque d'Etude, 64/3, 275–277.
Dunand, M. and Duru R., 1962. *Oumm el-'Amed, Une ville de l'époque hellénistique aux échelles de Tyr*, 2 vol., Paris.
Dunand, M. and Saliby, N., 1985. *Le temple d'Amrith dans la Pérée d'Aradus*, BAH 121, Paris : Geuthner.
Duru, R., 1976. "Techniques de construction orientales (à propos du temple de Bel)", in *Palmyre, Bilan et perspectives Colloque de Strasbourg (18–20 Octobre 1973)*, Strasburg, 69–74.
Empereur, J.-Y., 1998. *Alexandrie redécouverte*, Paris.
Eristov, H., Seigne, J. et al., 2002. "Le Naos de Théon à Jérash", *Archéologia*, 285, Janvier 2002, 26–35.
Fakhry, A.,1951. *The Necropolis of el-Bagawat in Kharga Oasis*, Cairo.
Fedak, J., 1990. *Monumental Tomb of the Hellenistic Age: A Study of Selected Tombs from the Pre-classical to the Early Imperial Period*, Toronto.
Fiema, Z.T., 1998. "The Roman Street of the Petra Project, 1997: A Preliminary Report", *ADAJ*, 1998, 395–424.
–, 2001. "Remarks on the Urbanistic Development of Petra's Center in the Nabataean and Roman Periods", *SHAJ*, VII, 433–436.
Förtsch, R., 1996. "The residences of King Herod and their Relations to Roman Villa Architecture", in Fitteschen, K. et Foerster, G., *Judaea and the Greco-Roman World in the Time of Herod in the Light of Archaeological Evidence, Acts of a Symposium Organized by the Institute of Archeaology, The Hebrew University of Jerusalem and the Archaeological Institute, Georg-August-University of Göttingen at Jerusalem, November 3rd–4th 1988*, Göttingen, 73–119.
Gawlikowski, M., 1989. "Les temples dans la Syrie à l'époque hellénistique et romaine", in

Dentzer, J.-M. and Orthmann, W., *Archéologie et Histoire de la Syrie, II, La Syrie de l'époque achéménide à l'avènement de l'Islam*, Saarbrücken, 1989, 323–346.
–, 1998. "Les sanctuaires du Proche-Orient romain dans la recherche récente", *Topoi*, 8, 31–52.
–, 1999. "Motab et hamana. Sur quelques monuments religieux du Levant", *Topoi*, 9.2, 491–505.
–, forthcoming. "The Nabataean Temple at Qasrawet", *Proceedings of the Egyptological Congress, April 2000*, Cairo.
Ginouvès, R., 1992. *Dictionnaire méthodique de l'architecture grecque et romaine, II, Eléments constitutifs: supports, couvertures, aménagements intérieurs*, Rome.
Griesheimer, M., "Cimetières et tombeaux des villages de la Syrie du Nord", *Syria*, 74, 1997, 165–212.
Grimm, G., 1998. *Alexandria, Die erste Königsstadt der Hellenistischen Welt*, Mainz.
Hammond, Ph. C., 1965. *The Excavation of the Main Theatre at Petra, 1961–1962*, London.
–, 1996. *The Temple of the Winged Lions, Petra, Jordan, 1973–1990*, Fountain Hills.
Healey, J.F., 1993. *The Nabataean Tomb Inscriptions of Mada'in Saleh*, Oxford.
–, 2001. *The religion of the Nabataeans, A Conspectus*, Religions in the Graeco-Roman World, 136, Leiden.
Hebsberg (von), H., 1996. "The significance of the Cities in the Kingdom of Herod", in Fitteschen, K. and Foerster, G., *Judaea and the Greco-Roman World in the Time of Herod in the Light of Archaeological Evidence, Acts of a Symposium Organized by the Institute of Archeaology, The Hebrew University of Jerusalem and the Archaeological Institute, Georg-August-University of Göttingen at Jerusalem, November 3rd–4th 1988*, Göttingen, p. 9–25.
Haeny, G., 1985. "A Short Architectural History of Philae", *BIFAO*, 85, 197–233.
Hammond, P.C., 1996. *The Temple of the Winged Lions, Petra, Jordan, 1973–1990*, Fountain Hills.
Hinkel, F.W., 1997. "L'Architecture méroïtique", in Wildung, D. (ed.), *Soudan, Royaumes sur le Nil*, Paris-München, 391–416.
Hittorff, I.J., 1866. *Mémoire sur Pompéi et Pétra* , Mémoire de l'Académie des Inscriptions, Paris.
Holthoer, R. and Altvist, R., 1974. "The 'Roman Temple' at Tehna el-Gebel", *Studia Orientalia*, 43/7, Helsinki, 4–24.
Horsfield, G., and Savignac, R., 1935. "Le Temple de Ramm", *RBi*, 44, 245–278.
Humbert, J.-B. (ed.), 2000. *Gaza Méditerranéenne, Histoire et archéologie en Palestine*, Paris.
Jaussen, J. and Savignac, R., 1914. *Mission archéologique en Arabie. II. El-Ela, D'Hégra à Teima, Harrah de Tebouk*, Paris.
Jones, R.N., 2001. Nabataean Inscriptions, in Fiema, Z.T., Kanellopouls, Ch., Waliszewski, Th. and Schick, R., *The Petra Church*, Amman, 346–349.
Joukowsky, M. Sharp, 1998. *Petra Great Temple, I. Brown University Excavations 1993–1997*, Providence.
–, 2001. "Petra: Brown University Excavations of the Great Temple. Questions about Functional Analysis", *SHAJ*, 7, 447–455.
Joukowsky, M. Sharp and Basile, J., 2001. "More Pieces in the Petra Great Temple Puzzle", *BASOR*, 234, 43-58.
Kohl, H., 1910. *Kasr Firaun in Petra*, Leipzig.
Knudstad J. E. and Frey, R. A., 1999. "Kellis: The Architectural Survey of the Romano-Byzantine Town at Ismant el-Kharab", in Churcher, C.S. and Mills, A. J. (éds), *Reports from the Survey of Dhakleh Oasis, 1977–87, Dakhleh Oasis Project*, Monograph 2, Oxford, 208–213.
Krencker, D. and Zschietzschmann, W., 1938. *Römische Tempel in Syrien*, 2 vol., Berlin-Leipzig.
Laroche-Traunecker, F., 1982. "Données nouvelles sur les abords du temple de Khonsou", *Karnak*, VII, 313–337.

Lenoble, P. (et al.), forthcoming. "Le cimetière au sud du Wadi Sharheh" in Villeneuve, Fr. and al-Muheizen, Z., "Fouilles de Kh. edh-Dharih", *Syria*, forthcoming.
Leriche, P., 1999. "Salle à gradins du temple d'Artémis à Doura-Europos", Topoi, 9.2, 719–739.
Lewis, N., 1989. *The Documents from the Bar-Kochba Period in the Cave of Letters: Greek Papyri*, Jerusalem, 1989.
Lyons, H.G., 1897. *A Report on the Island and the Temples of Philae*, London.
Lyttelton, M., 1974. *Baroque Architecture in Classical Antiquity*, London.
Lyttelton, M. and Blagg, Th., 1990. "Sculpture in Nabataean Petra, and the Question of Roman Influence", in Henig, M. (ed.), *Architectur and Architectural Sculpture in the Roman Empire*, Oxford University Committee for Archaeology Monograph No. 29, Oxford, 91–107.
Matthiae, K., 1991. "Die nabatäische Felsarchitektur in Petra", *Klio*, 73–1, 226–278.
McKenzie, J., 1990. *The Architecture of Petra*, BAMA 1, Oxford.
–, 2001, "Keys from Egypt and the East: Observations on Nabataean Culture in the Light of Recent Discoveries", *BASOR*, 234, 97–112.
Mouton, M., 1997. "Les tours funéraires d'Arabie, *Nephesh* monumentales", *Syria*, 74, 81–98.
Negev, A., 1988. *The Architecture of Mampsis. Final Report, I: The Middle and Late Nabataean Periods*, Qedem, 26, Jerusalem.
–, 1993a. "Elusa", in *NEAEH*, 1, 379–383.
–, 1993b. "Nessana", in *NEAEH*, 3, 1993, 1145–1149.
–, 1993c. "Sobata", in *NEAEH*, 4, 1993, 1404–1410.
–, 1997. *The Architecture of Oboda, Final Report*, Qedem, 36, Jerusalem.
Nehmé, L., 1998. "Une inscription nabatéenne de Bosra (Syrie)", *in* Amphoux, Ch.-B., *et al.* (éds)., *Études sémitiques et samaritaines offertes à Jean Margain*, Lausanne, p. 63–73.
Nehmé, L. and Villeneuve, F., 1999. *Pétra, Métropole de l'Arabie Antique*, Paris.
Nordiguian, L., 1997. "Le temple de Marliyyat (Chhîm) à la faveur de nouvelles fouilles", *Topoi*, 7, 945–964.
Oleson, J.P., 1995. "The Origins and Design of Nabataean Water-Supply Systems", *SHAJ*, V, 707–719.
–, 2001. "King, Emperor, Priest and Caliph: Change at Hawar (Ancient al-Humyama) in the First Millenium AD", *SHAJ*, VII, 569–580.
Oleson, J.P., et al., 1994. "Humeima", *AJA*, 98, 548–549.
Oren, E.D., 1993. "Qasrawet", in *NEAEH*, 4, 1213–1218.
Pantalacci, L. and Traunecker, Cl., 1984–1985. "Premières observations sur le temple coptite d'El-Qal'a", *ASAE*, 70, 133–141.
–, 1990. *Le Temple d'El-Qal'a, I. Relevé des scènes et des textes, Sanctuaire central, Sanctuaire nord – Salle des offrandes 1 à 112*, IFAO, Cairo.
Paradise, Th.R., 1998. "Sandstone weathering, Petra", *AJA*, 102.3, 1998, 576–578.
Parker, S.Th., 1998. "The Roman 'Aqaba Project: the 1996 Campaign", *ADAJ*, 42, 375–394.
Parr, P.J., 1960. "Excavations at Petra 1958–1959", *PEQ*, 92, 124–135.
–, 1996. "The Architecture of Petra: Review Article", *PEQ*, 128, 64–70.
Parr, P.J., Harding, G.L. and Dayton, J.E., 1971. "Preliminary Survey in N.W. Arabia, 1968", *BIAUL*, 10, 1971, p. 23-61.
Pensabene, P., 1993. *Elementi architettonici di Alessandria e di altri siti egiziani*, Repertorio dell'egitto greco-romano, Serie C – Vol. III, Rome.
Perdrizet, P., 1938. "Le monument de Hermel", *Syria*, 19, 47–71.
–, 1941. "Temples et maisons funéraires d'époque gréco-romaine", in Gabra, S., Drioton, E., – Perdrizet, P. and Waddel, W.G., *Fouilles de l'Université Fouad el Awal à Hermoupolis ouest (Touna el-Gebel)*, IFAO, Cairo, 51–105.
Pesce, G., 1950. *Il "Palazzo delle Colonne" in Tolemaide di Cirenaica*, Rome.
Potts, D.T., 1990. *The Arabian Gulf in Antiquity, II. From Alexander the Great to the Coming of Islam*, Oxford.

Renel, Fr., 2001. "Preliminary report ont the results of the excavations of the Qasr el-Bint in Petra", *Majalat athar*, 4, 29–30 (in arabic).

Rey-Coquais, J.-P., 1999. "Qalaat Faqra: un monument du culte impérial dans la montagne libanaise", Topoi, 9.2, 629–688.

Roussel, P. and de Visscher, 1942–1943. "Les inscriptions du temple de Dmeir", Syria, 22, 177–200.

Salles, J.-F., 1996. "Al-'Ula – Dédan. Recherches récentes", *Topoi*, 6, 565–607.

Sartre, M., 1985. *Bostra, des origines à l'Islam*, BAH, 117, Paris.

–, 1996. "La *Mission en Arabie* des pères A.Jaussen et R.Savignac. Historique et bilan scientifique", *Topoi*, 6, 1996, 533–552.

–, 2001. *D'Alexandre à Zénobie, Histoire du Levant Antique, IVè s. avant J.-C. – IIIè siècle ap. J.-C*, Paris.

Sartre-Fauriat, A., 2001. *Des tombeaux et des morts, Monuments funéraires, société et culture en Syrie du Sud du Ier s. av. J.-C. au VIIème s. apr. J.-C.*, BAH 158, 2 vol., Beirut.

Schmid, S., 2001a. "The "Hellenisation" of the Nabataeans: A New Approach", *SHAJ*, VII, 407–419.

Schmid, S.G., 2001b. "The International Wadi Farasa Project (IWFP), between microcosm and macroplanning, a first synthesis", *PEQ*, 133, 159–197.

Schmidt-Colinet, A., 1980. "Nabatäische Felsarchitektur, Bemerkungen zum gegenwärtigen Forschungsstand", *BJ*, 80, 189–230.

–, 1983. "A Nabataean Family of Sculptors at Hegra", *Berytus*, 31, 95–102.

–, 1991. "Aspects of "Hellenism" in Nabataean and Palmyrene Funerary Architecture", in *Ο ΕΛΛΗΝΙΣΜΟΣ ΣΤΗΝ ΑΝΑΤΟΛΗ, International Meeting of History and Archaeology, Delphi 6–9 nov. 1986*, Athens, 131–144.

–, 1993. "Der Ptolemäische Eckgebel, Ursprung und Wirkung eines Architekturmotivs", in Invernizzi, A. and Salles, J.-F. (eds.), *Arabia Antiqua, Hellenistic Centres around Arabia*, Serie Orientale Roma, 70.2, Rome, 1–13.

Schmidt-Colinet, A., Weber, Th., and Zangenberg, J., 1997. "Arabischer Barock, Sepulkrale Kultur in Petra", in Weber, Th. and Wenning, R. (eds)., *Petra: antike Felsstadt zwischen arabischer Tradition und griechischer Norm*, Mainz, 87–98.

Seigne, J., Morin, Th., 1995. "Preliminary Report on a Mausoleum at the Turn of the BC/AD Century at Jarash", *ADAJ*, 39, 175–191.

Seigne, J., 1997. "De la grotte au périptère, le sanctuaire de Zeus Olympien à Jérash", *Topoi*, 7, 1997, 993–1004.

Seyrig, H., Amy, R. et Will, E., 1975. *Le temple de Bêl à Palmyre*, BAH 83, Paris, 2 vol..

Siegler, K.G., 1970. *Kalabsha. Architektur und Baugeschichte des Tempels*, Berlin.

Starcky, J., 1966. "Pétra et la Nabatène", in Cazelles, H. and Feuillet, A. (eds.), *Supplément au Dictionnaire de la Bible*, 7, Paris, col. 886–1017.

–, 1985. "Les inscriptions nabatéennes et l'histoire de la Syrie méridionale et du Nord de la Jordanie", in Dentzer, J.M. (éd.), *Hauran, I*, BAH, 124, Paris, 1985,167–182.

Thiersch, H., 1911. An den Rändern des römischen Reichs, München.

Tholbecq, L., 1997. "Les Sanctuaires des Nabatéens: État de la question à la lumière de recherches archéologiques récentes," *Topoi*, 7.2, 1069–1095.

–, 1998. "The Nabataeo-Roman Site of Wadi Ramm (Iram): a new Appraisal", *ADAJ*, 42, 241–254.

Traunecker, Cl. and Willems, H., 1998. "Chenhour, Rapport des travaux de 1996 et 1997", *CRIPEL*, 19, 111–146.

True, M. and Hamma, K., 1996. *Alexandria and Alexandrianism. Papers Delivered at a Symposium Organized by The J. Paul Getty Museum and The Getty Center for the History of Art and the Humanities and Held at the Museum April 22–25, 1993*, Malibu.

Tsafrir, Y., and Holum K.G., 1993. "Rehovot-in-the-Negev", in *NEAEH*, 4, 1993, 1274–1277.

Turcan, R., 1985. *Héliogabale et le sacre du soleil*, Paris.

Villeneuve, Fr., and al-Muheisen, Z., 1988. "Fouilles à Khirbet edh-Dharih (Jordanie), 1984–

1987: Un village, son sanctuaire et sa nécropole aux époques nabatéenne et romaine (Ier – IV[è] siècles ap. J.-C.)", *CRAI*, avril–juin 1988, 458–479.

Waliszewski, T., 1999. "Découvertes récentes sur le sanctuaire romain de Chhîm (Liban du Sud)", *Topoi*, 9.2, 1999, 595–606.

Watterson B., 1998. *The House of Horus at Edfou, Ritual in an Ancient Egyptian Tempie*, Stroud.

Wenning, R., 2001. "The Betyls of Petra", *BASOR*, 234, 79–95.

Will, Er., 1949. "La tour funéraire de la Syrie et les monuments apparentés", *Syria*, 26, 3–4, 258–313 = Will, Er., 1995. *De l'Euphrate au Rhin*, Beirut, 629–686.

–, 1986. "Du môtab de Dusarès au trône d'Astarté", *Syria*, 63, 343–351 = Will, Er., 1995. *De l'Euphrate au Rhin*, Beirut, 269–277.

Will, Er. et Larché, Fr., 1991. *'Irak al Amir, Le château du Tobiade Hyrcan*, BAH 132, Paris.

Wright, G.R.H., 1961. "Petra-the Arched Gate, 1959–60", *PEQ*, 93, 124–135.

Zayadine, F., "Die Felsarchitektur Petras, Orientalische Traditionen und hellenistischer Einfluss", in Lindner, M., *Petra und das Königreich der Nabatäer*, Nürnberg, 39–69.

–, 1979. "Excavations at Petra (1976–78)", *ADAJ*, 23, 185–197.

–, 1987a. "Les sanctuaires nabatéens", *La Jordanie, de l'âge de la pierre à l'époque byzantine,* Rencontres de l'École du Louvre. Paris, 93–108.

–, 1987b. "Decorative Stucco at Petra and other Hellenistic Sites", *SHAJ*, 3, 131–142.

Zayadine, F. and Farajat, S., 1991. "The Petra National Trust Site Projects: Excavation and Clearance at Petra and Beida", *ADAJ*, 35, 275–312.

Zayadine, F., Larché, Fr. and Dentzer-Feydy, J., (Forthcoming). *Le Qasr el-Bint de Pétra, L'architecture, le décor, la chronologie et les dieux*, Beyrouth.

Zivie Ch. M., et al., 1992. Le Temple de Deir Chelouit, IV, Étude architecturale, IFAO, Cairo.

Nabataean Private Architecture

Bernhard Kolb

Introduction

The monumental architecture of Petra, cut from rock and built of stone, has held Nabataean scholars spell-bound ever since it was discovered. However, their interest in the 'Houses of the Dead' and the 'Houses of the Gods' did not include a discussion of the 'Houses of the Living' for quite a long time – rather astonishingly so as already in the late 1920s and the 1930s a series of rock-cut houses at the periphery of the town was investigated and published within the scope of the first archaeological digs in Petra (Horsfield 1983; Murray – Ellis, 1940). A scientific discussion of the built private architecture in Petra only began in the course of the last few decades, even though small parts of pri-vate buildings were published as 'incidentals' within the scope of some extensive, on-going excavation projects since the 1960s (Hammond 1977/78, 81–84; Russell 1980, 48–49)[1]. In fact, Peter Parr already drew attention to this lacuna in the respective research about 40 years ago, though nobody listened to him for decades to come (Parr 1965, 527). Given the aforementioned preconditions, it may not seem all that surprising that any attempt at establishing an overview of Nabataean residential building is hindered by the little evidence published to date: in Petra itself as well as in other Nabataean settlements, only a very few systematically studied private buildings can be listed that brought to light ground-plans and a dating of a certain evidential import. Due to the reasons mentioned above, the following explanations will have to be considered an attempt to de-velop the characteristic features of Nabataean residential structures quoting selected examples. Based on the private buildings studied in Petra, we aim to show that the private architecture of the Nabataeans is characterized by *autochthonous*, regional units and, to a varying degree, by foreign influences.

If we ignore the walls and floors uncovered by Peter Parr in Trench III on the Colonnaded Street in Petra that are provisionally dated to the 3rd to 1st century B.C. (Parr 1960, 130–131), the earliest datable residential structures of Petra first appeared in the course of the 1st century B.C.[2]. The much discussed descriptions

[1] For a summary of the rock-cut and built private houses of the Nabataeans cf. e.g. McKenzie 1990, 105–108; Netzer 2003, 124–130, 142–152; Schmid 2001, 374–376; Nehmé 1997.

[2] On the EZ IV dig, we found clues to a partly commercially used structure dated, due to excavated fragments of Black-Glazed ware, to the 1st century BC. Cf. Kolb – Keller 2001, 311, 317–319. On the EZ I terrace, two walls of Nabat. Phase II from the late 1st century BC have been reliably identified. Cf. Stucky 1996, 17–21, 48–49, and note 195 including some references to buildings not discussed here.

of Petra by Diodoros (19. 94.1–100.3) and Strabon (16. 4, 21) are to be seen against this background. In book 19 of his history written in the 1st century B.C., Diodorus mentions that one of Antigonos Monophtalmos's generals tried in vain to conquer, or rather, plunder Petra. For this description, Diodorus relies on an eyewitness account by historian Hieronymos of Kardia who not only reported on the unsuccessful raids on the Nabataeans but also gave a detailed description of the no-madic tribe (cf. Hackl – Jenny – Schneider 2003, 439–453). Hieronymos characterised the Nabataeans as nomads who were forbidden to build houses under threat of death. Hieronymos describes the strategically good terrain of the later town of Petra not as a settlement but a storage and market site. An entirely diffe-rent picture is drawn by Athenodoros, the source and friend quoted by Strabo. He describes the metropolis of the Nabataeans as a wealthy town of nicely built houses and gardens. The change from nomadic to settled life of, at least, part of the Nabataeans, therefore had to have happened somewhere between the 3rd and 1st century B.C.[3]. We also have to take into account that proven archaeological data on the Nabataean culture in general and their private architecture in particular only go as far back as the 1st century B.C. and that the cultural acme was already reached in the 1st century A.D. (cf. Schmid 2001, 402–404). This short time frame and the low number of dated buildings render a developmental analysis of the private architecture difficult or hardly possible at all. The known private buildings primarily document a strong social stratification of the urban population and less of a sequence of development in the sense of a history of architecture.

If we consider the totality of all known residential buildings in Petra, we can roughly and conceptually divide them into structures cut from the living rock on the one hand and built houses on the other one. For obvious reasons, the rock-cut houses concentrate on the eastern or western side of the basin-shaped site of Petra, where the rising rock flanks offered the necessary pre-conditions. Contrary to this, the stone-built houses are situated at more central urban locations, on the naturally terraced slopes above the Civic Centre (cf. fig. 9).

Concerning the size, ground-plan organization, and interior decoration, the rock-cut as well as built houses show a relatively large variety. Contrary to the richly decorated and large rock-cut houses, the stone-built ones show not only traces of foreign influence in their decorative aspects (paintings and stuccoes) but also regarding the room types and configurations.

The Rupestrian Houses

As a result of their field work in 1929, Conway and Horsfield realised that the rocky slopes of Petra did not exclusively house sepulchral structures but also quite a substantial number of rock-cut residential houses[4]. Unlike the numerous

[3] Stucky 1996, 14–17.

[4] The Horsfields documented rock-cut houses on the eastern flank turned towards the town of the el-Habis as well as in Wadi Siyyagh (Horsfield 1938).

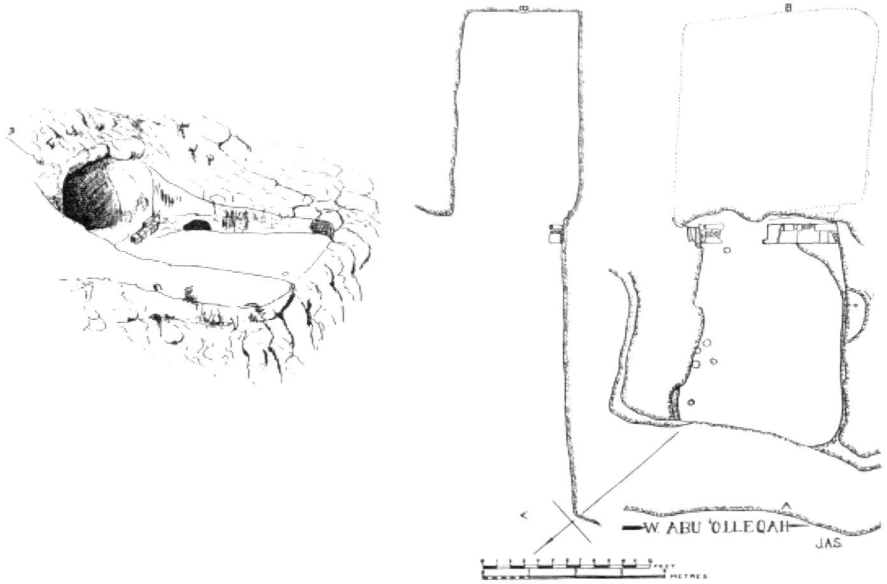

fig. 1 Petra. Wadi Abu ‘Olleqah, North Cave, plan and section.
(Murray – Ellis 1940, pl. V)

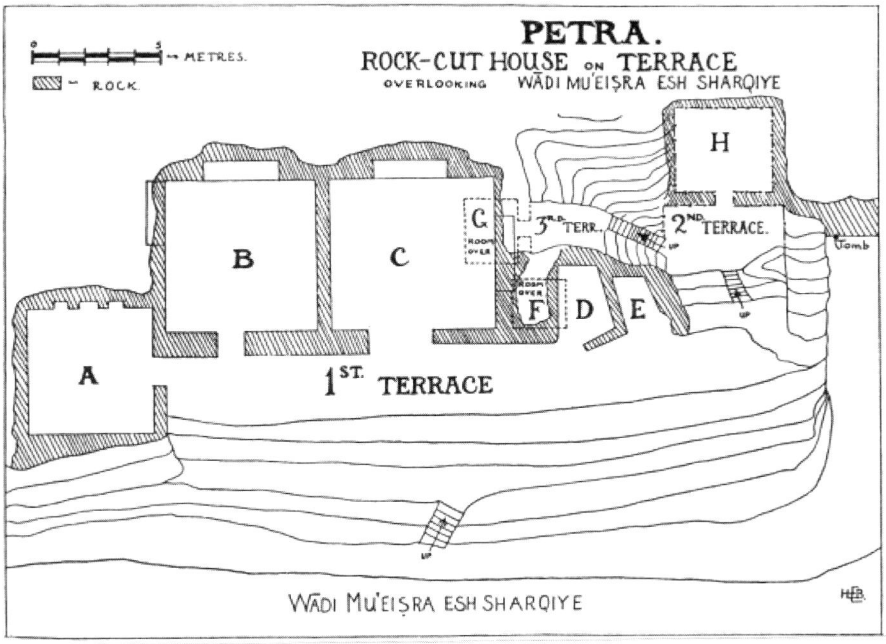

fig. 2 Petra. Wadi Mu’eisra esh-Sharqiye, rupestrian house.
(Horsfield 1938, 17 fig. 1)

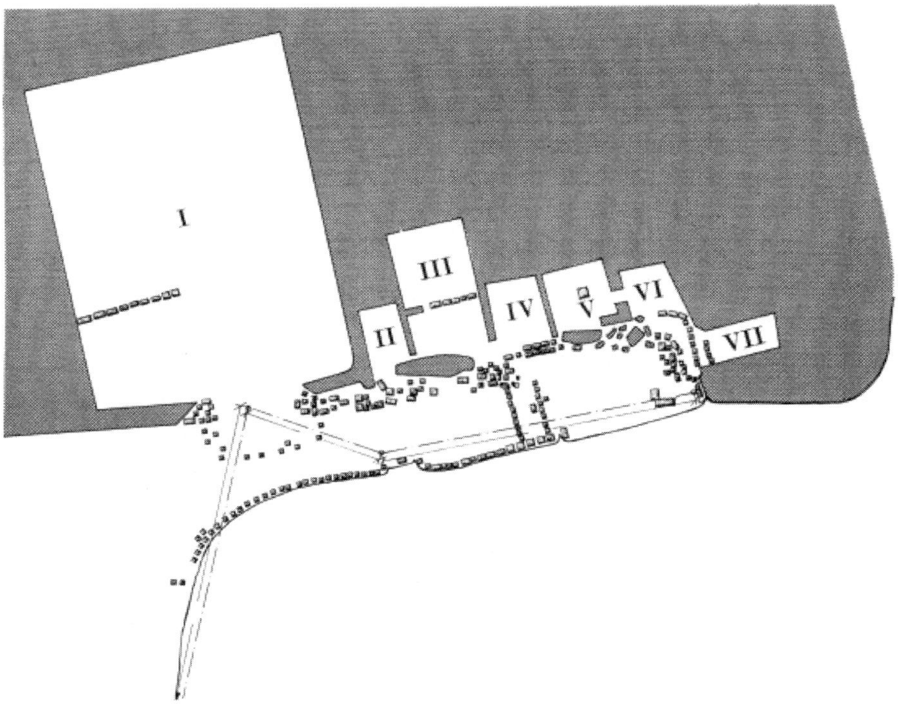

fig. 3 Petra. Umm el-Biyara, North Terrace, rupestrian house.
(Lindner 1980, 286 fig. 11)

graves, the rock houses have no monumental façades – the cave rooms of the residential houses were cut into the living rock over their entire width, then walled off, leaving free door openings and adding lean-ons. These mostly lost walls of the porches and, in particular, the rock terraces in front, that broke off due to rock falls, turned the rock houses into a seemingly bizarre series of yawning holes, which, without recognisable integration into the urban system, are positioned in rows along the rock face. Shortly after the first cave houses were published by the Horsfields in 1938, a team of the British School of Archaeology headed by M. Murray published additional rock dwellings[5]. In the following decades, the number of reliably identified and published structures has only slightly been increased[6].

The time the rock-cut houses were built could not yet be securely dated, not even in a single instance. Systematic excavation work at best allows a dating of the last period of utilisation of a antique structure. In many cases, dating is

[5] Murray – Ellis 1940, 3–13, with the North and South Cave in Wadi Abu-ʻOlleqah.

[6] Zayadine 1974, 135–139; idem 1986, 254–257. The exact location of the cave house is shown in fig. 6 in Lindner – Zeitler 1991, 5. Also see Lindner 1980, 282–290 including the survey report on the rupestrian house on the North Terrace of Umm el-Biyara.

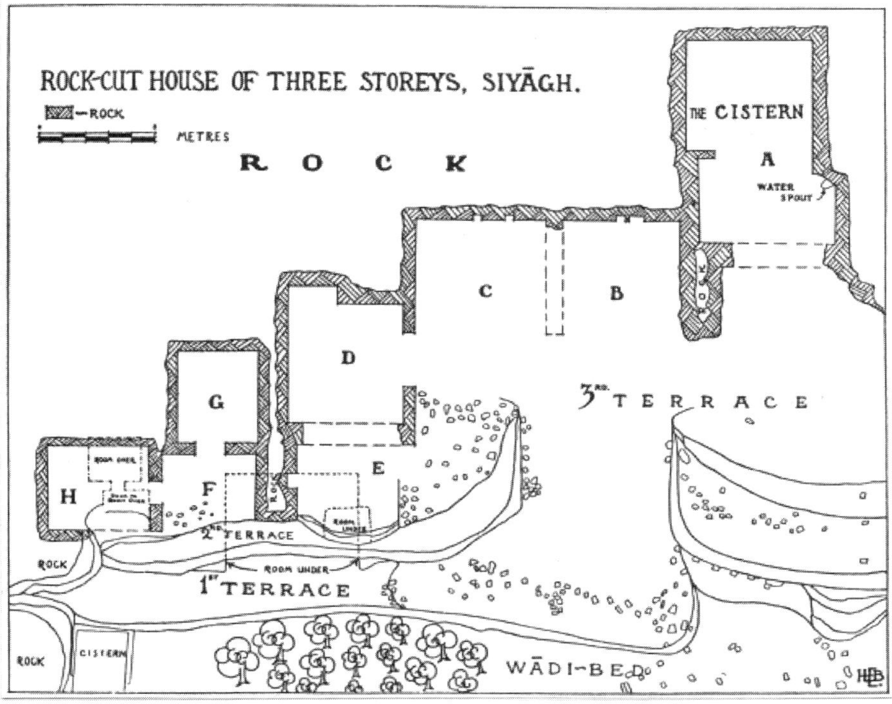

fig. 4 Petra. Wadi Siyyagh, rupestrian house, general plan.
(Horsfield 1938, 19 fig. 2)

rendered impossible as these rock spaces were used by local Bedouins until the most recent past[7]. Exceptions include some rock-cut spaces with well-preserved wall-paintings and stuccoes that may be dated approximately because of style criteria. Particularly beautiful remains of stuccoed and painted interior decorations of Hellenistic times, provisionally dated to the 1st century B.C., are extant on the rear wall of an otherwise lost two-storey, rock-cut house on the eastern flank of el-Habis (Zayadine 1987, 136) and in a house in Wadi Siyyagh[8].

Naturally, the rock houses are much more characterized by the lay of the land than the built ones. Three ground-plan variants can be distinguished: on the steep rock faces, a serial positioning of rooms along a rock terrace must be considered the most widely-spread solution (figs. 1–3). The vertical staggering of the spaces spread over two to three terraces is another variant of the spatial arrangement evidenced in several places (fig. 4). The scope is rounded off by the most lavish type of rock house which, to all purposes, takes up the ground-plan of a built house cut into the living rock (fig. 5).

[7] Bienkowski 1989.

[8] Zayadine 1987, 140–141; Kolb 2001, 443–444; Augé – Dentzer 1999, 72; Nehmé 1997, 285, fig. 7.

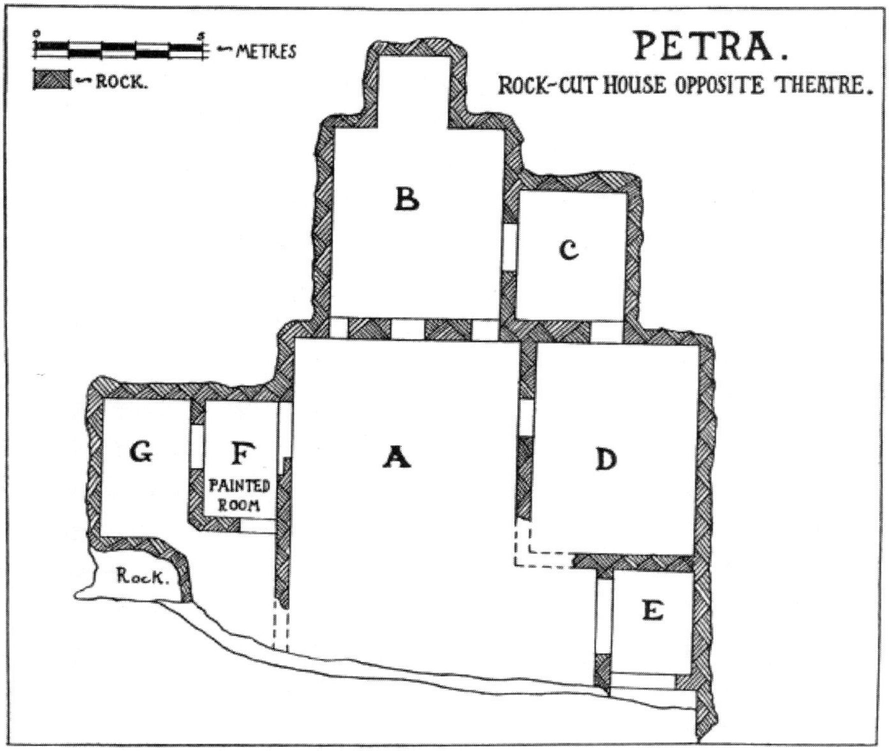

fig. 5 Petra. Opposite theatre, rupestrian house, general plan.
(Horsfield 1938, 20 fig. 3)

The size of the structures greatly varies and ranges from very small units consisting of a single rock-cut room with a courtyard framed by built walls to dwellings composed of many rooms extending over several terraces. Given the small number of documented houses, the broad range of variations of ground-plans may not be interpreted in a chronological-developmental manner. It rather seems as if this very variety was an expression of a pronounced social stratification of the urban population.

Among the most modest representatives belongs the North Cave published by Murray on the steeply jutting south-eastern side of Wadi Abu ‘Olleqah some 100 metres to the north of the Civic Centre (fig. 1)[9]: a natural cave space was expanded into a surface of about 4.85m x 4.25m though the low ceiling of about 2.5m was left unchanged. The lowest course of the closing wall with a rebate for a door was preserved *in situ*. In front of the cave room, there is a courtyard (app. 6m x 4m) slightly deepened into the rock. A similarly small structure was

[9] Murray – Ellis 1940, 3–5.

revealed by F. Zayadine beneath the Urn Tomb that was used until the earthquake of A.D. 363. The building consisted of a small cave room with a partially roofed-over courtyard in front[10]. On the east side of the courtyard, a staircase cut into the rock led to terrace room above the cave that can hardly be recognized any longer.

A good example of the serial positioning of rooms along a rock ledge is provided by the house in Wadi Mu'eisra esh Sharqiye (fig. 2)[11]. It consists of three large rooms, A (4.8m x 4.8m), B (app. 6.5m x 6m), and C (app. 6m x 6m) as well as two small secondary rooms, D and E, with polygonal ground-plans. Apart from room A, the rooms are placed shotgun-type along a small rock terrace in front. Room A closes off one of the narrow sides of the terrace; however, it remains unclear whether rooms F-G, positioned laterally above the main structure on two smaller rock terraces, belonged with the original house or have to be considered later additions. Along half the length of the terrace, some few steps of the former access stairs leading to the house are extant.

Just as M. Linder assumed, the serial cave rooms II–VII on the so-called North Terrace of Umm el Biyara may be allocated to this 'serial type', too (fig. 3)[12]. With room VII, positioned at a right angle to the row of rooms II–VI, the rock terrace is closed off in the shape of an L on one of its narrow sides. It remains unclear however whether Rock Hall I measuring 14m x 18m, was part of the house or not. The complex of rooms on the North Terrace proves how very difficult it is to categorize such structures without excavating the remaining building debris. Thus, fig. 3 documents a variety of ashlar that are left as rubble and debris on the terrace. Without a respective excavation, we cannot possibly determine whether there was a partitioning wall with a door between Hall I and the adjacent rooms II–VII. The allocation of the remains of columns and entablature observed by Lindner that might have belonged equally as well to a portico in front of Hall I or a gallery-type porch within the area of the smaller rooms has not been confirmed either. This point should be particularly interesting because, for the first time, we should be confronted with a built columnar architecture in connection with the rock house. This and additional basic problems will only be cleared up by systematic excavations and detailed reports on the respective findings.

A good example of the vertical staggering of the rooms is offered by the terrace house on the northern flank of Wadi Siyyagh (fig. 4)[13]. The structure comprises room ensembles consisting of three superimposed terraces accessed by way of staircases cut into the rock that are no longer extant. The upper terrace is enclosed by three rooms on the side of the slope arranged in the shape of an L: rooms B (app. 5m x 5m), C (app. 5.5m x 5m), and D (app. 5m x 5.2m). The next lower terrace is located to the west of room D and consists of rooms F, G (app. 3.4m x 4m) and H (app. 4.3m x 3.6m). On the lowest terrace, a room measuring 3m x 3m with an alcove opens up, already mentioned by Horsfield but only

[10] From the lowest layer 6, remains of burnt wood and tiles were excavated that imply a partial roofing of the courtyard. Also see Zayadine 1974, 135–139 and 1986, 254.

[11] Horsfield 1938, 17–18.

[12] Lindner 1980, 279–290.

[13] Horsfield 1938, 18–19.

examined by F. Vibert some few years ago, which brought to light one of the best-preserved murals in the greater Petra area[14]. With the observation already made on the so-called North Terrace of Umm (II–VII) and the house in Wadi Mu'aisra (B–D) and the two-room deep excavation of the rock for rooms F and G, the striving to provide the rock house with a centre becomes recognizable such as it is so clearly visible in the built houses with a central courtyard. Already Horsfield saw that this tendency to free the rock house from the linear serial arrangement of rooms was realised most consistently in the rock house across from the theatre, at the foot of the western flank of Jebal al-Khubtah (fig. 5)[15]. With a lot of effort, the rooms were cut up to 20 metres deep into the living mountain – probably to use already existing erosion caverns – to be able to realize a ground-plan that practically negates the rock as a natural barrier. The same as with a built house, rooms B–G line Rock Hall A recalling a Tuscan atrium (app. 6.7m x min. 10m). The largest and most important room B (app. 5.1m x 5.7m without the alcove) extends over the entire width of the hall. The position of the head end of the hall as well as the three entrances on the hall side leave no doubts as to its function as a reception or banquet room[16].

If we consider the entirety of the cave houses, the following points in common become visible in addition to the ground-plan versions: each structure, may it be ever so small, is graced by a courtyard – preferably in front of the cave room. The larger the house, the more its organisation approaches the ground-plan of a built house with courtyard. The various extant remains of the original, painted and stuccoed wall decoration of the rooms provide further evidence that, firstly, the interior furnishings of the rich rock houses met the same demands as those in the houses as yet to be discussed and, secondly, that the rock houses, too, hardly existed before the 1st century B.C.

Rock-cut residential buildings are also known from the Nabataean settlement of Oboda in the Negev. On the steep western slope of the settlement hill, countless buried cave rooms may be recognized which originally were the mountain-side ends of projecting residential and economy buildings (Negev 1997, 157, photo 242). The only better studied, partially rock-cut, partially built structure is the so-called 'Byzantine House' (fig. 6)[17]. Rooms 2–5 of this residential house are placed along the two sides of the small courtyard 1. The lost storey rooms were accessible by way of a staircase placed at the southern wall of the courtyard. Towards the east, rock rooms identified by A. Negev as a economic wing are adjacent to the residential space. At an unknown point in time, the building was extended by rooms 6–12 placed on a terrace some 2.5m lower. There are obvious parallels in the built private architecture of Petra of the clear division of economic and residential rooms visible in the ground-plan (Stucky 1996, 48; Zeitler 1991), however not for the exclusive economic utilisation of the cave rooms.

[14] Cf. Zayadine 1981, 355, Pl. CIII; idem 1987, 139–141; Augé – Dentzer 1999, 72; Kolb 2001, 443–444.

[15] Horsfield 1938, 19–20; Pl. XLVII.

[16] Cf. fig. 19 with room 6 on EZ IV.

[17] Negev 1997, 157–169.

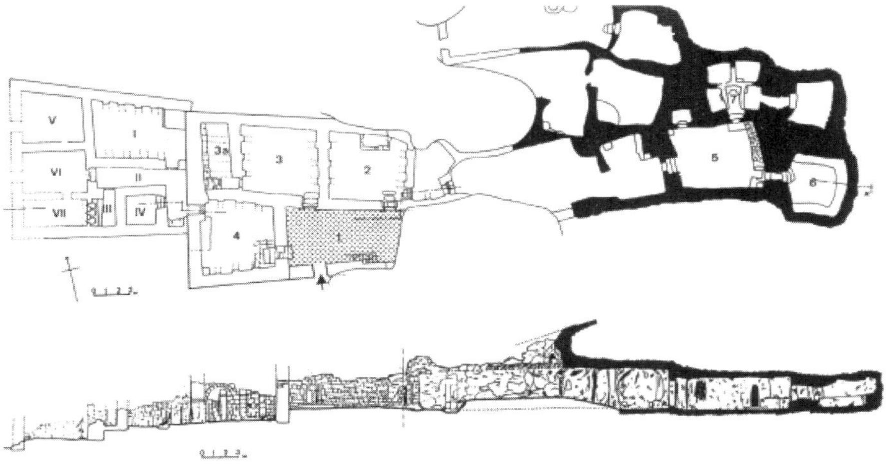

fig. 6 Oboda. Northwestern slope of the acropolis, Byzantine dwelling.
(after Negev 1997, 158 fig. 25)

Cave houses are well evidenced for the Nabataean core region, however may not be misunderstood as a purely Nabataean phenomenon. Thus, e.g. the cave houses in the rocky cliff above the Qasr al-Abd palace of Tobiade Hyrkan at Irak el Emir are known, that were described by Josephus (*Ant.* 12.231). Quite recently, F Zayadine has been able to prove that the Aramaic inscriptions in the cave rooms date from the late 4th century B.C. and, therefore, clearly from the time before the Nabataeans became settlers[18].

The Free-Standing Houses

I. The courtyard houses in Southern Transjordan and in the Negev desert – the Nabataean *commoners'* houses?

Among the most modest private buildings of Petra is the small House II situated on a natural rock terrace to the west and below the Urn Tomb from the middle of the 1st century A.D. excavated on behalf of the Naturhistorische Gesellschaft Nürnberg (fig. 7)[19]. The house has a surface of 160m^2 and is superimposed on the remains of a previous one-room structure I from the 1st century B.C.[20]. In the north, lower rooms are put in front of the three living-rooms A–C in the south – a rock-cut cistern and an economy room with the remains of an olive press. A

[18] Zayadine 1991, 20; cf. the Hellenistic "Cave City" of Marisa (Kloner 1993, 952–953; Kloner – Sagiv 1993).

[19] Zeitler 1990; idem 1991, 74–76; idem 1993, 255.

[20] House I consisted of a single room of 2.8m x 2.6m; cf. Zeitler 1990.

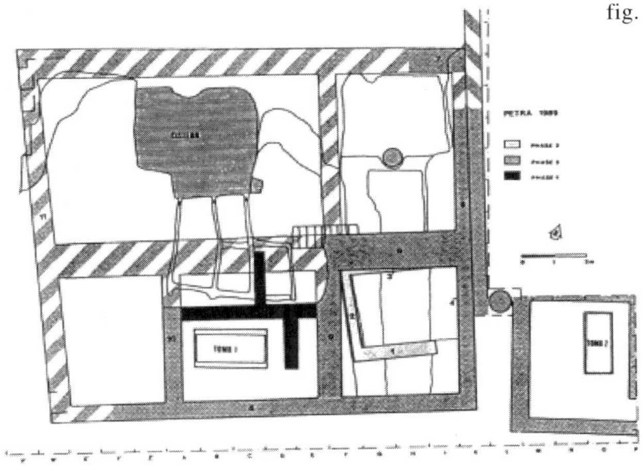

fig. 7a Petra. House II on the western foot of Khubtah, general plan. (Zeitler 1990, 402 fig. 2)

fig. 7b Petra. House II on the western foot of Khubtah, reconstruction. (Lindner – Zeitler 1991, 75

staircase cut into the rock connected the two areas of the house. A clear separation of private and economy rooms can be observed, which is emphasised by the staggering of levels between the southern and the northern rooms. The courtyard was not an integral element of the built structure but put in front of the southern façade of the house. Without any recognisable structural changes, House II was lived in from the 1st century AD until its destruction by an earthquake in A.D. 363[21]. In the following and last utilisation phase, the living-room C as well as room D with the oil press were abandoned. The heavily damaged middle room B of the residential wing was given a new northern wall after A.D. 363 and remained in use, though with a reduced surface, while the surface of the cistern room was changed into a garden with irrigation ditches. The end of the settlement period on the small terrace in the early 5th century is quite similar to that found on

[21] Zeitler 1993, 256; cf. idem 1991, 75. On the earthquake of 363 cf. Russell 1980; Amiran – Arieh – Turcotte. 1994, 265.

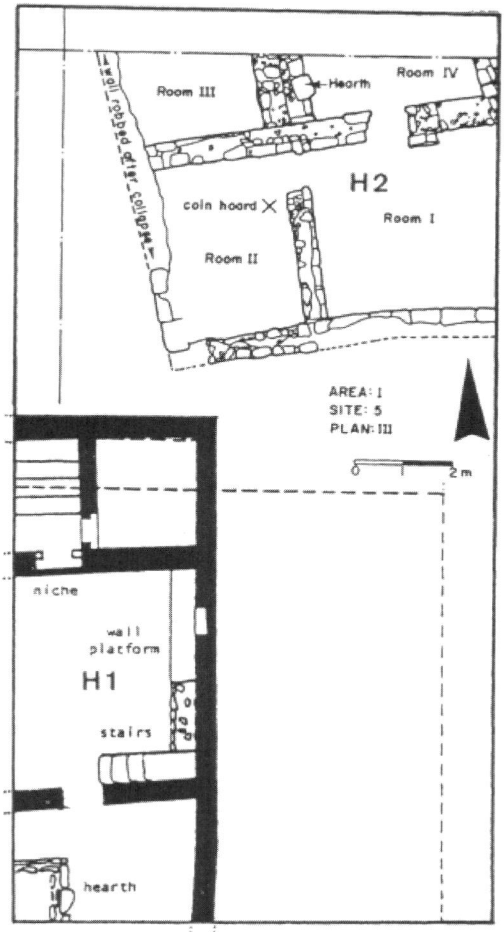

fig. 8 Petra. Area 1, Earliest House (H1) and Middle House (H 2). (after Hammond 1977/78, 230 pl. XLIV, Russell 1980, 49 fig. 2)

the Swiss excavation site EZ I; presumably, the earthquake of A.D. 419 destroyed House II at the Urn Tomb as well as the two sub-Nabataean houses of ez-Zantur (HE I and II)[22].

The excavations in Area I headed by Ph. Hammond (between the Temple of the Winged Lions and the so-called Petra Church) brought to light a sequence of different house structures ranging from the 1st century A.D. to Byzantine times (fig. 8)[23]. In the western half of Area I.2, four rooms of the so-called Early House (H 1) were broached, that – as far as recognizable – consisted of a central court-yard area with a staircase accessing the lost upper floor, a hearth room opening

[22] Sources on the earthquake of A.D. 419 compiled by Russell 1985, 42–43; Amiran – Arieh – Turcotte. 1994, 266. On the destruction of the houses on EZ I, cf. Kolb 2000, 238.

[23] The results of the excavation in Area I as summarised by Hammond 1977/78, 81–84; idem 1986, 22–23; Russell 1980, 48–49.

fig. 9 Petra. Aerial view of the Swiss excavation sites EZ I, EZ III and EZ IV south above the Civic Centre. (Photo B. Kolb)

towards the courtyard in the south and two smaller rooms in the north. The almost square northern room was not accessible from the middle one. In 1976, excavators uncovered additional Nabataean structures in the southern part of Area I.5, which were destroyed like the Nabataean house (H 1) in the early 2nd century[24] A.D. The Nabataean architectural findings in Area I.5 already mentioned have, to date, not been published.

The so-called Middle House of Phase XII is situated to the north of the preceding Nabataean building and could be examined partially within Area I.5 (fig. 8, H 2). The rectangular design of the walls define four rooms. The large room I with the secondary room II formed the southern end of the house. The hearth at the foot of the western wall and the – presumable – central position of room IV seem to recall a courtyard area. A coin-hoard found in room II is evidence of the destruction of the Middle House II by the earthquake of 363[25].

The same earthquake also damaged the two sub-Nabataean courtyard houses EH I and EH II on the Swiss dig of EZ I to the north of the rocky spur of ez Zantur (figs. 9–11)[26]. The two two-storey buildings were erected on the terrain of a large Nabataean dwelling in the early 4th century[27] destroyed in the early 2nd century A.D., will be discussed below.

[24] See Russell 1985, 41; Hammond 1977/78, 83–84, Phase XV.

[25] Russell 1980, 48–49; on EZ I, a hoard of coins was found in room 1 which is practically identical as to its composition to that of the Middle House. Cf. Peter 1996, 100–103.

[26] Kolb 2000, 243–244.

[27] Idem, 237–265.

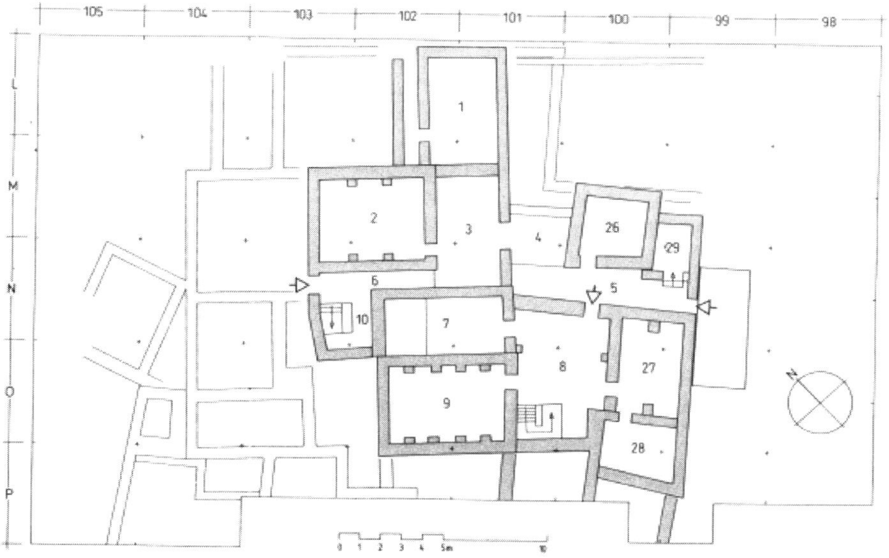

fig. 10 Petra. EZ I, Schematic plans of the sub-Nabataean dwellings HE I and HE II. (Kolb 2000, plan 5)

House I includes rooms 2–4, 6, and 10, House II the rooms 5, 7.9, and 27–28. Although the two houses formed part of a single polygonal block, they were two clearly separate units. The entry to House I was in the north-west, while that of House II was in the south-east of the terrace. Based on the archaeological data, both houses can be rated as non-commercial, residential buildings. Between the dwellings, detached from the actual building complex, there is baking house 26 with two ovens for bread baking. The isolated position of this facility, and that of the adjacent room 29, can be explained by the fire hazard such a building implies and by the communal use by the residents of both houses. While the rooms of House II (app. 105m^2 without rooms 4–5, 26) line the long sides of the centrally situated courtyard 8, the smaller House I (app. 70 m^2 without rooms 4–5, 26) boasts the lateral courtyard 3 in front of room 2. In the eastern corner of courtyard 8 (House II), a twin-flight staircase is preserved, originally leading up to an L-shaped gallery made of wood. The still traceable pillars of a former arch carried the gallery that provided access to rooms 9 and 27 on the upper floor. The staircase of House I was located next to the main door in the annex-like expansion 10 of corridor 6. The first flight of steps was constructed of stone, while the second flight must have been a wooden construction leading to the upper floor of room 2.

Three hoards of coins were uncovered, giving testimony to the fact that some of the rooms were completely destroyed by the earthquake disaster of the year A.D. 363. About 10 years later, the greater part of the rooms was re-used until the final destruction of the houses in the early 5th century – probably by the earthquake in A.D. 419 (cf. above, note 22).

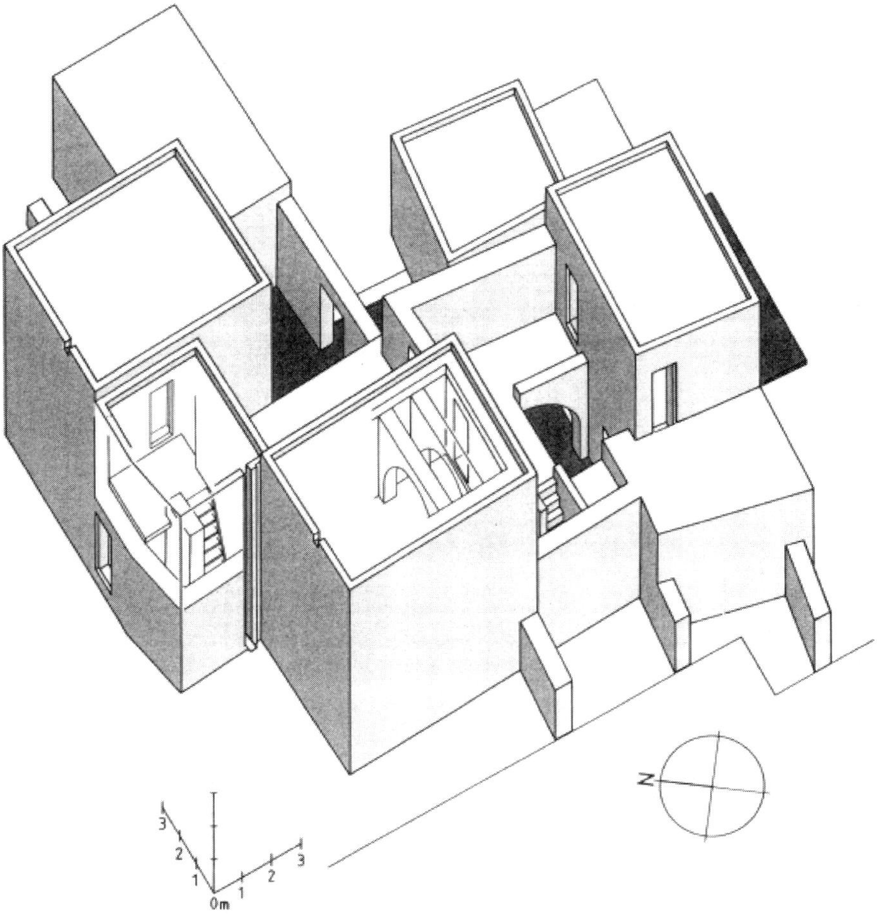

fig. 11 Petra. EZ I, Isometric reconstruction of the sub-Nabataean dwellings HE I and HE II. (Kolb 2000, plan 6b)

The earliest example known to date of a Nabataean courtyard house of the type of House I on EZ I with few residential rooms but a generously dimensioned lateral courtyard was built in the 1st century A.D. and examined in Khirbet edh-Dharih by a joint Jordanian-French venture (fig. 12, 1–3)[28]. Interestingly, this building consisting of a large courtyard and two square rooms is combined with a residential building with more or less the same ground-plan from the 3rd to 4th centuries A.D. (fig. 12, I–III). The same basic module of a courtyard with two square rooms along one side of the courtyard is also recognisable in the much larger, still to be discussed House V 1 (cf. fig. 20, rooms 1–2 with an adjacent courtyard in the north).

[28] Al-Muheisen – Villeneuve 1994, 752–754.

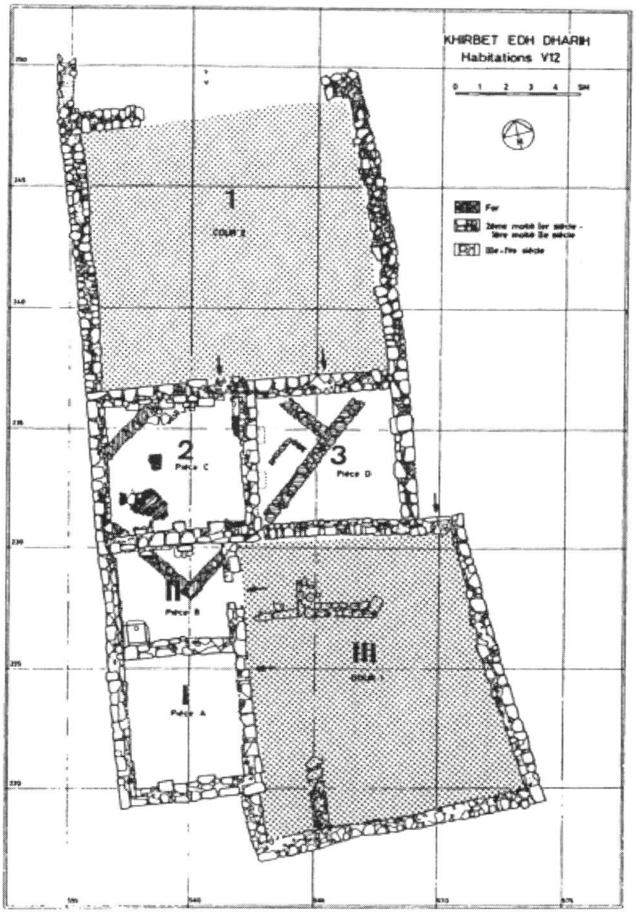

fig. 12 Khirbet edh-Dharih. House complex V12 with three-room houses. (Al-Muheisen – Villeneuve 1994, 753 fig. 9)

But let us once more return to House II on EZ I (figs. 10–11): the L-shaped gallery above courtyard 8 remains unique in the private architecture of Petra to this day, though several instances are known for residential buildings in Mampsis. The well-preserved houses of Mampsis that were occupied in until Byzantine times are dated to the late Nabataean period from about A.D. 70–150 by excavator and researcher A. Negev[29]. The building substance was only changed to a small degree over the centuries which, primarily, points to a stronger division of the houses and a changed utilisation[30].

Courtyard House Va with its surface of app. 250m^2 belongs among the few buildings of Mampsis that can safely be dated to the 1st century A.D. (fig. 13)[31].

[29] The most synoptic presentation of Negev's classification of eras in Negev 1983, 249; also cf. idem 1988.

[30] Negev 1988, 146.

[31] Ibid. 34–37. For a dating of the bath-rooms, cf. Shereshevski 1991, 34.

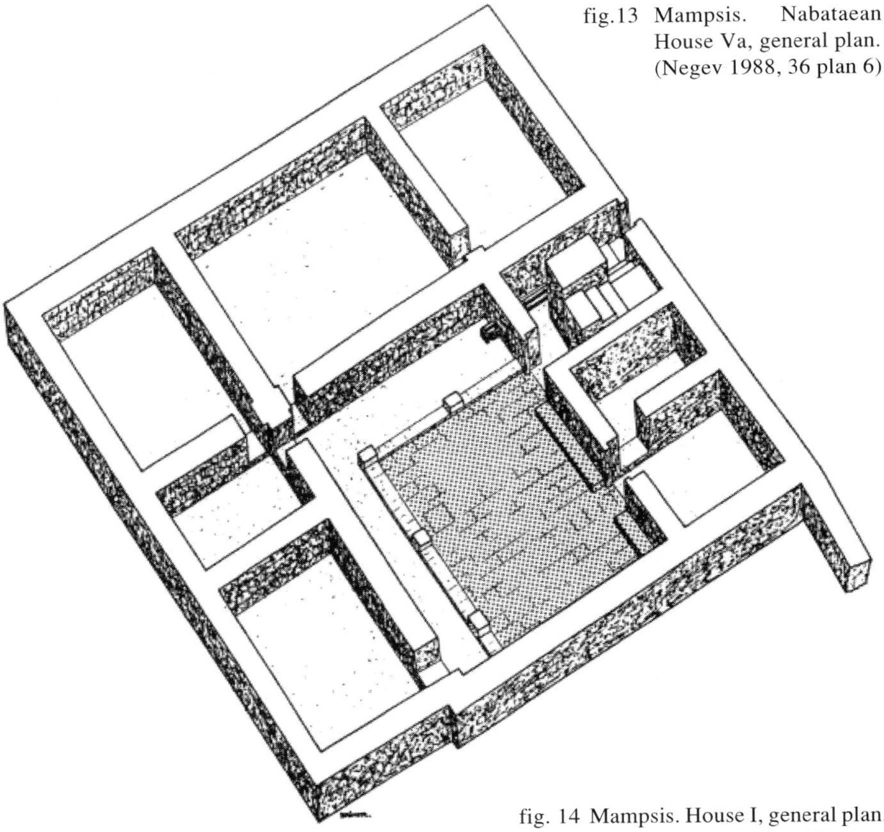

fig.13 Mampsis. Nabataean House Va, general plan. (Negev 1988, 36 plan 6)

fig. 14 Mampsis. House I, general plan. (Negev 1988, 53 plan 12)

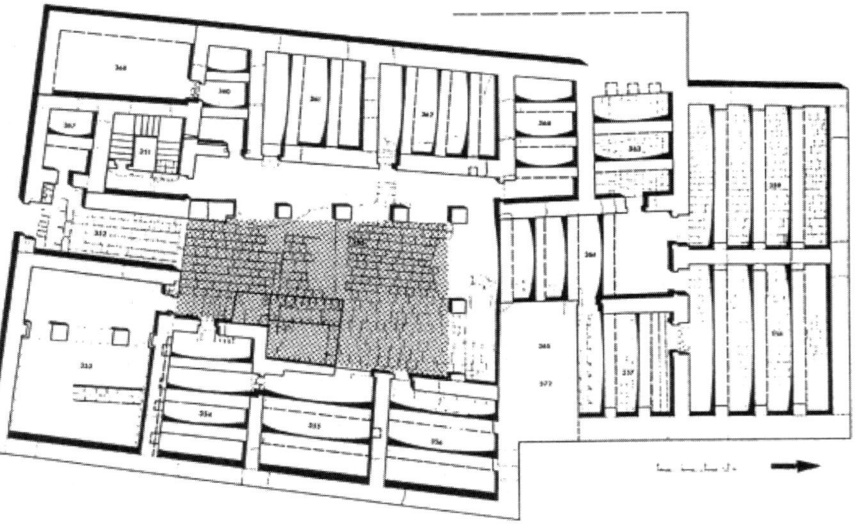

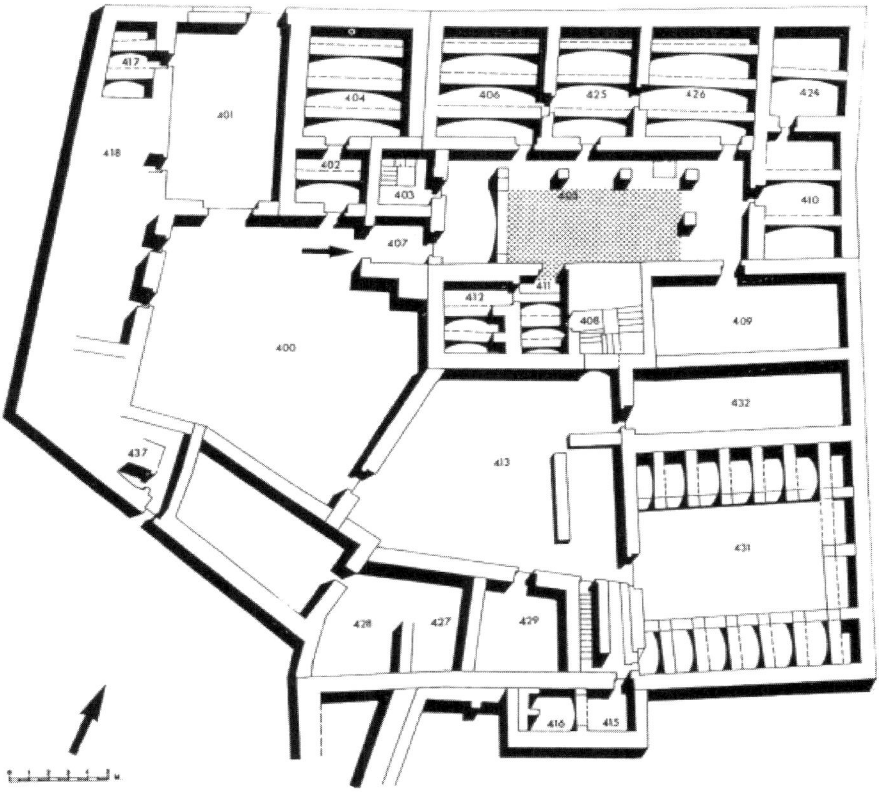

fig.15 Mampsis. House XII, general plan.
(Negev 1988, 113 plan 27)

The house entrance in the east opened onto a vestibule with staircase and the central courtyard. Six or seven rooms placed in a Pi-shaped? pattern frame the paved courtyard on three of its sides. Stylobates on the western and northern side of the courtyard are evidence of an L-shaped gallery linked to the two-flight stairs in the vestibule and provide access to the upper-storey rooms. An analogous gallery is shown in the much larger House I with its 620m^2 in the western part of town (fig. 14)[32]. The 100m^2 surface of the courtyard was framed along its western and northern side by pillars supporting a gallery leading away from the staircase to the west of the vestibule. The same as in House Va, the staircase is positioned close to the main entrance. Two groups of three rooms opened towards the courtyard. The largest room 353 – probably a reception room – was to the east of the vestibule. Two columns *in antis* show an organization of the room quite close to that in the Nabataean house on EZ I in Petra from the 1st century A.D. (cf. figs.

[32] Ibid. 50–77. Negev defines House I as a palace.

16–17 with rooms I–II)[33] probably based on a Herodian room concept the same as was realised in room 456 of Herod's Western Palace on Masada already in the 1st century B.C.[34].

With its surface of app. 1600m², House XII is once again clearly larger than House I because a generously proportioned stable and economy wing occupied the entire southern, western, and eastern area of the lot (Negev 1988, 111–147; fig. 15). The residential and representational wing is situated in the northern part of the complex and, with a surface of app. 450m², even smaller than that of House I. The distribution of rooms around the central courtyard on the ground-floor shows the very same ground-plan as Houses Va and I, and the two-storey design of the rooms, staircase 403, and the gallery repeat the spatial concept of Houses Va and I.

The described parallels between the private architecture in Transjordan and the Negev zone are confirmed by the data included in papyrus 22 from Nessana – a document detailing the distribution of an inheritance dating from the year A.D. 566 (Kraemer 1958, 70–74). This papyrus describes a two-storey dwelling of the now well-known type, with a central courtyard and rooms on the first floor opening onto a balcony above the courtyard.

The correspondence between the residential buildings of the 1st and 6th century A.D., as outlined, shows that a building tradition for residential homes covered the mentioned Negev area as well as southern Transjordan including Petra[35]. All buildings shown are more or less rectangular, built with the same wood-saving construction technology[36] and characterised by a lack of Graeco-Roman room-types and figurations. Exceptions, if any, include the representational room 353 with its double columns in House I as well as the portico in front of the stables of House XII in Mampsis.

It is important though that even the largest and most richly decorated House XII of Mampsis shows evidence of an extensive adherence to traditional construction styles. Therefore, any choice of the type of house was not contingent on the financial possibilities of the client but is to be considered a conscious decision in favour of tradition.

The presented houses situated in the core area of the Nabataean rule show that – widely independent of the size of the actual buildings – there are hardly any discernable changes as to the ground-plans of simple courtyard houses within the period from the 1st century BC till the early 6th century A.D. Free of any characteristics, these residential houses represent a regional, that is, Nabataean building tradition that remained untouched by political or economic changes.

[33] Negev 1988, 57–58, is probably correct in assuming a wooden roof here, due to the size of the room and the lack of a transversal arch, construction. His reconstruction of a covered western part (entrance area) and an open, that is, roofless eastern one seems questionable given the function of this room. Much more convincing is the reconstruction by R. A. Stucky such as for rooms I and II on ez Zantur, cf. Stucky 1996, 21–23.

[34] Netzer 1991, 241, plan 18, and 249, fig. 393.

[35] The architectural tradition restricted to the mentioned geographical region is discussed in detail in Kolb 2000.

II. On Mansions and Villas: the Homes of the Social Elite at Petra

In the course of the last few years, two rich Nabataean private houses were exposed in Petra whose architecture distinguishes itself from all buildings already discussed insofar as it shows distinct Hellenistic and Roman influences[37].

Between 1988–1994, the University of Basel, headed by Rolf A Stucky, excavated on terrace EZ I, immediately to the north of the ez-Zantur hilltop, a one-storey Nabataean private home with a surface of about 900m² (fig. 9)[38].

The house was erected during the early 1st century A.D. on top of a badly preserved earlier structure (fig. 16–17)[39]. After a phase of minor alterations in the late 1st century, the house burnt down in the early 2nd century A.D. In the early 4th century, the remains of the dwelling were plundered, re-used, and built up by new settlers (see above HE I and II). Despite this, the ground-plan of the Nabataean house could be reconstructed to a large extent. It consisted of the north-western rooms I–IX and XI which served representational purposes, while the south-eastern rooms X, XII, and XIII were used as private living quarters and working areas.

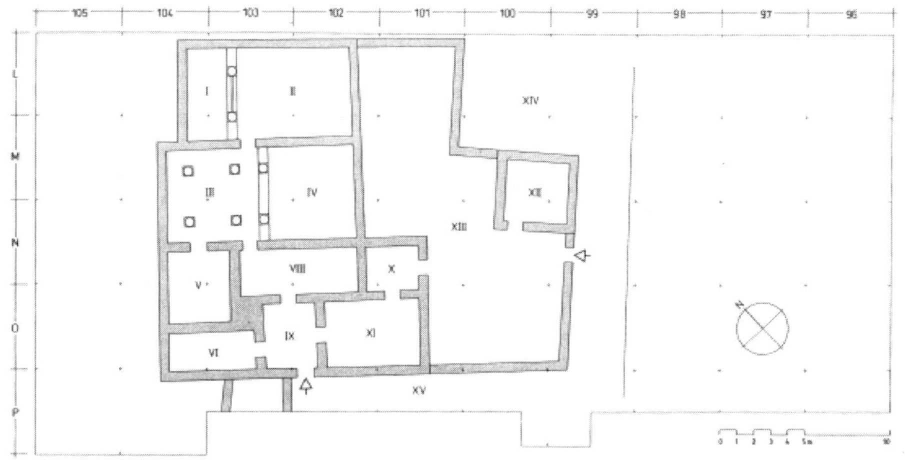

fig. 16 Petra. EZ I. Schematic groundplan of Nabataean dwelling. (Stucky 1996, 18 fig. 15)

[36] For a summary of building technology, cf. Kolb 2000, 295–296.

[37] Most probably the Nabataean structure comprising a large peristyle partially exposed by N. Khairy on el-Katuthe in 1981 must be added to the list on the rich dwellings in Petra; cf. Khairy 1990.

[38] Stucky 1996. The excavations by the University of Basel in Petra of 1988–2001 were executed under the patronage of the Swiss-Liechtenstein Foundation of Archaeological Research Abroad (SLFA) domiciled in Zürich.

[39] The remaining two walls AG and CU of a former building may be dated to the late 1st century B.C.; cf. Stucky 1996, 17–21.

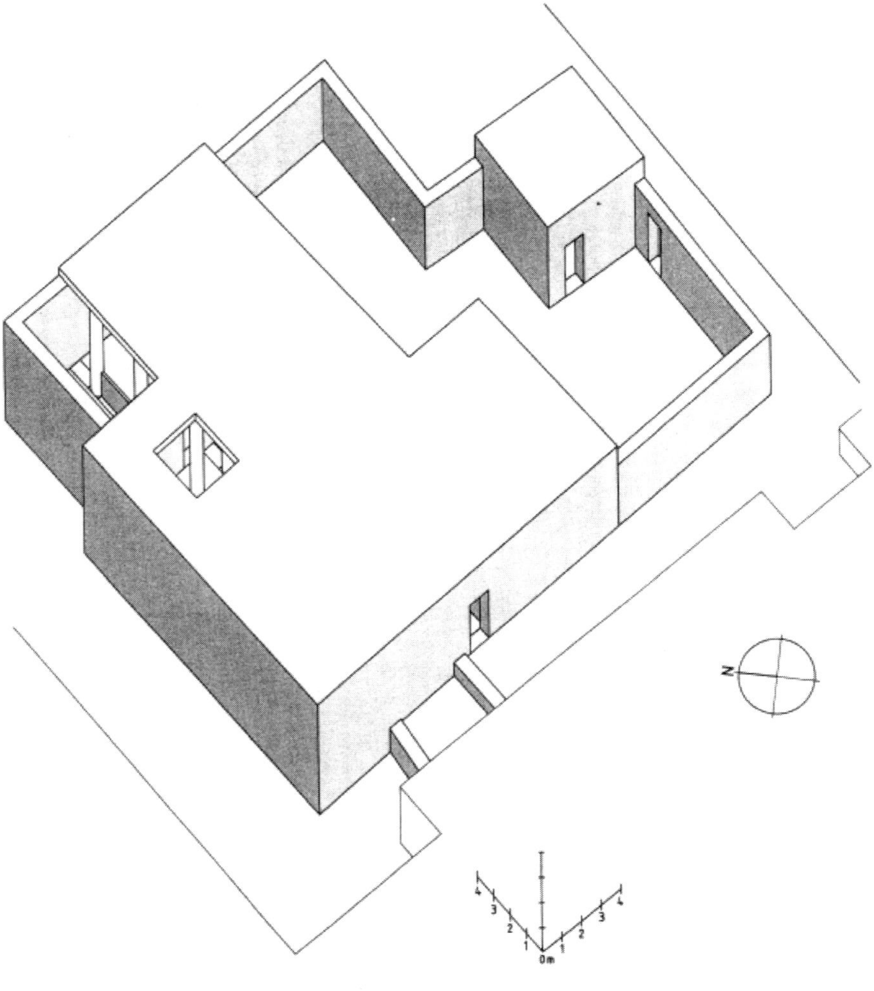

fig. 17 Petra EZ I. Isometric reconstruction of the Nabataean dwelling. (Stucky 1996, 42 fig. 69)

The stately part of the building included the receptions rooms II and IV which, originally, were decorated with linear polychrome murals[40]. Air and light for rooms II and IV were provided by the tiny courtyard I and the small peristyle III respectively. The two columns between courtyard I and room II, as well as the columns of the peristyle, were crowned by Corinthian capitals in the local style. The peristyle and the Corinthian capitals make clear that from the 1st century A.D. at the latest, high-ranking Nabataeans at Petra were familiar with the Graeco-Roman standards of house planning.

[40] Stucky 1996, 23 and pl. 1.1.

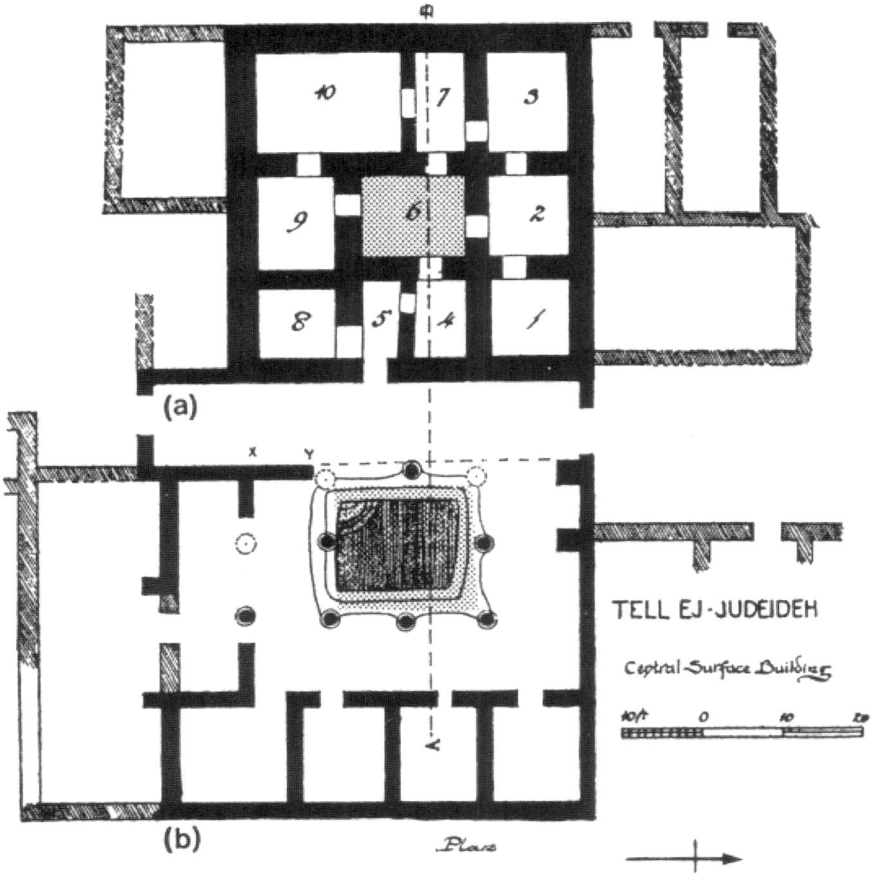

fig. 18 Tell ej-Judeideh. Governor's Palace, plan .
(Horowitz 1980, 110 fig. 15, after Bliss – Macalister 1902, pl. 12)

In contrast to the reception and banquet rooms, no indications of "Hellenization" could be found in the living and working area: in Phase Nabat. III–1, the comparatively small rooms of the private tract (X and XII) lie on the western and eastern side of the polygonal paved courtyard XIII with a second main entrance in its south-eastern wall. An almost independent private section is discernible, which was connected by room XI to the vestibule and the main entrance respectively. The rooms and courtyard of the private area seem to belong to a different tradition than the representational rooms of the building[41]. They define an architectural and functional unit in its own right, which seems to be rooted in the traditional regional architecture discussed in the preceding chapter.

There are only a few parallels for this juxtaposition of different building traditions in the building on EZ I. In Judea, the same phenomenon may be

[41] Ibid., 48–49.

fig. 19 Petra. EZ IV. Schematic plan of the Nabataean mansion.
(Kolb – Keller 2002)

observed in the so-called Governor's Palace on Tell ej-Judeideh. This building, excavated by Bliss and Macalister between 1898 and 1900 covers a surface of 460m², comprises two quite different wings (fig. 18)[42] and originated in the second half of the 1st century B.C. In the eastern stately wing, the small peristyle and the main room with *distylos in antis* show types of rooms that are well-known from Graeco-Roman architecture. A completely different picture shows the western wing, whose cell-like rooms open on a small interior courtyard. The concept of the ground-plan of this – possibly private – area of the 'Governor's Palace' is quite obviously in the tradition of the neo-Babylonian house construction and may have been influenced by the Hellenistic private architecture as is particularly well known in Dura Europos[43].

[42] Bliss – Macalister 1902, pl. 12; Horowitz 1980, 109–110; Broshi 1993, 838; Nielsen 1994, 160 dates the building somewhat earlier, without giving any reason. Also cf. Gibson 1994, 213–215.

[43] Cf. houses of the Merkes residential district in the Babylon of the 7th–6th centuries BC in

Let us turn to the palatial mansion on the EZ IV terrace south of ez-Zantur at Petra (figs. 9 and 19). The Nabataean building excavated under the author's direction from 1996 to 2001, was built in the early decades of the 1st century A.D.[44]. A few structural repairs and alterations were most probably necessitated by the impact of a minor earthquake in the early years of the 2nd century[45]. In the 3rd and 4th centuries, the building only underwent minor alterations and was ultimately destroyed by the disastrous earthquake of A.D. 363 that abruptly terminated the building and settlement history of this terrace[46].

The ground-plan of the residential house comprises three main areas: the eastern wing housed the servants' rooms (rooms 16, 35–37), the central and southern area the stately rooms (rooms 28, 25, 15, 1, 19, 6–7, 17, and 14) while the western wing housed some private rooms (30, 27, 22).

Black and white-mosaic fragments as well as fragments of marble tiles of former *opus sectile* coverings in the debris above the paved floors of the ground-floor clearly refer to the fact that the most attractive private rooms were placed on the first floor that has been confirmed above the three southern rooms 6, 7, and 17, above the eastern wing, and the central rooms 15 and 1. Two staircases provided access to the upper floors: the generous staircase 8 was probably reserved for the owners, while the servants had their own – and much more modest – staircase between rooms 35 and 37. The useful surface of the two-storey building amounted to a minimum of 1,200m^2.

The southern part of the rock terrace is built up by the three block-type, linked stately rooms 6, 7, and 17. To the north, these rooms are connected to the 'spine' of the mansion, i.e., the axially constructed courtyard 19, plus rooms 15 and 28 with the main entrance. In order to reach the reception rooms at the southern limit of the building, visitors had to walk down corridor 25 and cross courtyard 19 adorned with *distyloi in antis* with Corinthian capitals of a floral type on its northern and southern side. *Exedra* 7 is flanked in the east and west by the two reception rooms 6 and 17. Room 6 is connected to *exedra* 7 by an open passageway and two lateral doors, while room 17 has only a single access that relates to the axially opposed passageway leading to room 6. The floors in rooms 6 and 7 are paved with flagstones, while the floor of room 17 was originally covered with a sumptuous *opus sectile* pavement of imported marble and alabas-

Hoepfner-Schwandner 1994, 288–291 with fig. 284. Around a central courtyard, there is a simple sequence of 'girdling' rooms. If you reduce these ground-plans by the stately wing – that is designed as a separate unit on Tell ej Judeideh – this creates, the same as in the private wing of Tell ej-Judeideh, units composed of a great number of stunted individual rooms. The characteristic basic design of a unit is already discernible in the structures of the southern castle of Nebuchadrezzar II in Babylon; see in particular the courtyard houses 8–12 (Heinrich 1984, 203–207, figs. 122–123). Hellenised representatives of the described type are found in Dura Europos (Hoepfner-Schwandner 1994, 274–287).

[44] Kolb – Gorgerat – Grawehr 1999, 269.

[45] Kolb – Keller 2002, Squares 86–87/AN.

[46] Kolb – Keller – Fellmann Brogli 1997, 234; Kolb – Keller – Gerber 1998, 262, 267–275; Kolb – Keller 2000, 366–370; Kolb – Keller 2001, 321–323; Kolb – Keller 2002, glass table ware of the mid-4th century on EZ IV.

ter. Quantities of fragmented murals as well as architectural stucco indicate that rooms 6 and 17 were decorated with elaborate systems of stuccoed architecture and murals respectively.

The three-room-configuration with its central exedra and two lateral wing rooms is repeated in rooms 27, 22, and 30 in the north-western residential area of the building. Here, the main difference between the mansion on EZ IV and the house on EZ I is discernible that is based on the overall architectonic concept comprising the representative as well as the private areas of the building.

The mentioned room-configuration with the exedra and lateral wing rooms is not a Nabataean invention but can, as proposed in other places, be traced to Macedonian and later Ptolemaic models such as in the late Hellenistic Palazzo delle Colonne in Ptolemais/Cyrenaica[47]. In this respect, it is revealing that this characteristic sequence of rooms is confirmed in a slightly varied form on Masada in the early Herodian Western Palace which, seen from EZ IV in Petra, had an interim position in the chronological and geographical process of tradition[48].

In the south-western corner on EZ IV, a small private bath and heatable winter triclinium confirms a clearly Roman component. These structures belong to the second building phase provisionally dated to the early 2nd century A.D. and, thus, approximately equal to the Roman annexing of the Nabataean Empire in 106. Room 10 belongs to the bath area as do room 52, of which only the foundations are extant, room 40, with its floor heating (*caldarium*) as well as the furnace room 39 (*praefurnium*). From the adjacent furnace room 29, the hypocaust of the winter triclinium 14 was supplied with warm air. Our building on EZ IV with its bath-house is not the only one in Petra. Some years ago, K. ‘Amr was able to examine partial areas of a villa from the 1st century A.D. in Wadi Musa, the village just outside Petra, that was also equipped with a bath wing[49].

At the end of this article, I do not wish to discuss another building of Petra but House V 1 of the 1st century A.D. in Khirbet ed Darigh about 70 km to the north (fig. 20)[50]. At the south-eastern side of the originally rectangular large courtyard are rooms 1 and 2 identified by the excavators as stately rooms. These two rooms of equal size form a block-type unit along with the courtyard just as we saw at the same place in the house complex V 12 (fig. 12). During a second construction phase, room group 7–14 placed obliquely adjacent to the courtyard as well as rooms 16 and 17 were added. A well-preserved hypocaust in room 17, heated from corridor C, is interpreted by the excavators as the extant remains of a small private bath[5] .

Its surface of app. 1,200m^2 is comparable to EZ IV as well as the private bath of the second building phase. Here, the common features end however. In the

[47] Kolb 2001, 439–441.

[48] As to the close technical references to Roman models as described by Vitruvius 5. 10, 2–3, cf. Kolb – Keller 2000, 361-362.

[49] ‘Amr – Al-Nawafleh – Qrarhi 1997, 470–473.

[50] Al-Muheisen – Villeneuve 1994, 751–752.

[51] Ibid., 751.

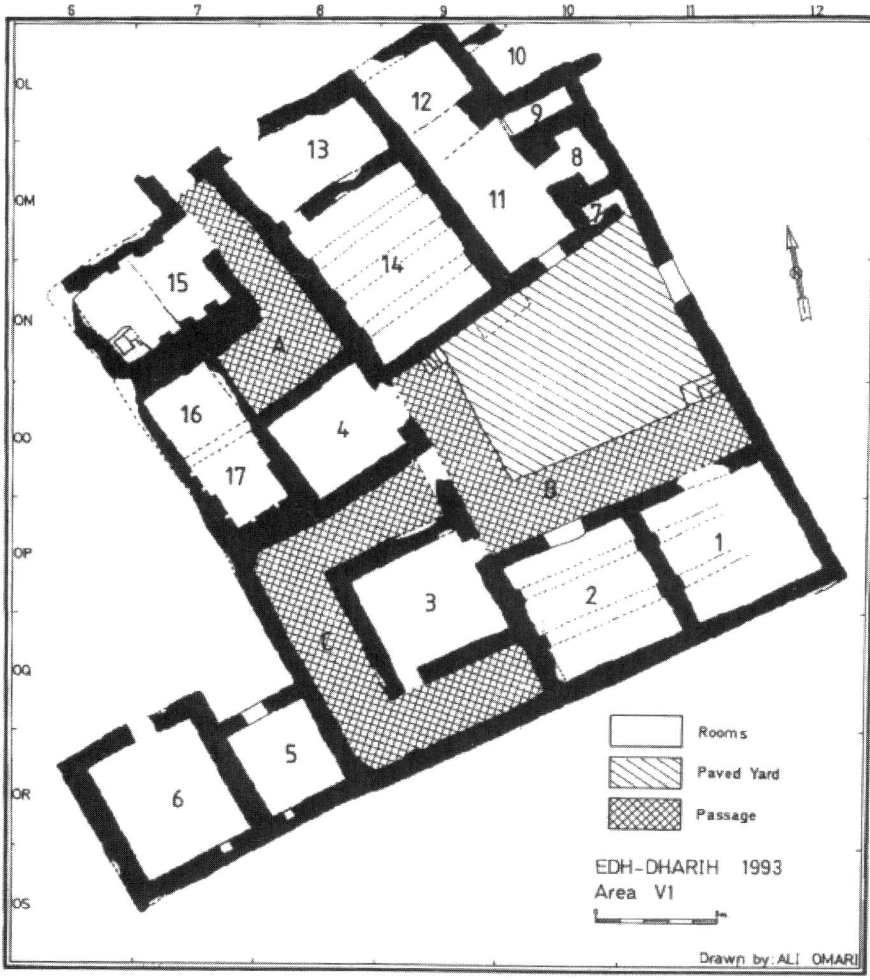

fig. 20 Khirbet edh-Dharih. mansion V 1, general plan.
(Al-Muheisen – Villeneuve 1994, 750 fig. 7)

architecture of House V 1, there are none of the typical western influences characterizing the rich Petraean private architecture. The room configuration of a courtyard and two almost square reception rooms is neither based on Hellenistic nor Roman models but on the regional, i.e. Nabataean building tradition defined in the preceding chapter.

The clearly discernible and characteristic Hellenistic influence (peristyle, three room-configuration, *distylos in antis*) of the private architecture of the social elite in Petra is non-existent in Kirbeth ed-Dharih. Obviously, the process of acculturation was mostly restricted to the economically and culturally outstanding capital. The ultimately low spreading radiation of the sophisticated private architecture is, on the one hand, to be read in the buildings of neighbouring Nabataean settlements and, on the other one, the later private buildings of the town proper.

Bibliography

Al-Muheisen, Z – Villeneuve, F., 1994. "Découvertes nouvelles à Khirbet edh-Dharih (Jordanie), 1991–1994: Autour du sanctuaire Nabatéen et Romain", *CRAI* 735–757.

Amr, K. – Al-Nawafleh, S.– Qrarhi, H., 1997. "A Preliminary Report on the Wadi Musa Salvage Excavation 1996", *ADAJ* 19, 469–473.

Amiran, D.H.K. – Arieh, E. – Turcotte, T., 1994, "Earthquakes in Israel and Adjacent Areas: Macroseismic Observations since 100 B.C.", *IEJ* 44, 261–296.

Andreou, A., 1988. *Griechische Wanddekorationen*, Michelstadt: Neuthor-Verlag.

Augé, Chr. – Dentzer, J.M., 1999. *Pétra. La cité des caravanes*, Paris: Gallimard.

Bernard, P., 1976. "Campagne de fouilles 1975 à Aï Khanoum (Afghanistan)", *CRAI*, 287–322.

Bienkowski, P., 1989. "Architecture of the Petra Beduin: A Preliminary Report", *ADAJ* 33, 335–343.

Bliss, F.J. – Macalister, R.A.S., 1902. *Excavations in Palestine during the years 1898–1900*, London: Palestine Exploration Fund.

Broshi, M., 1993. "Tell Judeideh", in E. Stern (ed), *The New Encyclopedia of Archaeological Excavations in the Holy Land*, Israel: Israel Exploration Society & Carta, 837–838.

Gibson, S., 1994. "The Tell ej-Judeideh (Tel Goded) Excavations: A Re-appraisal based on archived records in the Palestine Exploration Fund". *Journal of the Institute of Archaeology of Tel Aviv University* 21, 194–234.

Hackl, U. – Jenni, H. – Schneider, Chr., 2003. *Quellen zur Geschichte der Nabatäer*, Freiburg and Göttingen: Universitätsverlag Freiburg Schweiz and Vanderhoeck & Ruprecht.

Hammond, Ph.C., 1975. "Survey and Excavation at Petra 1973–1974", *ADAJ* 20, 5–30.

–, 1977/78. "Excavations at Petra 1975–1977", *ADAJ* 22, 81–101.

–, 1986. "Die Ausgrabungen des Löwen-Greifen-Tempels in Petra (1973–83)", in M. Lindner (ed), *Petra – Neue Ausgrabungen und Entdeckungen*, Munich and Bad Windsheim: Delp, 16–30.

Heinrich, E., 1984. *Die Paläste im alten Mesopotamien*, Denkmäler antiker Architektur Bd. 15, Berlin: Verlag Walter de Gruyter.

Hoepfner, W. – Schwandner, E.L., 1994. *Wohnen in der klassischen Polis I. Haus und Stadt im klassischen Griechenland*, Munich: Deutscher Kunstverlag.

Khairy, N., 1990, *The 1981 Petra Excavations I* Abhandlungen des Deutschen Palästinavereins, vol 13, Wiesbaden: Harrassowitz.

Horowitz, G., 1980. "Town Planning of Ancient Marisa: A Reappraisal of the Excavations after Eighty Years", *PEQ* 112, 93–111.

Horsfield, G. and A., 1938. "Sela-Petra, the Rock, of Edom and Nabatene", *QDAP* 7, 1–42.

Kloner, A., 1993. "Maresha (Marisa)", in E. Stern (ed), *The New Encyclopedia of Archaeological Excavations in the Holy Land*, Israel: The Israel Exploration Society & Carta, 948–957.

Kloner, A., – Sagiv, N., 1993. "Olive Presses of Hellenistic Maresha, Israel", in M.-C. Amouretti & J.P. Brun (eds), *La production du vin et de l'huile en Méditerranée*, BCH Suppl. 26, 121–135.

Kolb, B., 2000. Die spätantiken Wohnbauten von ez Zantur in Petra und der Wohnhausbau Palästina vom 4.–6. Jh. n.Chr. *Petra. Ez Zantur II*. Teil II. Ergebnisse der Schweizerisch-Liechtensteinischen Ausgrabungen, Terra Archaeologica IV, Mainz: Philipp von Zabern.

–, 2001. "A Nabataean mansion at Petra: Some Reflections on its Architecture and Interior Design", in G. Bisheh (ed) *SHAJ* 7, 437–445.

Kolb, B. – Keller, D. – Fellmann Brogli, R., 1997. "Swiss-Liechtenstein Excavations at az Zantur in Petra 1996. The Seventh Season", *ADAJ* 41, 231–254.

Kolb, B. – Keller, D. – Gerber, Y., 1998. "Swiss-Liechtenstein Excavations at az-Zantur in Petra 1997", *ADAJ* 42, 259–277.

Kolb, B. – Gorgerat, L. – Grawehr, M., 1999. "Swiss-Liechtenstein Excavations on az Zantur in Petra, 1998". *ADAJ* 43, 261–277

Kolb, B. – Keller, D., 2000. "Swiss-Liechtenstein Excavations at az Zantur/Petra: The Tenth Season", *ADAJ* 44, 355–372.

–, 2001. "Swiss-Liechtenstein Excavation at az Zantur/Petra: The Eleventh Season", *ADAJ* 45, 311–324.

–, 2002. "Swiss-Liechtenstein Excavations at az Zantur/Petra: The Twelfth Season", *ADAJ* 46, forthcoming.

Lindner, M. (ed), *Petra und das Königreich der Nabatäer*, Munich: Delp.

–, 986 (ed), *Petra – Neue Ausgrabungen und Entdeckungen*, Munich and Bad Windsheim: Delp.

Lindner, M. – Zeitler, J.P., 1991. *Petra, Königin der Weihrauchstrasse*. Exhibitioncatalogue Nürnberg: VKA-Verlag.

McKenzie, J., 1990. *The Architecture of Petra*, Oxford: Oxford University Press.

Murray, M.A. – Ellis, J.C., 1940. *A Street in Petra*, Norwich: Jarrolds & Sons.

Negev, A., 1983. *Tempel, Kirchen und Zisternen. Ausgrabungen in der Wüste Negev. Die Kultur der Nabatäer*, Stuttgart: Calwer Verlag.

–, 1988. *The Architecture of Mampsis. Final Report. Volume 1: The Middle and Late Nabatean Periods*, Qedem 26.

–, 1997. *The Architecture of Oboda. Final Report*. Qedem 36.

Nehmé, L., 1997. "L'habitat rupestre dans le bassin de Pétra à l'époque nabatéenne", in G. Bisheh, I. Kehrberg & M. Zaghloul (eds) *SHAJ* 6, 281–288.

Netzer, E., 1991. *Masada III. The Yigael Yadin Excavations 1963–1965. Final Reports. The Buildings: stratigraphy and architecture*, Jerusalem: Israel Exploration Society.

–, 2003. *Nabatäische Architektur*. Insbesondere Gräber und Tempel, Sonderbände der Antiken Welt, Mainz: Philipp von Zabern.

Nielsen, I., 1994. *Hellenistic Palaces. Tradition and Renewal*. Studies in Hellenistic Civilization V, Aarhus: Aarhus University Press.

Parr, P.J., 1960. "Excavations at Petra", 1958–1959, *PEQ* 92, 124–135.

–, 1965. "The Beginning of hellenisation at Petra", in: Le rayonnement des civilisations grecque et romaine sur les cultures périphériques, VIIIe Congrès International d'Archéologie Classique, Paris, 1963, Paris: Boccard, 527–533.

Peter, M., 1996. "Die Fundmünzen", in A. Bignasca – N. Desse-Berset – R. Fellmann Brogli – R. Glutz – S. Karg – D. Keller – B. Kolb – Ch. Kramar – M. Peter – S. G. Schmid – Ch. Schneider – R. A. Stucky – J. Studer – I. Zanoni, *Petra ez Zantur I. Ergebnisse der Schweizerisch-Liechtensteinischen Ausgrabungen 1988–1992*. Terra Archaeologica II. Monographien der Schweizerisch-Liechtensteinischen Stiftung für Archäologische Forschungen im Ausland (SLSA), Mainz: Philipp von Zabern, 91–127.

Russell, K. W., 1980. "The Earthquake of May 19 A.D. 363", *BASOR* 238, 47–64.

–, 1985. "The Earthquake Chronology of Palestine and Northwest Arabia from the 2nd through the Mid-8th Century A.D.", *BASOR* 260, 37–59.

Schmid, St.G., 2001. "The Nabataeans: Travellers between Lifestyles" in B. MacDonald, R. Adams & P. Bienkowski (eds), *The Archaeology of Jordan*, Sheffield: Sheffield Academic Press, 367–426.

Shereshevski, J., 1991. *Byzantine Urban Settlements in the Negev Desert*, Beer-Sheva V, Israel: Ben-Gurion University of the Negev Press.

Stucky, R.A., 1996. "Die nabatäischen Bauten", in A. Bignasca – N. Desse-Berset – R. Fellmann

Brogli – R. Glutz – S. Karg – D. Keller – B. Kolb – Ch. Kramar – M. Peter – S. G. Schmid – Ch. Schneider – R. A. Stucky – J. Studer – I. Zanoni, *Petra ez Zantur I. Ergebnisse der Schweizerisch-Liechtensteinischen Ausgrabungen 1988–1992*. Terra Archaeologica II. Monographien der Schweizerisch-Liechtensteinischen Stiftung für Archäologische Forschungen im Ausland (SLSA), Mainz: Philipp von Zabern, 13–50.

Zayadine, F., 1974. "Excavations at Petra 1973–1974", *ADAJ* 21, 135–150.

–, 1981. "Recent Excavations and Restorations of the Department of Aniquities (1979–1980)", *ADAJ* 25, 341–355.

–, 1986. "Tempel, Gräber, Töpferöfen. Ausgrabungen des Department of Antiquities in Petra", in M. Lindner (ed), *Petra – Neue Ausgrabungen und Entdeckungen*, Munich and Bad Windsheim: Delp, 214–269.

–, 1987. "Decorative Stucco at Petra and Other Hellenistic Sites", in A. Hadidi (ed) *SHAJ* III, 131–142.

Zeitler, J., 1989. "Die Siedlungsabfolge am Fusse des el-Hubta-Massivs von Petra (Jordanien)", in M. Lindner (ed), Petra und das Königreich der Nabatäer, Munich and Bad Windsheim: Delp, 307–318.

–, 1990. "A Private Building from the First Century B.C. in Petra", *ARAM* Periodical 2:1&2. First International Conference, The Nabataeans (Oxford, 26–29 September 1989), 385–420.

–, 1991. "Gebäude, Gewerbe und Geschirr", in M. Lindner & J.P. Zeitler (eds), *Petra, Königin der Weihrauchstrasse*. Exhibitioncatalogue Nürnberg: VKA-Verlag, 71–78.

–, 1993. "Excavations and Surveys in Petra 1989–90", *Syria* 70, 255–265.

The Nabataeans under Roman Rule (after AD 106)

David F. Graf

After the annexation of the Nabataean kingdom in AD 106, the "Nabataeans" fall into obscurity and their mere existence becomes enigmatic. With the loss of independence, they become submerged into the larger framework of *provincia Arabia*. The affairs with the Jews and Romans that attracted the interest of Strabo and Josephus are no longer. Not only is their name not retained in the name of the province ('Arabia'), but even the military units drawn from the Nabataean royal army – the *cohortes Ulpiae Petraeorum* – lack any reference to Nabataea. All traces of the royal dynastic family also disappear, even though the Babatha archive that sweeps across the transition between independence and provincialization, makes it clear that Rabbel II had an heir-apparent and that several members of the royal family must have survived into the annexation era.[1] But they pass out of existence without even a whimper or whisper. Roman imperial policy normally involved the enfranchisement of the local dynastic members, at least to some degree, but if this was the case with the Nabataean dynasty, it goes unmentioned in our extant sources. As Bowersock has observed, "Roman practice elsewhere might have suggested senatorial status for the remains of the royal house of the Nabataeans at least, but one looks in vain for a senator or even a citizen with the resplendent name of Rabbel or Aretas."[2] Nor is the explanation that the annexation represented a clash between the Nabataean royal family and Roman authorities a satisfactory explanation for the silence. The few signs of any confrontation in the annexation by Cornelius Palma the governor of Syria in 106, have escaped any consistent pattern by either the archaeological spade or historical inquiry.[3] The Nabataean kingdom remains *Arabia adquisita* and not *Arabia capta*.

[1] Y. Yadin, " Expedition D – The Cave of Letters," *Israel Exploration Journal* 12 (1962) 239–240, and "The Nabataean Kingdom, Provincia Arabia, Petra and En-Geddi in the Documents from Nahal Hever," *Ex Oriente Lux* 17 (1963) 230, w'l ḥyy 'bdt br rb'l mlkw nbt, 'in the times of Obodas the son of Rabbel king of the Nabataeans.' The papyrus is to be published in Y. Yadin, J. C. Greenfield, A. Yardeni and B. Levine, *The Documents from the Bar Kokhba Period in the Cave of Letters*, Vol. II: *Hebrew, Aramaic and Nabataean Documents*. Rabbel had two wives during his reign, Gamilat and Hagiru, as known from numismatic and epigraphic evidence, who produced other chikdren: See Y. Meshorer, *Nabataean Coins* (Qedem 3; Jerusalem, 1975) 70–79, especially 78–79.

[2] G. W. Bowersock, "Roman Senators from the Near East: Syria, Judaea, Arabia, Mesopotamia," *Epigrafia ordine senatorio* II (Rome, 1982) 656.

[3] S. G. Schmid, "Nabataean Fine Ware Pottery and the Destructions of Petra in the Late Frst and Early Second Century," *SHAJ* 6 (Amman, 1997) 413–420; cf. P. Freeman, "The Annexation of Arabia and Imperial Grand Strategy," *The Roman Army in the East*, ed. D. L. Kennedy (Ann

Even the Nabataean capital at Petra witnesses only expansion and remodeling in the early second century, not any major conflagration. The excavations at Petra thus far reflect only a smooth transition to Roman rule. Acculturation and assimilation to Roman culture appears to be dominant theme. Any signs of the survival of the Nabataean cultural tradition are few. The quest for Nabataean presence becomes primarily a search in the Greek and Aramaic epigraphic record of the new Roman province for "Nabataean" names, and it is not a futile search. As one may anticipate, hundreds appear in Greek texts that can be dated from the period of the annexation to the dawn of Islam and beyond.[4] Many of these are basileophoric names composed with the names of the former Nabataean kings (*'bdt*, *ḥrtt*, and *mlkw* or *mnkw*) or theophoroic names composed with Dushares. They appear in the Greek onomasticon of funerary stelae scattered across the old Nabataean realm, from Nessana to Avdat in the Negev, from the Ḥaurān through Transjordan to Aqaba. But none contain any assertions of "Nabataean" ethnicity. "Nabataean" pottery continues to be produced after the annexation into at least the fourth century although in diminished quantities,[5] but it was never coterminous with the borders of the kingdom, and consists more of a cultural vestige than an expression of ethnicity. In sum, the "identity" label of "Nabataean" virtually disappears after the annexation. Any assertions of "Nabataean" ethnicity are found only in a Palmyrene text dated to 132 found on an island in the Euphrates, and three Safaitic pre-Islamic Arabic inscriptions from the *ḥarra* in the Syrian desert.[6] The visibility of the Nabataeans is virtually lost, except for the occasional appearances in literary and epigraphic records.

Literary References

None of the major sources for the post annexation period refer to the Nabataeans, but there are several references to the Nabataeans in Latin literary sources of the second century. Both have been obscured by poor translations and/or interpretations, and have consequently been virtually ignored, but they deserve mention.

First, in Juvenal's *Satires*, written in the reigns of Trajan and Hadrian, there is a reference to Nabataea: *et quos deposuit Nabataeo belua saltu* (XI, 126), which is rendered as "Tusks that those great beasts shed in some Arabian [sic!] wadi, So burdensome they'd grown, too big to support."[7] Since Arabia is without ele-

Arbor: 1996) 91–118. J. Taylor, *Petra and the Lost Kingdom of the Nabataeans* (London/New York: Tauris, 2001) 73, suggests a possible peaceful arrangement between Rabbel and the Romans to bequeath his kingdom to Rome at his death..

[4] See now M. C. A. Macdonald, "Personal Names in the Nabataean Realm," *Journal of Semitic Studies* 44 (1999) 251–289.

[5] S. G. Schmid, "Typologie und Datierung nabatäischer Keramik," *Petra: Antike Felsstadt zwischen arabischer Tradition und griechischer Norm*, ed. T. Weber and R. Wenning (Mainz: Philipp von Zabern, 1997) 135.

[6] For the texts and discussion, see M. C. A. Macdonald, "Some Reflections on Epigraphy and Ethnicity in the Roman Near East," *Mediterranean Archaeology* 11 (1998) 186.

[7] The translation is by P. Green, *Juvenal: The Sixteen Satires* (London: Penguin, 1974) 231.

phants, the mystifying reference has forced commentators to turn to an African context. As a result, *Nabataeo* has been emended to "Napata," the Ethiopian city, to suit the other allusions to Syene and the Moors that appear in the immediate context.[8] But the dramatic events that brought the Nabataean kingdom into recent Roman control are not to be dismissed so easily, and such an interpretation ignores the presence of India in conjunction with Juvenal's allusion to Nabataea. The stunning recent discovery of exquisitely sculpted "Elephant-headed" capitals of Indian style in the "lower temenos" of the so-called "Great Temple" at Petra certainly provides a degree of credence to the Arabian interpretation of the passage in Juvenal.[9] In the fourth century, Eusebius indicates that Aila lay adjacent to the Red Sea, to which boats sailed from Egypt and the Red Sea.[10] An apt illustration of this movement is an incident in 496 during the reign of Anastaius in which an elephant and two giraffes from India were transported by a man from Ayla to Gaza across the Nabataean Negev.[11] Juvenal's reference to Nabataea is then to be taken seriously.

Secondly, Apuleius, in about 160 CE, makes an allusion to Nabataean traders in a flashy description of the geographical remoteness of India in his *Florida*: "Far away lies India, beyond the learned Egyptians, beyond the superstitious Jews and the merchants of Nabataea [*Nabathaeos mercatores*], beyond the children of Arsaces in their long flowing-robes, the Ituraeans, to whom earth gives but scanty harvest, and the Arabs, whose perfumes are their wealth" (*Florida* 6). Apuleius conjures up here the Nabataeos mercatores with other comparable traditional ethnic images for the Egyptians, Jews, Parthians, and the Arabs of the peninsula. These fitting stereotypes lie embedded in a collection of similar declarations of exotic descriptions and picturesque anecdotes meant to display his extraordinary rhetorical skill. Such poetic allusions may be interpreted as merely standard tropes and stock metaphors drawn from past, not contemporary images, but they must have retained some viability for the current situation. A favorite theme of modern scholars is the decline in Nabataean trade after the Augustan era, since Strabo says the sea-trade from the Indian ocean was diverted to the Egyptian ports (XVI.2.20 [756]), but as the *Periplus Mari Erythraei* (19)

[8] J. Y. Nadeau, "Ethiopians," *Classical Quarterly* 20 (1970) 348, who notes the text of the Res Gestae Divi Augusti 26.5, where Napata is spelled Nabata. But cf. E. Courtney, *A Commentary on the Satires of Juvenal* (London, 1980) 506, who notes "no reader who had heard of Trajans annexation of Arabia Petraea would think of this."

[9] M. S. Joukowsky, "Exploring the Great Temple at Petra: The Brown University Excavations, 1993–1996," in *The Archaeology of Jordan and Beyond: Essays in Honor of James A. Sauer*, ed. L. Stager et al (Winona Lake: Eisenbrauns, 2000), 228. Cf. T. F. C. Blagg, "Column Capitals with Elephant-head Volutes at Petra," *Levant* 22 (1990) 131–137.

[10] Eusebius, *Onomastikon*, ed. Klostermann, p. 6.

[11] P. Michigan Inv. 4290; *Timotheos of Gaza, On Animals* 24.2, ed. F. S. Brodenheimer and Rabinowitz (Paris/Leiden, 1949) 31; and Marcellinus Cokes, *Chronikon*-94 = Chronikon Minora Saecula IV–VII, ed. T. Mommsen (Berlin, 1894). For discussion see S. M. Burstein, "An Elephant for Anastasius: A Note on P. Mich. Inv. 4290," AHB 6.2 (1992) = *Graeco-Africana: Studies in the History of Greek Relations with Egypt and Nubia* (New Rochelle, 1994) 215–229, and I. Shahid, *Byzantium and the Arabs in the Sixth Century* (Washington, D.C., 1995) 28–31.

written in the middle of the first century AD reminds us, this did not mean that the trade to Petra ceased. Even if the East Indian Companies of the seventeen century brought the decline of Asian caravan trade by a paradigmatic shift in institutional structures, the same can not be said for the Roman era.[12] The impression is rather that the trade was of sufficient volume that a series of both sea and land routes to the Mediterranean continued to exist in antiquity.[13] The appearance of *Petraean bdellium* in Diocletian's Edict on Prices indicates that the incense trade was still active in the fourth century.[14] Juvenal's allusion to the Nabataeans may then be assumed to be of contemporary relevance.

Nevertheless, it soon became clear that Nabataea becomes a distant and murky memory. During the fourth century, Sidonius in Gaul makes allusion to Nabataea, but in a distorted and mucked fashion as a metaphor in general for the East. In speaking of geographical incongruities, he says it as "if the boat built with timbers from the Hercynian forest sails the Eastern [Nabataean] Hydaspes instead of the Rhine," *Hercynii nemoris si stipite lintris texta Nabataeum pro Rheno sulcat Hydaspen* (*Carmina* V, 284,). Nabataea is now taken figuratively in the West for 'eastern' or 'oriental,' the result of ignorant literary topographical generalizations that have become stock motifs. What is sorely lacking is any literary materials from the Nabataeans themselves.

Epigraphic Testimony

Where the Nabataeans become really visible is in the epigraphic record. Of striking importance are the Greek and Latin inscriptions attesting the presence of Nabataeans in the Roman military. After the annexation of the Nabataean kingdom, Trajan drafted six auxiliary units from the Nabataean army and entitling them the *cohortes Ulpiae Petraeorum*. Each consisted of infantry (*pedites*) and cavalry (*equites*) contingents, and at least three or four of them were of *milliaria* strength. They were all also probably *sagittaria* or archer units and undoubtedly constituted the *corps d'élite* of the Nabataean royal army. The primary evidence for the units is dedications by or for ten of the equestrian commanders of the units, and six military diplomas. Four of the units are known only from their commander's inscriptions (I–III, V), and two of the units by *diplomata* or their commander (IV, and VI). From the specific dates of the *diplomata* (136/7, 139, 157, 160, 161), it appears the units were initially recruited between 111 and 114, the same dates as are found on the inaugural milestones of the *Via Nova Traiana* and on the first coins issued in the province of Arabia. This chronology suggests the units were all levied in conjunction with Trajan's preparation for the Parthian campaign of 114–116. The later diplomas suggest they were from soldiers drafted

[12] N. Steensgaard, *The Asian Trade Revolution of the Seventeen Century* (Chicago, 1973).

[13] F. Millar, "Caravan Cities: The Roman Near East and Long-Distance Trade by Land," *Modus Operandi: Essays in Honour of Geoffrey Rickman*, ed. M. Austin et al (London, 1998) 125, and G. Young, *Rome's Eastern Trade* (London, 2001).

[14] *Diokletians Preisedikt*, ed. S. Lauffer (Berlin: De Gruyter, 1971) section 36.54 (p. 197).

as replacements for casualties suffered during conflicts, such as the Bar Kochba revolt (132–135), in which some of the regiments served.

Most of the commanders of the units are from Italy or Asia Minor, but a few are from Syria including a Palmyrene native and a descendant of the royal house of Emesa. Since native Syrians also served as commanders of Syrian *auxilia*, it is entirely possible that a native Nabataean could have been appointed as a commanders of one of the *Petraeorum* units, but there are only a few hints that this may have been the case. A recently discovered Nabataean Aramaic building inscription found in the region of Ḥumayma in southern Jordan attests a Marcus Ulpius Suᶜaydu (*mrqs ʾlpys šᶜydw*).[15] The name of Ulpius with a Semitic name suggests he was one of the original recruits of one of the *Petraeorum* units under Trajan, perhaps even a veteran of one of the units returning to his homeland for retirement. It may also be ventured that his name is the result of his command of one of the units during the Parthian campaign. The date of the inscription is lost, but the paleography suggests a date in the second quarter of the second century, precisely when the first retirements of the *Petraeorum* units were taking place. Another recent find is the shattered tombstone of an Aurelius Agrippa *ex Arabia* from the early third century found on the banks of the Drava river near Mursa in Pannonia. It had been set up by his grandfather or uncle, a M. Aurelius Bassus, who was an *eques Romanus*. Both are probably from the East, as the grandfathers name and village of Saharenus evoke parallels from southern Syria.[16] In similar fashion, a cavaryman of unknown rank and unit at the island fortress of Ana in the Euphrates identifies himself as a 'Nabataean' from the tribe of *rwḥy* (CIS 3973), a tribe known from a Nabataean Aramaic inscription at Umm al-Jimal, and Safaitic and Thamudic texts found recently in Transjordan to be published by Fawwaz al-Khraysheh and myself.

After Trajan's Parthian campaign, the *Petraeorum* units were assigned to garrison the eastern provinces of Cappadocia (III), Syria (I and V) and Palestine (IV and VI). Most of the units disappear by the middle of the second century. The *I Petraeorum* was still in Syria in 160 (CIL iii, 600), and the *cohortes IV* and *VI Ulpiae Petraeorum* in Palestine survive a little longer. After assisting in suppressing the Bar Kochba Revolt, it appears that the *Cohors VI Ulpiae Petraeorum* remained in Palestine. An inscribed brick tile attests to the legion at Emmaus, where it appears that it replaced the *legio V Macedonica*, which was stationed there during and after the First Revolt.[17] Talmudic literature suggests that Hadrian created a watch-post at Emmaus to guard the important pass leading from Jaffa

[15] H. Hayajneh, "Marcus Ulpius Su'aidu in einer nabatäischen Inschrift aus Süd-Jordanien," *Zeitschrift des Deutschen Palästina-Vereins* 117 (2001) 171–185.

[16] M. Šašel Kos, "M. Aurelius Bassus, eques Romanus, from Mursa," *ZPE* 91 (1992) 176–182 = *AE* 1992, no; 1454. For the name Bassus, see Cant. ii, 72, and Sartre, *Bostra* (1985) 188, and *IGLS* XIII/1 (1982) 9230, 9279–80, 9318, 9324, 9410, where it is regarded as the Hellenized form of Arabic *basa*, "cat."

[17] *Legio V Macedonica*: CIL iii 14155, 11, 12; 6646–47; J. H. Landau, Atiqot 11 (1976) 89–90. *Cohors VI Ulpia Petraeorum*: L. H, Vincent and F.-M. Abel, *Emmaüs, sa basilique et son histoire* (Paris, 1932) 427, no. 4 = *AE* 1924: 132.

via Lydda to Jerusalem, and that Arab horsemen were present in the region in the time of Rabbi Yohanan ben Zakkai.[18] It seems possible that this is a oblique reference to the unit. Dipomas attest that the unit was still in Palestine between 139 (CIL XVI, 87) and 160 (*RMD* 60 and 173), but not in 186 (*RMD* 69), when the provincial garrison was reduced from 15 to 9 *auxilia* units. Several inscriptions of praefects of the unit are known from Salona in Dalmatia around 200 AD, long after the other units disappear. Of the six units, only the *cohors III Ulpia Petraeorum* appears in the *Notitia Dignitatum* (38.27), now stationed at Metita in Armenia. But by this time, its ethnic constituency can no longer be considered as Nabataean.

Several Nabataeans also possibly emerged into the circles of the military elite. In the early second century, Trajan revived the imperial horseguard, which had been disbanded since AD 68. This elite army unity was recruited from the best men of the frontier cavalry (*alae*), and like Caesar and Augustus, drawn primarily from the German tribes on the Lower Rhine and Danube. The *equites singulares Augusti*, as they were known, constituted a force of 1,000 at the time of Trajan, and were doubled to 2,000 during the reign of Septimius Severus. More than 750 dedications and tombstones of this elite force are now known, the vast majority of which attest the Germanic origins of the recruits, but there are a few from various regions scattered across the empire. Among these, there are ten from Syria, including Damascus and Palmyra, and two from Arabia. Both of these are soldiers from Philadelphia (modern Amman). The first is from Mainz, the tombstone of a Flavius Proclus, and dates probably to the early years of Trajan's reign, the oldest known inscription of an *equites singulares Augusti*.[19] The other is from the catacombs of Rome, but lacks the name of the cavalryman, and appears to date to sometime in the second century.[20] Both of these elite cavalrymen may have been Nabataeans. A tombstone from Carnuntum in Austria dating to AD 69/70 mentions an *optio* in the *Cohors II Italica c*(*ivicum*) *R*(*omanorum*) named Proculus son of Rabilus, who is also from Philadelphia (CIL III 13483a). The patronymn discloses his Nabataean origins. Finally, a military diploma from Mauretania Tingitania in AD 88 lists another native of Philadelphia named Domitius Domiti, who was a member of the *Cohors II* (*Syrorum*) *sagittaria equitata milliaria* (CIL XVI, 159). His name is derived from his commander, Cn. Domitius Corbulo, so it is likely that he was also a native Nabataean. The region of Amman was known for its horsebreeding in the Hellenistic period, and it

[18] Mekhilta de Rabbi Ishmael, BaHodesh, 203–204 (ed. Horovitz Rabin) as cited with comments in B. Isaac, The Limits of Empire (Oxford, 1992) 293–294, and M. Fischer, B. Isaac and I. Roll, *Roman Roads in Judaea II: The Jaffa–Jerusalem roads* (Oxford, 1996) 155–155.

[19] M. P. Speidel, *Die Denkmäler der Kaiserreiter Equites Singulares Augusti* (Köln: Rhineland/Bonn: Rudolf Habelt, 1994) no. 684, *Flavius Procus, eq*(*ues*) *sing*(*ularis*) *Aug*(*usti*) *domo* [*P*]*hilodelpia, an*(*norum*) *XXV,* [*stip*(endorum) *h*(*eres*) *f*(*aciendum*) *c*(*uravit*). For a photo of the tombstone, see M. P. Speidel, *Riding for Caesar: The Roman Emperor's Horseguards* (Harvard, 1994) 16. no. 1.

[20] M. P. Speidel, *Die Denkmäler der Kaiserreiter Equites Singulares Augusti*, no. 265, [*...equ*(*iti*) *sing*(ularis) *Aug*(*usti*), *natione*] *Filadelp*[*ia*], *mil*(*itavit*) *an*(*nos*) *XVI, vix*(*it*) *an*(*nos*) *XXXV, ex tur*(*ma*)] *Caesorini Caius Charitonius Mercuriu*[*s*] *ex leg*[ato] *f*(*aciendum*) *c*(*uravit*).

seems likely that these recruits from Philadelphia were selected because of their skill as mounted archers in the Nabataean army. The *equites singulares Augusti* from Philadelphia in the second century only continued this tradition.

There is also some evidence that the Nabataeans at times fought *against* Rome. In September or early October of 135, during the last stages of the Bar Kokhba Revolt, one of the rebels named Soumaios sent a letter with his messenger Agrippa requesting wands and citrons for "the camp of the Jews." The letter is one of the papyri discovered in 1961 in Naḥal Ḥever on the western shores of the Dead Sea and is written in Greek because of the inability of Soumaios to write in Hebrew letters.[21] The name Soumaios appears elsewhere in the papyri for Nabataeans, and the writer's reference to "the camp of the Jews" and his inability to write in Hebrew script suggest he is a Nabataean, and that he and his comrades represent a Nabataean contingent among the rebels that fought with Bar Kokhba against the Romans.[22] In a rare allusion to the revolt in Roman literary sources, Cassius Dio mentions that "many outside nations" joined Bar Kokhba in the Jewish rebellion "through eagerness for gain" (69.13.2). It has been argued that the revolt transcended the borders of Judaea into the neighboring provinces of Arabia and Syria, since the governors of the adjacent provinces were granted *ornamenta triumphalia* after the rebellion had been quelled.[23] The governor of Arabia at the time was T. Haterius Nepos, and a Safaitic inscription discovered in the H5 'black desert' in northeast Jordan is by an individual who claims he "rebelled for three years against Nepos, who is a tyrant (*nfs zlm*)."[24] Just how extensive the rebellion may have been remains a matter of speculation, but some explanation should be offered for why the Nabataeans who appear to have accepted Roman rule so peacefully, should have become involved in the Bar Kokhba rebellion. Disenchantment over the fate of Petra and the Nabataean realm under Roman rule could be offered as an explanation, but any signs of such sentiment elsewhere are minimal. What can be assumed is that within the Nabataean community, there were diverse and different reactions to Roman rule. Moreover, as the Babatha archive from the same period attests, the Dead Sea

[21] H. Cotton, "Greek Letters: P. Yadin 52, Letter from Soumaios to Yonathes and Masabala in Ein Gedi," *The Documents from the Bar Kokhba Period in the Cave of Letters*, ed. by Y. Yadin, J. Greenfield, Ada Yardeni and B. Levine (Jerusalem: Israel Exploration Society,2002) 351–362.

[22] H.M. Cotton, "The Bar Kokhba Revolt and the Documents from the Judaean Desert: Nabataean Participation in the Revolt," in *The Bar Kokhba Revolt Reconsidered: New Perspectives on the Second Jewish Revolt Against Rome*, ed. P. Schäfer (Tübingen: Mohr/Siebeck, 2003) 133–152.

[23] W. Eck, "The Bar Kokhba Revolt: The Roman Point of View," *Journal of Roman Studies* 89 (1999) 76–89.

[24] S. Abbadi and F. Zayadine, "Nepos the Governor of the Provincia Arabia in a Safaitic Inscription," *Semitica* 46 (1996) 155–164. It should be noted that he name *nfs* appears at least a half-dozen times elsewhere in Safaitic and North Arabian texts as a personal name, so the identity of the *nfs* in this new text is not certain: G. Lankester Harding, *An Index and Concordance of Pre-Islamic Arabian Names and Inscriptions* (Toronto, 1971) 596. There are many other references to rebellion against Rome in the Safaitic texts, but none of them identify the specific ruler or governor.

community was "a society in which Arabs and Jews associated freely and in trust."[25]

Of course, there are also some 8,000 Nabataean Aramaic inscriptions scattered across their realm that bear testimony to Nabataean presence. But after AD 106, dated Nabataean Aramaic inscriptions appear infrequently until AD 356, when they cease altogether.[26] Prior to the annexation, there are more than 75 inscriptions dated to the reigns of the various Nabataean kings, extending from 96 BC to AD 106, a little over two centuries. For the post annexation period for the following two and a half centuries, there are only several dozen. In the second century, they appear scattered across the territory of the old Nabataean kingdom, at Bostra and Der el-Mešquq in the Ḥaurān of southern Syria, at Madaba in Moab, at Avdat in the Negev, at Wadi Ramm in the Ḥismā, Ruwwafa and Madāʾin Ṣāliḥ in the Ḥijāz, and at Wadi Mukatteb in the Sinai. Afterwards, they appear only on the periphery of the old Nabataean realm or outside its traditional territory. Most of these are concentrated in the southern Sinai, the eastern desert of Egypt, or at Madāʾin Ṣāliḥ. Not a single dated Nabataean inscription appears at Petra or in the Nabataean heartland after the annexation. This is usually explained as the result of the Greek language replacing the Nabataean language almost immediately after the annexation. The archive of Babatha clearly reflects this transition, at least for official legal documents. This transition is also reflected in the excavations at the temple at Oboda (Avdat) in the Negev.[27] All the Nabataean Aramaic inscriptions found in the environs of the acropolis and temple are assigned a pre-annexation date, with the exception of one dating to 126/7 and another to 204/5. In contrast, all the inscriptions of the second phase of the temple are in Greek ranging from 267/8 to 293/4. In spite of this transition, the personal names indicate the change has been with the language used, not in the ethnic composition of the community: the names are almost all of Nabataean character Nakebos, Ausos, Raisos son of Abdalgos, Abdomanos, Abdomaios, Souaidos, Ouallos, and Saadallas. The shift in cultural reflects an internal change in the indigenous population: accommodation to the language and culture of Roman administration by the provincial Nabataeans.

[25] G. W. Bowersock, *Roman Arabia* (Cambridge: Harvard, 1983) 75. For the Greek documents of the Babatha archive see N. Lewis, *The Documents from the Bar Kokhba Period in the Cave of Letters: Greek Papyri* (Jerusalem, 1989). The Nabataean Aramaic documents from the Babatha archive will appear shortly, but are available now in A. Yardeni, *Textbook of Aramaic, Hebrew and Nabataean Documentary Texts from the Judaean Desert* (Jerusalem, 2000). The contemporary archive of Salome Komaïse Daughter of Levi also reflects the friendly relations between Jews and Nabataeans at Maḥoza, a village southeast of the Dead Sea in the old Nabataean kingdom, where Babatha also resided. See H. M. Cotton and A. Yardeni, *Aramaic, Hebrew and Greek Documentary Texts from Naḥal Ḥever and Other Sites* (Oxford, 1997) no. 12 (Aramaic) and no. 60–65 (Greek). For dis-cussion of all these papyri, see, "Papyrology of the Judaean Desert," *Scripta Classica Israelica* 20 (2001) 113–181.

[26] For a list of the dated Nabataean inscriptions see R. Wenning, *Die Nabatäer. Denkmäler und Geschichte* (Göttingen: Vandenhoeck & Ruprecht, 1987) 305. The additions to the list are just a few texts primarily before the annexation.

[27] A. Negev, *Nabataean Archaeology Today* (New York, 1986) 109–111.

The several dozen dated post-annexation Nabataean inscriptions are sufficient for organizing the paleographical development and evolvement of the script in later centuries, as Grundler has demonstrated.[28] Inspection of non-dated texts indicates that many if not most can be dated from the second century to the fourth. For example, a recent text published from Riḥāb near Khirbet es-Samra has been assigned by Fawzi Zayadine to the last quarter of the third century.[29] At least one of the texts recently published from Siq Um El ʿAlda, just North of Petra exhibits similar late qualities of script, indicating a post-annexation date.[30] Almost forgotten in the literature are the Nabataean ostraca and stone inscriptions published by Franz Rosenthal from Nessana in the Negev, which he felt represented a transitional stage "between Nabataean and Arabic, and therefore were assigned a date between 150 and 350 of our era."[31] Nothing that has been published subsequently would dispel his conclusion. What is noteworthy is that the onomasticon of these texts is completely that of traditional Nabataean names, such as ʿAbd al-Gâ, ʿAbd-ʿObodat, Taymû, and Abdû. Clearly, Nabataean cultural conventions of script and language still apply in the Nabataean heartland. Finally, the vast majority of the more than 4,000 texts from the Sinai and eastern desert of Egypt are normally assigned a date after the annexation.[32] A steady stream of newly published texts from other regions continues to mount, but the general impression seems clear.

For the corpus of approximately 8,000 Nabataean texts, perhaps more than half are a product of the period after the annexation. Admittedly, it has been argued that not all of these texts should be considered 'Nabataean', as they represent only a number of local varieties of the Aramaic script which were not necessarily connected with the Nabataean people or state.[33] For example, it is argued that not all the so-called 'Nabataean' inscriptions from the Ḥaurān are necessarily to be considered Nabataean *per se*, since, as Starcky observed earlier, a variety of late Aramaic scripts existed in the region that was unrelated to the Nabataean chancellery.[34] The onomasticon and content of the thousands of Sinai inscriptions also suggest a cultural group that seems divorced from the Nabataean

[28] Gruendler, *The Development of the Arabic Scripts* (Havard Semitic Studies 43; Atlanta: Scholars Press, 1993).

[29] F. Zayadine, Inscriptions nabatennes de Riḥhāb des Banī Ḥasān et de irbat as SamrāΔ̃, in *Fouilles de Khirbet es-Samra en Jordanie*, Vol. I (Turnhout, BREPOLS, 1998) 542–543.

[30] M.–J. Roche and F. Zayadine, *Semitica* 49 (1999), 123–139, date all the texts to the first century BC to the end of the first century AD, but no. 3 (*yʿūˇtb*, appears later to me (see the *y*).

[31] F. Rosenthal, "Nabataean and Related Inscriptions," in *Excavations at Nessana*, Vol. I, ed. H. D. Colt (London, 1962) 198–210.

[32] M. E. Stone, *Rock Inscriptions and Graffiti Project: Catalogue of Inscriptions*, Volume 3 (Atlanta, 1994) 208, lists 3851 recorded from the Sinai. Taylor, *Petra and the Lost Kingdom of the Nabataeans*, p. 168, indicates there are 7,000 Nabataean inscriptions in the Sinai, but I do not know the basis for her figure.

[33] M. C. A. Macdonald, "Some Reflections on Epigraphy and Ethnicity in the Roman Near East," *Mediterranean Archaeology* 11 (1998) 186.

[34] J. Starcky, "Pétra et la Nabatène," *Supplment au dictionnaire de la Bible* VII (Paris, 1966) 930.

cultural tradition.[35] The Nabataean inscriptions from Ruwwafa from the Thamudic confederation dating to 166–169 also indicates that non-Nabataeans utilized the Aramaic script we identify as 'Nabataean.'[36] In essence, according to this argument, the vast majority of Nabataean inscriptions dating to after the annexation are not really Nabataean after all, but simply the absorption of what we call 'Nabataean' by other populations. In response, it must be insisted that this has always been the case even in the pre-annexation period. In the Augustan era, the dedicatory Nabataean-Greek bilingual inscriptions from the temple of Ba'al-Sham at Si' were by members of the local 'Ubayshat tribe, who represented the *koinon* and *dêmos* of the settlement (CIS II, 163–164). But members of the same tribe attached also to the same sanctuary inscribed their names in Safaitic some distance from the local sanctuary (CIS V, 3262; WH 1725a; CSNS 424). At about the time of the annexation, a Hellenized Ammonite man constructed a shrine to the local Zeus at Ziza that he identified in the Greek text as Beelphegor (IGLS XXI/2 [1986] no. 154). At the sanctuary of Khirbet Tannur, a Nabataean inscription indicates that "(This is stele) which Qosmalak made for Qos, the god of *ḥwrw*."[37] These examples could be multiplied, but they are adequate enough to illustrate the point that many ethnic groups within the Nabataean realm utilized what we call the Nabataean script both before and after the annexation.

Social diversity always existed in the Nabataean realm. The search for a common ancestry and ethnically pure Nabataean race is doomed to fail. It is best to understand 'Nabataean' as a political umbrella signifying those diverse Arabs groups who were subjects of the Nabataean king, not as a separate ethnic group. North Arabia was not the scene of a conquest that infused a new race of warriors into the region, replacing the existing population. What we call 'Nabataean' is better seen as the integration of various Arab groups into the political framework we call the 'Nabataeans'. The search for 'ethnicity' that has become the hobgoblin of trendy academic minds is in reality a product of post WWII urban sociologists. Prior to this period, such terminology rarely occurs if at all. The attempt to impose this category on the population and landscapes of antiquity is rarely successful, but such frustrations should not be considered a product of the exiguous nature of the evidence or the archaic concepts that existed in past cultures. As Clifford Geerz has put it, "All ethnography is part philosophy, and a good deal of the rest is confession."[38] A far better pursuit is to look for elements that we have identified as constituting a shared Nabataean culture.

[35] J. Starcky, "Les inscriptions nabatennes du Sinai," *Le Monde de a Bible* 10 (October 1979) 37–39.

[36] J. T. Milik, "Inscriptions grecques et nabatennes de Rawwafah," *Bulletin of the London Institute of Archaeology* 10 (1972) 54–57.

[37] J. T. Milik, "Nouvelles inscriptions nabatennes," *Syria* 35 (1958) 237–238.

[38] C. Geertz, "The Cerebral Savage: On the Work of Claude Lévi-Strauss," *The Interpretation of Cultures* (1973) 346. For further discussion on Nabataean ethnicity, see D. F. Graf, "Nabataean Identity and Ethnicity: The Epigraphic Perspective," in *Studies in the History and Archaeology of Jordan* VIII (Amman, 2004) 145–154.

Language and Culture

The end of the Nabataean *ethnos* has been seen in contrast to the proud survival of the Jews.[39] In essence, this requires a search for language and religion. To put it in the poignant words of Benedict Anderson, "What the eye is to the lover that particular, ordinary eye he or she is born with – language – whatever language history has made his or her mother tongue – is to the patriot. Through that language, encountered at mother's knee and parted with only at the grave, pasts are restored, fellowships are imagined, and futures dreamed."[40] For the Nabataeans, this means, for example, a search for such institutions as the royal dynastic Nabataean cult and the Arabic language. By including the latter, it should be clear that I am not sympathetic with the recent attempts to deny the 'Arabness' of the Nabataeans or the 'Arabicness' of their language. Enough of these elements are embedded in the epigraphic record of North Arabia to suggest that they existed in a larger scale than previously thought. Much of this evidence is fairly recent, and only the major aspects can be summarized here.

Of primary significance is the Nabataean community at Avdat on the opposite side of the Arabah from Petra, where abundant evidence of its peculiar cult has been found. The city was named after King Obodas, and this deceased king became identified as a god and the object of a cult. Inscriptions at the site are offered to Zeus Obodas, and as late as 267/8, a temple at Avdat was erected to him. The Greek inscription lists the dedicants, and the names are all traditionally Nabataean. Other dedications at the site are also offered to 'Zeus Oboda' or the 'God Oboda', exhibiting the prevalence and vivacity of the cult long after the annexation. As late as 293/4, the lintel of the tower in the south of the settlement indicates it was built by the aid of a Wailos from Petra. As noted above, of the 31 Greek names known from the pre–Byzantine period, only three or four are of Greek derivation; the rest are all typically Nabataean.[41] An undated graffito found near Avdat also records the erection of a statue to the god-king in a Nabataean Aramaic script that suggests a date around the time of the annexation.[42] Two lines of the Aramaic text are in Arabic, but of vexed interpretation and a matter of continuing controversy.[43] Nevertheless, the vibrant preservation of the native Nabataean dynastic cult in Roman Arabia centuries after the annexation is firmly established.

[39] G. W. Bowersock, "The Greek Moses: Confusion of Ethnic and Cultural Components in Later Roman and Early Byzantine Palestine," *Religious and Ethnic Communities in Later Roman Palestine*, ed. H. Lapin (Bethesda, 1998) 47.

[40] B. Anderson, *Imagined Communities: Reflections on the Origin and Spread of Nationalism* (London, 1983) 140.

[41] A, Negev, "The Greek Inscriptions from Avdat (Oboda)," *LA* 28 (1978) 87–126.

[42] A. Negev, "Obodas the God," *Israel Exploration Journal* 36 (1986) 56–64.

[43] The most recent discussions of the difficult text are M. Kropp, "A Puzzle of Old Arabic Tenses and Syntax: The Inscription of 'Avdat," *Proceedings of the Seminar for Arabian Studies* 24 (1994) 165–174, and D. Testen, "On the Arabic of the 'En 'Avdat Inscription," *Journal of Near-Eastern Studies* 55 (1996) 281–293.

There is also literary and numismatic evidence of the survival of the royal dynastic cult of Dushara after the annexation. Of primary importance here are two distinct groups of coins issued in Arabia, those from Adraa in the Ḥaurān and those from the region of Charach Moba (Kerak). The first have on the reverse a depiction of a hemisphere attached to a block; those issued in the reigns of Antoninus Pius and Marcus Aurelius have a legend with the name of the city and that of ΔΟΥΣΑΡΗΣ ΘΕΟΣ, 'The God Dushares.' At Charach-Moba, the reverse has a table or platform beneath a triangle, adjacent to which are two betyles. The issues in the reign of Elagabalus carry the same legend that appears on the Adra'a issues, ΔΟΥΣΑΡΗΣ ΘΕΟΣ.[44] There are also coins struck under Elagabalus that depict Dushares riding a camel. Both of these issues, of course, precede those of Bostra, in which Dushara appears in an even more elevated and different context. In the reign of Caracalla, similar coins appeared with the name of Bostra, followed by ΔΟΥΣΑΡΗΣ ΘΕΟΣ. But in the reigns of Philip the Arab and Trajanus Decius, during the mid-third century, coins of Bostra are struck with a Latin legend, *Actia Dusaria*, which suggests a festival with athletic and artistic competitions connected with Octavian's victory at Actium are held in association with the principal god of the Nabataeans.[45] In the fourth century, Epiphanius of Salamis indicates that at the temple of the idol at Petra, the people sing hymns to the virgin in Arabic (*Arabikêi dialektôi*), calling her 'Chaabos' which means 'virgin', and to the one born from her 'Dushares', which means 'only begotten of the Lord.' According to Epiphanius, the same rites are also performed in the city of Elusa as those at Petra (*Panarion* 51.22.11).[46] The remarkable description of the cult of a virgin goddess who was mother of Dushares has been viewed as an example of the transformation of a local cult by Hellenism, but it could just as well represent a confused account by a Christian outsider of the worship of Dushara and Allat. The Greek *Chaabos* probably reflects Arabic *kaʿb*, which generally means 'a virgin, a girl whose breasts are beginning to swell.'[47] Epiphanius' emphasis on Arabic in the ritual is important.

There are a handful of Aramaic texts in which there are Arabic loanwords or phrases that suggest Nabataean descendants preserved their speech and culture. In addition to the Arabic poetic phrases in the Avdat inscription mentioned earlier, there is another such Arabic poetic phrase embedded in a Nabataean

[44] P. Naster, "Le culte du dieu nabatéen Dousarès reflété par les monnaies d'époque impériale, *Proceedings of the 9th International Congress of Numismatics*, ed. T. Hackens and R. Weiller (Louvain-La-Neuve/Luxembourg, 1982) 402–403.

[45] A. Kindler, *The Coinage of Bostra* (Warminister, 1983) 58–59.

[46] Translated by O. R. Amidon, *The Panarion of St. Epiphanius, Bishop of Salamis* (Oxford, 1990) 182. For discussion see G. W. Bowersock, *Hellenism in Late Antiquity* (Ann Arbor, 1990) 21.

[47] Edward W. Lane, *An Arabic-English Lexicon* (London 1863–93; rp. Cambridge, 1984) 2616. The suggestion that *Chaabos* should be emended to *Chalmos* to reflect Aramaic *ġalmu* or *ʿalmah* "young woman" made by Fleischerus in the nineteenth century is normally still followed: see J. F. Healey, *The Religion of the Nabataeans: A Conspectus* (Leiden: Brill, 2001) 104. But Arabic, not Aramaic, is the language referred to, so I prefer maintaining the received text.

inscription from the eastern desert of Egypt.[48] There are also twenty-five or more Arabic lexical items in the Aramaic papyri from Naḥal Ḥever near the Dead Sea.[49] If these additions are added to the 'Arabic' known earlier from Nabataean inscriptions in the Ḥaurān and Hijaz, all the regions of the old Nabataean realm are represented by these mixed Arabic-Aramaic texts in the period after the annexation.[50] On this basis, it has been argued that Old Arabic was a purely spoken language that made only sporadic appearances in the epigraphic record until the fifth and sixth centuries, and then only in Aramaic and Greek, the scripts of prestige.[51] But this assessment must now be revised. Several Thamudic texts recently discovered at Mādabā and Uraynibah West in northern Transjordan near Amman are written completely in an Arabic that closely approximates what we designate as 'Classical Arabic.'[52] Both of these rather formulaic texts are lengthier than previously known Thamudic inscriptions, as well as syntactically and lexically more sophisticated. More importantly, both are petitions to the god Ṣa'b, the fortune deity of the Nabataeans, known previously only from Aramaic texts at Palmyra in Syria, Petra in Transjordan, and Madā'in Ṣāliḥ (Hegra) in the Ḥijāz. In addition, other Nabataean cultural items are embedded in the texts. These finds suggest some of the texts known by the inappropriate labels of 'Safaitic' and 'Thamudic' were scripts utilized by those we regard as Nabataeans. These texts can only be loosely dated from the first century BC to the fourth century AD, so it is possible that these formulaic texts are the product of local Nabataeans just before or after the annexation. The Mādabā and Uraynibah West also make it clear that Arabic was used in the local indigenous scripts of North Arabia, not just the prestige scripts of imperial nature. But the same must have be true elsewhere in Transjordan and other areas of the Nabataean realm. For example, the recently discovered Petra papyri from the sixth century, although written in Greek, are saturated with Arabic names for the districts, fields, orchards, and houses in the environs of the city.[53] The Nabataean names in the onomasticon of the papyri are reminiscent of the texts from the Negev of the same period. These signs of the survival of Nabataean culture and language into late

[48] E. Littmann and D. Meredith, "Nabataean Inscriptions from Egypt," *Bulletin of the School for Oriental and African Studies* 15 (1953)12, no. 23 [Umm Dummerana].

[49] See Y. Yadin et al (eds.), *The Documents from the Bar Kokhba Period from the Cave of Letters: Hebrew, Aramaic and Nabataean-Aramaic Papyri* (Jerusalem, 2002) 29–31 and 398–410.

[50] M. O'Connor, "The Arabic Loanwords in Nabataean Aramaic," *Journal of Near Eastern Studies* 45 (1986) 213–229.

[51] M. C. A. Macdonald, "Reflections on the Linguistic Map of Pre-Islamic Arabia," *Arabian Archaeology and Epigraphy* 11 (2000) 36.

[52] F. Al-Khraysheh, "An Arabic Inscription written in Thamudic Scrip[t] from Jordan," *Adumatu* 2 (2000) 59–70 [Arabic], and D. F. Graf and M. Zwettler, "The North Arabian Thamudic Inscription from Uraynibah West" *Bulletin of the American Schools of Oriental Research* 235 (2004) 53–89.

[53] L. Koenen, "The Carbonized Archive from Petra," *Journal of Roman Archaeology* 9 (1996) 187–188. See now Z. Fiema, "Late-antique Petra and its hinterland: recent research and new interpretations," *The Roman and Byzantine Near East Volume* 3, ed. J. H. Humphrey (Portsmouth, 2002) 191–252, fora fuller account.

antiquity must be considered as only the partial accidental record of the descendants of the Nabataean realm of the early Roman era. Future discoveries should provide even more such evidence.

Of course, for the present these scraps and pieces about the Nabataeans and Nabataea after AD 106 represent a fairly confusing and choppy picture. As a result, it is often lamented that the history of the Nabataeans suffers from their not having their own Josephus. But so much of what we know about the past is by accident, and so much has been lost. For example, during the Hellenistic period we know that treatises on *Arabika* were produced by Palaiphatos of Abydos and Teukros of Kyzikos, and during the Augustan era by Juba II of Mauretania. More importantly, for our purposes, an individual named Glaukos wrote an *Arabika* in the Antonine era. Thirteen fragments of his work survive, all of them preserved by Stephanus of Byzantium, who in the reign of Justinian produced an *Ethnika* a substantial list of almost 3,000 geographical names with commentary derived from excerpts from various earlier writers. What is preserved today is not his original work, but a severely epitomized version from later centuries that may have introduced distortions.[54] Stephanus himself is hardly uncritical – his work is filled with too many errors, but what he provides is a valuable and extensive compilation of more than 270 authors from antiquity whose works are now mainly lost. Among these is Uranius, who produced an *Arabika* in the middle of the fourth century at contained many valuable references to the Nabataean realm including the regions of Transjordan, the Negev, and the Arabian peninsula.[55] Of the 32 fragments preserved, 31 of them are contained in Stephanus' *Ethnika*.[56] What Uranius illustrates, and his *Arabika* is only one of a number that have disappeared, is just how much information we have lost in regard to the Nabataeans. It also should make it clear that writing the history of the Nabateans both before and after the annexation of AD 106 is an on-going process that will never be finalized.

[54] D. Whitehead, "Site-Classification and Reliability in Stephanus of Byzantium," *From Political Architecture to Stephanus of Byzantium: Sources for the Ancient Greek Polis* (Historia-Einzelschriften 87; Stuttgart: Franz Steiner, 1994) 101. For a brief discussion of Stephanus, see A. Khazdan, *Oxford Classical Dictionary* 3 (1991) 1953–54.

[55] J. M. I. West, "Uranius," *Harvard Studies in Classical Philology* 78 (1974) 282–284.

[56] F. Jacoby, *Die Fragmente der Griechischen Historiker* IIIC (Leiden: Brill, 1958) No. 675. The fragment not from Stephanus is from Chiliades of John Tzetzes in the middle of the twelve century.

Nabataean Cultural Continuity into the Byzantine Period

Konstantinos D. Politis

Introduction

The conventional view of historians of the Roman Near East has been that the Nabataean culture had died out by the second century A.D. However, recent archaeological discoveries have indicated that an indigenous Semitic people with a distinct 'Nabataean' identity persisted well into the Christian-Byzantine period in the southern Levant. The question remains therefore, how truly 'Nabataean' had their character remained?

By the time of the Roman conquest in the second century A.D. the Nabataeans were a cultural entity possessing their own Aramaic dialect and associated script, distinct religious pantheon, characteristic art style, architectural forms and a territory centred at Petra and Medai'n Salih.

It may be that the Romans planned to neutralise Nabataea by establishing a new capital of Arabia, encompassing most the Nabataean territory, at Bostra in the Hauran. Alternatively, the Nabataeans themselves may have decided by in the late 1st century A.D. to move northwards in order to remain competitive on the trades routes. In either case, the result of this northern relocation was to bring the Nabataean centre much closer to the Roman powerbase in Syria.

The succeeding Byzantine administration further fragmented the Nabataeans by dividing them into two separate provinces of Palestine. To a great extent these efforts succeeded, but the underlying response was that many of the indigenous Nabataean Arab people overcame these pressures and together with their physical survival managed to retain many of their cultural traits and customs. The objective of this paper is to highlight these by reviewing pertinent historical sources and presenting some of the latest archaeological discoveries in support of the mounting evidence for a Nabataean cultural continuity into the early Byzantine period.

Language and Inscriptions

Literature and epigraphy are often the best indicators for an ethnic group. Therefore, investigating the most recently found Nabataean inscriptions is crucial in determining the survival of the Nabataeans. Unfortunately, relatively few Nabataean inscriptions of the early Byzantine period have been found, and none at Petra.

A rock-cut tomb at the Qasr al-Bint in Meda'in Salih has a Nabataean inscription (JSNab 17) dated to A.D. 267 which indicates a continuous use of this important necropolis together with the Nabataean language into the later Roman period (Nehme 2005: 171–172). Furthermore, according to Nehme, another Nabataean inscription now stored in Jeddah, refers to a man with the title 'chief of Hegra' and is dated to A.D. 356. This may help to explain why early Byzantine-period (4th – 6th century A.D.) pottery sherds were also found at Meda'in Salih (see below) and substantiates the debate in favour of Nabataean cultural continuity.

Another late Nabataean inscription is an inked graffito on the wall plaster of a building at Oboda dating to the 4th century A.D. which invoked the Nabataean gods Oboda and Dushara (Erickson-Gini and Israel 2003: 11, fig. 30). This not only demonstrates the persistent use of the Nabataean language and script, but also a continued veneration of their original pagan religion, through Oboda who remained well-known in the late Roman period.

The survival of the Nabataean language and people is evident in Greek inscriptions of the Byzantine-Christian period which contain Nabataean personal and place names in Hellenised forms.

Amongst other significant literary discoveries there are three important collections of inscribed artefacts clearly demonstrating that whilst Greek persisted as the *lingua franca* of the Second and Third Byzantine provinces of Palestine (formerly part of the Roman Province of Arabia), Nabataean-Aramaic personal names remained predominant.

Avraham Negev's study regarding the usage of personal names in the Nabataean realm provides us with an invaluable insight into the survival of the Nabataeans. Although there was a marked decline from 81.8% in pre-Christian times, Nabataean names were still represented in the population. Information deriving primarily from the Nessana papyri shows that from A.D 350 to 650 the usage was 6.9% local and 18.1 common Nabataean names (Negev 1991: 206), and from A.D. 650 to 750 there were 5.9% local and 7.8% common Nabataean names (Negev 1991: 207). Although some scholars agree that the Nabataean language was in use until the 4th century A.D., this raises the question – what happened to it after this date? Negev concludes that "despite the five or six centuries which had elapsed since the middle Nabatean period, the original Nabatean ethnic element was still prominent" (Negev 1991: 3).

During the earlier part of the twentieth century, several inscribed and dated funerary stelae were collected from the cemetery of Zoara in the Ghor es-Safi (on the south-eastern shore of the Dead Sea). Subsequent excavations of the adjacent Sanctuary of Lot at Deir 'Ain 'Abata in the late 1980s and 1990s, and recent investigations in the Ghor es-Safi, have additionally provided over 400 early Byzantine-period inscriptions. These have shown that a vibrant early Christian community existed in this region from the 4th to the 7th centuries A.D. (Politis 2005a: 6). Although most of these inscriptions were written in Greek, roughly half of the personal names contained with in them were of Nabataean origin, though in Hellenised forms (Politis 2003: 366). These include, Alesos, Alfalas, Ameros, Arethas, Asemos, Avavi, Avavios, Avdalgis, Avdomanis, Avdoulas, Avdoys, Avoybathi, Avvivas, Azizios, Dusarios [Fig. 1], Keamos, Malehathis, Mosalemas, Nesarios, Netiros, Obodas, Ouardos, Pavivlos, Sadallas, Savas, Selamanos, Siltha and Themallas.

Fig. 1. Tombstone inscribed with the Hellenised version of Dushara (Z-48), Ghor es-Safi (photo: T. Springett)

In 1993 a cache of 152 charred papyri scrolls were found in a room adjacent to a large triple-apsed basilica church in the centre of Petra. All of these scrolls were written in Greek (excepting one line in Latin), and their dates range from A.D. 537 to 593 (Frosen and Fiema 2002:19). The documents were primarily contracts and land deeds pertaining to the Petra region (one specifically mentions Petra). [Fig. 2]

Fig. 2. The word *Petra* in Greek on a papyrus from the Church of the Virgin, Petra

However, another of these papyri refers to the seat of a bishop and specifically to a 'Theodoros son of Obodianos, archdeacon of the Church of the Virgin Mary' (presumably the church mentioned above where the scrolls were found). The name Obodianos is a Hellenised adaptation of the notable Nabataean name *Oboda*. Alternatively, the Nabataean name *Dusarios* is retained in preference to it's Greek form, *Dionysos*, the use of which might have been expected during the later Roman and Byzantine periods when Greek was the *lingua franca*.

Whilst enduring use of Nabataean personal names should not be surprising in it's capital city of Petra, the fact that these Nabataean names persisted for almost 500 years beyond the fall of the Nabataean kingdom is culturally very significant. Obviously, there must have remained a strong ethnic consciousness despite the earlier Roman hegemony and later Byzantine-Christian cultural influence.

However the survival of Nabataean place-names, such as Zadakothon and Berosaba, mentioned in the Petra papyri, is less surprising than personal names because place-names tend to survive despite the varying ethnic influence of usurping populations. This may also imply a continued occupation of these important urban centres by Nabataeans well into the Byzantine period as artefacts with Nabataean affinities have been recovered from these sites. All this archaeological evidence demonstrates that there remained a Nabataean ethnic tradition in Petra and its' environs until the late 6th century A.D. leading to the conclusion that these people had not been entirely assimilated even though they adopted the Greek language and later the Christian faith.

Religion

The cult of the most important Nabataean god Dushara seems to have persisted into the mid-3rd century A.D. at Bostra with the athletic and artistic festival of *Actia Dusaria* (Graf 2007: 184). Also, as late as the 4th century A.D. Epiphanius of Salamis claims that the people of Petra sang hymns in Nabataean to 'Chamu' (the virgin) and her child named 'Dusares'. Graf interprets this title as 'only begotten of the lord'. This not only confirms the survival of the Nabataean language but is also evidence of an amalgamation of their indigenous pagan religion with the now-dominant Christian faith. This is further proof that the Nabataean population had not disappeared but were merely undergoing a cultural transition.

There is also numismatic evidence for the cult of Dushara in the late Roman period, with some coins depicting *betyls* (Graf 2006:184).

Excavations at the cemetery of Khirbet Qazone revealed burials of a Nabataean community on the south-eastern shore of the Dead Sea (Politis 2005b: 149–151) which is identified as Mahoza in the Babatha archive. Exceptionally well-preserved textiles, wood and leather has greatly assisted in visualising the apparel of ordinary Nabataean men, women and children of the 1st – 2nd centuries A.D. (Politis and Granger-Taylor 2003: 108). Stones with engraved *betyl* and *nefesh* signs recovered from the site also testify to a continuity of the Nabataean religion. [Fig. 3] Furthermore, 3rd century A.D. pottery sherds of drinking bowls, fine cups and imported filter jugs found strewn around the graves allude to the Nabataean custom of funerary meals. [Fig. 4]

Fig. 3. *Betyl* stone (KQ 2) from Khirbet Qazone (photo: T. Springett)

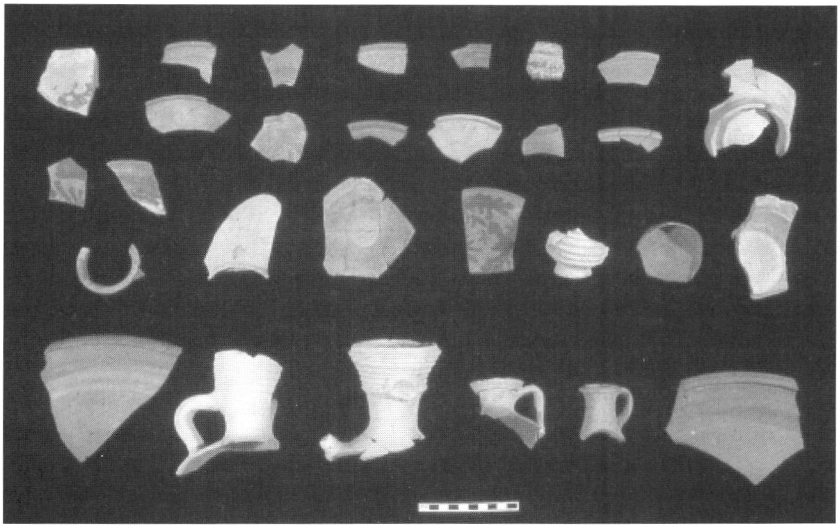

Fig. 4. Nabataean pottery sherds from Khirbet Qazone (photo: T. Springett)

In the northern extension of the Khirbet Qazone cemetery, three tombstones were recovered in association with 4th century A.D. pottery (Politis et al 2005: 327–337). These stones were decorated with crudely engraved crosses contained in a square [Fig. 5], the earliest known such finds. Another tombstone (KQ 37) similarly dated, is decorated with a roughly-etched palm branch design flanked by the Greek letters *alpha* and *omega*, which are typical early Christian symbols. [Fig. 6] Considering the immediate proximity, of these burials to those of the 1st – 3rd century, it is likely that these also belonged to the same Nabataean community that had, by the 4th century, converted to Christianity. DNA studies currently being conducted on the human remains from Khirbet Qazone and other Nabataean sites may shed more light on this, possible, religious transition of these particular people.

Fig. 5. Cross engraved on tombstone from Khirbet Qazone (photo: T. Springett)

Fig. 6. Palm branch flanked by *alpha* and *omega* on tombstone (KQ 37) from Khirbet Qazone (photo: T. Springett)

During excavations at Wadi Farasa in Petra, stone tablets inscribed in Greek from the early Byzantine period (5th – 6th century A.D.) together with tombstones engraved with crosses and palm branches have been discovered (Schmid 2002: 273, figs. 33, 34). Although of a finer workmanship, these closely parallel decorated stones found at Khirbet Qazone and Deir 'Ain 'Abata [Fig. 7], and may also indicate that Petraeans were converting to Christianity during this period.

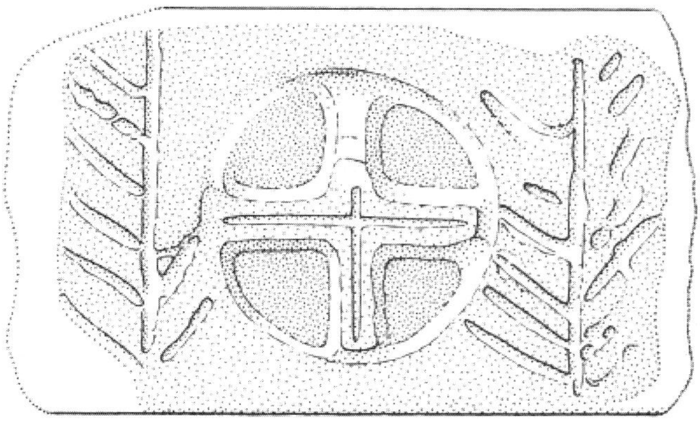

Fig. 7. Cross engraved on stone (DAA 29, 1445) from Deir 'Ain 'Abata (by J. M. Farrant)

A unique Christian tombstone found at Mampshit in the Negev, depicts a *betyl* design (Negev 1988: 88, fig. 6.64). This is the latest evidence of such a characteristically Nabataean sacred symbol which also demonstrates an attempt to integrate a pagan Nabataean symbol into the new religion's iconography.

There is a colourful account of the Nabataean conversion to Christianity in the story of the zealous monk Bar Sauma, famous for never sitting or lying down. In A.D. 423 he arrived at Petra with forty monks with the intention of destroying that city's pagan temples and Jewish synagogues. To prevent this, the inhabitants closed the city gates against them. In response, Bar Sauma threatened to attack the city and burn it down if they did not let him enter. Petra was then suffering from a four-year drought, but coincidentally when Bar Sauma arrived it began to rain heavily and the flood waters washed away the city walls. The pagan priests were amazed by this seemingly miraculous inundation which they interpreted as a divine intervention and promptly converted to Christianity. Intriguingly, there are no references to pagans being present in Petra after that date.

The Christianisation of the Nabataeans can be seen in Petra by the conversion of the 'Urn' tomb into a church in A.D. 446. Niches were carved into the eastern wall of the tomb in order to create apses, and the western end was extended by adding a series of subterranean arches. The growth of Christianity in Petra is also evident by the construction of new churches. In the 6th century a large basilica church with a sizeable adult baptistery was built and dedicated to the Virgin Mary. Immediately to the north-east of this structure the smaller 'Blue chapel' and the 'Ridge church' were also erected. A large monastery was founded and dedicated to Aaron's tomb on the heights of Jebel Haroun (biblical Mt Hor) just south-west of Petra, as mentioned in the burnt papyri from the basilica church. These building projects not only attest to the conversion of the indigenous Nabataean population to the new religion, but also to their physical survival.

A similar situation is mirrored at Nabataean sites and towns in the Negev and elsewhere.

There is some evidence that suggests an enduring influence of Nabataean religious practices on later creeds. For instance, it can been postulated that Nabataean 'high places' not only continued to be used for religious purposes during the early Christian-Byzantine period, but also that they may have become the inspiration for the raised chancel or *bema* in church architecture. A similar Nabataean origin can be claimed for the omphalos-shaped chancel post tops in early Byzantine-period churches.

The aniconic representation of gods by the Nabataeans seems to have had an influence on early Byzantine-Christian dogma with the iconoclastic movement of the 7th century A.D. This is particularly apparent in Judaism and Islam which still retain similar prohibitions relating to the realistic representations of human or animal forms.

Although these religious traits may not be exclusively 'Nabataean', they do show that their Arabian-based influence continued well into the Christian societies of the 7th and 8th centuries A.D.

Art and Architecture

Excavations of the ancient Zurrabah pottery kilns near Petra revealed that Nabataean pottery proto-types were being made from the 1st to 6th centuries A.D. (Amr 1991: 321). [Fig. 8] Excavations at ez-Zantur inside Petra unearthed Nabataean pottery from late 4th contexts (Schmid 1996: 240–241). More recently, excavations at Humeima, Wadi Mousa, Mada'in Salih and Deir 'Ain 'Abata have also brought to light the continuous production of pottery in the Nabataean tradition during the 5th and into the 6th centuries A.D. (Politis et al 2007).

Fig. 8. Nabataean painted bowl dated to that 3rd – 4th century A.D. (Petra Museum)

Architectural elements have been found at several early Byzantine churches in *Palestinae Tertia* which share close affinities to classical Nabataean styles (Patrich 1988: 105, ill. 152). At Elusa in the Negev (Negev 1986: 128, fig. 66) and at Deir 'Ain 'Abata characteristically Nabataean 'dogtooth' designs together with Christian crosses are found on capitals and lintels. [Figs. 9, 10] Nabataean 'horned' capitals also continued to be carved in the Byzantine period. [Fig. 11]

Fig. 9. Elusa capital no. 4005 (Negev 1986, fig. 66)

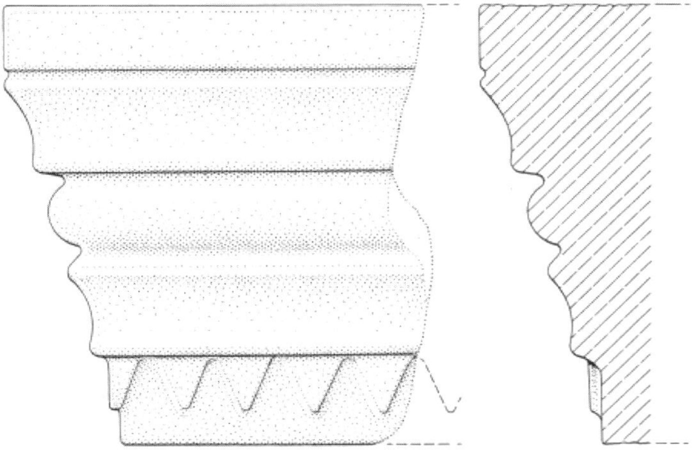

Fig. 10. Architectural stone from Deir 'Ain 'Abata (by J. M. Farrant)

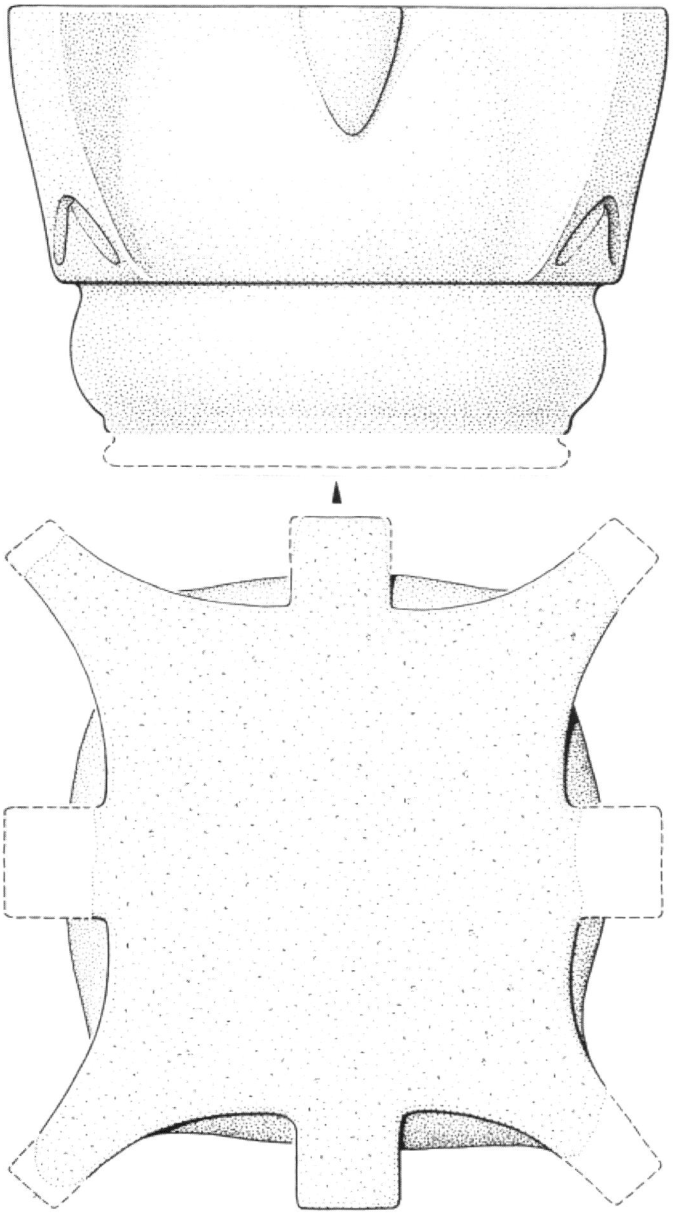

Fig. 11. Horned' capital (DAA 23 1555) from Deir 'Ain 'Abata (by J. M. Farrant)

Seventh century A.D. mosaic pavements have been uncovered in the churches of St Lot at Deir 'Ain 'Abata and Moses on Mt Nebo, Siyaga which exhibit floral patterns reminiscent of painted decoration on Nabataean fine-ware pottery. The mosaic at Deir 'Ain 'Abata is inscribed and dated to A.D. 691, well into the Umayyad period. [Fig. 12] It is intriguing to consider this as the result of an earlier Nabataean artistic influence.

Fig. 12. Mosaic pavement in nave of church of St Lot, Deir 'Ain 'Abata (photo: T. Springett)

Conclusion

Recent archaeological surveys and excavations at Petra, the Negev, Meda'in Saleh and the Dead Sea region have shed more light on the twilight of the Nabataeans. They have revealed some compelling evidence for 'Nabataean' cultural continuity beyond the 2nd century A.D. which has been the generally accepted date for it's termination. As evidenced here, these include religious practices, funerary customs, language, inscriptions, art, architecture and apparel.

It is now becoming apparent from the archaeological record that some 'Nabataean' traditions persisted well beyond the second century A.D. These, together with the literary testimony, combine to make a compelling argument for a Nabataean cultural continuity into the early Byzantine period. Perhaps the most conclusive evidence for this is from the continuous occupation of Nabataean sites into the early Byzantine period, indicating that the subordinated Nabataean people did not just disappear but had the tenacity to adapt to their new circumstances and thus were able to continue to express many of their remarkable cultural values. Appropriately, many modern Jordanian Arabs are proud to identify with the Nabataeans as being their ancient ancestors.

Bibliography

Amr, Khairieh (1991) *The Petra National Trust Site Projects: Preliminary Report on the 1991 Seasaon at Zurrabah.* A.D.A.J. 35: 313–323

Graf, David (2007) *Nabataeans under Roman Rule (After AD 106).* in (ed.) Politis, Konstantinos D., The World of the Nabataeans. Proceedings of the conference on the 'World of the Herods and Nabataeans', held at the British Museum in London 17–19 April 2001. Steiner Verlag, Stuttgart

Erickson-Gini, Tali and Yigal Israel (2003) *Recent Advances in the Research of the Nabatean and Roman Negev.* pp. 9–14 in The Nabateans in the Negev. ed. Renate Rosenthal-Heginbottom, Reuben and Edith Hecht Museum, University of Haifa, Haifa

Frosen, Jaakko and Zbigniew T. Fiema (2002) Petra- A City Forgotten and Re-discovered. Helsinki University Press, Helsinki

Negev, Avraham (1991) Personal Names in the Nabatean Realm. QEDEM 32, Institute of Archaeology, Hebrew University of Jerusalem, Jerusalem

Negev, Avraham (1988) The Architecture of Mampsis. Final Report. Volume I: The Late Roman and Byzantine Period. QEDEM 27, Institute of Archaeology, Hebrew University of Jerusalem, Jerusalem

Negev, Avraham (1986) Nabatean Archeology Today. New York University Press, New York

Nehme, Laila (2005) *Towards an understanding of the urban space of Mada'in Salih, ancient Hegra, through epigraphic evidence.* Proceedings of the Seminar for Arabian Studies. 35 (2005): 155–175.

Patrich, Joseph (1988) *Architectural Sculpture and Stone Objects.* Pp. 97–133, in Yoram Tsafrir et al, Excavations at Rehovot-in-the Negev. Volume I: The Northern Church. QEDEM 25, Institute of Archaeology, Hebrew University of Jerusalem, Jerusalem

Politis, Konstantinos D. *et al* (2007) Excavations at the Sanctuary of Lot at Deir 'Ain 'Abata in Jordan. British Museum Press, London

Politis, Konstantinos D., Amanda M. Kelly and Lisa Usma (2005) Survey and Excavations at Khirbet Qazone 2004. Annual of the Department of Antiquities of Jordan. 49: 327–337.

Politis, Konstantinos D. (2005a) *Introduction.* in Meimaris, Yannis E. and Kalliope I. Kritikakou-Nikolaropoulou Inscriptions from Palaestina Tertia. Vol. Ia. The Greek Inscriptions from Ghor es-Safi (Byzantine Zoora). National Hellenic Research Foundation, Athens

Politis, Konstantinos D. (2005b) *The Discovery and Excavation of the Khirbet Qazone Cemetery and its Significance Relative to Qumran.* Pp. 149–151, figs. 10.1–6, in (ed) Galor, Katherina Qumran – The Site of the Dead Sea Scrolls: Archaeological Interpretations and Debates. Proceedings for Conference held on November 17–19, 2002 at Brown University, Providence, Rhode Island. Brill Academic Publishers, Boston

Politis, Konstantinos D. (2004) *Ancient Arabs, Jews and Greeks on the Shores of the Dead Sea.* Pp. 361–370, in: F. al-Khraysheh *et al.* (eds.), Studies in the History and Archaeology of Jordan VIII. Department of Antiquities, Amman

Politis, Konstantinos D. and Hero Granger-Taylor (2003) *Nabataeans on the Dead Sea Littoral.* Pp. 106–108, in The Splendors of the Caravan Kingdom. (ed.) Glenn, Markoe, Abrahms, New York

Schmid, Stephan G. (2002) *The International Wadi Farasa Project (IWFP) Preliminary report on the 2001 season.* Annual of the Department of Antiquities of Jordan. 46: 257–277.

Schmid, Stephan G. (1996) *Die Feinkeramik*. Pp. 151–173, in A. Bignasca et al, Petra Ez Zantur I. Ergebnisse der Schweizerische-Liechensteinischen Ausgrabungen 1988–1992. Verlag Philip Von Zabern, Mainz

The Spice Trade from South Arabia and India to Nabataea and Palestine

Fawzi Zayadine

Abstract

South Arabia was renowned for its excellent quality gum-resins, frankincense and myrrh. These aromatic trees grow in western Ḥaḍramawt, eastern Dhufār and in the province of Mahra. Other countries on the western coast of Africa, namely Somalia and Ethiopia were also rich in groves of gum-resin trees. Similarly, India produced frankincense and myrrh, although of inferior quality when compared to the Arabian aromatics.

Other spices however were produced in India and were highly appreciated in the ancient world: cassia, cinnamon, cardamom, nard, in addition to the much coveted pepper. A variety of precious stones, shells and metals were a1so exported from India. But, the aromatics had the greatest demand. In the *Song of Songs*, the much-loved woman is compared to a closed garden where a variety of exotic aromatic plants grow: 'nard and saffron, calamus and cinnamon, with incense of every kind. Myrrh and aloes grow there with all of the most fragrant perfumes' (IV. 14). Most of these aromatics were alien to Palestine, and may account for the remark of Pliny about the 'surprising demand in Arabia for imported scents' (*NH*, XII). In Palestine, on the western shore of the Dead Sea, 'En-Gedi was famous for its balsam groves and perfume was produced at the workshop of 'En Boqeq (Diagi Mendels 1993: 96, Freedman 1992: 574). When the Nabataean caravaneers took over the spice trade from the Minaeans, probably as ear1y as the fourth century B.C., they became the middlemen of this lucrative commerce and transported the aromatics from al-Jawf of Yemen or the Arabian-Persian Gulf to the ports of Gaza or *Rhinocolura* (Al-'Arîsh).

Introduction

The production and sale of aromatic gums were, according to the classical authors, the origin of the legendary wealth of the Arabs. Pliny asserts: 'They are the richest race in the world, because vast wealth from Rome and Parthia accumulates in their hands, as they sell the produce they obtain from the sea or their forests and buy nothing in return' (NH, VI, XXXII, 162). When Pliny mentions the 'produce they obtain from the sea', he probably refers to the pearls the Arabs collected in the Arabian-Persian Gulf. As for the 'forests', this is no doubt an allusion to the frankincense and myrrh of Arabia. But who were those 'Arabs' who were involved in the trade of precious stones and aromatics? Salles has drawn the attention to the use of aromatic resins in Mesopotamia at the end of the third millennium B.C. (2004: 553ff). But he notes the difficulty in identifying the gum-resins in Akkadian; *riq-murru* is identified with the myrrh and *riq-kanaktu* attested in the second millennium B.C. could be identified with frankincense. At the beginning of the first millennium B.C., a new term appears in Mesopotamia to designate frankincense: *lubanatu* (Salles *eod. loc.* 554). The continuity of the trade of aromatics in the Arabian-Persian Gulf from the 3rd–2nd millennium B.C. to the Seleucid period indicates that the provenance of these spices was not from Arabia but rather, from India; the trade was in the hand of the Gerrhaeans, an Arab people who settled east of the Euphrates and spread-out to the region of al-Hasa and al-Hufuf in the area of Dhahrān. They are mentioned by Diodorus of Sicily and Strabo who reports that they 'traffic by land, for the most part in the Arabian merchandise and aromatics' (*Geog.* 16, 3). The same author reports that, Gerrha 'is situated in a deep gulf; it is inhabited by Chaldaeans, exiles from Babylon' (*eod. loc.*), confirming the Mesopotamian origin of the Gerrhaeans. In this case, the frankincense and myrrh of Gerrha was most probably of Indian origin (Salles 2004: 554), because it is unlikely that the aromatics crossed the desert from south Arabia to the Arabian-Persian Gulf, and again from that area to the port of Gaza (Salles *eod. loc.* 552). This assumption is reasonable and Diodorus confirms that the Nabataeans were only 'middlemen' who 'bring down to the sea frankincense and myrrh and the most valuable kinds of spices which they procure from those who convey them from what is called Arabia Eudaemon (*Felix*)' (XIX, 94, 5).

The uses of myrrh and frankincense

As early as the third and second millennium B.C. the Pharaohs of Egypt mounted regular expeditions to 'God's Land', the Punt, which was situated according to Leclant (1976: 39–46), from the valley of Baraka in Eritrea to the valley of Gash and river Atbara (in Sudan) (see the well documented analysis of Sayyed 2005: 203–233). There is no doubt that this region was situated along the Red Sea Coast and could be reached by sea and land through the Nile Valley. Queen Hatchepsut of the New Kingdom mounted an expedition to the Punt in 1,493 B.C. which was recorded in her temple of Deir al-Bahri (Dayagi-Mendels 1993: 113–115). [see figs. 1 a, b] The Egyptians brought back myrrh and myrrh seedlings to replant them in the temple of the queen. But the operation was not successful probably because the climate of Egypt was not suitable for the growing of those resin trees, since they naturally flourish prosper in a mountainous environment at least two kilometres above sea level, as it is the case in Dhufār or Somalia.

It is known that myrrh was used in Egypt for mummification. According to Herodotus, 'the body was emptied of the viscerals, except for the heart and filled with pure bruised myrrh, cassia and other aromatics, with the exception of frankincense' (*Hist.* II, 86). But Diodorus, who describes the eruption of asphalt in the Dead Sea, reports that the Arabs sell this product to the Egyptians for embalming

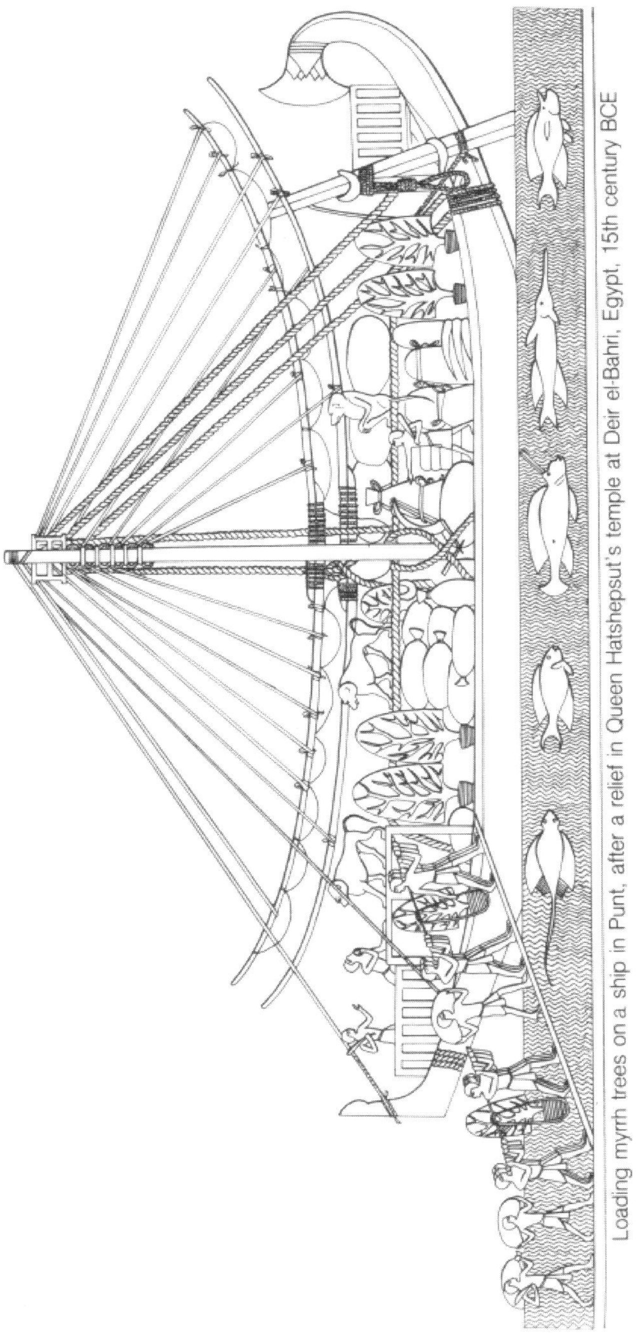

Fig. 1.a. Wall relief representing the loading of myrrh trees in Queen Htashepsut's Temple at Deir al-Bahri in Egypt. Fifteenth century B.C. (Diagi-Mendels, 1993: 113)

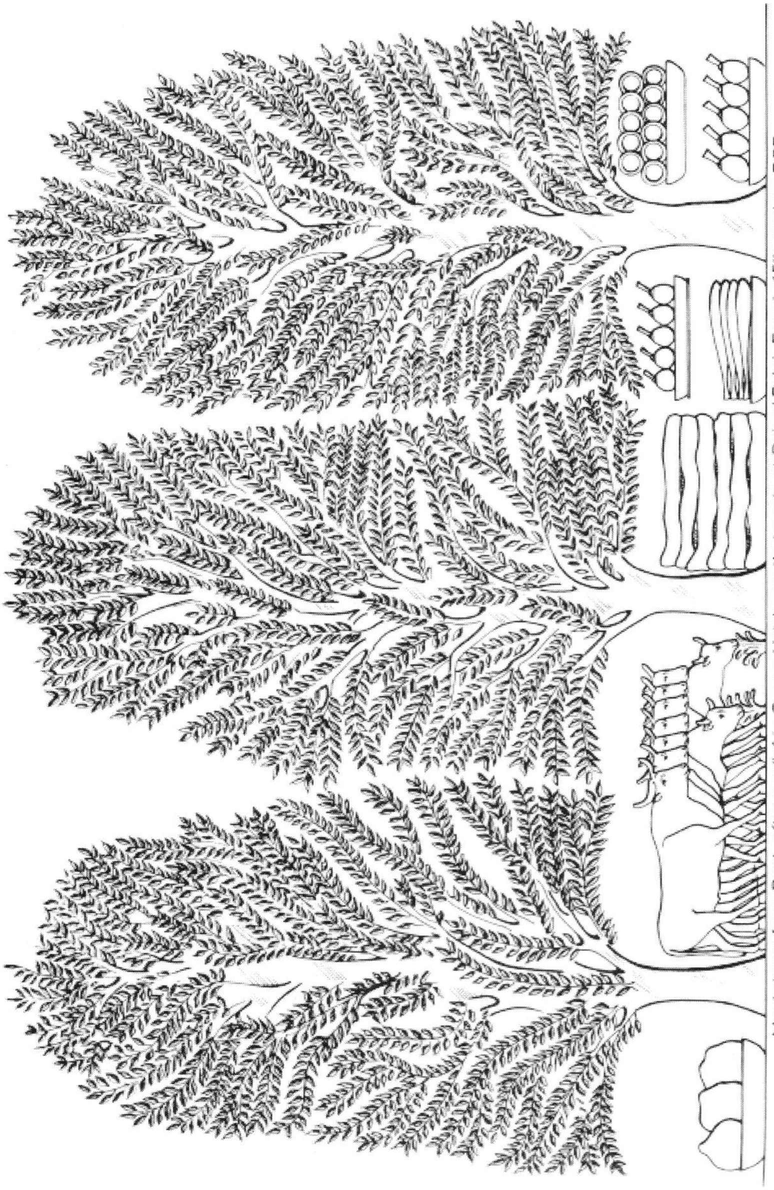

Myrrh trees from Punt, after a relief in Queen Hatshepsut's temple at Deir el-Bahri, Egypt, 15th century BCE

Fig. 1.b. Wall relief of Myrrh trees in the Temple of Queen Htashepsut at Deir al-Bahri in Egypt. Fifteenth century B.C. (Diagi-Mendels, 1993: 115).

their dead. He points out that 'unless this is mixed with the other aromatic ingredients, the preservation of the bodies cannot be permanent' (XIX, 98, 3). In the biblical narratives, Jacob and Joseph only were mummified. The operation lasted forty days (*Gen.* 50: 2–3, 26). But usually the corpse was soaked in *natron* for seventy days (Groom, 1981: 20). Then the eviscerated and cleansed body was rubbed with myrrh. Spices were added in the wrapping sheets of the dead. But myrrh had other medicinal uses. Before being crucified, Jesus Christ was offered wine mixed with myrrh (*Mark* 15, 23) probably as an analgesic to alleviate his pain. This gum-resin is also effective in the treatment of ear and eye infections, blains and chilblains and relieves liver pain (Groom 1981: 20). In this case, myrrh is usually mixed with frankincense for these prescriptions.

A special issue of the Omani periodical *Ḥasad* is dedicated to popular medical prescriptions and the healing virtues of plants. Frankincense for example, is recommended as a good drug 'to stimulate the stomach and liver, to revive the strengths, the intelligence and memory' (1980 5: 123–124). Red myrrh is indicated to cure diabetes, paralysis, migraine, conjunctivitis, rheumatism etc. (*Ḥasad* 5; 129). Of particular interest is a report of the International Institute for Cancer Research, that some herbs are effective in curing forms of skin cancer. More than fifty medical references prove the curative effects of frankincense for skin infections, mainly those of cancerous origin (Kessler, 1991: 40).

How myrrh and frankincense were collected in Arabia

The myrrh tree, *murr* in Arabic, is a *commiphora* in botanical terminology, and *qafal* in the *Shihri* dialect of Yemen. It grows from a central trunk which may reach six metres in height and is covered with foliage after the monsoon at the end of August or the beginning of September. It blossoms in spring time (van Beek 1960: 71–73). The western part of south Arabia, from Somalia to Ma'in, Ḥaḍramawt, Qataban and Ausan are rich in myrrh groves. However, Somali-land preserves the richest growth of this resin tree, as it was confirmed by Balsan in 1965. For this reason the pharaohs of Egypt, as mentioned above, organised expeditions to this country during the third and second millennium B.C. It was also noticed that Somali workers were specialised in the tapping of the trees and collecting the gum-resins. But according to Monod (1979: 149) the Bedouins of Dhufār in 'Oman were professionals in this practice. This modern-day French botanist from the *Jardin des Plantes* in Paris is also a celebrated explorer who investigated 16 stations of aromatic trees on foot in Yemen (1979: 146 150).

The frankincense plant, *Boswellia sacra*, or *luban* in Arabic and *mughur* in the *Shihri* dialect of Dhufār grows up from the ground to form a shrub, while the other variety, the *boswellia carteri* develops from a central trunk and may reach three to six metres in height. It grows naturally in the mountains at an altitude more than two kilometres. The usual method of obtaining the gum-resin is to incise the trunk of the tree with the *mengueb* or *mengueff* in the local dialect. This instrument is provided with two blades, the lower one is pointed to practice the incision while the upper one is rounded to collect the gum tears (see Zayadine 1995: 71, Fig.7). The frankincense tears are yellowish-translucent when they are freshly gathered, while myrrh is reddish-brown and turns to greyish-opaque when it hardens. Two harvests were possible in the time of Pliny the Elder, in the first century A.D. At that time, frankincense production was estimated at 2,500 tons to 3,000 tons, but myrrh averaged only 450 to 600 tons. In 1936 the British traveller Freya Stark, recorded that 1,200 tons of frankincense was exported from Dhufār and 800 from Somalia (the Arabian gum-resin being of superior quality). The production of the gum-resins is in decline today in the Arabia. Monod registered that in six months only 4,180 kilograms reached the port of Mukalla in 1967.

The caravan roads of the Nabataeans [Fig. 2]

In the Assyrian Annals, the Arabs were in possession of aromatics as early as the eight-seventh centuries B.C. In his campaign against Samsi, queen of the Arabs, Tiglat-Pileser III (745–727 B.C.) recorded 'a booty of 500 (bags) of all kind of spices' (*riqqu*). But it is difficult to guess what kind of aromatics the king received. Was it frankincense, was it myrrh or was it some other aromatic substances imported from India, such as nard, cinnamon or cassia?

In any case, if the queen of the Arabs could afford to offer to the Assyrian king such a large amount of spices, this means that the Arabs were active in the trade of aromatics during that period. They probably could procure the gum-resins either from south Arabia or from India. It was probably through the Gerrhaeans that Queen Samsi could obtain the spices. Later in the fifth century B.C., Herodotus (III, 97) asserts that the Arabs rendered a yearly gift of 1,000 talents of aromatics to the Achaemenid king. This was a huge amount equalling 26 tons of spices. It was not a tribute, but rather a present to the Persian king as a sign of loyalty to the Achaemenid Dynasty, because in 538 B.C. the edict of Cyprus the Great authorised the return of the exiles in their countries. The Arabs assisted Cambyses during his conquest of Egypt, and the Israelites were allowed to rebuild the walls and their Temple in Jerusalem, under the leadership of Nehemia, a cupbearer of the great king. The restoration of Salomon's Temple under Artaxerxes I in 428 B.C., required a good supply of frankincense and myrrh for the needs of the cult, and consequently the trade of aromatics flourished in Palestine. At Tell Jemmeh, ancient Yursa, on the south bank of Wadi al-Ghazzeh, an assemblage of thirty one incense-burning altars were found by Flinders Petrie (1928: 18–19). The site was located in a place in order to control the caravan routes from south Arabia to Egypt, Jerusalem, and markets in Phoenicia and from there to the Mediterranean (cf. Hassel 2005: 133). The chronology of the incense altars from Tell Jemmeh was estimated 'to have spanned the latter part of the seventh century to the middle of the fourth century B.C.' (Hassel *eod. loc.* 152). This period extended from the Assyrian campaigns of Palestine to the expedition of Nabonidus to Tayma in 552 B.C. The conquest of this city in north-west Arabia was decided by the last king of the Neo-Babylonian dynasty in order to divert the trade routes towards his capital Babylon. From that

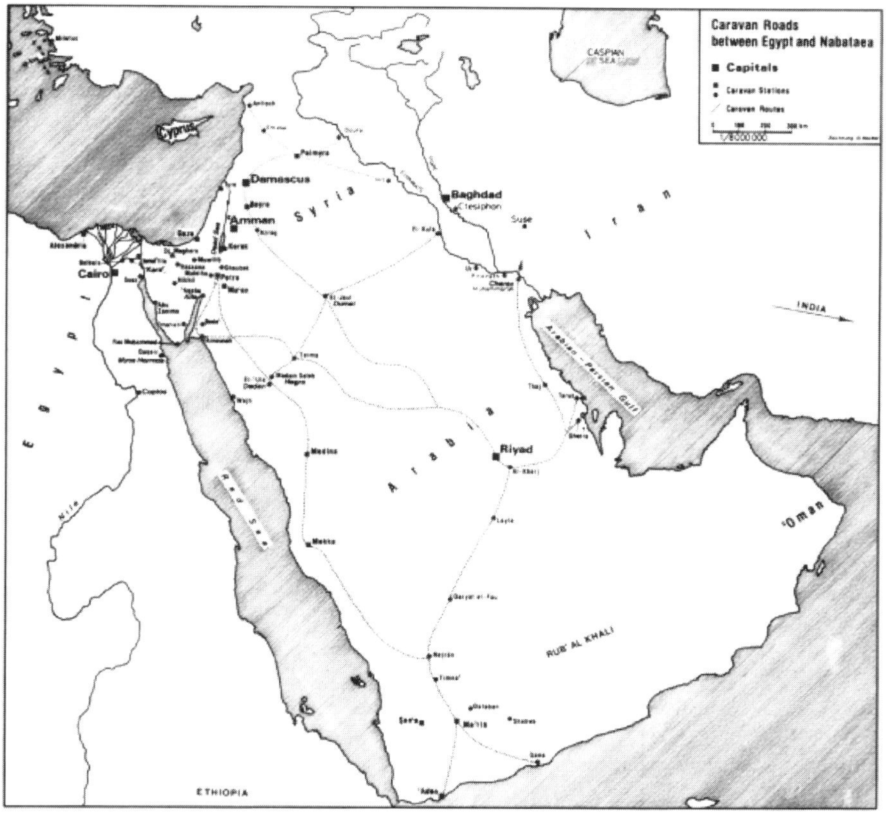

2. Map of sea and land trade routes of the Nabataeans

period on, many incense altars have been found in southern Mesopotamia, namely at Ur, the most southerly Babylonian city where Woolley unearthed many, incense altars (Wolley 1962: 103). The architectural context of these finds suggests that it was not a temple, but rather a domestic residence. (Russel *op.cit.* 156).

In his volume on the Palestinian incense altars, Stern distinguished four different groups (Stern 1973: 187–195). The first group, A, is decorated with a geometric design alone and exhibits strong Mesopotamian influence of the Assyrian-Babylonian periods in the sixth-fifth centuries B.C. The second group is decorated with 'reliefs of statuettes and represents the last phase of decline in the production'. The last group of Stern's examples in undecorated. In fact, Rahmani demonstrated that not all of the incense burners described by Stern are dated to the Persian period (Rahmani 1980: 116–122). One example, decorated with 'chip-carved triangles', is similar to Stern's type 22 and was dated by Rahmani to the sixth-eight centuries A.D. (1973: 195). As a matter of fact, several incense burners from the Umayyad period were discovered at Umm al-Walid, south of Madaba and at al-Fudein near

Mafraq (Humbert 1986: N° 353), and from the Amman Citadel (*La Voie Royale*, Luxembourg Exhibition: Paris, 1986, N° 369). [Fig. 3]

3. Incense burner from Umm al-Walid

The fifth to the fourth centuries B.C. is the period when the Arab-Nabataeans in southern Transjordan first appear. They resisted the attack of Athinaeus, the general of Antigonus in 311 B.C., but he was able to loot from their 'Rock' (probably as-Sela', near Tafileh) a large amount of frankincense and myrrh (Diodorus, XIX, 95: 3). The Nabataean caravaneers obtained the aromatics from South Arabia, mainly from western Hadramawt and from eastern Dhufār, in the district of Mahra. The gum-resins were stocked in large storage bins, called *mohr/mohor* in the local dialects, at the end of the monsoons in September. From there the aromatics were transported to the port of Mocha (ancient Musa) or to Ra's Fartak (Syagros) and to the major harbour of Qana, modern Bîr 'Ali, where excavations have been recently conducted by a Russian team (Sedov 1992: 110–137).

In a tomb at Umm Udheina in western Amman several bronze vessels were discovered, among which was a unique bronze censer carried by a caryatid figure dressed with a long tunic decorated by incisions and fastened by a tasselled belt [Fig. 4]. This censer was found amongst Attic *lekethoi* dating to the 5th century B.C. during the Persian period. [Fig. 5] It can be compared to a bronze incense burner which is supported by a woman dressed with a long folded *chiton* [Fig. 6]. This was found at Delphi in Greece and dates to the mid-5th century B.C. (Greek Art of Aegean Islands, 1979: fig 184).

4. Bronze censor supported by a caryatid figure from a tomb at Umm Udheina in western

5. Attic lekethos dating to 5th century B.C. found at Umm Udheina.

6. Bronze censor from Delphi in Greece. Mid-5th century B.C. (Greek Art of the Aegean Islands, New York 1979, fig. 184).

Shabwa, the capital of Hadramawt was reached by an overland track. The excavations and epigraphic research at Shabwa were undertaken by a French team (see Pirenne 1990 and Breton 1991). From this city the caravans proceeded to Ma'rib, the *Marsiaba* of Strabo (*Geog*., XVI, 4.24) and on to al-Jawf of Ma'in, the land of the Minaeans. If they continued north, they could reach Najran on the Yemeni-Saudi Arabia borders. From Medina Yathrib, the caravan road arrived at al-'Ula/Dedan and at Hegra/Mada'in Saleh. The caravan track headed north to Tabuk, in the Hisama of the Hijaz and reached Ma'an and Petra in southern Transjordan. A road through the Negueb started from Bîr Madhkur in the 'Araba Valley and Mayyet 'Awwad (possibly identified as 'Moa' on the mosaic map at Madaba), an important station with a spring and a large cistern. A fort on the hilltop protects a caravanserai, a hostel and 'cultural centre' (see Goren 2000: 110). This road was visited in 1998 via caravan from Petra reaching Gaza in four days. The road follows Wadi Omer and reaches the citadel of Qasra on a high knoll controlling the caravan tracks in to the deep depression of Ramon, an ancient crater 40 kms long and about 10 kms wide, formed along with the Jordan Rift Valley. The next station is the city of Avdat, ancient 'Obodat, named after the Nabataean King 'Obodat I (96–85 B.C.) who died at this station after his victory over King Antiochus XII in 87 B.C. (Bowersock 1983: 24). There is a large military camp at the site, as well as a temple and military barracks. 'Obodat was occupied during the Roman period but even more densely in the Byzantine period. After 'Obodat, al-Khalassa can be found at the beginning of the cultivated zone. An abundance of Nabataean pottery was discovered at the site. The last station passed before reaching Gaza was Rohobot, Nabataean Ruḥayba. Following the Besor, the road arrives at the port of Gaza. In ancient times the journey from Shabwa to Gaza lasted from 69 to 88 days.

A much-loved woman has been compared to a closed garden with all kinds of aromatic plants. The nard, from the Sanskrit *naladā* is of Indian origin (Robert, Tournay 1963: 87). It arrived in Europe through Persia (*eod. loc.*). The nard was known in Palestine as a very expensive perfume.

When Jesus was invited to the house of Lazarus, his sister Mary 'took half a litre of a very expensive perfume made of pure nard, poured it on Jesus' feet'. Judas Iscariot complained: "Why wasn't this perfume sold for three hundred silver coins and the money given to the poor?" One silver coin was the daily wage for a worker (*Good News Bible*, *Jn*, 12, 3–6; 6, 7). One may wonder how this costly Indian perfume could reach Palestine along with the other aromatic substances.

Saffron, *Crocus sativus*, is a perfumed plant which can grow in Syria-Palestine and the Lebanon but the calamus (*acorus calamus*) was found in Arabia and India. Cinnamon is the inner bark of a tropical tree of India. The trade with India was active in the first century B.C.-A.D. through the Red Sea or the Arabian Persian Gulf.

The Periplus Maris Erythraei is a precious document written in the mid-first century A.D. by a Greek sailor from Egypt as a handbook to supply information on the trade routes to India, the ports and the products which could be purchased or exchanged there (Casson 1989). On the western coast several harbours were frequented by Roman and Egyptian ships to obtain various spices. The two important ports on the northwest coast, Barbarikon and Barygaza were referred to in the *Periplus*. To reach them, ships had to leave the Red Sea in July to catch the monsoon which would convey them in twenty days (Casson 1989: 289). The return trip was in December or January (Pliny, *Natural History*, VI, 26; 101). The goods which could be obtained in these ports were: metals, corals, wine, glass and frankincense. This gum-resin was not brought from Arabia as it was assumed by Young (2001: 28), but was certainly a native product of India. This gum-resin was well known in India under the botanic terms of *Boswellia Serrata* (Salles 2004: 554). Ctesias, a Greek physician and historian of the 5th–4th century B.C., was captive at the royal court of Susa and produced his history, *Persika* in 23 volumes. He described an aromatic tree called rose-myrrh which produced very delicate aromatic tears. The king alone with his revenue could acquire this perfume. This remark of the Greek historian probably refers to a monopoly of the aromatic products by the king (cf. Salles 2004: 556, n.50). The other aromatic products which were obtained at the two ports were bdellium and nard.

Chinese silks were conveyed via the Indus River to those ports where they were purchased by Palmyrenes and Nabataeans. The Kitot tower tomb of Palmyra dated

A.D. 40 revealed textile finds that were either imported from China or woven locally in similar patterns as the Chinese silks (Stauffer 1996: 427). The Elahbel Tower Tomb dated. A.D. 103 was remarkable for the discovery of several fragments of textiles. One example was made of 'purple wool, whose quality is as fine and shining as silk'. Some weaving structures of silk fragments found in the same tomb 'is derived from the Han damaks' (Stauffer 1996: 427 and 429, fig.4; see also Pfister 1937: 1:35ff, note 2, and pl. 9a-d). The project for the study and analysis of the textiles of Palmyra was initiated by the Berne University, the German Archaeological Institute, and the German Cultural Aid Funds in cooperation with the General Directorate of Antiquities and Museums in Syria (cf. Schmidt-Colinet 1996: 418 and n.10). According to Schmidt-Colinet, 'the original textile finds from Palmyra prove that indeed local or oriental textiles patterns were transferred on stone sculpture and then architecture. But this assumption is unlikely. Whereas weavers followed patterns from workshop cartoons, stone masons and sculptors had different sources of designs.

It should be noted here, that no silk textiles have been found at Petra, even though the city was one of the major destinations of the 'silk road', according to Chinese documents. As recorded by the *Wei Lüleh* in a *Summary of the Wei Dynasty*, the regions of the far west (from the Chinese point of view) were designated as *Li-Kan* or *Li-Kien*. The German scholar Hirth (1885, reprinted in 1975) identified *Li-Kan* or *Li-Kien* with Petra (Graf 1996: 207), because this capital was known as *Reqem*, in a Nabataean inscription of Petra (Starcky 1965: 44–45). The letter R is missing in the Chinese alphabet and is usually substituted by L, transcription of a final M by N is common in the Chinese dialects (Graf 1996: 208). Since the Nabataeans were active on the Arabian/Persian Gulf, where the silk of China arrived, and succeeded to the Minaeans from at least the second century B.C. in the trade of spices, it is not surprising that Petra was recorded in the Chinese documents of the Han Dynasty in the second century B.C. and later.

In the first century B.C., the activity of the Nabataeans is illustrated by the arrival of the Magi in Bethlehem to offer to the child Jesus 'their gifts of gold, frankincense, and myrrh' (*Mt.* 2: 11). The gold is believed to be a variety of frankincense (Ryckmans 1951: 372–76). St Justin Martyr, a native of Neapolis (Nablus) identified the Magi as 'Arabian Princes' (*Dialogue*, LXXVII, 9). His assumption is reasonable when we consider that the Nabataeans were in control of the aromatic trade in the first century B.C.-A.D. The visit of the Magi was allegoric, and the intention of the Evangelist Matthew was to confirm the divine birth of Jesus Christ. It also reflects the active trade of spices from the east.

In Petra, several altars for incense burning have been recovered in the 'Winged Lions' temple (Hammond, 1994: 335, Fig. 3), together with unguentaria for the trade of perfumes (Johnson 1990: 235–248). From east of the Jordan, several artefacts have been discovered from the Persian period. At Tell al-Khaleifeh, near Ayla/'Aqaba, a large ovoid jar 'with short neck, collared rim and high ring base' and incised with two Minaean characters was discovered on the floor of a room belonging to level IV, dated to the sixth century B.C. (Fig 3a; cf. Glueck 1967: 22–23, Fig. 7). From a long inscription discovered at Yathil (modern Braqish), it can be

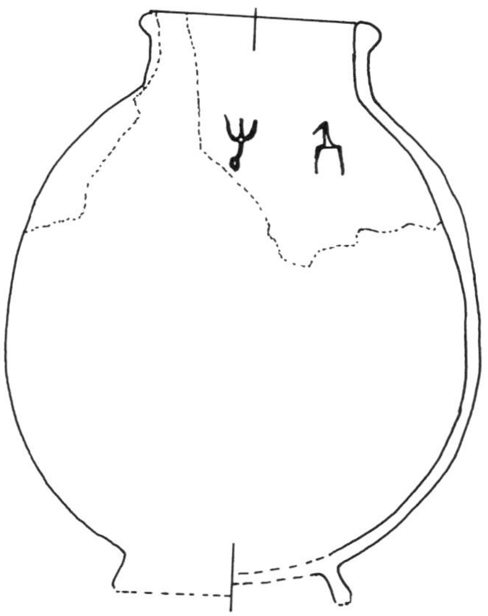

7. A jar with South Arabian letters from Tell el-Khaleifeh near Ayla/'Aqaba. 6th century B.C.

deduced that the Minaeans were active in the caravan trade in the sixth century B.C. (Robin 1991–93: 58–63). Other inscriptions from Yemen attest that the tribe of 'Amir, who was based in al-Jawf of Yemen controlled the spice trade.

After the conquest of Alexander the Great, the Minaeans were established in most of the emporia of the Mediterranean basin, from Gaza to Tyre, Sidon, to Delos where a dedication was found to the South Arabian god Wadd (*RES*, 3570=M 349). Their caravan tracks passed certainly by Ayla/'Aqaba, Petra, Gaza and through the Palestinian coast to Delos. They could cross the lower Galilee, at Dothan, as it was attested by the biblical narratives of *Genesis* (37) where the saga of Joseph, son of Jacob and his brothers is reported. The brothers were jealous of Joseph. When he came to visit them at Dothan, south-west of Beisan, in lower Galilee, they plotted to get rid of him, but finally they threw him in an empty cistern. When they noticed some Ismaelites (=Arabs), coming from Galaad, in northern Transjordan, with their camels laden with gum-resin, balsam and ladanum, which they transported to Egypt, they sold their brother to the Ismaelites for 'twenty pieces of silver' (*Gen.* 37: 2528). In verse 28 of the same chapter, the Ismalites are called 'Midianites'; they are Arabs from the Ḥisma of the Hijaz, in the area of Tabuk and Mad'in Shu'ayb. The changing of 'Ismaelites' by 'Midianites' was intentional to account for their load of Arabian spices.

The Book of Genesis is often dated to the 8th–7th centuries B.C., during the Assyrian period, when the Arabs, as noted above, were involved in the trade of aromatics (see Finkelstein, Silberman 2001: 66–69). But what is surprising in this narrative is the mention of 'balsam' coming from 'Galaad', when we know that this perfume was collected in the Jordan Valley, around Jericho and in the area of 'En-Gedi (Strabo, *Geog.*, 16,2:41; Pliny, *NH*, 12,III:123; Diodorus, 19, 98).

The Balsam of 'En Gedi

The plantation of balsam in the Jericho and 'En-Gedi areas were famous in antiquity and recorded by classical authors as mentioned above. Diodorus of Sicily reported valuable information about this aromatic plant: 'In a certain valley (Jericho) in this region there grows what is called balsam, from which there is a great income since nowhere else in the inhabited world is this plant found, and its use as a drug is very important to physicians' (19,198, 1).

It is not sure that balsam was growing only in the Jordan Valley. This perfume plant was so coveted by Cleopatra VII that she obliged King Herod the Great to give her the balsam groves of Jericho in 34 B.C. (Starcky 1966, col. 910). A workshop for the production of perfume was actually found at 'En Boqeq (Dayagi-Mendels 1993: 107–109). In a cave near Qumran, a very interesting discovery was made by Joseph Patrich. He found a first century A.D. juglet wrapped in palm fibre which contained an oily substance, most probably *apersemon* which derives from balsam plants (Diayagi-Mendels op. cit.: p. 10 and fig. 107 on the same page). Finally, it was recorded that the army of Vespasian who occupied Palestine and destroyed the Temple of Jerusalem in A.D. 69, raised the groves of balsam in the Jordan Valley.

References

Balsan, F. (1965) *A pied au nord Somalie*. Vichy.

Jérusalem Bible (1973) Paris, Cerf.

Breton, J.-F. ed. (1991) *Fouilles de Shabwa* 11, Rapports préliminaires (extraits de Syria T. LXVIII). Geuthner, Paris

Casson, L. (1989) *The Periplus Maris Erythraei*. Princeton Univ. Press.

Diagi-Mendels, M. (1993) *Perfumes and Cosmetics in the Ancient World*. The Israel Museum, Jerusalem.

Diodorus of Sicilus (1962) *Library of History*. Trans. Geer, R.M., Loeb, Class. Lib., London

Freedman, David Noel ed. (1991) Balsam, Balm. *The Anchor Bible Dictionary*. Volume 1: A-C. pg. 574, Doubleday, New York.

Glueck, N. (1967) Some Edomite Pottery from Tell el-_heleifeh. *BASOR* 188, 8–38.

Graf, D. (1996) The Roman East from the Chinese Perspective, in Palmyra and the Silk Road. *AAAS*, 42, 199–214.

(1979) Greek Art of Aegean Islands. The Metropolitan Museum of Art, New York

Groom, N. (1981) *Frankincense and Myrrh. A Study of the Arabian Incense Trade*. London and New York.

Hammond, Ph. (1994) The American Expedition to Petra, 1990–1993 seasons. *ADAJ*, 38: 335, fig. 3, ceramic incense burner.

Hasad (1980) at-tib al-Sha'bi. nadwat al-dirasat al- 'umaniyeh, 5 (in Arabic), al-Ghul, M., ed.

Johnson, D.J. (1990) Nabataean Unguentaria. *Aram*, 2, 1&2,235–248;

Hassel, D. J. (2005) A re-examination of the cuboid incense-burning altars from Flinders Petrie Palestinian excavations at Tell Jemmeh. *Levant*. 37: 133–162 ;

Leclant, J. (2005) *Dictionnaire de l'Antiquité*. art Pount, Paris, Puf.

Monod, TH. (1979) Les arbres à encens (Boswellia sacra Flükinger, 1967), dans le Hadramaout, *Bulletin du Musée National d'Histoire Naturelle* 4/1: 131–160.

Pfister, R., 1934, Textiles de Palmyre, id. 1937, Nouveaux textiles de Palmyre, id. 1940, Textíles de Palmyre 111 (in AAAS, 42, 1996: 427, n. 2).

Pliny (1989) *Natural History*. 11, trans< ; Rackam, R., London, Loeb, Clas. Lib.

RES, Répertoire d'épigraphie sémitique. Paris.

Robin, C., 1991–1993, cités; royaumes et empire de l'Arabie avant l'islam, in *l'Arabie de antique de Karb'il à Mahomet*, 61.

Robin, Ch. (1994) Les plantes aromatiques que brûlaient les Sabéens. in *Saba* 1.

Ryckmans, G. (1951) De l'or (?), de l'encens et de la myrrhe. *RB*, 58: 372–376.

Salles, J.-F. (2004) La péninsule arabique dans l'organisation des échanges du royaume séleucide, *Topoi*, Suppl. 6, 2004: 545–568.

Sayed, A.N., A.H. (2002) On the geographic location of the Land of Punt, *Aegyptus ad Pannonia* II: 203–237.

Schmidt-Colinet, A., Stauffer, A., Al-As'ad, Kh. (2000) *Die Textilen auf Palmyra, Neue und alte Funde, Mainz von Zabern*: Silk: 19, 142, 172, etc.

Smith, A. M. (2005) *Bir Madhkur Project: A Preliminary Report on Recent Fieldwork*. B.A.S.O.R. 340: 57–75.

Stark, F. (1936) *The Southern Gates of Arabia*. Great Britain.

Stauffer, A., Schmidt-Colinet, A. (2001) Zénobie et la richesse des tissus de Palmyre, Catalogue *Moi, Zénobie, reine de Palmyre*. Paris, Skira.

Stern, E. (1973) *Material Culture of the Land of the Bible in the Persian Period*, 538–332 B.C. Jerusalem.

Strabo, *Geography*, Trans. Jones (1966) London, Loeb, Classical Library

Woolley, L. and Mallowan, M.E.I. (1976) *Ur Excavations VII, The Old Babylonian Period*. British Museum Press, London.

Young, G. (2001) *Rome's Eastern Trade*. London and New York.

Zayadine, F. (1995) Cosmetic Techniques. A Historical and Botanical Approach. *SHAJ* V: 67–75.

Nabataean Water Supply, Irrigation, and Agriculture: An Overview

John Peter Oleson

The Nabataeans and their Environment

A full understanding of Nabataean society, economy, and settlement strategies depends in large part on a thorough knowledge of the way in which the Nabataeans dealt with the problems of water supply and agriculture in all regions of their largely desert kingdom. These technologies, of course, varied across time and space within the Nabataean kingdom. In much of the northern Nabataean territory or at higher altitudes, for example near Wadi Musa or around Amman, annual direct precipitation was sufficient to allow drought farming without extensive human intervention. But elsewhere, as at Petra or around ancient Hawara (modern Humayma),[1] all crops required direct irrigation or the harvesting of local run-off water. The provision of drinking water for humans and their domestic animals relied everywhere on some combination of cisterns, wells, springs, and aqueducts, but the character of each system varied according to local circumstances of topography and water sources, and techniques naturally evolved over time.[2] Nabataean hydraulic techniques were based in part on regimes inherited from their Bronze Age and Iron Age predecessors, and on some Hellenistic Greek accomplishments, but the final systems bear an unmistakable local stamp. Both large settlements such as Petra and small ones like Hawara depended on water-supply and agricultural systems that were the result of numerous interrelated decisions. The final arrangements were determined not only by local topography, geology, and hydrology, but also by size of population, character of the economic system, choice of crops and domestic animals, and political and cultural forces. This paper will present a brief account and analysis of the various water-manipulation regimes now documented for the Nabataeans before and after the Roman conquest, and their relationship to agriculture and irrigation. Unfortunately, we still know very little about many other issues associated with Nabataean water-supply: for example, the way in which projects were planned; the source of funding; the composition and organization of teams of designers and builders; construction procedures; the local administration of water and the ways in which consumption was metered or apportioned; the approach to ownership of run-off

[1] For an account of the excavations at Humayma, see now Oleson et al. 1999, 2003; Oleson 2001, 2003a.

[2] For a general study of ancient hydraulic technology, see now Wikander 2000. Oleson 1995 provides a survey of Nabataean hydraulic technology, and Oleson 2001b a survey of ancient hydraulic technology in Jordan; cf. also Oleson 1992, 2003b.

potential or the output of springs or the contents of pools and cisterns; responses to variation in precipitation, run-off, or spring flow; religious beliefs and rituals surrounding consumption; and actual consumption rates for humans, large and small livestock, and crops. Nevertheless, survey, excavation, and historical analysis all continue to contribute to advances in our knowledge of Nabataean water systems. This brief account will culminate in the summary analysis of the water-supply system at Hawara, as an example of the progress that has been made.

In the late first century B.C., Diodorus of Sicily, using information from the third-century historian Hieronymos of Kardia, wrote a striking and controversial description of the Nabataeans (19.94.2–10):

> "They live in the open air, claiming as native land a wilderness that has neither rivers nor abundant springs from which it is possible for a hostile army to obtain water. It is their custom neither to plant grain, set out any fruit-bearing tree, use wine, nor construct any house... Some of them raise camels, others sheep, pasturing them in the desert. ...Whenever a strong force of enemies comes near, they take refuge in the desert, using this instead of a fortress. For the desert lacks water and cannot be crossed by others, but to them alone it furnishes safety, since they have prepared subterranean reservoirs lined with plaster... After filling these cisterns with rain water, they close the openings, making them even with the rest of the ground, and they leave signs that are known to themselves but are unrecognizable to others..."

Archaeological research suggests that this passage, although romanticized for the sake of historiographical contrast, reflects fairly accurately the character of early Nabataean society, and the resources upon which it depended.[3] The early Nabataeans were wandering pastoralists who lived largely off the land and shifted their flocks of sheep, goats, and camels from place to place depending on season and the condition of the pasturage. The water that sustained them in the desert was for the most part run-off from the meager precipitation that fell in the winter months and was stored in plastered cisterns cut in the bedrock. There were no rivers in Edom, the arid Nabataean heartland, and the infrequent springs seldom flowed in significant volume; often they were no more than seepages. Except for a few small areas around the peaks of the mountains towering over the Wadi Arabah, precipitation is less than 100 mm per year, and for most of Edom it ranges between 25 and 75 mm. Because of the strong, constant sunshine and the low humidity, the rate of evaporation is very high.[4]

Nevertheless, according to Diodorus' source – confirmed by recent archaeological surveys – this dramatically beautiful desert landscape supported a significant human population and their animals.[5] The Nabataeans clearly were able to make the best of their meager resources. In another well-known passage, the historian Strabo, writing a generation after Diodorus, ostensibly describes Nabataean society of the late first century B.C. (16.4.26):

[3] There is a long discussion of the descriptions of the Nabataeans by Diodorus and Strabo in Dijkstra 1995, 297–307, with citation of previous literature; also Hackl et al. 2003.

[4] National Atlas 1984, Salameh & Bannayan 1993, Henry 1983.

[5] E.g. Jobling 1986, 1989.

"The Nabataeans are a sensible people, and they are so much inclined to acquire possessions that they publicly fine anyone who has diminished his possessions and also confer honours on anyone who has increased them... They prepare common meals together in groups of thirteen persons, and they have two girl-singers for each banquet. The king holds many drinking-bouts in magnificent style, but no one drinks more than eleven cups of wine, each time using a different golden cup. Their homes, through the use of stone, are costly; but on account of peace, the cities are not walled. Most of the country is well supplied with fruits except the olive; they use sesame oil instead. The sheep are white-fleeced and the cattle are large, but the country produces no horses. Camels afford the service they require instead of horses."

The striking differences between Diodorus' lean, foxy nomads and the hedonistic, settled Nabataeans described by Strabo are usually attributed to social and economic changes that transformed Nabataean society between the early third and the first centuries B.C. According to Strabo's sources, the new culture included a developed monarchy, small-scale urbanism with elaborate stone houses, agriculture (including fruit trees and vineyards), more diverse herds of animals-including cattle, a very demanding addition – and luxurious possessions associated with sophisticated manufacture and long-distance trade. There were also new social habits such as the consumption of alcohol, most spectacularly at the symposium, or public drinking party on the Greek model. The technology of water supply is not mentioned, but implicit in the overall picture are more sophisticated structures and techniques than the rock-cut cisterns mentioned by Diodorus. Although this model of two comprehensive, monolithic stages in Nabataean cultural development has now been challenged,[6] the reality of an arid environment is not in doubt. How were these materialistic wine-drinkers and flute girls, their homes, herds, and fields supplied with water in an environment just as arid in the first century B.C. as it had been in the third and as it is today? The higher standard of living may have been in large part the result of the switch from a mainly nomadic way of life to a settled one, a process that has worked in both directions in this region for millennia in response to political and environmental conditions. But this settled life depended both on the more intensive application of traditional Iron Age water-harvesting techniques and on the introduction of new techniques from the Hellenistic world. In addition, it is possible that Strabo or his source is describing or conflating information concerning Nabataeans encountered farther north, in Moab or Ammon, where the soil was richer, precipitation more abundant, and farming was possible without any form of irrigation. By the mid-first century A.D., some form of Nabataean political control or influence extended as far as Damascus, and inscriptions document the spread of Nabataean individuals throughout the Hauran.[7] In a period of relative stability, these individuals would have been living off the fat of the land, compared with the clans in the south. Strabo's comment about the absence of olive

[6] Dijkstra 1995, 297–307 proposes that both authors present selective visions of a society that was in fact more diverse, and that sedentarization was already well underway in the fourth century B.C. Schmid 2001, however, marshals convincing evidence that sedentarization in fact only commenced about 100 B.C.

[7] Wenning 1987, 22–75.

trees says more about Nabataean culinary tastes than about the location of his sample population, since the olive tree can flourish in the desert if a run-off field is provided, and they are mentioned in documents concerning Nessana and Hawara.[8] Horses, of course, would have been an enormous luxury in the desert regions of the kingdom, but it is also difficult to envisage the raising of "large cattle" with the fodder available there.[9]

Nevertheless, much of Strabo's account concerns Edom and the Hijaz, and archaeological research has proven that Petra developed into an urban site only in the course of the first centuries B.C. and A.D., and that many smaller settlements flourished in the southern desert regions.[10] It is important to try to reconstruct the mechanisms and the extent of this dramatic social change, along with its motivations. The development of appropriate water-supply techniques and systems clearly must have constituted an important factor.

Early Techniques of Water Management in Trans-Jordan

The techniques of water management can be grouped under the headings of collection, transport, and storage. For most of the desert areas of the Nabataean kingdom, collection of water was the most important consideration. One characteristic of a desert landscape is that precipitation runs off the surface unimpeded and collects in short-lived torrents that fill the wadis and grow in force until they empty into mud flats or cross permeable geological strata. Although meager and very localized, precipitation does fall reliably in the desert areas of the former Nabataean kingdom nearly every year, and the secret of survival was the knowledge of how to harvest it. The obvious techniques had been discovered by the Late Bronze and Iron Age and put to work throughout the arid areas of the Near East. The terracing of hillsides is the most visible of these early methods: heavy stone walls built across the slope of a hill captured both run-off water and the particles of earth it carried.[11] The deposit of soil gathered and protected in this fashion served in turn as a sponge to hold moisture to sustain the crops planted on the level surface. In a variation of this technique, walls were built across wadis that carried the occasional run-off from a catchment area.[12] Although vulnerable to damage, walls and fields in such a location were more likely to receive significant run-off and alluvial soil than the terraces on the slopes above.

The containment dam, in contrast to the wadi barrier that merely slowed down the water flow, was designed to trap and hold a pool of water. This type of dam was attempted in arid regions of the Near East as early as the Early Bronze Age, but seldom with much success.[13] The barrier wall had to be impermeable,

[8] Evenari, Shanan, Tadmor 1982, 122, 208; Mayerson 1961, 17–21; Hawara, below, n. 57.

[9] Jobling 1989 proposes that the representation of what may be bovine animals in rock art in the Hisma points to the existence of a better grazing regime in antiquity than today in that region.

[10] Stucky et al. 1996, Schmid 2001.

[11] Ron 1966, Bruins 1990.

[12] Evenari, Shanan, Tadmor 1982, *passim*.

[13] Hodge 2000, Garbrecht 1987–1991.

Fig. 1: Water collection channel and cistern opening, Umm Biyara (Petra).

capable of withstanding the shock of the water's sudden arrival, its erosive action as it poured over the spillway, and the weight and percolation of the standing pool. The bedrock, too, had to be more or less impermeable. Some ancient dams were spectacular failures, such as the Old Kingdom, Egyptian Wadi Garawi dam, which seems to have collapsed at its first filling.[14] Even when structurally successful, containment dams provided a pool of water that was subject to evaporation and to pollution by bird and animal droppings and by plant, insect, and animal life in the pool itself. Nevertheless, large dams were built in the Early and Middle Bronze Age at Jawa, Tel el-Handaquq and other sites in the region.[15]

From the Early Bronze Age on, cisterns have been the preferred method for storing drinking water in the Near East.[16] The entry of water was controlled, and the captured water was protected from evaporation and pollution. Hand in hand with advances in cistern design, the archaeological record shows progress in the creation of plasters resistant to the percolation and erosive effect of the water. By the Iron Age, the Edomites, who gave their name to the Nabataean heartland, had adopted a rock-cut, bottle-shaped cistern appropriate to their needs, and examples can be seen in large numbers at habitation sites such as Umm Biyara above Petra (Fig. 1) and es-Sil' near Buseirah. Such cisterns were cut into the bed-rock close to the focus of a natural catchment and provided with small feeder channels to

[14] Garbrecht 1984, 5.
[15] Mabry 1989.
[16] Brinker 1990.

Fig. 2: Pool of 'Ain Abu an-Nusur Spring, northwest of Hawara.

lead the water into the draw-hole or a special intake hole, which expanded into a circular tank three to four metres wide. This type of cistern remained in use among the early Nabataeans and is described by Diodorus (19.94.7): "They have prepared subterranean cisterns lined with plaster... As the landscape in some places is...of soft stone, they make great excavations in it, the mouths of which they make very small, but by constantly increasing the width as they dig deeper, they finally make them up to one plethron wide." The dimension cited, approximately 27 m, is a gross exaggeration.

The infrequent springs and seepages of Edom, for the most part found among the strata exposed by the al-Shera escarpment or the Dead Sea rift, were always a focus for human activity. At 'Ain al-Jammam and nearby 'Ain Abu an-Nusur (Fig. 2) north of Hawara, occupation dates from the Pre-Pottery Neolithic B.[17] As pools became muddy from frequent use, they would be cleared out, eventually lined with stone, and earth channels or, less often, conduits cut in stone blocks, provided to carry the overflow to adjacent artificial access basins or fields. The qattar, or site where water seeps from an exposed aquifer, is exploited by trimming back the original face and by cutting runnels and basins to concentrate and collect the water. (Fig. 3) A natural basin below the Muqawwar cascades at the foot of the al-Shera escarpment southeast of Ras en-Naqb was enlarged at some time during the Edomite or Nabataean periods to accommodate both sur-

[17] Waheeb 1996: 342.

Fig. 3: Enhanced water seep (*qattar*), Petra.

face run-off water and the seepage from an aquifer.[18] The numerous pictographs and inscriptions cut on the bedrock in the area of the basin highlight the high level of human and faunal activity this water source attracted.

Some of the wells that survive in this region may well go back to the pre-Nabataean period, but it is often difficult to date this type of structure. The Old Testament and other early sources certainly mention the use of wells, sometimes at sites later occupied by Nabataeans, such as Rehovot (Gen 26:22) and Be'er Sheva ("Well of Seven" or "Well of Oath", Gen 21.28–31, 26.33).[19]

Water transport was less well developed in this early period. Although conduits might be used for restricted local distribution around a spring, extensive aqueduct systems to not seem to have existed in the area of the kingdom prior to the first or second century B.C. Earthen channels can serve local needs, but over long distances in a hot climate they are not efficient for the transport of the small volumes of water available in Moab or Edom. The stone conduit blocks with deep longitudinal channel invariably used in Nabataean aqueducts (Fig. 4) can be found in various eastern-Mediterranean and Near Eastern water-systems as early as the Late Bronze Age, but they do not appear to have been used to transport water more than a few metres.

[18] Jobling 1989: 18–23.
[19] Oleson 1992, 885–87.

Fig. 4: Conduit channels of 'Ain Ghana aqueduct, Hawara.

Nabataean Water-Supply Techniques and Systems

These were the techniques and resources available to the early Nabataeans as they moved into the southern desert and Edom-possibly from northeastern Arabia and possibly as early as the fifth century B.C. Judging from the rapidity with which their culture spread through a large new territory, the Nabataeans undoubtedly already knew the appropriate methods of harvesting the scanty desert precipitation. But in the course of the second and first centuries B.C., new techniques and administrative approaches appeared, probably first in response to a growing population and more frequent transit through the desert, then in response to the shift to a more settled, agricultural economy. Since many of these techniques-such as the arch-roofed cistern-remained in use through the Byzantine period throughout the area occupied by Nabataean communities – from the Hauran on the north to the Hejaz on the south, and west across the Negev to the Mediterranean coast – it is very difficult to document the precise time and place of their introduction. Nevertheless, excavations at Humayma, ancient Hawara, a Nabataean settlement in southern Jordan, and recent surveys at Petra, suggest that the first century B.C. was a period of particularly rapid innovation. This period, of course, also saw the appearance of Nabataean coins, inscriptions, and Hellenized art styles.[20]

[20] Schmid 2001.

Fig. 5: Rock-cut channel feeding Nabataean cistern, Hawara.

Although we do not know many details, the Nabataeans also developed their own administrative systems for the crucial water supply. An inscription dated 6 B.C. found at the cult centre of Khirbet at-Tannur, for example, mentions an individual with the title "Master of the spring of La'ban," a nearby site.[21] The title is generally taken to refer to a government official appointed to supervise distribution of spring water at La'ban; the water conduits can still be seen around the site. On a higher administrative level, it has also been suggested that the titles bestowed on King Aretas IV, "He who loves his People," and on King Rabbel II, "He who brought life and deliverance to his people," had their origins in the enthusiastic support of these monarchs for agricultural development and water-supply systems.[22] An inscription found at Petra indicates that either King Malichos II or King Rabbel II built the dam and tunnel that diverted run-off water around the Siq, and it is clear that the complex, interrelated water-control and water-supply systems that can still be traced around the large area of the ancient city must have been the result of careful planning, funding, and administration at a high social level.[23] Such structures included several spring-fed aqueduct systems, numerous reservoirs, containment and retention dams, run-off collection fields, qattars, wadi barriers, and agricultural terraces. Smaller complexes of

[21] Glueck 1965, 138, 512–14.

[22] Negev 1963, Hillel 1982, 124.

[23] Parr 1967. On the urban water-supply system of Petra, see al-Muheisen 1990; the important survey and restoration of the Siq and its water system appears in Bellwald and al-Huneidi 2003.

Fig. 6: Wadi barrier fields, and run-off water collection channels on valley slope, Avdat.

terraces, run-off fields, and cisterns could also be the result of individual initiative. A Dedanite inscription in Wadi Ramm records the efforts of two individuals who built some sort of structure that "collected rain water at Diwah."[24] In any case, the repertoire of structures and techniques available to the Nabataeans for the collection, transport, and storage of water from the second century B.C. onward was more sophisticated than that of their Iron Age predecessors.

Bed-rock or earthen catchment areas could be adapted to human needs by the construction of containment walls or the cutting of channels to catch water at the edges of a slope or to divert it towards a cistern intake. Features of this type were relatively easy to arrange on bedrock slopes, and around Petra and Hawara many of them still function today. (Figs. 1, 5) The enhancement of run-off on earth slopes, however, required more careful management. Original earth conduits have survived at a few sites, most notably at Avdat and Subeita in the Negev, and reveal the character of the system, which must have required frequent maintenance.[25] Shallow trenches were cut across the slope and reinforced on the down-slope side with field stones. (Fig. 6, across the hillside) These features intercepted the run-off water and channeled it at a gentle fall rate (to avoid excessive erosion) to the target field or cistern.

It was also possible to increase the run-off yield of an earthen slope. Large areas of the gravelly slopes around many of the Nabataean sites in the Negev are

[24] Farès-Drappeau 1995.
[25] Evenari, Shanon, Tadmor 1982, 103.

covered with geometric patterns formed by field stones piled in regular heaps or lines.[26] (Fig. 7) Removal of the surface stones on these slopes allowed the soil to crust over when it was moistened by rain and thus increased the yield of run-off water. Erosion of the exposed soil by wind and water meant that continued clearing of exposed stones was essential, and today the surface soil has largely disappeared under the accumulation of exposed gravel and cobbles. It has not been possible to date these features precisely, but it is usually assumed they were created during the flowering of the major Nabataean settlements of the Negev in the first century B.C. or A.D.; they may, however, belong to the agricultural florescence of the Byzantine period.[27] The excellent preservation of the archaeological landscape has allowed calculation that the ratio of the area of a catchment field to its targeted agricultural field could range from 1:17 to 1:30, which-allowing for absorption and other losses – might multiply the local precipitation by a factor between 2 and 5.[28] In the Nabataean territories of Jordan, catchment fields enhanced in this way are very rare, either because of differences in local rainfall patterns and crops, or because of the absence of a Byzantine agricultural boom there. One example of such a field can be seen near Hawara.

Fig. 7: Run-off enhancement field with stone piles, Wadi Laban near Subeita

[26] Evenari, Shanon, Tadmor 1982, 127–48,

[27] Rosen 2000.

[28] The ratio of catchment field area to cultivated field area varies from site to site, probably because of differences in local topography, soils, crops, and precipitation: Rosen 2000, 21:1; Hillel 1982, 146–47, from 1:17 to 1:30. Kedar 1957, 184 estimates the run-off from this type of slope at 10 to 15 percent of the precipitation.

Another advance of the Middle Nabataean period was the application of wadi barriers to divert excess water flow into channels that carried it to fields above the unpredictable wadi bed proper.[29] This arrangement both expanded the area of watered fields and avoided the loss of soil and moisture that resulted when the rush of water down a wadi breached a barrier wall. There are spectacular examples in the Wadi Laban near Subeita and Nahal Zin near Avdat. (Fig. 8)

Fig. 8: Terraced fields fed by Wadi Laban near Subeita.

Containment dams represented a different approach altogether. Small dams built across steep-walled gullies to form cisterns or detainment pools to slow the arrival of flood water are common in the sandstone topography of Petra and other Nabataean settlements in southern Jordan, but these small barrier walls do not involve the engineering difficulties of large containment dams. The best examples of large dams in this region are three at Mampsis in the Negev which barred the main wadi and created pools holding 10,000 cubic metres of water. (Fig. 9) The date of their construction is still not certain, but an origin in the first or second century has been proposed on historical grounds.[30] The containment walls, built of mortared blocks, had vertical faces upstream and sloping walls downstream for buttressing. Recent rebuilding has concealed the original spillway arrangement. A smaller dam (10.7 m long, 4.4 m thick) at Hawara had a

[29] Evenari, Shanon, Tadmor 1982, 95–119.

[30] Kloner 1973; Rubin 1988; Lindner 1987 provides a survey of Nabataean containment dams, including these.

Fig. 9: Nabataean or Roman dam, Mampsis.

Fig. 10: Nabataean dam south of Hawara.

narrow enough span and was thick enough that buttressing was not necessary.[31] (Fig. 10) On this structure, the spillway, always the most vulnerable point on a containment dam, was cut in the bedrock to one side of the mortared masonry wall. The reservoir held approximately 1400 cubic metres of water, made accessible by steps cut in the steep rock wall of the canyon at one side. The pools behind the dams at both Mampsis and Hawara are now filled to the brim with silt and sand, reminding us that constant maintenance by interested parties was necessary to keep this sort of structure functioning properly. The dam across the upstream end of the Siq at Petra was designed simply to divert the water through a tunnel, leaving the original wadi bed free as a road.

Water held behind dams or stored in cisterns had to be lifted out by hand in containers and carried to its place of use. There is so far no evidence that mechanical water-lifting devices were used in the Nabataean world, although the application of the shaduf to low lifts is very likely. This device would have been suitable at Nessana, for example, where papyri record the presence of cisterns and irrigation channels serving an agricultural field.[32] Spring water usually flows of its own accord and could be carried down-slope in aqueducts to a location more convenient for use or storage. Nabataean aqueducts, unlike Roman systems, were almost entirely ground level structures, dependent on natural slopes to provide their fall. The water was carried in a channel usually about 12 cm wide and 15 cm deep cut lengthwise into blocks of sandstone, marl, or limestone 60 to 90 cm long. (Fig. 4) The blocks were placed end to end and held in position by framing walls. This type of water channel was used in the area of the Nabataean kingdom from at least the first century B.C. through the Early Islamic period.[33]

Aqueducts of this type were constructed at most major springs in the region, varying in length from several metres to the record 26.5 km documented for the system serving Hawara. The aqueduct that carried the water from 'Ain Musa to Petra was approximately 8 km long, while the 'Ain Brak aqueduct was slightly shorter. The conduit carrying the water from 'Ain Shellaleh in Wadi Rum to the adjacent sanctuary was only 1.5 km long.[34] These conduits fed reservoirs either along their courses or at their termination. Because of the exiguous water supply in Nabataea and the smaller population, aqueduct systems were constructed even when the discharge would be a tiny fraction of the amount carried by the typical Hellenistic or Western Roman aqueduct. While the water channel of the Pont de Gard near Nîmes was approximately one metre wide and deep, and its flow 20,000 cubic metres per day, the channel of the main aqueduct serving Petra was 15 cm square and had a maximum flow of no more than 500 cubic metres per day.[35] The long conduit serving Hawara could have discharged at most 148.6 cubic metres per day. The date of the introduction of the qanat to this region, a

[31] Oleson 1991a.

[32] Kraemer 1958: no. 31, 32; for a survey of water-lifting devices, see Oleson 2000a.

[33] Eadie and Oleson 1986, 61–70; Oleson 1995.

[34] Petra, see Lindner and Hübl 1997; Ramm, Savignac 1932.

[35] Nîmes, Hodge 1992, 347; Petra, U. Bellwald, Oral Communication, March 2001.

subterranean conduit excavated by means of the chain of access shafts, is still uncertain. It may belong to the Islamic period, but in any case, it was rarely used in Arabia Petraea. There are examples at Udruh southeast of Petra, and at Yotvata in the Wadi Araba.[36]

Several well preserved stretches of a typical ground-level conduit along the Hawara aqueduct have been excavated and provide useful information on design and construction.[37] The conduit blocks were laid end-to-end in a bedding of crumbly mortar and fist-sized rubble, framed by roughly trimmed blocks and boulders. (Figs. 4, 11) A course of small stones set in plaster ran along either side of the channel to support heavy, partly trimmed cover slabs, intended to prevent obstruction, the entry of pollutants, evaporation, and diversion of the water. There is evidence that during the last years water flowed through the aqueduct to Hawara, portions of the conduit were left uncovered, allowing algae or grass to grow in the channel. The tiny stalks attracted calcium carbonate deposits, which grew rapidly until they blocked the channel with a mass of worm-like concretions. Aqueducts are always expensive and difficult to build, required constant observation and maintenance, and are easily disrupted. It is no wonder that public reservoirs and private cisterns filled by run-off water remained important to the people of Hawara even after the construction of the aqueduct system and the reservoir it fed. To Nabataean eyes, harvesting desert precipitation was a more dependable form of water-supply than reliance on a long, spring-fed conduit. Many of the cisterns remain in use today, while the aqueduct has been dry for 1,500 years. The same dependence on cisterns fed by local run-off water can be seen even at Petra, which was served by a shorter conduit fed by a far more generous spring.

Because of their smaller scale, the design requirements of Nabataean aqueducts were more flexible than those of Roman aqueducts, but the rugged landscape nevertheless presented challenges. Where necessary, Nabataean engineers supported their ground-level aqueducts with heavy support walls, viaduct bridges, slab bridges over small gullies, channels cut across bed-rock cliffs, and-at Petra, arched bridges over gorges or run-off channels. (Fig. 12) Although the Nabataean aqueduct system at Petra incorporated terracotta pipelines for part of its course, and at Hawara for the local distribution system, so far, there is only one documented example of an intentionally pressurized section along the main line of a Nabataean aqueduct (as opposed to a terminal distribution system): a 60 m stretch at the end of the 'Ain Brak aqueduct at Petra.[38] A conduit of heavy ceramic pipes carried water down the right side of the Siq at Petra, but it is unlikely to have been a pressurized system, since it continued to function after the tops of the pipes had been cut off to allow removal of sinter. Because the carrying capacity of their conduits was relatively small, Nabataean hydraulic engineers could lay out channels down slopes that were unthinkable to Roman engineers,

[36] Kennedy and Riley 1990, 70–76; Killick 1987; Graf 1997, 129; Goblot 1979.

[37] Oleson 1988, 158–60.

[38] U. Bellwald, Oral Communication, March 2001.

Fig. 11: Preserved section of 'Ain Ghana aqueduct, Hawara.

Fig. 12: Arch carrying northern al-Hubtha aqueduct over Se'b Qes, Petra.

and they readily incorporated into their systems sharp bends and sudden changes in level. Vitruvius proposes a slope of 0.5 percent as appropriate for a aqueduct channel, and surviving Hellenistic and Roman aqueducts typically have slopes between two percent and 0.03 percent.[39] The overall slope of the aqueduct leading to Hawara is 2.5 percent, but at points where the channel descends the al-Shera escarpment, the channel slope varies from an impressive ten to an astonishing fifty percent! Although the technology is typically Nabataean, the scale of the Hawara aqueduct project may reflect a familiarity on the part of King Aretas III – who boasted the title "Philhellene" – with Hellenistic aqueduct systems in the eastern Mediterranean, particularly that of Pergamon.[40] It certainly represents an impressive investment of social resources.

When an aqueduct arrived at the target settlement, metering tanks divided the water up among various sub-conduits or pipelines leading to public reservoirs and cisterns, public baths, and possibly to private cisterns and agricultural plots. In the Nabataean region, these are large basins, either block built or monolithic, with three or four discharge holes or spouts at a slightly lower level than the intake hole. A particularly well-preserved basin of this type is still in situ at the end of the water system feeding the main cistern at Subeita. A distribution basin identical in function but slightly different in design appears toward the end of the 'Ain Brak aqueduct at Petra.[41] (Fig. 13) The Romans, who termed this feature a *castellum aquae* or *dividiculum*, installed them at the terminus of an aqueduct to divide the water up in carefully calculated proportions among conduits serving a variety of public and private purposes, or simply to allow intermittent delivery to various mains throughout the day.[42] At Hawara, after passing through a small monolithic division basin of this type (D 0.50 m), the aqueduct filled a large, shallow reservoir with a capacity of 633 cubic metres on the edge of the settlement centre. (Fig. 14) It is unclear what other destinations the tank might have served, but the continuous stream of overflow water leaving the reservoir was carried off in conduits and terracotta pipelines to serve a bath building, private cisterns, a shrine, and possibly small orchards and vegetable gardens south of the settlement. At Petra, the 'Ain Brak system fed a large reservoir or swimming pool 23 by 46 m, built in the monumental centre of the city in the first century A.D. Although the water was undoubtedly meant for use, the reservoir accommodated an island retreat and was connected with a public garden, providing a striking spectacle of watery abundance in the centre of this desert city, and publicly reaffirming the royal competence in hydraulic technology.[43] The Hawara pool may have had a similar symbolic function.

[39] Hodge 1992, 171–91, 347.

[40] Garbrecht 1987, Fahlbusch 1982, 34–93.

[41] Similar basins were found beneath downspouts in the water-collecting system of the North Church complex at Nessana; Eadie and Oleson 1986: 63–64. 'Ain Brak, Lindner and Hübl 1997.

[42] See discussion in Hodge 1992: 279–91. The more explicit term castellum divisorium is modern.

[43] Bedal 1999, 2000.

Fig. 13: Aqueduct water distribution basin, 'Ain Brak aqueduct, Petra.

Fig. 14: Nabataean reservoir (no. 63) served by 'Ain Ghana Aqueduct, Hawara.

Reservoirs with constantly flowing water do not need roofs, but dead-end cisterns do. Otherwise, the water is lost to evaporation, infested with plant and insect life, and polluted by the excrement of animals brought there to drink from troughs. The traditional bottle-shaped cistern cut into bedrock, or course, was well protected from the sun and pollution, but it had to be located where suitable bedrock was available in conjunction with an appropriate run-off field. The roofing of built cisterns, however, was a problem in Arabia Petraea, since slabs of the friable sandstone typical of the desert regions could not span any significant distance, and timber was unavailable. The solution was adoption of a Hellenistic Greek cistern design, in which the cistern was spanned with transverse arches, of which the extrados were leveled off with filler blocks to support roofing slabs.[44] (Fig. 15) This design, probably seen in use by Nabataean merchants visiting Delos and other arid Aegean islands, allowed the construction of cisterns wherever they were needed, and wherever the catchment area was most suitable, such as at the site of Hawara. The two public cisterns there were roofed with 16 arches, carrying a roof of heavy stone slabs well chinked and sealed with mortar, so that people and animals could move around and even over them without hazard to themselves or the precious water within. (Fig. 16)

Fig. 15: Theatre reservoir, Delos.

[44] Oleson 1995, 716–18.

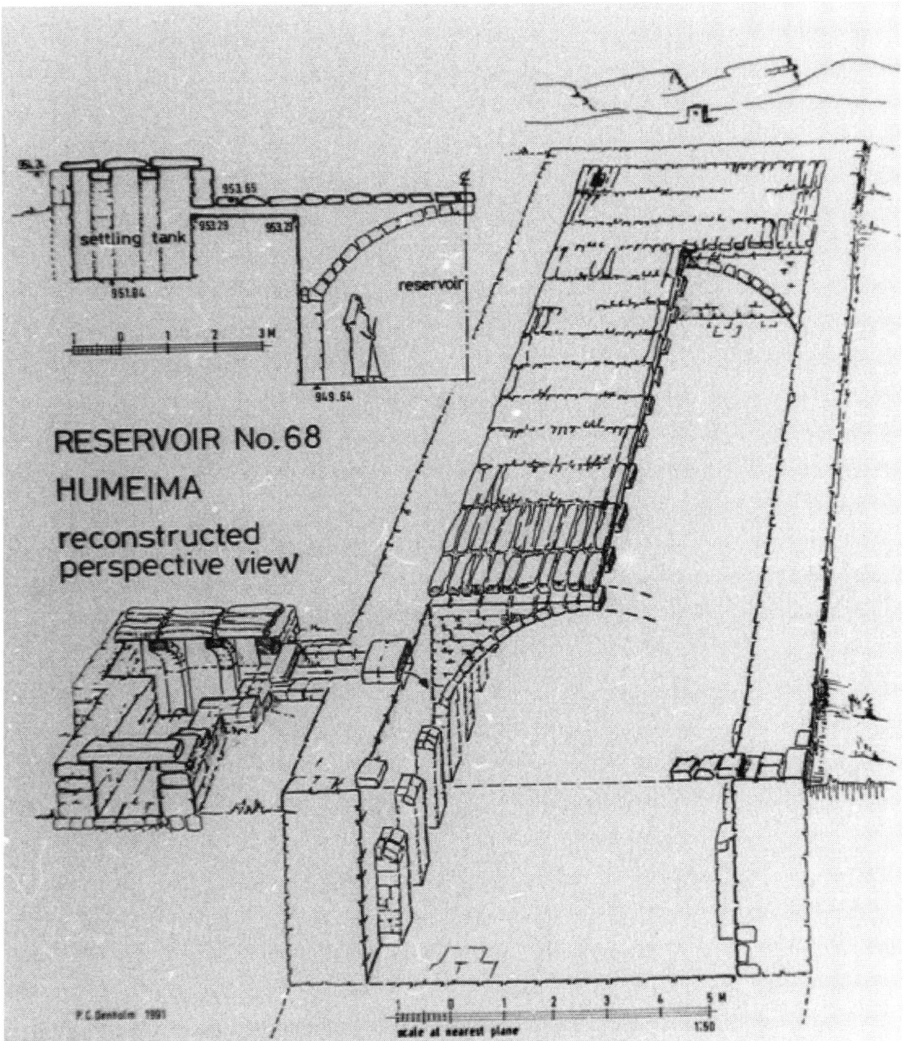

Fig. 16: Nabataean reservoir no. 68, Hawara, reconstruction.

This cistern design, applied to both rectangular and round plans, quickly became typical of virtually every Nabataean site, and the method of roofing was soon applied to the stone houses of which the newly sedentarized Nabataeans were so proud, as at Avdat and Mampsis. Cisterns and houses continued to be roofed in this manner throughout the region until the early modern period. The design was applied to rock-cut cisterns as well, and there are numerous surviving examples, many still in use, around the area of the former Nabataean kingdom. All cisterns needed a settling tank near the intake, which allowed the debris carried by the run-off water to settle out before the water spilled over into the main tank.

In Arabia Petraea the topography and geology did not favour the use of wells, but where conditions were appropriate, the Nabataeans did dig them. In the western and southern parts of the Negev, where the sandy soil made the collection of run-off water impossible, wells appear at Nessana, Eleusa, and Rehovot. At Avdat a very deep well (60 m) was dug through solid rock to reach an aquifer to supplement locally available run-off water. The well at Rehovot, which may go back to the Late Bronze Age, was even deeper (100 m).[45]

The Water-Supply System of Hawara

The enormous water-control and water-supply system serving Petra is still being explored, but the water-supply system at the small desert settlement of Hawara has been thoroughly studied and can serve as an example for most of the techniques and structures used by the Nabataeans in the first centuries B.C. and A.D.[46] As at Petra, some sort of royal involvement is implicit. Hawara most likely was founded in the 80s B.C. by King Aretas III (possibly before his accession to the throne) halfway between the port of Aila (Aqaba) and Petra, on the caravan route that later became the Via Nova Traiana.[47] The king probably intended the new settlement to facilitate caravan trade and to begin a process of sedentarization through exploitation of the fertile soil of the adjacent plain, and it is likely that the main elements of the indispensable water-supply system – the aqueduct and the public reservoirs – are the product of royal patronage and belong to the town's formative period. Although a small settlement, Hawara flourished and apparently exerted enough influence over an otherwise sparsely inhabited region that the Romans felt it advisable to install a legionary unit in a large fort built at the site soon after the absorption of the Nabataean kingdom into the Provincia Arabia in 106. Hawara continued to grow as an agricultural, pastoral, trading, and administrative centre through the Byzantine and Early

[45] Shereshevski 1991, 47, 59–60, 89, 102. Although the well at Avdat served a Byzantine bathhouse, it may well have been dug much earlier.

[46] Oleson 1991b, 1992, 1995, 1997. Oleson is preparing a monograph on the water system which will appear in 2006.

[47] The foundation story is reported in Ouranios' Arabica (fragment A.1, FGrH IIIC, p. 340), which states that King Obodas sent out "his son Aretas" in response to an oracle. The reigns of both Aretas III (85–62 B.C.) and Aretas IV (9/8 B.C.–A.D. 40) followed those of kings named Obodas (I and III, respectively), but Aretas IV was not in fact the son of Obodas III. The ceramics found in the earliest occupation levels at the site also suggest that Aretas III was the founder. For the Nabataean king list, see Starkey 1965, 907–9, 913–14; Fiema and Jones 1990.

Islamic period.[48] During the Nabataean and Roman periods, numerous privately owned cisterns were constructed to take advantage of run-off water, and the Roman military unit took care to provide a reservoir inside the walls of the fort. Nevertheless, the additions were all supplementary to a system essentially Nabataean in character, and it remains an excellent example of the Nabataean capacities in hydraulic technology.

The diagram (Fig. 17) presents the main features of the system, which includes the full panoply of Nabataean water-supply techniques. Circles represent the sources of water: only precipitation and springs, since the geology and topography are not conducive to wells. Single lines with arrows represent either the natural movement of water through the landscape or the consumption of water by groups of people and their animals, while boxes represent structures built as part of the water-supply system. Triangles represent both natural water loss and human consumers. The double line represents the aqueduct channels.

Even without topographical indicators, this chart makes clear the regional character of the water system supplying the small settlement of Hawara, and the interdependence of village and countryside. Run-off from precipitation on the mountainous or hilly periphery of the roughly triangular, 250 square kilometer water catchment area around Hawara fed terraced fields and wadis, open lowland fields below catchment slopes, local catchment fields for 48 rural cisterns, and three impoundment dams. These structures were constructed and controlled by families or clans living for a significant portion of the year in tents in the countryside, grazing their flocks on vegetation in the stony hills during the moist winter and spring, while grain grew in the low-land fields, then on the stubble in these fields after the early summer harvest. The flocks may have been moved to pastures high in the al-Shera escarpment later in the summer, before the cycle began again. Although the average rainfall in this part of the Hisma is only 80 mm/year, the 250 square kilometer area of the catchment around Hawara might theoretically receive as much as 20,000,000 m^3 of precipitation in an average year. Of this enormous amount, only 4,415.2 m^3 could be accommodated in the rural cisterns, 3,469 m^3 behind the dams, and perhaps fifty times those combined amounts was held in the soil of prepared fields to sustain crops. The rest was "lost" to uncultivated soil and the geological strata below it, to evaporation, and as run-off down the main regional water-course, the Wadi Gharid.

The aqueduct system also passed through the countryside, carrying to the village the discharge of the 'Ain Ghana, 'Ain Sara, and 'Ain al-Jammam. The maximum possible flow into the terminal reservoir (calculated on the basis of slope, channel cross-section, and roughness of the conduit walls) was approximately 1.72 lt/sec (6.192 m^3/hr), and it is clear that filling reservoir no. 63 in the village (Fig. 14) was the major original goal of the 26.508 km of aqueduct channel. Nevertheless, two rock-cut tanks which drew water from the main Ghana aqueduct at km 6.512 (Fig. 18) and 9.597 (measured from 'Ain Ghana) clearly were intended to provide access to the water-supply for rural dwellers and

[48] Oleson 2001a.

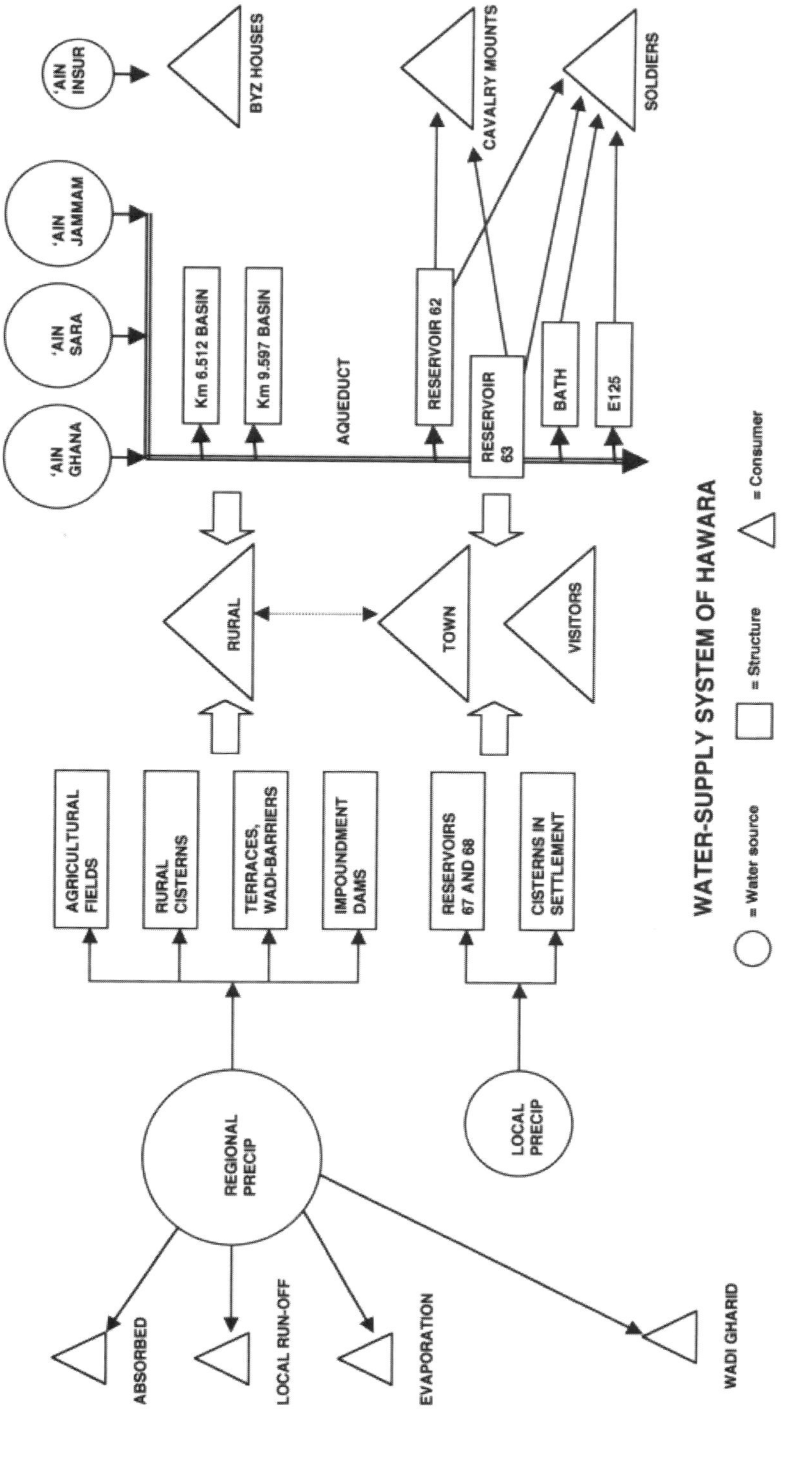

Fig. 17: Diagram of water system of Hawara.

Fig. 18: Draw tank fed by 'Ain Ghana aqueduct, Hawara.

their flocks as well. The foothills where these tanks occur would have been prime grazing area, and it is probably significant that no cisterns filled by run-off water were cut in the rock nearby. The tanks tapping the aqueduct flow apparently were sufficient for the resident population. The conduit tapping the smaller flow of the 'Ain Abu an-Nusur (Fig. 2), in contrast, conducted the water only a few hundred metres, to a small cluster of Byzantine houses.[49]

The Nabataean reservoir (no. 63) fed by the aqueduct had a capacity of 633 m^3, but of course water constantly flowed through it in the original configuration. (Fig. 14) The aqueduct could provide up to 148.6 m^3 of water every 24 hours. The outflow aqueduct carried the water toward the village centre, probably serving a small bath building (Field E077) on the way, but the ultimate fate of the outflow is not known. In the Late Roman period the overflow conduit was replaced by a stopcock feeding a lead pipe that served the re-built bath, and the surplus water was taken off before the reservoir by a terracotta pipeline serving habitations and a shrine (Field E125) 90 m southeast of the reservoir. Roman engineers also tapped the aqueduct in the early second century, 400 m north of the Nabataean reservoir, with a branch channel diverting water to a large reservoir (no. 62) built just inside the northwest corner of the nearby fort (capacity, 1273.3 m^3). Some sort of tapping arrangement or water-lifting system at this last reservoir fed a pressurized terracotta pipe system within the fort which probably

[49] Waheeb 1996, 345.

was connected to drinking basins serving the needs of the soldiers and their mounts, and possibly latrines. Since this reservoir does not seem to have had an overflow that would have allowed it to be constantly refreshed with flowing water, the soldiers undoubtedly made use of the water in the Nabataean reservoir as well, and, of course, they drew on the outflow of that reservoir for their bath.

The aqueduct, already made accessible to rural inhabitants at two tanks in the countryside, serviced a wide variety of users in the settlement centre. The main clients were the local inhabitants and their flocks, a group that would change in composition and number as nomadic or semi-nomadic families moved between the countryside and the village. They accessed the water at the Nabataean reservoir, and possibly at a Nabataean bath building below the Roman bath. The presence of this constantly refreshed pool of water (and perhaps a bath) must also have attracted travelers moving along the old King's Highway, which passed close by.

But the village was provided as well with a run-off water supply, used to fill a pair of large public reservoirs in the settlement centre (nos. 67 and 68, each with a capacity of 488 m^3). (Fig. 16) These reservoirs, which had slab roofs supported by arches to protect their contents from pollution and evaporation, were built early on in Hawara's history. Presumably their clients were the local inhabitants and their flocks, along with occasional residents and visitors. Subsequently, smaller, usually cylindrical, cisterns were constructed around the edges of the same run-off area by families or clans for their private use. The two run-off reservoirs had a combined capacity of 976 m^3, while the 13 private cisterns could hold a total of 1473 m^3 of water.

The storage capacity of the public reservoirs and private cisterns in the area of the settlement centre of Hawara was 4,355.3 m^3, to which should be added the maximum figure of 148.6 m^3 that could be delivered daily by the aqueduct. It is interesting that the calculated total capacity of the rural cisterns (4,315.2 m^3) is quite close to that of the water storage facilities in the settlement centre. It is tempting to suggest that the two systems were meant to function in parallel, providing water to the same groups of humans and animals as they moved from the centre to the periphery of Hawara's territory and back, pursuing various activities throughout the year. The soldiers, however, are unlikely to have spent as much time living outside the fort as within it, and their reservoir represents 29 percent of the total storage capacity in the settlement. In any case, it is likely that our sample, particularly of the rural cisterns, is incomplete. I have calculated elsewhere that these resources of water could have supported a population of 163 persons, 163 camels, and 1,469 ovicaprids in the countryside and 654 persons, 20 camels, and 180 ovicaprids in the village.[50] The proportions of humans and the various animals can be juggled by taking account of estimated water consumption of each category, but the overall impression is one of a significant regional population.

Given the infrequent rainfall, and the porous character of the sandy soil, it is not surprising that only one drainage channel has been found in the village of

[50] Oleson 1997: 176–77.

Hawara (site no. 76).[51] The 17 m long channel, however, was large (W 0.30 m, H 0.34 m), well constructed, and associated with a settling or collecting basin. Because of the high proportion of paved and roofed areas, and probably as a result of cultural habit, the interior of the fort had its own drainage system. Collector drains and perforated stone gratings channeled run-off water inside the fort to drains running under the centre of the Via principalis (E/W road), which emptied into a heavily built main drain (W 0.35 m, H 0.35 m) extending under the Via praetoria (N/S road) and out the south gate.

Water-Supply and the Foundation of Hawara

Clearly the inhabitants of Hawara in antiquity depended both on run-off water and on water brought to the site by the aqueduct. Each of these supply systems has its own advantages and disadvantages. In collecting run-off water for cisterns or reservoirs, it is important to strike a balance between too large a catchment, which might yield a torrent very difficult to control, and one too small, which might be missed altogether by localized desert rain storms. The potential for excess flow was less important in situations where the water was to be conducted across sturdy wadi barriers or terraces to moisten agricultural soil than where it was meant to fill cisterns close to habitation areas, particularly where the cisterns were built of blocks rather than cut in the bedrock.

The settlement of Hawara is interesting in this regard. There is no obvious strategic reason for its location at this point in the Hisma, or any obvious relationship to a node in the regional transport network. If the founder had placed the settlement centre 5 km farther north, or 10 km farther east or south, the inhabitants would still have had easy access to their agricultural land and routes of travel. In the Middle East, cereal growing typically extends 3–4 km out from a settlement, tree crops are farther away, and grazing land beyond that.[52] It seems that the advantage of this precise spot was the presence of a potential water-catchment field particularly well suited to supply the public run-off reservoirs and family-owned cisterns that were one of the two pillars of Hawara's water-supply system. This field, approximately one square kilometer in area, slopes gently from north to south towards a natural outlet approximately 50 metres across, framed by the low ridges along which the village was built. (Fig. 19) If only half the field received the 80mm of rain which the region averages through the year, and even if as much as 85 percent of that were absorbed, 6,000 cubic metres would still run through this gap-enough water to sustain approximately 2,400 persons for a year. The settlement was designed to depend on the two large public reservoirs (nos. 67 and 68; discussed above), built as a pair 50 m west of the gap – close enough to be filled through collection channels, but out of harm's way. One (no. 67) been cleared out for reuse and still serves as the major public water source at the site. Of course the run-off field might well not yield 6,000

[51] Oleson 1996.

[52] Beaumont, Blake, Wagstaff 1976, 164–65.

Fig. 19: Run-off catchment field north of Hawara.

cubic metres of water every year, and during a recent drought the one cistern put back into use has remained dry for five years. Nevertheless, the prosperous history of Hawara shows that the safety margin was sufficient. During the 800 years of the settlement's existence, more than 30 houses were built on the low slopes surrounding these public cisterns. Some of them tapped the same run-off course to fill smaller, circular cisterns below their private courtyards. Many of these cisterns are still in use today, filled by the sparse, but usually predictable desert rainfall. As far as we can tell, the adjacent wadi bed, which drains approximately 200 square kilometres of the Hawara catchment, was used only to water agricultural fields, as its flow was too violent, at too low a level, and the wadi bed too mobile for the water to be diverted easily into cisterns.

It is unlikely to be a coincidence that the site of Hawara also represents the southernmost point an aqueduct system fed by the Ghana and Jammam springs could reach without requiring the use of substructures far more extensive than those seen in this or other Nabataean aqueduct systems, or without attempting a hazardous crossing of the unstable bed of the Wadi Gharid. Although the Nabataeans probably regarded a well-designed water-supply system dependent on run-off water as more reliable than one dependent on a long, spring-fed aqueduct, the future King Aretas and his scouts seem to have selected a site where both types of system could converge. In addition, Hawara was adjacent to arable fields, was located on the King's Highway (or soon attracted the nearby track to it), and some paths to the west allowed access to the Wadi Arabah. Finally, the southern half of the regional catchment consisted of a shallow basin of fertile loessal soil surrounded by sandstone hills that could provide a reliable source of run-off water for fields and cisterns. The comprehensive and regional character of the water-supply system may be the reason Hawara/Humayma survived for so many centuries as the single significant habitation centre in the Hisma.[53]

Nabataean Agriculture and Irrigation

Since agriculture and irrigation are less dependent on monumental structures than water-supply systems, less evidence survives for Nabataean agricultural practices other than wadi terraces.[54] The Nabataean kingdom or areas of Nabataean cultural influence included regions that varied enormously in resources of arable soil and annual precipitation. The Mediterranean coast of the Near East is well watered. Inland, where precipitation tapers off very quickly in the rain shadow of the coastal ranges, the situation was (and remains) very different. The Hauran, Decapolis region, and Ammon caught some precipitation and were fairly well watered. The Hauran, however, abuts the eastern desert, and to the south, in Moab and the Edom, farming of grain crops without irrigation was possible only along the higher elevations of the inland ranges, where annual precipitation exceeded 250 mm. In the deserts of Syria and Arabia, occasional springs – sometimes very large, as at Azraq – allowed local irrigation or a wide variety of crops and fostered thriving trade and agricultural centres such as Petra, Azraq, Jericho, Damascus, and Palmyra. Elsewhere the scale was more restricted, but in nearly all circumstances the spring water was distributed to these fields in earth channels, a simple arrangement used throughout the ancient Near East. The Babatha archive found near the Dead Sea includes at least two late first-century A.D. papyri that specify the days and hours the owner of agricultural plots near the Dead Sea was legally permitted to irrigate his crops.[55] Fines for violation were owed to the Nabataean king, indicating some type of royal authority over water use. Public control is also seen at Palmyra, where a Roman period inscription specifies the amount of the municipal tax on irrigation water. Private contracts specifying irrigation practices have survived in papyri found at Petra and at Nessana in the Negev; they belong to the Byzantine period but probably reflect unchanging practices that go back at least to the first century B.C.[56] The main crops were always various types of wheat and barley, but grapes were also important, particularly in the Negev, along with chick peas, various root and leaf vegetables, and fruits such as the olive, fig, date, plum, and apple. Several early

[53] The settlement at Wadi Ramm was smaller, and more of a sanctuary or pilgrimage site than a settlement and trading centre.

[54] On irrigation, see Oleson 2000b; for Nabataean and Byzantine agriculture in the region, Aresvik 1976, Barker et al. 1997, 1998, 1999, Evenari, Shanon, Tadmor 1982, Mayerson 1961, 1967, Rosen 2000. For pre-Nabataean agriculture in the region, see Levy and Alon 1987, Stager 1976.

[55] Bowersock 1983, 77–78, 1991, 340; the papyri are also discussed in Isaac 1992.

[56] Palmyra, Teixidor 1984; Petra papyri, Koenen 1996; Nessana, Kraemer 1958, Mayerson 1961; Babatha Greek papyri, Lewis 1989.

Islamic historians report that 'Ali ibn 'Abd Allah, who purchased the site of Hawara/Humayma in the late seventh century, tended a grove of 500 olive trees at the site.[57] A pressing installation, probably for wine, can be seen cut into the bedrock 1.8 km west of the site.

In the absence of flowing spring water, however, irrigation of anything but small crops of vegetables, or spot irrigation of newly planted trees or vines, was a laborious luxury possible only where cistern water was particularly abundant. One of the Nessana papyri mentions a cistern in the context of a plot of land with figs and vines.[58] Hand irrigation of grain crops, the staple food, was impossible. As we have seen, however, even in extremely arid regions of Nabataea, run-off water from local precipitation constituted a substantial resource that could be used to augment the moisture in carefully prepared, dyked or terraced fields. As noted above, the Nabataeans were particularly adept at water-harvesting and would focus on one field the precipitation from an area 17 to 30 times its size. (Figs. 6–8) This procedure made the production of grain crops possible even with annual precipitation as low as 80 mm, as one can see from the Bedouin grain fields around Humayma today (Fig. 20), and at a reconstructed Nabataean farm of this type near Avdat (where precipitation is higher). In antiquity, as today, it is likely that each landowner, family, or clan held title to fields scattered around their usual haunts, thus increasing the chances that at least a portion of a family's plots would receive water. The same redundancy was used with cisterns fed by run-off. During the winter the owners would observe which fields received sufficient moisture to allow production of a crop or wheat or barley. Once the seed had been sown, no further water was applied to the field, and the owners simply protected the crop from grazing and returned to harvest it in the late Spring. Micro-catchments could also be prepared, to funnel run-off water to a single olive or fruit tree.[59] Trees, however, also required additional irrigation by hand for the first few years, in order to become established. Run-off water from the Jebel Druze was very important to the many Nabataean and Roman settlements in the Hauran, and the same system of terraced and diked fields and earthen channels has continued in use up to the present.[60] Because of the continued, intensive occupation, no actual Nabataean or Roman fields have survived in the Hauran, but ancient earth and stone block channels and fields can still be seen at numerous sites in the thinly populated and more arid region of the Negev, as at Avdat, and in the Wadi Araba.[61] The large fields around the mining settlement of ancient Phaeno in the Wadi Faynan were sustained by water diverted from the main wadi course. The small square plots still visible at et-Telah depended on run-off from the local wadi, probably supplemented by spring water stored in a nearby cistern.[62] Although most of the farms in the Araba probably engaged in

[57] al-Balâdhurî 1978, III, 74; al-Dûrî 1971, 135, 144–45.

[58] Kraemer 1958, 102–3, no. 32.

[59] Evenari, Shanon, Tadmor 1982, 220–28.

[60] Braemer 1990.

[61] Evenari, Shanon, Tadmor 1982, 103; Barker et al., 1997, 1998, 1999.

[62] al-Muheisin 1992.

Fig. 20: Modern Bedouin earthen water barrier and wheat field, Humayma.

subsistence farming, estates in the Negev, which received a bit more rainfall, exported wine on a large scale in the Byzantine period.[63]

Conclusion

For thousands of years before and after the period of Nabataean cultural domination, the ways of life in the region encompassed by their kingdom have oscillated between the extremes of desperately poor nomadism and relatively comfortable settled life. The major Nabataean accomplishment is that their culture, in both its nomadic and settled form, lived in harmony with the resources of the unforgiving desert environment. Although the Nabataeans do not seem to have been exporters of food stuffs, neither do they seem to have depended significantly on imports of food. The corresponding, and dependent social accomplishment is that the ancient Nabataeans, like their modern descendants in Jordan over the last century, managed to develop a stable and accepted monarchy in a period of challenging, often chaotic regional political developments. One is reminded of Athenodorus's comments, preserved in Strabo (16.4.21): "The outside parts [of Petra] have springs in abundance, both for domestic purposes and for watering gardens. Outside the circuit of the rock, most of the territory is desert... Petra is always

[63] Mayerson 1985.

ruled by a king from the royal family, and the king has as administrator one of his companions, who is called 'brother'. It is extremely well governed." It was only in the face of the pan-Mediterranean power of the Romans that the Nabataean kingdom, one of the very last client kingdoms of the Roman world, was transformed into the Provincia Arabia.

Bibliography

al-Dûrî, 'Abd al-'Aziz, and 'Abd al-Jabbâr al-Mutallabî, eds., 1971. Akhbâr al-Dawla al-'Abbâsiya, Beirut: Dâr al-Talî'a.

Aresvik, O., 1976. The Agricultural Development of Jordan, New York: Praeger.

al-Balâdhurî, 1978. Ansâb al-Ashraf, pt. 3, 'Abd al-'Aziz al-Dûrî, ed., Wiesbaden: Franz Steiner.

Barker, et al., "The Wadi Faynan Project, Southern Jordan: A Preliminary Report on Geomorphology and Landscape Archaeology", Levant 29, 19–40.

–, 1998. "Environment and Land Use in the Wadi Faynan, Southern Jordan: the Second Season of Geoarchaeology and Landscape Archaeology (1997)." Levant 30, 5–25.

–, 1999. "Environment and Land Use in the Wadi Faynan, Southern Jordan: the Third Season of Geoarchaeology and Landscape Archaeology (1998)." Levant 31, 255–92.

Beaumont, P., G.H. Blake, J.M. Wagstaff, 1976. The Middle East: A Geographical Study, London: John Wiley & Sons.

Bedal, L.-A., 1999. "A Paradeisos in Petra: New Light on the 'Lower Market'", ADAJ 43, 227–39.

–, 2000. The Petra Pool Complex: A Hellenistic Paradeisos in the Nabataean Capital, PhD diss., University of Pennsylvania.

Bellwald, U., al-Huneidi, M., 2003. The Petra Siq: Nabataean Hydrology Uncovered. Amman: Petra National Trust.

Bowersock, G., 1991. "The Babatha Papyri, Masada, and Rome", JRA 4, 336–44.

Braemer, F., 1990. "Formes d'irrigation dans le Hawran (Syrie du sud)", in B. Geyer, ed., Techniques et Pratiques hydro-Agricoles Traditionnelles en domaine irrigué, vol. II, Paris: Paul Geuthner, 453–74.

Brinker, W., 1990. "Wasserspeicherung in Zisternen. Ein Beitrag zur Frage der Wasserversorgung früher Städte", Mitteilungen, Leichtweiss-Institut für Wasserbau, 109, 1–155.

Bruins, H.J., 1990. "Ancient Agricultural Terraces at Nahal Mitran", Atiqot 10, 22–28.

Dijkstra, K., 1995. Life and Loyalty, Leiden: Brill.

Eadie, J., and J.P. Oleson, 1986. "The Water-Supply Systems of Nabataean and Roman Humayma", BASOR 262, 49–76.

Evenari, M., L. Shanan, N. Tadmor, 1982. The Negev: Challenge of a Desert, 2nd ed, Cambridge: Harvard University Press.

Fahlbusch, H., 1982. Vergleich antiker griechischer und römischer Wasserversorgungsanlagen. Mitteilungen, Leichtweiss-Institut für Wasserbau, 73, Braunschweig: Leichtweiss-Institut.

Farès-Drappeau, S., 1995. "L'inscription de type dédanite de Abu ad-Diba'/Wadi Ramm. Une nouvelle lecture", ADAJ 39, 493–97.

Fiema, Z., and R.N. Jones, 1990. "The Nabataean King-List Revised", ADAJ 34, 239–48.

Garbrecht, G., 1984. "Geschichtliche Talsperren im östlichen Mittelmeerraum", Mitteilungen, Leichtweiss-Institut für Wasserbau, 82, 1–21.

–, 1987. "Die Wasserversorgung des antiken Pergamon", Die Wasserversorgung antiker Städte, 2, Mainz: von Zabern, 11–48.

–, 1987–1991. Historische Talsperren, 2 vols., Stuttgart: Wittwer.

Glueck, N., 1965. Deities and Dolphins: The Story of the Nabataeans, New York: Farrar, Straus and Giroux.

Gobot, H., 1979. Les qanats: Une technique d'acquisition de l'eau, Paris: Mouton Éditeur.
Graf, D., 1997. "The Via Militaris in Arabia", DOPapers 51, 271–81.
Hackl, U., H. Jenni, C. Schneider, 2003. Quellen zur Geschichte der Nabatäer, Göttingen: Vandenhoeck & Ruprecht.
Henry, D.O., 1983. "An Investigation of the Prehistory of Southern Jordan", PEQ 115, 1–24.
Hillel, D., 1982. Negev: Land, Water, and Life in a Desert Environment, New York: Praeger.
Hodge, A.T., 1992. Roman Aqueducts and Water Supply, London: Duckworth, 1992.
–, 2000. "Reservoirs and Dams", in Wikander 2000, 331–39.
Isaac, B., 1992. "The Babatha Archive: A Review Article", IEJ 42, 62–75.
Jobling, W.D., 1986. "Prospection archéologique et épigraphique dans la region d'Aqaba-Ma'an, 1984–85", Syria 63, 405-15.
–, 1989. " 'Aqaba-Ma'an Archaeological and Epigraphic Survey", in D. Homès-Fredericq, J.B. Hennessy, eds., Archaeology of Jordan: II1. Field Reports, Leuven: Peeters, 1989, 16–24.
Kedar, Y., 1957. "Ancient agriculture at Shivtah in the Negev", IEJ 7, 178–89.
Kennedy, D.L., and D. Riley, 1990. Rome's Desert Frontier from the Air, Austin: University of Texas Press.
Killick, A., 1987. Udhruh. Caravan City and Desert Oasis, Romsey.
Kloner, A., 1973. "Dams and Reservoirs in the North-Eastern Mountains of the Negev", Eretz Israel 11, 248–57 (in Hebrew).
Koenen, L., 1996. "The Carbonized Archive from Petra", JRA 9, 177–88.
Kraemer, C.J., 1958. Excavations at Nessana, III: Non-Literary Papyri, Princeton: Princeton University Press.
Levy, T.E., and D. Alon, 1987. "Settlement Patterns along the Nahal Beersheva-Lower Nahal Besor: Models of Subsistence in the Northern Negev", in T.E. Levy, ed., Shiqmim, I, British Archaeological Reports, Intl. Ser., 356, Oxford: BAR.
Lewis, N., ed., 1989. The Documents from the Bar Kokhba Period in the Cave of the Letters, Greek Papyri. Jerusalem: Israel Exploration Society.
Lindner, M., 1987. "Nabatäische Talsperren", in Garbrecht 1987, 147–74.
–, and H. Hübl, 1997. "Where the Pharao's Daughter got her Drinking Water From. The 'Ein Brak Conduit to Petra", ZDPV, 113, 51–67.
Mabry, J., 1989. "Investigations at Tell el-Handaquq, Jordan (1987–88)", ADAJ 33, 59–95.
Mayerson, P., 1961. The Ancient Agricultural Regime of Nessana and the Negev, Jerusalem: Colt Archaeological Institute.
–, 1967. "A Note on Demography and Land Use in the Ancient Negeb", BASOR 185, 39–43.
–, 1985. "The Wine and Vineyards of Gaza in the Byzantine Period", BASOR 257, 75–80.
al-Muheisen, Z., 1990. "Maîtrise de l'eau et agriculture en nabatène: L'exemple de Pétra", Aram 2, 205–20.
–, 1992. "Modes d'Installations agricoles nabatéennes dans la region de Petra et le wadi Arabah", in M. Zaghloul et al., SHAJ, IV, Amman: Department of Antiquities, 215–19.
National Atlas, 1984. National Atlas of Jordan, I: Climate and Agroclimatology, Amman: Jordan National Geographic Centre.
Negev, A., 1963. "Nabataean Inscriptions from 'Avdat (Oboda)", IEJ 13, 113–24.
Oleson, J.P., 1988. "Humayma Hydraulic Survey: Preliminary Report of the 1987 Season", ADAJ 32, 157–69.
–, 1991a. "Eine nabatäische Talsperre in der Nähe von Humeima (das antike Auara) in Jordanien", in Garbrecht, 1991, 65–71.
–, 1991b. "Aqueducts, Cisterns, and the Strategy of Water Supply at Nabataean and Roman Auara (Jordan)", in E.T. Hodge, ed., Future Currents in Aqueduct Studies, Bristol: Francis Cairns, 45–62.
–, 1992. "Water Works", in D.N. Freedman, ed., Anchor Bible Dictionary. New York: Doubleday, vol. 6, pp. 883–93.

–, 1995. "The Origins and Design of Nabataean Water-Supply Systems", in SHAJ, V, Amman: Department of Antiquities, 707–19.
–, 1996. "Surface Water Management at an Ancient Site in Jordan's Southern Desert", in Acts, 16th Congress of the International Commission on Irrigation and Drainage, Cairo, 1966, Cairo, 1996, 141–56.
–, 1997. "Landscape and Cityscape in the Hisma: The Resources of Ancient Al-Humayma", in SHAJ, VI. Amman: Dept. of Antiquities, 175–88.
–, 2000a. "Water-Lifting", in Wikander 2000, 217–302.
–, 2000b. "Irrigation", in Wikander 2000, 183–215.
–, 2001a. "King, Emperor, Priest, and Caliph: Cultural Change at Hawara (Ancient al-Humayma) in the First Millennium AD", in SHAJ, VII. Amman: Department of Antiquities, 569–80.
–, 2001b. "Water-Supply in Jordan", in B. MacDonald et al., eds., The Archaeology of Jordan, Sheffield: Sheffield Academic Press, 603–14.
–, 2003a. "'Romanization' at Hawara (Humayma)? The Character of 'Roman' Culture at a Desert Fortress," in SHAJ, VIII, Amman: Department of Antiquities, 353–60.
–, 2003b. "Nabataean Water Supply," in R. Rosenthal-Heginbottom, ed., The Nabataeans in the Negev. Haifa: Hecht Museum, 39–42, 55–60.
–, K. ,Amr, R. Foote, J. Logan, M.B. Reeves, R. Schick, 1999. "Preliminary Report of the al-Humayma Excavation Project, 1995, 1996, 1998", ADAJ 43, 411–50.
–, M.B. Reeves, B. Fisher, 2002. "New Dedicatory Inscriptions from Humayma (Ancient Hawara), Jordan," Zeitschrift für Papyrologie und Epigraphik 140, 103–21.
–, G.S. Baker, E. de Brujin, R.M. Foote, J. Logan, M.B. Reeves, A.N. Sherwood, 2003. "Preliminary Report of al-Humayma Excavation Project, 2000, 2002." ADAJ 47, 37–64.
Parr, P., 1967. "La date du barrage du Siq à Pétra", RBib 74, 45–49.
Ron, Z., 1966. "Agricultural Terraces in the Judean Mountains", IEJ 16, 33–49.
Rosen, S.A., 2000. "The decline of desert agriculture: a view from the classical period Negev", in G. Barker, D. Gilbertson, eds., Archaeology of Drylands: Living at the Margin, London: Routledge, 45–62.
Rubin, R., 1988. "Water Conservation Methods in Israel's Negev Desert in Late Antiquity", Journal of Historical Geography 14, 229–44.
Salameh, E., and H. Bannayan, 1993. Water Resources of Jordan: Present Status and Future Potential, Amman: F. Ebert Stiftung.
Savignac, M.R., 1932. "Notes de voyage. Le sanctuaire d'Allat à Iram", RBib 41, 581–97.
Schmid, S., 2001. "The Hellenisation of the Nabataeans: A New Approach", in SHAJ VII, Amman: Department of Antiquities, 407–19.
Shereshevski, J., 1991. Byzantine Urban Settlements in the Negev Desert, Be'er Sheva: Ben-Gurion University of the Negev Press.
Stager, L., 1976. "Farming in the Judean Desert during the Iron Age", BASOR 221, 145–58.
Starkey, J., 1965. "Pétra et la Nabatène", in Dictionnaire de la Bible, Supplément, Paris: Letouzey et Ané, 886–1017.
Stucky, R. et al., 1996. Petra: az-Zantur, I, Mainz: von Zabern.
Teixidor, J., 1984. Un port romain du desert: Palmyre et son commerce d'Auguste à Caracalla, Paris: Librarie Adrien-Maissoneuve.
Waheeb, M., 1996. "Archaeological Excavation at Ras an-Naqab-Aqaba Road Alignment: Preliminary Report (1995)", ADAJ 40, 339–48.
Wenning, R., 1987. Die Nabatäer-Denkmaler und Geschichte, Göttingen: Vanderhoeck & Ruprecht.
Wikander, Ö., ed., 2000. Handbook of Ancient Water Technology, Leiden: Brill.

Animal Exploitation in the Nabataean World

Jacqueline Studer

Introduction

The Greek historian Diodorus of Sicily noted that although many Arabian tribes exploited the desert for pasture, the Nabataeans surpassed all others in wealth "*although they are not much more than 10,000 in number*". This picture of the Nabataeans as nomads dates to 312 B.C., but definitive evidence of a Nabataean culture with a sedentary infrastructure, does not occur before the late second century B.C.[1]. Even as nomads, the Nabataeans dominated trade in spices, incense, perfumes, medicinal products as well as other goods, from the Arabian Peninsula to the ports of the eastern Mediterranean. They continued to engage in this form of trade following sedentization although, as suggested by Rosenthal-Heginbottom[2], this led to a division in the society between the nomadic sector of the po-pulation (traders, caravan guides) and the settled population, with the latter dependent on the former. Throughout the Levant, way stations, administrative centres and settlements were established by the Nabataeans along their trade routes[3]. The settlement of Petra evolved to become the capital of the Nabataean Kingdom[4], although Negev[5] claims that this settlement was of minor economic importance and served primarily as the religious centre of the Kingdom. By A.D. 106 the Nabataean kingdom lost its independence and was incorporated into the Roman Empire as part of the Province of Arabia.

Most publications describe the impressive Nabataean architectural remains and their material culture, but little is known about their daily life, subsistence and diet. Classical sources provide some insights into these subjects. In the oldest description of the Nabataeans by Diodorus of Sicily, the nomadic character of the society is emphasised: "some of the Nabataeans keep camels, others sheep that feed in the desert. And when they fly away in the desert, they live on meat [of small ruminants], milk and wild plants[6]." From the second half of the first century BC, the Greek geographer Strabo provides an extensive description of animals kept by the Nabataeans: *"The sheep are white-fleeced and the oxen are*

[1] The description of Diodorus of Sicily was written during the first century BC, but it refers to an event dated to 312 BC (cf. Hackl *et al.* 2003). For an overview of Nabataean culture see for example Fiema 1996; Hackl 1993; Negev 1988a; Schmid 2001; Zayadine 1992.

[2] Rosenthal-Heginbottom 2003, 23.

[3] Bignasca *et al.* 1996; Schmid 2001.

[4] Bignasca *et al.* 1996; Schmid 2001.

[5] Negev 1988a.

[6] cf. Hackl *et. al.* 2003, 444–5 and note 1.

large, but the country produces no horses. Camels afford the service they require instead of horses[7]." Further information is derived from an inscription on a cuneiform tablet found in the Edomite site of Tawilan in Jordan dating to the Persian period (5th– 4th centuries B.C.), which refers to the sale of livestock by people identified as Nabataeans[8]. Together these sources provide a general picture of the Nabataean economy as based on domestic stock raised for meat and milk, while the camel provided the main means of transport. Camel raising and the exploitation of small stock in the desert, are both elements, which would accord well with the nomadic character of the Nabataeans.

Despite the large number of Nabataean sites that have been excavated in the Near East[9], there is little primary information available from archaeozoological studies on the range of species exploited, extent of hunting, strategies of herd management and methods of food preparation. Moreover, in many sites the faunal samples from the Nabataean period are described together with those from later Roman levels. The few archaeozoological studies of Nabataean settlements currently available include a description by Zeitler[10] of remains recovered from the foot of Jabal el-Khubta in Petra, a general publication on fauna from Nabataean through early Abbasid levels from Al-Humayma[11], another from Nabataean-Roman in the Negev[12], a very small faunal sample (25 bones) from the settlement of Deir 'Ain 'Abata near the Dead Sea[13], another small collection from Rujm Beni Yasser[14], 45 identified bones from a private rural house or a farm house in the small village of Quseima in northern Sinai[15], an assemblage of some 1000 bones from Avdat[16] and a small sample of bones from a sanctuary on Jebel Serbal (Sinai Peninsula)[17]. The most comprehensive archaeozoological information presently available is derived from az-Zantur[18] (or EZ), a domestic quarter of Petra. However, even this data-set is biased and does not necessarily reflect the food habits of the general population as no data are currently available on animal remains from Nabataean pastoral encampments, way stations, farms and villages in the outlying regions.

[7] Geographica 16, 4, 26, cf. Hackl *et al.* 2003, 615–617.

[8] Bennett cf. Browning 1989.

[9] for example Erickson-Gini & Israel 2003; Hackl 1993; Negev 1988; Schmid 2002.

[10] Zeitler 1990.

[11] Oleson 1997. The bone assemblages are not separated into periods.

[12] Hakker-Orion 1993, 78. Three sites are mentioned, Mo'a, Sha'ar Ramon and Mesad Dafit.

[13] Beech in press, 2007

[14] Toplyn 1994.

[15] Hellwing & Agiman 2000.

[16] Horwitz & Lernau in prep.

[17] Horwitz in prep.

[18] Studer 2002.

Species Representation

As it is the largest Nabataean archaeozoological assemblage studied to date, the ez-Zantur sample serves as the focus of this paper. Where pertinent, additional information is given on fauna from other Nabataean sites in the region.

Figure 1 lists the total number of identified bones and the relative frequencies of mammalian species from Nabataean strata on the small hill of ez-Zantur, a domestic quarter of the city of Petra. Nearly 10,000 animal remains were recovered during excavations of three terraces. Terrace EZ I contained a large Nabataean house with two phases of occupation, terrace EZ III represents domestic structures, while terrace EZ IV yielded a mansion initially constructed during the first century A.D.[19].

		NISP		% mammals
Sheep, goat	*Ovis aries, Capra hircus*	4540		91%
Camel	*Camelus dromedarius*	188		4%
Pig	*Sus domesticus*	74		2%
Cattle	*Bos taurus*	13		<0.5%
Donkey, horse	*Equus asinus, E. caballus*	14		<0.5%
*Dog**	*Canis familiaris*	*16*		*<0.5%*
Gazelle	*Gazella sp.*	39		1%
Wild boar	*Sus scrofa*	13		<0.5%
Hare	*Lepus capensis*	5		<0.5%
Hyrax	*Procavia capensis*	1		<0.5%
*Small carnivores**		*6*		*<0.5%*
*Rodents**		*48*		*1%*
total mammals		**4887**	**83%**	**100%**
Birds		477	8%	
Fish		145	2%	
Molluscs**		406	7%	
TOTAL (identified)		**5985**	**100%**	

Figure 1
Nabataean fauna from ez-Zantur.
Total number of identified bones (NISP) and the relative frequencies of the different mammalian species.
* not considered as food remains
** only two molluscan species are considered as food remains (see text)

At ez-Zantur, domestic mammals served as the mainstay of the Nabataean economy and comprised 83% of all identified remains. Sheep (*Ovis aries*) and goat (*Capra hircus*) were the most common taxa, supplemented by pig (*Sus domesticus*), chicken (*Gallus gallus*) and cattle (*Bos taurus*) as well as three

[19] For information on the Nabataean house at EZ I, see Stucky 1992, 1996. The bone material from EZ I can be separated into two phases: first century B.C. and first century A.D. For descriptions of the archaeology of the terrace EZ IV, see Kolb 1998 and Kolb *et al.* 1999.

beasts of burden: camel (*Camelus dromedarius*), donkey (*Equus asinus*) and horse (*Equus caballus*). Hunting appears to have been a minor activity as attested to by the paucity of remains of wild animals – gazelle, wild boar, hare, hyrax, carnivores and birds. However, consumption of fish was relatively common, and there are some indications that marine molluscs were also consumed. A similar range of domestic species as well as fish are reported from Jabal el-Khubta[20] and Avdat[21].

The ez-Zantur assemblage also bears a close resemblance to faunal remains derived from other Hellenistic and early Roman sites in the region. For example, Tell Hesban in Jordan[22], Tel Anafa in northern Israel[23] and Horbat Rimmon in southern Israel[24]. All contain a similar spectrum of domestic animals, a predominance of sheep and goat and paucity of hunted species. In addition, traded items such as fish are found in all sites. Therefore, in these features, the ez-Zantur Nabataean animal economy is not markedly distinct.

(a) Sheep and goat

Remains of both domestic sheep and goat have been identified from ez-Zantur. Based on bone counts (NISP), together they constitute 90–94% of all mammalian remains in the three terraces studied and served as the major source of protein for the inhabitants of the site (Figure 1). This is not surprising as following their domestication in the Neolithic period, these two species have played a major role in human subsistence in the Near East, and this continued to be the case in the Nabataean period. It is possible that for Nabataeans, herd size served as a source of wealth and status as it does for Bedouin today[25].

At ez-Zantur, sheep are more common than goat, with a ratio of 2:1. The detailed study of skeletal elements is still underway but preliminary findings indicate that caprines are represented by all portions of the carcass, head to foot, suggesting that householders at ez-Zantur had access to complete animals.

Reconstruction of mortality profiles for sheep and goat remains combined was based on the state of tooth eruption, dental attrition scores and bone fusion. Results indicate that the majority of caprines were slaughtered as adult animals i.e. over 3.5 years. The age profile based on attrition scores of teeth in jaws show that 9% of the animals were killed before their first year of life, 20% between 1 and 2 years, 28% between 2 and 3 years and 44% were older than 3 years (Figures 2 and 3). In addition, the last class is represented by a majority of very old individuals, with a mandible wear stage of over 40 following Grant[26]. Cull

[20] Zeitler 1990.
[21] Horwitz & Lernau in prep.
[22] von den Driesch & Boessneck 1995.
[23] Redding 1994.
[24] Horwitz 1998.
[25] Abu-Rabia 1994.
[26] Grant (1982).

SHEEP AND GOAT MANDIBLES			
MWS	Age	Nb	%
1-14	< 1 year	6	9%
15-27	1-2 years	13	20%
28-34	2-3 years	17	28%
> 35	> 3 years	28	44%
	TOTAL	64	100%

Figure 2
Age distribution of Nabataean sheep and goat from ez-Zantur.
Mandible Wear Stage (MWS) follows Grant 1982. The estimation of age for sheep and goats is based on tables given in Habermehl (1975), which correspond to wear stages in unimproved breeds from protohistoric sites (Méniel 1987). Silver's tables (1969) give older age classes for similar wear stages such that instead of 44% as reported here, using Silver's method the frequency of caprines older than 3 years would be as high as 70% (equivalent to Grant 1982 MWS >25).

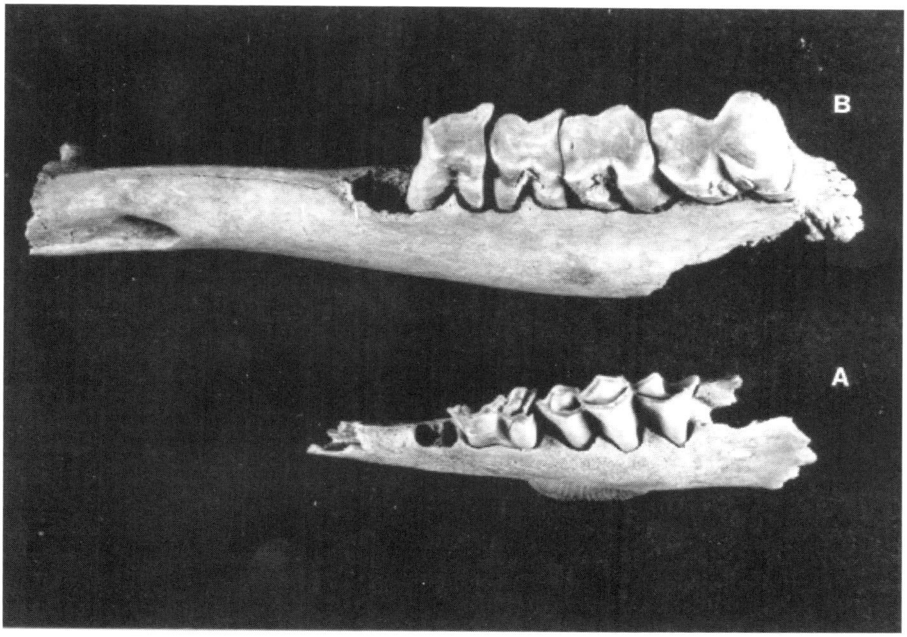

Figure 3
Age estimation on caprines mandibles.
(A) Mandible of a goat lamb of about 3 months. The 6 cusps of the milk teeth D4 are in wear, with one dentine union (Tooth Wear Stage = c, Grant 1982). The first molar has begun to erupt (see the cavity in the bone behind the D4; TWS = 1/2 or U) which corresponds to a Mandible Wear Stage of 4 or 5 (Grant 1982).
(B) Mandible of an old caprine of 6 years or more. Premolars and molars show an advanced wear stage which corresponds to a MWS of at least 46 (TWS: M1=m, M2=m, M3 (missing)= at least g). (Photo by C. Ratton).

patterns reconstructed from bone fusion do not give such detailed results as the last long bone in the skeleton fuses at 3.5 years, while dental attrition continues into adulthood. However, even in the data-set based on bone fusion, adult animals predominate. When only the distal part of the radius is considered, which fuses at the age of 3.5 years, it is evident that 54 % of the remains have fused distal epiphyses[27]. While for the distal end of the tibia (which fuses at about 15–20 months), 80% of these ends are fused[28]. Of course, the sample may have been biased with unfused elements from immature animals under-represented due to carnivore (dog) gnawing or differential attrition due to diagenesis of their more fragile bones. However, considering the low rate of carnivore damage on bones in the ez-Zantur sample, as well as the presence of abundant and well preserved fragile bones of birds and fish, carnivore ravaging and diagnesis appear to have had a limited impact on this assemblage.

Payne[29] has proposed that a management strategy for caprines aimed at meat production will be characterised by a peak cull of immature animals of both sexes at circa 2 years of age. In contrast, for milk production only immature surplus males will be preferentially culled at 2 years while a maximum number of females will be kept into adulthood. For wool production the majority of animals of both sexes will be kept into adulthood. Based on the predominance of adult animals in the ez-Zantur assemblage, it is suggested that sheep and goats were exploited not only for their meat but primarily for their milk and fibre (and kept as a sign of richness). Unfortunately the available data are insufficient to examine caprine age in relation to sex and species attribution (sheep or goat) in order to examine inter-species differences in herding strategy.

Butchery damage and other anthropogenic modifications visible on bones offer insights into the manner in which animals were slaughtered and their carcasses prepared for consumption. These include cut marks on the bones, evidence for their intentional fragmentation and burning, as well as the presence of human tooth marks. Caprines in the ez-Zantur assemblage were slaughtered by having their throat cut as attested to by the presence of fine incisions on the ventral face of the atlas, the first vertebra (Figure 4). Other cut marks observed on the bones are characteristic of skeletal disarticulation with the carcass initially divided into two equal halves by severing the vertebral column (Figure 5). This resembles the pattern of goat butchery undertaken by Bedouin today. Fine filleting marks for the removal of meat from the bone are also evident in this sample, while both sheep and goat bones and horns were modified and used in the manufacture of artefacts.

Due to the exceptionally good conditions of preservation, unique remains of textiles have been discovered in Nabataean sites in the Negev desert. Analyses of the animal fibres used in their manufacture have shown that not only sheep wool

[27] According to Habermehl 1975, the distal part of the radius fuses at the age of 3.5 years. The sample from ez-Zantur comprised 28 fused distal radius out of a total of 52 (54%).

[28] According to Habermehl 1975, the distal end of the tibia fuses at the age of 15–20 months. The sample from ez-Zantur comprised 68 fused remains out of a total of 85 (80%).

[29] Payne 1973.

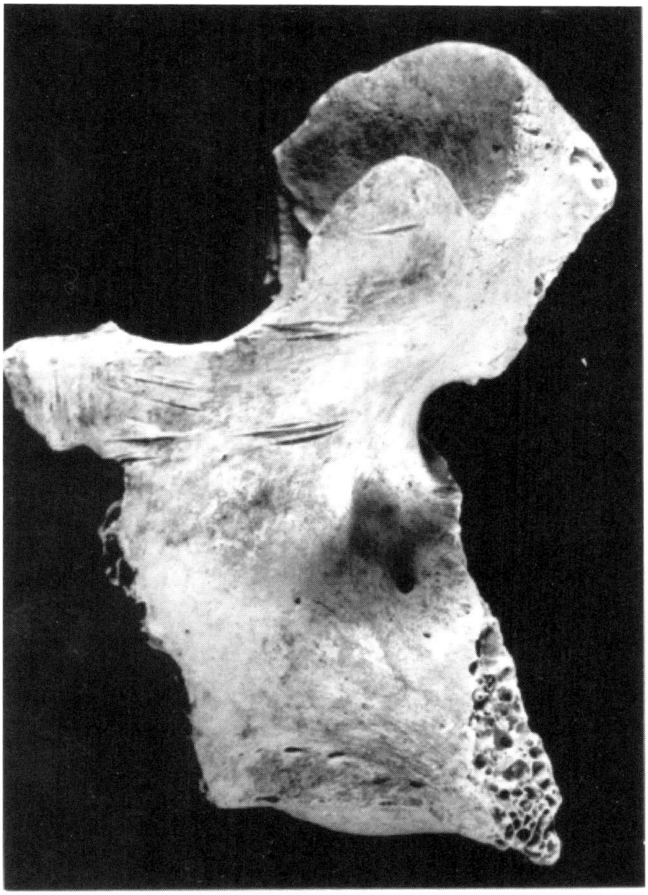

Figure 4
Atlas (first vertebra) of a caprine with butchery marks.
The Nabataeans slaughtered caprines by cutting their throat with a knife. This technique left typical cut marks on the ventral face of the atlas. (Photo by C. Ratton).

and goat hair were used but also camel hair. Natural fibres of goat hair range in colour from cream to dark brown while those of sheep were cream or light brown indicating the natural pelage of animals at this time[30]. These findings corroborate Strabo's description of the Nabataeans having 'white-fleeced' sheep.

[30] Shamir 2003, 36.

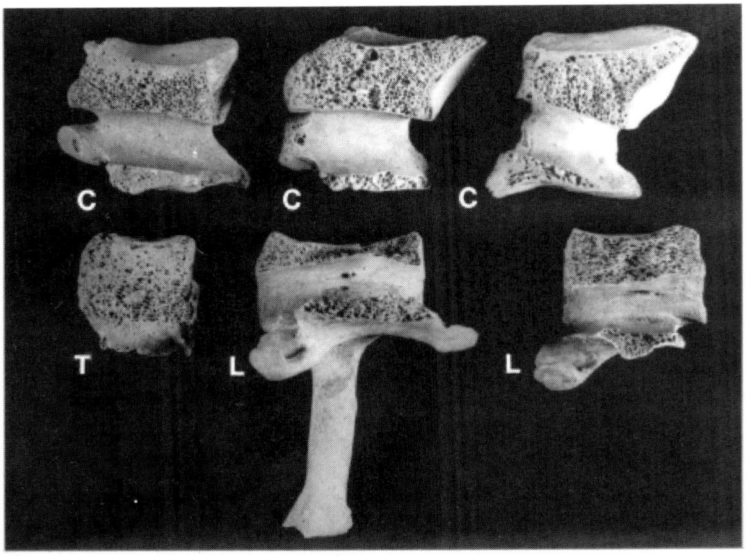

Figure 5
Caprine cervical (C), thoracic (T) and lumbar (L) vertebrae severed through the middle of the centrum.
The majority of the vertebrae at ez-Zantur have been cut through the centrum to form into two equal parts. This shows that during butchery, the carcass was initially separated into two parts by sectioning the vertebral column down the centre. (Photo by C. Ratton).

(b) Other domestic mammals

Although camel is the next most frequently represented mammalian species after sheep and goat, its remains only constitute 4% of the identified mammal bones. It is represented by all skeletal elements: cranium, trunk, limbs and feet. Butchery marks, especially on vertebrae, ribs and toe bones are common, attesting to the consumption of camel meat (Figure 6). However, the paucity of camel remains indicates that it was not regularly eaten. It is possible that this species was also exploited for milk, but it is not possible to test this claim based on the faunal record currently available. The majority of bones are fused, representing adult individuals. One unfused pelvis indicates the presence of a very young juvenile, while a small proportion of young adults are represented by phalanges which are in the process of fusing. The camel, being well adapted to sandy areas, was essentially used for riding as well as a pack animal and not for food. Classical sources, for example Strabo, describe the use of camel riders in the Nabataean army, such as in the Arabian campaign with the Romans (Negev 1988a). The importance of camels in trade may explain why, despite its relative scarcity in the archaeozoological record, the camel was commonly represented in Nabataean terracottas[31] as well as in reliefs such as that in the Siq at Petra.

[31] Bignasca 1993, 66.

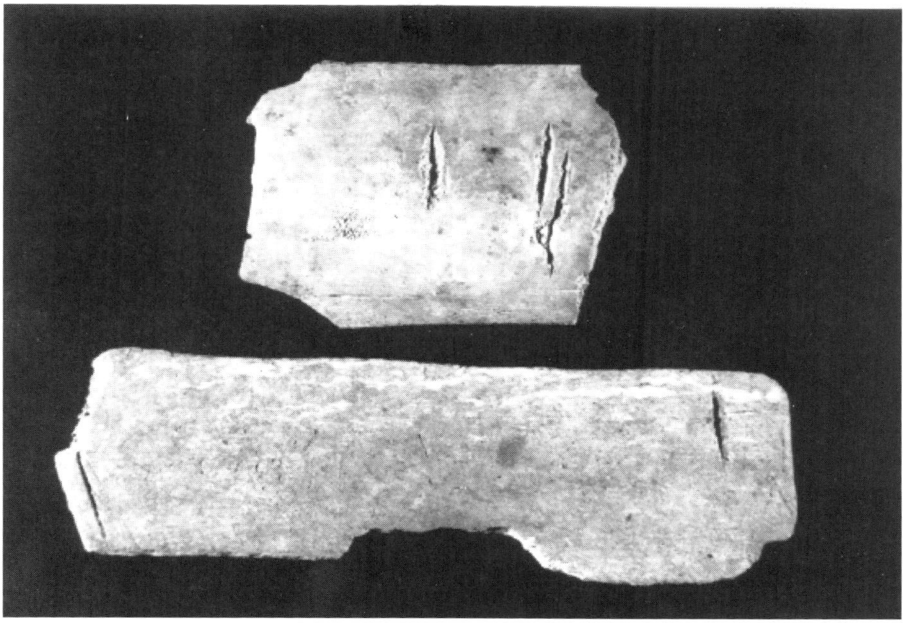

Figure 6
Butchery marks on camel ribs.
Repetitive chop marks reflect the difficulty faced in sectioning the thick ribs of adult camels. (Photo by C. Ratton.)

Camel bones were used in the manufacture of bone artefacts as attested to by the presence of sawn diaphyses in the ez-Zantur assemblage[32] while at the sites of Avdat, Nizzana and En Rahel camel scapulae were used as writing tablets[33]. Herodotus[34] describes the Nabataeans as having camel-skin water containers, a further indication of the multiple forms of exploitation of this species and its products. Shamir[35] reports that natural fibres of camel hair found in Nabataean sites in the Negev, were light yellow in colour, which is similar to animals found in the region today.

Among the equids (0.3% of mammal remains, Figure 1), which include donkey, horse and maybe even mule, all bones were derived from adult animals. Like the camel, donkey bones show butchery marks indicating that they were also exploited for food. This does not appear to be the case of the horse, although to date only three horse bones have been identified in this sample. Clay figurines of

[32] Bone artefacts will be studied by A. Schneider-Naef.

[33] Negev (1977) has originally described the camel scapula from Avdat (subsequently mentioned by Hakker-Orion 1984: 210), and that from Nizzana (Negev 1988). The scapula from En Rahel is referred to by Hakker-Orion (1993).

[34] In Hackl *et al.* 2003, 462.

[35] Shamir 2003, 36.

horses and riders are commonly found in Nabataean sites[36], while at several settlements in the Negev desert, remains of stables have been found which have been associated with the keeping of horses[37]. At least two Classical texts support this claim; Josephus[38] mentions that Malchos I gave four riding horses to Hyrkanos II, while in the *Epigram* of Poseidippos of Pella it is stated that horses were ridden by the Nabataeans during combat[39].

Cattle are poorly represented at ez-Zantur (0.3%), and only by toe bones and cranial elements. In this very small assemblage, two fragments exhibit cut marks resulting from butchery. The few cattle remains found till now represent a gracile and relatively small-sized animal that does not tally with the large Nabataean oxen described by Strabo[40]. Although far less important than the camel in the Nabataean economy, cattle could have provided a similar variety of secondary products. Following Herodotus's description that Arabs of the fifth century B.C. used containers made of camel and cattle hide[41], it is likely that Nabataeans favoured cattle skin to manufacture leather.

Pigs constitute 2% of the domestic fauna. They are primarily represented by juvenile individuals and even piglets. This slaughter pattern and the presence of all elements of the skeleton indicate that they were raised locally for meat rather than preserved joints of pork being imported.

Remains of dogs are rare. Their bones are generally complete and in two instances several bones were discovered in anatomical connection. This, as well as the fact that there are no butchery marks on the bones, indicates that they were not eaten but rather kept as pets. Few of the 10,000 bones in the assemblage of ez-Zantur exhibit carnivore damage that may reflect the limited number of dogs kept at the settlement.

(c) Wild mammals

Relative to the domestic fauna, hunted mammals are rare. They are mainly represented by gazelle (*Gazella* sp.), which even nowadays can be seen in the Wadi Araba a few hours walk from Petra, and wild boar (*Sus scrofa*), a species now extinct in the area. Remains of hare (*Lepus capensis*) as well as hyrax (*Procavia capensis,* Figure 7) have been identified but it is uncertain whether they were consumed. Several species of wild carnivore are found including the weasel (*Mustela nivalis).* They too may not have served as dietary items. The weasel is found in the Levant up until the Byzantine period after which it became extinct in the region[42].

[36] Bignasca 1993, 66.

[37] Rosenthal-Heginbottom (2003, 26) notes that Nabataean stables were uncovered at Mampsis, Oboda, Sobata and Rehovot-in-the-Negev.

[38] Josephus *Antiquities of the Jews* 15, 165–179, cf. Hackl *et al.* 2003, 505–509.

[39] Hackl *et al.* 2003, 587.

[40] Geographica 16, 4, 26, cf. Hackl *et al.* 2003, 615–617.

[41] Hackl *et al.* 2003, 462.

[42] Boessneck 1977 has discussed the osteological remains of weasels from archaeological

Figure 7
Hyrax (*Procavia capensis*).
This small mammal of about 3kg is found in Africa, the Arabian Peninsula and the Levant where it lives in colonies and inhabits rocky. Hyrax occurs today in the mountainous region of Petra. (Photo by M. Ruedi).

All these wild mammals could have been hunted in the vicinity of the city, even the wild boar (see below). There is only one species commonly hunted in the area today which is not represented in the Nabataean levels at Petra (nor in the Late Roman or Byzantine period), the ibex (*Capra ibex nubiana*). It is difficult to imagine that this well-adapted cliff dweller did not inhabit this region in the past, a feature highlighted by the presence of terracotta statuettes depicting ibex from Nabataean levels at ez-Zantur[43]. However, as it is difficult to distinguish skeletal elements of goat and ibex (except for the horn cores), this methodological issue may account for the absence of ibex in the faunal record.

sites in the region, while Harrison and Bate 1991 have described the present-day species from Arabia.

[43] Bignasca 1993, 66: the ibex statuettes are easily identifiable due to the ringed-form of their horns.

(d) Birds

Despite their small size and fragility, bird remains are well represented and comprise 8% of the identified species (Figure 1). A total of 755 bird bones were recovered from the three terraces at ez-Zantur of which over half (477) could be identified to family and/or species. Bones of chicken were the most abundant and fragments of their eggshells were also represented in large quantities. The domestic goose (*Anser anser*) is also found, but represented by only 2 bones. Remains of pigeon (*Columba livia*) were identified but their status as wild or domestic could not be determined.

Wild birds constitute between 11–28% (116 bones) of the identified bird remains from the three terraces. The most common species is the chukar partridge (*Alectoris chukar*), whose bones exhibited numerous cut marks associated with skeletal disarticulation. This bird species is still hunted in the Petra area by Bedouin. After the partridge, the most common game bird represented is the water rail (*Rallus aquaticus*). Other species like the corncrake (*Crex crex*), the moorhen (*Gallinula chloropus*), the sand partridge (*Ammoperdix heyi*) and the quail (*Coturnix coturnix*) are present but in low numbers. Remains of small songbirds (Passeriformes) were also found but may represent non-dietary items that were accidentally included in the archaeological deposits.

Several fragments of ostrich eggshell – all without decorations, and an atlas vertebra attest to the presence and hunting of ostrich (*Struthio camelus*)[44]. The ostrich is now extinct in the Near East, since the last individual was killed in 1939 near the pipeline between Iraq and Saudi Arabia[45]. The discovery of ostrich eggshell suggests that ostrich eggs may have been consumed, but these items have also been the object of extensive trade in the Near East and were used as receptacles, decorative elements or ritual objects[46]. Therefore they should be considered as both raw material (maybe even trade objects) and dietary remains.

(e) Fish

Though not found in large quantities, fish remains are regularly recovered from Nabataean layers at ez-Zantur[47]. Tuna and mackerel (Scombridae, 33%) and Emperors (Lethrinidae, 30%) dominate the sample, followed by groupers (Serranidae, 14%). Parrotfish, which becomes the major fish species consumed in later periods and reaches 80% of the fish remains during Byzantine time[48], is only poorly represented in the Nabataean layers (4%). Snappers (Lutjanidae), barracudas (Sphyraenidae), seabreams (Sparidae), trevallies (Carangidae) and probably grunts (Haemulidae), complete the variety of marine fish eaten by the Nabatae-

[44] Studer 1996, 368–9.
[45] Jennings 1986, 445.
[46] Caubet 1983.
[47] Desse-Berset & Studer 1996.
[48] Studer 2001, 385.

ans. All the fish identified to species level were imported from the Red Sea, which could suggest that no fish were imported from the Mediterranean Sea.

A single species of freshwater fish, the catfish (*Clarias gariepinus),* is also found at ez-Zantur. As yet we do not know from which large river it originates, the nearest being the Jordan River, but a recent study has shown that long distance trade in catfish took place from the Nile River to the town of Sagalassos in Turkey during the Roman period[49].

(f) Molluscs

Marine, freshwater and terrestrial molluscs were recovered from ez-Zantur[50]. The marine shells are the most abundant (more than 400 pieces) and originate from both the Red and Mediterranean Seas. There are at least 30 species of seashell at the site, but the assemblage is dominated by two species: the wedge clam (*Donax trunculus*) and the top shell (*Tectus dentatus*). The presence of a large quantity of wedge clams regularly found *in situ* at the site with the two valves still together, and apparently not used as raw material in the preparation of ornaments, indicates that these shells should be interpreted as dietary residues. This contention is supported by the presence of damage on the ridge of the shells and cut marks on their internal surface. This species is a common bivalve from the Mediterranean Sea. The second common mollusc, the top shell, originates from the Red Sea. Because of the presence of decorative elements made from the top shell, there is some doubt as to whether it served as a dietary item. Further studies will probably resolve this question. The other marine shells were most probably been used as ornaments or decorative items. Some, like the pearl oyster (*Pinctada margaritifera*), spider conch (*Lambis truncata*) and cowries (Cyprinidae) include specimens that have been modified, while others were left intact .

An edible landsnail, *Helix* sp., appears to have been consumed by the Nabataeans. Twelve *Helix* shells were found on a floor next to a pottery assemblage dated to the first century A.D.[51]. Previously a few fragmented shells of this species were found on-site but were thought to represent recent intrusions. The current finds and their particular context shows without doubt that the Nabataeans consumed landsnails. Remains of freshwater bivalves were also found at ez-Zantur, but as yet have not been identified to species such that their use cannot as yet be interpreted. To summarise, it seems that the molluscs found at ez-Zantur were essentially used for ornamental purposes, except for the wedge clams and *Helix* which were eaten.

[49] Arndt *et al.* 2003.

[50] The study of molluscs from ez-Zantur has been undertaken by the author in collaboration with Yves Finet.

[51] Gorgerat 1999, 272.

Chronological Variation

An earlier study on dietary differences between the Nabataean and Roman periods at az-Zantur has shown that variation between bone assemblages may in fact reflect differences in socio-economic status between areas of the same site rather than chronological change[52]. Examination of diachronic trends within the Nabataean sample is less complex as the two Nabataean phases can be separated only on one terrace, EZ I. However, the assemblages from each are not large. Of the total 5,985 identified animal bones recovered from the three terraces at ez-Zantur, only 2,914 remains can be more precisely dated: 1,862 bones can be attributed to the earliest Nabataean phase (first century B.C.) and 2,702 to the 2nd Nabataean phase (first century A.D.).

The frequency of sheep and goat remains is similar in the two phases, comprising 93% of the bones. However, the other mammals exhibit markedly different frequencies (Figure 8). When sheep and goat remains are excluded from

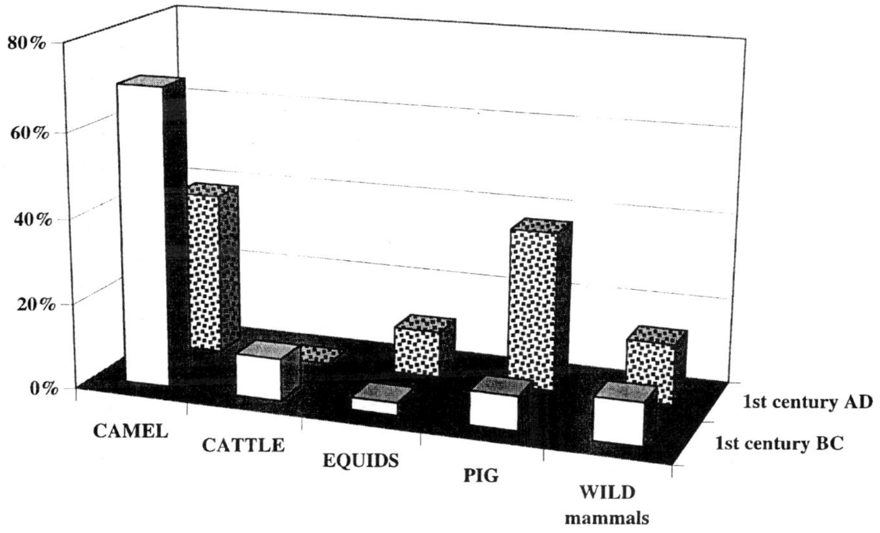

Figure 8
Chronological variation at ez-Zantur.
A comparison of the relative frequencies of edible mammals (excluding caprines) from the two Nabataean phases in Terrace EZ I.

the calculations, camel remains constitute 69% of all other mammals during the earliest phase at EZ I and only 39% in the later phase. In contrast, pig frequencies increase from 8 % to 37% and equids from 3% to 11%. This may be a reflection of a trend towards increased sedentism and urbanisation at the site as camels are a quintessential nomadic species while pigs are generally associated with sedent-

[52] Studer 2002.

ism[53]. Furthermore, the increase in equids is primarily due to the abundance of donkeys. This may reflect their replacement of camels as beasts of burden in the city or for trade.

The freshwater catfish, *Clarias gariepinus,* is the only fish species found in the Nabataean levels at ez-Zantur that does not originate in the Red Sea[54]. Of the 7 bones of this species, 4 were found in the first century A.D. sample in three different localities and as such do not constitute a localised deposit. There is no precise chronological information concerning the other 3 bones. Most importantly, no other remains of catfish or of any other freshwater fish species have been recovered from later periods at Petra or sites such as Jabal Harun in its immediate vicinity. Their presence in the later Nabataean levels at the site may reflect the increased wealth of the settlement and the importation of luxury items.

Spatial Variation

To date, dietary information is only available for one quarter of the city of Petra. As noted above, even in the same part of the town, bone remains from the different terraces separated from each other by only 100m may reflect variation in the social status of the inhabitants[55]. Although Nabataean diet, as reflected in bones recovered from all three terraces at ez-Zantur, was dominated by meat and secondary products derived from sheep and goats, the inhabitants of terrace EZ IV consumed a far greater quantity of birds than those of terrace EZ I (32% compared to 9%). This concerns not only domestic chicken but also wild birds (Figure 9). Chicken represent 23% of the remains at EZ IV compared to 8% at EZ I. Similarly, the inhabitants of EZ IV consumed much more game birds (9%), namely chukar partridge and Rallidae than their neighbours on EZ I (1%). In addition, although based on small numbers, the remains of gazelle on EZ IV are double those of EZ I. These results, combined with the more complex architecture and wall decorations found on terrace EZ IV might reflect the greater wealth of the inhabitants of this terrace. It appears then that, as in the subsequent Roman period, poultry and game birds as well as venison were luxury items already in Nabataean times.

Evidence for trade

Renowned as traders, the Nabataeans built and developed their Kingdom thanks to the wealth resulting from trade in luxurious products and aromatics. Some ceramics from ez-Zantur reflect their trade links essentially with the Mediterranean world[56]. Architectural elements were also brought to the city, like marble and

[53] Grigson 1995; Hesse & Wapnish 1996; Horwitz & Studer in press.

[54] Desse-Berset & Studer 1996, 386.

[55] Studer 2002, 279–280.

[56] Schneider 1996, 142: different kinds of imported ceramics, especially amphora from

Figure 9
Spatial differences at az-Zantur (in %).
The Nabataeans living on terrace EZ IV consumed more chicken as well as wild birds than their neighbours on terrace EZ I. This may reflect social differences between the inhabitants of the two areas. (Drawings by E. Studer.)

balks. It is evident that pack animals, the dromedary and equids, facilitated this endeavour as reflected in the presence of both these species at ez-Zantur. Examination of the age of camels and donkeys found at ez-Zantur indicates that mostly adult animals are represented. As yet no information is available on sex ratios, but these data correspond well with the age profile expected for pack animals[57].

In addition to the presence of beasts of burden, the most tangible evidence for trade provided by archaeozoological studies lies in the identification of the goods transported. Many of the imported animal products represent food items. The diet of Nabataeans living in the city of Petra included fish from the Red Sea which lies some 150 km to the south. Hundreds of fish bones were recovered from all three terraces of ez-Zantur, and Red Sea fish were also present in the houses in front of Jabal el-Khubta (Zeitler 1990) and at Avdat (Horwitz and Lernau in prep). The consistency of their presence and the quantity of these remains suggest that they were consumed not only as a supplement, but on a regular basis, at least for the

Rhodes, confirm the contacts with Greeks and Romans from the Mediterranean area. Direct evidence of trade with Aqaba is only shown by one piece of amphora (Keller and Schneider in prep.).

[57] Kohler-Rollefson 1989.

wealthier inhabitants. In addition, the presence of freshwater fish reflects trade from either the Levant or Egypt. Similarly, the presence of marine shells indicates trade with both the Mediterranean and Red Seas. An additional non-dietary faunal item brought to Petra was elephant ivory, imported in the form of finished products.

Animals and ritual

On Mount Serbal in western Sinai, a Nabataean sanctuary, dating to the 2nd century B.C. through to the early part of the 2nd century AD, was excavated by U. Avner (Israel Antiquities Authority). Some 70 animal bones were recovered from the site of which 51 represented burnt and unidentifiable fragments (Horwitz in prep.).

The bones were recovered from a passage some 50 cm wide situated between the inner and outer courtyards of the sanctuary, as well as from the outer courtyard. They were found together with a rich assemblage of cultural items. Of the 19 bones that could be identified to species, 5 were burnt but no butchery marks were evident. Taxa identified were a small sized fowl (*Gallus gallus*), gazelle, probably *Gazella dorcas* and sheep/goat (*Ovis/Capra*). With the exception of a small fragment of sheep/goat jaw, all bones represent limbs, suggesting selection of meat-rich bodyparts. Only the gazelle bones could be aged, and these are derived from an immature animal. According to Horwitz (in prep.), the assemblage from Jebel Serbal is reminiscent of a temenos deposit comprising remains of animals sacrificed or dedicated to the deity of a sanctuary. Following ritual activities, which often including burning, the bone remains were discarded on or near the sanctuary grounds.

Another example of animal remains derived from Nabataean ritual contexts are the bones of camel and horse which were found in a Nabataean tomb during recent excavations under the Khazneh carried out by the Jordanian Department of Antiquities. It is not clear whether these represent remnants of a funerary banquet or offerings interred with the deceased.

Paleoclimate and animals

There are some species found in the assemblage of ez-Zantur which do not inhabit the Petra region nowadays and whose presence two thousand years ago can be related to the less arid environmental conditions prevailing during the Nabataean and Roman periods (see summary in Horwitz and Studer 2005). In addition, the irrigation system created by the Nabataeans to provide water for the town of Petra, as well as numerous cisterns, water canals and dams that were built throughout the landscape to facilitate cultivation, would have created mesic micro-environments[58]. For example, the water rail (*Rallus aquaticus)* is the

[58] Oleson 1997, 2001.

second most common wild bird found on each of the three terraces. This species is adapted to marshes and a small number of resident birds augmented by a large winter influx were found at the Azraq oasis north-east of Jordan 40 years ago, when the marshes were still extant[59]. The semi-arid conditions around Petra today do not offer a suitable habitat for this species. In addition, other avian species that are associated with wetland sites have been identified, but are only represented by a few bones, such as the grey heron (*Ardea cinerea*), the moorhen (*Gallinula chloropus*) and, in some extent, the corncrake (*Crex crex*). The hypotheses that these game birds were trade products and not hunted in the area cannot entirely be discounted, but given the presence of relatively high quantities of water rails, their presence in the region is viable.

A further indication of more mesic environmental conditions during the Nabataean is the presence at ez-Zantur of wild and domestic mammals with a high water dependency, such as the wild boar, domestic pig and cattle. In the past, raising of swine in the Levant would probably not have been viable in areas which received less than 300 mm of rainfall per annum[60], unless a sufficient supply of water was guaranteed through investment in special hydraulic systems[61]. Petra is situated today below the 200 mm isohyte, such that even if the climate was slightly less arid 2,000 years ago, this would still not have been sufficient to support extensive pig husbandry. The presence at ez-Zantur of relatively few pig remains during the first century B.C. (0.5 %) followed by an increase during the first century A.D. (2.4%) may be related to the increased precipitation in the region and the development of wide-scale hydraulic technology[62].

Conclusions

The faunal data currently available for the Nabataeans is primarily based on remains from Petra. They document an economy similar to that found in other contemporaneous Near Eastern settlements, namely one based on sheep and goat herding supplemented by the exploitation of other domestic animals, hunted game as well as fish. Sheep and goat served as the primary source of animal protein, with a focus on the exploitation of milk and probably also fibre. Camels and equids provided transport with camels more common indicating their relative importance in the economy. Donkeys as well as horses were exploited, the latter documented in the epigraphy, iconography and architecture. A substantial part of Nabataean diet was comprised of birds especially chicken and their eggs, and fish. Increasing frequencies of pig, presence of cattle as well as imported fish, molluscs and luxury items, point to the increasing wealth and sedentism of this population. The Classical texts then provide only a partial picture of Nabataean

[59] Andrew 1995: 76.
[60] Grigson 1995.
[61] Hesse & Wapnish 1996.
[62] Horwitz & Studer in press.

diet, and may in fact reflect only the pre-sedentary phase of this community. Given the limited archaeozoological material available, it is not possible as yet to assess the economic relationship between town and countryside, but it appears that animals were kept by the town dwellers who did not rely solely upon markets and traded items for their food.

Acknowledgements

The work on the fauna from ez-Zantur is part of the Swiss-Liechtenstein Research project undertaken under the direction of Rolf Stucky and Bernhard Kolb since 1988. I would like to express my gratitude to them as well as all other members of the team for their assistance in the fruitful and friendly collaboration which continues. The sorting of small bones from sieved deposits as well as cleaning of all the bones from the excavation was carried out with the precious and patient help of Jean-Marie Zumstein to whom I'm deeply grateful. I would also like to thank the excavators of the Khazneh from the Jordanian Department of Antiquities, for allowing me to study the faunal material from this site. I am especially grateful to Liora Kolska Horwitz for facilitating access to her unpublished data, and her useful comments on this manuscript.

The excavation of ez-Zantur was supported by the Swiss-Liechtenstein Foundation for Archaeological Research Abroad (Zurich) and work on the fish remains from this site was supported by a grant from the G. and. A. Claraz Foundation (Switzerland) for the creation of a reference collection of species from the Red Sea. The fish were prepared with the assistance of Jean-Marie Zumstein and Catherine Masserey at the Marine Science Station of Aqaba (Jordan) to whom I offer my sincere thanks.

References

Abu-Rabia, A., 1994. *The Negev Bedouin and Livestock Rearing*, Oxford: Berg Publishers.

Andrews, I.J., 1995. *The Birds of the Hashemite Kingdom of Jordan*, Scotland: Burns and Harris Ltd.

Arndt, A., van Neer W., Hellemans B., Robben J., Volckaert F. & Waelkens M., 2003. "Roman trade relationships at Sagalassos (Turkey) elucidated by ancient DNA of fish remains", *JAS* 30, 1095–1105.

Beech, M., 2007. "The mammal bones", in K.D. Politis et al, *Excavations at the Sanctuary of Lot at Deir Ain Abata*, The British Museum Press, London.

Bignasca, A., Desse-Berset N., Fellman Brogli R., Glutz R., Karg S., Keller D., Kolb B., Kramar Ch., Peter M., Schmid S.G., Schneider Ch., Stucky R.A., Studer J. and Zanoni I., 1996. *Petra. Ez Zantur I. Ergebnisse der Schweizerisch-Liechtensteinischen Ausgrabungen 1988–1992*, Mainz: von Zabern.

Bignasca, A., 1993. "Die Terrakotten", in *Petra und die Weihrauchstrasse*, Exhibition Catalogue for "Le Point", Zurich, 65–67.

Boessneck, J., 1977. "Funde vom Mauswiesel, Mustela nivalis Linné, 1766, auf dem Tell Hesbon, Jordanien", *Säugetierkundliche Mitteilungen* 25, 1/77, 44–48.

Browning, I., 1989. *Petra.*, London: Chatto & Windus.

Caubet, A., 1983. "Les oeufs d'autruche au Proche-Orient ancien", *Annual Report of the Department of Antiquities of Cyprus*, 193–198.

Dar, S., 2003. "The Nabateans in the Hauran", in R. Rosenthal-Hegingbottom (ed.), *The Nabateans in the Negev*, Hecht Museum Exhibition Catalogue: Haifa University, 45–46.

Desse-Berset, N. & Studer J., 1996. "Fish Remains from Ez Zantur (Petra, Jordan)", in A. Bignasca *et al.*, *Petra, Ez Zantur I. Ergebnisse der Schweizerisch-Liechtensteinischen Ausgrabungen 1988–1992*, Terra Archaeologica II, Monographien der Schweizerisch-Liechtensteinischen Stiftung für Archäologische Forschungen im Ausland (SLSA/FSLA), Mayence: von Zabern, 381–387.

Driesch, A. von den & Boessneck, J., 1995. "Final report on the zooarchaeological investigation of animal bone finds from Tell Hesban, Jordan", in O. S. LaBianca and A. von den Driesch (eds) *Faunal remains: taphonomical and zooarchaeological studies of the animal remains from Tell Hesban and vicinity*, Hesban 13: Andrews University Press, 67–108.

Erickson-Gini, T. and Israel, Y., 2003. "Recent advances in the research of the Nabatean and Roman Negev" in R. Rosenthal-Hegingbottom (ed.), *The Nabateans in the Negev*, Hecht Museum Exhibition Catalogue: Haifa University, 9–13.

Fiema, Z.T., 1996. "Nabataean and Palmyrene commerce – The mechanisms of intensification", *Annales archeologiques arabes syriennes* 42, (Palmyra and the silk road), 189–195.

Gorgerat, L., 1999. "Nabataean Fineware from Room 15", in B. Kolb, L. Gorgerat and M. Grawehr, Swiss Liechtenstein excavations on Az-Zantur in Petra, 1998, *ADAJ* XLIII, Amman, 270–272.

Grant, A., 1982. "The use of tooth wear as a guide to the age of domestic ungulates", in B. Wilson, C. Grigson and S. Payne (eds.), *Ageing and Sexing Animal Bones from Archaeological sites*, British Archaeological Reports, British Series 109, 91–108.

Grigson, C., 1995. "Plough and Pasture in the early economy of the southern Levant", in T.E. Levy (ed.), *The Archaeology of Society in the Holy Land*, London: Leicester University Press, 245–268.

Habermehl, K.-H., 1975. *Die Altersbestimmung bei Haus- und Labortieren*, Berlin & Hamburg: Paul Parey.

Hackl, U.,1993. "Die Geschichte der Nabataer", in Petra und die Weihrauchstrasse, Exhibition Catalogue for "Le Point", Zürich, 5–13.

Hackl, U., Jenni H., Schneider C, 2003. *Quellen zur Geschichte der Nabatäer: Textsammlung mit Übersetzung und Kommentar*, Freiburg, Schweiz: Universitätsverlag.

Hakker-Orion, D., 1984. "The role of the camel in Israel's early history", in J. Clutton-Brock and C.Grigson (eds.), *Animals and Archaeology*, vol. 3, BAR International Series 202, Oxford, 207–210.

– 1993. "Faunal remains from sites along the Frankincense and Myrrh route", in H. Buitenhuis and A.T. Clason (eds.), *Archaeozoology of the Near East*, Leiden: Universal Book Services, 77–87.

Harrison, D.L. & Bates P.J.J., 1991. *The Mammals of Arabia*, Seven Oaks, Kent: Harrison Zoological Museum.

Hellwing, S. & Agiman I. 2000. "G. Animal bones", in Z. Meshel, *Sinai. Excavations and Studies*. BAR International Series 876, Oxford, 14–16.

Hesse, B. & Wapnish P., 1996. "Can pig remains be used for ethnic diagnosis in the Ancient Near East ?", in A.S. Silberman and D. Small (eds.), *The Archaeology of Israel*, Journal for the Study of the Old Testament, Supplement Series 237, 238–270.

Horwitz, L.K., 1998. "Animal bones from Horbat Rimmon: Hellenistic to Byzantine periods" *Atiqot* XXXV, 65–76.

Horwitz, L.K. & Lernau O., in prep. "Fauna from Avdat", in T. Erickson-Gini (ed.), *Avdat*, Israel Antiquities Authority Monographs.

Horwitz, L.K., in prep. *A Diachronic Study of Patterns of Animal Exploitation in the Sinai Peninsula*, Ph.D. Thesis, University of Tel Aviv.

Horwitz, L.K. & Studer J., 2005. "Pig production and exploitation during the Classical periods in the Southern Levant", *Archaeozoology of the Near East* VI., H. Buitenhuis, A. M. Choyke, L. Martin, L. Bartosiewicz and M. Mashkour (eds.), Groningen: ARC-Publicaties, 222–239.

Jennings, M. C., 1986. "The distribution of the extinct arabian ostrich *Struthio camelus syriacus*, Rothschild, 1919". *Fauna of Saudi Arabia* 8, 447–461.

Kolb, B., 1998. "Swiss-Liechtenstein excavation at Az Zantur in Petra 1997", *ADAJ* XLII, 259–277.

Kolb, B., Gorgerat L. & Grawehr M. 1999. "Swiss-Liechtenstein excavations on az-Zantur in Petra, 1998". *ADAJ* XLIII, 261–277.

Kohler-Rollefson, I., 1989. "Zoological Analysis of camel skeletons", in *Pella of the Decapolis*,vol. 2, Final Report of Wooster Excavations in Area IX, The Civic Complex, 1979–1985, The College of Wooster, 142–164.

Méniel, P., 1987. "Les dépôts d'animaux du fossé chasséen de Boury-en-Vexin (Oise)", *Revue archéologique de Picardie*, 1/2, 3–26.

Negev, A., 1977. "Excavations at Avdat 1975–1976", *Qadmoniot* 10, 27–29. (in Hebrew)

– 1988a. "Understanding the Nabateans", *Biblical Archaeology Review*, November/ December, 27–45.

– 1988b. "Nabatean Cities in the Negev", *Ariel* 62/63, 126. (in Hebrew)

Oleson, J.P., 1997. "Landscape and cityscape in the Hisma: the resources of ancient Al-Humayma", *Studies in the History and Archaeology of Jordan* VI, 175–188.

– 2001. "Water supply in Jordan through the ages", in B. MacDonald, R. Adams and P. Bienkowski (eds.), *The Archaeology of Jordan*, Sheffield Academic Press, 603–619.

Payne, S., 1973. "Kill-off patterns in sheep and goats: the mandibles from Asvan Kale", *Anatolian Studies* 23, 281–303.

Peters, F.E., 1977. "The Nabataeans in the Hauran", *Journal of the American Oriental Society* 97, 263–277.

Redding, R.W., 1994. "The vertebrate fauna", in S.C. Herbert (ed.), *Tel Anafa I, i. Final Report on Ten Years of Excavation at a Hellenistic and Roman Settlement in Northern Israel*, Journal of Roman Archaeology Supplementary Series 10 (I,i), Michigan: Ann Arbor, 279–321.

Rosenthal-Heginbottom, R., 2003. "Artists and artisans: Reflections on Nabatean minor art – clay, metal and stone", in R. Rosenthal-Hegingbottom (ed.), *The Nabateans in the Negev*, Hecht Museum Exhibition Catalogue: Haifa University, 23–29.

Silver, I. A., 1969. "The ageing of domestic animals", in D. Brothwell and E.S. Higgs (eds.), *Science in Archaeology*, second edition, London: Thames and Hudson, 282–302.

Schmid, S.G., 2001. "The Nabataeans: Travellers between lifestyles", in B. MacDonald, R. Adams and P. Bienkowski (eds.) *The Archaeology of Jordan*, Sheffield: Sheffield University Press, 367–426.

– 2002. "From Aretas to the annexation: Petra and The Nabataeans", in J. Frosen and Z.T. Fiema (eds.), *Petra. A City Forgotten and Rediscovered*, Helsinki: Helsinki University Press, 44–59.

Schneider, Ch., 1996. "Die Importkeramik", in A. Bignasca *et al. Petra, Ez Zantur I. Ergebnisse der Schweizerisch-Liechtensteinischen Ausgrabungen 1988–1992*, Terra Archaeologica II, Monographien der Schweizerisch-Liechtensteinischen Stiftung für Archäologische Forschungen im Ausland (SLSA/FSLA), Mayence: von Zabern, 129–149.

Shamir, O., 2003. "Textiles, basketry and cordage from Nabatean sites along the spice route between Petra and Gaza", in R. Rosenthal-Hegingbottom (ed.), *The Nabateans in the Negev*, Hecht Museum Exhibition Catalogue: Haifa University, 35–38.

Stucky, R. A., 1992. "Das nabatäische Wohnhaus und das urbanistische System der Wohnquartiere in Petra". *Antike Kunst* 35, 2, 129–140.

– 1996. "Die nabatäischen Bauten", in A. Bignasca *et al. Petra, Ez Zantur I. Ergebnisse der Schweizerisch-Liechtensteinischen Ausgrabungen 1988–1992*, Terra Archaeologica II, Monographien der Schweizerisch-Liechtensteinischen Stiftung für Archäologische Forschungen im Ausland (SLSA/FSLA), Mayence: von Zabern, 13–50.

Studer, J., 1996. "La faune romaine tardive d'Ez Zantur, à Petra", in A. Bignasca *et al.*, *Petra, Ez Zantur I. Ergebnisse der Schweizerisch-Liechtensteinischen Ausgrabungen 1988–1992*, Terra Archaeologica II, Monographien der Schweizerisch-Liechtensteinischen Stiftung für Archäologische Forschungen im Ausland (SLSA/FSLA), Mayence: von Zabern, 359–375.

– 2001. "Observations on Animal Bones from Jabal Harûn", in J. Frösen *et al.*, The 1998–2000 Finnish Jabal Harûn Project: Specialized Reports, *ADAJ* 45, 384–386.

– 2002. "Dietary differences at Ez Zantur Petra, Jordan (1st century BC – AD 5th century)", in H. Buitenhuis, A.M. Choyke, M. Mashkour and A.H. Al-Shiyab (eds.), *Archaeozoology of the Near East* V, Groningen, The Netherlands: ARC-Publicaties 62, 273–281.

Toplyn, M. R., 1994. *Meat for Mars: Livestock, Limitanei, and Pastoral Provisioning for the Roman Army on the Arabian Frontier (A.D. 284–551)*, Unpublished PhD Thesis, Harvard University.

Zayadine, F., 1992. "L'espace urbain du grand Pétra, les routes et les stations caravanières", *ADAJ* 36, 217–233.

Zeitler, J.P., 1990. "Houses, sherds and bones: aspects of daily life in Petra", in S. Kerner (ed.) *The Near East in Antiquity*, vol I., Goethe-Institut, Amman: Al Kutba Publishers, 39–51.

The Urban Development of Petra

Peter J. Parr

Recent decades have witnessed a remarkable increase in archaeological activity at Petra, compared with the neglect the site suffered following its initial scientific exploration in the early 20th century. In addition to the continuing excavation of the Temple of the Winged Lions, and the perennial work of clearance and restoration at the Qasr el-Bint, there has been the uncovering of domestic architecture on ez-Zantur, the renewed investigation of the Colonnaded Street, the exposure of the spectacular Great Southern Temple, the revealing of several churches, and the discovery that the 'Lower Market' is an elaborate ornamental garden. Further reference to this work will be made later; for the moment suffice it to stress – what hardly needs stressing – how it has revolutionised our appreciation of the sophistication of Nabataean culture and our understanding of its affinities to that of the wider Greco-Roman world.

It is therefore all the more disappointing to realise that, despite these advances, the problem of dating the Petra free-standing monuments, and thus the history of the urban development of the city, remains as unresolved as it was when Judith McKenzie summarised the evidence available in 1990 in her book on *The Architecture of Petra*. Like Rome, Petra was not built in a day, but precisely when it was built is still not very certain. It is true that those – myself amongst them – who once assumed that many of the surviving major civic buildings could best be attributed to the period after the Roman annexation of AD 106, have been conclusively proved wrong. But who was responsible for each of the individual monuments and what was the appearance of the city at various times in its history, are questions to which at present no answer can be given with any degree of confidence.

The principal reason for this state of affairs is, of course, the almost complete lack of building inscriptions. The contrast in this respect between Petra and comparable sites in the region is striking, even allowing for the fact that these sites have been more extensively surveyed and excavated. The reason for this lack of inscriptions in Petra is obvious: the local building stone, sandstone, is conducive neither to the carving nor the preservation of good legible epigraphy. It is true that limestone and even marble were used on occasion in Petra for inscriptions, as they were for sculpture and architectural decoration, but this material must have been too rare and expensive to have been used liberally, and the fragments that escaped the lime-burner and survived to be found by the excavator are invariably small. In the circumstances, the architects of the free-standing monuments may well have been prompted to use alternative materials, such as metal or stucco, for any dedications, as they regularly were for funerary texts, as close study of the tomb façades makes clear.[1, 2]

In view of the paucity of epigraphic evidence for dating the free-standing monuments we are left with the archaeologist's traditional tools, pottery and coins. There are well known problems with both as dating material – coins can remain in circulation for a long time and pottery fashions usually change gradually – but at Petra they have special weaknesses. Regarding coins, the sandy soils of the site do not favour their preservation; of the one thousand or so coins found in the excavations of the British School of Archaeology there between 1958 and 1964, less than half were legible and many of these only uncertainly so, and the same seems to be true, for example, of the coins found in the first five seasons of Joukowsky's excavations of the Great Temple and of Khairy's excavations on el-Katute.[3] Coins can also easily become displaced from their original contexts, especially at Petra because of the soft, dry, sandy nature of the archaeological deposits there, and this is a problem which also affects potsherds, perhaps to an even greater extent.[4] Over the centuries the torrential winter rains and floods and the strong summer winds in the Petra valley have undoubtedly removed and re-positioned the unstable deposits, leaving behind the artefactual material which now lies in heterogeneous profusion on the surface, to be further disturbed by animal or human activity. Intrusive and extrusive material is the bane of the excavator's life, and it, and the dangers arising from it, are probably more pronounced at Petra than at most other archaeological sites in the region. Extreme caution thus has to be observed in using ceramic and numismatic evidence, even from reliable contexts, to establish dates for the excavated monuments.

Bearing these initial cautionary comments in mind, I intend, in the following paragraphs, to review the evidence currently available for constructing a chronology of the urban development of Petra, concentrating on the physical remains and ignoring the social, political and institutional aspects of urbanism. I shall also largely ignore the literary evidence bearing on the historical and economic development of the Nabataeans and their capital, since it is important to keep this and the archaeological data separate, if circularity of argument is to be avoided, and I shall refer to literary sources only in so far as they inform us directly about the appearance of the capital. I shall focus on the objective dating evidence, and treat very cautiously arguments based on stylistic and typological grounds, since these can only be valid if supported by an objective chronological framework. I shall deal with four issues: the date and nature of the original settlement of the Nabataeans; the Petra of Athenodorus and Strabo; the Roman impact; and the

[1] Parr 1968, 12, 14–15.

[2] McKenzie 1990, 33, suggests that tomb inscriptions may have been painted directly onto the stucco with which many of the façades were rendered. It is hard to agree with Joukowsky that "the Nabataeans did not intend to leave a written record – obviously, it did not matter to them if inscriptions could be seen, read, or understood" (Joukowsky 2001a, 3).

[3] Barrett 1998, 317; Khairy 1990, 7.

[4] Parr 1986, 193–194. On the problems at Petra of dating with coins and pottery. see also the sensible remarks of Hammond and Johnson (2000, 26–27).

decline of the city. And if I sometimes appear to take an unduly sceptical approach, I can only appeal to Abelard's well known dictum: "By doubting we come to inquiring, by inquiring we come to perceive the truth."

The date and nature of the initial settlement

The earliest free-standing structure in Petra which can be dated with reasonable accuracy is represented by the walls assigned to Phase (v) of the stratigraphic sequence beneath the south portico of the Colonnaded Street, Trench III of the British excavations.[5] Of these, only Walls A and E appeared in the section then published, but a number of other walls and associated surfaces, including patches of stone paving can certainly be attributed to the same phase, while south of the Portico Wall two further stretches of wall are also certainly contemporary (Fig. 1). An analysis of the stratigraphy shows that there are in fact several sub-phases to Phase (v), representing a number of repairs and modifications to a single structure, the size and plan of which are impossible to judge owing to later building activities and disturbances and to the restricted area of excavation. However, that it was a fairly substantial building cannot be doubted. Although the walls are made of only irregularly coursed limestone boulders taken from the nearby *wadi* and packed with smaller stones and clay, they are sturdy, being between 0.85 m. and 1.0 m. in thickness, and their rough construction was originally concealed by a surface rendering of clay. Although now largely broken or destroyed, the contemporary stone paving was originally regular and carefully laid (Fig 2).

An indication of the approximate date of this building is afforded by the twenty or so coins found on associated surfaces, including, most significantly, a group of seven, probably a dispersed hoard. The coins are all of the uninscribed type sometimes called Early Nabataean but now recognised as being the first true Nabataean issue, originating in the reign Aretas II (c.100–96/92 BC).[6] However, Meshorer has argued that they could still have been minted by Aretas' successor, Obodas I (c.96/92–86 BC) and possibly even by Aretas III (c.86–62 BC).[7] It is also probable that they continued in use for a lengthy period, for, as Meshorer points out, Aretas III's own coinage – the first fully inscribed Nabataean issue – was minted in Damascus and primarily intended for circulation in the north.[8] In view of the uncertainties, therefore, we must exercise caution in using the coins from Phase (v) to establish a precise date of the building. Nevertheless, the fact that no examples of later issues were found amongst the relatively large number of coins from the relevant contexts strongly suggests that its construction and occupation are to be placed no later than the first decades of the 1st century BC.

[5] Parr 1965, 528; 1970, 357–358, 369–370, fig.1.

[6] Bowsher 1990, 232. Bowshers's attribution of these coins to Phase IV must now be corrected to Phase V.

[7] Meshorer 1975, 12.

[8] Meshorer 1975, 14.

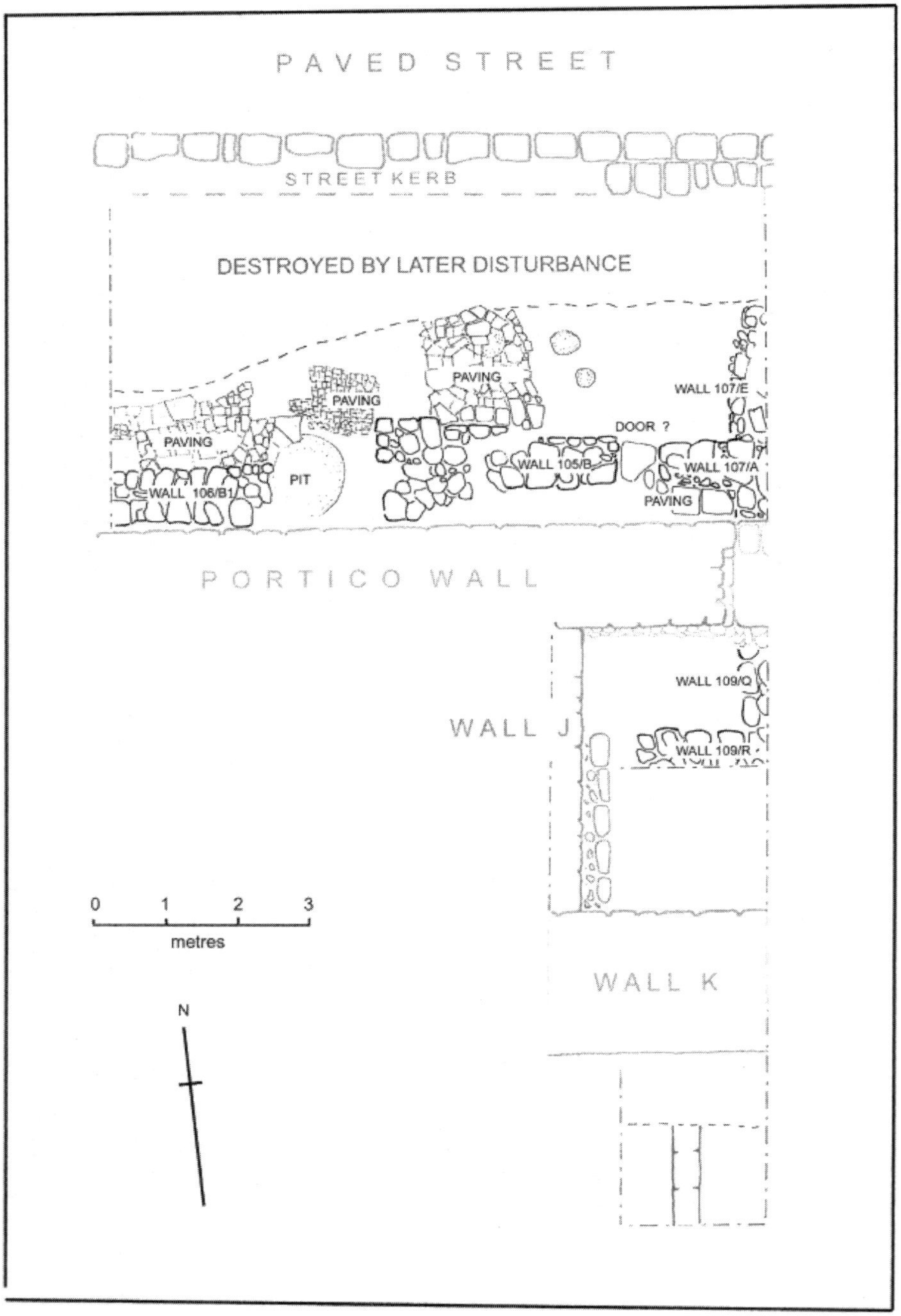

Figure 1: Plan of Trench III (South), Phase V

Figure 2: Trench III (South), Phase V, stone paving

This date is supported by the presence in Phase (v) – for the first time in the sequence – of a few examples of fine Nabataean pottery, including one sherd painted in the simple linear style [9] which is generally agreed to belong at the beginning of the stylistic development of the Nabataean painted ware.[10]

[9] Parr 1970, 358 and Fig.2:16.

[10] Parr 1965, 530–531; 1978, 203; Schmid 1995, 640, 645 and Fig. 9. On the basis of his analysis of the large quantities of painted Nabataean pottery from the Swiss-Liechtenstein excavations on ez-Zantur, Schmid concludes that this linear style precedes the naturalistic floral style of painting; he suggests a date of the late 2nd and early 1st century BC for the linear style and the later 1st century BC for the floral. This sequence and chronology accords well with that derived from the much smaller amount of material from the Trench III sounding, where examples of the floral style first appear in Phase VI and continue until at least Phase IX, which has a *terminus post quem* of 9 BC, based on coins of Aretas IV (Parr 1970: 358, 370). However, dating the linear style earlier than the floral gives rise to a problem concerning the stylistic origin of this pottery. It is generally accepted that the shapes and fabrics of the earliest Nabataean fine wares derive from Hellenistic prototypes, and I have argued elsewhere that the same is true of the painted floral decoration, for the naturalistic style of which there are many Hellenistic analogies (Parr 1978: 206). However, if the linear patterns are earlier than the floral, though on similar shapes and in a similar technique, serious difficulties of understanding arise. There are no obvious antecedents of the linear decoration in either the Hellenistic repertoire or in the local Near Eastern repertoire, and it would be strange if the Nabataean potters adopted Hellenistic pottery shapes, to which they applied their own simple linear designs, first, only adding the Hellenistic floral motifs later. It is surely more logical to suppose that the inspiration for both shapes and decoration occurred at one and the same time, and in an earlier paper I have suggested how and why this might have occurred. But the matter certainly needs further consideration.

However, this is not the earliest building beneath the Colonnaded Street. As the interim report on this sounding makes clear,[11] there are four earlier phases of occupation, the earliest of which, Phase (i), is characterised by walls of similar construction, though apparently incorporating fewer large boulders and having clay floors rather than stone paving, resting directly on the natural undisturbed gravel of the *wadi* bank. Subsequent to this is at least one other major building phase, and perhaps two, with walls on a slightly different alignment and more similar in construction to those of Phase (v) than those of Phase (i) (Figs. 3 and 4). The stratigraphy here is very compressed and has been disturbed by later building, while to complicate matters further there are indications of occupation phases having been entirely removed by human or natural agencies; the detailed structural sequence here is thus far from certain, although the outlines are clear.

Unfortunately there is no direct dating evidence for the phases prior to Phase (v). The suggestion in the original report and elsewhere[12] that the earliest structures should be dated to the middle or end of the 3rd century BC was based largely on the recovery in the excavations of a number of coins of this date minted at Aradus in Phoenicia, but further analysis has shown that most of these come from secondary deposits – pits or fills – and of the very few found in primary occupation levels the earliest belongs to Phase (v). The coins may have been in circulation for a long time, therefore, and they thus provide no firm basis for ascribing the earliest occupation to the 3rd century BC. The same applies to an uninscribed fragment of an imported amphora handle fragment in one of the Phase (i) occupation levels; amphorae of mid- and late-3rd century date were certainly in use in Petra, but, like coins, this type of vessel could have a long life. In the absence of concrete evidence, therefore, we are obliged to use the rule of thumb: such is the clear impression from the stratigraphy that building activities extended over a considerable period of time prior to the construction of the Phase (v) building, to be measured in decades and perhaps in generations, that the assumption that the earliest occupation here dates back to the early 2nd or even the late 3rd century BC cannot be far wrong.

So far we have been dealing with the early structures south of the Colonnaded Street, and now a few words are necessary concerning similar remains on the opposite side of that thoroughfare. Direct stratigraphic links for this period between the two sides of the street have been destroyed, by the deep foundations of the street itself and by a previous large disturbance – perhaps the result of flood erosion or the collapse of a retaining wall – visible in the published section.[13] However, at the base of the sounding on the northern side, resting on the natural *wadi* gravel, are remains of walls of the same rough boulder-and-clay construction as those we have been considering (Fig. 5). It is impossible to say precisely to which phase of the southern sequence they belong, but in view of their structural similarity and their position at the base of the archaeological deposits, it is certain that they date to the same general period. Although they are too

[11] Parr 1970.

[12] Parr 1965, 528; 1970, 369–370.

[13] Parr 1970, 353, fig.1.

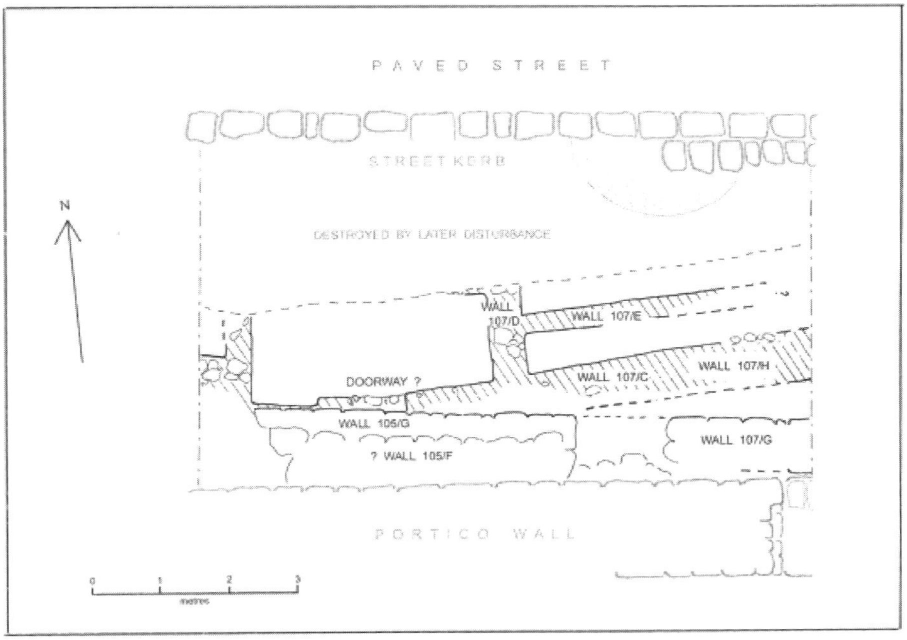

Figure 3: Plan of Trench III (South), Phases i–iv

Figure 4: Trench III (South), Phase i, walls

Figure 5: Trench III (North), walls and oven of earliest phase

exiguous to provide a coherent plan, they are significant because they considerably enlarge the area covered by these early structures on the *wadi* bank, and because the presence of a clay oven indicates that the structures were houses and not storerooms, as has recently been suggested. [14]

We must now consider the two other areas in Petra where there appears to be evidence for relatively early structures. The first is on a terrace overlooking the Wadi Musa due west of the Urn Tomb. Here Zeitler has exposed a room of a house with walls built of undressed medium-sized wadi stones resting more-or-less directly on the rock surface.[15] No mention is made in the reports of clay packing or surface rendering – in fact, the excavator says a dry stone walling technique was used – or of stone paving, but despite this the similarities with the walls from the early phases in Trench III are striking. A domed clay oven found within the room also recalls that at the bottom of the northern part of that Trench. As for date, no legible coins were found, but Zeitler's study of the Terra Sigillata and Nabataean pottery (in the case of the latter mostly based on comparisons with the Trench III sequence, most analogies being with material from Phases v–viii) lead him, justifiably, to ascribe this building to the 1st century BC, though later than 30 BC, since it overlies a rock-cut tomb containing a coin of Obodas II (or

[14] Taylor 2001, 82.
[15] Zeitler 1989, 307–318; 1990, 386–387.

III, depending on whether an earlier ruler of this name existed, as some believe).[16] The house is thus considerably later than the earliest structures we have been considering beneath the Colonnaded Street, and it is interesting that such simple domestic architecture was still being employed in Petra at this time.[17]

The third locality where evidence for early Nabataean occupation has been found is just below the ridge of ez-Zantur, south of the Colonnaded Street. According to the excavators, the earliest stone structure so far discovered here comprises two stone walls (Walls AG and CU) of ashlar masonry forming a corner of a large building (Haus I) – of the plan of which nothing further is known – stratified below a much more complete building (Haus II) with a *terminus post quem* of 9 BC established by coins of Aretas IV.[18] There is apparently no numismatic evidence for the date of Haus I, and its construction in the late 1st century BC or the early 1st century AD is postulated on the evidence of the associated Eastern Sigillata and Nabataean painted ware (Schmid's chronology of which is also essentially dependent on the dating of the Sigillata).[19] The situation on ez-Zantur prior to this is known only from soundings, none of which reached bedrock, and is not without ambiguity. Beneath Haus I there is a sequence of occupation material and living surfaces, interspersed with sterile deposits, dating – again on the evidence of the pottery – to between the late 2nd and the late 1st centuries BC. There is no direct evidence for contemporary stone-built structures, and Stucky therefore suggests that the settlement was composed of tents, occupied on a seasonal basis by an essentially nomadic population. However – and somewhat contradictorily – it is reported that there is some circumstantial evidence, in the form of stone chippings in some of the deposits, which might indicate building activity prior to the construction of Haus I, and thus contemporary with the tented settlement.[20] On the basis of these discoveries, Stucky concludes that it was "during the late first century BC [that] the first humble stone-built dwelling was erected on the [ez-Zantur] terrace", and, further, that "for the first time in Petra it is possible to conceive the change from nomadism to a settled way of life, a process which before was only documented by the authors of antiquity." [21]

Although there are aspects of this reconstruction which are not entirely convincing – for instance, the fact that the layers interpreted as tent floors hardly seem, in the published section, sufficiently horizontal to have served that purpose – it is the chronology with which we are concerned. Two points need to be noted: first, that pottery attributed to the late 2nd-early 1st centuries BC was found throughout the soundings beneath Haus II, and, second, that at the very base of

[16] Zeitler 1990, 395–396. For the problem of Obodas see McKenzie 1990, 34 and references.

[17] From the sequence in Trench III it would appear that ashlar sandstone masonry had already come into use by Phase vii (Parr 1970: 358).

[18] Stucky 1995, 194–195; Schmid 1995, 640.

[19] Schmid 1995, 640–641.

[20] Stucky 1996, 17.

[21] Stucky 1995, 198.

one of the soundings, A, there appear to be the remains of another stone structure, which would thus presumably date to early in this period.[22] No mention seems to be made of this possible structure in the excavation report, and its presence must thus remain problematic. But, taken together with Stucky's suggestion that stone structures existed contemporaneously with his presumed tents, and the fact that bedrock was nowhere reached, it is surely premature to assume that the earliest settlement was tented, ignoring the possibility that permanent stone architecture was to be found on ez-Zantur earlier than the late 1st century BC.

So far we have confined our attention to the stratigraphic and structural evidence for early Nabataean settlement in Petra, referring to the artefactual evidence only in so far as it helps to establish a relevant chronology. Two groups of artefacts, however, the coins and imported amphorae dateable to before the 1st century BC, need further consideration. A review of the published evidence[23], together with that from the unpublished British excavations of 1958–1964, reveals that the earliest coins so far excavated at Petra comprise one Carthaginian of c. 310–280 BC, twelve Ptolemaic of between c. 300–221 BC, and fifteen from Aradus on the Phoenician coast of c. 240–187 BC.[24] These are all single finds and are of very limited use for dating purposes, since not all were found in primary deposits and many could have been in circulation for a long time. But it is significant that all but one of the Aradus coins, seven of the twelve Ptolemaic coins, and the Carthaginian issue, came from the sounding beneath the Colonnaded Street, where we have argued on other grounds for a 2nd or even a 3rd cen-tury settlement. (The fact that such a large proportion of the early coins are from Aradus is also interesting, but is a matter best considered elsewhere.) As for the published early amphorae, these appear to be rather more evenly spread throughout the excavated areas of Petra; of the thirty-seven stamped examples from known provenances, nineteen come from the various excavations on el-Katute (where, however, much of the archaeological deposits are fills derived from elsewhere), thirteen from ez-Zantur, two from the Temple of the Winged Lions (but again in a fill), two from beneath the Colonnaded Street, and one from the Great Temple. The earliest of the dated examples is from c. 240 BC[25], the rest belonging to the following decades down to the early years of the 1st century BC. However, as with coins, amphorae have to be used for dating with great caution. It is impossible to agree with Schneider[26], who believes that even though all the examples from ez-Zantur were found in levels of the 1st century BC they

[22] Stucky 1996, 14, Abb. 11.

[23] The reports consulted are those of Murray and Ellis 1940, Horsfield and Horsfield 1941, Hammond 1965, Zeitler 1989, 1990, Khairy 1990, Hammond and Johnson 1995, Hammond 1996, Bignasca and Desse-Bersel 1998, Fiema 1998, and Joukowsky 1998.

[24] The Carthaginian coin, and all of the Aradus coins are from the British excavations. The coins from the British excavations were originally partly identified by the late Fr. A. Spijkerman, and the complete catalogue is now being prepared for publication by J. M. C. Bowsher, to whom I am greatly indebted for the information utilised here.

[25] Schneider 1996, 129, No. 1.

[26] Schneider 1996, 142.

neverthless testify to a settled population in Petra already in the second half of the 3rd century, or with Stucky, who writes that they "prove that even in the early third century BC the Nabataeans drank wine imported from the West".[27] Virginia Grace has noted that Egyptian papyri record many commodities other than wine being stored and transported in foreign jars, and recalls Herodotus' story (*Histories* III: 5–7) of how the mayor of each town in Egypt was required to collect empty wine jars and send them to Memphis, to be refilled with water and taken to the desert between Syria and Egypt in order to provide refreshment for travellers, a service which the Persians had apparently introduced.[28] Like coins, therefore, amphorae could enjoy a long life expectancy. It will not pass unnoticed that the desert region Herodotus mentions is precisely that with which the nomadic Nabataeans, or their immediate ancestors, would have been familiar at the time of his writing in the mid-5th century BC, and it is very possible that the first Nabataean settlers in Petra brought with them the habit of using recycled jars.

In summary, therefore, although the early coins and stamped jar handles cannot be used to prove the existence of a permanent Nabataean settlement, or even a Nabataean presence, in Petra as early as the 3rd or 2nd BC, other considerations make such a settlement extremely likely. On present evidence this settlement seems to have been restricted to a relatively small area on the banks of the Wadi Musa in the centre of the site, though the existence of contemporary buildings spreading up the slopes of ez-Zantur to the south cannot be discounted. But although small, the settlement on the *wadi* bank was not insubstantial; right from the beginning it comprised solidly built, if architecturally unremarkable, structures. It is possible, of course, even probable, that less permanent, seasonal, of the type envisaged by Stucky, had taken place earlier than this, especially if Zayadine is correct in suggesting that 'the Rock' of the Nabataeans to which Hieronymus of Cardia referred was located at Sela^{c} near Tafileh, and that Petra itself was in the 4th century BC the site of the 'great fair' to which they were accustomed to attend periodically, and which was thus already likely to have been a religious centre.[29] But if so, no trace of such an occupation has survived. It is also by no means unlikely that during the late-3rd and 2nd centuries BC, when a tradition of solid architecture was becoming established, a tented settlement existed side-by-side with the permanent buildings, and that vestiges of some later examples of these, dating to the 1st century BC, may indeed have been found on ez-Zantur; there is plenty of historic and ethnographic evidence for such a juxtaposition, as Stucky notes, and the practice may well have continued even longer in Petra, throughout the remainder of its history. But already during the 1st century BC a new development was taking place in the architecture of Petra: the introduction of sandstone ashlar masonry, the first use of which in Trench III can be assigned to Phase vii–viia, dating probably to not long after Phase v.[30] How this corresponds in date with the signs of stone working noted by Stucky on ez-

[27] Stucky 1995, 194.
[28] Grace 1962, 107–108.
[29] Zayadine 1999.
[30] Parr 1970, 358–360.

Zantur prior to the construction of Haus I cannot be said, but it is surely no coincidence that this initial use of quarried and shaped masonry seems to occur at a time not far removed from the first incontrovertible evidence for the excavation of rock monuments at the site – the very simple Triclinium 21,dated to the first year of Obodas I (96/92 BC).[31]

Before leaving the 2nd and early 1st centuries BC to consider the Petra of Strabo, we must confront the problems raised by two early literary references – or supposed references – to the site. The first is unconvincing and may be dismissed. It occurs in the pseudepigrahical Book of Enoch, the composition of which is probably dates to the 3rd – early 2nd century BC. In a paper on the fragments of Enoch from Qumran, Milik has argued that the author was a merchant participating in the spice trade, and thus familiar with Nabataean merchants and with Petra.[32] This, according to Milik, he describes in chapters 28–29:

> And thence I went towards the east, into the midst of the mountain range of the desert, and I saw a wilderness and it was solitary, full of trees and plants. And water gushed forth from above. Rushing like a copious watercourse [which flowed] towards the north-west it caused clouds and dew to ascend on every side.
> And thence I went to another place in the desert, and approached to the east of this mountain range. And there I saw aromatic trees exhaling the fragrance of frankincense and myrrh, and the trees also were similar to the almond tree. (Trans. H. R. Charles 1913)

Whether Milik's understanding of Enoch is justified or not is not our concern, but it is surely rash in the extreme to identify Petra in the lines quoted above, and to write of the author that "il admire surtout l'aqueduc de la capitale des Nabateens, dont on peut voir encore aujourd'hui des restes imposants dans la gorge d'es-Siq au Wadi Musa."[33] If the author had indeed travelled along the trade routes towards the aromatic regions, there would have been many other fertile oases, such as Dedan or Tayma in northern Arabia, to which his words would equally apply. Although – as we have argued above – there probably was a settlement of some kind at Petra in the 3rd and 2nd centuries BC, the Book of Enoch cannot be cited in its support.

The second literary reference to Petra prior to Strabo's cannot be dismissed. According to an inscription from Priene in Asia Minor (to which attention was first drawn by G. W. Bowersock[34]), in 129 BC an ambassador from that city travelled to a number of places in the region, including Alexandria and Petra. Clearly, as Bowersock notes, the Nabataean kingdom must have been widely recognised then as of considerable importance, and Petra must have been the seat of its ruler – whoever that was.[35] But what kind of place was it? Unfortunately

[31] McKenzie 1990, 33–34.

[32] Milik 1971.

[33] Milik 1971, 346–347.

[34] Bowersock 1983, 32.

[35] There is a gap in the known list of Nabataean rulers between Aretas I, usually placed c.168 BC on account of a reference in the Book of the Maccabees, and Aretas II, ruling around the end of the 2nd and the beginning of the 1st century BC. A putative king Rabbel (I) might fit somewhere in the gap.

Moschion, the ambassador, left no description of his visit, but the archaeological evidence we have reviewed above seems to indicate that the Nabataean capital was little more than a small cluster of unpretentious buildings, together with perhaps a collection of tents or similar impermanent structures – hardly to be compared with Alexandria! But this reference does not necessarily invalidate the testimony of the archaeology. There is nothing inherently improbable about a harbour city such as Priene wishing to establish, or strengthen, good relations with a group of Arabian merchants as vital to the Mediterranean economy as the Nabataeans, whatever the level of their material culture; after all, Antigonas Monophthalmos had thought it necessary two centuries earlier to send emissaries – though more belligerent ones – to the same people. Nevertheless, Moschion's visit is intriguing, and reminds us that archaeological evidence, even when unequivocal, never tells the full story.

Strabo's Petra

Strabo's description of Petra as a bustling, cosmopolitan, wealthy commercial city, is well known, as is the fact that he derived his information in part, at least, from his friend the Stoic philosopher Athenodorus, who had lived there. For the archaeologist using this information, however, there are a number of problems. In the first place, although it is generally agreed that the *Geography*, in its received form, dates from the author's declining years before his death in c. AD 23, it may be presumed that the material had been collected, and perhaps partly written down, some time previously. Strabo also received some information from another friend, Aelius Gallus, the Roman prefect of Egypt who, in c.26 BC, had led the joint Roman-Nabataean expedition to southern Arabia, and with whom Strabo travelled up the Nile a little later. Some second- or third-hand account of the Nabataean capital may well have been passed on then. As for his first-hand informant, Athenodorus (c.73 BC – AD 7), the details of his life are too meagre to indicate the date of his sojourn in the city, or when he talked about it to Strabo; both, it appears, lived in Rome intermittently from c. 44 BC onwards, and there would have been many opportunities for conversations to have taken place.

A second difficulty with Strabo as a source is his reliability, and that of his informants. This has already been questioned by David Graf[36], who has drawn attention to many apparently misleading statements in the *Geography* that seem to fly in the face of the evidence: for example, that the Nabataeans cared nothing for their dead; that they did not themselves produce sculptures and paintings; that they worshipped the sun; that their towns were unfortified. These may well all be errors, as Graf believes, resulting from false information or defective memories. Furthermore, the fact that only the stone houses of the inhabitants, and not their public buildings and tomb façades – so obvious to us today – are ignored in Strabo's description, does not inspire confidence. But, on the other hand, some of

[36] Graf 1994, 266–268.

these 'errors and omissions' might well be true of the Petra to which his description refers; until we know whether that is the Petra of Malichus I (59–30 BC), Obodas II/III (30–9 BC) or Aretas IV (9 BC – AD 40) – to name the obvious possibilities – we cannot be sure, and we certainly cannot use Strabo as a guide in our attempt to trace the urban development of the site. Can we, on the other hand, use the archaeological evidence to give us a closer date for the period to which Strabo is referring?

There can certainly be no doubt that during the final decades of the 1st century BC and the early decades of the 1st century AD an enormous amount of building activity took place in Petra, not only in the centre but also on the peripheries, resulting in the city more-or-less as we know it from its ruins today. It is true that the only direct contemporary evidence for this activity is the newly discovered fragmentary inscription of the eleventh year of Aretas IV (AD 2/3), referring to the building of a '*theatron* to Dushara', the value of which is, however, severely reduced by the uncertainty as to what monument is meant, a problem to which we shall return.[37] Somewhat less direct evidence is provided by the incomplete inscription relating to temple offerings dated to the same king's thirty-seventh year (AD 26/27), found in a workshop associated with the Temple of the Winged Lions and – if we accept the excavator's assumption – intended to be attached to a wall of the temple at around the time of its construction .[38] Coins of Aretas IV also come from the fill beneath this building, providing a *terminus post quem*.[39] As for other monuments in the city centre, the Portico Wall revealed in Trench III of the 1958–1964 excavations also has a *terminus post quem* of 9 BC established by a coin of Aretas IV found in what is probably a level associated with its contruction, and this would also apply to the structurally contemporary terrace retaining wall and associated rooms (Walls K and J on the plan, fig. 1).[40] Furthermore, Bedal has recently claimed that the Portico Wall and Wall K form an integral part of the impressive ornamental garden and pool which she has discovered in the so-called 'Lower Market', which must therefore also date to the reign of Aretas IV or later, and she also proposes that this entire complex is contemporary with the first phase of the Great Temple to the west, to which we shall return.[41] A critical evaluation of this work must await its more detailed publication, but her preliminary conclusions seem plausible. The fact that the dating for this massive urban development seems at present to rest entirely the evidence of a single coin from Trench III, is a vivid indication of the dificulty of establishing a close chonology for the urban history of Petra.

Evidence for building activity away from the city centre at about this time is provided by the Theatre, for which Hammond has proposed a date of c. 25 AD, partly on stylistic and historical considerations (which, however, can easily result in circularity of argument), and partly on the palaeography of builders' marks on

[37] Jones 2001, 346–349; Joukowsky and Basile 2001, 54–57.
[38] Hammond and Johnson 2000, 31.
[39] Hammond 1996, 5.
[40] Parr 1970, 364 and Fig.1.
[41] Bedal 2001, 30–31.

architectural elements – evidence which is not as solid as could be desired.[42] As for less monumental buildings, Haus II on ez-Zantur and the houses on the lower slope of el-Katute excavated by Khairy, also have coins of Aretas IV in levels either pre-dating or contemporary with their construction; in the case of one of the el-Katute houses (Area B) the relevant coin is of Aretas and Shaqilat, and the building is thus later than AD 18.[43] These coins, of course, only indicate the earliest possible dates for the construction of these buildings, and there is nothing to prove that they were not, in fact, built some time later; it may be noted that, of the very small amount of painted pottery published from the el-Katute houses, none is of the early 'naturalistic' floral style; and the same is true of the (equally sparse) material from the Theatre. But the wide distribution elsewhere in Petra of this style of ceramic – Schmid's Phase 2 –can be taken as an indication, if not a very precise one, of the urban spread during the later decades of the 1st century BC and the beginning of the 1st century AD, since it is clear that this style was in fashion then, giving way to what I have termed the 'formal' or 'classic' style – Schmid's Phase 3 – sometime during the reign of Aretas IV.[44] It is this naturalistic style which characterises the levels underlying Haus II on ez-Zantur the Portico Wall (Phase IX of the Trench III sequence), both of which have *termini post quem* of 9 BC. This style is also found in stratified contexts at a number of the widely separated areas away from the city centre excavated by the 1958–1964 British expedition, associated, for example, with a large house on the southern edge of the site (Trench I)[45], and with houses overlooking the Wadi Turkmaniyeh on the north (Trenches V and XXI: see Fig. 6 for the location of these areas of excavation.) It is abundantly evident that Petra was expanding considerably at this period., and it is most likely that it was now, also, that the first defensive system – the Conway Tower and its accompanying walls, where the associated painted pottery is also of the early floral style – was built.[46]

So far this evidence, limited and imperfect though it is, points to the reign of Aretas IV as the time of accelerated urban development at Petra; can anything be said of the building activities of his predecessors? The two free-standing monuments which are becoming generally accepted as dating to before Aretas's reign are the Qasr el-Bint and Great Temple, and these must now be considered.

We have seen that investigation of 'Lower Market' has prompted Bedal to assign a date in the reign of Aretas IV for the Great Temple, but we have proposed reserving judgement on this until more details of her work are available. Not all the evidence from the excavation of the temple itself is published, either, since the work is still in progress, and any comments must be provisional. In the first volume of her 'final' report (which is in fact no more than a series of interim reports), Joukowsky tentatively assigns the original building to the reign of either Malichus I (59–30 BC) or Obodas II/III (30–9 BC), or perhaps both.; in her latest

[42] Hammond 1965, 65, 78.
[43] Khairy 1990, 5–6.
[44] Schmid 1995, 640–644 and figs 8–9. Cf. already Parr 1978, 203 and fig. 1.
[45] Parr 1960, 126–130.
[46] Parr 1962.

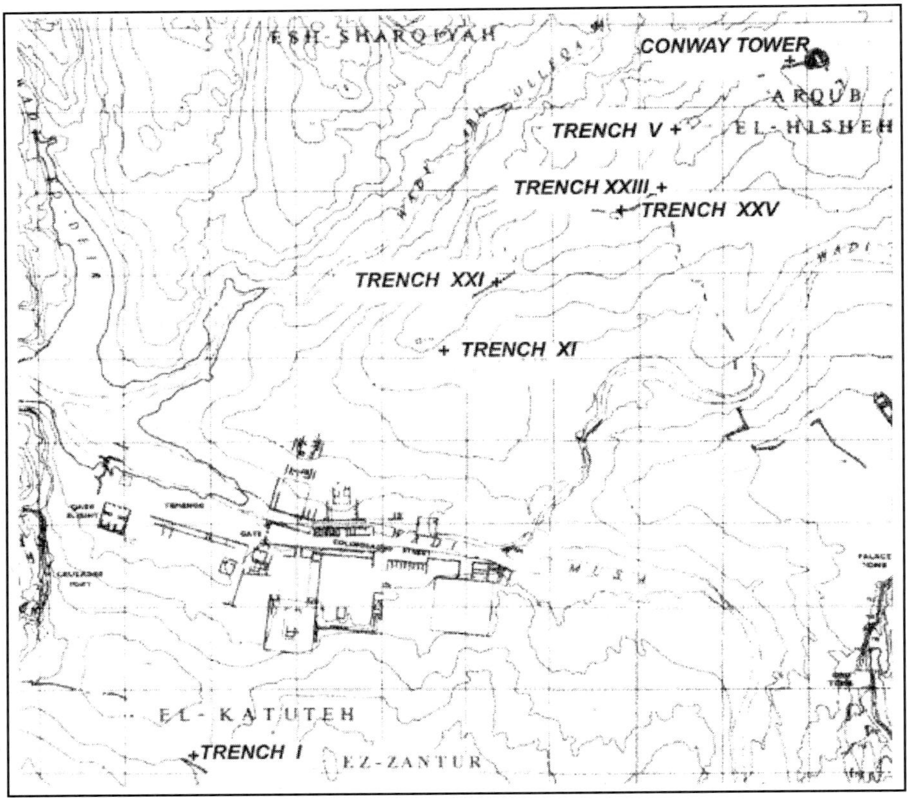

Figure 6: Plan of Petra, showing location of excavations of British School of Archaeology, 1958–1964

review she dates it less specifically to the last quarter of the 1st century BC.[47] This conclusion seems to be based largely on the observation that "from the style of the floral decoration, especially the limestone capitals, the Petra Great Temple iconographic evidence appears to be similar to that of Al-Khazna", a monument which she follows McKenzie (and indeed most other scholars today) in dating to before the beginning of the 1st century AD.[48] In a more detailed discussion, Basile draws attention also to similarities of design between the Great Temple and the Qasr el-Bint which, he states, is "canonically ... dated with a *terminus ante quem* of the 1st century CE, roughly contemporary with at least some of the remains at the Great Temple".[49] More objectively, he argues that the Propylaeum

[47] Joukowsky 1998, 136; Joukowsky and Basile 2001, 50.
[48] Joukowsky 1998, 136.
[49] Basile 1998, 206.

steps of the Temple are, in origin, earlier than the extant Colonnaded Street. Until more of the evidence is published – particularly detailed plans and sections – this conclusion cannot be properly evaluated, but it has to be noted that it hardly helps with chronology, since the date of the Colonnaded Street in its present form is far from being settled. Basile is mistaken when he writes that I have suggested that "the extant Colonnaded Street was built over the foundations of a Nabataean predecessor sometime between 9 BCE and 76 CE"[50]; what I wrote, on the basis of my interpretation of the stratigraphy and of the numismatic evidence from the 1958–1964 excavations, was that "the construction of the paved street ... is clearly later than *circa* AD 76, when Rabbel II and Gamilath began to reign."[51] That conclusion was contested by McKenzie,[52] who proposed a possible alternative *terminus post quem* for the paving of the beginning of the reign of Aretas IV, suggesting that the Colonnaded Street was built sometime after *either* 9 BC *or* after 76 AD – which is not at all the same as saying that it was built *between* 9 BC and 76 AD.[53] The recent work of Fiema further east along the Street seems to support the post-AD 76 date of the paving, but closer investigation of the situation directly in front of the Great Temple is necessary before the chronological relationships here are satisfactorily elucideted. Finally, with regard to the Great Temple, we must note that if the *theatron* inscription of AD 2/3, mentioned above, could be shown to refer to major alterations within the Great Temple, as has been suggested[54], then its original contruction prior to Aretas IV's reign would be certain.

Surely we are on firmer ground with the Qasr el-Bint, for which (as Basile states) a *terminus ante quem* of the beginning of the 1st century AD has become part of the accepted wisdom? Provided that the *theatron* inscription does not refer to this building (as has also been suggested), the only hard evidence for this date is the statue base of Aretas IV, build into a kind of plinth above a short (c. 6 m.) row of benches (called here the West Benches) against the southern enclosure wall of the Qasr *temenos*.[55] A short distance away to its left a similar block of stone carries a few letters of an illegible Greek text, while to the right two larger blocks each have holes for the fixing of plaques of a different material, now missing. The benches are likely to have formed a kind of royal portrait gallery, though whether devoted just to Aretas IV or to a number of other rulers cannot be said. The fact that the Aretas text (dated on palaeographic grounds to around the beginning of the era) and the illegible Greek text are both engraved directly onto the masonry of the plinth, while the other two could have been added later, does not necessarily indicate that they are original, since they too could have been engraved on the blocks after the benches had been built. But the Aretas inscrip-

[50] Basile 1998, 190–191.

[51] Parr 1970, 370.

[52] McKenzie 1990, 36.

[53] The statement in Joukowsky and Basile 2001, 44, that the street was constructed in 9 BCE *and* [my italics] 76 C., does not make sense, and must be an editorial error.

[54] Joukowsky and Basile 2001, 7–8.

[55] Starcky and Strugnell 1966, 236–244; Parr 1967–1968, 2–3, 11–13.

Figure 7: Qasr el-Bint *temenos*: view of benches from west

tion does provide an incontrovertible *terminus ante quem* for the West Benches. The question is, what is the relationship of the West Benches to the Qasr el-Bint?

They have, initially, all the appearance of being later than the much longer row of benches (the East Benches) adjacent to them, which are of the same masonry as the *temenos* wall and are certainly contemporary with it, while the wall is presumably (though this has not been conclusively proved) contemporary with the Qasr. At the time of the inscription's discovery, therefore, I had little doubt that it provided a *terminus ante quem* for the Qasr, which – since it was unlikely that the addition of the West Benches would have happened almost immediately after the original construction of the *temenos* – would thus necessarily date to the reign of Aretas's predecessor at the latest; and a few years later, following further limited investigation, I reaffirmed this, although I pointed out that the situation was by no means straightforward and that there remained a number of problems which needed resolving.[56] Further relection has convinced me that these problems are more significant than I originally thought, and that solutions are required before we can be certain of all the chronological relation-

[56] Parr 1967–1968, 13.

ships. Since I have discussed this matter recently elsewhere[57] I will only mention here some of the main points. The accompanying illustrations – a general photograph of the West Benches (Fig. 7) and two hitherto unpublished plans (Figs. 8 and 9) – are relevant.

First, if benches already existed, why was a short length of them removed and replaced with new benches, and why are these – the 'portrait gallery' – of such different (and inferior) workmanship, as the illustrations show? (It may also be noted in passing that the supposedly later Western Benches are furnished with a more elaborate *cyma reversa* moulding than the simple bevelled moulding of the East Benches, this being contrary to the usual 'complex to simple' progression which McKenzie has shown to be the general rule in Nabataean architectural decoration.[58]) Why were the statues and their inscriptions not simply placed on the plinth crowning the existing benches? In some ways a more logical explanation here would be that, when the *temenos* wall and the Eastern Benches were constructed, the Western Benches with their 'portrait gallery' were an earlier feature that needed to be preserved, a feature perhaps contemporary with the earlier building – almost certainly an earlier temple – on the site of the Qasr which is known to have existed.[59] The structural evidence is ambiguous; there is no obvious reason why the Eastern Benches could not have been built up against the Western Benches, rather than *visa versa,* while the extant *temenos* wall could have been built behind the Western Benches with little difficulty. There is, to be sure, one argument against this reconstruction of the sequence of events, namely the fact that the paving slabs of the *temenos* immediately in front of the Western Benches having been very untidily cut and removed, as seen in the photograph, Fig. 7. The obvious explanation is that this was connected with the removal of earlier benches and the erection of new ones, thus supporting the accepted view that the Western Benches were a later addition. But the new benches would not have needed foundations, had there been pre-exiting paving slabs on which to lay them directly, as the Eastern Benches are, and it is at least possible that the slabs may have been cut in order to avoid disturbing the foundations of an already existing 'portrait gallery'. Even though these questions cannot be answered without further fieldwork, neither can they be ignored. Although it remains most likely from the evidence currently available that the *temenos* wall and thus the Qasr are, as generally agreed, earlier than the beginning of the 1st century BC, the matter should not be considered closed.

Let us return to Strabo. The few buildings to which we have been able to assign actual dates, even though mostly on the admittedly not very robust evidence of a handful of numismatic *termini post quem* – the Portico Wall (and presumably a comparable structure on the opposite side of the main thoroughfare, protecting it from the *wadi*, as well, perhaps, as bridges), the Terrace Wall, the 'Lower Market' complex (and the Great Temple, if Bedal is right), the Temple of the Winged Lions, the Theatre, and the houses on ez-Zantur and el-Katute –

[57] Parr 1996, 65–66.

[58] McKenzie 1990, 121.

[59] Zayadine and Farajat 1991, 292.

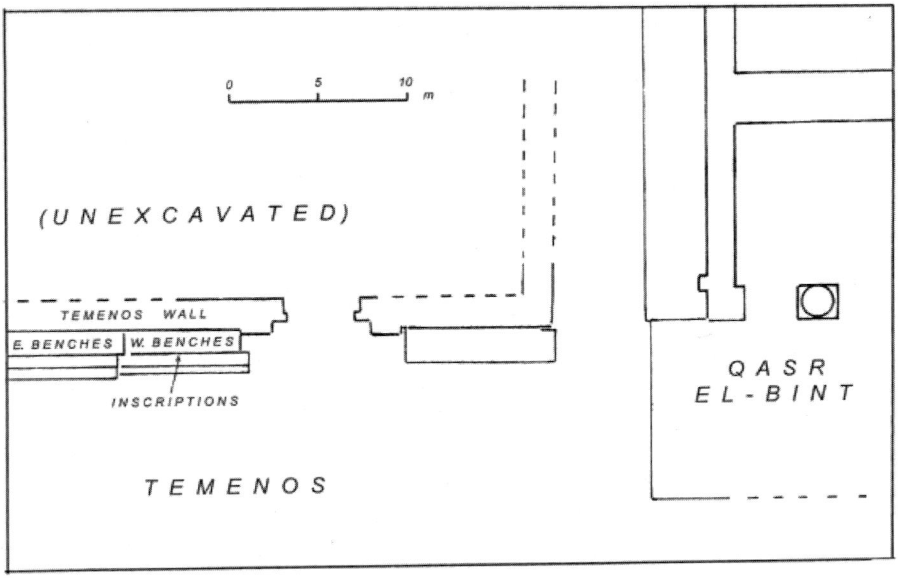

Figure 8: Qasr el-Bint *temenos*: location of western and eastern benches

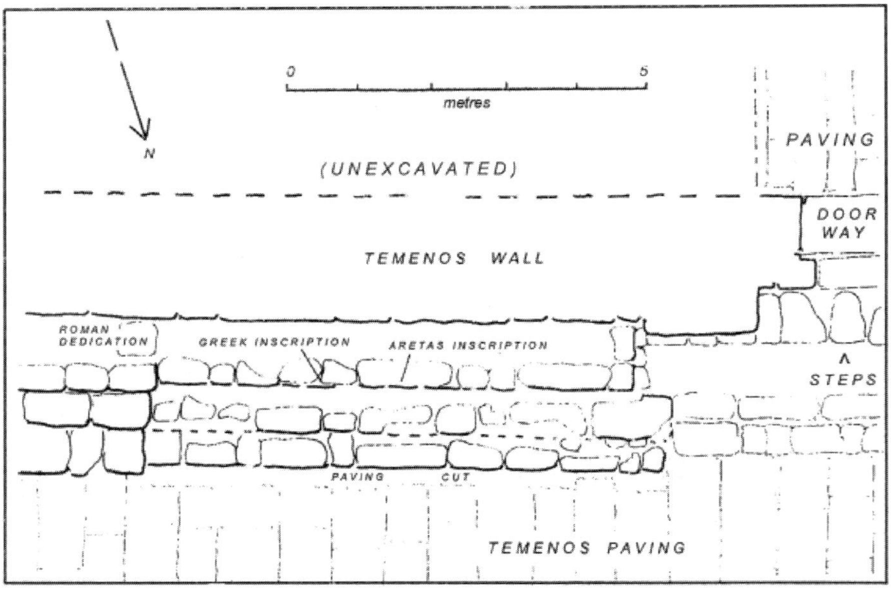

Figure 9: Qasr el-Bint *temenos*: detail of benches and location of inscriptions

would all seem to belong to the reign of Aretas IV. Was this the Petra of Strabo? Could his information have been as up to-date as this? It seems most unlikely, considering that his death occurred in about AD 23. What then do we know of an earlier Petra? Of the major free-standing monuments only the Qasr el-Bint and, perhaps, the Great Temple belong to the time of Aretas' predecessors, and could have been seen by Athenodorus (though he does not mention them); apart from these archaeology has so far revealed only the traces of buildings already mentioned, dating to the middle of the 1st century BC and before, which, although certainly of stone, would hardly seem worthy of Strabo's description. But although clear structural evidence for the Petra as described by Strabo remains disappointingly elusive, we should not allow this to negate the other archaeological evidence – particularly the high quality pottery, imported and local – for increasing wealth, technological competence, and international contacts during the 1st century BC. Strabo may not be too far wrong, after all.

The Roman impact

With one major exception – to which we shall return – hard evidence for changes to the urban landscape of Petra in the years immediately following the Roman annexation is hard to find. Schmid's argument that the destruction of the Nabataean buildings on ez-Zantur was a result of violence accompanying the arrival of the Romans depends largely upon his belief that it can be dated on ceramic grounds to more-or-less precisely around AD 106 rather than earlier or later, and ignores the fact that severe structural damage results from natural causes or domestic accidents as often as it does from military conflict[60]. Nevertheless, the subsequent abandonment of ez-Zantur throughout the 2nd and 3rd centuries is paralleled by a similar situation elsewhere on the southern side of the city: the buildings excavated by Khairy on the slopes of el-Katute were abandoned until at least the end of the 3rd century [61], while the house overlooking the Wadi Farasa in Trench I of the 1958–1964 excavations was also destroyed and the site never re-used, except as a cemetery.[62] Neither is there evidence of 2nd century or later occupation along the northern limits of the city, though there has been excessive erosion here, which may have removed the relevant material. Whether or not as a direct result of Roman military activity in AD 106, it does seems certain that a contraction in the city area took place after the annexation.

The situation in the city centre was different. Hammond's attribution of the extensive alterations in Phase Ic of the Theatre to the early years of the Roman period is based on little more than historical plausibility[63]; and the same may be said of Schluntz's proposal that the insertion of the *cavea* into the *cella* of the Great Temple occurred now, as a result of the new political situation, reflecting a change in the function of that building from royal Nabataean audience hall –

[60] Schmid 1997, 418.
[61] Khairy 1981, 7–8.
[62] Parr 1960, 129.
[63] Hammond 1961, 64

which is how she interprets it – to Roman civic *boulteuterion*, coincident with the granting of the title *of metropolis* to the city by Trajan.[64] This is not the place to discuss her argument; since our preoccupation is with chronology it is sufficient to note that objective evidence for dating the changes to the *cella* is lacking, the excavator indicating no more than that they could have happened anywhere between the last years of Aretas IV and AD 106.[65] (Of course, if it could be shown that the new *theatron* inscription of AD 2/3 does actually refer to the *cavea*, Schluntz's interpretation would be proved wrong; but, as we have seen, this interpretation of the inscription is only one option of several.) As for the Temple of the Winged Lions, this experienced repairs and remodelling from time to time, but no significant changes to its fabric or function seem to have occurred before its destruction by earthquake in AD 363.[66] No doubt builders were active in Petra during the 2nd and 3rd centuries AD, but on present evidence they were far less involved with major monumental works than their predecessors under the Nabataean rulers of earlier centuries had been – with the possible exception mentioned above.

The only direct proof of major building works in Petra immediately following the Roman annexation is to be found in the monumental Greek inscription of Trajan, dated to AD 114, found during the clearance of the Colonnaded Street at the foot of the steps leading to what is traditionally called the Upper Market.[67] On the basis of his recent excavations Fiema is inclined to agree with the original discoverer of the inscription, Diana Kirkbride, that it comes from a monumental arch fronting the steps, and, further, that she is correct in supposing that the present paving, the portico, and the steps themselves, are all contemporary with the arch.[68] The suggestion, that this impressive embellishment of the city centre accompanied the conferring on Petra of the status of Metropolis, is very attractive, and one which I am inclined to accept, but it has to be admitted that the only solid evidence for dating the paving comprises two coins of Rabbel II, one found in Trench III of the British excavations in a level cut by the foundation trench of the street, and the other by Fiema in the bedding of the flagstone paving.[69] Although the latter coin would seem to remove the doubts expressed by McKenzie concerning the validity of the evidence from Trench III (see above and notes 46 and 47), it remains true that the construction of the Colonnaded Street in its surviving form could just as easily have taken place during the final years of the independent Nabataean kingdom as they could after the annexation, as many scholars have supposed.[70] Neverthless – and even if Tracy is correct in dissociating the Trajanic inscription from the postulated arch [71] – there is clear evidence for some monumental construction in the aftermath of the annexation.

[64] Schluntz 1999.
[65] Joukowsky 1998, 139.
[66] Hammond 1966, 11–14.
[67] Tracy 1998, 370–375; Joukowsky and Basile 2000, 51.
[68] Fiema 1998, 418–419. See also Kanellopoulos 2000.
[69] Parr 1970, 370; Fiema 1998, 419.
[70] For example, Starcky 1964, col. 944.
[71] Tracy 1999, 53.

This leads us to the monumental Temenos Gate, about which the one thing that is certain is that, in its present form, it is later than the Street – that is later than AD 76 – on the stratigraphic and structural evidence set out in the interim excavation report.[72] Unfortunately the excavations carried out between 1958 and 1964 around the its foot produced no direct dating evidence, while the nature and date of the structure which undoubtedly underlies it – presumably an earlier entrance to the Qasr el-Bint *temenos* – are quite unknown. Strictly speaking, therefore, it is possible, on the available evidence, that the extant Gate was built between AD 76 and AD 106, but it is surely most unlikely that the changes to the layout of the city plan which its erection entailed would have taken place so soon after the Colonnaded Street itself had been built, and even if the Street was built during the final years of the Nabataean kingdom, a Roman date for the Gate seems indicated. Although arguments based on stylistic analysis have been mostly and deliberately eschewed in this paper, Wright's conclusion[73], that the overall proportions of the Temenos Gate and the free-standing columns flanking its eastern face are features more characteristic of monumental gates of the later 2nd or 3rd centuries AD than earlier, cannot be ignored, and is not in conflict with McKenzie's assessment of its decorative features, since these have analogies on rock-cut monuments in Petra ranging from the 1st century BC to the 2nd century AD, their eclectic nature being itself, perhaps, an indication of the Gate's relatively late date.[74]

The urban decline of Petra

It is universally accepted that Petra was severely ruined by the well documented earthquake of AD 363. In an earlier paper I argued that, following the disaster, the inhabitants lacked the desire or the will or the resources to restore the city to its former condition, and that only limited clearance and restoration was attempted, even in the city centre, where the Colonnaded Street and the Temenos Gate were allowed to remain encumbered. Other parts of the city were abandoned, only to be used eventually as rubbish dumps and cemeteries.[75] Recent excavations – on the Street at the foot of the steps to the 'Upper Market', at the Great Temple and 'Pool Complex', at the Temple of the Winged Lions, on ez-Zantur and el-Katute – have confirmed these conclusions.[76] There can be no doubt that after the early summer of AD 363 Petra was not the place it had been.

But what sort of place was it? Was this the beginning of the decline of Petra? 'Decline' is a subjective, not to say an emotive, word, and Fiema has urged

[72] Parr 1960, 131–132; Wright 1967–69, 20. In the absence of more recent excavations near the Monumental Gate, I consider Kader's (1996) recent attempt to analyse its chronological development entirely hypothetical.

[73] Wright 1966.

[74] McKenzie 1990, 19, 50; Parr 1996, 67–68.

[75] Parr, 1986.

[76] Fiema 1998, 419; Hammond 1996, 14; Joukowsky 1998, 139; Bedal 2001, 32; Gerber 1998, 274–275.

caution in using it in connection with the undoubted changes that took place in Petra from the 4th century onwards. He has pointed out that, "the cultural patterns of the Byzantine period ... reflect a reality different from that represented by the norms of classical aesthetics and orderliness", and that features such as "the encroachment of private structures into public space, blocking and/or disuse of earlier public buildings, abandonment of whole areas within city limits, spontaneous development of suburbs, massive reuse of construction materials, are all well attested in the urban contexts of the Near East, specially in the sixth centrury and later. It is therefore debatable whether the urban features observed in Byzantine Petra or elsewhere may be considered as realistic disagnostics of the economic standing of a city."[77] Elsewhere he writes that "instead of viewing the late history of Petra as a decline, one might see a transformation from the status of an internationally recognized metropolis into a provincial town." [78]

In general terms he is correct. Changes had been taking place to the urban ammenities of Petra before the earthquake: areas had been abandoned already under the Roman administration, the Theatre had ceased to be used as such, the Great Temple and 'Pool Complex' had also suffered damage and perhaps temporary abandonment.[79] Neither is there proof that other changes, such as the encroachment onto the Street of shoddily built shops and the construction of the Inner Town Wall on the north of the site, had not occurred before the earthquake, though the re-use of earlier architectural material in their construction argues very much against this. But even if the new concepts of urbanism – the transformation of a Graeco-Roman metropolis into a Late Antique country town – to which Fiema refers, may have been emerging in the decades prior to the 4th century disaster, that disaster must surely have dramatically accelerated the process of change.

The history of Petra in the Byzantine period has recently been reviewed by Fiema and Schick in their contributions to the report on the excavation of the Petra Church.[80] It is obvious that Petra did revive following the disaster of AD 363, though the nature and speed of the recovery are unclear. The fact that it retained its status of provincial capital may not mean very much in the context of urbanism, if the provincial governor and administration was resident elsewhere, as Fiema suggests may have been the case.[81] But if the account of Bar Sauma's visit to Petra in c. 420 is at all reliable, it indicates that the town was by now refortified (presumably the 'Inner Wall') since the citizens are said to have closed the gates against the beligerent monk, and converted to Christianity only when 'miraculous' rain storms washed away the walls. However, it is the churches that are the most obvious testimony to Petra's revival. Although first mentioned by Eusebius, it is not until the middle of the 5th century that archaeological evidence

[77] Fiema 1998, 398.

[78] Fiema 2001, 425.

[79] Hammond 1965, 11–13; Joukowsky and Basile 2001, 50; Bedal 2001, 32.

[80] Fiema 2001, 425–436; Schick 2001, 1–5. These surveys were published after the original version of this conference paper was delivered, and the text has accordingly been amended.

[81] Fiema 2001, 426.

for their presence in Petra is found, with the recently discovered Petra Church, Ridge Church, Blue Chapel and the apsidal building excavated by Khairy (if it is a church), now joining the re-modelled Urn Tomb in the list of Christian buildings.

The unexpected discovery of substantial ecclesiastical architecture in Petra, together with that of the late 6th century Petra Papyri, should not, however, be allowed to obscure the fact that Byzantine Petra is otherwise very poorly represented in the archaeological record. Many other remains of the town at this period may have been removed by erosion or may still await discovery, of course, and until they are any discussion can only be speculative. But a few comments are necessary. First is the fact that, whatever church building was taking place, there was no restoration and re-occupation of the ruins of earlier monuments; only their debris was robbed for reusable building material. Nor does any effort seem to have been made to re-establish the Colonnaded Street as a main thoroughfare, though it remained in use as a trackway. Numismatic evidence suggests that even the poor structures built over it after the earthquake were not much frequented later on; of the identifiable coins from various stratified locations in the 1958–1964 excavations along the street and around the Temenos Gate, only three of the 5th century and one of the 6th century were found, compared with thirty of the late 4th century, after AD 363. These figures agree reasonably well with those recorded by Kirkbride for the coins found during her clearance of the Colonnaded Street, of which only eight could be identified as 5th or 6th century, compared with fifty-five 4th century[82], and with Fiema's initial analysis of fifty-three coins from the floor of one of the rooms (Room XXIX) excavated by him at the foot of the steps to the Upper Market, of which only seven were minted after AD 363.[83] In contrast, of the 239 identifiable coins from the Petra Church, 25% are of the first sixty years of the 6th century, and less than 1% are post-Justinianic.[84] Imprecise though these statistics are, they do not, in my view, lend much weight to the argument that Petra was still a flourishing market town in the later Byzantine period. To this evidence we may add the fact that (according to Fiema) there is no reference in the Petra Papyri to "any form of trade or commerce, local or international" and no indication that any of the wealthy landowners from the Petra countryside mentioned in them were involved in civic activities: "specific information relative to the city itself, whether its administration or economy, is negligible."[85] This is negative evidence and therefore suspect, but it at least warns us to be cautious until more positive evidence is available.

To return to the physical remains: Kanellopoulos and Akaseh have already drawn attention to the fact that "the three known freestanding churches are together on the slope north of the Wadi Musa", a statement which – if not strictly accurate, in view of the possible church excavated by Khairy on the opposite side of the *wadi* – nevertheless makes a significant point.[86] Given the lack of evidence

[82] Kirkbride 1960, 121.
[83] Fiema 1998, 414.
[84] Fiema 2001, 428.
[85] Fiema 2001, 426–427.
[86] Kanellopoulos and Akasheh 2001, 7.

for Byzantine occupation over much of the site, particularly in and south of the central valley, it suggests that Christian Petra may have been largely concentrated around the three churches on and below the northern ridge. It is also here, close to the ecclesiastical centre, that whatever secular buildings there were are most likely to have been found. If this asumption is correct, it is all the more unfortunate that it is here, on the northern periphery of the site, that evidence for erosion is most pronounced – excavation has shown, for example, that levels contemporary with the construction of the Inner Wall have been completely removed.[87] In the circumstances, the true nature of Byzantine Petra may never be revealed to the archaeologist, and we may never know whether or not it deserved to retain the title of city that it had previously enjoyed.

References

Barrett, D. G., 1998. "The Coins", in Joukowsky, M. S., 1998, 317–324.

Basile, J. J., 1998. "The Lower Temenos", in Joukowsky, M. S., 1998, 189–206.

Bedal, L-A., 2001. "A Pool Complex in Petra's City Center", *Bulletin of the American Schools of Oriental Research* 324, 23–41.

Bignasca, A. N. *et al.* 1996. *Ez-Zantur, I: Ergebnisse der Schweizerischen-Liechtensteinischen Ausgrabungen 1988–1992* (Mainz:Von Zabern).

Bowersock, G. W., 1983. *Roman Arabia.* (Cambridge Mass. and London: Harvard University Press).

Bowsher, J. M. C., 1990. "Early Nabataean Coinage", *ARAM* 2, 221–228.

Charles, H. R., 1913. *The Apocrypha and Pseudepigrapha of the Old Testament* (Oxford: The Clarendon Press).

Fellman Brogli, R., 1996. "Die Keramik aus den spätrömischen Bauten", in Bagnasci , A. N., 1996, 219–281.

Fiema, Z. T., 1998. "The Roman Street of Petra Project, 1997. A preliminary Report", *Annual of the Department of Antiquities of Jordan* XLII, 399–424.

Fiema, Z. T., 2001. "Historical Conclusions", in Fiema, Z. T. *et al.*, 426–436.

Fiema, Z. T., Kanellopoulos, C., Welisnewski, T. and Schick, R., 2001. *The Petra Church* (Amman: American Center of Oriental Research).

Gerber, Y, 1998. "Coarse Ware Pottery from Room 6", in Kolb, B., 1998, 272–275.

Grace, V., 1962. "Stamped Handles of Commercial Amphoras", in Colt, H. D. (ed.) *Excavations at Nessana I* (London: Colt Archaeological Institute and British School of Archaeology in Jerusalem), 106–130.

Graf, D. F., 1994. "The Nabataean Army and the *Cohortes Ulpiae Petraeorum*", in Dabrowa, E. (ed.), *The Roman and Byzantine Army in the East* (Krakow: Uniwersytet Jagiellonski), 265–311.

Hammond, P. C., 1965. *The Excavation of the Main Theater at Petra, 1961–1962* (London: Colt Archaeological Institute and Bernard Quaritch).

Hammond, P. C., 1996. *The Temple of the Winged Lions, Petra, Jordan. 1974–1990* (Fountain Hills, Arizona: Petra Publishing).

Hammond, P. C. and Johnson, D. L., 2000. *Survey and Excavations: 'Temple of the Winged Lions', Petra (Jordan)* (CD-ROM) (Fountain Hills, Arizona: Petra Publishing).

Horsfield, G. and Horsfield, A., 1941. "Sela-Petra, the Rock, of Edom and Nabatene IV. The Finds", *Quarterly of the Department of Antiquities in Palestine*, IX/2, 3–4.

[87] Parr 1986, 200.

Jones, R. N., 2001. "Nabtaean Inscriptions", in Fiema, Z. T. *et al.*, 2001, 346–349.

Joukowsky, M. S., 1998. *Petra Great Temple. Volume I: Brown University Excavations 1993–1997* (Providence: Brown University).

Joukowsky, M. S., 2001. "Nabataean Petra", *Bulletin of the American Schools of Oriental Research*, 324, 1-4.

Joukowsky, M. S. and Basile, J. J., 2001. "More Pieces in the Petra Great Temple Puzzle", *Bulletin of the American Schools of Oriental Research*, 324, 43–58.

Kader, I., 1996. "Propylon und Bogentor", *Damaszener Mitteilungen*.

Kanellopoulos, C., 2001. "The Architecture of the Shops and Colonnaded Street in Petra", *Bulletin of the American Schools of Oriental Research*, 324, 9–22.

Kanellopoulos, C. and Akasheh, T. S., 2001. "The Petra Map". *Bulletin of the American Schools of Oriental Research*, 324, 1–7.

Khairy, N. I., 1990. *The 1981 Petra Excavations (Abhandlungen des Deutschen Palästina-vereins 13)* (Wiesbaden: Otto Harrassowitz).

Kirkbride, D., 1960. "A Short Account of the Excavations at Petra in 1955–56". *Annual of the Department of Antiquities of Jordan*, IV–V.

Kolb, B., 1998. "Swiss-Liechtenstein Excavations at Az-Zantur in Petra 1997". *Annual of the Department of Antiquities of Jordan*, XLII, 259–277.

Meshorer, Y., 1975. *Nabataean Coins (Qedem 3)* (Jerusalem: Hebrew University Institute of Archaeology).

Milik, J. T., 1971. "Problèmes de la Littérature Hénochique à la Lumière des Fragments Araméens de Qumrân", *Harvard Theological Review*, 64, 333–378.

Murray, M. A. and Ellis, J. C., 1940. *A Street in Petra* (London: British School of Archaeology in Egypt and Bernard Quaritch).

Parr, P. J., 1962. "Le 'Conway High Place' à Pétra: une nouvelle interprétation", *Revue Biblique* 69, 64–79.

Parr, P. J., 1965. "The Beginnings of Hellenisation at Petra", in *Le Rayonnment des Civilisations Grecque et Romaine sur les Cultures Périphériques. Huitième Congrès International d'Archéologie Classique, Paris, 1963* (Paris: Éditions E. De Boccard), 527–53.

Parr, P. J. 1967–68. "Recent Discoveries in the Sanctuary of the Qasr Bint Far'un at Petra I. Account of the Recent Excavations", *Annual of the Department of Antiquities of Jordan* XII–XIII, 5–19.

Parr, P. J., 1968. "The Investigation of some 'Inaccessible' Rock-Cut Chambers at Petra", *Palestine Exploration Quarterly PEQ* 1968, 5–15.

Parr, P. J., 1970. A Sequence of Pottery from Petra", in Sanders, J. A. (ed.), *Near Eastern Archaeology in the Twentieth Century. Essays in Honor of Nelson Glueck* (New York: Doubleday), 348–381.

Parr, P. J., 1978. "Pottery, People and Politics", in Moorey, P. R. S. and Parr, P. J. (eds.), *Archaeology in the Levant. Essays for Kathleen Kenyon* (Warminster: Aris and Phillips), 203–209.

Parr, P. J., 1986. "The Last Days of Petra", in Bakhit, M. A. and Asfour, M. (eds.), *Proceedings of the Symposium on Bilad al-Sham During the Byzantine Period,* Vol. II, English Section (Amman: University of Jordan/Yarmouk University), 192–205.

Parr, P.J., 1996. "The Architecture of Petra: Review Article". *Palestine Exploration Quarterly*, 128, 63–70.

Sartre, M., 1993. *Inscriptions de la Jordanie. Tome IV (Inscriptions Grecques et Latines de la Syrie, Tome XXI)* (Paris).

Schick, R., 2001. "Ecclesiastical History of Petra", in Fiema, Z. T. *et al.*, 2001, 1–5.

Schluntz, E., 1999. *From Royal to Public Assembly Space: The Transformation of the "Great Temple" Complex at Petra*. Unpublished PhD dissertation, Brown University (Providence, Rhode Island).

Schmid, S. G., 1995. "Nabataean Fine Ware from Petra". *Studies in the History and Archaeology of Jordan, V* (Amman: Department of Antiquities), 637–647.

Schmid, S. G., 1996. "Die Feinkeramik", in Bignasca, A. N. *et al.*, 1996, 151–172.

Schmid, S. G., 1997. "Nabataean Fine Ware Pottery and the Destructions of Petra in the Late First and Early Second Century AD." *Studies in the History and Archaeology of Jordan, VI* (Amman: Department of Antiquities), 413–420.

Schneider, C., 1996. "Die Importkeramik", in Bignasca, A. N. *et al.*, 1996, 129–142.

Starcky, J. and Strugnell, J., 1966. "Pétra: deux nouvelles inscriptions nabatéenes". *Revue Biblique* 73, 236–247.

Stucky, R. A., 1995. "The Nabataean House and the Urbanistic System of the Habitation Quarters in Petra". *Studies in the History and Archaeology of Jordan, V* (Amman: Department of Antiquities), 193–198.

Stucky, R. A. *et al.*, 1991. "Swiss-Liechtenstein Excavations at ez-Zantur in Petra 1989. The Second Campaign". *Annual of the Department of Antiquities of Jordan* XXXV, 251–273.

Stucky, R. A., 1996. "Die Nabataischen Bauten", in Bignasca, A. N. *et al.* 1996, 13–49.

Taylor, J., 2001. *Petra and the Lost Kingdom of the Nabataeans* (London and New York: I. B. Tauris).

Tracy, S. V., 1998. "An Imperial Inscription in Petra", in Joukowsky, M. S.,1998, 370–375.

Tracy, S. V., 1999. "The Dedicatory Inscription to Trajan at the 'Metropolis' of Petra", in Humphrey, J. H. *The Roman and Byzantine Near East,* Vol. 2 (Portsmouth, RI: Journal of Roman Archaeology Supplement 31).

Wright, G. R. H., 1966. "Structure et Date de l'Arc Monumental de Petra." *Revue Biblique* LXXIII, 404–419.

Wright, G. R. H., 1967–1968. "Recent Discoveries in the Sanctuary of the Qasr Bint Far'un at Petra II. Some Aspects concerning the Architecture and Sculpture". *Annual of the Department of Antiquities of Jordan,* 20–27.

Wright, G. R. H., 1970. "Petra – the Arched Gate, 1959–1960: some additional drawings." *Palestine Exploration Quarterly* 1970, 111–115.

Zayadine, F., 1999. "Le relief neo-Babylonien a Sela' pres de Tafileh: interpretation historique." *Syria* 76: 83–90.

Zayadine, F. and Farajat, S., 1991. "Excavation and Clearance at Petra and Beida." *Annual of the Department of Antiquities of Jordan* XXXV, 275–311.

Zeitler, J. P., 1989. "Die Siedlungsabfolge am Fuss des el-Hubta-Massives von Petra (Jordanien)", in Lindner, M. (ed.), *Petra und das Königreich der Nabataer* (München), 307–318).

Zeitler, J. P., 1990. "A Private Building from the First Century B.C. in Petra", *ARAM* 2, 385–420.

Textiles of the Herodian, Nabataean and Roman periods from the Dead Sea area

Hero Granger-Taylor

The desert around the Dead Sea, by providing conditions that are both dry and stable, has proved an excellent environment for the preservation of textiles. Discoveries have been made at many sites and are particularly rich from the Herodian, Nabataean and Roman periods. Despite the inhospitable desert climate, people were attracted to the area at this time for a number of reasons: two local crops were economically significant, dates and the still-somewhat-mysterious balsam; raw materials were derived from the Dead Sea itself, most famously asphalt/bitumen but probably also sulphur; major trade routes from the Red Sea and Petra ran nearby, across the southern end of the Dead Sea westwards to Gaza and, on the plateau to east, northwards to Syria (during winter months, when the temperatures in the valley are not so high, some of this northwards trade may well have been carried by boat on the Dead Sea); political events caused people to seek refuge in the desert, most importantly Jews fled here during the First and Second Revolts against the Romans; finally, variously-expressed religious beliefs led people to the desert for the purposes of prayer and self-denial.

The following sites are the most important in terms of the discovery of textiles: 1) Khirbet Qazone, a cemetery site on the eastern littoral with finds of clothing from around the 1st to 4th centuries A.D.; 2) Masada, where the material is all fragmentary but richer and broader in type – it dates mostly from the occupation by insurgents during the First Revolt but some textiles were found in Herodian contexts; 3) the Cave of Letters, one of a number of hiding places in the Wadi Saiyâl/ Nahal Hever used during the Second Revolt and where the textiles, mostly from burials, compare closely with those from Khirbet Qazone; 4) Qumran, famously the site of the discovery of the Dead Sea scrolls, where the occupation probably ended with the First Revolt – textiles have been discovered at the settlement as well as in the caves.

At Qumran, most of the finds are of linen, a reflection of the fact that most had been used as scroll wrappers or jar covers. At the other sites, the great majority are of wool and are mostly the remains of clothing. At Khirbet Qazone, Masada and Qumran, a small number of cotton items have also been discovered. At Masada, thicker utilitarian textiles include many of goat-hair or goat-hair combined with camel-hair. No silk fibre or gold thread has so far been identified but the wool textiles from Masada include many that are very fine: fragments of a purple-dyed wool textile from a Herodian context at Masada may be the remains of a cloak that had belonged to Herod or to a member of his family (the ground is a red shade of shellfish purple, *argaman* in Hebrew, the colour that was particularly associated with kings). On average, the quality of wool textiles had lowered by the Second Revolt, but the standard remained very good: textiles were largely made by women, using simple technology but with a great deal of skill. Dyed colour is often excellent. Bright red is most common, achieved by mordanting wool fleece with alum salt and then dyeing it with madder root.

Complete items of clothing have been found at the Cave of Letters and at Khirbet Qazone. Together with the more fragmentary finds from Masada, these allow us to build a fairly detailed picture of dress at the time. Men and women both wore tunics, usually of wool and usually with contrasting shoulder stripes, or *clavi*. In the Hellenistic tradition, civilian dress consisted of such a wool tunic combined with a draped mantle, a large rectangle of wool worn without fastenings. Mantles of this sort are the only sort of male outer garment found in the burials. However, fragments of cloaks from Masada show that, outside the city (and, we should add, outside the grave), men frequently wore a pinned cloak in place of a mantle. The majority of cloaks used at Masada were semi-circular, in the Roman style.

Women's dress also varied between two principal combinations. Many women undoubtedly also wore the Greek-style mantle (the woman's version often has a coloured ground). But a local alternative was a large-head veil, also often coloured but of a much looser weave than the mantle and covering only the head and the upper part of the body (this garment is seen in representations of the Virgin Mary who, in eastern Christian art, almost invariably wears such a head-veil). Complete examples of head-veils have been found at the Cave of Letters and Khirbet Qazone and fragments of a further 70 or so at Masada. For the meantime, the combination of tunic and veil can be described as the traditional women's dress of the Dead Sea area. But it may have been worn across a much wider region, as much Arab as it was Jewish. Outside the Roman Empire the head-veil seems to have been combined with a plain tunic rather than the tunic decorated with *clavi*.

At Masada, where the textiles mostly come from accumulations of rubbish rather than from burials, fragments of many minor garments have been discovered: hair-nets, socks, belts, breast bands (*strophia*), loincloths, leg bindings and head-bands. Also present among the Masada finds are fragments from domestic and utilitarian textiles.

Figure a)
Khirbet Qazone, Textile 17, one piece from a two-piece tunic, here for a small child, all wool, undyed with purple-coloured *clavi*, c.30 x 35 cm (with fringes, c.46 cm). Photograph: British Museum

Figure b)
Masada, Textile 92-113/1, fragment from a semi-circular cloak, all wool, undyed lightly pigmented, c.7.5 x 6.5 cm (the sewn finish to the curved edge dates from an ancient 'reconditioning').
Photograph: Hero Granger-Taylor

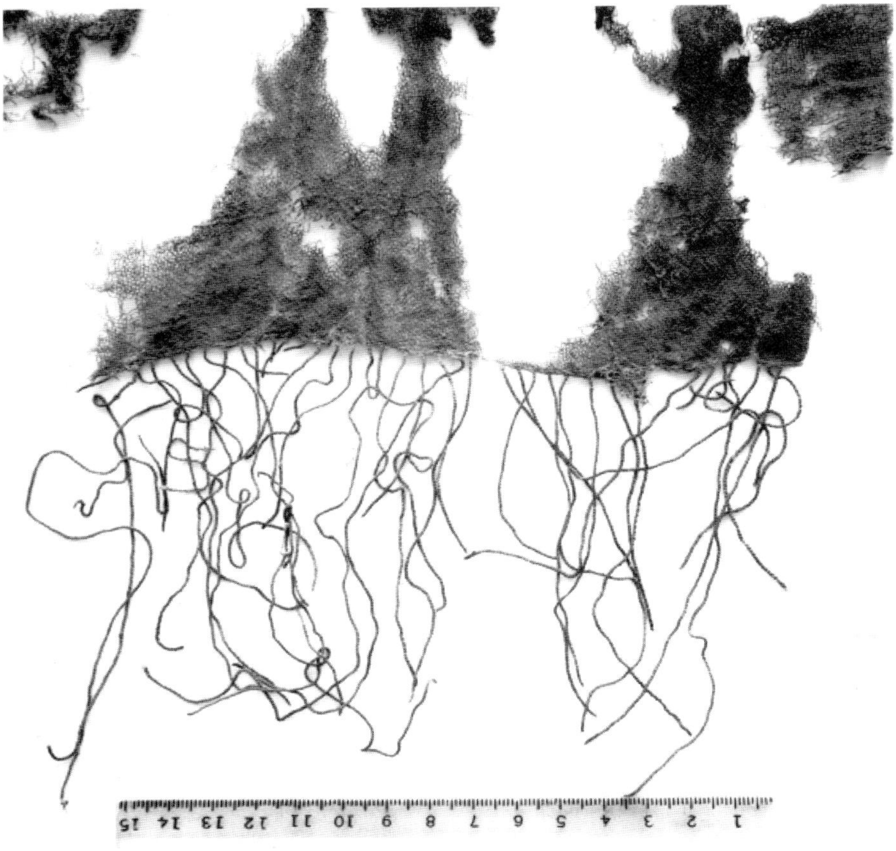

Figure c)
Cave of Letters, Textile 53 (2/18), fragmentary woman's head veil (detail), all wool, undyed or yellow.
Photograph: Hebrew University of Jerusalem

Bibliography

Khirbet Qazone

a) the textiles

Granger-Taylor, Hero, "The Textiles from Khirbet Qazone (Jordan)" in *Archéologie des Textiles – des origines au Vème siècle* (Actes du Colloque de Lattes, Octobre 1999), edited by Dominique Cardon and Michel Feugère, (Monographies Instrumentum 14), Montagnac 2000: 149–62 (a full study of the textiles will be included as part of a Final Report on the site).

Saito, Masako, and Nana Kasasaku. "Identification of the Fibers and Dyes on the Khirbet Qazone Textiles (Unpublished)." Kyoritsu Women's University, 2001 (Professor Saito and her team will be publishing complete dye results as part of the Final Report).

Cruickshank, Pippa, Anna Harrison, and John Fields. "Conservation of the Textiles and Leather from Khirbet Qazone, Jordan: From Excavation to Display (Unpublished)." Department of Conservation, British Museum, 2001.

Fields, John A. "Analysis of Dyes on Jordanian *(sic)* Textiles from Khirbet Qazone", *Dyes in History and Archaeology* 19 (2003): 94–99 (this work was not carried out as part of the study of the textiles and is therefore not recommended)

Granger-Taylor, Hero. "Textiles from Khirbet Qazone and the Cave of Letters, Two Burial Sites near the Dead Sea: Similarities and Differences in Find Spots and Textile Types." *Riggisberger Berichte* 13 (2006), 113–131.

b) general

Politis, Konstantinos , Amanda Kelly, Lisa Usman, and "Survey and Excavations at Khirbat Qazone, 2004." *Annual of the Department of Antiquities of Jordan* 49 (2005), 327–337.

Politis, K.D. "Rescue Excavations in the Nabataean Cemetery at Khirbat Qazone 1996–1997." *Annual of the Department of Antiquities of Jordan* 42 (1998): 611–14.

Politis, K.D. "Rescuing Khirbet Qazone: The Struggle to Save a Unique Nabataean Cemetery." *Minerva* 13/2 (2002): 27–29.

Politis, K.D., and H. Granger-Taylor. "Nabataeans on the Dead Sea Littoral." in *Petra Rediscovered: Lost City of the Nabataean Kingdom*, edited by G. Markoe, New York: Abrahms, 2003: 110–12 [11].

Shanks, H. "Who Lies Here? Jordan Tombs Match Those at Qumran." *Biblical Archaeology Review* 25/5 (1999): 48–53.

Zangenberg, J. "The 'Final Farewell': A Necessary Paradigm Shift in the Interpretation of the Qumran Cemetery." *QC* 8/3 (1999): [what is QC?] [pp?]

Masada

a) the textiles

Sheffer, Avigail and Hero Granger-Taylor, "Textiles from Masada – a Preliminary Selection." in *Masada IV – the Yigael Yadin Excavations 1963–65*, edited by Joseph Aviram, Gideon Foerster and Ehud Netzer, Jerusalem, 1994: 149–256

forthcoming

Hero Granger-Taylor and Vogel, Tal, with contributions by Ehud Netzer, Guy Stiebel and Martin Ciszuk, *The Textiles from Masada* (Masada VIII- the Yigael Yadin Excavations 1963–1965), edited by Joseph Aviram, Gideon Foerster and Ehud Netzer, Jerusalem (Israel Exploration Society and Hebrew University of Jerusalem) 2007

b) general

Yadin, Yigael. *Masada: Herod's Fortress and the Zealot's Last Stand.* London, 1966

Yadin, Yigael. "The Excavations of Masada, 1963–4, Preliminary Report." *Israel Exploration Journal* 15 (1965): 1–120, map opposite 121, 24 pls

The Cave of Letters

a) the textiles

Yadin, Yigael. *The Finds from the Bar-Kokhba Period in the Cave of Letters.* Jerusalem, 1963: 169–279 and pls 58–102

Granger-Taylor, Hero. "Textiles from Khirbet Qazone and the Cave of Letters, Two Burial Sites near the Dead Sea: Similarities and Differences in Find Spots and Textile Types." *Riggisberger Berichte* 13 (2006), 113–131.

b) general

Lewis, Naphtali. *The Documents from the Bar-Kokhba Period in the Cave of Letters I, Greek Papyri* (Judean Desert Studies II) Jerusalem, 1989.

Cotton, H.M., and J.C. Greenfield. "Babatha's Patria: Mahoza, Mahoz 'Eglatain and Zo^{c}ar", *Zeitschrift für Papyrologie und Epigraphik* 107 (1995): 126–133

Freund, Richard A. *Secrets of the Cave of Letters: Rediscovering a Dead Sea Mystery*: Amherst, 2004[?] (does not in fact supplant Yadin's discussion of the finds)

Qumran

a) the textiles

Crowfoot, G.M., "The Linen Textiles." in *Qumran Cave I*, (Discoveries in the Judaean Desert I) edited by D. Barthélemy and J.T. Milik, Oxford 1955: 18–38 and Pls.

Bélis, Mireille, "Des Textiles – Catalogues et Commentaires." In *Khirbet Qumrân et* ^{C} *Aïn Feshkha II: Études d'anthropologie, de physique et de chimie,* edited by Jean-Baptiste Humbert OP and Jan Gunneweg,.Fribourg and Göttingen 2003: 207–88

Taylor, Joan E., Kaare L. Rasmussen, Gregory Doudna, Johannes Van der Plicht, and Helge Egsgaard. "Qumran Textiles in the Palestine Exploration Fund, London: Radiocarbon Dating Results." *Palestine Exploration Quarterly* 137/2 (2005): 159–67

b) general

Cansdale, Lena, *Qumran and the Essenes: A Re-Evaluation of the Evidence*. Tübingen 1997

Magness, Jodi, The Archaeology of Qumran and the Dead Sea Scrolls, Grand Rapids, 2002

Nabataean Pottery

Stephan G. Schmid

I. Introduction

This contribution deals with one of the most characteristic products of Nabataean material culture, their pottery, particularly the plain and painted fine ware[1]. The first modern scholar to mention Nabataean pottery was G. Dalman who in 1908 described large quantities of broken vessels which he saw all over Petra[2]. In 1930 A. Conway and G. Horsfield were the first to explicitly associate this pottery with the Nabataeans[3]. Since then studies on Nabataean pottery have developed in different ways. Some works focussed on stylistic analysis of the painted ware, which mostly lack chronological elements supported by excavation data[4]. Other contributions concentrated on typological studies, producing catalogues of different types, which also lack a connection with excavation data in order to establish a firm chronology, though the material was found, at least partially, in regular excavations[5]. Finally, scientific analyses were used in order to examine questions related to the production of Nabataean pottery[6].

It would follow that a combination of the described approaches would be most promising, especially if large quantities of pottery are recovered from well stratified contexts during excavations. The first such approach was employed during the 1950s by the excavators of Dibon (Dhibân), though the quantities of pottery found were not great and the stratigraphy of the excavation was difficult to interpret[7]. Recently, field work still suffers from relatively small quantities of pottery, though stratigraphically dated finds allow an improvement in determining the chronology[8]. The following remarks on Nabataean pottery are mainly based on the rich material from the Swiss-Liechtenstein excavations at az-Zantur at Petra where Nabataean pottery was found in abundance and in well stratified contexts. However, cross-checks showed that the results obtained so far are valuable for other sites as well, as shall be demonstrated with a few selected cases[9].

[1] For a detailed study of Nabataean fine ware pottery, dealing in a more extensive way with the points mentioned here, see Schmid 2000A.

[2] Dalman 1908: 357.

[3] Conway – Horsfield 1930: 386; Conway 1930: 160.

[4] Schmitt-Korte 1968; 1989A; 1989B.

[5] Hammond 1957; 1959; 1962; Khairy 1975, working on pottery from Peter Parr's excavation at the paved street in Petra; cf. f. ex. Parr 1970; 1978.

[6] 'Amr 1987; Gunneweg *et al.* 1988.

[7] cf. below III. 1.

[8] See Weippert 1979 and especially Zeitler 1990A; 1990B.

[9] In general see Schmid 2000A, on comparisons with results from other sites especially 93–105.

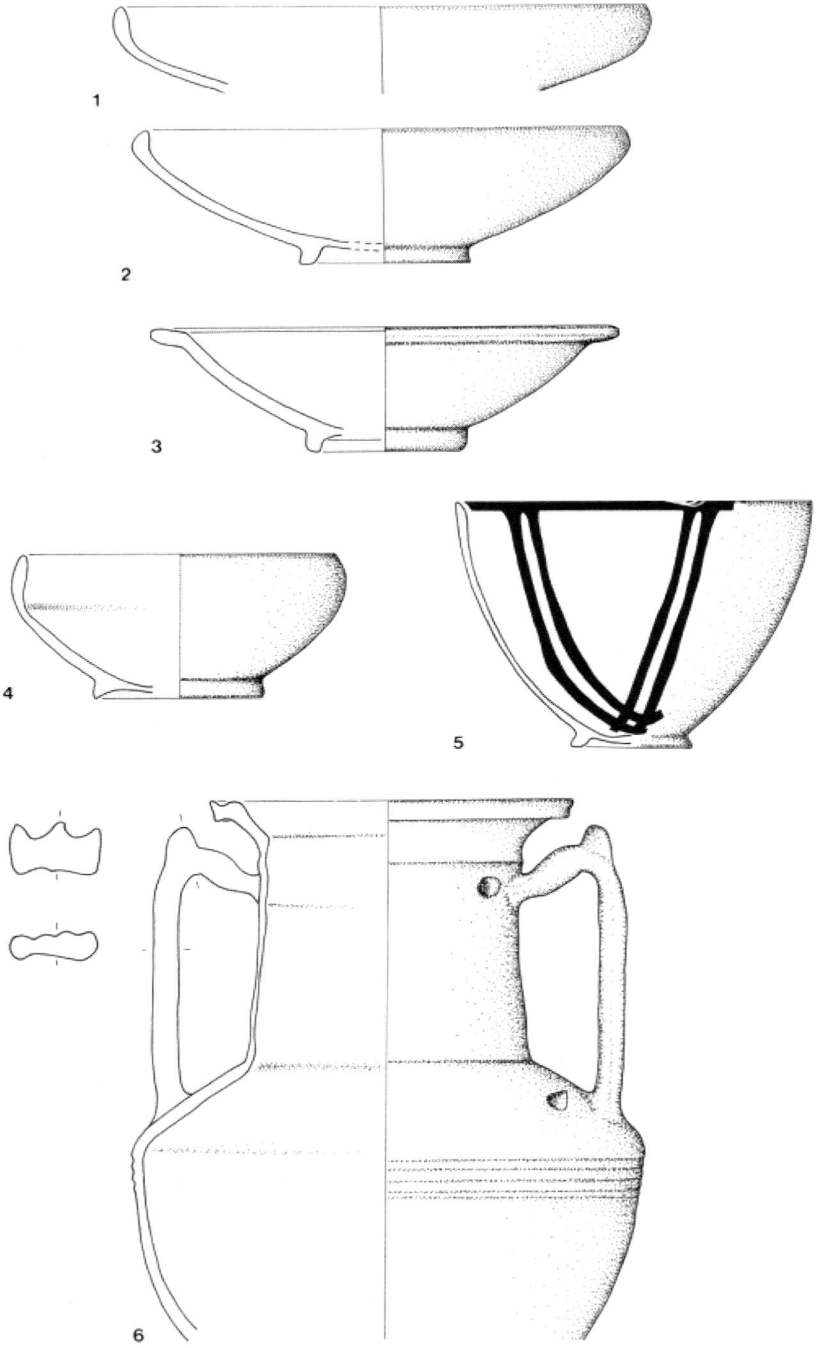

Fig. 1, 1–8: Plain and painted pottery of phase 1 (c. first half of 1st century BC). Drawings Schmid

II. Main types and chronology

II. 1. Phase 1 (c. 100 – c. 50 BC)

The first strata at az-Zantur that contained what can be called 'Nabataean' pottery also contained fragments of Eastern Sigillata A (ESA), dating the beginning of this phase to about 100 BC. The most frequent forms in terms of statistics, are open shapes (i.e. different types of plates and bowls, fig. 1, 1–4). They show a common thickness of their walls of about 4–6 mm, and a light red to orange fabric. Furthermore, they often display a red slip applied to the inner and/or outer surface. Although these shapes are by far the most frequent ones, there are also occasionally other forms, such as amphorae (fig. 1, 6) or other closed shapes. This shows that the different vessels belong to a kind of service, meeting all the demands of a rather profane use of pottery: A large number of platters and drinking bowls, as well as a few bottles, amphorae and other forms for serving and storage purposes[10].

It is remarkable that this pottery does not differ from what could be called the Hellenistic *koiné* of pottery in the Near East[11]. The shapes, the red slip and the thickness of the walls correspond to pottery standards attested to contemporary Judaea, Syria and other regions of the ancient Near Eastern. The only difference seems to be the occasional application of red paint, consisting of simple or double lines, straight or wavy, on the inside of a specific type of bowl (fig. 1, 5). As a matter of fact, this type of painting has no parallels within the immediate surrounding regions, but only in areas around the Arab-Persian Gulf and in Iran[12]. Whether this is an indication of early Nabataean contacts in these regions, or whether it might even be a vestige of the presumed Nabataean origins from that wider area, is an other question[13]. According to the latest ESA finds from strata containing pottery of phase 1, this comes to end towards the middle of the 1st century BC.

II. 2. Phase 2 (c. 50 BC – c. AD 20)

For the dating of phase 2 we can again refer to a considerable number of ESA sherds found in the same contexts as well as to Nabataean coins and occasionally other finds, such as Pompeian red ware or Italian Terra Sigillata[14]. In general terms two main tendencies can be observed within the roughly three quarters of a century that are covered by this phase: An evolution of the shapes from phase 1 towards finer and more delicate forms (fig. 2, 1. 2), with an average wall

[10] To these shapes of fine ware should be added coarse ware pottery, used for preparing and storing of food and beverages.

[11] On this see also Schmid 2000A: 111–118; Hannestad 1990; 1983: 83ff.

[12] Schmid 2000A: 119–121.

[13] Graf 1990; Schmid 2000A: 133–137, both with the older literature.

[14] Schmid 2000A: 23–25. 37–39 figs. 420. 421; Schneider 1996: 136f.; Peter 1996: 93f.

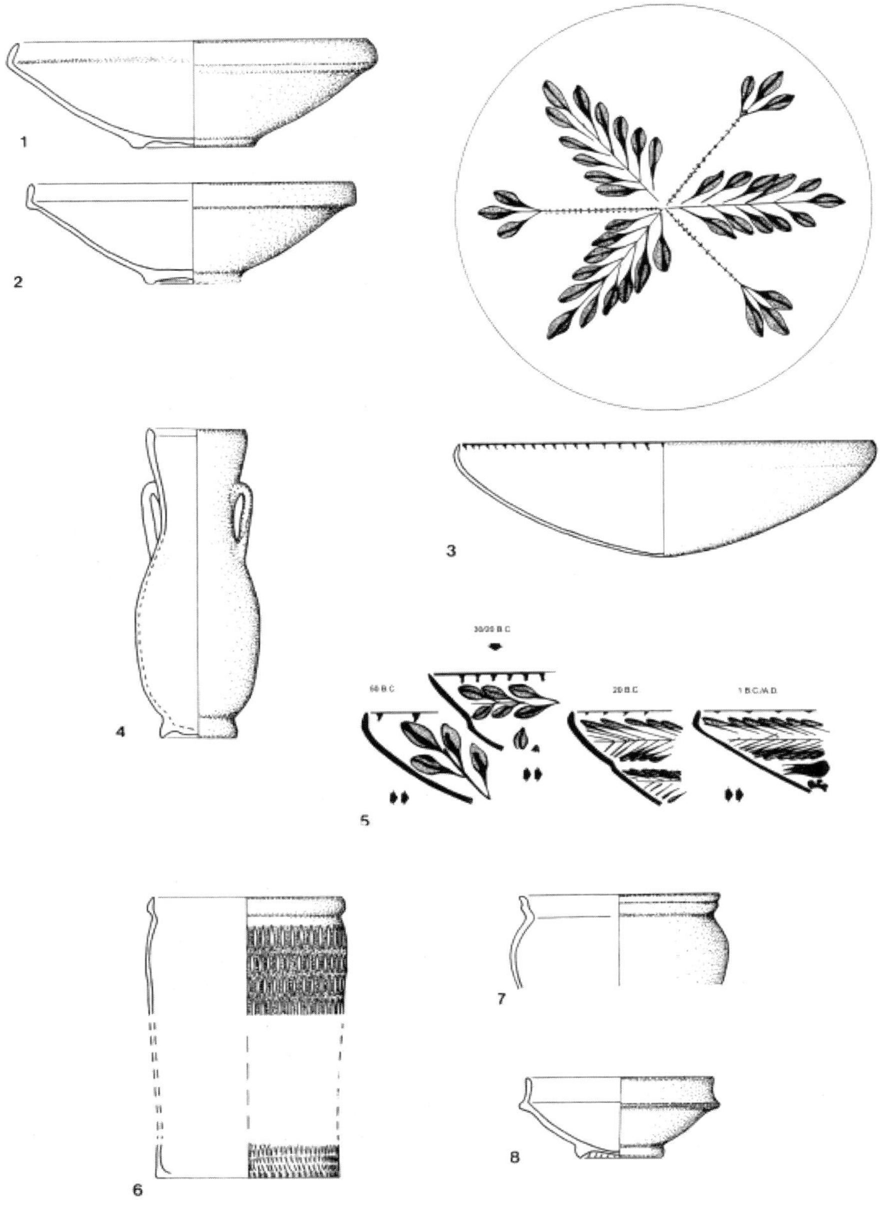

Fig. 2, 1–8: Plain, painted and rouletted pottery of phase 2 (c. 50 BC – AD 20). Drawings Schmid

Fig. 3: Painted pottery of phase 2a (above, c. 50-25 BC) and 2b (below, c. 25 BC – 1 BC/AD). Photograph Swiss-Liechtenstein excavations at az-Zantur, Petra.

Fig. 4: Fragments of painted bowl of phase 2c (c. 1 BC/AD – AD 20). Photograph Swiss-Liechtenstein excavations at az-Zantur, Petra.

thickness of 2 to 3 mm on the one hand, and the introduction of occasionally new shapes and decoration elements (fig. 2, 3–8) on the other hand.

Again, in terms of statistics the most frequent shapes are open plates and bowls. Contrary to phase 1, the beginning of a stronger separation between plain and painted types is now evident. The plain plates and bowls (fig. 2, 1. 2) stand in a close tradition of corresponding forms from phase 1 (fig. 1, 1. 2) and again their main use was probably for eating. The painted forms usually do not have any standing devices such as feet or rings on their bottom (fig. 2, 3). This is a typical characteristic of drinking vessels that are supposed to be constantly held in the hand. The shape of these painted bowls clearly derives from drinking vessels of precious metals or glass, typical luxury items of the Hellenistic and early Roman Near East[15]. The same seems true for the painting which consists mostly of floral motifs such as palmettes and leafs (figs. 2, 3; 3).

Some observations on minor changes in shapes but especially in decoration motifs allow a further subdivision of phase 2 into sub-phases 2a, 2b and 2c, each lasting for 20 to 30 years (cf. fig. 2, 5)[16]. Sub-phase 2a shows rather substantial leafs, applied concentrically on the inner side of the vessels body (fig. 3 above). In sub-phase 2b these become finer and radially applied (fig. 3 below). Especially from sub-phase 2c onwards (into sub-phase 3a; cf. below) one witnesses increasing attempts by Nabataean potters and painters to completely cover the entire inner part of the shallow bowls using, beside the radial palmettes, small clusters of leafs and "peacock eyes" (fig. 4). Specific shapes such as the small bowls and beakers on fig. 2, 6–8 are clearly influenced by Roman or Italian pottery production, while others, such as the shallow bowl with a step in the wall (fig. 2, 5 second from left) indicate Iranian prototypes, illustrating the distant geographic relations but also the open-minded spirit of Nabataean potters and, of course, their clients.

II. 3. Phase 3 (c. AD 20 – early 2nd century AD)

Phase 3, comfortably dated by ESA, coins and occasionally other imported pottery types, spans most of the 1st century AD. The tendencies observed above also also apply with this period. Again, there is an evolution of the shapes into finer forms, usually not thicker than 1 to 2 mm (fig. 5, 1–8). Like in phases 1 and 2, in phase 3 as well the open plates and the painted drinking bowls are the most frequently found shapes (fig. 5, 1. 2. 8). However, within phase 3 there is an increasing production of a very rich selection of small closed shapes (as illustrated on fig. 5, 3–7), some of them decorated with stamped and rouletted motifs, mostly referring to Roman prototypes[17].

[15] See Schmid 2000A: 147–150 for further references and parallels.

[16] The decoration motifs even point to a more detailed sub-division such as sub-phases 2a early and 2a late, as well as 2b early, middle and late; on this see Schmid 2000A: 28–39.

[17] Schmid 2000A: 123–125.

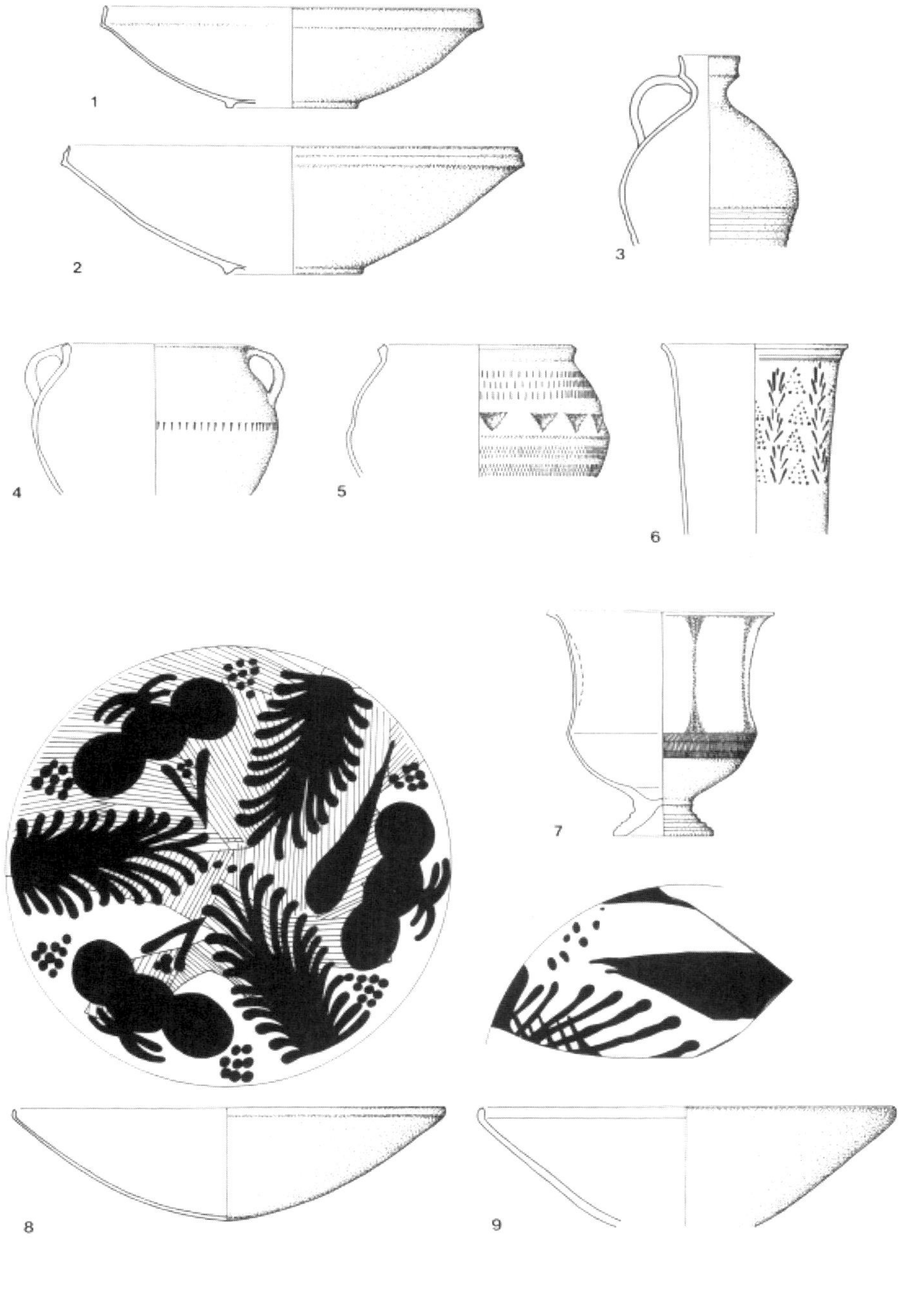

Fig. 5, 1–8: Plain, rouletted, stamped and painted pottery of sub-phases 3a–b (c. AD 20–100); 9: Painted bowl of the 2nd/3rd century AD. Drawings Schmid

The paint of the open bowls becomes darker in phase 3, pointing to a change in firing techniques. This is also supported by the observation that, contrary to phases 1 and 2, the fractions of pottery frequently show a core of dark fired clay, while the inner and outer surfaces are still in the same bright red to orange colour. The motifs of the decoration also undergo some changes. In phase 3a (c. AD 20 – 70/80) they present similar patterns than in the previous phase 2c (fig. 6) as well as some new patterns, including rather realistic floral motifs (fig. 7). In phase 3b (c. AD 70/80 – 106) the detailed and small scale floral motifs are replaced by larger and more stylised ones, such as somewhat clumsy palmettes and geometric motifs (figs. 5, 8; 8. 9), usually on a background of fine lines.

In the huge destruction layers at az-Zantur and other sites in and outside Petra that can be dated to the early 2nd century AD, the main component in terms of painted pottery belonged to phase 3b. However, there was always a smaller percentage present of a very similar decoration system that we call sub-phase 3c. It shows basically the same patterns as described above for sub-phase 3b, but somewhat carelessly applied and without the background lines. According to the archaeological evidence, the change from sub-phase 3b to 3c should have occurred by around AD 100[18].

III. The use of Nabataean pottery for further studies

Although some important progress has been made recently, increasing our knowledge about a precise typology and chronology of Nabataean pottery, there is still much to be done in this field. First of all, the precise recording of excavation contexts will probably lead to a finer tuning and minor changes in terms of chronology. In addition, the production of 'Nabataean' pottery does not stop with the annexation of Nabataean kingdom by the Roman emperor Trajan in 106 AD. Finds from the necropolis of Mampsis, from Petra and elsewhere show that this characteristic pottery continues without interruption well into the late Roman period (cf. fig. 5, 9)[19]. So far the picture related to this later phases of Nabataean pottery is not very precise and further studies hopefully will help to sharpen it[20]. Some other possibilities of how to use the results related to Nabataean pottery shall be demonstrated below.

III. 1. The dating of structures

Pottery, since the later Neolithic period has been a main product of most cultures, and is consequently one of the primary tools for identifying, and especially for dating all kind of remains of material culture. Nabataean pottery is no exception

[18] Schmid 2000A: 38; cf. below.

[19] Mampsis: Negev – Sivan 1977; cf. Schmid 2000A: 101f.; on the finds from the Petra area see below n. 53.

[20] See also the remarks in 'Amr – al-Momani 1999: 191f.

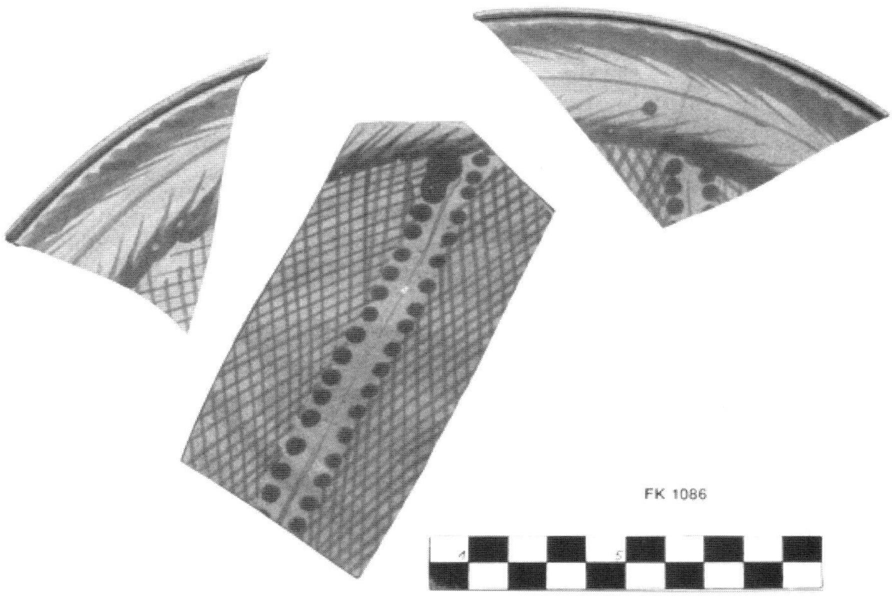

Fig. 6: Fragments of painted bowl of sub-phase 3a (c. AD 20–75). Photograph Swiss-Liechtenstein excavations at az-Zantur, Petra.

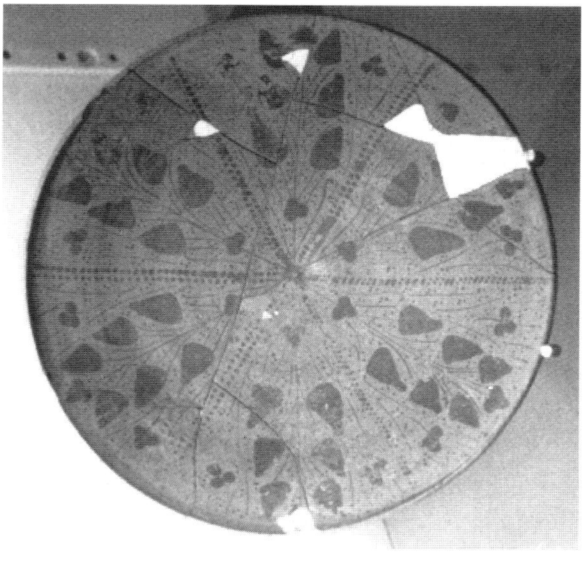

Fig. 7: Petra, Museum. Painted bowl of sub-phase 3a (c. AD 20–75). Photograph Schmid.

Fig. 8: Fragmented painted bowl of sub-phase 3b (c. AD 75–100). Photograph Swiss-Liechtenstein excavations at az-Zantur, Petra.

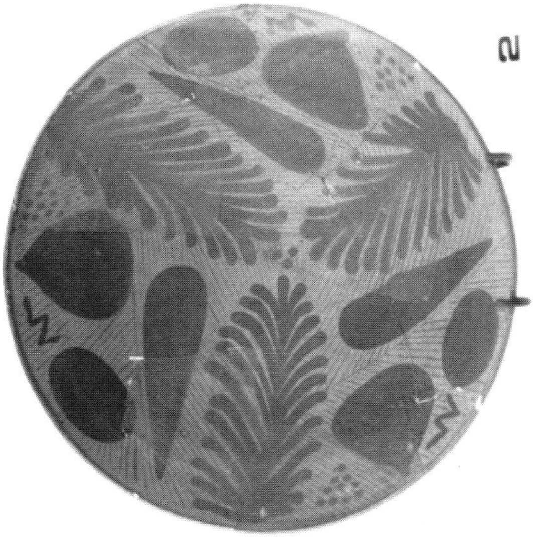

Fig. 9: Petra, Museum. Painted bowl of sub-phase 3b (c. AD 75–100). Photograph Schmid.

to that rule and particularly since it was produced in abundant quantities, since it follows a strong typification (cf. above) and since recently it was possible to establish a firm chronology, it is probably in dating of related structures that lies the most important value for further occupation with Nabataean pottery.

In some cases this kind of analysis can even be undertaken retrospectively, as is demonstrated by the excavation of the Nabataean settlement of Dibon (Dhibân), mentioned above[21]. The American excavations created as early as the 1950s a good foundation for the study of Nabataean pottery, which is hardly ever mentioned in recent research[22]. The analysis of decoration patterns led A. D. Tushingham to a sub-division that corresponds quite well with what has been proposed above in chapter II[23]. Therefore, his group A (1) corresponds to the main unpainted types of several of the phases at az-Zantur[24]. Tushingham's group A (2) a covers the painted pottery of az-Zantur phase 1; group A (2) b is equal to phases 2c and 3a, while group A (2) c corresponds to painted pottery of phase 2b middle; A (2) d are phases 2b late and 2c in our terms, group A (2) e covers just phase 2c; finally, group A (2) f corresponds to phase 3a while A (2) g covers phases 3b and 3c.

The excavators suppose – with reservation – an early Nabataean settlement, followed by the construction of a temple, a first destruction, a re-construction and shortly afterwards a final destruction[25]. However, A. D. Tushingham had already realised by analysing the pottery, that the first and the second destruction would be extremely close to each other in terms of chronology[26]. This can be underlined today by completing and comparing his chronological table with the phases as obtained by the analysis of Nabataean pottery from az-Zantur (fig. 10). In assemblage C and D, representing the end of phase I, as well as in assemblage A, that supposedly was deposited only after the final destruction, there is definitely painted pottery from az-Zantur phase 3c[27]. This means that we are most probably not dealing with two phases and two destructions, but just with one building and occupation phase and one destruction. This can be confirmed by the analysis of Eastern Terra Sigillata A (ESA) found in the destruction level at Dibon, profiting from the progress in dating ESA compared to the situation 25 years ago[28]:

[21] Tushingham 1972; cf. Schmid 2000A: 104f.

[22] Wenning 1987: 62 and 1990: 393 is one of the rare exceptions.

[23] Tushingham 1972: 51ff. with table X.

[24] Above chap. II; in Dibon the unpainted pottery was not further differentiated and, therefore, several of our chronological phases belong to A (1).

[25] Tushingham 1972: 27ff. 49ff.

[26] Tushingham 1972: 50: "On the basis of this dating of the terra sigillata in Assemblage D, we cannot posit much lapse of time between the destruction of period I and the final destruction...". In the following he proposes a dating within the third or fourth quarter of the 1st century AD for the first destruction, while he sees the final destruction related to the Roman annexation of the Nabataean kingdom in AD 106.

[27] On phase 3c see above II. 3.

[28] ESA is identified following the typology and chronology of Hayes 1985.

ESA from layers "end of phase I":	Hayes 1985	formdating
Dibon I Pl. 70, 14 (assemblage D)	51(?)	AD 70–120
Dibon I Pl. 70, 19 (assemblage D)	59	AD 100–150

ESA from final destruction	Hayes 1985	formdating
Dibon I fig. 71, 7 (assemblage A)	58	AD 100–150
Dibon II fig. 3, 31 (casemate)	50	AD 60/70–100
Dibon II fig. 4, 60	50	AD 60/70–100

Therefore, the two levels can not be separated based on ESA finds, as the fragment of a Hayes 59 from assemblage D give the same *terminus post quem* of around AD 100 as does the fragment of a Hayes 58 from assemblage A. Both, Nabataean pottery and ESA of assemblages A, C and D show exactly the same picture as does a huge destruction level found at az-Zantur in Petra and elsewhere in the Nabataean kingdom and that can most probably be connected with the Roman annexation of AD 106[29].

An other point that needs to be examined is the interpretation of the contexts that are called "in front of wall III" in the Dibon publication (cf. fig. 10). At this

Nabataean Pottery by Locus

	plain pottery	phase 1	phases 2c and 3a	phase 2b middle	phases 2b late and 2c	phase 2c	phase 3a	phases 3b and 3c	phases after az-Zantur		
Locus	A (1)	A (2) *a*	A (2) *b*	A (2) *c*	A (2) *d*	A (2) *e*	A (2) *f*	A (2) *g*	A (3)	B	C
Nab. Temple FTs and Podium Fill	Fig. 3.3,4, 6,7,8,14	Fig. 3.12	Fig. 2.59	1 (unillustrated)	Figs. 2.60; 3.9,10				Fig. 3.5,13, 15,16,20,26	Fig. 3.1,2	
Assemblage C	*Dhiban* I, pl. 68.1							*Dhiban* I, pls. 62B.2,3, 10?,13,15; 68.7,9			*Dhiban* I, pl. 69.11
Assemblage D	*Dhiban* I, pl. 70.15						*Dhiban* I, pl. 62B.9	*Dhiban* I, pl. 68.8			*Dhiban* I, pl. 69.10
Casemate		Fig. 3.34							Fig. 3.35,36		
T 1, Sounding A			*								
T 1, Sounding B	Fig. 4.40, 46,47			Fig. 4.48		*			*		Fig. 4.43,44, 45
R 31	Fig. 4.58	Fig. 4.55	Fig. 4.57	Fig. 4.56						Fig. 4.59	
Assemblage A	*Dhiban* I, pl. 70.8							*Dhiban* I, pl. 62B.5,14, 16	*Dhiban* I, pl. 68.3		*Dhiban* I, pl. 71.12
In front of Wall III	Fig. 4.4,5,7	Fig. 4.12, 14,15,26		Fig. 4.19, 13?,18?					Fig. 4.6,16		Fig. 4.8,9,10

* Indicates the presence of one or more sherds but no indication, if more than one, of the number of separate vessels represented.

Fig. 10: Dibon, sub-division of phases with corresponding sub-phases according to results of az-Zantur. After Tushingham 1972.

29 See Schmid 2000A: 20f. 34–36. 40f. 141–146; cf. Schmid 1997.

spot a sounding was carried out that brought to light Iron Age material from its lower levels as well as later finds from the upper levels[30]. This later pottery seems to be exclusively Nabataean and points to an early Nabataean settlement prior to the construction of the temple. However, two coins dated to the 4th and the 14th centuries AD respectively also are said to come from this trench[31]. The Mameluk coin was only found on the excavation dump and the trench supervisor already suspected it might be intrusive[32].

Apart from these two coins, the Nabataean pottery seem homogeneous and leads to a final interpretation of structures and phases from Dibon as follows: At the beginning we can place the material from the sounding in front of wall III, containing painted Nabataean pottery from our phases 1 and 2b middle (cf. above) as well as a ESA of Hayes form 11, dating to 50–20/1 BC[33], which would perfectly fit the dating of phase 2b from az-Zantur, ranging from 30/20–1 BC/AD[34]. The following construction phase of the temple contained painted Nabataean pottery from az-Zantur phases 1 to 2c[35]. Tushingham proposes an approximate date of AD 10 for the construction of the temple, a fragment of a so-called Herodian lamp being the only chronological indication[36]. Again this date can be confirmed by Nabataean pottery, as phase 2c dates from 1 BC/AD to AD 20 on az-Zantur[37]. The final (and only) destruction level of the Nabataean settlement at Dibon contained Nabataean pottery from az-Zantur phases 3b and 3c with very few earlier fragments. This, together with the fragments of ESA, points to a date of around AD 100 for the destruction.

It is, of course, much easier and effective to use the known results about Nabataean pottery in new field work. Given the statistical value that has been established within large and even enormous quantities from well stratified contexts, even small amounts from new excavations can give precise information. Such is the case with a recent project in the Wadi Farasa East in Petra[38]. The main monuments of that area – the so-called 'Soldier Tomb' and the opposite triclinium 235 on the lower terrace, as well as the so-called 'Garden Triclinium' and related installations on the upper terrace – always were somewhat enigmatic within Nabataean culture, especially, though by no means exclusively, in terms of chronology[39]. Already during the first field seasons of the International Wadi Farasa

[30] Tushingham 1972: 48f.

[31] Tushingham 1972: 49 coin catalogue nos. 12. 89.

[32] *Ibid.*

[33] Tushingham 1972: fig. 4, 30; Hayes 1985: 19.

[34] cf. above II. 2.; Schmid 2000A: 38.

[35] The latest element seems to be the bowl Tushingham 1972: fig. 2, 59 which corresponds to Schmid 2000A: 28 type E 2a 356 fig. 88 color plate 1, 1–3.

[36] Tushingham 1972: 32f. fig. 4, 19; these lamps cover the period from the last quarter of the 1st century BC until around the middle of the 1st century AD; see Negev 1974: 27f.

[37] Schmid 2000A: 38.

[38] On the project see Schmid 2000B; 2001A; 2001B.

[39] On these monuments, beside the works referred to in n. 38, see further Wenning 1987, 249–253 with the older bibliography.

Project (IWFP) considerable progress was made. Small amounts of pottery sherds found under the pavement of the courtyard between the 'Soldier Tomb' and the opposite triclinium, as well as from the hydraulic mortar of the huge water basin next the 'Garden Triclinium' presented a homogenous picture, dating these monuments to the second or third quarter of the 1st century AD[40].

III. 2. The settlement of the Nabataeans and the evolution of their material culture

As stated above (chap. I) the first pottery that can so far be connected to the Nabataeans stands in a proper Hellenistic tradition and covers the laps of time between the end of the 2nd and the middle of the 1st century BC (cf. fig. 1). This leaves us with the problem that between the first historical reference of the Nabataeans, locating them in central and southern Jordan in 312 BC[41], and this pottery there is a difference of 200 years[42].

Although occasionally pottery finds – mostly stamped amphora handles – with an earlier date are reported and almost exclusively from Petra, compelling evidence for a well established production of ceramics is lacking[43]. Furthermore, the same picture occurs in other categories of Nabataean material culture, for instance, no coin minting can be associated to the Nabataeans before the end of the 2nd or the beginning of the 1st century BC.

Though this seems puzzling at first, an explanation can be found by closer examining the relevant historical sources referring to the Nabataeans. On the one hand, Diodorus of Sicily, writing in the mid 1st century BC while referring to events of the very late 4th century BC, depicts the Nabataeans as nomads or semi-nomads without permanent installations or built structures. On the other hand, the Roman general M. Aemilius Scaurus reportedly did not destroy their *cultivated* land in 64/3 BC after being paid a huge sum by the Nabataeans (Josephus, Ant. 14, 5, 1). This, together with the account of Strabo (Geogr. 16, 4, 21), describing Petra as a flourishing city with plenty of well irrigated gardens, indicates that during the 1st century BC the Nabataeans definitely adopted a sedentary lifestyle. The sudden beginning of material culture, best represented by the pottery production, at around 100 BC points to some decisive changes within the Nabataean socio-economy at this time, probably the change from a nomadic to a more settled lifestyle, at least in and around Petra[44].

A future task of Nabataean pottery studies should be, therefore, the careful observation of whether there is pottery that can be securely attributed to the Nabataeans and dates before the late 2nd century BC.

[40] Schmid 2000B: 343f.; 2001A: 176. 179; 2001B: 349.
[41] Diod. 19, 94, 1; 95, 2ff.
[42] On this see also Schmid 2001C and in a broader frame 2001D.
[43] Schneider 1996: 130-132. 141f.; see also Parr 1960: 135.
[44] Beside the works quoted in n. 42 see also Dentzer 1999: especially 237–239 for Petra.

III. 3. The presence of Nabataeans and Nabataean commercial connections

The fact that Nabataean pottery follows a rather strict typology with very characteristic main shapes and decoration patterns makes it an ideal tool for identifying Nabataean settlements or tracing, for example, the presence of Nabataean traders at sites outside the proper Nabataean area[45].

Already Nelson Glueck used the characteristic pottery as an indication for Nabataean settlements during his surveys in the 1930s[46]. But also more recent survey projects rely on pottery for identifying Nabataean settlements[47]. It is clear that with the progress in dating and identifying also not so common types of Nabataean pottery[48], there should be a considerable improvement related to distribution patterns and chronology of Nabataean settlement activities within the proper Nabataean area.

Although of remarkably high quality, Nabataean pottery apparently never was used as a trading good itself for export. This can be shown by the fact that no such pottery has yet been identified in the Mediterranean area (i.e. the Aegean islands, Greece or Italy), although we know that these were areas frequented by Nabataean traders and ambassadors[49]. On the other hand, on the Arabian peninsula Nabataean pottery is found along the trading routes as well as on port sites in modern Yemen, Oman and the Gulf Emirates[50]. This means that in addition we can probably conclude that there was a certain social differentiation within Nabataean society, as obviously the people carrying out the trade on the Arabian peninsula were not the same that travelled to the West.

III. 4. Workshops and production centres

The high quality and the immensely large number of Nabataean pots that were produced, at least within phases 2 and 3 (cf. above chap. I) clearly point to professional potters and a well organised craftsmanship. Unfortunately, little information about workshops exists. A. Negev claims to have excavated a potter's workshop at Oboda[51], however, the evidence related to the presumed kiln is not very convincing[52]. The environs of Petra clearly must have been a major production centre of Nabataean pottery. At least for the later phases this is well attested by a series of kilns and related structures excavated at az-Zurraba[53].

[45] Some more detailed reflections on the distribution pattern of Nabataean pottery are presented in Schmid 2004 and, therefore, here just some general thoughts are presented.

[46] Glueck 1933/34; 1934; 1934/35; 1937; 1937/39; cf. Iliffe 1934.

[47] Politis 1997; Mattingly 1990; Hart – Falkner 1985; Hart 1985; 1986; 1987.

[48] So for around 400 different types of Nabataean pottery were identified and integrated in a precise chronological frame; Schmid 2000A: 43–84.

[49] Wenning 1987: 22–24; Roche 1996: 73–99.

[50] Schmid 2000A: 127–131; 2004.

[51] Negev 1974; 1986.

[52] ʿAmr 1987: 17.

[53] ʿAmr 1991; ʿAmr – al-Momani 1999; ʿAmr – al-Momani 2001: 261f.

However, their major period of production seems to date from the later 1st century AD onwards. Therefore, for a period of c. 150 years we are lacking compelling evidence of how and where the Nabataeans produced their characteristic pottery. We can only assume that Petra must have been a major centre of these crafts, as is indicated by scientific analysis proving that the clay used for producing Nabataean pottery did come from the same deposits for all of the 1st centuries BC and AD[54].

Occasionally, smaller pottery production is referred to for other and somehow more peripheral sites[55]. To which extent the pottery production must have been a well organised craft or even industry, may be deduced by pottery finds from the Hawran[56]. The local clay which contains large amounts of quartz was inappropriate for the production of the fine, plain and painted pottery as represented on figs. 2–9. This is why only the thicker shapes and the coarse ware are apparently produced from local clay, while the fine ware found in the Hawran surely is imported. This means, that the Nabataeans not only specialised in long distance trade but also had organised their interior exchanges and economics very well.

This brief overview will hopefully help to stimulate interest for further studies on Nabataean pottery, a field that still needs much research to be clearly understood.

IV. Bibliography

For a detailed bibliography on Nabataean pottery and related fields see Schmid 2000A: 163–177.

'Amr 1987: K. 'Amr, The Pottery from Petra: A Neutron Activation Analysis Study, BAR Int. Series 324 (Oxford 1987).

'Amr 1991: *eadem*, The Petra National Trust Site Projects: Preliminary Report on the 1991 Season at Zurrabah, ADAJ 35, 1991, 313–323.

'Amr – al-Momani 1999: K. 'Amr – A. al-Momani, The Discovery of Two Additional Pottery Kilns at az-Zurraba/Wadi Mousa, ADAJ 43, 1999, 175–194.

'Amr – al-Momani 2001: *idem*, Preliminary Report on the Archaeological Component of the Wadi Musa Water Supply and Wastewater Project (1998–2000), ADAJ 45, 2001, 253–285.

Barret *et al.* 1985: M. Barret – L. Courtois – D. Orssaud – F. Villeneuve, Le metériau céramique, in: J. M. Dentzer (ed.), Hauran I. Recherches archéologiques sur la Syrie du Sud à l'époque hellénistique et romaine (Paris 1985) 223–234.

Conway 1930: A. E. Conway, Exploring a City of Mystery. The First Excavations at Petra: Discoveries in the Remains of the "Built" City, and a New Explanation of the Rock-Cut "Sanctuaries", ILN 1. Feb. 1930, 160–161.

[54] Schmid 2000A: 136f.

[55] Wenning 1987: 298.

[56] See f. ex. Dentzer 1985; Barret *et* al. 1985: 229f. I would like to thank J.-M. Dentzer and P.-M. Blanc (Paris) for having showed me samples of Nabataean pottery found in their excavations in the Hawran.

Conway – Horsfield 1930: A. Conway – G. Horsfield, Historical and Topographical Notes on Edom: With an Account of the First Excavations at Petra, The Geographical Journal 76, 1930, 369–390.

Dentzer 1985: J.-M. Dentzer, Céramique et environnement naturel: la céramique nabatéenne de Bosrà, in: SHAJ II (Amman 1985) 149–153.

Dentzer 1999: *idem*, L'espace des tribus arabes à l'époque hellénistique et romaine. Nomadisme, sédentarisation, urbanisation, CRAI 1999, 231–261.

Graf 1990: D. F. Graf, The Origin of the Nabataeans, ARAM 2, 1990, 45–75.

Gunneweg *et al.* 1988: J. Gunneweg – I. Perlmann – F. Asaro, The Origin, Classification and Chronology of Nabataean Painted Fine Ware, JbRGZM 35, 1988, 315–345.

Hannestad 1983: L. Hannestad, Ikaros. The Hellenistic Settlements 2, 1. 2: The Hellenistic Pottery from Failaka (Aarhus 1983).

Hannestad 1990: *idem*, Change and Conservatism. Hellenistic Pottery in Mesopotamia and Iran, in: Akten des XIII. Internationalen Kongresses für Klassische Archäologie, Berlin 1988 (Mayence 1990) 178–186.

Hammond 1957: P. C. Hammond, A Study of Nabataean Pottery (unpubl. PhD Yale Univ. 1957).

Hammond 1959: *idem*, Pattern Families in Nabataean Painted Ware, AJA 63, 1959, 371–382.

Hammond 1962: *idem*, A Classification of Nabataean Fine Ware, AJA 66, 1962, 169–180.

Hayes 1985: J. W. Hayes, Sigillate Orientali, in: EAA, Atlante delle forme ceramiche II. Ceramica fine romana nel bacino mediterraneo (Rome 1985) 1–96.

Glueck 1933/34: N. Glueck, Explorations in Eastern Palestine I, AASOR 14, 1933–34, 1–113.

Glueck 1934: *idem*, Explorations in Eastern Palestine and the Negeb, BASOR 55, 1934, 3–21.

Glueck 1934/35: *idem*, Explorations in Eastern Palestine II, AASOR 15, 1934–35, 1–202.

Glueck 1937: *idem*, Explorations in Eastern Palestine III, BASOR 65, 1937, 8–29.

Glueck 1937/39: *idem*, Explorations in Eastern Palestine III, AASOR 18/19, 1937–39, 1–288.

Hart – Falkner 1985: S. Hart – R. Falkner, Preliminary Report on a Survey in Edom 1984, ADAJ 29, 1985, 255–277.

Hart 1985: S. Hart, Survey and Soundings between Tafileh and Ras en-Naqb 1985, Liber Annuus 35, 1985, 412–414.

Hart 1986: *idem*, Some Preliminary Thoughts on Settlement in Southern Edom, Levant 18, 1986, 51–58.

Hart 1987: *idem*, Five Soundings in Southern Jordan, Levant 19, 1987, 33–47.

Iliffe 1934: J. H. Iliffe, Nabatean Pottery from the Negeb. Its Distribution in Palestine, QDAP 3, 1934, 132–135.

Khairy 1975: N. I. Khairy, A Typological Study of the Unpainted Pottery from the Petra Excavations (unpubl. PhD, London 1975).

Lindner 1989: M. Lindner (ed.), Petra und das Königreich der Nabatäer. Lebensraum, Geschichte und Kultur eines arabischen Volkes der Antike (5th ed., Munich 1989).

Mattingly 1990: G. L. Mattingly, Settlement on Jordan's Kerak Plateau from Iron Age IIC through the Early Roman Period, ARAM 2, 1990, 309–335.

Negev 1974: A. Negev, The Nabatean Potter's Workshop at Oboda, ReiCretRomFautActa Suppl. I (Bonn 1974).

Negev 1986: *idem*, The Late Hellenistic and Early Roman Pottery of Nabatean Oboda. Final Report, Qedem 22 (Jerusalem 1986).

Negev – Sivan 1977: A. Negev – R. Sivan, The Pottery of the Nabataean Necropolis at Mampsis, ReiCretRomFaut Acta 17/18, 1977, 109–131.

Parr 1960: P. J. Parr, Excavations at Petra, 1958–59, PEQ 92, 1960, 124–135

Parr 1970: *idem*, A Sequence of Pottery from Petra, in: J. A. Sanders (ed.), Essays in Honor of Nelson Glueck: Near Eastern Archaeology in the Twentieth Century (New York 1970) 348–381.

Parr 1978: *idem*, Pottery, People and Politics, in: R. Moorey – P. J. Parr (eds.), Essays for Kathleen Kenyon: Archaeology in the Levant (Warminster 1978) 202–209.

Peter 1996: M. Peter, Die Fundmünzen, in: Petra ez Zantur I. Ergebnisse der Schweizerisch-Liechtensteinischen Ausgrabungen 1988–1992, Terra archaeologica II (Mayence 1996) 91–127.

Politis 1997: K. D. Politis, Rescue Excavations in the Nabataean Cemetery at Khirbat Qazone 1996–1997, ADAJ 42, 1998, 611–614.

Roche 1996: M.-J. Roche, Remarques sur les Nabatéens en Méditerrané, Semitica 45, 1996, 73–99.

Schmid 1997: S. G. Schmid, Nabataean Fine Ware Pottery and the Destructions of Petra in the Late First and Early Second Century A.D., in: G. Bisheh – M. Zaghloul – I. Kehrberg (eds.), Studies in the History and Archaeology of Jordan VI (Amman 1997) 413–420.

Schmid 2000A: *idem*, Die Feinkeramik der Nabatäer. Typologie, Chronologie und kulturhistorische Hintergründe, Petra – Ez Zantur II 1. Ergebnisse der Schweizerisch-Liechtensteinischen Ausgrabungen (= Terra archaeologica IV. Monographien der Schweizerisch-Liechtensteinischen Stiftung für Archäologische Forschungen im Ausland [SLSA/FSLA]) (Mayence 2000).

Schmid 2000B: *idem*, The International Wadi Farasa Project (IWFP). Exploration Season 1999, ADAJ 44, 2000, 335–354.

Schmid 2001A: *idem*, The International Wadi Farasa Project (IWFP). Between Microcosm and Macroplanning – A First Synthesis, PEQ 133, 2001, 159–197.

Schmid 2001B: *idem*, The International Wadi Farasa Project (IWFP). 2000 Season, ADAJ 45, 2001, 343–357.

Schmid 2001C: *idem*, The Impact of Pottery Production on the Sedentarization of the Nabataeans, in: J. R. Brandt – L. Karlsson (eds.), From Huts to Houses. Transformations of Ancient Societies. Proceedings of an International Seminar organized by the Norwegian and Swedish Institutes in Rome, 21–24 September 1997 (= ActaRom 56/ActaAArtHist 13) (Stockholm 2001) 427–436.

Schmid 2001D: *idem*, The Nabataeans. Travellers between Lifestyles, in: B. MacDonald – R. Adams – P. Bienkowski (eds.), The Archaeology of Jordan (Sheffield 2001) 367–426.

Schmid 2004: *idem*, The Distribution of Nabataean Pottery and the Organisation of Nabataean Long-Distance Trade, in: F. al-Khraysheh et al. (eds.), Studies in the History and Archaeology of Jordan, VIII (Amman 2004) 415–426.

Schmitt-Korte 1968: K. Schmitt-Korte, Beitrag zur nabatäischen Keramik, AA 83, 1968, 496–519 (for a shortened english version see ADAJ 16, 1971, 47–60).

Schmitt-Korte 1989A: *idem*, Die bemalte nabatäische Keramik: Verbreitung, Typologie und Chronologie, in: Lindner 1989: 205–227.

Schmitt-Korte 1989B: *idem*, Die Entwicklung des Granatapfel-Motivs in der nabatäischen Keramik, in: Lindner 1989: 228–232.

Schneider 1996: Ch. Schneider, Die Importkeramik, in: Petra ez Zantur I. Ergebnisse der Schweizerisch-Liechtensteinischen Ausgrabungen 1988–1992, Terra archaeologica II (Mayence 1996) 129–149.

Tushingham 1972: A. D. Tushingham, The Excavations at Dibon (Dhibân) in Moab, The Third Campaign 1952–53 (= AASOR 40, 1972).

Weippert 1979: M. Weippert, Nabatäisch-römische Keramik aus Hirbet Dor im südlichen Jordanien, ZDPV 95, 1979, 87–110.

Wenning 1987: R. Wenning, Die Nabatäer – Denkmäler und Geschichte. Eine Bestandesaufnahme des archäologischen Befundes, Novum Testamentum et Orbis Antiquus, 3 (Freiburg/Göttingen 1987).

Zeitler 1990A: J. P. Zeitler, A Private Building from the First Century B.C. in Petra, ARAM 2, 1990, 385–420.

Zeitler 1990B: *idem*, Houses, Sherds and Bones: Aspects of Daily Life at Petra, in: S. Kerner (ed.), The Near East in Antiquity, German Contributions to the Archaeolgy of Jordan, Palestine, Syria, Lebanon and Egypt, Vol. I (Amman 1990) 39–51.

Experimenting the Manufacture of Nabataean Fine-ware Pottery

James R. B. Mason

Introduction

The question of where Nabataean pottery might have been manufactured was not clear until archaeological excavations at Udruh and Zurrabeh, and to a lesser degree, Oboda, provided evidence for pottery production. At these sites kilns have been unearthed shedding light on Nabataean pottery activity. A Nabataean-period kiln was found at Udruh (Killick 1987: 7–8). At Oboda a structure was excavated which may have been a kiln. But the most exciting discovery was five kilns found at Zurrabeh near Petra (Zayadine 1982: 365–393). The range of Nabataean vessels and objects from the excavations demonstrates the wide range of wheel-made pots. To date though, no potters' wheel has been discovered. The only related finds are spindle sockets, a trimming knife and bronze spatula from Udruh and a small tool from Zurrabeh.

The forms of the earlier bowls appear to be influenced from Iron Age shapes followed by Hellenistic and Roman styles. The bowls and dishes however, can be described as characteristically Nabataean because of the standard to which they progressed beyond any earlier influence.

The Zurrabeh kilns were first discovered in the early 1980s when bulldozers cut a road to the Bdul village at Umm Sahun. Altogether four kilns were excavated with substantial workshop and storage space adjacent to Kiln 1. Kilns 3 and 4 were re-buried in 1980 but in 1991, re-exposed for further study by Khairieh Amr. At this time, a fifth kiln was discovered dating to the sixth century AD.

The importance of this 'potter's complex' illustrates a manufacturing area producing specialised wares for some 600 years. The earliest excavated kilns (3 and 4) according to Amr were not used later than the 2nd century A.D. These two kilns were abandoned and pottery activity then continued in the fourth century when Kilns 1 and 2 were constructed along with the large workshop.

Fine-ware painted bowls seem to be the type of pottery which has drawn the most attention. The reasons for this are due to the thin delicacy of the ware, their light-weight and careful craftsmanship. The thin lines and geometric dots demonstrate an expressive confidence during this peak and gives an insight into the potters. This is apparent through the inspiration, sensitivity and handling of the material. They depicted the flora and fauna in the Petra environs in a stylised manner on the pottery.

Reconstructing Pottery Manufacture

1. Clay sourcing

Clay deposits exist in great quantity in the regions surrounding Petra. Extensive work has been carried out on clay samples, as well as possible clay sources involving neutron-activation analysis (Amr 1987). By way of learning more about the clay used in this research, practical tests carried out at Yarmuk University, investigating the following characteristics of how the clay performed: Porosity of fired samples, shrinkage rates, hardness comparisons as well as the mechanical abilities of the clay to be 'thrown' on a wheel to fine sections, or as thinly as possible. Firing tests sought to find clay samples which fired to a similar colour and hardness achieved by the ancient Nabataean potters.

Gradually a fair working knowledge of what type of clay the Nabataeans had chosen for the manufacture of their bowls and an approach towards a fair approximation of their work was understood.

Sources of water-borne clay which had been deposited at 'Ain Tineh was initially used. This was the clay source closest to the workshop complex at Zurrabeh. There are also areas on the escarpment going from Wadi Musa to Ra's al Naqb which contain suitable clay deposits. Many samples tested were fired to colours ranging from deep pink-reds to orange-reds. However, they varied in shrinkage rates, a crucial aspect of working with clays if cracking and warping are to be avoided, either upon drying or firing, especially when making thin-bodied ware.

The clays were identified as a mixture of smectite and illite, clays which are predominantly formed in a sea-bed environment during the Lower-Cretaceous period in the Petra region. Such clays require care when firing because they are known as a three-body layered clay so that carbons 'trapped' within this matrix require more time to burn out if the full expression of the red colour is to be achieved. Indeed, whether by trial or error, or intentionally, the Nabataean potters brought the clay to such a level of maturity in their firings.

2. Surface Treatment

None of the pottery associated to the Nabataeans is glazed. There are however, two very distinctive attributes. First is the painted treatment of the surfaces executed on the best examples with an ease and confidence in dark brown/black or ranges of deep red.

The second characteristic, and one which again applies to the better 'classical' samples, is a surface sheen closely resembling a burnishing technique. Burnishing is a term applied to a technique of surface treatment whereby the outer surface is gently rubbed with for example, a smooth pebble stone. This technique coaxes the silica particles to the surface giving a shiny patina. Attempts at following this method failed, though one not without some clues. Many ores and minerals can be found in the southern region of Jordan amongst them haematite, copper ore, and manganese, south at Wadi Khrusheibeh and north at Wadi Dana. When carrying out work on the painted surfaces a Bdul friend gave us a heavy black stone which when rubbed with water produced a strong red pigment. This was identified as a form of haematite.

The coloured sandstones and ochre which exist naturally in the Petra region were an obvious choice. When tested, the fired results were disappointing, giving weak, 'watery' shapes and lines.

In the hills surrounding Petra a deposit of debris twelve centimetres thick had been left down at the bottom of the Petra basin surrounding the paved area next to the Qasr Al Bint. The clay from the uppermost surface, some three or four centimetres thick, was fired along with other clays in a small electric kiln at the temperature ascertained as being a favourable working temperature (850'–900' C). The top surface possessed an orange rich sheen. An extremely thin layer identifiable through the section possessed the qualities present on the classical bowls which was the goal. Another sample, when cleaned and mixed with water so that the clay was mixed together did not perform the same way. However it could be explained in terms of how the clay was first prepared. It can be argued that the finest particles of clay had migrated to the surface before settling.

3. Clay preparation

One method of preparing clay involves washing, whereby clay and water are mixed together after which the heavier particles drop to the bottom of the mixing pan. Afterwards, the upper levels of the clay/water mixture are siphoned-off and allowed to settle. The water is then removed and the deposit collected. This method is known as levigation. Samples of levigated clay found in excavations of kilns at Udruh and Oboda clearly show that this method was favoured by the early Nabataean potters. It was hoped thereby to keep the majority of the smaller particles in the mixture. Although this method was followed 'washing' was repeated three or four times, the 'sheen' remained illusive. It was considered to try and identify the clay-types which had contributed to a 'flood' sample collected some months earlier, but this would have been an extremely difficult task, since the soils and clays that had contributed to the 'flood' sample would have come from a wide area and from many different wadis.

The Faculty of Research Studies at Yarmuk University in Irbid, Jordan supported the second phase of the experiment which involved reconstructing a kiln based on the archaeological record of the kilns excavated at Zurrabeh. The type of fuel which may have been used by the Nabataeans was also considered. The effects of the firings on the bowls using traditional firing methods needed study.

Initially, the consensus amongst archaeologists about how Nabataean pottery was produced was generally guarded. One prevailing idea was that they had been made in some kind of mould and that they could never have been wheel-made. It

1. Example of spalling on early test bowl (photo: J. R.B. Mason)

2. 'Dry crack' at base join on early test bowl (photo: J. R.B. Mason)

was decided quite early on that the approach would have to consider whether or not they could have been made on a wheel. There is no archaeological evidence of potters' wheels or moulds. The first step was to ascertain how the clay from 'Ain Tineh performed.

Several test strips 10 x 2 cms were produced of varying thicknesses to approximate to the thinness of the sections of the bowls and fired at a range of temperatures between 7SO'C and 950'C. Changes were evident between these firings temperatures in colour, hardness and percentages of overall shrinkage, as could be expected. [fig. 1]

When these tests were satisfactory, a few small pots were thrown on the wheel to find out how vertical samples would perform. For the first batch of bowls thirty kilos of clay were brought from 'Ain Tineh, to the Ceramic Department at Yarmuk University. These first samples were made from clay which had been washed, mixed with water and sieved through a 40 mm mesh sieve. These were clumsy and heavy the majority of them being warped and cracked at the

3. 'Dry crack' at base join on early test bowl (photo: J. R.B. Mason)

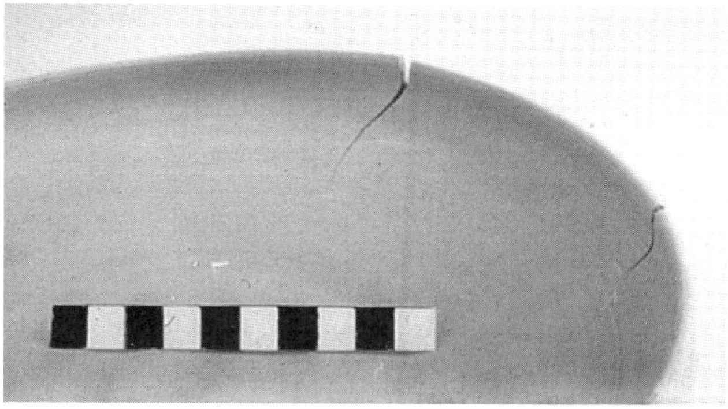

4. 'Dry crack' on rim of early test bowl (photo: J. R.B. Mason)

drying stage. [figs. 2, 3, 4] The mistake was trying to throw them as thin as possible at one go, and making them far too flat. One important aspect of how a potter works is to internalise the shapes to be made in the minds eye and through a working knowledge of what the clay allows is guided by that inner form. Unfamiliarity enough with the clays or the forms and subtleties of the bowls were problems.

For a second attempt the bases of the bowls were made thicker and the inward facing lip as thin as possible. Furthermore original Nabataean pottery was studied. An examination of the bases showed a rougher surface than the inner one, with slightly incised lines and the drag effect of small particles inscribed in a circular way. Put simply, the bottom third section of the bowls had been 'turned', that is clay had been removed with a sharp tool, or paired away. Another factor was that some, but not all had foot-rings, a round section cut away to form a base. [fig.]

The second batch of some 20–30 pots were made in this manner. The next problem was dealing with the cracking and warping. It was decided that a slower drying period was required and a more uniform section through the pots was needed. With these changes improvements slowly became evident.

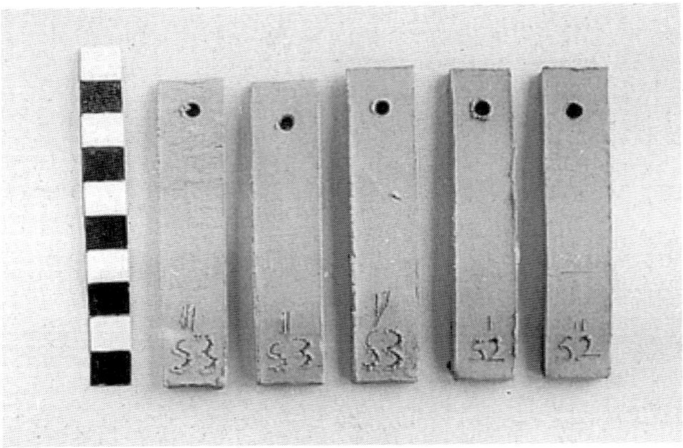

5. Clay test strips (photo: J. R.B. Mason)

4. Constructing the kiln

Altogether five kilns were discovered at Zurrabeh dating from the 1st century B.C to the 6th century A.D. The kilns' construction apparently evolved from a narrower-deeper to a wider-shallower design. The reconstruction was based on the largest kiln excavated. However this was considered too large to replicate on a 1:1 scale, primarily because of the impracticality of filling it with pottery to be fired. The test kiln was therefore scaled-down to one third the size. All that remained of the Zurrabeh kiln was a large oval hole in the ground with the bricks of four arch-springers embedded into the sides of the kiln, presumably the firebox. An entrance at ground level existed with a stone arch *in situ*.

A site to build the kiln was chosen in ancient Jerash. Construction of the kiln was from hand-made bricks of local Jerash clay. Experimenting with different clay mixtures, testing them in an electric kiln at Yarmuk University, at temperatures above requirements – to 1200' C, estimating the bricks used to build the firebox would need greater working temperatures than in the firing chamber itself.

The dimensions of the brick sizes had been estimated based on bricks from the larger kiln at Zurrabeh, and like the kiln, reduced the size by a third. They were made in wooden moulds of two sizes; one size for the bricks and the other for the tiles onto which the ware would be stacked and for the arches.

Several versions were tried using different amounts of local clays, as well as clay used in a modern brick factory. To adapt those varying amounts of crushed pottery sherds were added. After several trials a suitable recipe for the brickwork, kiln shelves and the mortar were reached.

The kiln was built with unfired bricks since it seemed more sensible as well as providing an opportunity to trim off edges or fit bricks in using a sureform to re-shape them. [fig. 6]

6. Early examples of successful painted bowl reproductions (photo: J. R.B. Mason)

Fuel

Since the kiln had been excavated nine years earlier identifying ash deposits from the ancient firings was not possible to verify what fuel type the Nabataeans potters had used.

The hardwoods that grow naturally in the Petra region include sycamore fig, olive and oak. In the past, evergreen oak, deciduous oak, Aleppo pine, juniper, hawthorn, almond and pistachio were also present.

The hardwoods would have been too precious to use as fuel. Therefore in the first experiment dead walnut and pine was used as fuel. In subsequent firings palm branches and olive waste were used.

On examination of the ancient ash waste taken from one of the later kilns, olive pips were identified. A lorry-load of olive waste from a recent pressing was obtained for future experimental firings. A square wooden brick-mould was constructed to make several hundred briquettes from the waste mixture, and when dried, effectively used as fuel.

The olive waste proved highly successful; it gave heat and created very little ash deposit. This replicated the design of the original kiln which also showed no signs of containing an ash-pit.

7. Applying iron ore pigment on a reproduced bowl in 1993

Conclusions

In general the kiln was under-fired and the ware was not hard-fired; many bowls showed effects from surface smoking. Of the 19 wasters the cores were not coloured, and it was estimated that no true reduction had occurred. The highest fired ones were in the stack that had collapsed. Bowls at the front gave a dull ring on tapping; those in the stack, protected by ones above and below were redder. The sandstone pigment tests were unconvincing, and none had the lustre effect that we sought for. About 17–18 bowls had broken or were cracked, mainly due to the stack which collapsed.

Bibliography

'Amr, K. (1987) *The Pottery from Petra. A Neutron Activation Analysis Study*. B.A.R. International Series, Oxford

Killick. M. *Nabataean Pottery*. (1978) Pp. 7–8 in A. Killick (ed.) *Udruh: Caravan City and Desert Oasis*.

Mason, J. R.B, & K. Amr (1990) *A study of Nabataean Pottery Manufacturing Techniques: an experiment for reconstructing the production of fine-ware bowls*. ARAM 2/1 & 2: 287–307.

Mason, J. R.B, & K. Amr (1992) *An Investigation into the Firing of Nabataean Pottery. Studies on the History and Archaeology of Jordan V*. pp. 629–636

Mason, J. R.B, & K. Amr (1988) *Remaking Nabataean Fine-Ware bowls. Ceramic Review* 134: 11–12

Mason, J. R.B, & K. Amr (1993) *Nabataean bowl production: interim summary of developments. Levant* 25: 207

Mason, J. R.B (2000) *Discovering Nabataean Pottery*. J.R.B. Mason, Bembridge, Isle of Wight
Zayadine, F. (1982) *Recent Excavations at Petra (1979–81)*. *A.D.A.J.* 26: 365–393

8. The completed experimental kiln in Jerash (photo: J. R.B. Mason)

Monetary Interchange in Nabataean Petra[1]

Julian M.C.Bowsher

This discussion comprises a brief survey of coins that have been found at Nabataean sites, principally Petra, and an overview of our current state of knowledge. Much of the information used in this paper is based on the major excavations in Petra conducted by the British School of Archaeology at Jerusalem by Peter J. Parr. The coins from these excavations are, at last, about to see the light of day.[2] Scientific excavations at Petra began in the late 1920s,[3] but it is only recently – with increased archaeological activity there – that coins have been published in larger numbers.[4] Nevertheless, coin material from a number of other excavations and explorations within Petra still await detailed publication.[5]

Numerous sources describe Nabataean society as wealthy but the use of the numismatic data has often been limited.[6] For example the report on the 1981 Katute excavations notes that "The dating of our stratigraphy depends mainly on coins."[7] with little intrinsic detail. The study of Nabataean coins themselves goes back to the 19th century although the standard catalogue by Meshorer dates only to 1975, with new types published by Schmitt-Korte in 1990.[8] Nabataean coins are numerous at Petra but are increasingly found farther afield within and beyond the Nabataean realm. [9]

[1] I am grateful to Konstantinos Politis for asking me to provide a "work-shop talk" on Nabataean coin finds, albeit then persuading me to write up my notes as the present "paper". I am also grateful to Andy Meadows who shared much information on Nabataean coinage in another workshop session.

[2] Bowsher forthcoming A. Mention of coins in the preliminary reports by Parr is superseded by this forthcoming study.

[3] For an account of archaeological exploration at Petra from 1929 to 1989, see Parr 1990; for work since, see reports in the *Annual of the Department of Antiquities of Jordan*.

[4] Coins from the Swiss excavation have been published by Peter 1996; American excavations by Betlyon 2001, Sokolov 2001, Barrett 1998 (rather user *un*friendly) and Bowsher forthcoming B. A discussion on circulation also based on coins from the Brown University excavations around the "Great Temple" and the IFAPO excavations around the Qasr el-Bint has been presented by Augé, forthcoming.

[5] Coins are barely mentioned in the reports of Professor Hammond, or of Dr Lindner, but basic details are found in Dr Zayadine's reports for the Department of Antiquities.

[6] Noted in Bowsher 1990.

[7] Khairy 1990, 7. The corpus of coin finds from these excavations appears to comprise issues of Aretas IV, Malichus II and Rabbel II as well as some Byzantine pieces. No statistical details are given other than the information that about 1/3 of the (unknown) total were fully identified.

[8] Meshorer 1975; Schmitt-Korte 1990.

[9] For a more comprehensive survey of Nabataean coin finds, and research, see Wenning 1991.

The plethora of coins to be found at Petra is well known; Murray and Ellis for example noted that "coins of both silver and bronze are not uncommon".[10] Kirkbride reported in 1939 that "many of the new types of Nabataean bronze were obtained at Petra by means of mass searches".[11]

This paper focuses on the 1st centuries BC and AD, the period during which the Nabataeans themselves produced great quantities of coinage. The Hellenistic period at Petra is dominated by imported coins, mostly Ptolemaic, Phoenician and a sprinkling of others, and from c. 110 BC, by the first Nabataean issues attributed to Aretas II.[12] These, latter, coins continued to circulate – or, at least, continued to be lost – into the 1st century AD. None of the Damascene issues of Aretas III have been found in Petra and their circulation was almost certainly limited to Syria.[13] At the other end of the period, the use and probable continued circulation of Nabataean coins after their absorption into the Roman Empire in AD 106 forms another element outside the scope of the present discussion.

The Nabataeans did not produce a gold coinage and apparently did not need a silver coinage (of their own) until the 60s BC. Few of these early silvers have been recovered, one example being an issue of Obodas III found in a tomb at al-Khutba.[14] The archaeological and architectural record for this period is slender compared to the 1st century AD. Very few Nabataean coins of the 1st century BC have been recovered archaeologically.

It might be noted here that silver coins are often found in funerary contexts: two issues of Aretas IV from shaft tomb B1,[15] Malichus II from the courtyard of Tomb 813,[16] and Rabbel II from Tomb IX, south of Umm el Biyara (BSAJ). The reuse of Nabataean tombs in the Roman period may even have been accompanied by the same custom; a denarius of Septimius Severus was found in Tomb 64B, locus 5.[17]

Nevertheless, of the 9 Nabataean silvers found in the BSAJ excavations, most came from Trench I, on the Katute ridge. This collection included a fine silver of Syllaeus and even a new type being, as far as one can determine, a fraction of Aretas IV.[18]

[10] Murray & Ellis 1940,3; Despite this claim Murray & Ellis describe only one coin find, an issue of Hadrian minted in Gaza. Their discussion of coins of Obodas and Malichus was for stylistic comparative purposes only.

[11] Kirkbride 1939, 54

[12] Partly discussed in Bowsher 1990 and in Parr (this volume). A greater discussion will appear in Bowsher forthcoming A

[13] Meshorer 1975, 13–14. For a discussion on monetary interchange in the Nabataean Hauran, see Augé 1985, 208–209.

[14] Zayadine 1973, 82 and 1974,140 – with photograph pl. LXIV.2. Although published as Obodas II, the description and photograph can be clearly identified with the Obodas III, defined by Meshorer 1975, and a type – jugate heads / single head – dated to the second part of his reign.

[15] Zayadine 1979, 189

[16] ibid. 192

[17] Zayadine 1982, 369

[18] Just the sort who's (hitherto) absence was decried by Schmitt-Korte & Price 1994,103 "We find it difficult to understand that Aretas IV minted no fractions of silver coins".

A Roman Republican denarius of Manius Cotta, 46 BC, was found on the surface at Petra during the BSAJ excavations. It is in good condition and it is unlikely to have stayed in circulation for long. Nabataean acquaintance with Roman silver can be seen from the composition of a hoard of 227 (silver) coins from the Wadi Murabbat, 25 kilometers south of Jerusalem, thought to have been deposited during the second Jewish Revolt of the 130s AD.[19] Although just over half were Nabataean (from Aretas IV to Rabbel II), there were also 54 Roman denarii, including interestingly, another example of the same Manius Cotta issue as that found at Petra, and 57 Roman provincial drachmae. Nevertheless, it may be remembered that the widespread circulation, and archaeological deposition, of Roman silver accompanied heightened expenditure caused by civil wars.

At the turn of the millennium Nabataean silver bore some relationship with Roman denarii, but by the end of the 1st century AD it had dropped in weight and in silver content. After the Roman annexation, a new provincial mint was established by Trajan at Bostra, and this has produced numerous examples of drachmae overstruck on silver, of Rabbel II (at least), indicating some acceptance of this lower standard.[20] A number of these have been found in hoards at Mampsis[21] and at Tell Kalaf[22]. One such drachma from Petra (BSAJ) is also possibly overstruck on a Nabataean issue but its details are obscure. It is assumed that reserves of Nabataean silver coin were seized by the Roman authorities, although their circulation, as determined by losses revealed in the archaeological record, was limited.

Bronze Nabataean coins from the later 1st century BC found at Petra also appear to be rare. One example of Obodas III was found at Zantur,[23] and another from the BSAJ excavations came from Trench XXI on the north wall. However "a few specimens" (of Obodas III) have also been found in the centre of the city.[24]

From the 1st century AD, there is a wealth of data and Nabataean coins are by far the largest number, being found in virtually every investigation and many in contemporary contexts.[25] The largest percentage of coins from this period is those of Aretas IV and it is clear that they continued to circulate throughout the century. Coins of Rabbel II usually come second, but a tomb on the North Ridge clearly dating from the mid century produced a large number of Malichus II issues, altering, on that particular site, the usual statistics.[26] Early British excavations produced only two of Aretas IV, two of Malichus II and one of Rabbel II, thought

[19] Milik & Seyrig 1958

[20] Kindler 1983, 95–103

[21] Negev 1978

[22] Metcalf 1975

[23] Peter 1996, 93 no.3

[24] Augé forthcoming

[25] A rough calculation suggests that some 70 % of 1st century AD Nabataean coins come from contemporary deposits.

[26] Bowsher forthcoming B

at the time to be within contemporary deposits.[27] The first American excavations, at the "Conway High Place" (now referred to as Tower), produced 18 Nabataean coins which comprised two coins of "Aretas II", Aretas IV – including four "whole" units (Meshorer 112–114), three "commemoration" issues (Meshorer 97) and two "quarter" units, one Malichus II "whole" unit and a number of illegible "probably Nabataean" pieces. Nevertheless, the report also contains the caveat "The eighteen coins described below are almost certainly all from the [Conway] High Place, but this cannot be absolutely guaranteed."[28] From the BSAJ excavations, the coins of Aretas IV form 36% of all the Nabataean coins, with Rabbel II at 25.5% and Malichus II at 5.5%.[29] One coin of Rabbel II is reported from a late phase in the Temple of the Winged Lions.[30]

The predominance of Aretas IV issues lies not just in the plethora of types produced under his reign, but the variety of denominations. Most of these are the "quarters", with fewer of the "halves". The apparent rarity of lower denomination coins produced by his successors ensured that the Aretan fractions continued to serve an economic function for the rest of the Nabataean period. The brief description of coins of Aretas IV found at the Katute in 1981 is restricted to a dating before and after the marriage to Shaqilat II in 18 AD.[31] But there appears to be no recognition that those pre 18 pieces are fractions and likely therefore to have circulated for longer than the new 'whole' units that appeared after 18.[32] Of all the coins of Aretas IV discovered in the BSAJ excavations, 27.5% were "quarter units" (Meshorer types 62–78). A later Aretan series of "quarters" (Meshorer types 119–122) formed 12% and also seemed to circulate for quite a period. It is difficult therefore to agree with Karl Schmitt-Korte's reassignation of these particular "quarters" to the one year (c. 9 BC) "joint reign" of Aretas IV and Syllaeus.[33] Amongst the few later fractions found at Petra were two examples of a "half" issue of Malichus II, hitherto thought to be unique.[34]

Foreign bronze coins of this period (later 1st c. BC and 1st c. AD) found at Petra are few and were probably not accepted economically. Nevertheless, the extent of their geographical origin is of interest. The earliest such coin found in

[27] Horsfield 1942, Ar.IV – 115, no.14, 201. no.460; M II – 115, no.13, 126, no.67; R II – 126, no. 68 (other coins include a possible Ptolemaic p. 136, no. 121, and two 4th century pieces p. 167, nos. 293a and b).

[28] Cleveland 1960, 72–73. The only non-Nabataean coin was described as Late Roman – AD 348–361.

[29] Nabataean coins comprise 53.3% of the BSAJ excavation corpus, of which "Aretas II" forms 13.3%, Obodas III – 1 coin, Syllaeus 1 coin, Aretas IV – 36%, Malichus II – 5.5% and Rabbel II – 26.5%.

[30] Hammond 1975, 16

[31] Schmitt-Korte would reassign the date of this marriage to 16 AD, Schmitt-Korte 1990, 129–130.

[32] Khairy 1990, 7–8.

[33] Schmitt-Korte & Price 1994, 103.

[34] Bowsher forthcoming B, this type (Meshorer 141) was noted as "rare" (Meshorer 1975, 65), and then as "unique" (ibid. p. 68).

the BSAJ excavations was an issue of John Hyrcanus I of the late 2nd c. BC.[35] The absence of further Hasmonaean or any Herodian issues is puzzling for coinage was minted in profusion by both dynasties throughout the first centuries BC and AD. It may be assumed therefore that the Nabataean and Jewish realms were exclusively independent financially. However, two coins from the 1st (Jewish) Revolt; Year 2 (AD 67) (BSAJ) and Year 3 (AD 68),[36] may be connected with the widespread *volkwanderung* that the disturbances caused.

Roman Imperial coins from this period are rarely found at Petra for they were of little use in a Nabataean context and were probably random losses. A coin of Augustus was found in a 1st century context in Room RN2 behind the paved street in the mid 1950s[37] and a quadrans of Caligula (in good condition) was found on the surface during the BSAJ excavations.[38] Roman provincial coins however, are more commonly found; a coin of Augustus from (probably) Asia[39] and coins of Galba[40] and Nerva (BSAJ) both from Antioch. Again these might reflect the most important Roman city in the east rather than economic ties although plenty of smaller cities to the north and west of Petra were minting their own coins in the 1st century AD.[41]

Nearby sites of Nabataean origin have produced only limited numismatic material. At Udhruh, there was clearly some Nabataean presence before the construction of the Roman fortress and Nabataean coins from the 1st century form 13% of coins from the site, the only other 1st century piece was, surprisingly, a silver denarius of Vitellius minted in Spain.[42] The Nabataean temple complex in the Wadi Rumm has produced few (published) coins. Only one to date has been described as possibly Nabataean,[43] but renewed French excavations at the site may reveal more. Similarly, the Nabataean settlement at Khirbet ed-Dharih has produced five poorly preserved Nabataean coins of the 1st century, but a piece from Ascalon dating to between 76 and 86.[44] The great southern entrepôt of Hegra (modern Medain Saleh) had the distinction of being named on a coin of Aretas IV (Meshorer type 87), which, however, is absent from the archaeological record. At the beginning of the 20th century, French explorers at the site recorded a silver piece of Obodas III as well as "un grande nombre d'autres monnaies de

[35] Meshorer 2001, 42 Type E.

[36] Barrett 1998, 317

[37] Kirkbride 1960,119. It is not recorded whether this Augustan coin was imperial or provincial. There was also a coin of Aradus dating to the 2nd c. BC as well as later pieces from later phases of occupation.

[38] cf. Bowsher 1987a on Roman small change in the area – written before this piece was seen.

[39] Betlyon 2001, p. 385, no. 21 – perversely called "late Roman"!

[40] Barrett 1998, 318

[41] It might be noted that such local coinage forms the majority of retrieved coins from the 2nd century AD at Petra.

[42] Bowsher 1987B, 12

[43] Described as a 14mm dia bronze; Kirkbride 1960A, 83f. Later issues included a bronze coin of Marcus Aurelius – Savignac & Horsfield 1935, 259.

[44] Villeneuve 1990, 370–371

bronze deja connues", mostly, it would appear, of Aretas IV, but all from the surface.[45]

Petra was regarded as a cosmopolitan place, full of "Romans and other foreigners" (Strabo *Geog.* 16.4.21) and one might have expected more foreign currency than appears to be the case. However, this limited survey of coin finds suggests that the Nabataean monetary system was strong enough to withstand the use of foreign coins in Petra at least. Furthermore, inscriptions from the Nabataean site of Medain Saleh specify that fines (for tomb violation) must be paid in Nabataean state currency.[46] Stratigraphic data, showing a continued circulation into the early 2nd century, would suggest a confidence in Nabataean money that was slow to change. It is just such statistical analysis of stratified coin finds that could answer many questions of ancient coin use, such as attribution and date as well as circulation.[47]

Bibliography

Augé, C., 1985. "Les monnaies de fouilles de Si' et la circulation monétaire antique dans le Hauran", in Dentzer, J.M., (ed.) *Hauran I.* Paris: IFAPO, BAH CXXIV, 202–217

– forthcoming. "Coin Circulation from Recent Excavation Finds". Second Conference on Nabataean Studies. Petra, October 2002. *Bulletin of Nabataean Studies.*

Barrett, D.G., 1998. "The Coins", in Joukowsky, M.S. (ed), *Petra Great Temple: Brown University Excavations 1993–1997. Vol. 1.* New Haven, Brown University Petra Exploration Fund, 317–324.

Betlyon, J.W., 2001. "Coins from the 1992–93 Excavations", in Fiema, Z.T., et al., *The Petra Church.* Amman, A.C.O.R., 384–390.

Bowsher, J.M.C. 1987a. "Trajanic Quadrantes from Arabia", *Num Chron* 147, 166–168

– 1987b. "Coins", in A.Killick (ed). *Udhruh, Caravan City and Desert Oasis. A Guide.* Romsey, privately published, 12–13.

– 1990. "Early Nabataean Coinage", *ARAM*, 2:1&2, 221–228

– 1998. "Coins from Excavation to Publication", in Goodburn-Brown, D., & Jones, J., (eds), *Look after the Pennies; Numismatics and Conservation in the '90s.* London, Archetype Publications, 81–84

– forthcoming a. "The Coins", in Parr P.J., (ed) *Excavations at Petra by the British School of Archaeology at Jerusalem, 1958–1964. Vol. I.*

– forthcoming b. "The Coins", in Bikai, P.M., (ed.) *Petra: The North Ridge.*

Cleveland, R.L., 1960. "The Conway High Place at Petra", AASOR, XXXIV–XXXV, 53–97.

Hammond, P.C., 1975. Survey and excavation at Petra, *ADAJ*, 20, 5–30.

Healey, J.F., 1993. *The Nabataean Tomb Inscriptions of Mada'in Salih.* Journal of Semitic Studies, Supplement 1. Oxford, Oxford University Press (on behalf of the University of Manchester).

[45] Jaussen & Savignac 1909, 441, 136. Although described as Obodas II, the description, and drawing can be clearly identified with the Obodas III, defined by Meshorer 1975, and a type – jugate heads / single head – dated to the second part of his reign. There is some discrepancy with the recorded inscription – Obodas, king of the Nabataeans – and restored date which appears to be written rather than numeric.

[46] On the inscriptions see Healey 1993, and on the monetary value and significance – Naster 1986, Schmitt-Korte & Price 1994, 90f.

[47] See the discussion in eg. Bowsher 1998

Horsfield, G., & Horsfield, A., 1942. "Sela-Petra, The Rock, of Edom and Nabatene: Pt. 4, The Finds", QDAP, IX, 105–204
Jaussen, A., & Savignac, R., 1909 *Mission Archéologique en Arabie*, (Vol. I), Paris.
– 1914, *Mission Archéologique en Arabie*, (Vol.II), Paris.
Khairy, N.I., 1990. *The 1981 Petra Excavations*, Abhandlungen des Deutschen Palästinavereins, Band 13. Wiesbaden.
Kindler, A., 1983. *The Coinage of Bostra*, Warminster, Aris & Phillips.
Kirkbride, A.S., 1939. "Currencies in Transjordan", *PEQ*, 152–161.
– 1947. "Some rare coins from Transjordan", BASOR, 106, 4–9.
Kirkbride, D. 1960 a. "Le Temple Nabatatéen de Ramm; son evolution architecurale", *Rev. Bib.* 67, pp. 65–92.
– 1960 b. "A Short Account of the Excavations at Petra 1955–1956", ADAJ, IV & V, 117–122
Meshorer, Y., 1975. *Nabataean Coins*. Jerusalem. Qedem 3.
– 2001. A Treasury of Jewish Coins. Yad ben-Zvi, Jerusalem.
Metcalf, W.E., 1975. "The Tell Kalak Hoard and Trajan's Arabian mint", *ANS Museum Notes*, 20, 87–108.
Milik, J.T., & Seyrig, H., 1958. "Trésor monétaire de Murabba'at", *Rev Num* I (nouv ser), 11–26
Murray, M.A. & Ellis J.C., 1940. *A Street in Petra*, London, British School of Archaeology in Egypt / Bernard Quaritch Ltd.
Naster, P., 1986. "De Munten van Nabataea in de Nabatese Opschriften", *Acta Orientalia Belgica*, 4, 101–104
Negev, A., 1971. "Notes on the Trajanic drachms from the Mampsis hoard", *Jahrbuch für Numismatik und Geldgeschichte*, XXI, 115–120. (Reprinted in Spijkerman, A., 1978, *Coins of the Decapolis and Provincia Arabia*, Jerusalem, Franciscan Printing Press, 32–35.)
Parr, P.J., 1990. "Sixty years of excavation in Petra: a critical assessment", *ARAM* 2:1&2, 7–23
Parr, P.J., forthcoming / this volume i.e. pp.xxx. "The Urban Growth of Petra",
Peter, M., 1996. "Die Fundmünzen", in Bignasca, A., et. al. *Petra. Ez Zantur I. Ergebnisse der Schweizerische-Liechtensteinischen Ausgrabungen 1988–1992*. Mainz, Verlag Philipp von Zabern, Terra Archaeologica II, 91–127. 1996.
Robinson, E.S.G., 1936. "Coins from Petra Etc", Num *Chron*, xvi, 288–91
Savignac, M.R., & Horsfield, G., 1935, "Le Temple de Ramm", *Rev. Bib.* 44, pp. 245–278.
Schmitt-Korte, K., & Cowell, M., 1989. "Nabataean Coinage – Part II: The silver content measured by X-Ray fluorescence analysis", *Num Chron*, 149, 33–58.
Schmitt-Korte, K., 1990. "Nabataean Coinage – Part II: New Coin Types and Variants", *Num Chron*, 150, 105-133.
Scmitt-Korte, K., & Price, M.J., 1994. "Nabataean Coinage – Part III: The Nabataean monetary system", *Num Chron*, 154, 67–131.
Sokolov, H., 2001. "Coins from the 1996 Season", in Fiema, Z.T., et al., *The Petra Church*. Amman, A.C.O.R., 391–394.
Villeneuve, F., 1990, The pottery from the oil-factory at Khirbet edh-Daharih (2nd century A.D.). A contribution to the study of the material culture of the Nabataeans. *ARAM*, 2:1&2. 367–484.
Wenning, R., 1991. "Die Nabatäische Münzprägung", in Hackens, T., et. al. (eds). *International Numismatic Commission: A Survey of Numismatic Research 1985–1990*. Brussels, International Association of Professional Numismatists, Special Publication No.12, 108–110.
Zayadine, F., 1973. "Excavations at Petra", ADAJ, 18, 81–82.
– 1974. "Excavations at Petra (1973–1974)", ADAJ, 19, 135–150.
– 1979. "Excavations at Petra (1976–1978)", ADAJ, 24, 185–197.

The Nabateans as Pastoral Nomads: An Archaeological Perspective

Steven A. Rosen

Introduction

The oft repeated observations of Diodorus Siculus, in turn citing Hieronymus of Cardia, that the Nabateans had no permanent homes and engaged in no agricultural activities, have long served as the primary documentary evidence that Nabatean origins are to be found in a Bedouin-like adaptation in the deserts of Near East (Diodorus Siculus XIX.93; also see Strabo 16.4.2 for the lifeways of other Arabian tribes). Although the tenuousness of this rather limited literary base has been acknowledged (e.g., Graf 1990), in the absence of more texts and greater detail, and the assumed difficulties of the archaeological data in dealing with nomadic systems (e.g., Kenyon 1980: 177; Finkelstein and Perevoletsky 1990), there has been little attempt to explore the issue of Nabatean pastoral nomadism in greater depth. While there is little that can be done to address the absence of a detailed literary record, the past two decades of research in the deserts of the southern Levant have demonstrated the great potentials of archaeology for exploring ancient pastoral nomadic societies (e.g., Cribb 1991; Banning 1986; Rosen 1992; Avni 1996; Haiman 1995; Bar-Yosef and Khazanov 1992; Saidel 1998).

Analysis and synthesis of archaeological survey and excavation data from the Central Negev provide new perspectives on the Nabateans as pastoral nomads. Briefly stated, these materials seem to reflect a pastoral nomadic system based on seasonal movement, tethered to the more sedentary Nabatean system which developed as a result of Nabatean trade. Although too late in date to provide direct information on origins, these data also suggest that there are great potentials for further archaeological investigations, both in the Negev and elsewhere.

The Region and the Survey

The Central Negev, or Negev Highlands, is a region defined by five parallel anticlinal ridges running NE-SW, with broad synclinal valleys between them, located southwest of the Dead Sea and west of the Rift Valley (the Wadi Araba, or the Arava) (Fig. 1). It is marked by degraded Irano-Turanian steppe vegetation, grading into Saharo-Arabian desert vegetation in the southern areas (Danin 1983). Average rainfall varies between 150 and 75 mm per year, falling exclusively in the winter months. The peaks of the anticlinal ridges achieve altitudes of

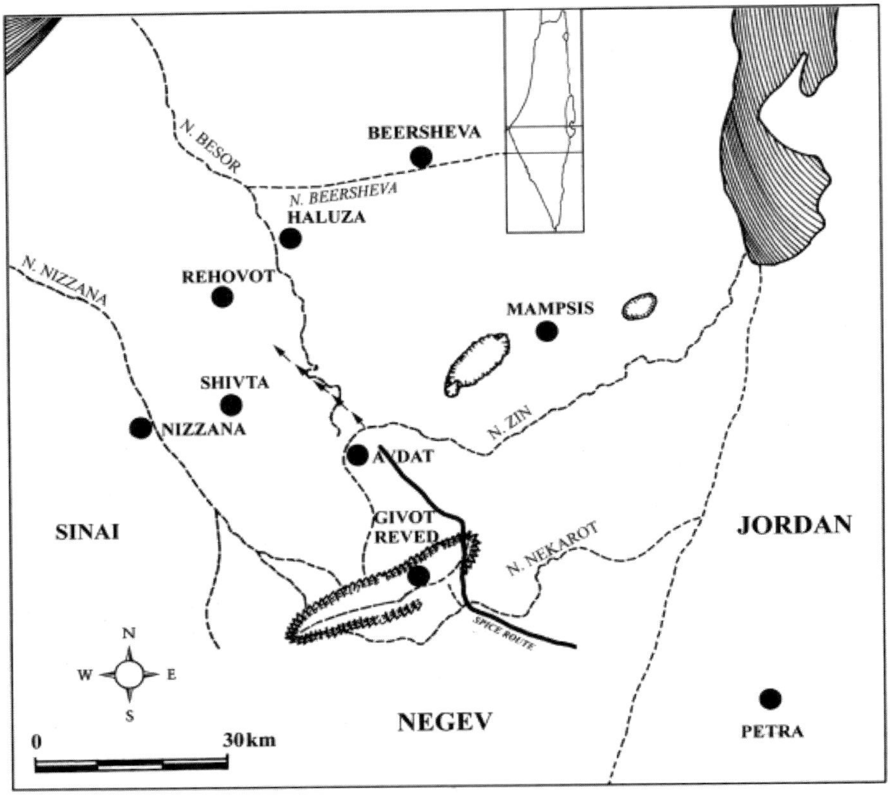

1. Map of region showing selected sites.

greater than 1000 m in the southwest, but the ridges in the northeast are lower, and the valleys are typically between 500 and 700 m above sea level. Geomorphologically, the region is also notable for the existence of *makhteshim*, large erosional cirques the result of a rather rare combination of softer substrata (sandstones and clays) capped by harder upper strata (limestones and dolomites), geological uplift, erosion, and undercutting (e.g, Evenari et al. 1982; also Orni and Efrat 1980: 15–34 for geographic reviews).

In antiquity, the area was a major component of the Roman province Palestina Tertia. It is especially notable for the desert urban settlements of the Byzantine period (Late Roman in European terminologies), supported by sophisticated runoff agricultural systems (e.g., Evenari et al. 1982; Kedar 1967; Mayerson 1960). With respect to Nabatean civilization, the Negev Highlands constituted a major portion of the Nabatean kingdom (e.g., Negev 1983). During the later stages of the kingdom, the famous Nabatean spice route traversed the Negev Highlands from Petra to the Mediterranean (e.g., Cohen 1982; Negev 1966; Meshel and Tsafrir 1975).

The Negev Emergency Survey, on which most of this study is based, was established in 1979, and continued actively in the field until 1982, one of the dividends of the peace agreement with Egypt. Its primary goal was salvage survey and excavation, in light of the planned (and later completed) redeployment of the Israel Defense Forces from Sinai back to the Negev. On the order of 3000 previously unreported sites were registered in the Negev Highlands, and to date nine survey monographs from the Negev Highlands , each covering a 100 sq. km. block, have been published (Cohen 1981, 1986; Lender 1990; Haiman 1986, 1991, 1993, 1999; Rosen 1994; Avni 1991). This study incorporates data from the published work, and one as yet unpublished volume compiled by the author.

Methodological Issues

The primary methodological issue underlying the settlement pattern analysis, which constitutes the first part of this study, is site attribution. The first step in addressing this issue is the actual definition of Nabatean pottery (cf. Negev 1986). Although the analysis presented here is based on each surveyor's ceramic readings, the overall high level of integration of the Negev Emergency Survey ensured that the great majority of ceramic readings are indeed comparable. Thus, pottery was considered Nabatean when it was a red ware, fine grained matrix, highly fired, often with red paint designs, commonly floral. Of course, specific morphologies are also considered (Fig. 2), but survey data are often lacking in numerous diagnostics. There is some overlap with Early Roman ceramics in the region, but given the use of the ceramics here primarily as a chronological indicator, and not as an ethnic one, this overlap is not especially important. In fact, chronologically, virtually all of the pottery found in the Negev surveys reviewed here attributed to the Nabateans can be dated to the first and second centuries CE, perhaps stretching back to the first century BCE. There is a general scarcity (indeed, near absence) of ceramics attributable to the preceding Hellenistic phase, although the succeeding Roman and Byzantine phases are well represented (e.g., Rosen 1987a; also see survey volumes indicated above).

Given this definition of Nabatean pottery, for those sites where only Nabatean pottery was recovered it was assumed that the sites could be attributed primarily to Nabatean period occupation. It should be noted here that unlike sites in the Mediterranean zone, or sites which have been the subject of intensive reoccupation (like tells), in the Negev Highlands the vast majority of sites are small, with little accumulation of fill, alluvium, or occupation debris. This allows reasonable characterization of sites without excavation. Personal experience also indicates that surface artifacts are usually representative of the occupation history of the site.

For sites with multiple ceramic period presence, the attribution of specific features or characteristics of a site to a particular period is often difficult without excavation. For the purposes of this analysis, sites with a clear dominance of Nabatean ceramics, or whose architectural character was 'Nabatean' (according

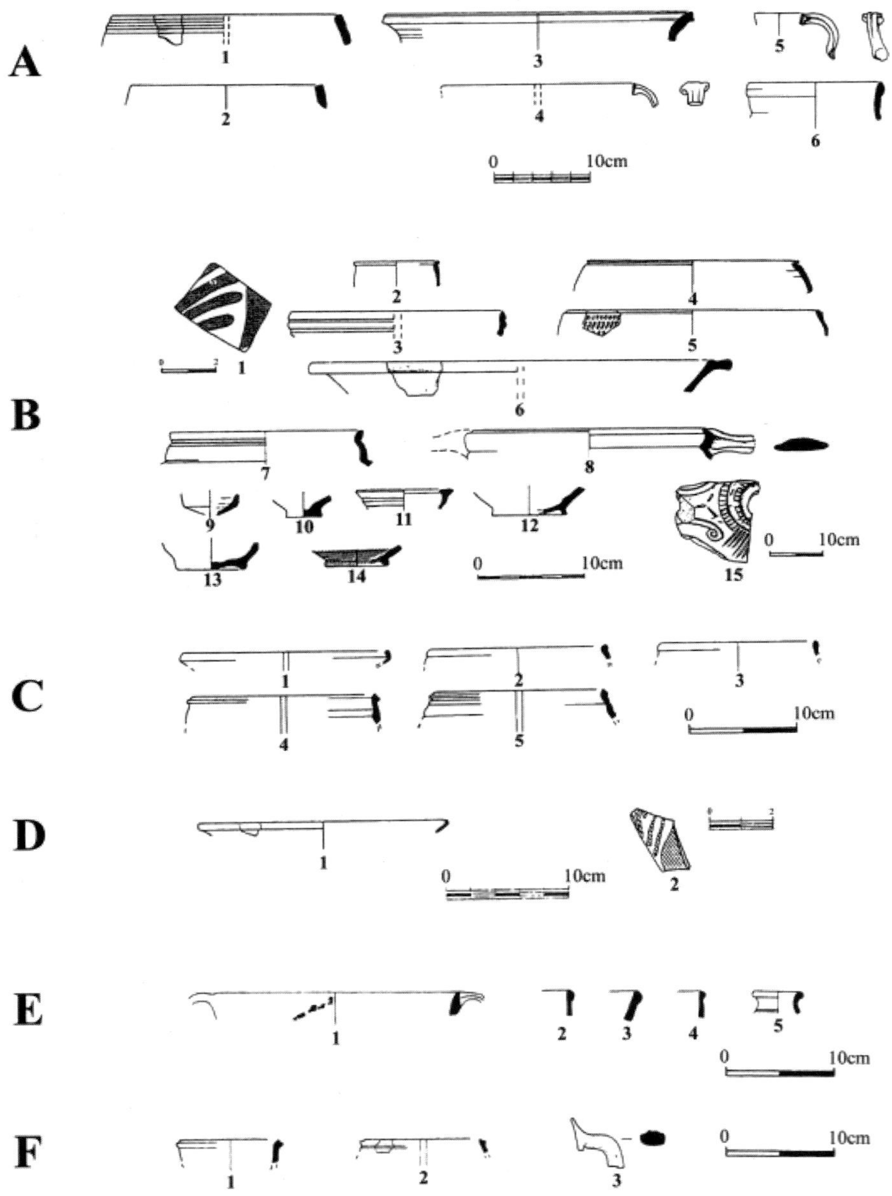

2. Nabatean pottery from selected sites from the Negev Archaeological Survey publications. A. (Cohen 1981: site 30): 1–2. bowls, 3. basin, 4. juglet, 5. cooking pot, 6. jar; B. (Lender 1990: site 75): 1. decorated bowl, 2–5. bowls, 6. basin, 7–8. cooking pots, 9–10. juglets, 11–14. jugs, 15. lamp; C. (Haiman 1991: site 118): 1. small bowl, 2–3. bowls, 4–5. cooking pots; D. (Haiman 1986: site 256): 1. bowl, 2. decorated bowl; E. (Haiman 1993: site 13): 1. cooking pot, 2–4. jars, 5. juglet; F. (Rosen 1994: site 205): 1–3. cooking pots.

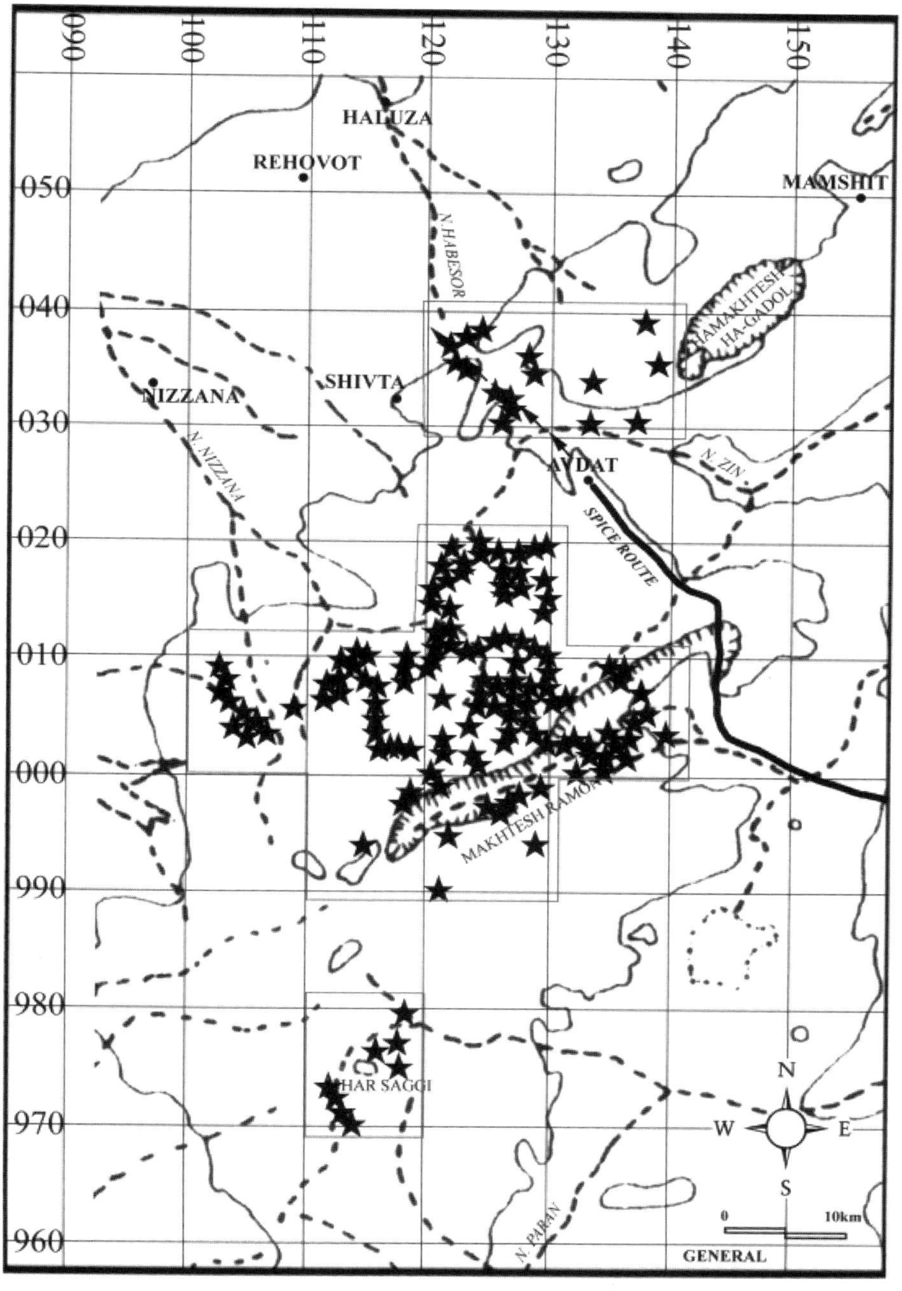

3. Distribution of all Nabatean occurrences in the survey region.

to the judgment of the surveyor) were attributed to Nabatean period occupation. Sites that could be characterized as Nabatean based on later excavations (especially sites from Cohen 1981, 1986 and Lender 1990) were also included. Other sites, with Nabatean ceramics but with other ceramics as well, such that it was not possible to characterize or classify the Nabatean period presence at the site, were excluded from the analysis. Thus, Fig. 3, which presents the total distribution of Nabatean period occurrences in the surveyed areas (also Table 1), included more sites than the total sites from Figs. 10 and 11, reflecting only those sites whose Nabatean component, that is, the architecture, could characterized functionally or classified typologically.

Beyond the problem of site attribution, the issue of field survey compatibility must also be addressed (see Rosen 1994; Avni 1991 for reviews of field and recording methods). Although the site distribution patterns defined in this study seem to be quite strong, there is always the question of whether they might not be an artifact of differential field recognition and recording – that different surveyors may have observed and recorded sites according to different definitions. The problem is most evident, of course, in the recognition of the smallest and most non-descript sites, i.e., the campsites with no architecture.

There are two lines of evidence suggesting that potential differences in field recognition do not affect the basic site distribution patterns as analyzed here. First, all surveyors recorded reasonably high numbers of prehistoric sites (Table 1), ranging in date from the Middle Paleolithic through the Neolithic. These sites show little architecture and if they are found then one can reasonably assume that roughly analogous historic period sites were found as well.

Second, the settlement pattern analysis rests on the presence/absence of architectural sites as well as campsites. Even if campsites are removed from the analysis, the geographic contrast between rectilinear and curvilinear architectural features, the basic site types utilized in this analysis, still holds. Given the pedestrian nature of all the surveys, and the fact that numerous curvilinear *Bronze Age* sites were registered by all surveyors (Table 1), it can be considered unlikely that there are significant biases in this realm of the data. It must be emphasized that survey data are always only a sample of a larger historical universe, and the issue is not the recovery of all sites, but the representativeness of the patterns revealed from the sites recovered.

The second part of the analysis of the survey data indicates the existence of quantitative and typological trends in the ceramic samples collected in the course of field work and published in the survey monographs. Simply stated, surface sherding in the Negev Emergency Survey was undertaken in order to provide chronological indicators for site attribution. Collection was neither systematic nor exhaustive. For example, my personal policy was to collect only enough sherds to compose an illustrative plate, so as not to harm the sample for possible later systematic collection or excavation. In many cases, even such minimal quantities could not be collected.

Sample size obviously constitutes a genuine problem. Thus, only nine Nabatean sherds were published from all the campsites together, and only 11 from the southern survey blocks. Any typological trends based solely on such numbers are, of course, suspect. However, the numbers for other site types and areas are larger.

The selection of sherds for illustration in the publications, on which the following analysis is based, constitutes another possible source of bias. Basically, all indicative sherds – rims, handles, bases, and decorative elements – were illustrated and most were published. Body sherds, on which site attributions were sometimes based, were not illustrated.

In spite of these limitations, there is little evidence to indicate that the ceramic collection is fundamentally biased in a way that would affect the relative proportion of types. Obviously, sherds break in different proportions, but this should not affect secular trends in the proportions of types found at different sites since patterns of sherd breakage should remain constant between sites. Although one can argue that differences in collection methods between surveyors affected these secular trends since different archaeologists have surveyed in different areas, in fact it is hard to argue that there is a difference in collection between, for example, cooking wares and bowls. In fact, if on one hand sampling was not neither controlled nor systematic, on the other hand there is nothing to indicate that it was not random or representative. Finally, the strength of the patterns established, and their accordance with the settlement distribution, is a strong argument for their relative reliability.

Survey Analysis

Examination of settlement pattern data derived from the Negev Emergency Survey conducted in the 1980s (Cohen 1981, 1986; Haiman 1986, 1991, 1993, 1999; Lender 1990; Avni 1991, Rosen 1994, n.d.) results in a set of 182 sites or occurrences attributable or partially attributable to the Nabatean period (Table 1). Although some of these cannot be classified functionally due to the presence of other cultural remains, a rough typology based on architectural remains (no structural remains, curvilinear architecture, rectilinear architecture, rectilinear towers) shows clear geographic patterning. Summarizing the results before detailed explication, the rectilinear architectural remains, clearly more substantial, cluster in the northern part of the surveyed region, closer to Avdat, the Byzantine town founded by the Nabateans as a nexus for the spice trade, and the area most suitable for run-off farming. The distribution of the less substantial sites, consisting of non-architectural camps and sites with curvilinear architecture, overlaps with that of the rectilinear in the center of the survey region, but also continues in significant density farther south, beyond the apparent hinterland of either Avdat or the Spice Route, and beyond the Irano-Turanian vegetation zone into the Saharo-Arabian zone, less appropriate for run-off agriculture. These patterns can be most parsimoniously interpreted as reflecting a system of complementary pastoral and agricultural zones. These geographic-architectural contrasts (cf. Rosen 1987b) are further supported by analysis of ceramic distributions.

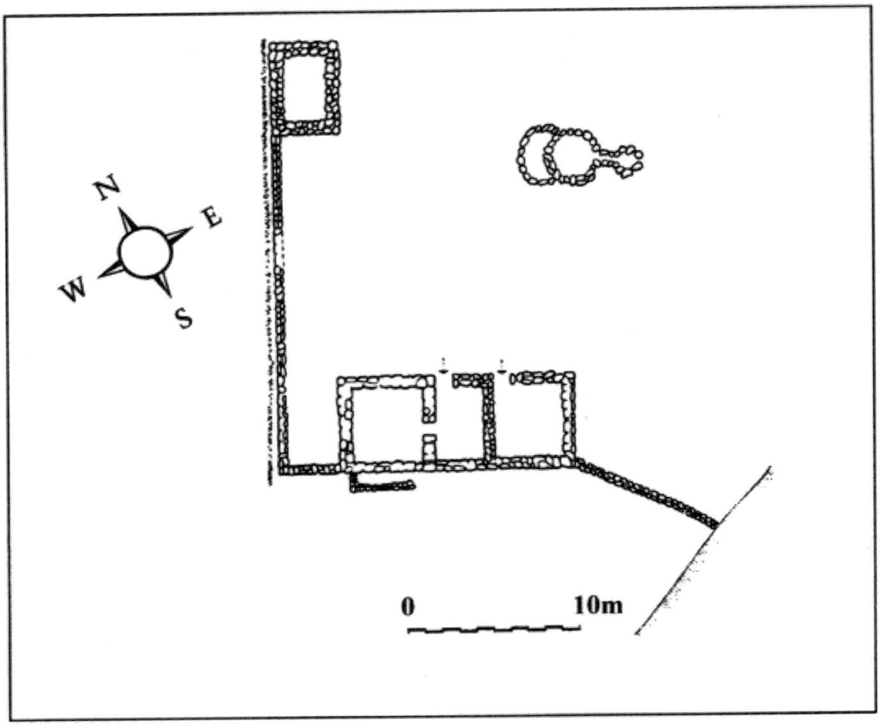

4. Lone rectilinear structure (Cohen 1986: site 22).

5. Village with rectilinear structures (Haiman 1991: site 202).

Sites with rectilinear architecture vary in size from single structures (e.g., Fig. 4), perhaps to be characterized as lone farm houses, to large clusters of 10 or more such structures, hamlets or indeed villages (Fig. 5). Some of the rectilinear structures have been classed by their surveyors as towers (e.g., Fig. 6; Lender

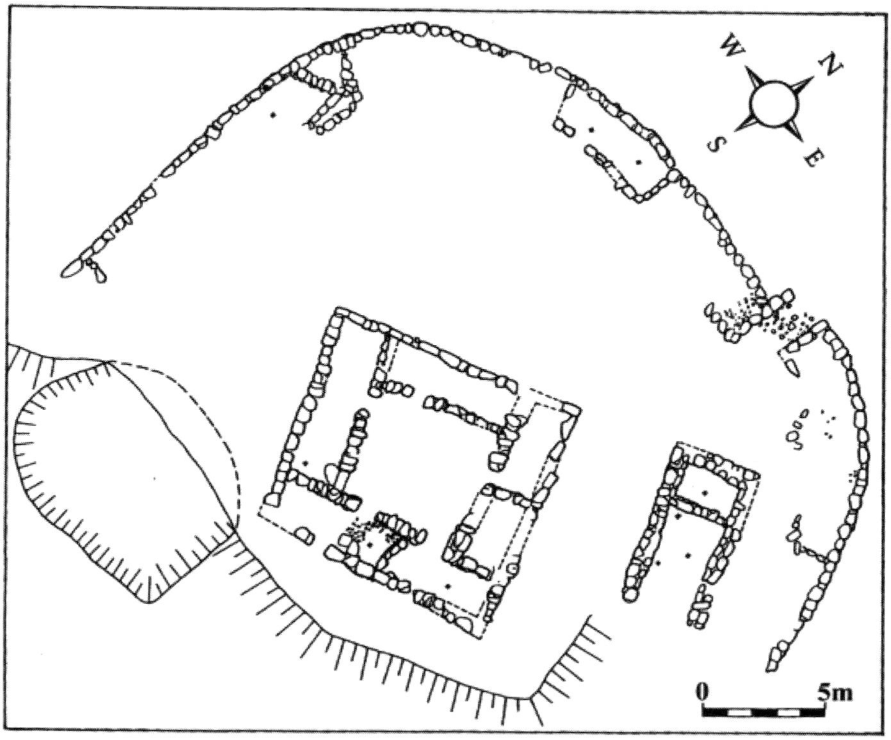

6. Tower (Lender 1991: site 406).

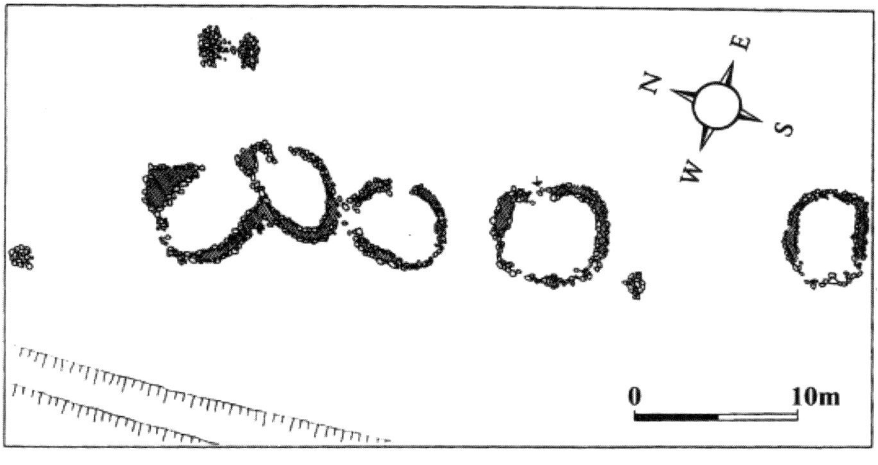

7. Plan of site with curvilinear structures (Rosen 1994: site 93).

1991: site 406) with an implication of defensive function. Aside from the rectilinear nature of the architecture, construction is marked by the use of hewn blocks of stone, with walls occasionally preserved almost up to original roof height, two meters high. Doorways with thresholds and lintels have been noted at some sites, as have windows.

Although many of these sites may be associated with terraced fields, the problem of the chronological attribution of dam systems remains intractable. Based on geographic proximity, and the absence of other (non-Nabatean) sites in the vicinity of some dam systems, it seems likely that run-off agriculture played a role in at least some of these settlements. However, direct proof is simply difficult. In fact, in this context, it seems reasonably clear today that much of the agricultural development initially assumed to be Nabatean (e.g., Glueck 1959: 191–243) is best attributed to the Byzantine and Early Islamic periods (e.g., Haiman 1995; Bruins 1986).

The curvilinear (round) architectural type differs in almost all its particulars from the rectilinear. The type has been described for the Byzantine and Early Islamic periods (Rosen 1987b, Rosen and Avni 1993; Avni 1996), and the Nabatean differs little from its successors. Structures are round or oval, usually 2–5 m in diameter, and often open at one end (Fig. 7). They rarely stand more than three courses high (0.5–0.75 m), and probably were never much higher. Construction is of unmodified wadi cobbles or bedrock slabs. In some cases the structures show excavation to a depth of ca. 0.4 m, followed by the lining of the pits with stones and further courses laid on top of this. In others, the structures are surficial. It seems reasonably clear that superstructures were either tents or perhaps brush.

The sites themselves are often aligned along the alluvial terraces of secondary wadis in a linear pattern. The size of the sites varies from lone circles to up to 20 structures. Some seem to be associated with small-scale terrace systems (Fig. 8), but to a lesser extent than the rectilinear structures. The same problems of association apply.

Camps are non-architectural in the sense that obvious habitation structures are not present (Fig. 9). Nevertheless, these sites show a wide range of features, allowing their general definition with little problem. Aside from the background scatter of ceramics which allows chronological attribution, these sites include hearths, stone lines, stone piles, cleared areas, and other miscellaneous installations. The stone lines and cleared areas often strongly suggest tent remains, the stones presumably used to hold down tent flaps. Numerous ethnoarchaeological studies have shown similar phenomena (e.g., Avni 1992; Banning and Kohler-Rollefson 1992; Cribb 1991; Eldar et al 1992; Simms 1988). Like the curvilinear sites, campsites are almost always located on flat wadi terraces. They rarely seem to be associated with agricultural dam systems. The more ephemeral curvilinear sites, with only surface structures, grade into the more substantial campsites with more defined stone lines.

The architectural variability described above by itself seems to imply contrasts between a pastoral nomadic system and a sedentary-agricultural one (e.g., Flannery 1972 for interpretation of similar architectural contrasts in the Neolith-

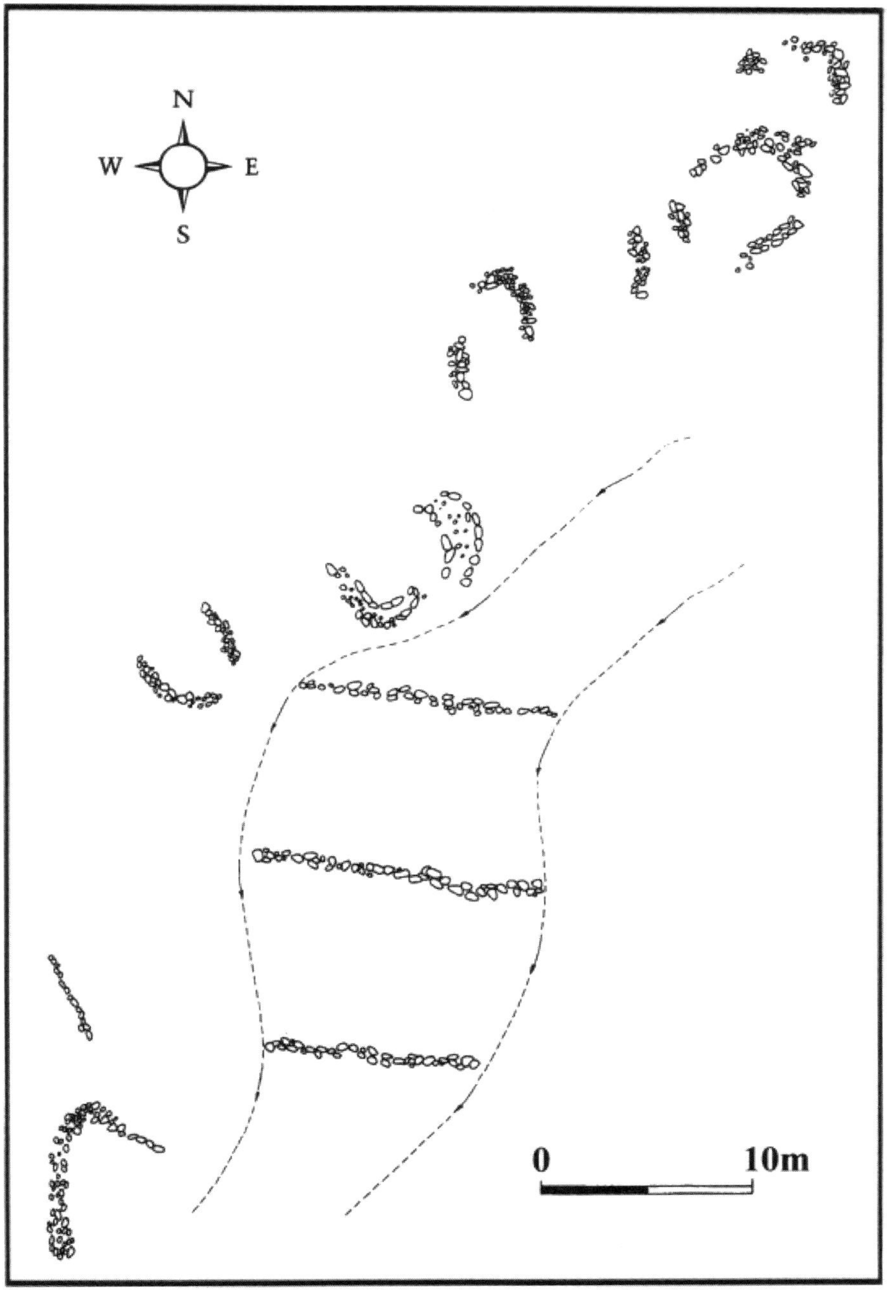

8. Plan of site with curvilinear structures associated with terrace dams (Rosen 1994: site 64).

9. Camp, part of the Giv'ot Reved site.

ic). However, without supporting analyses such an interpretation remains at the level of rather simplistic one-to-one analogy. For example, reasonable counter interpretations might be that the campsites and round structures represent caravan or trade camps, military patrol camps, or simply herdsmen camps tied to village farms (although the large size of some of the curvilinear sites would argue against the simple herdsmen hypothesis).

Two analytic procedures, based on site type distribution and ceramic frequency analysis, support the idea of a contrast between pastoral nomadic and sedentary agricultural systems. First, examination of site type distributions (Figs. 10, 11) reveals significant geographic contrasts in location of the rectilinear sites (villages, towers, and farmhouses) on one hand, and curvilinear and camp sites on the other. Fig. 10 presents the distribution of rectilinear structures and sites (including towers) and exhibits a high density of sites in the northern survey areas, north of Avdat in the Sede Boker area, and in the center of the survey regions. There are virtually no rectilinear sites in the southern survey areas. In direct contrast, the distribution of curvilinear and camp sites (Fig. 11) is clearly skewed to the south, with virtually no such sites in the northernmost survey areas.

These contrasting distributions correspond to the environmental transition from Irano-Turanian steppe zone in the center and northern part of the areas surveyed, to the Saharo-Arabian desert zone in the Makhtesh Ramon and southern areas. In this light, it should also be noted that the run-off agricultural systems

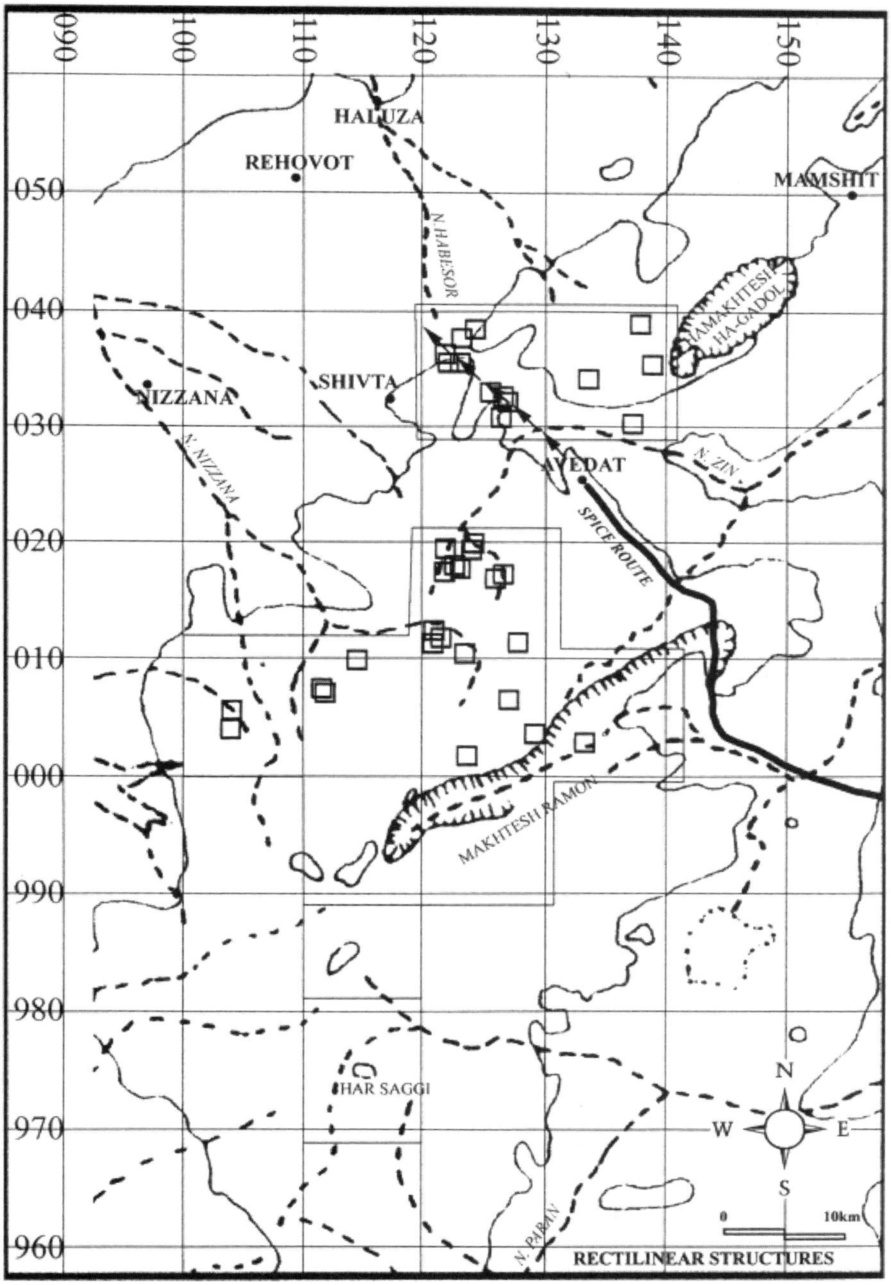

10. Distribution of rectilinear sites (farmhouses, villages, towers).

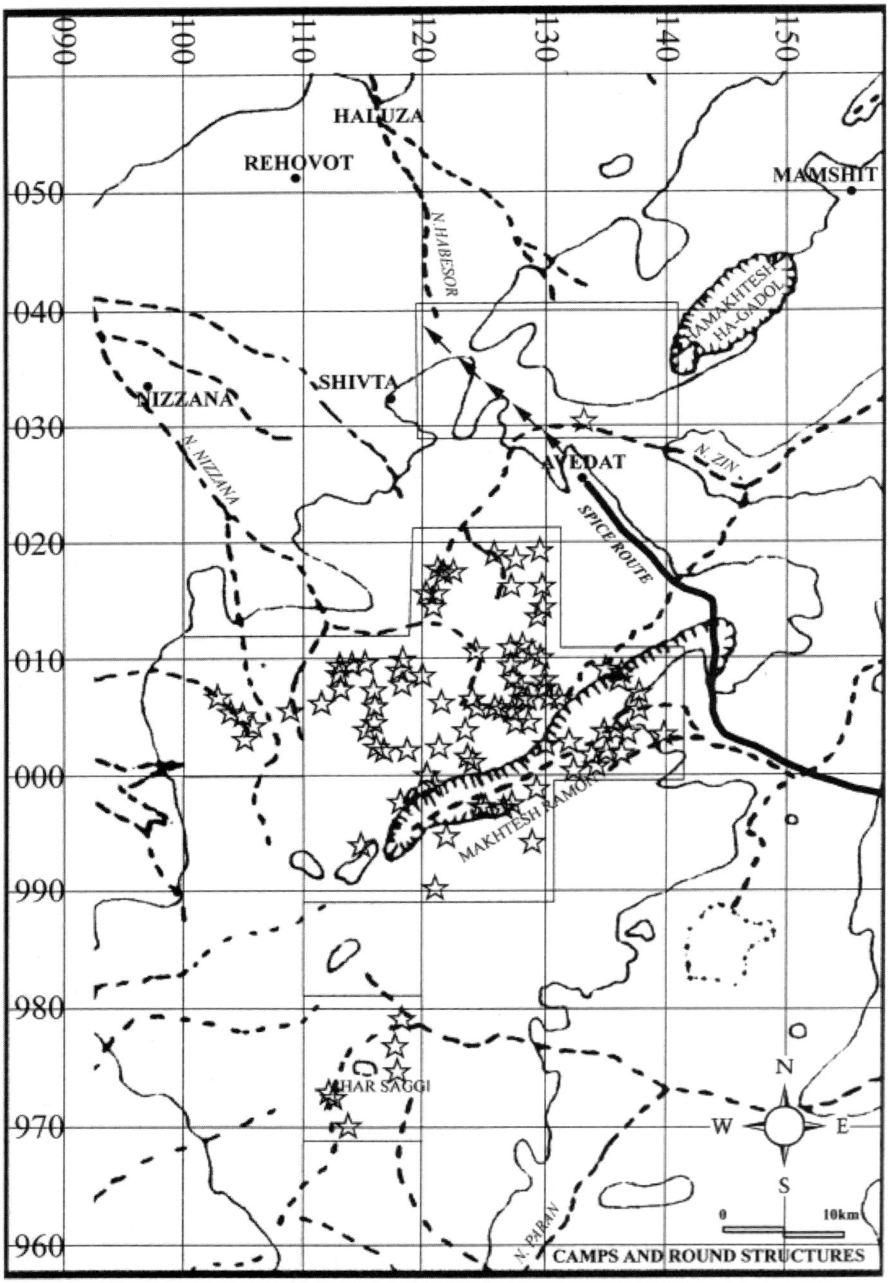

11. Distribution of nomadic sites (camps and curvilinear sites).

are to be found almost exclusively in the steppe zone, and are nearly absent farther south (e.g., Rosen 1987b; also see Kedar 1967; Haiman 1995). The only exceptions to this are the highest areas of the Negev, southwest of the Makhtesh Ramon. It is also clear that the core zone of the Nabatean trade system, as based at Avdat (e.g., Cohen 1982; Negev 1986: XV–XVI), is to be found in the northern steppe zone, such that the rectilinear (village, etc.) sites are to be tied to that system, and the increase in camp and curvilinear sites corresponds to increasing distance from that core.

Although Lender (1991: xxiii) has suggested that the Nabatean settlement pattern in Nafha area can be tied to the existence of secondary trade routes, the strength of the overall geographic patterning argues against the particularistic interpretation of a single survey block. The combination of architectural variability with contrasting type distributions, tied to specific environmental zones, seems to best fit a model of interaction between complementary and contrasting pastoral nomadic – sedentary agricultural lifeways.

Ceramic frequency analysis of the survey materials also supports the idea of a functional differentiation between the pastoral sites (camps, curvilinear sites) and the settled sites (rectilinear villages and farmhouses, towers). Figs. 12 and 13, (also Tables 2 and 3) present total ceramic frequencies and selected ceramic type frequencies according to A. architectural type and B. north-south location (by survey map). There is a striking decrease in number of (published) sherds[1] per site according to site type, from the rectilinear farms, villages, and towers to the more ephemeral curvilinear sites and camps. In complement, there is a similar decrease from the northern survey areas to the southern. It seems quite plausible to interpret these trends as reflecting greater or lesser tendencies toward settlement or mobility.[2]

The trend toward increasing relative frequency of cooking ware as one moves south, and the increased proportions of bowls farther north (Fig. 13B, Table 2), lends itself well to the nomadic-sedentary hypothesis as well. The same trends are evident when ceramic type frequencies are examined against camps, curvilinear structures, and rectilinear structures (Fig. 13, Table 3). In essence, cooking wares are utilitarian items whose relative importance in a ceramic assemblage would be expected to increase given the need to jettison less functional items as a result of increased nomadism. Bowls can be interpreted as precisely those items that one might expect to reflect more sedentary living.

[1] Clearly one cannot actually date sites which average less than a single sherd per site. These numbers relate to sherds published in the survey volumes. Dating of the sites was based on the entire surface collection, including body sherds, which were never illustrated, but which can indeed be indicative as general chronological indicators.

[2] Obviously the problem of non-systematic collection may affect the proposed trends. Even given this problem, all surveyors attempted to find enough sherds to provide reasonable illustrative and dating materials and the declines probably do indeed reflect lesser quantities of materials on the less permanent sites. For example, my own training in prehistoric archaeology would suggest that I would perhaps be expected to find a greater number of small sherds, yet my surveys resulted in some of the lowest numbers of sherds per site. This is true regardless of my policy of limiting collection, since I never achieved more than the minimum necessary for attribution and illustration.

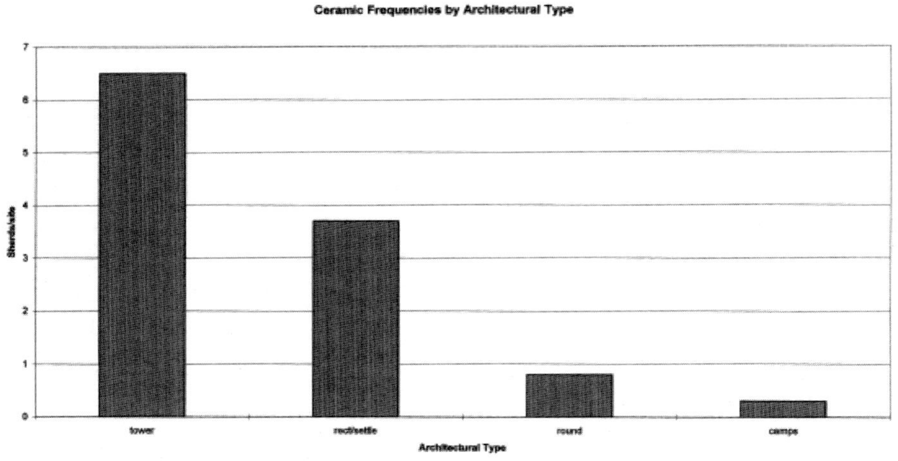

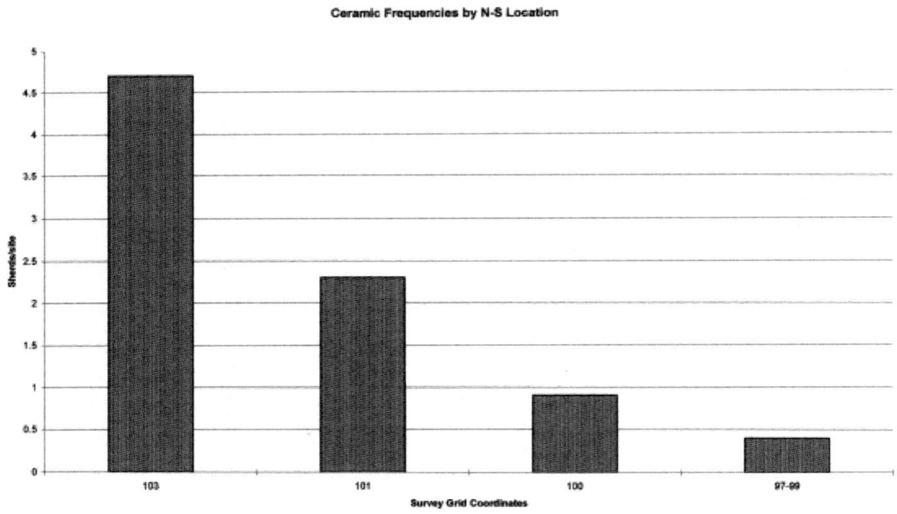

12. Histograms of total ceramic frequencies according to architectural type (A), and north-south location (by Israel Grid) (B).

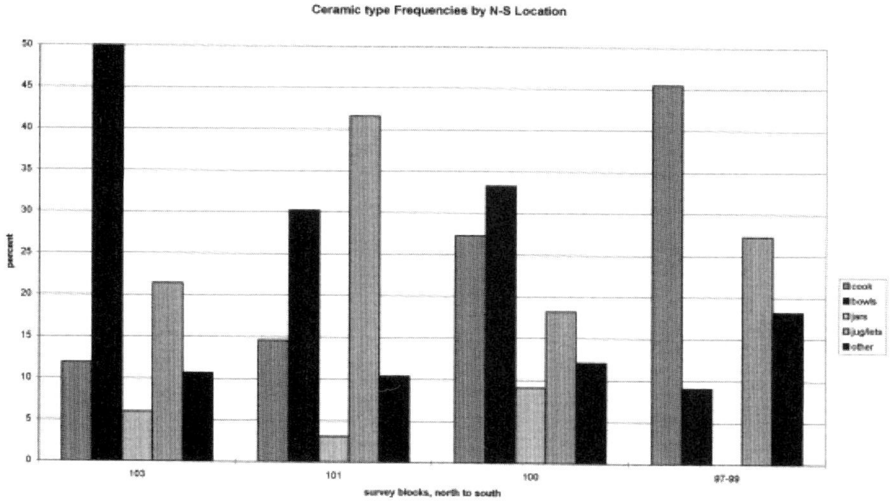

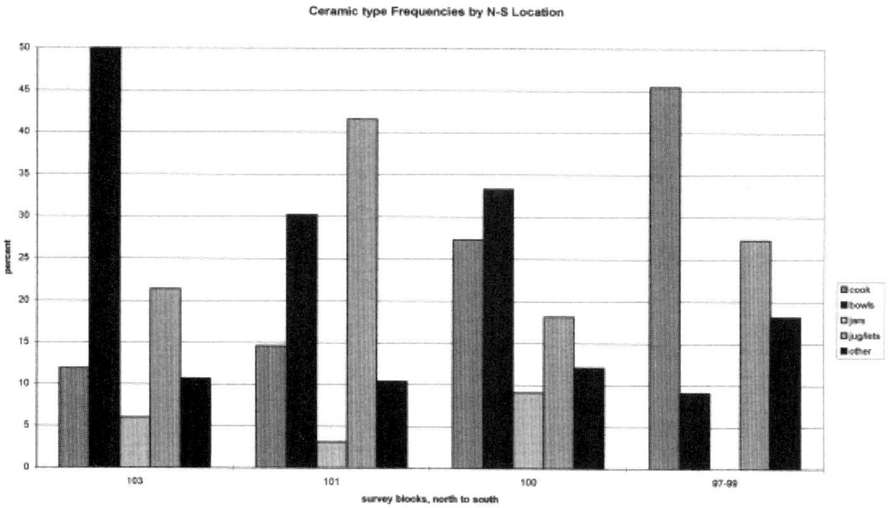

13. Histograms of selected ceramic type frequencies according to architectural type (A) and north-south location (by Israel Grid) (B).

Excavations at Giv'ot Reved

Excavations at the site of Giv'ot Reved (Rosen 1993)[3] were conducted in order to explore the potentials of in depth investigations at classical period nomadic encampments. The site is in the eastern section of the Ramon Crater, 8 km west of the Nabatean Spice Route, on the terrace of a secondary tributary of Nahal Ramon (Fig. 1). The region is particularly arid, receiving on average 75 mm of rainfall per year, and is characterized by a low density of Saharo-Arabian vegetation.

The site stretched over approximately 250 m of wadi terraces. It is difficult to estimate its precise size at any one time since it is impossible to establish the contemporaneity of its different components except in a very gross sense. In general, remains covered an area of one to one and one-half hectares, but unlike a dense urban archaeological setting, occupation was extensive and patchy.

The site was comprised of five areas, separated one from the other by the physical features of the wadis and a (modern) quarry spoil heap (Fig. 14). These are the Northwest Terrace, the Southwest Terrace, the Northeast Terrace, the Southeast Terrace, and the Main Excavation Area, located between the Northwest and Southwest terraces. Both of the latter areas primarily reflect recent and sub-recent Bedouin occupation, as evidenced by scatters of Gaza Ware pottery (cf. Rosen and Goodfriend 1993; Rosen and Avni 1997: 70, Fig. 7.6)[4], and a scarcity of earlier ceramics. The other three areas show higher densities of Nabatean pottery, and a scarcity of Gaza Ware.

The Northeast Terrace contained numerous small stone piles, sometimes forming crude elongate circles. These may have marked burials. The Southeast Terrace had typical round structures reflecting tent bases, with a possible pen built against a bluff of the terrace. In addition to the Nabatean ceramics, millstone fragments were also noted, in spite of the total absence of terraced fields in the vicinity. In fact, it is hard to even imagine where agriculture might have been carried out in this area, and the millstones most likely reflect the processing of imported grain.

The Main Excavation Area includes a minimum of 6-8 round structures (Fig. 15), clearly to be interpreted as tent bases. These are aligned along the length of the wadi terrace, in a linear pattern. Excavations were conducted in this area because it exhibited the highest density of ceramics and contained the greatest number of 'domestic' structures.

Excavation of this area consisted of initial surface scraping and sieving of all sediments through 2–3 mm mesh to ensure recovery of even the smallest artifacts, and to 'clean' the architecture. In essence, all fist-sized stones or larger were left in situ, resulting in a 'cleaned' surface which allowed easy delineation of structural remains. Excavation then proceeded to a depth of 10 cm in one area

[3] The site was destroyed in the course of quarrying activities before a detailed overall plan could be completed.

[4] Note to be confused with Byzantine Gaza Jars, these are Ottoman in date, and extend into the British Mandatory period.

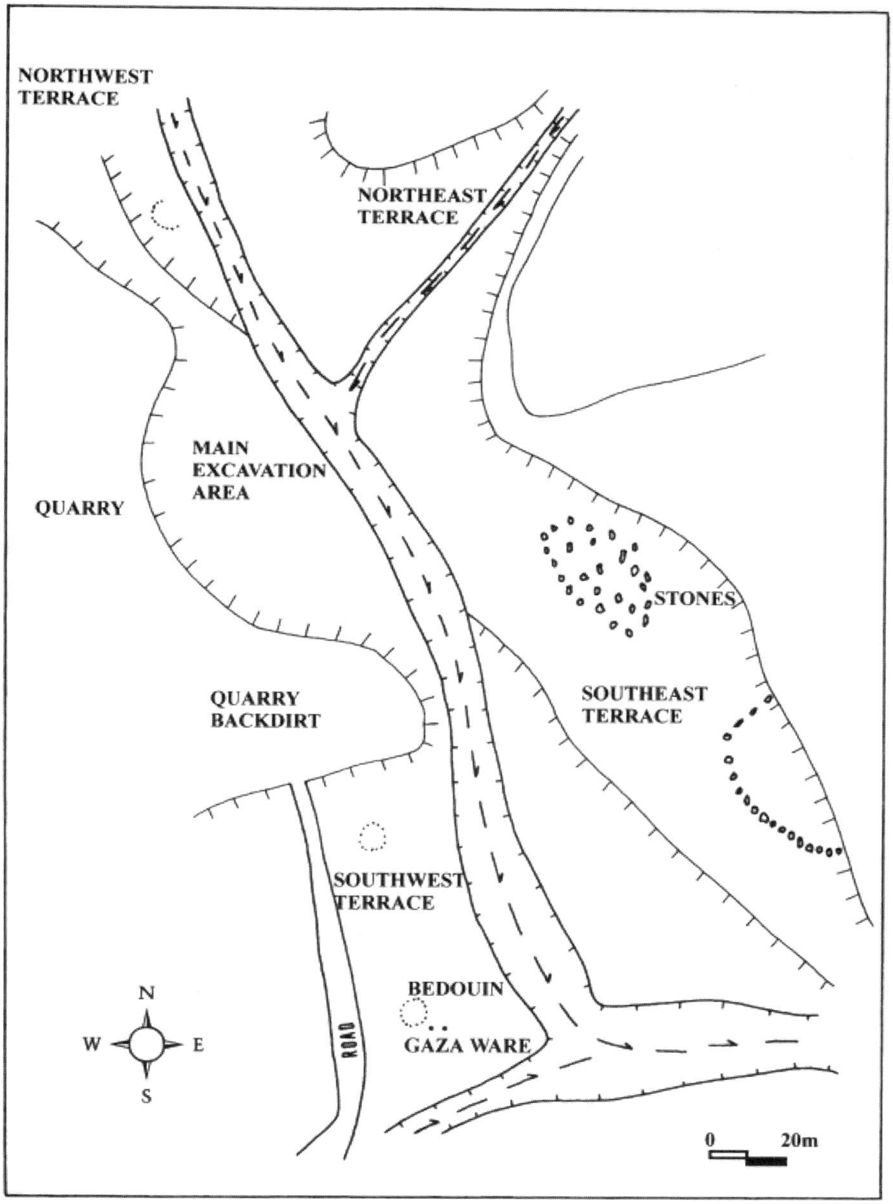

14. Sketch plan of Giv'ot Reved (Rosen 1993).

15. View of Main Excavation Area at Giv'ot Reved, looking northeast. (S. Rosen)

(Locus 201, Fig. 16), resulting in the conclusion that no subsurface deposits were present on the site, and the surface scraping would suffice. In addition to surface scraping, parts of the site not showing structures requiring clearer definition were collected systematically without scraping.

Three structures were thus investigated (e.g., Fig. 17), covering a total of 275 sq.m., with an additional 250 sq.m. collected systematically. These structures were built of unmodified wadi cobbles, in arc-shaped walls, 2–4 m in length, preserved no higher than two courses (25–50 cm). The dearth of stone fall precludes significantly greater original height. Some of the walls are of double, parallel rows of stone, the intent perhaps to create storage areas between the stone lines. It seems reasonably clear that these structures represent the remains of tents, the stones used either to hold down tent flaps or lines, the result of stone clearance for tent placement, or, as noted above, for site furniture.

In addition to these tent remains, other built features included hearths, storage bins, small stone piles or platforms, and smaller stone circles. The general pattern in the location of these features suggests domestic activities in and around the tents. Similar general patterns are evident in ethnoarchaeological studies of Bedouin sites (e.g., Eldar et al. 1992; Simms 1988; Cribb 1991) and indeed they are similar in this sense to the Bedouin remains found on other parts of the site itself.

The ceramic assemblage from the Main Excavation Area at Giv'ot Reved consisted of 212 sherds, of which only 20 are morphologically diagnostic (Fig.

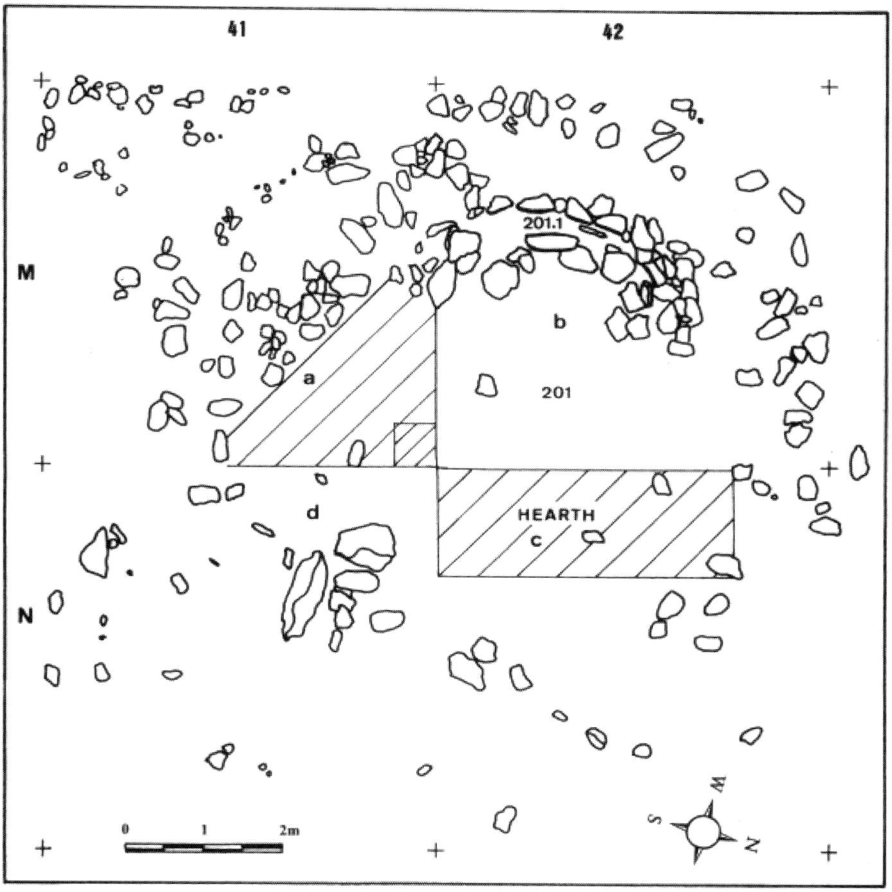

16. Plan of Locus 201, Giv'ot Reved.

18), although all but one fall into the general Nabatean/Early Roman framework. More specifically, the lamp fragments in particular suggest a 1st–2nd century AD date (c.f. Negev 1986: figs. 1163–1189). Many of these sherds are quite small, measuring less than 5 cm in maximal dimension.

In an effort to enhance the information that could be obtained from such a small ceramic assemblage, refitting analysis was conducted, resulting in 42 conjoins producing 11 larger sherds. Using the refitting analysis, typological examination, and the general spatial clustering of the pottery on the site, reasonable estimates of numbers of vessels could be derived: 2–3 cooking pots, 2–3 oil lamps, 2 jugs, 1 juglet, 1–2 bowls, 1–2 jars, and 1 bowl/cup (of body sherds, not drawn), either an Early Bronze Age intrusion, or perhaps a contemporary crude local ware (cf. Rosen and Avni 1997: 69–70; Haiman and Goren 1992). Thus, the maximum number of vessels represented on the site is only 14, and a more likely

17. View of Locus 203, looking southwest. (S. Rosen).

number is 10–12. This figure is important since is renders unlikely an ephemeral caravan stop interpretation of the site, and accords well with the pastoral nomadic hypothesis. It is hard to imagine so many broken pots from an overnight caravan stay or a military patrol. The functional configuration, small as it is, fits nicely into the picture obtained from the larger survey materials. Finally, it is further to be noted that the ceramics found at Giv'ot Reved are clearly all imports (except possibly the cup/bowl). There is no evidence for ceramic manufacture at the site. Given the proximity to Avdat with its pottery workshop, the identity of ceramic types, and nomadic aspect of the site, it seems a reasonable hypothesis that Avdat was indeed the source of the pottery recovered from Giv'ot Reved.

Even these pilot excavations at Giv'ot Reved provide a more detailed view of Nabatean pastoral nomadism than previously obtainable. Accepting that the potentials of any single such site are limited given the basic poverty of the remains, such sites have tremendous potential when viewed in aggregate.

Discussion

The presence of pastoral nomads in the Negev Highlands at the end of the 1st millennium BC and the beginning of the 1st millennium AD comes as little surprise historically. The archaeological picture presented here confirms what we thought we knew all along, and, of course, if this is the case, why bother? In fact,

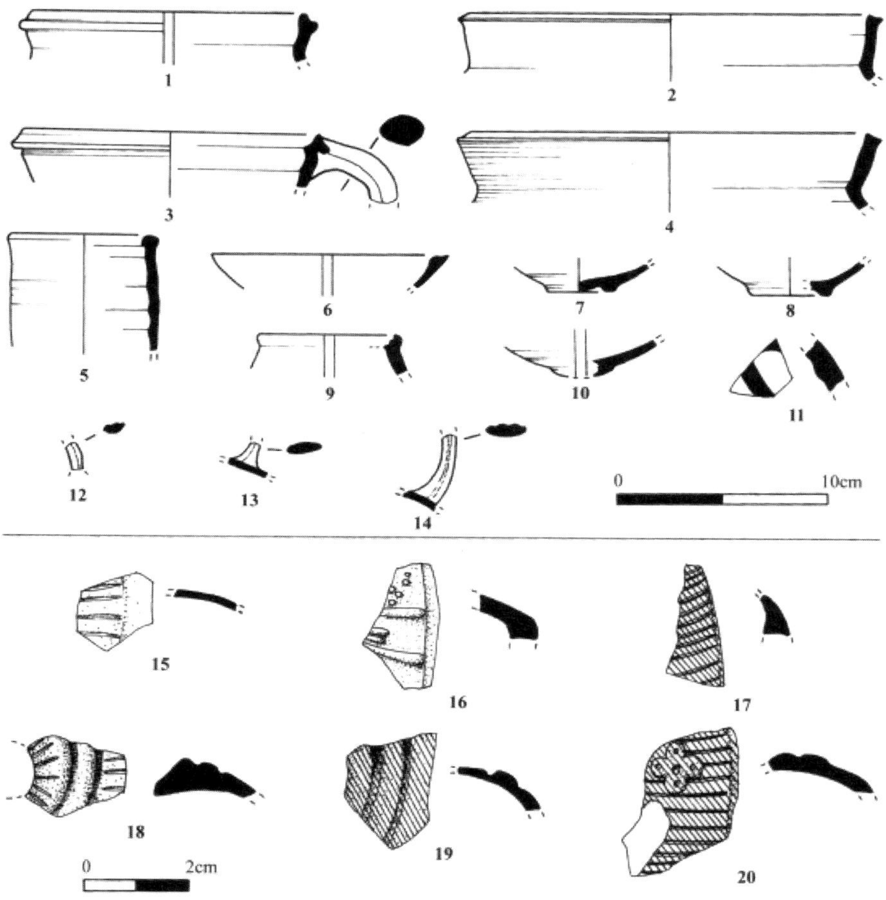

18. Ceramics from Giv'ot Reved (Rosen 1993): 1,3. Cooking pots; 2,4. Jars; 5,9. Jugs; 6–8. Bowls; 10. Juglet base; 12–14. Handles; 15–20. Lamps.

the archaeological picture extends well beyond the hints gleaned from the texts and our assumptions based on imperfect ethnographic analogies.

It appears that the pastoral nomadic presence in the central Negev is a late occurrence in the general Nabatean system, as least as far as the areas surveyed here are concerned. There is virtually no pastoral nomadic presence, as reflected in the camps and curvilinear structures, that can be attributed to the earlier Hellenistic period, preceding the 'classic' Nabatean of the first centuries BC and AD. In this light it is important to note that if we find ephemeral sites from the later Nabatean phases, it makes sense to assume that we would find them from the earlier as well, if they were present. They are not.

Given the later date of the southern Avdat phase of the Spice Route (Cohen 1982), and the historical contexts surrounding the shift from the northern route, through the Scorpion Pass, to the southern (e.g., Cohen 1982; Gichon 1980), it seems reasonable to tie the rise of the pastoral nomadic system to the development of the southern route. This connection is maintained through the first millennium AD, as the Spice Route sedentizes, transforms into the Limes, urbanizes into the periphery of the Byzantine Empire, and finally into the periphery of the Ummayad Caliphate. Throughout these periods a pastoral nomadic complement at edge of the empire can be traced archaeologically. This component disappears only with the ultimate collapse of the Ummayads, and the degeneration of the Levant into an economic and cultural backwater (Rosen and Avni 1993, 1997; Rosen 2000).

The problem of the ethnic identity of the nomads revealed in the archaeological record of course remains difficult. Although I have referred to them as Nabateans (cf. Healey 1989), this identification is based primarily on ceramics, a notoriously poor means of identifying ethnicity. In fact, nomads almost invariably import their pottery from their settled neighbors. Thus, the nomads of the succeeding Byzantine period, identifiable in the texts as ethnically distinct Saracens (or not so distinct, e.g., Mayerson 1986, 1989) and clearly present in the archaeological record (Rosen 1987b; Rosen and Avni 1993, 1997; Avni 1996; Haiman 1995), all utilized typical Byzantine ceramics almost exclusively. In fact, the presence of Thamudic inscriptions in the region (e.g., Halloul 1990) suggests the possibility that groups other than the Nabateans were also present. On the other hand, the vast majority of the Thamudic inscriptions were found in the northerly part of the surveyed regions, the settled zones most closely associated with the Nabateans. The issue awaits more investigation.

In this historical context, the nature of the relations between the nomads and the settled zone requires some detailed explication. Archaeology can and does provide the only tool, imperfect as it is, for critically examining the historical reconstructions and anthropological models of such relations. There are three important issues here.

First, the rather intense spatial interfingering of the pastoral nomadic sites with the sedentary system must, of necessity, reflect a working relationship between the groups. Anthropologically, nomads and farmers accommodate themselves to each other through any number of mechanisms, allowing relatively peaceful co-existence and prosperity (e.g., Barth 1961; Banning 1986 with references). The geographic overlap between the systems would be difficult to sustain given hostile relations.

Second, the fact that the nomadic presence in the region seems to be the result of the prior establishment of the sedentary system implies an economic asymmetry. The nomads seem to have followed the sedentary infrastructure, and abandoned it hundreds of years later when that infrastructure finally disappeared. This nomadic dependence on settled systems has been the theme of much recent anthropological literature on pastoral nomads (e.g., Khazanov 1984).

Third, beyond the conclusions that can be drawn from analyses of settlement patterns, it is significant that the material culture recovered from the pastoral nomadic sites undoubtedly derives virtually in its entirety from the sedentary centers. Certainly Nabatean pottery is not the product of some ad hoc pastoral kiln, but of skilled craftsmen, most likely centered at Avdat. The presence of milling stones in non-agricultural sites also implies trade in grain, although a paucity of evidence renders this conclusion more speculative. These types of connections fit well with the conclusions concerning economic asymmetries reviewed above.

At another level, beyond nomad-settled relations, the documentation of ancient pastoral nomads archaeologically is not less important than the archaeological study of any other culture. The description of habitation sites, subsistence, seasonality, cult, social organization, and general lifeways, is inherently important. Any interpretations of historical causality must ultimately rest on precisely such details.

Conclusions

Archaeologically, the Nabateans are well known from the impressive remains of the Petra necropolis and town, the spice route caravanserai, and from the somewhat more difficult to characterize remains of the large settlements of the Central Negev. Although these large scale remains have shed much light on numerous aspects of Nabatean culture and history, they have, in fact, provided virtually no data on the Nabateans as pastoral nomads. Our knowledge of the social and economic origins and development of the Nabateans continues to suffer from a dearth of relevant data. Undoubtedly part of the problem has been the perception that nomads do not leave remains, and that even if they do, given their basic poverty few cultural or historical conclusions can be rendered from them. Hopefully, the above discussion will help dispel some of this myth. Rigorous survey and careful excavation can indeed reveal ancient nomads in the deserts of the Near East.

In a very real way, the analyses presented here, based as they are on painfully problematic data, can only be considered preliminary. The list of lacunae is long, including most especially a lack of systematically collected ceramics, problems of comparability in site descriptions, and a scarcity of detailed site plans. The near absence of excavations also limits our understanding of the phenomenon. On the other hand, the conclusion that nomads were present historically and are present archaeologically, is inescapable. The continuing publication of the results of intensive salvage surveys and associated excavations in the Negev during the past twenty years has provided a first opportunity for looking at the Nabateans as nomads through their archaeology. The stress here is on 'first'. Archaeological surveys, excavations, and analyses of nomadic remains from all over the Nabatean realm hold great promise for new and exciting discoveries and insights into this ancient desert civilization.

Acknowledgments

I am most grateful to Peter Fabian for helping me understand more of Nabatean history and material culture than I would otherwise have understood. Haim Goldfus also corrected some of my naive assumptions concerning the Nabateans. I discussed various elements of this work with Itzhak Gilead, Sorin Hermon, Gunnar Lehmann, Shaike Lender, Ofer Marder, Arlene Rosen, Benjamin Saidel, and Yuval Yekutieli. Patrice Kaminsky prepared the distribution maps. Rudolf Cohen's technical expertise as my supervisor in the Negev survey will forever be appreciated. And of course, such work is always the result of the team effort of all members of the Negev Emergency Survey, both the team leaders cited in the body of this study, and our dozens of volunteers. Excavations at Giv'ot Reved were funded in part by the Wenner-Gren Foundation for Anthropological Research, the Jo Alon Center for Bedouin Studies, and by the Archaeological Survey of Israel. The preliminary draft of this paper was written while I was the Cotsen Fellow at the UCLA Cotsen Institute of Archaeology.

Table 1: Comparison of surveys conducted by different researchers according to general period of attribution, with site totals from selected periods. As a rule prehistoric sites show little or no architecture. Bronze Age sites show curvilinear architecture.

Surveyor	prehistoric sites		Bronze Age sites		Nabatean sites		total sites
Cohen 1981	13	10%	35	19%	6	5%	129
Cohen 1985	2	2%	39	30%	12	9%	131
Haiman 1986	7	2%	76	20%	11	3%	386
Haiman 1991	5	1%	78	22%	35	10%	353
Haiman 1993	8	2%	43	12%	26	7%	373
Haiman 1999	26	10%	43	17%	3	1%	252
Lender 1990	5	1%	55	11%	42	8%	500
Avni 1992	4	1%	72	26%	10	4%	282
Rosen 1994	24	9%	54	20%	12	4%	271
Rosen n.d.	20	8%	27	11%	25	10%	244

Table 2: Ceramic frequencies by architectural type.

site type	# sites	cook %	bowls %	jars %	jug/lets %	other %	total sherds	sherds/ site
towers	4	12	62	8	12	8	26	6.5
rect/settle	32	13	35	5	37	10	117	3.7
round	79	23	39	5	18	10	66	0.8
camps	30	44	0	33	22	0	9	0.3

Table 3: Ceramic frequencies according to n-s location , arranged north (top) to south according to Israel Grid horizontal coordinate

grid #	total sites	cook %	bowls %	jars %	jug/lets %	other %	total sherds	sherds/ site
103	18	11.9	50	6	21.4	10.7	84	4.7
101	42	14.6	30.2	3.1	46.6	10.4	96	2.3
100	72	27.3	33.3	9.1	18.2	12.1	66	0.9
97–99	25	45.5	9.1	0	27.3	18.2	11	0.4

References

Avni, G. 1991. *Archaeological Survey of Israel Map of Har Saggi North-East (225)*. Israel Antiquities Authority, Jerusalem.

Avni, G. 1992. Survey of Deserted Bedouin Campsites in the Negev Highlands and its Implications for Archaeological Research. In *Pastoralism in the Levant*. Editors: Bar-Yosef, O. and Khazanov, A.M. Pp. 241–254. Prehistory Press, Madison.

Avni, G. 1996. *Nomads, Farmers, and Town-Dwellers*. Israel Antiquities Authority, Jerusalem.

Banning, E.B. 1986. Peasants, Pastoralists, and *Pax Romana*: Mutualism in the Southern Highlands of Jordan. *Bulletin of the American Schools of Oriental Research* 261: 25–50.

Banning, E.B. and Kohler-Rollefson, I. 1992. Ethnographic Lessons for the Pastoral Past: Camp Locations and Material Remains near Beidha, Southern Jordan. In *Pastoralism in the Levant*. Editors: Bar-Yosef, O. and Khazanov, A.M. Pp. 181–204. Prehistory Press, Madison.

Barth, F. 1961. *Nomads of South Persia*. Little Brown, Boston.

Bar-Yosef, O. and Khazanov, A.M.1992. (eds.) *Pastoralism in the Levant*. Prehistory Press, Madison.

Bruins, H.J. 1986. *Desert Environment and Agriculture in the Central Negev and Kadesh Barnea during Historical Times*. Nijkirk, Netherlands, Midbar Foundation:.

Cohen, R. 1981. *Archaeological Survey of Israel Map of Sede Boqer-East (168) 13–03*. Archaeological Survey of Israel, Jerusalem.

Cohen, R. 1982. New Light on the Date of the Petra-Gaza Road. *Biblical Archaeologist* 45: 240–247.

Cohen, R. 1985. *Archaeological Survey of Israel Map of Sede Boqer-West (167) 12–03*. Israel Department of Antiquities, Jerusalem.

Cribb, R. 1991. *Nomads in Archaeology*. Cambridge Univ. Press, Cambridge.

Danin, A. 1983. *Desert Vegetation of Israel and Sinai*. Cana, Jerusalem.

Eldar, I., Nir, Y., and Nahlieli, D. 1992. The Bedouin and their Campsites in the Dimona Region of the Negev: Comparative Models for the Study of Ancient Desert Settlements. In *Pastoralism in the Levant*. Editors: Bar-Yosef, O. and Khazanov, A.M. Pp. 205–219. Prehistory Press, Madison.

Evenari, M., Shanan, L., and Tadmor, N. 1982. *The Negev: The Challenge of a Desert*. Harvard University Press, Cambridge, Mass.

Finkelstein, I. and Perevoletsky, A. 1990. Processes of Sedentarization and Nomadization in the History of the Negev and Sinai. *Bulletin of the American Schools of Oriental Research* 279: 67–88.

Flannery, K.V. 1972. The Origins of the Village as a Settlement Type in Mesoamerica and the Near East. In *Man, Settlement and Urbanism*. Editors: Ucko, P., Tringham, R. and Dimbleby, G. Pp. 23–56. Duckworth, London.

Gichon, M. 1980. Research on the Limes Palaestinae: A Stocktaking. In *Roman Frontier Studies, 1979*. Editors: Hanson, W.S. and Keppie, L.J.F. Pp. 843–63. British Archaeological Reports International Series S71, Oxford.

Glueck, N. 1959. *Rivers in the Desert*. Jewish Publication Society, Philadelphia.

Graf, D..F. 1990. The Origins of the Nabateans. *ARAM* 2: 45–75.

Haiman, M. 1986. *Archaeological Survey of Israel Map of Har Hamran Southwest*. Israel Dept. of Antiquities, Jerusalem.

1991. *Archaeological Survey of Israel Map of Mitzpeh Ramon Southwest (200) 12–00*. Israel Antiquities Authority, Jerusalem.

Haiman, M. 1993. *Archaeological Survey of Israel Map of Har Hamran Southeast (199)*. Israel Antiquities Authority, Jerusalem.

Haiman, M. 1995. Agriculture and Nomad-State Relations in the Negev Desert in the Byzantine and Early Islamic Periods. *Bulletin of the American Schools of Oriental Research* 297: 29–54.

Haiman , M. 1999. *Archaeological Survey of Israel Map of Har Ramon (203)*. Israel Antiquities Authority, Jerusalem.

Haiman, M. and Goren, Y. 1992. "Negbite" Pottery: New Aspects and Interpretations and the Role of Pastoralism in Designating Ceramic Technology. In *Pastoralism in the Levant. Archaeological Materials in Anthropological Perspectives*. Editors: Bar-Yosef, O. and Khazanov, A.M. Pp. 143–152. Prehistory Press: Madison.

Halloul , M. 1990. New Thamudic Inscriptions from the Negev. In *Ancient Rock Inscriptions, Supplement to Map of Har Nafha (196) 12–01*. Sharon, M. and Halloul, M. Pp. 36–45. Archaeological Survey of Israel, Israel Antiquities Authority, Jerusalem.

Healey, J.F. 1989. Were the Nabateans Arabs? *ARAM* 1: 38–44.

Kedar, Y. 1967. *Ancient Agriculture in the Negev Highlands*. Jerusalem, Bialik Insitute (Hebrew).

Kenyon, K. 1980. *Archaeology in the Holy Land*. Benn Norton, London.

Khazanov, A.M. 1984. *Nomads and the Outside World*. Cambridge Univ. Press, Cambridge.

Lender, Y. 1990. *Archaeological Survey of Israel Map of Har Nafha (196) 12–01*. Israel Antiquities Authority, Jerusalem.

Mayerson, P. 1960. *The Ancient Agricultural Regime of Nessana and the Central Negev. Excavations at Nessana* Vol. I. Colt Institute, London.

Mayerson, P. 1986. The Saracens and the *Limes*. *Bulletin of the American Schools of Oriental Research* 262: 35–47.

Mayerson, P. 1989 Saracens and Romans: Micro-Macro Relationships. *Bulletin of the American Schools of Oriental Research* 274: 71–79.

Meshel, A. And Tsafrir, Y. 1975. The Nabatean Road from Avdat to Sha'ar Ramon. *Palestine Exploration Quarterly* 107: 3–21.

Negev, A. 1966. The Date of the Petra-Gaza Road. *Palestine Exploration Quarterly* 88: 89–98.

Negev, A. 1983. *Masters of the Desert*. Keter, Jerusalem. (Hebrew).

Negev, A. 1986. *The Late Hellenistic and Early Roman Pottery of Nabatean Oboda*. Qedem 22, Monographs of the Institute of Archaeology. Hebrew University, Jerusalem.

Orni, E. And Efrat, E. 1980. *Geography of Israel*. Israel Universities Press, Jerusalem.

Rosen, S.A. 1987a. Demographic Trends in the Negev Highlands: Preliminary Results from the Emergency Survey. *Bulletin of the American Schools of Oriental Research* 266: 45–58.

Rosen, S.A. 1987b.Byzantine Nomadism in the Negev: Results from the Emergency Survey. *Journal of Field Archaeology* 14: 29–42.

Rosen, S.A. 1992. Nomads in Archaeology: A Response to Finkelstein and Perevoletsky. *Bulletin of the American Schools of Oriental Research* 287: 75–85.

Rosen, Steven A. 1993. A Roman Period Pastoral Tent Camp in the Negev, Israel. *Journal of Field Archaeology* 20: 441–451.

Rosen, Steven A. 1994 *Archaeological Survey of Israel Map of Makhtesh Ramon – 204*. Israel Antiquities Authority, Jerusalem.

Rosen, S.A. 2000. The Decline of Desert Agriculture: A View from the Classical Period Negev. In *The Archaeology of Drylands*, Editors: Barker, G. and Gilbertson, D. Pp. 45–62. One World Archaeology 39, Routledge, London.
Rosen, S.A. n.d. Archaeological Survey Map of Mitzpe Ramon East. Israel Antiquities Authority, Jerusalem. Unpublished.ms.
Rosen, S.A. and Avni, G. 1993. The Edge of Empire: The Archaeology of Pastoral Nomads in the Southern Negev Highlands in Late Antiquity. *Biblical Archaeologist* 56: 189–199.
Rosen, S.A. and Avni, G. 1997. *The 'Oded Sites: Investigations of Two Early Islamic Pastoral Camps South of the Ramon Crater*. Beersheva, Beersheva XI, Studies by the Department of Bible and Ancient Near East, Ben-Gurion University Press.
Rosen, S.A. and Goodfriend, G.A. 1993. An Early Date for Gaza Ware from the Northern Negev. *Palestine Exploration Quarterly* 125: 143–48.
Saidel, B. 1998. *Arid Zone Pastoralists in the Early Bronze Age in the Southern Levant*. Unpublished Ph.D. dissertation, Harvard University, Cambridge.
Simms, S.R. 1988. The Archaeological Structure of a Bedouin Camp. *Journal of Archaeological Science* 15: 197–211.

The Cultural and Heritage Management of Petra

Zaki Aslan

The protection of the ancient ruins of Petra is of great interest to all scholars of the ancient Nabataean world. This paper focuses on the responsibility which field archaeologists take after excavating archaeological sites at Petra, combining site-presentation and protection for future generations. This endeavour concerns many modern archaeologists in a way that complements their work in addressing issues and responsibilities in both fields of heritage management and public archaeology. The core of this discussion will cover various current management issues facing the site of Petra, and on illustrating present efforts to save the cultural values inherent at this important Nabataean site from disturbance associated with urban expansion, touristic development and archaeological activities. In my capacity as a conservation architect and heritage manager (of the International Conservation Centre in Petra), I hope to demonstrate problems and efforts made by collaborative projects with the Jordanian Government.

First it should be emphasized that the methodology used at Petra intended to establish conservation and protection strategies for the site and its monuments in a 'holistic' approach. At present, strategies are based on careful review of the following:

1. the cultural values of the site, its identity, or its significance among various interest groups.
2. its administrative context relevant to financial and human resources and regulations.
3. its physical conditions.

In line with contemporary conservation approaches, all these three aspects are to be based on present socio-economic and cultural dimensions in the context of integrated urban/ territorial conservation.

The Significance of the Site of Petra

All scholars of the Nabataean realm accept the great significance of the site of Petra. Indeed, cultural and natural characteristics of that site are apparent, exemplified by monuments sculpted in the rock and free-standing buildings, as well as natural geological formations comprising a distinct cultural landscape of human occupation for over 8,000 years. All these features make present-day Petra the 'jewel' of Jordan.

The Petra site is relatively extensive. The area of the archaeological park is about 264 square kilometres and the area of the Petra region is about 900 square kilometres.

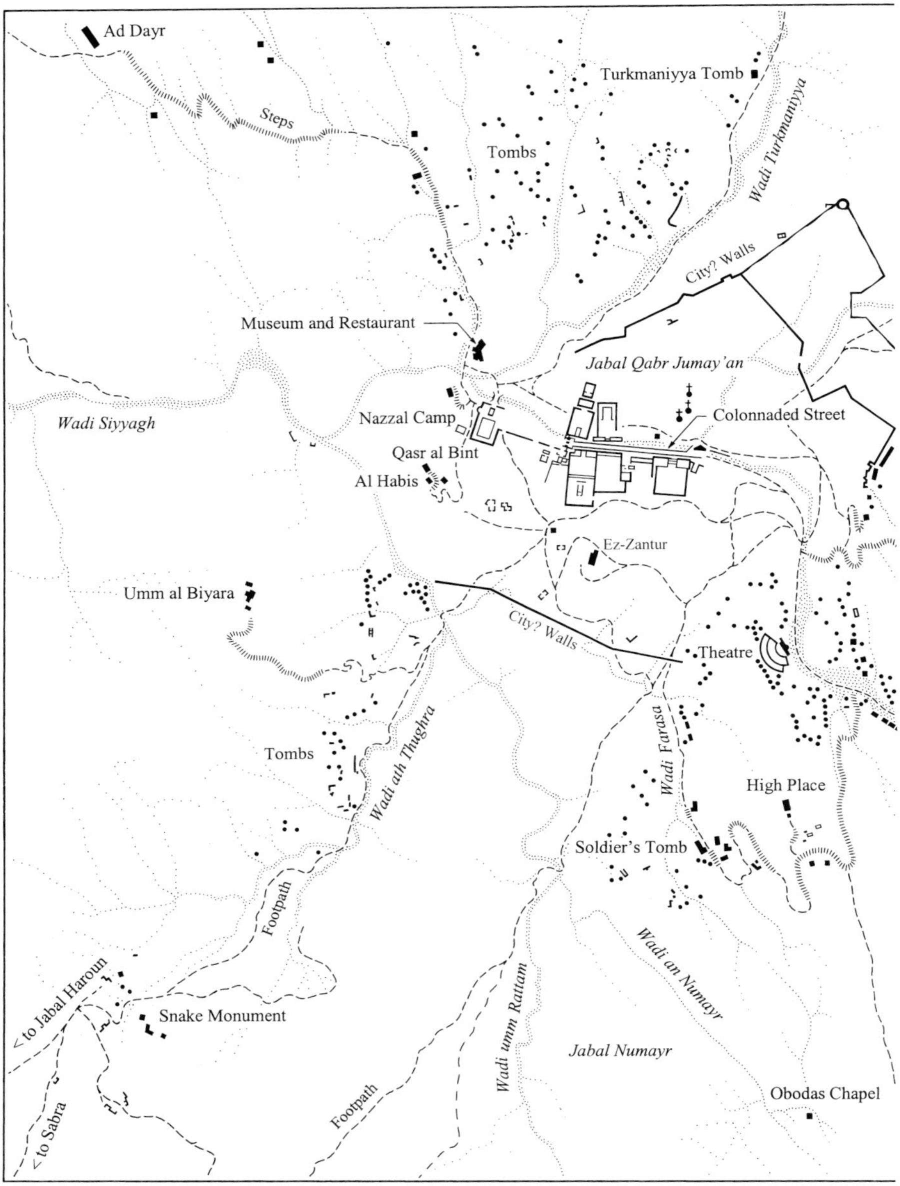

Plan of Petra region by J. M. Farrant

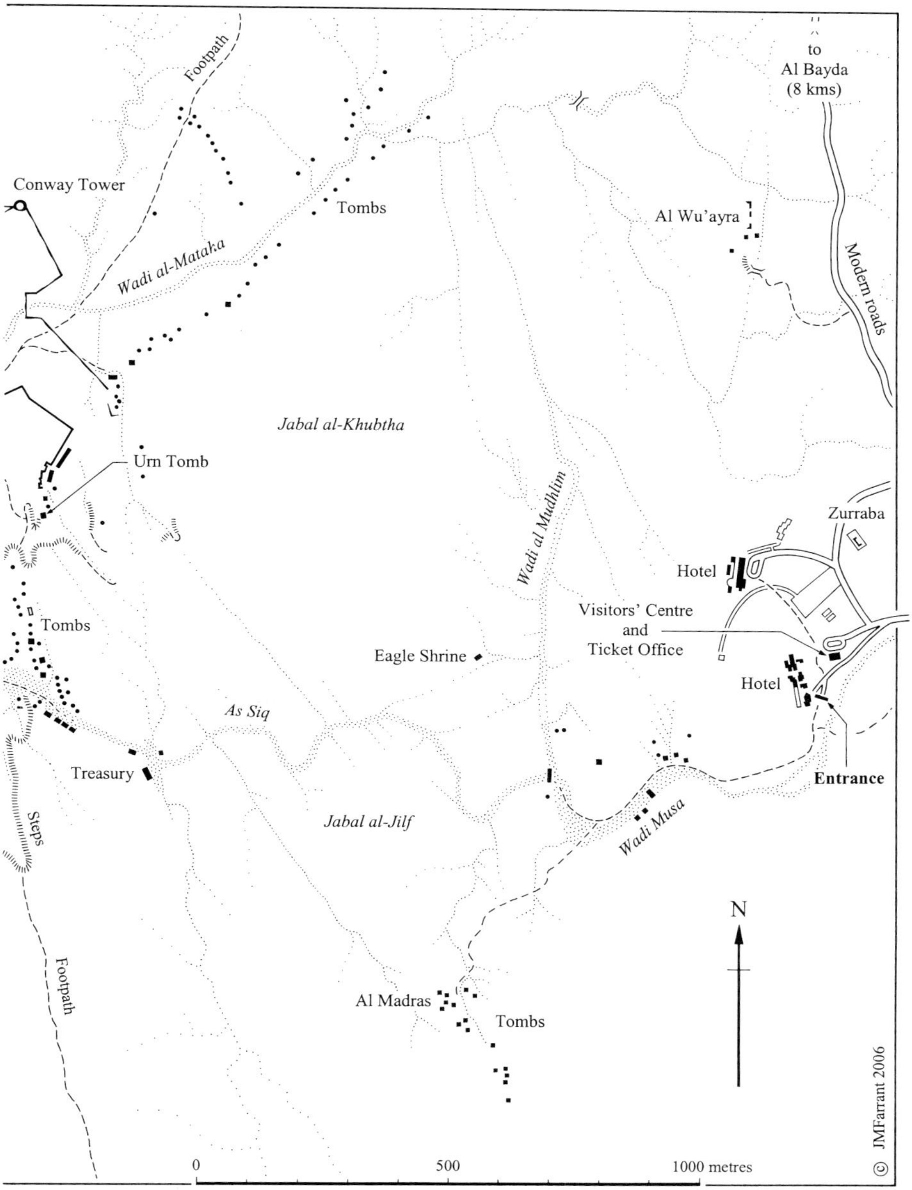
to
Al Bayda
(8 kms)
Footpath
Conway Tower
Tombs
Al Wu'ayra
Wadi al-Mataka
Modern roads
Jabal al-Khubtha
Urn Tomb
Wadi al Mudhlim
Zurraba
Hotel
Tombs
Visitors' Centre
and
Ticket Office
Eagle Shrine
Hotel
As Siq
Treasury
Entrance
Jabal al-Jilf
Wadi Musa
Steps
N
Footpath
Al Madras
Tombs
© JMFarrant 2006
0
500
1000 metres

Petra was listed as a World Heritage site in 1985 according to the first and third criteria of the World Heritage convention. The first is related to the creative work of humanity and the second to the testimony of a unique and exceptional work of a cultural tradition and of an extinct civilisation. In fact, these criteria clearly define the quality of the site. The cultural and historical qualities of the site are related to the periods of human occupation and interaction between man and nature. Effectively, the monuments and excavated finds at Petra represent the history of nearly all human civilisations in the area. However, the majority of the present extraordinary architecture of Petra dates primarily to the wealthy period of the classical Nabataeans. Nevertheless, it should be noted that while natural, historical, socio-anthropological and economic values are recognised by specialists, members of the public and visitors consider values of Petra for quite different reasons. For tourists Petra has an exceptional cultural and natural landscape. For the majority of local inhabitants and some other Jordanians, Petra is primarily a major source of income for the local and national economy. It therefore becomes crucial that archaeologists be fully involved in the interface between archaeology and the local public, whose main interest is on financial gains.

Effectively, during the last ten years, Petra has become the chicken that laid the golden eggs, thus creating a situation that requires several sustainable planning measures to maintain the spirit of this place and preserve its identity for future generations. This protection obliged the government to take specific measures and implement the appropriate methods described in this paper.

Tourist development at Petra with regard to its conservation and protection

Since the signing of the Jordan-Israel peace treaty in 1994, the number of tourists visiting Petra have increased considerably. Between 1994 and 1996 the number of tourists grew from 200,000 to 415,000. The income from entrance fees correspondingly increased from 1.6 million dollars in 1994 to 9.4 million dollars in 1996. The figures in 1997 however revealed a drop of 8.25% over 1996 and continued fluctuating around the figure of 1997 until 2000 due to political problems in the region.

The economic boom of the mid-nineties fuelled the speculative purchase of land for development as people from outside the region tried to capitalise on the potential of tourism. This led to a host of problems such as the construction of new hotels in the town of Wadi Musa, adjacent to Petra, and along the panoramic Wadi Musa-Taybeh highway.

Tourist development also necessitated taking measures to develop visitor services around and in the archaeological park.

At the entrance of the site, the visitor centre area had to be upgraded, the traffic and the parking lots had to be re-designed, and inside the site the tents and vendors' kiosks had to be reorganised or relocated.

Around the site, four areas or villages were to be planned in the context of physical sustainable urban and socio-economical development:

- The town of Wadi Musa, near ancient Petra providing the main access to the site.
- The entrance area to the site and the visitor centre zone.
- The scenic route from Wadi Musa to Taybeh
- The village of Umm Sayhoun, where the Bedouin tribe of the *Budul* were relocated in 1985. Before their transferring, the *Budul* inhabited caves in the archaeological site, and their transfer out of there was only decided following the recommendations of the first management plan of the American Parks Service in 1968. The life-style of the *Budul* was deemed incompatible with the preservation of the ancient monuments.

Several elaborate management plans before and after the Jordan-Israel peace agreement anticipated the tourist crisis at Petra. However, the plans before 1994 were neither comprehensive nor detailed. They included:

- The plan of the American Parks Service of 1968 was the cause of the problem of creating the village of Umm Sayhoun after 1985 to house the *Budul*. The problem of the visual impact of Umm Sayhoun is apparent from the site. In addition, the selected location of the village is problematic for it is at the future visitor exit route from Petra. There were also problems of land procession and movement around the actual boundaries of the village, which should be resolved to avoid the uncontrolled expansion of the village into the site. The problem of the Umm Sayhoun is a long-lasting one. Efforts have already been made to mi-nimise the visual impact, and there is a plan to oblige the *Budul* to paint the outer walls of their houses with a sandy-beige colour.
- A master plan developed in 1989 by the Ministry of Municipal and Rural Affairs permitted the construction of hotels just outside the main entrance of the site and accepted developing hotels in the residential zones. The Ministry of Tourism was responsible for issuing construction permits for these hotels, but there was unfortunately no co-ordination between ministries at the time. This resulted in constructing various hotels at the entrance of Wadi Musa thus creating congestion in this zone without adequate provision of infrastructure for sewage and wastewater. The government therefore stopped further development in this area in both Wadi Musa and the route to Taybeh. In 1992, the effects of increasing tourism in Wadi Musa and surrounding areas of the site and the lack of effective local management and planning institutions in the area were recognised. At this time the establishment of a Petra Regional and Planning Council was deemed necessary upon the recommendations of the UNESCO to develop a master plan for the site.
- The plan of the UNESCO was directed by various experts. The recommendations of this plan emphasised the creation of an independent institution manage the region of Petra. The plan equally recommended the establishment of zones, to provide sufficient infrastructure, to control urban development, to define the limits of a buffer zone to the archaeological park, to limit the number of hotels, and to ameliorate visitor management and flow. This plan

was not officially endorsed but the documents which were developed at a later stage were based on its directives.

- The action plan of the 'World Bank' in 1996 provided a study of options and solutions addressing environmental problems at the region of Petra, and elaborated an urban planning study of four areas around the archaeological site: Wadi Musa, 'Entrance area', Umm Sayhoun and Taybeh. The plan established new zoning at the scenic view routes of Umm Sayhhon and Taybeh. The plan equally addressed management problems of the physical environment (Limitation of sewage impact, reforesting agricultural terraces, and introduction of sewage treatment system at the area of Beida in the west. In addition, the plan provided a design of the entry route to the site and visitor services facilities. At Dara, near the entrance of the site, the plan proposed a co-operation constituting of landowners to solve problems of ownership and development there. The plan provided architectural solutions at the area of the entrance of the site to minimise motor vehicle traffic impact. At Umm Sayhoun, which will eventually be a zone of an exit of one way traffic for the tourist route, the plan suggested a compromise to control future construction and physical development inside the actual limits of the village and to enhance the traffic route at this zone.

Before conducting these studies, problems of planning and management around Petra can be summarised in the following:

- Uncontrolled urban expansion at the areas surrounding the archaeological site Hotel capacity quadrupled in 1996.
- The absence of infrastructure to tackle the needs of urban expansion (traffic flow and road conditions, sewage, water and waste water services and environmental degradation)
- The lack of a detailed plan for visitor management inside the archaeological park. For example, pedestrian traffic was hampered by horse traffic. This situation was modified by limiting access of horses just to the entry gate of the *siq*. However, carriages are only allowed for handicaps and elderly. Additionally, camels and donkeys could be used at the urban centre of the ancient site. It is to be mentioned that sign problems to guide access and access control to avoid wear and tear in isolated areas are being studied by a USAID-funded project co-ordinated by the Petra National Trust.

Carrying Capacity of the site and visitor management

The policy adopted in Petra strictly allows pedestrian access to the site. Car and bus parking are located at the immediate vicinity of the site. In the future, it is envisaged that a shuttle service is provided for tourists to leave the site from the central area to Umm Sayhoun. The access control in the site which is monitored by about 100 guards is inadequate. The visitor centre may play a role to delay the flow of visitors. On the other hand, activities inside the site are reduced to minimum to preserve the historic image of the place. Although local guides are being hired by tourist companies, it is still possible to visit the site unaccompanied. However, a comprehensive visitors' study has not yet taken place.

Despite the absence of such studies to date, a 1994 UNESCO management plan of Petra gave an indication of the general carrying capacity of the site and at a few specific locations, such as the *siq* and the Khazneh, where there is a visitor overflow. This preliminary study was based on general criteria related to the cultural and ecological impact of overflow, and to the development of tourism activities. Two hypotheses on long and short terms were envisaged. The first considered a one-way access to the site from the *siq* to Umm Sayhoun. The second considered several access points to the site. The evaluation was based on a theoretical maximum carrying capacity of 4,420 simultaneous visitors in the site. In fact, this figure obtained in the study reached 3,000 to 3,500 visitors simultaneously, considering the daily and hourly fluctuation. However, each area of the 'Petra park' must be studied independently.

Nevertheless, the general figure of the carrying capacity of the site is a useful tool for comprehensive planning of the region, notably to determine the maximum number of hotel rooms. Consequently, the study recommended a strict control of construction for tourist accommodation. However, studies on the carrying capacity at fragile areas of the site are still needed.

Administrative Context/ Infrastructure for the Physical Protection of the Site

As it was recommended in the UNESCO plan of 1994, a new regional institution was established in 1995 to resolve the host of problems on a local level. The main tasks for this institution entitled the 'Petra Regional Planning Council' were:

- the protection of the site from urban development
- the enhancement of the quality of visitor experience
- Maximising economic benefit for the country

The institution has constituted of government representatives from various ministries and departments, and the Petra National Trust. It was effectively established in 1997. Until the beginning of 2001, it was presided over by the Minister of Tourism and Antiquities. It then became an autonomous entity accountable to the Prime Ministry. Its budget is based on various contributing institutions and 25% of entrance fees in to Petra. In 1998 a loan of 24 million U.S. dollars was given to the Petra Regional Planning Council by the 'World Bank' to implement the plans of action of 1996 prepared by the same funding body.

In addition to a USAID and GTZ (German Technical Cooperation) grants to develop water related infrastructure in the surrounding areas of the site, other several major projects, which are in the process of establishment, are being developed in collaboration with local governmental institutions inside the site:

- The GTZ has spent 8 million DM for the establishment of a conservation centre in Petra. The project, in its final stages, has provided equipment, laboratory facilities, and training as well as implementation measures for a sustainable centre that is the first of its kind in the region. In collaboration of the Department of Antiquities, physical presence of this centre in Petra will eventually be a nucleus of a 'Park Management Entity' for the archaeological park as such. It is envisaged that this centre provide technical as well as managerial assistance for the many sites in the country. However, the focus remains for the protection of the monuments in Petra. The main goal of the centre is to plan, supervise and execute conservation work of stone monuments.

- In addition, there are been numerous conservation projects aimed for Nabataean Petra. These include short term projects for the implementation of actions outlined in the UNESCO report of 1994. For example, USAID involvement in the conservation of the 'Petra Church', the Roman Street and the 'Great Temple' projects. Swiss involvement focused in the conservation of the *siq* and water systems flanking it for the security of visitors, as well as the protective shelter for the frescoes in the ez-Zantur building. These are only few examples of the efforts to document, protect and plan the safeguard the monuments of Petra for future generations.
- In the near future the Conservation Centre in Petra will co-ordinate all these efforts to avert decay of the site.

As far as the present socio-economic context is concerned, it has to be said that despite the absence of studies, surveys and participation of local social conditions in Petra. New efforts focus on further community involvement in the management and protection processes. For example, not only are local technicians and inhabitants being trained in monument conservation and site management though the Conservation Centre in Petra, but also further studies are underway to develop better communication possibilities between residents of the area and the Petra Regional Planning Council. It is a challenge that effective participation in activities and decisions related to the site has to take place with institutional collaboration in the area.

Conclusion

It should be stressed, that after a tardy and sluggish beginning, there is now increasing awareness of the importance of effective local administrative presence to protect and manage the site in an efficient manner. The work selected here for presentation is testimony to the concern which the Jordanian Government as well as other parties have in relation to the protection of Petra. Despite these efforts there are some weaknesses, notably in the management policies of the site, the inadequate co-operation among all parties involved, and the participation of the local community. In spite of these shortcomings, the site-management of Petra is definitely improving thanks to the collaborative efforts of archaeologists and heritage conservators together with external technical and financial assistance. These have all assisted newly created local institutions to implement plans and strategies for the protection of the world heritage site of Petra, for the people of Jordan and humanity in general.

Bibliography

Petra National Park Management Plan (1964) UNESCO
Master Plan for the Protection and Use of the Petra National Park (1968) United States National Park Service
The Study on the Management Analysis and Recommendations for the Petra World Heritage Site (1996) US ICOMOS
The Management of the Petra Archaeological Park (1999) UNESCO

Epilogue

Providing an epilogue to such a rich and varied offering of papers on the Nabataeans was hard enough in April of 2001, but it is even harder now. Although I retain the remarks that I delivered at the end of the conference, it would be folly to publish them as they were, when six years, full of important new discoveries and publications, have already passed. Accordingly, this epilogue seems to me the appropriate place to signal progress since the international conference at the British Museum and to demonstrate the extraordinary vigour and fecundity of Nabataean studies today.

First, the Petra exhibition, organized by Glenn Markoe for an opening at the New York Museum of Natural History in 2003, served as the occasion for a publication, like the present one, with contributions from many of the leading *nabatéologues* on current work: *Petra Discovered. Lost City of the Nabataeans* (Cincinnati Art Museum, 2003). It is to this volume that one will turn for supplementary studies of the Nabataean language (by Michael Macdonald), the sculpture (by Judith MacKenzie), the excavations at the Great Temple (by Martha Joukowsky), the Petra papyri (by Ludwig Koenen, Robert Daniel, and Traianos Gagos), and the Nabataeans in the Hawran (Jean-Marie Dentzer).

The Markoe book appeared too soon to take account of the extraordinary discoveries made by Jordanian archaeologists in front of the Khazneh and on a level below it. A group of evidently royal tombs, to which access was maintained through stairs, was clearly preserved after the construction of the Khazneh itself. The level of the original tombs implies a plaza at the end of the Siq below the current level. We await publication of these tombs.

The full publication of Martha Joukowsky's work came in a volume that she edited: *Petra Great Temple,* volume 1, Brown University Excavations 1993–1997 (Providence, RI, 1998), and Peter Parr had access to this work in writing his chapter. It contains the definitive account of the astonishing elephant capitals and the equally astonishing theater or bouleuterion in the interior of the Great Temple, but it appeared too soon to accommodate the water installations and pool on which Leigh-Ann Bedal spoke at the British Museum. Her paper does not appear in this publication volume, but her analysis can be read in her book, *The Petra-Pool Complex: A Hellenistic Paradeisos in the Nabataean Capital* (Gorgias Press, Piscataway NJ, 2004). It is worth adding now that in the *ACOR Newsletter* 17.2 (Summer 2006), under the title "The Petra Great Temple – A Final Chapter," Prof. Joukowsky concludes, on p. 2, "Elaborate floral friezes and acanthus-laden limestone capitals suggest the temple was constructed in the last quarter of the 1st century BC by the Nabataeans after which it was enlarged with the theater in the 1st century AD. The precinct was in use until the 6th century AD, the Byzantine period." In other words, it was still in use at the time when the papyri were written.

An unexpectedly early reference to the Nabataeans has brought sudden illumination to the darkest period of Nabataean history. It appears in the new collection of epigrams by Posidippus, published by Colin Austin and Guido Bastianini: *Posidippi Pellaei quae supersunt omnia* (Milan, 2002), referring to a "Nabataean king of Arab cavalry." This must refer to some time in the early third century BC.

At the opposite end of recorded Nabataean history the Petra Papyri from the sixth century AD have documented an urban community that no one had even imagined until the papyri were discovered in late 1994. Finnish colleagues have already produced the first volume in their series on the papyri entrusted to them: *The Petra Papyri*, ed. J. Frösén, A. Arjava, and M. Lehtinen (Amman, 2002). Another is on the way. Inventory no. 10, the longest and most informative of the documents (more than 200 lines, with a treasure of onomastic information and Arabic toponyms) is still eagerly awaited from the Michigan team that is working on it. The complete publication of the Petra Church appeared in a handsome volume under the authorship of Zbigniew Fiema with many collaborators: *The Petra Church* (Amman, 2001).

Even as they labored on the decipherment and interpretation of the papyri, the Finns simultaneously supported an excavation at Petra itself on the Mount of Aaron, the Jebel Haroun, where they have discovered the monastery mentioned by the papyri, an inscription with Aaron's name on it, and a midden that reveals a fish diet that is reminiscent of the molluscs described at Zantur. Pending the full publication of the Jebel Haroun excavation, the reports in the catalogue of an exhibition at the Amos Anderson Art Museum in Helsinki provide basic information: *Petra – A City Forgotten and Rediscovered*, ed. J. Frösén and Z. Fiema (Helsinki, 2002).

Another paper presented at the British Museum but not included in this volume is the authoritative publication of 120 clay bullae from Petra with the city's titles. This exceptional accretion to our knowledge of Petra's self-representation, particularly on coins, may be found in Haim Gitler's publication, "A Group of 120 Clay Bullae from Petra with Titles of the City," *The Numismatic Chronicle* 2005, pp. 183–92, with plates 16 through 26. These bullae provide the first attestation of the title *Antoniniana* for Petra before the sixth-century papyri. The title seems to have been granted under Caracalla.

New light on the Nabataean city of Mada'in Salih in the Hijaz has come recently from the collaborative work of a French and Saudi team, which has so far done surveying as reported in "Mission archéologique de Mada'in Salih (Arabie Saoudite): recherches menées de 2001 à 2003 dans l'ancienne Hijra des Nabatéens," *Arabian Archaeology and Epigraphy* 17 (2006), 41–124. Plans for excavation at the site were accepted by the Saudi government in December 2006.

Norman Lewis' important contribution to this volume on the travels and notebooks of John Bankes is now amply supplemented through the article by Lewis and Michael Macdonald, Maurice Sartre, and others: "W. J. Bankes and the Identification of the Nabataean Script," *Syria* 80 (2003), 41–110, and above all by the magnificent publication by Annie Sartre-Fauriat, *Les voyages dans le Hawran (Syrie du sud) de William John Bankes (1816 et 1818)*, Ausonius éditions – Mémoires 11 / IFPO Biblioth. 169 (Bordeaux and Beirut, 2004).

Finally, the author of this epilogue has endeavoured to interpret the precious information about Nabataeans in the fragments of the lost historians, Glaucus and Uranius, who both wrote works on the Arabs. The initial publication of this study was so full of typographical errors that it is best consulted in G. W. Bowersock, "Two Greek Historians of Pre-Islamic Arabia," *Selected Papers on Late Antiquity*, Munera 16 (Edipuglia, Bari, 2000), pp. 12–34.

Clearly the World of the Nabataeans is growing in size and clarity with every passing year, and the conference documented here will stand as a milestone in this progress.

G. W. Bowersock

Contributors' Addresses

Dr Zaki Aslan
ATHAR Programme
ICCROM
Via di San Michele 13
Rome 00153
Italy
za@iccrom.org

Revd Professor John R. Bartlett
102 Sorrento Road
Dalkey, County Dublin
Ireland
jrbartlett@eircom.net

Professor Glen W. Bowersock
Institute for Advanced Study
School of Historical Studies
Einstein Drive,
Princeton, NJ 08540
U.S.A.
gwb@ias.edu

Mr Julian M. C. Bowsher
Museum of London Archaeology Service
Mortimer Wheeler House
46 Eagle Wharf Road
London. N1 7ED
England
jbowsher@museumoflondon.org.uk

Professor David F. Graf
Department of Religious Studies
College of Arts and Sciences
521 Ashe Building
P. O. Box 248264
University of Miami
Coral Gables, Florida 33124-4651
U.S.A.
dgraf@miami.edu

Ms Hero Granger-Taylor
hero@granger-taylor.com

Professor John Healey
School of Languages, Linguistics and Cultures
University of Manchester
Oxford Road
Manchester M13 9PL
England
john.healey@manchester.ac.uk

Dr Bernhard Kolb
Archaeologisches Seminar
Schoenbeinstrasse 20
CH-4056 Basel
Switzerland
Bernhard.kolb@unibas.ch

Mr Norman Lewis
35 Stanhope Road
Croydon CR0 5NS
England

Mr James R. B. Mason
7 Westfield Road
St Helen's, Ryde
Isle of Wight PO33 1UZ
England
jim_in_iow@hotmail.com

Professor John Peter Oleson
Dept of Greek and Roman Studies
P. O. Box 3045
University of Victoria
British Columbia V8W 3P4
Canada
jpoleson@uvic.ca

Professor Peter J. Parr
Flat 5, 8-10 Arlington Road
London NW1 7HX
England
pjparr@qadesh.freeserve.co.uk

Professor Joseph Patrich
Institute of Archaeology
Hebrew University of Jerusalem
Mt Scopus
Jerusalem 91905
ISRAEL

Dr Konstantinos D. Politis
Hellenic Society for Near Eastern Studies
B. Mela 10
Athens 15562
Greece
kdpolitis@hsnes.com

Professor Steven A. Rosen
Archaeology Department
Ben Gurion University
P. O. Box 653, Beersheba
Israel
rosen@bgumail.bgu.ac.il

Professor Stephan G. Schmid
Université Paul Valéry - Montpellier III
CNRS UMR 5140
Route de Mende
Montpellier 34199
France
stephan.schmid@univ-montp3.fr

Dr Jacqueline Studer
Muséum d'histoire naturelle
Département d'archéozoologie
CP 6434
CH-1211 Genève 6
Switzerland
jacqueline.studer@ville-ge.ch

Professor Laurent Tholbecq
Université Laval, Département d'Histoire
Pavillon Charles-De Koninck
Québec G1K 7P4
Canada
laurent.tholbecq@hst.ulaval.ca

Professor Robert Wenning
Pienersallee 34
D-48161 Muenster
Germany
robwenn@uni-muenster.de

Dr Fawzi Zayadine
Department of Antiquities
P.O. Box 88, Amman
Jordan